THE Consumer BIBLE

1001 WAYS TO SHOP SMART

BY MARK GREEN

WITH NANCY YOUMAN

AND GLENN VON NOSTITZ AND OLIVIER SULTAN

ILLUSTRATIONS BY MICHAEL SLOAN

WORKMAN PUBLISHING, NEW YORK

ALSO BY MARK GREEN

Changing America: Blueprints for the Clinton Administration (1993, editor)

Reagan's Reign of Error: The Instant Nostalgia Edition
(1987, 2nd Edition, with Gail Macoll)

The Challenge of Hidden Profits (1985, with John Berry)

Who Runs Congress? (1984, 4th Edition)

Winning Back America (1982)

The Other Government: The Unseen Power of Washington Lawyers (1975)

Corporate Power in America (1973, edited with Ralph Nader)

The Monopoly Makers (1973, editor)

The Closed Enterprise System
(1972, with Beverly C. Moore, Jr. & Bruce Wasserstein)

Library of Congress Cataloging-in-Publication Data

Green, Mark J.
The consumer bible : 1001 ways to shop smart / by Mark Green with Nancy Youman. — Completely rev.
p. cm.
Includes bibliographical references and index.
ISBN 0-7611-1227-8
1. Consumer education—United States. 2. Shopping—United States.
I. Youman, Nancy. II. Title.
TX336.G74 1998
640'.73'0973—dc21   98-40308
                                     CIP

Workman books are available at special discounts when purchased in bulk for premiums and sales promotions as well as for fund-raising or educational use. Special editions or book excerpts also can be created to specification. For details, please contact the Special Sales Director at the address below.

Workman Publishing Company, Inc.
708 Broadway
New York, NY 10003-9555

Manufactured in the United States of America

First Printing September 1998
10 9 8 7 6 5 4 3 2

The views expressed in this book are those of Mark Green and not those of either the Office of the Public Advocate or the Government of New York City.

In loving memory of
Ann and Irving Green

ACKNOWLEDGMENTS

The Consumer Bible is, in effect, the product of thousands of advocates in hundreds of organizations over scores of years. So from Upton Sinclair to, of course, my friend and mentor Ralph Nader, I'm a megaphone for countless predecessors who spoke up and out for consumer justice.

This volume's midwives have been my extraordinary collaborators—co-author Nancy Youman and contributors Glenn von Nostitz and Olivier Sultan—who invested a quantity and quality of effort that have distinguished their careers. They all worked with me at the Department of Consumer Affairs and helped produce the pioneering studies and actions that comprised the cornerstone of our office and this book.

Others who assisted so ably in their respective specialties to *The Consumer Bible* include Philip Higgs, Jennifer Kohn, Amy Karas, Andy Eiler, Michael Alcamo, and Norman Schreiber.

I very much want to thank friends Victor Navasky and Esther Margolis, of *The Nation* and Newmarket Press respectively, who brought me and Peter Workman together to produce this collaboration. Along with Peter's early confidence, it was Suzanne Rafer's and Margot Herrera's close editing and advice that indispensably contributed to the book's coherence (such as it is).

Finally, a special note of love and appreciation to Deni, Jenya, and Jonah, a very patient family who tolerated—even encouraged!—a book and a campaign in the same year. I hope they use the result to stretch the family budget as $marter consumers should.

—M.G.

Contents

SHOPPING SMARTER IN THE NEW CONSUMER CENTURY

When Ralph Nader jump-started the consumer movement in 1965 with *Unsafe at Any Speed,* the consumer's world was seemingly a much simpler place. There was only one kind of mortgage (fixed), one telephone company (AT&T), and just three TV channels (ABC, CBS, and NBC). And you didn't pay a dime to keep your money in the bank—or take it out. But then again, the Corvair was killing people; you practically had to be an intelligence officer to break the date code on a carton of milk; and nobody had ever heard of a Freedom of Information request.

The succeeding three decades have been years of incredible and lasting change for consumers: Air bags are now standard equipment on all cars sold in the U.S.—and the U.S. Consumer Product Safety Commission has significantly improved the safety of many products. "Nutrition Facts" have replaced nutrition fiction on food labels. And credit and leasing terms are now clearly spelled out on contracts.

Ralph Nader's consumer call to arms in the late 1960s has also spawned a sophisticated cadre of activists and groups in Washington, DC, local and federal consumer protection officials and agencies, and a nationwide network of grassroots advocates focused on everything from utility rates and banking fees to health care quality and access.

And it's a good thing. For despite the headway, new and old problems continue to vex consumers and consumer advocates.

■ *More choices than ever.* The consumer marketplace has become a teeming Tower of Babel, with not only many more choices overall but also more complicated and specialized options. Now consumers have to figure out which of myriad long-distance plans is best for their phoning patterns. Which mutual fund or portfolio of funds will get them to their retirement goals. Which HMO best fits their family's medical needs. Whether to take a 30-year, 15-year, or 10-year term on their fixed mortgage, or whether to go for an adjustable rate. And soon, many will be asked to choose an electricity provider the same way they choose a long-distance company.

■ *More information than ever.* Meanwhile, consumers are being deluged with advertising (in some supermarkets you can't buy a banana without a sticker on it advertising Blockbuster Video) and consumer information that can be confusing, conflicting, and overwhelming. I don't know if I've ever seen a mutual fund ad that *didn't* say it was #1. How could *all* of them be the best? Have you ever tried booking an airline flight at the incredibly low price advertised in the newspaper? More likely than not, the teaser fare was already sold out.

■ *More threats to competition.* After several decades of mergers, larger and larger companies are flexing their corporate muscles and using their market power to crush smaller competitors. The Justice Department's investigation of Microsoft has been widely reported, and regulators are also looking at Anheuser-Busch to see whether it has been discouraging distributors from selling small microbrew brands. Big airlines have been accused of using predatory pricing on selected routes to squeeze out start-up regional airlines and the competition from low fares. And the 1990s witnessed the greatest bank consolidation in American history—and bank fees, not coincidentally, accelerated as fast.

Using President Kennedy's 1962 proclamation of four consumer rights—the right to be heard, the right to be informed, the right to safety, and the right to choose—as a yardstick shows that the Consumer Movement's work isn't done . . . and perhaps never will be.

Until that Nirvana when the market performs perfectly for consumers, we have a choice with every purchase—get smart or get taken. Because of advancing technology, fraud, complexity, and demand, you can pay 100% more for the same VCR, over-the-counter drugs, or jewelry, depending on whether you invest your time before you invest your money.

Hence, *The Consumer Bible.* It's designed to be the only consumer book you'll need. It tries to tip the scales—and the odds—in favor of average shoppers by gathering in one place the best available information about your choices and rights in 65 different consumer categories.

The book is an outgrowth of my 28 years' experience as a consumer advocate, from a decade spent as a public interest lawyer with Ralph Nader in Washington, DC, to my years as the Consumer Affairs Commissioner of New York City to my present role as the elected Public Advocate, or ombudsperson, of the City. And based on the 50,000 consumer complaints my consumer office received over three years, as well as my several hundred investigations, reports, and lawsuits, I've come to the following conclusions about our consumer economy: Scams are extensive and expensive—and penalties are weak. Nonetheless, smarter consumers can fight back—and, in the coming consumer century, we increasingly will.

Scams and Schemes

Although opinion leaders with cushy incomes often seem to shrug off marketplace fraud or manipulation, the average consumers whose calls flooded the hot line at the New York City Department of Consumer Affairs (DCA) and now my Office of Public Advocate were not so dismissive. Their concerns were well warranted. During my tenure, for example, the DCA found:

- Electronics store employees red-handedly using razors to cut out the word "refurbished" from cardboard boxes containing old VCRs.
- Two-thirds of all home-improvement contractors failed to obtain legally required licenses.
- In an inspection sweep of 150 gas stations, one in six was caught committing "octane fraud"—deceptively selling inexpensive regular gas as the pricier premium (average overcharge per tank: $2.70).
- Supermarket scanners charged regular prices for advertised sale items 10% of the time.
- 90% of independent pay telephones illegally failed to disclose information required by the state's Public Service Commission—such as their exorbitant hidden rates.

Obviously, no one of these abuses equal the billions of dollars looted in the Savings & Loan scandal. But corner-cutting stores know that it's far easier to trick a dime out of 100,000 customers than to cheat one of $10,000 outright.

Indeed, all those dimes and dollars add up to huge consumer losses: In my 1985 book, *The Challenge of Hidden Profits: Reducing Corporate Waste and Bureaucracy* (with John F. Berry), I gathered the leading studies from around the country on the costs of price-fixing, securities fraud, auto repair fraud, product defects, pollution, bribery, and kickbacks, etc. The rough total: Consumers lost $862 billion a year (in 1985 dollars) to waste, abuse, and outright fraud—a sum equal to 20% of consumer purchasing.

Suppose workers were told that, starting tomorrow, their pay would be cut by 20%. They would strike, or worse. So why should consumers in the marketplace tolerate a reduction in spending power they would never put up with in the workplace? Why work 2,000 hours a year for, say, $40,000 and then squander $8,000 on fraud and waste?

Becoming a Smarter Consumer

Consumers have two resources to get a fair deal in the free marketplace: the law and self-help.

The law, of course, consists of the rules and regulations that prohibit deceptive ads, rigged scales, phony warranties, and defective products . . . or that require price-posting, truth-in-lending, and auto performance standards.

But the law alone is not sufficient to protect buyers in the marketplace. No matter how strong a few *hundred* consumer officials or laws may be, they are no substitute for alert, educated consumers engaging in *billions* of weekly point-of-purchase interactions with sellers. Consumer self-help is essential.

Over the years, *Consumer Reports,* Ralph Nader, the federal Consumer Information Center, Better Business Bureaus, and national and local consumer organizations have helped to correct the traditional information imbalance between sellers and buyers in the marketplace. By synthesizing so many of these advocates' money-saving suggestions into one volume—combined with insights gleaned from years of consumer advocacy and law enforcement—*The Consumer Bible* seeks to turn readers into "$marter Consumers" and to help convert *caveat emptor*—let the buyer beware—into *caveat vendor.*

Each chapter provides an overview of a type of product or service, along with warnings on "What to Watch Out for." Every chapter also includes specific advice and tips on how to be a $marter Consumer and ends with a HELP box containing resources that will enable consumers to access services, get further information, or take action.

Consumer Century

A revolution is like waves lapping at a cliff, wrote French historian Henri Seé. For decades, nothing happens . . . and then the side of the cliff falls in.

A trend is setting the stage for a consumer revolution that is potentially as dramatic as the creation of advertising itself in the mid-1800s—electronic shopping.

As the Internet links buyers and sellers world-wide, couch-cozy consumers can access essential informa-tion about goods and services with the flick of a remote or the click of a mouse. At the most innovative Worldwide Web sites, you can both gather and efficiently sift through product offerings and specifications to put together the perfect computer system for your needs, identify, outfit and learn which dealer has the best price on your next car, and sort through hundreds of mutual funds to find reliable ones that fit your investment goals.

True, computer- or cable-illiterate consumers will not easily—or ever—change their buying habits. But the younger generation, at ease using computers, are more capable of launching themselves into consumer cyberspace and using new, high-tech services.

■ Consumers who currently have the ability to go online can sample a whole range of products from the comfort of their home before deciding whether to buy. For example, a number of Web sites let you download samples of new recordings and many book and magazine companies allow you to read excerpts. At carpoint.com you'll find three-dimensional, interactive pictures to show you the interiors of dozens of cars.

■ Once you've sampled, you can also buy. Searching for a hard-to-find rose gardening guide? Amazon.com will do the searching for you. Unable to get to the grocery store before it closes? Peapod.com will do the shopping for you and drop the groceries off at your door. Hate car salespeople more than the dentist? CarBargains will haggle with car dealers for you. Not sure your travel agent is working hard enough to find the lowest airfare? If you tell priceline.com how much you want to pay for two tickets to Tahiti, they'll try to find an airline that'll take you for what you're offering.

Aside from taking the schlepping out of shopping, the Internet is also a powerful defense against fraud. If you think somebody's trying to scam you, check what the Federal Trade Commission and other government consumer agencies have to say about the outfit (www.consumer.gov), or check with the Better Business Bureau (www.bbb.org) or the National Fraud Information Center (www.nfic.inter.net). And if you're dissatisfied with your purchase, you can bypass customer service and phone-mail jail by firing off an e-complaint to the chief executive of the company.

Hence, the coming consumer century. America's first century was agrarian-based; small farmers were the vertebrae in the spine of our economy. Our second was factory-based; the belching smokestack became the metaphor for production of goods, regardless of their net social costs or desirability. And now, with the dawning of our new information-based global economy, buyers have the prospect of evening the odds with sellers.

As we approach the era of interactive TV and computers-as-showrooms, *The Consumer Bible* provides the essential information—product by product and service by service—you need to talk back and fight back in the marketplace.

Mark Green
New York City, August 1998

PART 1

Food

CHAPTER 1

GROCERIES

Some Thought for Food

No matter how often you cook meals at home, whether you favor cooking from scratch or simply microwaving a frozen dinner, you must shop for food. You can save time, money, and your health if you learn to steer your way around the marketing traps of food shopping. From advertisements on television to the layout of supermarkets to marketing schemes, all of us are being urged constantly to spend our money on food that we—like Steve Martin in the remake of *Father of the Bride*—might be happier and healthier without.

Martin's character escapes from prewedding chaos by going to the supermarket to pick up something for dinner. He gets arrested in the bread aisle for refusing to pay for *twelve* hot dog buns when hot dogs come in packages of only *eight*. Martin rants about his theory of the mismatched frank and bun quantities:

"Some big shot over at the wiener company got together with some big shot over at the bun company and decided to rip off the American public because they think the American public is a bunch of trusting nitwits who'll pay for things they don't need rather than make a stink."

An extra bun here or there probably won't break your budget, but these and other marketing gimmicks can add up. According to *Today* show grocery-shopping guru Phil Lempert, you can probably save hundreds of dollars a year on your grocery bill: Use just 10 manufacturer's coupons a week, and you'll save $300 a year (the average coupon saves you about 60 cents). Be alert for store specials, which usually add savings of 15%, store coupons, and

> "**B**igger is not always cheaper. Grocery stores know shoppers automatically associate a larger size with a lower cost per ounce, so they've begun to price some popular middle-sized containers higher than both the small and the large."
>
> — "Tightwad Tips for Millionaires," in *Worth* magazine

3

special sale items, and a family of four can easily save another several hundred dollars a year. And if you switch to less-expensive store brands, you'll add another few hundred dollars to the cookie jar.

There's other key advice to follow, such as never shopping when you're hungry—it invariably leads to overbuying, especially of food that can be quickly unwrapped and gobbled up. But there's also much more that everyone who eats can't afford *not* to know.

THE BASICS

Supermarket Shopping

Store layout. Supermarket floor plans are carefully designed to force shoppers to walk to the back of the store to find staple items, such as milk or bread. All along the way to the rear of the store, consumers must pass—and try to pass up—enticements. Typical are displays of "special" seasonal or new products, and colorful, fragrant pre-cut (and more expensive) fresh produce, tactics stores use to slow consumers down so that they'll stick around and spend more money. Attractive displays at the ends of aisles, where consumers may expect to find sale items, are usually stocked with high-profit items that *aren't* on sale. And supermarkets often place their bakeries near the entrance, filling the air with the mouth-watering smell of freshly baked bread and pastries.

Shelf space is basically real estate. Stores place high-profit convenience foods, such as cans of pie filling and cake frosting, in prime locations at eye level, but require shoppers to bend way down to find such staples as flour and sugar on the bottom shelf. Foods that companies advertise to children are also placed at eye level—kid's-eye level, that is. In the cereal aisle, there's a good chance you'll find shredded wheat on an upper shelf and Cocoa Crispies down below.

Finally, the checkout counter is loaded with candy, magazines, film, and batteries—items that many grocery shoppers might not need right then or could normally buy for less elsewhere, such as at a discount store. "I can resist anything except temptation," wrote Oscar Wilde in an axiom supermarkets rely on when they appeal to unwary consumers.

Supermarket vs. national brands. Nationally advertised brands cost more than supermarket brands, mostly because manufacturers pass along the cost of expensive advertising campaigns. Americans could cut about 20% off their grocery bills and sacrifice little in quality by choosing supermarket and no-frills brands. That would amount to savings of more than $2,000 a year if you spend $135 a week on brand-name products.

Coupons and specials. Newspapers, store circulars, and Sunday-paper inserts are filled with promotions and coupons for food products. But unless an item meets your needs—budget-wise and nutritionally—a few cents off is really a lot of cents wasted. Store coupons

ORGANIC BOUNTY

Concerned about the effects of ingesting pesticide residue, many people are turning to organic food. And it makes sense to do so. Most pesticides are poisonous synthetic preparations. "No one really knows what a lifetime of consuming the tiny quantities of pesticides found on foods might do to a person," according to scientists interviewed by *Consumer Reports*. Safe levels are set by animal testing, not human evidence. And the allowed level may exceed the safe level, if the benefit to farmers outweighs the risk to consumers. In addition, safe levels are set based on ingestion of one pesticide alone—though even the government's own monitoring shows that most produce has traces of several pesticides.

Whatever the health effects of consuming pesticides, children are most vulnerable—the safety levels are geared to adults, and kids' small, developing bodies may be more susceptible to pesticides' ill effects.

No wonder so many parents these days opt for organic food. The foods most likely to contain unsafe levels of pesticides, even after washing, are peaches, apples, nectarines, popcorn, pears, and baby food containing peaches, pears, and apples.

Although organics comprise less than 1% of the U.S. market, the business is thriving and consumers' choices are increasing. Annual sales are projected to quadruple from $2.5 billion to $10 billion in the next five years. Long gone are the shriveled apples and crooked carrots of the 1970s. Stop by Fresh Fields or Whole Foods, two natural foods chains, and you'll find that organic harvests appear little different in size, color, or variety than conventional produce.

However, there is one big difference: price. Organic products cost an average of 57% more than their non-organic equivalents, according to a *Consumer Reports* survey.

The boom in organic foods prompted the U.S. government to institute federal standards for organic products in 1998—rectifying years of confusion, a patchwork of state laws, spotty enforcement, and self-regulatory efforts. The United States Department of Agriculture (USDA) certified organic seal on vegetables and grain products will assure you that the food or its ingredients were grown in soil untouched by synthetic chemicals for at least three years. Processed foods with the organic label were made without chemical additives or preservatives. Organic poultry and livestock were bred and raised without preventive antibiotics or hormones.

5

usually have small print on them, requiring consumers to purchase a minimum amount of groceries for each coupon they use, and limiting the quantity of the item that each shopper may purchase.

To lure shoppers, most stores advertise "loss leaders," such as milk or eggs sold at or below cost. Once the shopper is there, stores then hope to sell them a lot of other items with high profit margins.

Warehouse buying clubs. Warehouse buying clubs have sprouted up across the country, offering consumers who pay an annual fee of $25 or $35 huge savings on bulk items in a no-frills setting. Clubs sell all sorts of items, from appliances and tires to jewelry and books. Before buying, consumers should ask themselves a few questions: Do I have a lot of storage room in my pantry? Do I have plenty of refrigerator and freezer space to keep food fresh? Do I have a large family or friends to share bulk purchases with?

Those who answer "yes" to those questions can save a lot of money shopping at a warehouse club—but they should keep these points in mind:

- Unless they do a large amount of food shopping or plan to buy other non-food items at warehouse clubs, consumers may need to join only one club to make sure they save money beyond the cost of the membership fee.
- Because the warehouse atmosphere can encourage impulse purchases, shoppers have to work hard to stick to their shopping lists.

- If consumers want to buy something that's not on their lists, they should be sure that they can store or use it before it spoils. A five-pound bag of rice is a better long-term investment than a five-pound block of Swiss cheese.
- As always, shoppers need to know prices—a retail supermarket's store-brand items may be cheaper, on a unit-price basis, than the name-brand product sold at a warehouse store.

Supermarket "member" cards. Some supermarkets give free identification or check-cashing cards connected to frequent-shopper programs. Typically, these programs, similar to airline frequent-flier programs, reward loyal shoppers with discounts, prizes, and special services based on the volume of their purchases. Just remember that these programs track your purchases and demographics, and then can target you with specific advertising and promotions based on your buying habits. Shoppers should discuss any privacy concerns with the store manager *before* signing up.

Food Safety

Reports of outbreaks of food poisoning come all too frequently these days. Four children died and 144 were hospitalized after eating undercooked fast-food hamburgers in 1993. In 1997, thousands of Americans got sick from eating tainted raspberries, as did many children from drinking apple juice. Millions of pounds of ground beef that might have been contaminated with *E. coli* bacteria were recalled in

1997, the largest meat recall in history, after 17 people got sick.

As if these incidents weren't scary enough, they tell only part of the story. Public health officials estimate that thousands of people die each year from bacteria, viruses, and parasites in their food—and millions become ill. Exact figures do not exist: fewer than 5% of food-poisoning cases are recognized and reported. Here are the major foodborne bugs: Campylobacter, found in raw and undercooked poultry, unpasteurized milk, and untreated water, is the leading cause of food poisoning nationwide—responsible for 1.1 to 7 million infections and up to 1,000 deaths per year; salmonella, found in poultry, meat, eggs, dairy products, seafood and fresh produce, sickens 800,000 to 4 million people per year and kills up to 2,000; E. coli 0157:H7, found in raw and undercooked ground beef, unpasteurized milk, lettuce, untreated water, and minimally processed juices, infects 25,000 people each year and kills about 200.

Contamination is usually tasteless and odorless, and, contrary to what you might think, no less common in organic items than in mass-produced brands. But how common is it? When *Consumer Reports* tested 1,000 whole fresh chickens bought in 36 cities over a five-week period in 1997, including leading brands, premium brands (including "free-range"), and supermarket brands, they found campylobacter in 63% of the chickens, salmonella in 16%, and 8% had both. Just 29% were free of both. These levels are slightly below the levels the U.S. Department of Agriculture found during studies in 1994 and 1995.

When foods are cooked and handled properly, these bugs pose no problem at the dining table. However, research shows that people either don't know about or don't bother with easy food safety. When researchers at the University of Arizona studied people's homes, they found that bacteria levels were highest in the kitchen, higher even than in the bathroom. It turned out the toilet seat was cleaner than the counter.

The U.S. government's new inspection system should make the food supply safer, but there are several flaws. A serious one: there is no requirement that chicken producers test for campylobacter. "People have to eat—but they don't have to get sick or die while doing it," says the FDA. To be on the safe side, handle all raw meat, poultry, seafood, fruits and vegetables as though they contain disease-causing bacteria. Here are some ways to minimize your risk of food poisoning.

■ *Butcher blocks.* Pick well-wrapped packages from the bottom of the case, where it is likely to be coldest. Pick a "sell date" days away. Don't let raw meat or poultry or its germs come in contact with other food. Keep meat away from other foods, and wash cutting boards, plates and utensils used to prepare meat with hot, soapy water before reusing them. Marinate in the refrigerator. Thaw in the refrigerator or in a microwave. Use kitchen sponges and towels with care—you may want to

DANGEROUS DISHES

It's not only the foods you eat, it's also the dishes you eat your food *on* that affect your health. Many dishes are made with lead, a toxic substance that can leach from your plate into your food and your body. There is no safe level of lead.

Lead is a highly toxic metal that people absorb through eating and breathing. Lead accumulates in the body and can be stored in the bones for more than 20 years. Exposure can cause brain damage and impair IQ levels, short-term memory, and the ability to concentrate. Lead can damage every system in the body, including the immune system. Exposed adults can suffer from hypertension, reproductive complications, and loss of neuromuscular control. In extreme cases, lead poisoning can cause death.

Kids at risk. People of all ages are affected, but owing to their smaller size, children and fetuses are at the most risk because even small amounts of lead can harm them. A fetus exposed to low levels of lead in the mother's blood can suffer from impaired development and low birth weight. Children and adults—especially women who are or who expect to become pregnant—should minimize their exposure to lead.

Lead leachers. Some dish manufacturers add lead to some glazes, paints, and decals to create a shiny look and clear colors. The use of tiny amounts of lead is not necessarily hazardous if manufacturers properly formulate the glazes, paints, and decals; apply them correctly; and then fire the dishes at the right temperature for the right amount of time. Dishes can leach lead regardless of their color, where they were made, or how expensive they are. Tiffany and Company recalled lead-leaching plates that cost more than $1,200 for a single place setting. Unless a manufacturer tells you that it used only lead-free glazes, paints, and decals on its dishes, you can't be certain about the presence of lead without testing.

Be most concerned with the dishes you use most often—your coffee mug or a bowl used to store leftovers. Even though you can't tell whether lead is leaching just by looking—dishes must be tested to know for certain—there are some signs of higher-risk dishes that call for extra attention:

- Ceramic ware with a corroded glaze, or a dusty, chalky gray residue after you've washed it.
- Old china, made before the danger of lead was formally recognized by the FDA.
- Handcrafted china and pottery, whether made in this country or imported.

- Highly decorated surfaces, especially inside a bowl or in the center of a plate, where there is contact with food.
- Decorations applied on top of the glaze instead of beneath it (you may be able to check by running your fingers over the decorations or holding the item at an angle to the light).

If you're unsure about a certain item:

- Don't use it to heat food or drinks in conventional or microwave ovens.
- Don't use it to store acidic food or drinks.
- Serve only dry, acid-neutral food (such as pretzels) in it.
- Save it for special occasions.

Store food only in glass, plastic, or stainless steel containers. And minimize the three factors that cause lead to leach into food: length of contact time, heat, and acidity of the food. Acidic foods include fruit products; salsa; spaghetti sauce; such drinks as coffee, tea, and cola-type sodas; and salad dressings and sauces made with vinegar, wine, or lemon juice.

Testing your dishes. Consider testing your dishes with a home testing kit. These simple tests are useful for identifying items that leach at least a minimum amount of lead into food. The kits cost between $20 and $30, and use different methods to test

as few as eight or as many as 100 items. See the **HELP** section at the end of this chapter for the names and phone numbers of some companies that make them.

If you use a home test and find lead leaching from your dishes, it's best to stop using the dishes for food. If your newly purchased dishes release lead, report it to your local FDA office (listed under the Department of Health and Human Services in the government section of your phone book), or call FDA headquarters at (301) 443-3170.

Buying new dishes. Plain glass (not crystal) dishes are lead-free, and plain stoneware dishes are almost always made without added lead.

If you're not buying glass dishes, your best bet is to call or write ceramic manufacturers and ask whether all the pieces from the pattern can be sold without a special warning under the California Proposition 65 law. That proconsumer, proenvironment law requires manufacturers to either meet a much stricter lead-leaching standard than the FDA's, or to put a warning on the product. Don't be snowed by manufacturers who refer to the California Tableware Safety law, which basically mirrors the FDA's looser standards. Ask about a specific pattern to get the clearest answer.

use paper towel after working with raw meat or poultry. Cook beef, veal, and lamb to at least 145 degrees F and cook ground meat and pork to 160 degrees F. Cook poultry to 180 degrees F.

- *Dairy dos.* Do not drink unpasteurized milk. Take milk and other dairy items from the back of the dairy case at the supermarket. Keep your refrigerator below 40 degrees F and your freezer below 0 degrees F. Cook eggs until the white is no longer runny and the yolk has begun to firm up.

- *Something fishy.* Cook fish until it flakes with a fork. Cook shrimp until they turn pink and opaque; cook oysters until plump (about five minutes) and avoid raw oysters. Steam clams and mussels until the shells open, probably five to 10 minutes. Keep seafood salads cold until you serve them.

- *Produce protection.* No grabbing grapes to snack on while you shop (they haven't been washed and often have heavy pesticide residue). Wash *all* produce, including citrus fruits and melons—it will help remove germs that can migrate from the skin to the fleshy parts when you slice through a contaminated rind. Scrub with a vegetable brush where appropriate. Discard outer leaves of lettuce and other greens. Wash prepackaged greens, even if the label says they have been washed. Do not drink unpasteurized apple juice.

- *Leftovers.* Refrigerate or freeze leftovers within two hours of cooking. Store in shallow containers for quick cooling. Use them up within three to five days.

- *Sanitize for sanity.* Periodically sanitize cutting boards, knives, pots, and pans in a solution made of 1 quart water and 1 teaspoon chlorine bleach. Then rinse thoroughly with water. Keep in mind that antibacterial soaps and rinses on the market have not been approved by the federal government as effective in eliminating harmful bacteria.

For more information about food safety, go to www.foodsafety.org, or contact the USDA Meat and Poultry hotline (800) 535-4555, or visit the USDA Web site at www.usda.gov. You can also call the FDA Food Information and Seafood Hotline at (800) 332-4010, or go to www.fda.gov.

WHAT TO WATCH OUT FOR

Scanner Scams and the Case for Item Pricing

What if every time you went grocery shopping, you had to play *The Price Is Right* because there were no prices marked on any of the bottles, boxes, cans, or containers in the entire store? Actually, only a few states and localities—including California, Massachusetts, and Michigan—require stores to individually price most items.

Nearly all prepackaged food products have bar codes, also known as universal product codes (UPC), on their labels. Those codes are made up of a grid of lines representing a 10-digit number that's read by electronic scanners at the checkout counter. The scanner

BAD HABITS

Percentage of Americans who:

Eat raw or undercooked eggs	50%
Eat undercooked hamburger	23%
Eat raw clams or oysters	17%
Don't wash cutting boards after cutting raw meat or poultry	26%

Source: Food and Drug Administration, 1997

identifies the product and charges whatever amount the store has programmed the scanner to charge.

But unless the product also has a price marked *on the package,* known as an "item price," shoppers need the memory of an elephant to verify the price charged at the checkout counter. Comparison shopping becomes very difficult, since shelf-pricing is often out-of-date and misplaced. And then keeping within a budget takes a mathematical genius—or a handy calculator.

To err is not as common as shoppers might expect, but there can be mistakes at the checkout counter. In a 1996 study by the Federal Trade Commission, the National Institute of Standards and Technology, and several state attorneys general, grocery store consumers were charged the wrong price 3.5% of the time. And the study confirmed consumers' worst fear: they are more likely to be overcharged than

undercharged at the grocery store. The store benefited almost 2% of the time, while the consumer came out ahead 1.5% of the time.

Sale items present the overwhelming majority of errors. A New York City survey found that one in 10 times an item was supposedly on sale, the scanner charged the regular price.

To deter such problems, Michigan adopted a law requiring retailers to pay consumers who are overcharged 10 times the difference in price, requiring a minimum recovery of $1 and a maximum of $5. The law also provides that if the bounty is not offered to the consumer, the shopper can sue the store for the amount of the overcharge or $250, whichever is larger, and $300 in attorney's fees.

The Claim Game

To clear up confusing and sometimes misleading health claims on food labels, Congress passed a law in 1990 requiring the Food and Drug Administration (FDA) to strengthen its food-labeling regulations. The USDA, which regulates meat and poultry, joined with the FDA in requiring new food *labels* to provide shoppers with more accurate and relevant information. But there's still a loophole—some food *advertisements* continue to make product claims that could not be made on labels.

The Federal Trade Commission (FTC) is supposed to make sure that advertisements are neither deceptive nor misleading, but the FTC has a spotty record of acting against such food ads. And even though the FTC embraced the *principles* of consistent rules in 1994 when the agency announced an advertising enforcement policy on health and nutrition claims, the weak policy still allows claims that the FDA and the USDA do not permit on labels. Look to food labels—not ads—for reliable nutrition information.

Short-weighting and Downsizing

When the box says it contains 24 ounces but inside there are only 22, the company has short-weighted the package by almost 10%. Or when you ask the deli man for half a pound of ham and end up with a little less, owing to an inaccurate scale or to his not deducting the weight of the wrapping, that too is short-weighting. Every state, and many counties and cities, employs inspectors who check on the accuracy of packaged goods and grocery-store measuring devices, and these inspectors have cited large food companies and small independent grocers alike for short-weighting.

A 20-state enforcement sweep checking milk and juice containers in 1997 found the odds to be almost 50-50 that shoppers would get less than they paid for; 41% of the milk cartons, juice containers, and dairy products inspected contained 1% to 6% less than the package promised.

If it happens to you, complain to either your grocer or the producer of the product or to your local consumer officials.

Some food manufacturers engage in deceptive "downsizing"—selling food in packages that look and cost the same as the old ones but that really have less inside. Star Kist, for example, shrunk the contents of its tuna cans from 6.5 to 6 ounces but continued to charge the same price—which was, in effect, a quiet 7% price increase. Beech-Nut Nutritional Corp. downsized its Beech-Nut Stage 1 and Stage 2 baby foods from 4.5 to 4 ounces. Kal Kan Pedigree dog food is now sold in 13.25-ounce containers, 5% smaller than the former 14-ounce size.

None of the companies downsized their prices to match. To fight this economic deception, keep an eye on the content disclosure, which is required by law, and use unit-pricing calculations to compare among brands.

THE $MARTER CONSUMER

Supermarket Strategies

The Golden Rule: Comparison shop. The first question to ask yourself is whether the store where you shop gives the best value for your dollars. It's easy to check—make a list of the items you frequently buy, then go to your usual supermarket and at least one other grocery store, and compare. Chances are you'll find a difference of a few percent on several items, which can add up to many dollars over time.

Keep a running shopping list. Jot down items you're running low on to make your shopping more efficient. You'll spend less time in the aisles thinking about what you may need or what you forgot. A list will also help you avoid impulse purchases, which are often costly and unhealthful. And following a list will help you avoid time-consuming extra shopping trips, which can really bust your budget if you opt for a convenience store where prices are high.

Check out unit prices. A unit price is the cost for a small unit of measure, such as an ounce, that's used to compare the cost of differently priced items in differently sized containers. Some states and cities require grocery stores to put tags listing unit prices on the shelves beneath items. If your supermarket offers you this calculation, you'll easily find the best buys. Otherwise, a calculator will come in handy.

Usually, but not always, the larger the container, the lower the unit price. According to Jewel Supermarket's unit price tags in Munster, Indiana, a box of twelve 1-ounce packets of instant oatmeal costs $4.12 per pound, while an 18-ounce carton of loose oatmeal costs $1.68 per pound—and a 42-ounce carton costs only $1.25 per pound.

Unit pricing also helps you to compare similar items made by different manufacturers, who often package products in slightly different sizes, making cost comparisons tricky. Buy the food that sells for the least amount per unit, unless you know that the quality is poor or that you don't need or can't store a large amount.

Beware of so-called "specials." Food displayed in a store as "featured" or "new"—such as cookies, soda pop, paper towels—aren't necessarily bargains but may simply be promotions of regularly priced items—or products approaching their "sell by" dates. To save money, buy only the special items you know you will use. When items you use are on sale, stock up. And don't be lured into buying something you really don't need just because a sign says "Limit Four Per Customer"— consumers tend to buy more when the stores impose a limit.

Try no-frills and store brands. Remember, it's worth checking out alternatives to the priciest products. Buying items that are not nationally advertised but that are identical—or at least close enough—can save you a lot of money. At that Jewel Supermarket in Indiana, a gallon of Ocean Spray cranberry juice cocktail costs $3.59, 13% more than the Jewel Brand that costs $3.09, and 64% more than the store's no-frills Econo Buy brand that costs $2.19. Econo Buy saltines, toaster pastries, and pretzel twists, for example, cost only half the price of the national brand-name products Nabisco Premium saltines, Kellogg's Pop Tarts, and Frito Lay Rold Gold pretzels.

Staples such as no-name frozen vegetables or canned beans are often just as good as big-name products. Compare ingredients when they are listed on labels to determine how similar products are—sometimes, they're identical. Other items, such as dish soap, however, may be noticeably inferior. Still, take a chance; buy and try lower-cost foods—if you like them, your small "investment" will pay a high rate of return.

Scan the scanner. Scanners are fast, but you've got time on your side. If your store doesn't item-price, write on your shopping list the prices that you should be charged. Try to check the register as the cashier rings up your items, but a surer bet is to check the receipt against the items you bought when you get home. On your next visit, show any discrepancies to the store manager, who will at least correct your charge and—at some stores—may even give you the item for free.

Stick to food. Unless you know the prices are low, don't buy such health and beauty items as aspirin and toothpaste in grocery stores. You'll usually save money buying non-food items in a discount or drugstore.

Take rain checks. If your store doesn't have the advertised special you want, ask for a rain check. In some cities and states, you have a legal right to one. When the item is back in stock, you can buy it for the sale price.

Follow freshness dating. Some manufacturers put dates on food packages to ensure that their foods are not sold or eaten after they're stale or spoiled. Always buy food—especially dairy products—with the most distant date. After the date passes, the food may still be safe to eat, but be wary. And when in doubt, throw it out.

An "expiration" date indicates when the product should be thrown away. A "sell by" date is the last day a product should be sold. A "best if used by" date tells you when you can expect the quality to be at its peak.

Enjoy fresh produce. Everyone agrees that Americans need to eat more fresh fruits and vegetables—and to avoid dangerous pesticides. Yet much of the produce we buy has been treated with pesticides and coated with wax. Follow these tips to maximize the health benefits of a diet rich in fresh fruits and vegetables while minimizing your exposure to pesticides.

■ Buy local produce in season. It's easiest to avoid pesticides and waxes when you buy recently harvested produce from local farmers—particularly if you buy directly from them. Out-of-season produce may be imported and may contain pesticides that are restricted in the United States.

■ Buy produce that is organic, transitional, or grown under integrated pest management (IPM). Like organic fruits and vegetables, transitional produce may also be grown without synthetic pesticides, but on land where pesticides have been used too recently for the produce to be considered organic. To be sure, ask the grower or grocer what he or she means by "transitional."

Farmers who employ IPM minimize pesticide use through a variety of techniques, such as monitoring insect populations, using plants resistant to insects and disease, and

According to the *Today* show's food-shopping expert, Phil Lempert, the worst times to go food-shopping are afternoons between 4 PM and 7 PM, Sundays, Saturdays, Memorial Day weekend, the Fourth of July, Labor Day weekend, Thanksgiving Eve, the day after Thanksgiving, Christmas Eve, and the day after a major disaster (snowstorm, hurricane, earthquake). That leaves plenty of good, if less convenient, times.

releasing beneficial insects—like ladybugs and praying mantises—that eat pests on crops.

■ Buy unwaxed produce whenever possible. Waxes often seal in pesticides, and they can't be washed off—you have to peel the produce. According to a report by the New York State Attorney General's office, 85% of non-leafy produce sold in the United States is waxed. Some waxes are applied in a fine mist; even a peach that feels fuzzy can be sealed with wax. Ask your grocer to sell unwaxed produce.

■ Wash thoroughly or peel produce. To minimize your risk of eating pesticides on fruits and vegetables, wash all produce well in a pot of water with a drop of mild dishwashing detergent and rinse thoroughly.

Cherries, grapes, strawberries, cauliflower, green beans, lettuce, potatoes, sweet potatoes, and carrots are likely to have the highest levels of pesticide residue. Peel any non-organic fruit or vegetable, with an obvious wax coating; discard the outer leaves of leafy vegetables, such as cabbage and lettuce and the leaves on celery; and don't worry about wax on produce you peel anyway, such as bananas, melons, winter squash, and citrus fruit.

Seek out alternative grocery stores. If you're unhappy with the supermarkets near you—and even if you're not—look into other options. Farmers' markets, specialty grocery stores, and quality butchers sell assortments of food you may not see even at the largest supermarkets: freshly picked produce, ethnic items, organically grown foods, and high-quality meat, poultry, and fish. Prices may be competitive, or you may find that the products are worth the extra money. Also, check out whether there's a food cooperative nearby. Co-ops sometimes offer members great prices and hard-to-find items in exchange for dues, labor, or both.

Read and decode food labels. Why? To help choose foods that make up a healthful diet. Thanks to the revised nutrition label law, making healthy food choices has never been easier. Nearly every food sold in grocery stores must have a nutrition label and an ingredients list. And words such as "low fat" and "lite" can only be used if they describe a food that meets legal standards set by the federal government.

DAILY VALUES

To help consumers use food labels to plan a healthy diet, the FDA established a new term, *daily value*. These DV's are not exactly recommended intakes—use them as reference points for "average" adult diets.

■ Daily values are based on a 2,000-calories-a-day diet for adults and children over four years old for fat, saturated fat, cholesterol, total carbohydrates, fiber, sodium, and potassium.
■ The daily value for protein does not apply to certain populations for whom the government has established the following daily intakes: 16 grams for children one to four years old; 14 grams for infants under one year old; 60 grams for pregnant women; and 65 grams for nursing mothers.
■ Daily values for all other nutrients are based on the National Academy of Sciences' Recommended Dietary Allowances.

Food Component/ Nutrient	Daily Value
Fat	65 g
Saturated fat	20 g
Cholesterol	300 mg
Total carbohydrate	300 g
Fiber	25 g
Sodium	2,400 mg
Potassium	3,500 mg
Protein	50 g
Vitamin A	5,000 IU
Vitamin C	60 mg
Thiamin	1.5 mg
Riboflavin	1.7 mg
Niacin	20 mg
Calcium	1 g
Iron	18 mg
Vitamin D	400 IU
Vitamin E	30 IU
Vitamin B6	2 mg
Folic acid	0.4 mg
Vitamin B12	6 mcg
Phosphorus	1 g
Iodine	150 mcg
Magnesium	400 mg
Zinc	15 mg
Copper	2 mg
Biotin	0.3 mg
Pantothenic acid	10 mg

Source: *FDA Consumer*

Here are the established definitions for common words found on food labels. The words all pertain to one serving of the food. Key to understanding the terms is the concept of *daily values,* which was created by the FDA to provide a simplified interpretation of what a person eating a 2,000-calories-per-day diet should ideally aim for.

Daily values set maximum limits for fat and cholesterol, and minimum goals for essential vitamins and nutrients.

- *Free.* These foods can contain only a trivial amount of the nutrient. For example, "fat-free" and "sugar-free" foods can contain no more than a half-gram per serving; "calorie-free" means fewer than 5 calories per serving.
- *Low.* Foods with this term can be eaten frequently without exceeding the daily values. "Low fat" has 3 grams of fat or less; "low saturated fat" has 1 gram or less; "low sodium" has less than 140 mg; "very low sodium" has less than 20 mg; "low cholesterol" has less than 20 mg cholesterol; and "low calorie" has 40 calories or less per serving.
- *Lean* and *extra lean.* Used to describe the fat content of cheese, meat, poultry, and seafood. "Lean" means less than 10 grams fat, less than 4 grams saturated fat, and less than 95 mg cholesterol per serving; while "extra lean" means less than 5 grams fat, less than 2 grams saturated fat, and less than 95 mg cholesterol.
- *High.* Used when foods contain 20% or more of a daily value of a nutrient, as in "High fiber."
- *Reduced* and *less.* Generally, these foods have 25% less of a nutrient or calories than a comparable reference food; examples include "reduced-calorie salad dressing" or "less fat."
- *Light.* Basically, either one-third fewer calories or no more than one-half the fat (or no more than one-half the sodium) of the reference food. If "light" refers to texture or color, the label must say so, as in "light brown sugar" or "light and fluffy."
- *More.* These foods contain at least 10% more of the daily value of a nutrient than the reference food does, as in "more iron."

Understand the health claims. The government allows health claims on labels in instances when it has determined that the scientific community is in agreement on the relationship between particular nutrients and disease. Some examples:

- To make health claims about fat and heart disease, foods must be low in fat, saturated fat, and cholesterol.
- Food products that make favorable health claims regarding blood pressure and sodium must be low in sodium.
- To make claims about being cancer-fighting, foods must be low in fat and a good source, without fortification, of at least one of the following: dietary fiber or vitamins A or C.
- To make favorable health claims pertaining to heart disease, foods must be low in fat, saturated fat, and cholesterol *and* contain at least six-tenths gram soluble fiber, without fortification.

Make the grade. The grading system for produce, dairy products, meat, and poultry does *not* refer to nutritional quality. The voluntary grading information relates to any of the following characteristics: size, uniformity, smoothness, texture, and appearance. In the case of milk and dairy products, Grade A refers to the level of sanitary processing standards.

17

MAKING SENSE OF NUTRITION FACTS

Serving size. *If you plan to eat the amount listed as the serving size, then simply read the rest of the information. If you eat twice the amount, double all the rest of the information, including calories, fat, and vitamins.*

Calories. *Generally, women, the elderly, and less active people need fewer calories to maintain their weight than men, younger adults, and active folks. A 5'4", 138-pound active woman needs about 2,200 calories daily, while a 5'10", 174-pound active man needs about 2,900 calories.*

Calories from fat. *Keep it low. Each gram of fat equals 9 calories. You can multiply the grams of fat in a food by 9 and divide the total fat calories into the total calories to stay below the maximum of 30% recommended by the federal government—or better yet, the 20% many health advocates advise.*

Total fat. *Most Americans eat too much fat, which contributes to obesity and disease. Recommended maximum* **total fat** *intake for a 2,000-calorie-a-day diet is 65 grams, of which no more than 20 grams should be saturated fat. Saturated fat is the worst kind of fat, since it can raise your blood cholesterol level. Saturated fats—butter, lard, coconut oil, etc.—are solid at room temperature; better-for-you fats like olive, corn, and canola oils are liquid.*

Cholesterol. *Found only in animal products, such as meat, poultry, fish, dairy products, and eggs. Too much contributes to heart disease; try not to eat more than 300 mg a day.*

Sodium. *Another excess in most people's diets. Keep your intake below 2,400 mg a day. Eating too much salt can lead to high blood pressure.*

Total carbohydrate. *The basis of a sound diet is plenty of carbohydrates, such as whole grains, bread, potatoes, fruits, and vegetables. But when you scan for the number of "total carbohydrate," beware—you wouldn't want most of your "carbs" to come from sugars. Read both the total grams of carbohydrates and the grams of sugar. Also, check the dietary fiber count—an average goal is at least 25 g a day. Aim for 11.5 g per 1,000 calories. Eating adequate amounts of fiber can reduce your risk of heart disease and cancer.*

Protein. *Chances are you eat a lot more protein than you need. Unless you eat a very restricted diet, don't worry about getting enough.*

Vitamins and minerals. *Eat a variety of foods to get enough of what you need. Supplement pills and powders can't compensate for a poor diet.*

Daily values. *Daily values are an interpretation of what levels of nutrients a person eating 2,000 calories a day should aim for. Use the daily values as a guide to figure out if a food is a good—or bad—source of a nutrient. Aim for low daily values for fat, saturated fat, cholesterol and sodium. Choose high daily values for total carbohydrate, dietary fiber, vitamins, and minerals.*

Nutrition Facts

Serving Size 1 cup (228g)
Servings Per Container 2

Amount Per Serving

Calories 260   Calories from Fat 120

	% Daily Value*
Total Fat 13g	**20 %**
Saturated Fat 5g	**25 %**
Cholesterol 30mg	**10 %**
Sodium 660 mg	**28 %**
Total Carbohydrate 31g	**10 %**
Dietary Fiber 0g	**0 %**
Sugars 5g	
Protein 5g	

Vitamin A 4%	•	Vitamin C 2%
Calcium 15%	•	Iron 4%

*Percent Daily Values are based on a 2,000 calorie diet. Your daily values may be higher or lower depending on your calorie needs:

	Calories:	2,000	2,500
Total Fat	Less than	65g	80g
Sat Fat	Less than	20g	25g
Cholesterol	Less than	300mg	300mg
Sodium	Less than	2,400mg	2,400mg
Total Carbohydrate		300g	375g
Dietary Fiber		25g	30g

Calories per gram:
Fat 9 • Carbohydrate 4 • Protein 4

GOOD FATS, BAD FATS

Switching from butter to margarine may not be the health bargain it was once made out to be. In 1994, Harvard researchers reported that margarine and other foods with hydrogenated vegetable oils that contain trans fatty acids could actually be *worse* for you than the saturated fat in butter and meat. Trans fatty acids are formed when more healthful liquid vegetable oils are processed to make them solid at room temperature.

Diets high in trans fatty acids may be responsible for 30,000 heart disease deaths in the United States each year. What should you do? Try to accustom your taste buds to food with less fat of any kind, and when you do eat fat, stick to healthier fats, ones that are liquid at room temperature, such as olive, canola, or corn oil.

Ingredient listings. Federal law requires food manufacturers to list ingredients in descending order of predominance by weight. So, the earlier an ingredient is listed, the more of it is in the food.

Since the FDA improved its requirements, ingredient listings have become more common and more thorough. Many foods that were previously exempt must now disclose their contents. Certified Food, Drug and Cosmetic (FD&C) color additives must be listed by name (such as FD&C blue #1). And to help consumers who cannot easily digest dairy products, a milk derivative called caseinate must be listed on foods claiming to be non-dairy, such as coffee lighteners.

Serving sizes. The FDA has established uniform serving sizes that more nearly approximate the portions people eat—instead of the Lilliputian serving sizes that manufacturers used to cite in order to make their food look low-calorie and low-fat. Uniform serving sizes also make product comparisons easier. Another bonus of uniformity: Health claims and nutrient descriptions are more reliable.

How to Complain

Return spoiled food or any product you believe is short-weighted or expired to the store manager. In addition, you may want to report short-weighting and recurrent scanner overcharges to your state or local weights-and-measures department (sometimes called an agriculture, a markets, or a consumer-affairs department).

Report packaged food that is contaminated or spoiled to your local FDA office. You'll need as much of the packaging as possible, since the FDA requires certain coded information. A letter to the company is also a good idea. Products inspected by the USDA include eggs, meat, and poultry. Report any problems to the USDA office nearest you. Check the government office listing in your telephone book to find your local branch office.

H E L P

■ **A leading advocate** for good nutrition and health is the Center for Science in the Public Interest (CSPI), which publishes *Nutrition Action Healthletter*, a consumer-friendly newsletter filled with food facts, research updates, practical advice, product reviews, and recipes. Improving on the USDA food pyramid, which is really a triangle, CSPI produced a three-dimensional version that separates food into three categories: those suitable for eating anytime, sometimes, and seldom. To order a CSPI pyramid or to subscribe to the newsletter, write to CSPI at 1875 Connecticut Avenue NW, Suite 300, Washington, DC 20009-5728, call (202) 332-9110, or e-mail cspi@cspinet.org.

■ **Public Voice for Food and Health** Policy, a research and advocacy organization, promotes seafood safety, sustainable agriculture, pesticide reduction, healthier school lunches, and consumer education. For free tips on seafood safety, a booklet on nutrition labeling, or a list of publications, send a self-addressed, stamped envelope to Public Voice at 1101 14th Street NW, Suite 710, Washington, DC 20005, (202) 371-1840. Their Web site is at www.publicvoice.org/pvoice.html.

■ **To learn how to protect yourself** against pesticides, bacteria, and other hidden hazards in food, read *Safe Food: Eating Wisely in a Risky World,* by Michael F. Jacobson, PhD, Lisa Y. Lefferts, and Anne Witte Garland (Living Planet Press: Los Angeles, 1991).

■ **The FDA publishes useful pamphlets** on food labels, food safety, and other topics. To order, write to FDA, 5600 Fishers Lane, room 16-59, Rockville, MD 20857; call (800) 532-4440, or go to www.fda.gov.

■ **Direct your questions about the re-** lationship between nutrition and cancer to the American Institute for Cancer Re-

search Nutrition Hot Line, which operates Monday through Thursday from 9 AM to 10 PM EST, and Fridays from 9 AM to 6 PM: (800) 843-8114. Ask for a list of free brochures.

■ **The American Dietetic Associa-** tion sponsors the National Center for Nutrition and Dietetics Consumer Nutrition Hot Line, where registered dietitians answer calls Monday through Friday, 9 AM to 4 PM CST. Call (900) 225-5267; the call costs $1.95 for the first minute and 95 cents for each additional minute. You can also go to www.eatright.org.

■ **The USDA Meat and Poultry Hot** Line operates Monday through Friday from 10 AM to 2 PM EST. (800) 535-4555. Ask about free USDA brochures.

■ **For information and helpful advice** on good nutrition, equipping an efficient kitchen, and cooking healthful meals, read *Jane Brody's Good Food Book*, by Jane E. Brody (New York: Bantam Books, 1987), $16.95.

■ **To learn the location of the food** co-operative nearest you, write Co-op Directory Services, 919 21st Avenue F, Minneapolis, MN 55404. For a directory of over 300 food co-ops across the country, send $8.50 to National Co-op Directory, Box 57, Randolph, VT 05060. Get information on setting up a grocery co-op by writing to the National Co-operative Business Association, 1401 New York Avenue NW, Suite 1100, Washington, DC 20005, or by calling (202) 638-6222.

■ **Read what parents must know** about their children's diets and learn ways to get your kids to eat more healthfully in *What Are We Feeding Our Kids?*, by Michael F. Jacobson, PhD, and Bruce Maxwell (New York: Workman, 1994).

Continued on next page

Continued from previous page

■ **Learn how to select and store food** for maximum enjoyment, value, and safety in *Keeping Food Fresh,* by Janet Bailey (New York: Harper & Row, 1993).

■ **Find answers to nearly every nutri**tion question in *Total Nutrition: The Only Guide You'll Ever Need,* edited by Victor Herbert, MD, FACP and Genell J. Subak-Sharpe, MS (New York: St. Martin's Press, 1995), available in paperback for $16.95.

■ **For a free brochure on home test**ing tips for lead in water, paint, dust, soil, and ceramics, call "Get the Lead Out," a lead testing service sponsored by the Environmental Law Foundation (ELF) at (510) 208-4557.

■ **To get the Food and Drug Adminis**tration's free pamphlet on lead in ceramic ware, crystal, wine bottles, and cans, "What You Should Know About Lead in China Dishes," call (800) 532-4440 or go to www.fda.gov.

■ **All children between the ages of six** months and six years should be tested for lead at least annually. State and local health departments administer lead poisoning prevention programs and provide free educational materials and information on where to have children screened for elevated blood lead levels.

■ **For a list of ceramic ware pat**terns that meet the strict California Proposition 65 standards, send a self-addressed, stamped business-size envelope to Lead-Safe China Brochure, Environmental Defense Fund, P.O. Box 96969, Washington, DC 20090-6969

■ **For "Dishing Up Lead: A Guide** to Poisonous Ceramics," a full-color brochure showing patterns of dishes likely to leach excessive lead, send a self-addressed, stamped envelope (at least 6" by 10½") to Hawaii Department of Health, Food and Drug Branch, 591 Ala Moana Boulevard, Honolulu, HI 96813.

■ **If you want to check your dishes** for their lead content, call one of these companies.

Frandon Lead Alert Kit
Pace Environs, Inc.
(800) 359-9000

Lead Inspector
Michigan Ceramic Supplies
(800) 860-2332

LeadCheck Swabs
HybriVet Systems, Inc.
(800) 262-LEAD

LeadCheck Swabs,
Carolina Environment
(800) 448-LEAD

CHAPTER 2

FAST-FOOD OUTLETS

What Are You Getting Into and What's Getting Into You?

There was a time when most of the selection in fast-food restaurants would have warranted a Surgeon General's warning that "This Food May Be Hazardous to Your Health." In recent years, however, many fast-food restaurants have added healthier options to their menus. Subway's extensive "Light Menu" is a notable standout. Nonetheless, the bad stuff still lurks. Jack in the Box offers a low-fat, high-carbohydrate Chicken Teriyaki Bowl on the same menu as its Bacon Ultimate Cheeseburger, which contains more fat than most people should eat in an entire day.

But such contrasts aren't always that obvious. A grilled chicken sandwich may seem healthy, and probably is by itself, but when it comes under a sheen of mayonnaise, your heart and waist would be better off with a small burger. Sometimes it's virtually impossible to tell the good choices from the bad. Bet you didn't know that a single packet of salad dressing can have as much fat as a full order of fries.

Most fast food is fattier than ever. Ads brag about double and (triple!) meat burgers, extra-large fries, and jumbo sodas, all of which means more fat and cholesterol, more grease and sodium, and more empty or sugar-laden calories for those of us who choose to eat out. Here are some fast-food facts to digest.

THE BASICS

The $103-billion-a-year fast-food industry feeds a growing portion of the American appetite. About 20% of us eat at fast-food restaurants each day. And the U.S. Department of Agriculture (USDA) reports that half of every dollar we spend on restaurant food we spend on fast food. That adds up to an average of $340 a year—or almost a dollar a day—on fast food.

The USDA also found that Americans get nearly half their fat and calories while eating out. Despite some laudable recent efforts, fast food still generally tends to be high in calories, fat, cholesterol, and sodium, all of which promote obesity, heart disease, high blood pressure, and cancer.

Experts continue to focus on the relationship between diet and health and have repeatedly shown that cutting back on fat and salt can lower the risk of getting or dying from these conditions. Typically, fast-food meals are loaded with fat and sodium, but few diners realize that a fish or chicken sandwich can be worse than a burger. Rather than counting every single gram of fat in your favorite foods, you'll find it easier to identify and cut back on the major sources of fat in your diet. A few simple choices can help you avoid the fat trap:

- Opting for a sourdough roll or breadstick (2 or 3 fat grams) instead of cornbread (13 fat grams) or a biscuit (12 grams) at KFC.
- Holding off on the bacon-and-cheese potato topping (with 29 grams of fat) at Carl's Jr.
- Choosing grilled chicken instead of breaded chicken for your sandwich at Wendy's saves you 13 grams of fat.

A Numbers Game?

Consumer Reports analyzed samples of fast foods to test the accuracy of the nutrition information supplied by the companies in brochures and on posters. For the most part, the companies' numbers added up. However, some chicken salads contained several more grams of fat than the companies claimed, probably because of variations in portion size or the amount of cheese. You can avoid the extra fat by removing some or all of the cheese to make sure you don't get more fat than you want.

Consumer Reports also found fudging on milk shake data. Some shakes contained more saturated fat—the kind that raises blood cholesterol levels—than the nutrition brochures state. Arby's shakes had *twice* the amount of saturated fat as the company claimed.

Even so, the nutrition information offered by fast-food chains is more likely to be accurate than that of sit-down restaurants. Standardized menus and staff training ensure uniform serving sizes and recipes.

> "*Choosing healthy fast foods is like walking through a mine field—be careful. Most are loaded with fat, salt, and sugar, which cause everything from obesity to heart attacks.*"
>
> —MICHAEL F. JACOBSON, coauthor of the *Fast-Food Guide*

Kids' Meals

Kids eat fast food four out of every five times they eat out. And one quarter of all vegetables eaten by kids are french fries, according to the National Cancer Institute. (Could this be among the reasons that the percentage of overweight and obese children has doubled since 1980?) These meals are popular because they are quick and cheap and because fast-food chains spend millions of dollars advertising on Saturday-morning television—

QUICK CHOICES: THE GOOD, THE BAD, AND THE UGLY

Item	Calories	Fat	Sodium
THE GOOD			
Carl's Jr. BBQ Chicken Sandwich	310	6 g	830 mg
Carl's Jr. Hamburger	200	8 g	500 mg
Hardee's 3 Pancakes	280	2 g	890 mg
Jack in the Box Garden Chicken Salad	200	9 g	420 mg
McDonald's Grilled Chicken Salad Deluxe	120	1.5 g	240 mg
McDonald's Hamburger	260	9 g	580 mg
Subway Roasted Chicken Breast Salad	162	4 g	693 mg
Subway Roasted Chicken Breast 6-Inch	348	6 g	978 mg
Taco Bell Light Chicken Soft Taco	180	5 g	660 mg
Wendy's Grilled Chicken Sandwich	290	7 g	720 mg
THE BAD			
Burger King Big Fish	700	41 g	980 mg
Burger King Chicken Sandwich	710	43 g	1400 mg
Burger King Whopper	640	39 g	870 mg
Carl's Jr. Catch Fish Sandwich	560	30 g	1220 mg
Carl's Jr. Santa Fe Chicken Sandwich	530	30 g	1230 mg
Hardee's Works Burger	530	30 g	1030 mg
Jack in the Box Ultimate Breakfast Sandwich	620	36 g	1800 mg
McDonald's Big Mac	560	31 g	1070 mg
Taco Bell Chicken Club Burrito	540	31 g	1290 mg
Wendy's Big Bacon Classic	640	36 g	1500 mg
THE UGLY			
Burger King Croissan'wich with Sausage, Egg, and Cheese	600	46 g	1140 mg
Burger King Double Whopper with Cheese	960	63 g	1420 mg
Carl's Jr. Double Western Bacon Cheeseburger	970	57 g	1810 mg
Hardee's Big Country Breakfast with Sausage	1000	66 g	2310 mg
Jack in the Box Bacon Ultimate Cheeseburger	1150	89 g	1770 mg
Taco Bell Taco Salad	840	52 g	1670 mg

McDonald's spent over $20 million in 1996—and in collaboration with movie studios and toy makers. Free dolls, toys, and colorful cups make kids want to "collect the entire set." Plus, business from kids means business from parents, too.

Like adults, kids should eat less fat and salt and fewer calories than they typically do. Unfortunately, kids' fast-food meals aren't made up of the most healthful offerings. Ask if you can substitute juice or protein-rich milk for sugary sodas, avoid the fried stuff, and ask for extra lettuce and tomato on sandwiches. (And don't forget, finishing their meals for them when they're too full won't do *you* any good.)

Information, Please

Since the government advises Americans to eat less fat and sodium, consumers need basic information about what's in the food they eat in order to make wise choices about their dollars and their health. Many fast-food outlets provide nutritional analyses of the food they serve; some even provide a poster close to the register to help you choose—but you may need a magnifying glass, calculator, and a master's degree in nutrition to decipher the information. Check serving sizes closely—the chart may analyze a smaller serving than you've ordered. (If information isn't available at the branch you frequent, call the restaurant's consumer relations department line, and they'll send one to you.)

Under a new federal law, words such as "light" and "low fat" on menu boards must meet the same strict federal standards that apply to packaged food. (See "Groceries" page 17, for the definitions of these and other terms.)

WHAT TO WATCH OUT FOR

If it's fried, it's fatty. Just because it's fish or chicken doesn't mean it's better than a burger. A McDonald's Filet-O-Fish sandwich has 18 grams of fat—twice as much as a hamburger (9 grams) and nearly as much as a Quarter Pounder (20 grams). Remember that fried food, no matter what kind, is bound to be loaded with fat.

"Extra crispy" chicken equals extra fatty. A KFC Original Recipe thigh is already loaded with 18 grams of fat and 250 calories. Left to fry longer, the Extra Tasty Crispy thigh soaks up an extra 7 grams of fat and another 120 calories.

Hold the dressing. Heavy dressings turn healthy salads into fat mines. Same for plain mayonnaise and tartar sauce on chicken and fish sandwiches. And a little bit goes a long way . . . on our hips, butts, and bellies. The average American woman gets more fat from salad dressing than from any other food. Remove heavy dressings from your meal or opt for FDA-defined "light" substitutes.

There aren't many sure bets. Things you might think are healthy may not be so, and a good choice at one restaurant may not be so else-

CALCULATING YOUR FAT INTAKE

The Food and Drug Administration (FDA) advises Americans to limit their fat intake to fewer than 30% of their daily calories. "Average" adults eat 2,000 calories a day, and each gram of fat yields 9 calories, so a limit of 65 grams of fat a day (about 600 calories) is sensible. Many health experts believe that 20% fat—or about 44 grams—is a better ceiling. (See "Groceries," page 18, for more information on fat and calories.)

To calculate the proportion of fat calories in food, multiply the number of fat grams times 9 (for 9 calories in each fat gram) and divide that number into the total calories. For example, a 320-calorie Dairy Queen chili dog gets 53% of its calories from fat (19 fat grams × 9 calories/gram = 171, and 171 ÷ 320 calories = 53%)—nearly *double* the recommended guideline.

If your mind's not metric, picture teaspoons of fat. One tsp. equals close to 5 grams, and that chili dog contains almost 4 tsp. of fat; the recommended limit is around 10 grams (just 2 tsp.)

where. A healthy pita filled with salad, now popular at Wendy's, isn't all that healthy when you get it filled with too much cheese, marinated meat, and oily dressing. Chicken sandwiches, usually a good choice, range from KFC's Value BBQ sandwich with 8 grams of fat and 256 calories to Burger King's hefty Chicken Sandwich, with 710 calories and almost half a day's worth of saturated fat. (See the Quick Choices chart on page 24.) And don't assume "veggie" is short for vegetarian. Wendy's recently came under fire for advertising their Veggie Pita as vegetarian because the ranch dressing it came with contained gelatin, an animal by-product. Wendy's has switched the sauce, but some other vegetarian-esque items—such as Taco Bell's Veggie Fajita—contain animal extracts as well. (The fajita was never advertised as "vegetarian.")

Save your diet, not a few pennies. Ordering meal deals—usually a sandwich, large fries, and a large drink—will land you in the deep-frying pan. A combo with a large sandwich like Burger King's Double Whopper adds up to 1,500 calories and more than a full day's recommended intake of fat. And washing it down with 32 ounces of carbonated sugar-water doesn't give your body what it needs.

Calling a burger "made for grown-ups" doesn't make it good for you. McDonald's Arch Deluxe has almost three times the fat (31 grams) of the now defunct McLean Deluxe (its only "light" burger option with 12 grams of fat) and 300 more calories than a plain hamburger. And for what? A potato roll and extra mayonnaise.

Salt watchers beware. Even fast food with reduced fat and calories usually contains high levels of sodium. Some low-fat items at Subway are especially high in sodium. A Turkey Breast six-inch sandwich has 1,403 mg, nearly 60% of the daily recommended intake. If you're cutting down on sodium, you may have to cut out fast food altogether. Except for plain vegetable salads, nearly every fast food is high in salt.

THE $MARTER CONSUMER

The trick to eating well at fast-food restaurants is knowing how to spot the healthiest food. Choose restaurants that offer more control over your meal. Subway sandwiches are made right in front of you as you select fillings, and even Burger King lets you "have it your way." *Use* these options to create a healthier meal.

Following these general guidelines will help you eat meals that fit into the recommended lower fat diet you and your family should strive for.

■ Seek out innovative fast-food restaurants that feature more healthful food, such as grilled, skinless chicken and baked fish.

■ Skip the superlatives, such as "super," "extra," "grande," "big," "jumbo," "double," or "supreme." As a rule, smaller is always better.

■ Order baked, roasted, or broiled chicken if it's offered. Several fast-food chicken restaurants now sell rotisserie-roasted chicken. To avoid too much fat and salt in fried chicken, your best bet is to peel off and discard the fried coating as well as the skin.

■ Extras usually add up to more calories, sodium, and fat. Keep the bacon, double cheese, and special sauce off your sandwich. Instead, ask for extra lettuce, tomato, and onion for their flavor and nutrients.

■ Just because you crave a cheeseburger doesn't mean you have to get the jumbo triple deluxe with extra bacon. Order a regular-sized burger to satisfy your craving. If you're still hungry, order another. It takes more than three McDonald's hamburgers with 9 fat grams apiece to match the 31 fat grams in one Big Mac.

■ Choose side salads and plain baked potatoes instead of french fries and onion rings, but skip the sour cream, cheese, bacon bits, and heavy dressing.

■ Skip the saltiest and fattiest items at salad bars, which are often filled with as many nutritionally poor choices as good ones. Load up on low-fat bean salads in vinaigrette dressing, and fresh, sliced vegetables and fruit. Tomatoes, carrots, cauliflower, and such dark green vegetables as spinach and broccoli pack the most nutrients.

■ When you top your salad, use very little dressing. A single packet of McDonald's Bleu Cheese or Ranch dressing turns an otherwise healthful salad into the fatty equivalent of a cheeseburger and a medium order of fries. Better yet,

BEWARE OF TRANS FATS

In the 1990's, most fast-food restaurants were no longer using cholesterol-laden animal fats (such as beef tallow) and had switched to vegetable-based fats. That means that fried fast foods are now lower in *saturated* fats and cholesterol than they used to be. But fried foods are still laden with fat—including a kind called "trans fatty acids" that has been linked with an increased risk of developing breast cancer and may raise your blood cholesterol level as much as saturated fats do. Trans fats dole out a double whammy: They raise the level of "bad" LDL-cholesterol and lower "good" HDL-cholesterol levels.

The Center for Science in the Public Interest tested several fast foods and found that some chains that boast of using "100% vegetable oil" use vegetable *shortening*, which is high in trans fatty acids. According to the group's tests:

■ A large order of Burger King fries has more cholesterol-raising fat than a Whopper.
■ Two plain Dunkin Donuts contain as much cholesterol-raising fat as most people should eat in an entire day.

use a small amount of *lower fat* or *lower calorie* dressing. For example, McDonald's Lite Vinaigrette Dressing has only one-tenth the amount of fat as the Bleu Cheese or Ranch.

■ Instead of soft drinks—the single biggest source of sugar in our diets—wash down your meal with fruit juice, plain carbonated water from the soda spigots, low-fat or skim milk, or water. You'll avoid empty calories—a Burger King medium Sprite (18 ounces) has 14 teaspoons of sugar. Diet drinks don't offer any nutrients and are dangerous to people who can't metabolize the artificial sweetener properly.

■ If you want a shake or dessert, look for a skinny alternative to a high-fat milk shake or a piece of fried pie. Check the salad bar for fresh fruit or canned fruit in its own juice, not sugary syrup. If you do choose a low-fat frozen yogurt shake or cone, leave off the nuts, syrups, and whipped cream.

BREAKFAST OF CHAMPIONS

Many fast-food outlets have tapped into Americans' desire for a morning meal on the run. If you're a fast-food eater who wants to start your day on a firm nutritional footing, it's a challenge—but not impossible. If you're careful, you can keep your intake of fat, cholesterol, and sodium down—and you may even get some valuable nutrients, such as calcium and fiber.

■ If a breakfast sandwich is what you crave, don't start your day with any version of the egg, cheese, and sausage sandwich. Whether this concoction is served up on an English muffin, a croissant, or a biscuit, it's almost always the most high-fat, cholesterol-laden, sodium-soaked choice on the menu.

■ To cut back on fat and cholesterol, weigh your options. Canadian bacon has less fat than sausage; a meat-only sandwich has more fat than eggs, but eggs are crammed with cholesterol. Get your sandwich on an English muffin or bagel—they have much less fat than biscuits and croissants.

■ Better yet, opt for pancakes. You'll get plenty of complex carbohydrates, the foundation of a sound diet. Skip the butter or margarine, and go easy on the syrup, which is high in calories.

■ Avoid scrambled egg platters— they're loaded with cholesterol and fat, especially when they come with fried potatoes and sausage.

■ Your food probably already contains plenty of butter or margarine—so don't add more. Instead, use jam or jelly—a fat-free, lower-calorie choice.

■ Avoid hash browns, which are usually fried in the same vat as french fries. The same goes for "french toast" items. Burger King's French Toast Sticks have no eggs in their batter, and therefore zero cholesterol, but still outweigh an egg burrito from Taco Bell by 13 fat grams.

■ Watch out for the doughnuts: A single sugared cake doughnut from Dunkin Donuts has more fat than an entire Egg McMuffin—and who eats just one doughnut?

■ Choosing cold cereal and low-fat milk will start your day off on solid nutritional ground.

■ Orange juice and low-fat milk are the best ways to wash down your meal and get valuable nutrients, to boot.

HELP

For more nutrition information about the fast food you eat, consult:

■ *The Fast-Food Guide,* **2nd Edition,** Michael F. Jacobson, Ph.D., with Sarah Fritschner (Workman, 1991).

■ *Consumer Reports,* **"Fast, Yes,** But How Good?" December 1997.

■ **Center for Science in the Public** Interest's *Nutrition Action Healthletter* regularly reviews fast-food and other to-go items. Write CSPI, Suite 300, 1875 Connecticut Avenue NW, Washington, DC, 20009-5728. For subscriptions only, call (800) 237-4874.

■ **Fast Food Finder, an Internet** site sponsored by the Minnesota Attorney General's office, lets you plug in your favorite foods, then feeds you information on their nutritional content. Go to www.olen.com/food.

CHAPTER 3

WATER

Should You Be Worried About Yours?

Scary news reports like those about unsafe bacteria levels in Washington, DC's water in 1996 or the contamination of Milwaukee's municipal water supply in early 1993, which killed 100 people, have challenged people's faith in what comes out of the faucet. The slightest brackish color, fishy smell, or funny taste to the water makes people worry.

You can probably trust your tap, but don't do so blindly.

THE BASICS

Public water supplies are supposed to meet stringent standards of purity that were laid out in the Safe Drinking Water Act of 1974, which was beefed up in 1996. The Environmental Protection Agency (EPA) enforces the law and has set maximum levels for more than 100 possible chemical, bacteriological, radiological, and physical contaminants, including lead, mercury, and benzene. To meet the law's requirements, public water supplies must be either clean to start with or purified to register within the allowable range, and municipalities generally do a good job of maintaining standards. How-

ever, the EPA's safe drinking water program was said to be "approaching a state of disrepair" in 1990 by the General Accounting Office, the main investigative arm of Congress.

While most people's worries are unfounded, those with immune system disorders may be especially vulnerable to contaminants, even at low levels. The Centers for Disease Control and Prevention recommends that people at risk take zero chances: the elderly, those who are HIV positive, and transplant and chemotherapy patients should boil or filter their water or drink only bottled water from a clean source. The pressures of development threaten the purity of once protected water sources; contaminants can seep into the water as it courses through the pipes or sits waiting for you to turn on the tap; and water drawn from private wells may not be subject to any state requirements for treatment and testing. In 1997, the EPA found that more than half the nation's watersheds had pollution problems. And a 1994 study by Ronnie Levin, the EPA chief of water safety, came to the conservative conclusion that 2 million people a year get infectious diseases from drinking water—which manifest themselves as common, symptoms, including uncomfortable cramps, abdominal pains, diarrhea, and vomiting. "Many outbreaks are not identified as outbreaks," she told National Public Radio. "We learned about the Milwaukee outbreak of cryptosporidiosis from drugstores there, which started running out of Kaopectate and Immodium [diarrhea remedies]."

Thousands of contaminants have been identified as unsafe—heavy metals (such as mercury and lead), radon, microbes, and industrial and agricultural pollutants, to name a few. Of these contaminants, the most common and most worrisome is lead.

Lead, a toxic heavy metal, is now known to be both more widely present in water and more toxic than it was once believed. Drinking water accounts for 20% of our lead exposure, according to the EPA.

Lead exposure can affect every system in the body and may contribute to high blood pressure, reproductive complications, and loss of neuromuscular control in adults. However, infants, children, and pregnant women's fetuses are most vulnerable to lead poisoning. A small dose of lead that would have little effect on an adult is readily absorbed by a fetus or a young child and can impair their mental and physical development. Fetuses exposed to low levels of lead in the mother's blood may also suffer low birth weight. Naturally, infant formula that must be mixed with tap water presents a hidden risk to infants. And even tiny amounts of lead in infants' and children's systems can affect their ability to learn; in extreme cases, lead poisoning can cause death. The blood lead level of children at age two directly correlates to their intelligence at ages 10 to 13, according to Dr. Herbert L. Needleman of the University of Pittsburgh and Dr. David Bellinger of Harvard Medical School, who have been periodically testing the blood lead levels and abilities of a group of 200 middle-class Boston children born between 1979 and 1981. Elevated blood lead levels in children are also associated with the incidence of attention deficit disorder and hyperactivity.

> "Unfortunately, at this time we cannot take for granted the safety of our drinking water."
>
> —CAROL BROWNER, head of the U.S. Environmental Protection Agency

Are You Worried About Your Water?

Don't panic or make any rash purchases! First, you need to collect some information.

To find out what's in your water, request a copy of your utility company's annual water quality report. This will give you the average levels of any pollutants in the municipal water supply as well as the highest levels of any pollutants detected during the previous year.

Testing the water. Water safety problems, for the most part, escape amateur detection by sight, taste, or smell. Common complaints about unpleasant colors or tastes may be caused by such non-toxic substances as rust or sediment. Lead, however, is tasteless, colorless, odorless—and toxic. So is gaseous radon, which invisibly escapes from its benign form, in water, into the air in people's homes when they shower, wash dishes, or run a washing machine.

The only reliable way to find out whether you should be worried about your water is to test it. Since contaminants can enter the water supply anywhere along the route from the municipal source to your faucet, you will have to check every tap individually to fully understand what's in your water.

Look for a state-certified independent water testing company: Get a list from your water utility company or look in the Yellow Pages under "laboratories" or "testing." (You can also use mail-order testing companies listed in **HELP** at the end of this chapter, or call the EPA's safe drinking water hot line at 800 426-4791.) Labs will test for anything from one to hundreds of different contaminants. Since testing for a large number of contaminants will probably be expensive, narrow the list down to those you have good reason to believe may be in your water. Take into account reports from the local public works department, local news, and your neighbors.

For the test itself, send the lab two samples from each faucet: "first draw" water, which has been standing in pipes for several hours; and "purged line" water, which flows after the tap has run for a minute or two to clear out stagnant water. Depending on what you are testing for, you could pay from $20 to ten times that amount. Some municipal water suppliers, such as New York City, have begun offering free lead tests. And residents of San Diego, California, can get a free computer analysis of their water from the San Diego Water Utilities Product Division. If your local water supplier does not provide this service, you can get a reliable home lead test that costs $15 per faucet (plus $1.50 for postage and handling); write or call the Environmental Law Foundation. (See **HELP** at the end of this chapter for contact information.)

If the test comes back positive, don't take drastic, expensive measures—yet. Ask the lab to retest your water, or send a water sample to a different lab to confirm the diagnosis. Also remember that the mere presence of a contaminant in water is not necessarily anything to worry about. The concentration of the contaminant matters most, since some are harmless when diluted. Some labs discuss testing results with consumers, others are less forthcoming; to be sure, call your local health department or the state department of health to find out whether the concentration of contaminants in your water is harmful.

Hitting the bottle. If, after testing, you are convinced that your water is unsafe, one alternative is to buy bottled water for drinking.

Since July 1993, the FDA has required bottled water manufactur-

FRESH WATER AT VINTAGE PRICES

Americans buy about $2.6 billion worth of bottled water annually. In 1996 they each drank an average of 11 gallons, ten times what they were drinking two decades ago. But at least 35% of it is, essentially, Eau de Reservoir, according to the FDA. Bottlers simply draw water from municipal supplies, filter it, bottle it, and slap on a hefty price tag. Bottled water costs an average of only 50 cents a gallon to package, market, and distribute—and sells for anywhere from $1 to $4 a gallon. Compare those prices to the price of tap water: a New Yorker who simply turns on the tap gets 748 gallons for a dollar.

definitions for "spring," "mineral," "artesian," "well," "distilled," and "purified" water and require disclosure of the water's source. Federal rules also require standard nutrition labeling; but only a few states require manufacturers to freshness-date bottled water. The plan does not cover any carbonated beverages or tonic water, which the FDA considers, and regulates as, soft drinks.

As for choosing among bottled waters, it's all a matter of taste and price. The presence and quantity of various minerals distinguish the flavor of one bottled water from another. You'll have to choose for yourself which tastes best.

To treat or not to treat. Another alternative for dealing with tainted tap water is home water treatment.

Water treatment systems range from simple (and relatively inexpensive) carafe filters to major appliances that you'll need a professional to install. Since not every device treats every water problem, you will have to consider the nature of your particular water quality problem and the degree of the problem. The chart on page 34 should help you decide what you need.

When choosing among brands, keep an eye out for the National Sanitation Foundation's seal of approval. The independent research organization certifies water treatment devices for companies that volunteer to participate in the program and pay a fee. Products that lack a seal are not necessarily less effective than others, but the seal assures you that the device has met minimum standards of efficacy. You

ers to meet the same safety standards drinking water must meet for most contaminants and an even lower standard for lead. (Because much bottled water is bought by expectant and lactating mothers or to make infant formula, it can contain only 5 parts per billion of lead, lower than the tap-water standard of 15 parts per billion.)

The FDA also set truth-in-labeling regulations that should cut down on some of the confusion about where the water in the bottle came from. The rules set uniform

also might want to consult *Consumer Reports* for information and ratings about specific products.

Get the lead out. Even if your water is fine when it leaves the supplier, it can pick up lead as it makes its way to you. Lead leaches into water from pipes, chrome or brass faucets, and the solder used to join pipes. In fact, in newer homes, water is a greater source of lead contamination than paint. A University of North Carolina researcher tested 20 new faucets in 1990, and all 20 flunked. When evaluated against the stringent criteria of California's sweeping toxic-chemicals law, Proposition 65, a few of the faucets leached 50 to 250 times the legal amount of lead. This will not be the case for new faucets. The major faucet makers settled a California lawsuit in 1996 and agreed to make sure that 95% of new faucets meet that standard by 1999. Those that do not meet the standard will be labeled as such.

A high lead reading on the "purged line" sample of your water suggests that lead comes from a source outside your house. If the "first draw" sample of your water contains a high lead level but the "purged line" sample contains less, you probably have a problem with pipes or faucets inside the house.

If you have a lead problem, see the chart below for water treatment devices that effectively reduce lead.

FINDING THE RIGHT WATER TREATMENT DEVICE

Device	How It Works	Uses
CARBON FILTER	*As water flows through the filter, contaminants stick to the charcoal.*	*Improves taste; removes odors, rust, chlorine, and such organic compounds as pesticides and solvents.*
REVERSE OSMOSIS DEVICE (*most often includes a carbon filter*)	*Water is slowly forced, under pressure, through a filter.*	*Removes Giardia and crypto; removes such inorganic compounds as fluoride, lead, mercury, and nitrate.*
DISTILLER	*Boils water, then catches it as it cools and condenses.*	*Kills microbes; removes minerals and such heavy metals as lead and mercury.*

Source: California Public Interest Research Group

WHAT TO WATCH OUT FOR

Lead heads the list. Lead in water knows no boundaries—unlike lead in paint, which is a bigger problem in older housing than in newer housing. No matter where you live, city or suburb, apartment building or house, lead may be leaching into your water. Have your water tested.

Anyone who wants to test your water for free. Water treatment system salespeople may come to your door offering to test your water for free. Don't trust them or their tests. They'll almost certainly say you have something to worry about in order to sell you something. Eco Water Systems of Long Island, New York, was caught on tape scaring customers into buying thousands of dollars worth of water treatment equipment, when in fact their water was completely safe.

Devices that promise totally pure water. No device will provide totally pure water no matter what the manufacturer or salesperson claims. Nor are the devices "approved" by any agency of the federal government, which neither tests nor evaluates water treatment devices. If the device uses silver to inhibit the growth of bacteria in the unit, the entire unit must have been "registered" with the EPA. Registration simply means that the EPA is satisfied that excessive amounts of silver, a potentially dangerous pesticide, will not leak into your water.

Dirty filters. Don't forget upkeep. Most water treatment devices need periodic maintenance—such as cleaning or filter replacement—in order to continue doing what you installed them to do. The life expectancy of the filter depends on how much water you use and the level and number of contaminants.

Carbon filters. On their own and when they are included as part of other water treatment devices, carbon filters can be breeding grounds for bacteria—another reason to replace filters regularly. While the effects usually are not severe, bacterial contamination can lead to brief gastrointestinal distress.

Reverse osmosis. Don't waste money or water unless absolutely necessary. Reverse osmosis water treatment devices capture only 10% to 25% of the water that runs through them. The rest goes down the drain, a fact that most sales literature fails to divulge.

Expensive water. Bottled water can cost 200 times what you'd pay for tap water; some of the "fancier" waters cost 1,000 times more.

THE $MARTER CONSUMER

Let it run. When drawing water from a faucet that hasn't been used in a while, let the cold water run for a bit to flush out contaminants that may have leached into the water from pipes and plumbing fixtures. (So as not to waste water, use what you flush out to water your plants.) Let the water flow until it runs as cool as it gets. Then you will know the water is flowing from its source and has not been sitting in your pipes.

Cold, cold, cold. Since hot water picks up lead more easily, use only cold water for drinking, making baby formula, or cooking.

To get rid of the taste of chlorine, let water stand in an open pitcher in the refrigerator for a few days before drinking. You can also stir water briskly or put it in an uncovered blender at a low speed—aeration makes the chlorine in water evaporate, and the unpleasant taste exits with the vapors.

H E L P

■ **For general infor-** mation about drinking water, call the EPA safe drinking water hot line, (800) 426-4791, or go to http://www.epa.gov. The hot line provides information about regulations that apply to public water systems under the Safe Drinking Water Act, as well as publications; federal, state, and local contacts for information on local drinking water conditions; and EPA-certified drinking water testing labs. (Hot line staff cannot discuss manufacturers or recommend specific brands.)

■ **For information about the safety of** drinking water on the Worldwide Web, check out these sites: Natural Resources Defense Council, www.nrdc.org; Environmental Defense Fund, www.edf.org; and Environmental Working Group, www.ewg.org.

■ **Mail-order water testing services:**
Daily Analytical Laboratories
1621 West Candletree Drive
Peoria, IL 61614
(800) 752-6651

Spectrum Laboratories
301 West County Road E2
New Brighton, MN 55112
(800) 447-5221

Suburban Water Testing Labs
4600 Kutztown Road
Temple, PA 19560
(800) 433-6595
http:www.h2otest.com

■ **For a home lead** testing kit, call or write: The Environmental Law Foundation's Lead Testing Project, 1736 Franklin Street, 8th floor, Oakland, CA 94612; (510) 208-4557. Each kit costs $15, which includes materials and analysis. You'll need one kit for each faucet. No matter how many kits you order, add another $1.50 for postage and handling. Your water samples will be analyzed at one of the nation's best-regarded water testing facilities, University of North Carolina at Asheville's Environmental Quality Institute.

Clean Water Lead Testing, Inc., UNCA, 1 University Heights, Asheville, NC 28804, (704) 251-6800, sells tap water and well water kits for $17 each. Your samples will also be analyzed by UNC at Asheville's Environmental Quality Institute.

■ **To find out about the performance** of specific water treatment devices: *Consumer Reports* tested and reviewed them in July 1997. The National Sanitation Foundation, (800) 673-8010 or www.nsf.org, certifies water treatment devices and also provides information about them.

■ **For more information about the** hazards of lead exposure and how to avoid them, call the National Lead Information Center Hot Line, (800) LEAD FYI.

PART 2

Health

HEALTH INSURANCE

HMOs Are Great— If You Don't Get Sick

"Your money or your life" was the command barked by stagecoach robbers of old, but these days health insurers might as well say it, too. Because if you're one of the 41 million Americans without health insurance, you probably can't afford to get seriously ill.

Unfortunately, even having insurance coverage no longer guarantees avoidance of large medical outlays, what with growing co-payments, insurers' "reasonable cost" payments, and special rules on pre-authorization, second opinions, and excluded treatments.

How do you find affordable insurance if your job doesn't cover you or if you have been laid off? And if you now have insurance, how can you make sure you get everything you're entitled to?

The failure of Congress to enact President Clinton's health insurance plan or a credible alternative—other than limited stopgop measures—left the job of aiding and protecting health care consumers to the states, and no state has filled the breach. Some members of Congress now want to set Federal standards for health care

plans in order to ensure access to services and information nationwide. Public opinion is increasingly on their side and may force action. A Louis Harris poll in August 1997 found that 54% of Americans believed that they were harmed by the trend toward managed care, up from 43% only the year before.

THE BASICS

There are two basic types of health insurance coverage. With indemnity "fee for service" health insurance, you pay a separate fee for each service, which the insurer then reimburses after you complete a claims form. You may see any doctor you wish. In many cases the insurance company pays the provider directly—but you're ultimately responsible for payment. With health maintenance organizations (HMOs), and to a degree with their variant, preferred provider organizations (PPOs), all your medical care is overseen by a primary care doctor, who must approve visits to specialists. At the time of treatment you pay only a token amount and you don't have to fill out any paperwork.

Indemnity "Fee for Service" Health Insurance

Indemnity health insurance used to be the most common form of coverage, but many employers are finding that HMOs make more economic sense. But fee-for-service insurance is still available and consists of three separate coverages.

- *Surgical/medical.* This is your basic coverage for services provided by physicians and other health professionals. If you are hospitalized, surgical/medical coverage includes treatment by medical professionals that is not included in a hospital bill. So it could include fees for an ambulance, an anesthesiologist, and in-home care if needed after your operation. You will probably have to pay a portion of each bill yourself, called "co-insurance"—typically 20%—although there is usually an annual cap above which the insurance company picks up the entire tab. You will also be required to pay an annual deductible.

Although "reasonable and customary cost" payments supposedly reflect local costs, the amount on which the insurance company bases its 80% payment could be significantly less than the bill, leaving a hefty balance for you to absorb.
- *Hospitalization.* This covers bills incurred once you are admitted to a hospital, such as the charges for the room and the operating suite, basic nursing care, and stays in the intensive care unit. Only gold-plated insurance policies cover those luxury suites offering *pâté de foie gras* served on bone china that some hospitals have added to attract affluent patients.
- *Major medical, or "catastrophic," insurance.* This is supplemental coverage that kicks in once your hospitalization and surgical/medical plans have paid out $20,000 or so. It's important coverage to have, especially considering how quickly medical expenses add up. In the event you ever need long-term rehabilitation, you'll be glad you have major medical. These plans also typically have much higher lifetime limits than standard employer plans.

HMOs and PPOs

Health Maintenance Organizations (HMOs) are health insurance plans in which participating providers agree to take care of your health needs for a set, prepaid fee. Some 67 million Americans are enrolled in HMOs.

Instead of choosing a health service provider on your own and assuming direct responsibility for the bill, as with indemnity plan insurance, with an HMO you must use primary care doctors, specialists, laboratories, and hospitals in a prescribed network. If you go outside the network, you may not be covered or may have to pay a large share of the bill. If you stay within the network, you have no paperwork to complete; if you go out-of-network, there are claims forms to file.

A preferred provider organization (PPO) is an HMO variant. You can see any doctor without prior approval, but you avoid more than a token co-payment only by using participating doctors. Patients have to pay much of their bill out of pocket if they use outside providers. And if they do, there is typically an annual deductible.

With an HMO, you have to select a primary care physician (PCP) from the HMO's roster of participating doctors. Your PCP "gatekeeper" coordinates all your health care and authorizes specialist visits.

Strict specialist referral rules are starting to erode with the spread of "point-of-service" HMO plans, also called "open access" plans, which place no restrictions on seeing specialists without a referral. For doctors listed on the HMO roster, you pay only the usual nominal co-payment. You receive only partial reimbursement for non-network doctors.

Cost and Availability

Cost Factors. If you are buying an individual policy or work for a small company, the cost of your health insurance depends on several factors.

■ *Your health and age.* Insurance companies do whatever they can to avoid insuring or to charge extra those who are ill or who appear likely to become ill. If you are HIV-positive, or have cancer or another serious (and costly) chronic ailment, getting coverage will be extremely difficult no matter what your age. Insurers also charge higher premiums if you smoke. And since premiums rise with age, some people between 55 and 65 (when Medicare

coverage takes over) who know that they will have trouble affording insurance decide against retiring early and giving up their employer-sponsored plan.

Eighteen states are now trying to even out the premium differences—while retaining limited premium disparities for age and smoking—through a process called "community rating." Lawmakers saw that too many people were being priced out of health insurance as insurers "cherry picked" only the healthiest prospects and the cost of insuring everyone else went through the roof.

If you are insured through a medium- or small-size employer, the premiums and the extent of your coverage might be based on a procedure the industry calls "experience rating," under which the overall medical costs of a company's employees determines the insurance rates. If a few employees of a small firm have unusually expensive medical needs—such as regular kidney dialysis—the rates may be higher.

■ *Your occupation.* You may have little sympathy for doctors and lawyers, but did you know they can have trouble getting reasonably priced insurance? Seems the insurers think they might make waves. And among other occupations whose practitioners have trouble getting health insurance are long-distance truck drivers, bartenders, and workers in restaurants, convenience stores, and parking lots.

■ *The amount of your deductible.* Some comprehensive policies have deductibles as high as $2,500, which significantly reduces the premium while still protecting you from financial catastrophe.

Finding Insurance. How do you find the least expensive insurance if you aren't already covered on your job? The National Insurance Consumer Organization suggests that you first check out your local HMOs. Then you might try the "Blues," the non-profit Blue Cross/Blue Shield insurance company in your vicinity —although some "Blues" are converting to for-profit status and their cost advantages are ending. State insurance departments are beginning to publish cost comparison lists. New York State, for instance, makes available a guide listing the counties covered by each HMO and the premium each charges for an individual policy.

You also might find a lower premium through a group plan sponsored by your professional, trade, or alumni organization. One option if you can't get coverage anywhere else is one of the high-risk insurance pools sponsored by about half the states. As with high-risk pools for drivers, the premiums are expensive but at least you are covered. Your state insurance department can tell you if your state has one.

Ultimately, since it's a gargantuan task to compare premium quotes and policies, your best approach to finding an acceptable deal might be to seek the help of an independent insurance agent.

Insurance Legislation. Out of the wreckage of President Clinton's controversial 1994 health insurance proposal has emerged the Health Insurance Portability and Accountability Act of 1996—popularly known as Kennedy-Kassebaum. It attempts to soften the harshness of a health insurance system where many people stayed at the same job for fear of losing coverage. And it uses tax breaks to make it slightly easier to afford individual insurance. The basic provisions are:

- *Portability.* If you leave your job, were covered there for at least 18 months, and are ineligible for or have exhausted COBRA coverage, insurers must cover you without a waiting period. Important caveats:
- If your new employer doesn't offer employees insurance, the act is not required to cover you, although you have a right to purchase individual insurance on your own. The new law applies only to people moving from one group plan to another or from a group to an individual plan.
- The law doesn't regulate the cost of your new premium. It could well be unaffordable—a problem that 1998 studies indicate have weakened the law's impact.
- If your new employer has a less generous plan, it need not be upgraded to the level of your old plan, if it was better. As the law states, employers may limit "the amount, level, extent, or nature of the benefits."

If you're leaving your job, Kennedy-Kassebaum requires your employer to give you a document certifying whether you had health insurance and, in some cases, whether it covered mental health services, prescription drugs, and dental and vision care.

THE BASICS OF COBRA: IF YOU LOSE YOUR JOB

As America's employers continue to restructure, many people are finding themselves restarting their careers as freelancers or consultants, working for small companies that do not provide health insurance, or simply unemployed.

What can these folks do for health insurance? The insurance plan portability and tax break provisions of the 1996 Kennedy-Kassebaum law may help in purchasing an individual policy—although, as explained elsewhere in this chapter, this new law has serious limitations, such as no limit on the cost of premiums.

Of greater help might be COBRA, the Consolidated Omnibus Budget Reconciliation Act of 1985. COBRA requires that if your employer has 20 or more employees, you can continue under your group coverage for 18 months (29 months if you are disabled). You'll have to pick up your employer's premium payments (which can be considerable) to your policy plus another 2% to cover administrative expenses. Employers who go out of business have no obligation to continue coverage. You have 60 days from the date you leave your job to opt in.

COBRA isn't *always* a bargain. Regular non-group insurance or an HMO could be cheaper if you have no serious or chronic pre-existing medical conditions. If possible, shop around before writing your COBRA check.

■ *Preexisting conditions.* A preexisting condition is one for which medical help was recommended or received during the six months before enrollment (issuers can't impose a preexisting condition exclusion on pregnancy). A serious problem experienced by people with chronic conditions, such as HIV-positive status or heart disease, was the preexisting medical condition exclusion. This problem has been partially resolved under Kennedy-Kassebaum: health insurers and employers can delay your coverage for a pre-existing medical condition for only 12 months. But such delay must be reduced by one month for each month you were previously employed.

For example, if you worked nine months at your old job, the preexisting exclusion could delay coverage by your new insurer by only three months. As the congressional staff report on the new law explained, "Employers and insurers must credit coverage of less than 12 months toward any preexisting condition exclusion under a new health plan." Once the 12-month limit expires, no new preexisting condition limit may ever be imposed on you if you maintain your coverage, with no more than a 63-day gap, even if you change jobs or health plans.

■ *New tax breaks.* Kennedy-Kasse-baum allowed the self-employed to deduct 40% of their health insurance premiums in 1997, increasing gradually each year to 100% in 2007.

■ *Medical savings accounts.* If you work for yourself or for a small company (50 or fewer employees) and purchase a qualified health insurance plan with a high deductible, you may open a special medical savings account (MSA) to which you can deposit tax-deductible money. For individual coverage, 65% of the health insurance plan's deductible can be contributed to the MSA; for family coverage, 75%. Withdrawals from the account to pay for medical expenses are not taxed. You can use the money in the account to pay for day-to-day medical expenses—the doctor's bill from your flu visit, eyeglasses, the kids' orthodontist—and use the high-deductible insurance plan for expensive hospital stays. There is a tax penalty for using the money in the account for nonmedical purposes.

Utilization Review

Welcome to the age of "utilization reviewers," people who work for insurance companies—or for companies that work for insurance companies—and who have one major purpose: to save the company money. They are the front line troops in the nation's effort to reduce medical expenditures and the efforts of for-profit insurers to improve on the bottom line. These are their most important functions:

■ *Preauthorize hospitalizations/procedures/major tests.* Before proceeding with a hospitalization or expensive procedure, your doctor will probably be required to get the insurer's OK. Easier said than done. Newspapers and TV news magazines are full of horror stories in which the insurer said "no way" to an expensive treatment that the patient's doctors said was a matter of life or death.

Doctors say that it is an inherently frustrating exercise to try to justify a treatment over the telephone to a utilization reviewer who has never seen the patient. Chances are that the reviewer is applying rigid rules in a manual—for example, that there has to be 40% blockage in two arteries before bypass surgery can be approved.

At the initial determination level, reviewers typically aren't even doctors. We have heard physicians complain about utilization reviewers who can't pronounce the name of the procedure they are being asked to authorize. And physicians add that many of the "peer reviewers" to whom initial appeals are taken also aren't qualified, since their expertise is in a different field or they have had little clinical experience.

Disapprovals can be quite bizarre. An office manager working for a prominent New York City pediatric orthopedic surgeon told us about a child born with six fingers on each hand whose HMO would not cover corrective surgery because it would be merely "cosmetic." She called this story "not at all unusual," adding, "We have to fight the insurers every day."

HMOs: Ways Doctors Are Paid

Fee-for-service. Doctors are paid for each service according to a discounted fee schedule. This is how specialists are usually paid.

Capitated. Doctors receive a flat monthly fee per enrolled patient. But since the doctor gets no extra money if you visit more often, the effect of such a payment method is to encourage "assembly-line care" and discourage spending much time with you. Generally limited to paying primary care physicians, this method may soon be used for paying groups of specialists, too.

The group gets to pocket whatever it didn't spend on you.

Salaried. In a staff-model HMO, the doctors receive a paycheck that probably remains constant no matter how many patients they see. So they're under no pressure to show you the exit and get on to the next patient. Doctors in a group-model HMO may also be salaried, although they still might be pressured to limit their time with you if the group's contract with the HMO provides that they are paid extra if cost-containment targets are met.

■ *Decide whether to reimburse for emergency room visits.* In the middle of the night you are awakened by an intense pain in your chest. Since it feels just like what you've been told are classic heart attack symptoms, you rush to the emergency room. An ER doctor checks you out and tells you it was just gas and to see your doctor at your leisure. There's a good chance your insurer will pass the entire ER bill back to you because, after all, it wasn't really a heart attack.

In response to situations like this, several states are now enacting laws requiring application of a "prudent person" standard in determining whether an emergency room visit must be covered; if a "prudent person" would have thought the ER visit was necessary, the insurer must pay.

■ *Monitor your hospital stay.* When the insurance company preapproves a hospitalization, it also says for how many days. Then, once you're actually hospitalized, utilization reviewers make "concurrent review" calls to your doctor every few days. They'll ask about your progress, but they're not just concerned for your welfare. What they really want to know is if you're on schedule for discharge and, if not, why not.

Your doctor may be required to argue your case, faxing notes and test results to the HMO. A 1996 study prepared by the office of the New York City Public Advocate, *What Ails HMOs,* which relied on interviews with dozens of doctors, hospital administrators, and managed care consultants, found that the burden is on the physician to show why a longer stay is needed, not on the HMO's utilization reviewer to show why the patient should be discharged quickly. One major hospital's executives described attending physicians as being in a daily struggle with HMO concurrent review nurses (who are the HMO's front-line staff) with the HMO usually winning. A New York City vascular surgeon said, "They bug you a lot and form you to death. They are constantly at you to get the patient out. Sometimes you have to go back and forth with them several times, arguing your case."

Some HMOs apply "cookbooks"—guidelines prepared by consulting companies—to determine your maximum length-of-stay. Here are the number of hours or days of hospitalization one of these companies recommended in 1995, as reported in *What Ails HMOs*: tonsillectomy, 6 to 12 hours; modified radical mastectomy, appendectomy, gallbladder removal, one day; pneumonia, two days; double bypass surgery, four days. These stays are much shorter than national averages. HMOs respond that such limits are based on ideal, uncomplicated cases and that they are not strictly applied. But many doctors say that, in reality, even though few cases are "ideal," managed care insurers try to enforce "guidelines" more often than not.

Public backlash to utilization review excesses has come in the form of a new Federal law requiring insurers to cover at least 48 hours hospitalization after a delivery if the doctor says it is medically necessary. And various states have begun to legislate required stays for specific procedures; New York, has a law prohibiting outpatient radical mastectomies. Many states are also considering legislation to license utilization reviewers and set minimum qualifications for holders of this key health care position.

HMOs: Advantages and Disadvantages

The major advantages of HMOs are lower out-of-pocket costs and, with no claims to submit, no paperwork. Just show the doctor or hospital your membership card and pay only a $10 or $15 copayment. If your HMO is in a clinic, with a range of specialists under one roof, you also have the advantage of convenience.

Some HMOs also live up to the name "health *maintenance* organization" by emphasizing preventive care, such as regular cholesterol tests, flu shots, mammograms, and screening for high blood pressure and diabetes.

The biggest disadvantage to HMOs is that your selection of doctors is limited to those on the participating provider roster. It can get quite complicated when you are trying to locate an HMO that includes your own regular primary care doctor, the pediatrician your kids actually look forward to seeing, not to mention that trusted, sensitive gynecologist. It's also possible that your doctor could withdraw from an HMO after you've joined.

And don't forget that with an HMO, reimbursement may be next to nothing for a top specialist if he or she isn't on the roster. In a survey conducted at Georgetown Medical Center in Washington, D.C., of 39 doctors who saw both HMO and fee-for-service patients, the doctors were "more likely to refer an HMO patient to a specialist they didn't know" and "less likely to discuss patient care with specialists in HMOs." You can obtain special authorization to go outside this network only in very unusual cases where the HMO determines it is necessary because no network provider has the needed expertise.

HMOs also may limit your selection of hospitals to those on their participating provider roster. This means you might not have access to your preferred hospital. Practically speaking, if in an emergency the ambulance takes you to a nonparticipating hospital, your HMO will probably transfer you to one on their roster as soon as you are deemed (by the HMO) to be medially stable, even if you don't want to move or don't think you're ready to be transported.

As a rule of thumb, if you are not very old and are in very good health, an HMO might be appropriate (see the box on Medicare HMOs). Surveys have shown that people who seldom get sick or have uncomplicated medical issues—like a straightforward leg fracture—are the most satisfied with HMOs. After all, there is no paperwork and the basic out-of-pocket costs are incidental. But for people with complex or chronic illnesses, HMOs can be a nightmare, with the "gate-keeper" primary care doctor being pressured to carefully ration care.

So, when all is said and done, are HMOs better or worse than traditional fee-for-service indemnity plans? There is no answer yet. Until very recently, a disproportionate share of HMO members were younger and healthier, making it hard to make generalizations. So in most of the states that keep track, HMOs tend to receive fewer complaints to insurance or health departments than indemnity insurers. But this could change as more of the less-healthy population enrolls in HMOs. Indeed, complaints about HMOs doubled in 1996 in New Jersey, a trend also being seen in other parts of the country.

Comparing HMOs

Let's say you've decided to opt for an HMO instead of an indemnity insurance plan. How do you decide which one to join?

Compare coverage and rules. Start by carefully reading each HMO's literature. Ask to see not just the promotional flyer sent to anyone who inquires, but also the handbook given enrollees once they sign up. Demand to see the all-important subscriber agreement, which contains some of the nitty-gritty details about coverage and excluded procedures. Among the areas in which to compare coverage:

■ *Well-care.* How frequent are reimbursed periodic check-ups and what tests are covered? Sigmoidoscopies? Cholesterol screening? At what age does the HMO start covering regular mammograms? Some cover annual mammographies after 35, some after 40, and others not until age 50.

■ *Referral rules.* Some HMOs require a new primary care physician approval for each and every specialist visit, while others allow the primary care doctor to approve a block of five or even ten visits. The more visits, the easier for you.

■ *Mental health.* How many visits to a therapist will the plan cover per year and per lifetime? Ask if the HMO you are considering requires therapists to agree to HMO inspection of their files on very short notice. Must therapists send their session notes to the HMO or the HMO's behavioral health company?

■ *Gynecologists.* Does the plan allow women to choose and visit a gynecologist without a referral from the primary care physician? (Some states now require HMOs to allow women to designate a gynecologist of their choosing and to visit the gynecologist without first getting a primary care doctor referral.)

■ *Dermatologists.* Visits to dermatologists are closely scrutinized, especially since ABC-TV's *20/20* news magazine aired a report on how insurance companies reimbursed for fancy facials in exclusive salons that dermatologists prescribed as medically necessary.

■ *Childbirth.* Labor pains may not be the only pain you experience when giving birth. You could feel financial strains if your policy has unforeseen coverage exclusions, such as for diagnostic procedures like ultrasound or amniocentesis. There is also a chance that your policy covers only pregnancy *complications,* not routine costs.

Many states are beginning to require that plans disclose certain information beyond the basic coverage. For instance, a 1995 Arizona law requires HMOs to tell about rules such as whether coverage can be denied retroactively and how to get treatment from non-plan doctors and hospitals. New York State has gone further than just about anyone in requiring HMOs to disclose everything from the list of drugs they cover to their method for determining whether a particular treatment is experimental and therefore not covered.

Some state governments and medical associations publish HMO guides. For instance, in 1996 the Illinois State Medical Society started publishing an *Annual Guide to Illinois Health Maintenance Organizations,* comparing plans on everything from how much they spend on actual health care compared to administration to the number of complaints they received.

Compare participating doctor and hospital rosters. Does the HMO list an ample selection of primary care doctors and specialists? Does it include doctors you now see and want to continue seeing? One serious drawback to some HMOs is a limited list of participating specialists like gastroenterologists and endocrinologists. Find out how many pediatricians are on staff or in the network if you have children, and whether they are conveniently located. Older people might ask if any of the physicians have special training in gerontology.

When it comes to hospitals, try to opt for an HMO that lists the most prestigious medical centers in your region. You never know when you might require state-of-the-art care, and treatment could be delayed if you have to ask the HMO for permission to use a non-network hospital with the necessary expertise or equipment—and the answer could be "no." You should also check a plan's rules and coverage for care outside the basic service area, especially if you travel frequently.

Find out how the doctors are paid. The method the HMO uses to compensate doctors may affect your care. (See Box, HMOs: Ways to Pay.) Benefits consultant Arthur J. Dreschler gives this analogy: You can contract with your heating oil delivery company to perform oil burner repairs one of two ways: either by paying one set annual fee for service or a separate fee for each repair. Guess which method leads to frequent visits by the repairman and under which method he doesn't return calls?

Try to compare quality. Unfortunately, when it comes to quality, there isn't any definitive information out there. Still, you should try to find out:

■ *Accreditation status.* In June 1994 the National Committee for Quality Assurance (NCQA) began publicly disclosing the accreditation status of health plans. They examine HMOs for 50 different characteristics, such as quality improvement efforts, how well doctors' credentials are checked, responsiveness to mem-

bers, and the percentages of members who get various preventive services. Trouble is, since only HMOs that ask to be reviewed are reviewed, nearly half of the nation's HMOs are now omitted. And the NCQA does not yet measure medical outcomes—that is, which HMOs are better at keeping their members healthy and treating them when they are sick. The possible accreditation designations are:

1. "Full accreditation" for three years, received by 37% of the reviewed plans. These HMOs have "excellent programs" for continuous quality review and meet "rigorous standards."

2. "One-year accreditation," received by 39% of reviewed plans. They meet most NCQA standards. These HMOs are supposed to be busy implementing a list of NCQA recommendations, and they face a re-review in a year.

3. "One-year provisional accreditation," received by 11% of the reviewed HMOs. These HMOs meet some NCQA standards but need to demonstrate progress before they can be considered for the higher designations.

4. "Denial," for the 12% that do not meet the requirements for the first three designations.

5. "Under review" is the designation for HMOs that received an initial determination but have asked for another review.

■ *The percentage of participating doctors who are board-certified.* Board certification means that the doctor passed rigorous exams in a chosen field, such as family practice or car-

MEDICARE HMOS: TO JOIN OR NOT TO JOIN

Enrollment in Medicare HMOs is surging, registering a 25% increase in 1996 alone. In 1997, 13% of the 38 million people in Medicare were enrolled in HMOs. Although Medicare HMOs operate much like regular HMOs, there are some special considerations.

Probably the biggest benefit to joining a Medicare HMO is that it usually covers prescription medications, with co-pays of $5 to $20 per prescription, while regular Medicare generally does not. However, the Medicare HMO could limit you to anywhere from $500 to $3,000 worth of drugs a year, and not all drugs are covered—you should ask first. Some Medicare HMOs also offer low-priced eyeglasses.

Another plus is that you no longer need to buy a Medigap insurance policy, which covers Medicare deductibles and the 20% of doctor bills and lab tests (the "Part B" expenses) Medicare doesn't cover. Medigap policies cost from $300 to $3,000 a year, depending on coverage.

But Medicare HMOs have serious downsides. If you have chronic illnesses or multiple maladies, you may be ill-suited to HMO care. What are the chances that all of the trusted doctors you've been seeing for different medical problems are on the HMO's roster? Not good, meaning that you'd have to switch doctors, especially given that most Medicare HMOs don't cover non-network providers. In addition, following strict HMO rules of getting referrals from the "gatekeeper" doctor for specialist visits could prove cumbersome. And, as with regular HMOs, if the capitation payment method is used (see box, page 45), medical care providers may be encouraged to limit treatment—but for seniors, the resulting harm could be worse than for younger, healthier people.

If you decide to join a Medicare HMO, compare the copayments and the benefits beyond what Medicare requires. If you do join and decide you made a mistake, you can always go back to regular fee-for-service Medicare, although starting in 2002 you will be allowed to change plans no more than once a year.

diology. HMOs with board-certification rates in excess of 85% for both primary care doctors and specialists are preferred. Be wary if the rate is less than 70%.

■ *Complaints ratio.* The insurance or health departments of some states, like New York, issue an annual ranking of health insurers according to the complaints ratio.

■ *Member disenrollment rates.* A plan that sticks out because of a high annual disenrollment rate might have a lot of unhappy members who are voting with their feet. For Medicare HMOs, a 1997 study by Families USA found an average dropout rate of 13%, with the rate varying among HMOs from 2% to 81%.

Try to get your hands on any available quality-comparison surveys. Some major employers like Xerox, American Express, and GTE give their employees helpful information on their HMOs, such as the results of surveys of what their employees think of each offered HMO and the HMO's doctor turnover rates.

Call your state insurance and health departments to find out if your state has issued quality comparison reports. For instance, Maryland issues HMO report cards based in part on member surveys and the level of preventive care given by each HMO. In 1997, New Jersey released a report critical of many of the state's HMOs for lackluster preventive care. And in 1998, the U.S. Healthcare Financing Administration, the agency that runs Medicare, plans to release limited quality data on 350 HMOs that enroll Medicare members; among the helpful information the government is collecting is heart attack victims' follow-up care and mammography and flu vaccination rates.

Unfortunately, most of the current publicly available data is of limited use. Whether a plan screens most of its older members for colon cancer is somewhat telling. But much more helpful would be knowing from an independent monitor just how aggressively the plan tries to interfere in doctors' medical practice by shortening requested hospital stays and denying specialist referrals. The best way to measure quality would be with "outcomes" data, such as the risk-adjusted death and complication rates for various diagnoses. Release of this sort of data isn't imminent.

What to Do When Your HMO Says No

Beyond appealing to the HMO—and you should always pursue your case through the HMO's internal grievance system—there is no truly effective recourse because the final decision is ultimately the HMO's—which is akin to a losing defendant appealing to the plaintiff.

But you can improve your odds. For starters, ask the HMO for a complete written clinical explanation of their determination. Get your doctor's active and written support. If you feel comfortable disclosing your personal medical problems, you should also ask your employer's benefits administrator to assist. Ask office managers and nurses working in medical offices for advice, since they often know the in's and out's of a plan's procedures. And, as with any important consumer dispute, keep a log of all of your phone conversations and copies of all correspondence.

Get aggressive. Demand from the HMO the names of the utilization reviewers and their supervisors along with everyone's credentials, including their clinical experience. For how long did *they* practice medicine or nursing or whatever? Are they specialists in the particular field? Filing a complaint with your state insurance or health department sometimes does the trick; once the HMO knows you've gone "official," they might view the dispute differently. (In California the Department of Corporations, not the insurance or health departments, principally regulates HMOs.) Some states, like California and New York, have set up toll-free managed care complaint hotlines. Send copies of your complaints to state legislators and, in the most egregious cases, to the local media.

New Jersey is the state that has come closest to establishing an independent HMO appeals body. Under a new law, New Jersey residents may appeal coverage determinations to an independent review panel. A big loophole is that the panel's decisions are not binding, although it is assumed that HMOs will comply with them in the vast majority of cases. In California, a new external review board hears appeals from terminally ill patients when they are turned down for treatment, but these boards are actually hired by the HMO, tainting their objectivity. A presidential commission has recommended a Federal law requiring that, under certain circumstances, patients have the right to appeal to a neutral third party for a binding ruling.

You still can't sue an HMO for malpractice even if it refused to cover a procedure that your doctor insisted was absolutely crucial to your health. Employee benefit plans are governed by the U.S. Employee Retirement Income Security Act (ERISA), which prohibits state court malpractice suits against insurance carriers. Texas is the only state that allows HMOs to be sued for malpractice, but the industry is challenging this law in court.

WHAT TO WATCH OUT FOR

HMO promotional literature and advertising. HMOs spend a fortune on promotion. For instance, in 1994, CIGNA of New York spent $4.50 per member each month on marketing, 22% of the amount spent on inpatient hospital care and 27% of the expenditures on doctors. HMO ads picturing fathers rough-housing with their laughing children, healthy families running together through fields, and vigorous seniors out on the links are carefully designed to make you associate the HMO with good health. HMO brochures—sent to anyone who inquires—invariably tout their top-rate doctors and enormous breadth of coverage. To find out the real story, follow the recommendations in this chapter.

Internally generated HMO patient satisfaction scorecards. Dozens of HMOs have issued member satisfaction surveys, some claiming satisfaction rates in excess of 90%. It is indeed true that most HMO members are satisfied—after all, most people are healthy, don't visit doctors frequently, and appreciate the low co-payments for check-ups. The big flaw in these surveys is that relatively few respondents have sufficient experience with their HMO to comment on its willingness to refer to top specialists or to pay for hospitalizations or costly special procedures.

Many member surveys have methodological errors, such as not polling people who recently quit (maybe out of frustration with the HMO), inadequate response rates, leading questions, and limited range of available responses in the survey form. To be of any use, HMO surveys must be independently run and the questions must be standardized to allow comparisons with other HMOs. And remember, a survey company that gained a reputation for surveys casting its customers in an unfavorable light would soon have to find a new line of business.

Restrictive drug "formularies" and "therapeutic switching." If you have pharmaceutical coverage, there's an increasing chance that the drug your doctor really wants you to take is not going to be on the plan's "formulary"—the list of drugs the plan will cover. (To learn why and what this could mean to your health, turn to page 59.)

Emergency room preauthorization rules. Some plans require that you notify them within 24 hours of an emergency room visit; others require 48 hours. Some start the clock ticking at the time of your accident or when you realized you needed to go to the ER, others from when you

entered or left the emergency room. There also may be a requirement to seek aid within 12 hours of the first appearance of symptoms.

Obsolete participating provider lists. Before you join an HMO or PPO because your regular doctor is on the participating provider roster, first ask the doctor if he or she is still participating. Many rosters are not updated frequently enough.

Medicare HMO advertising. Some Medicare HMO promotions suggest that the Medicare Part B premium won't be deducted from your Social Security check if you join their HMO: not true. It's also not true, as some Medicare HMO ads imply, that they charge no premiums: all this claim really means is the Medicare HMO charges no *additional* premiums.

Coverage gaps when you travel outside your HMO region. If traveling to another city, you could find it difficult to get preauthorization to use a hospital there for non-emergencies.

THE $MARTER CONSUMER

Dicker with the doctor. If your insurance covers only a portion of the doctor's fee—that is, a portion of what the insurer considers the "reasonable and customary" cost—there is nothing to lose by asking the doctor to reduce the bill. With many of the best doctors, your insurance company's "reasonable and customary" allowances don't come near to covering the actual bill.

And be careful. Just because your insurer precertified a procedure doesn't mean that it agreed to pay the full cost.

Avoid duplicate coverage. If you or your spouse both work, figure out if you'll save money by dropping one of your coverages and joining the other's health policy. A little extra might be deducted from a paycheck if this requires conver-

sion from an individual to a family policy.

Find out about the HMO's grievance procedures. Are there time limits on rendering findings to make sure the process moves along quickly? Who makes the final decision?

For individual coverage, consider buying a policy with a high deductible. The premium savings may more than compensate for the additional medical bills you pay out of your own pocket.

H E L P

■ **To find out about** an HMO's accreditation status with the National Committee on Quality Assurance, call, toll free, 888-275-7585. To order a list of accredited HMOs, call 800-839-6487. Their Web site is at www.ncqa.org.

■ **The July 24, 1996, edition of** *Newsweek* rated more than 40 of the country's largest HMOs. The December 1996 issue of *Consumer Reports* has a very helpful story on HMOs.

■ **If you are self-employed or work-** ing for a company that does not offer insurance, you might want to check out the health insurance policy offered by Working Today, a new organization dedicated to organizing people working independently. They offer group rate health and dental coverage through the National Writers Union associate mem-

bership plan. It's a comprehensive, portable plan with competitive group rates. Call 212-366-6066 or visit their Web site at www.workingtoday.org.

■ **Useful state phone numbers:** New York State Managed Care Complaint Hotline, 800-206-8125; order the free *Annual Guide to Illinois HMOs* by calling the state medical society at 800-782-4767 or contact www.isms.org; order the *Consumers' Guide to Health Plans* in the Washington, DC, area by calling the Center for the Study of Services at 202-347-7283.

■ **Questions about Medicare HMOs?** Ask the Medicare Rights Center to send their brochure, *Medicare Health Maintenance Organizations: Your Rights, Risks and Obligations.* 1460 Broadway, New York, NY 10036. Costs $3.

PHARMACEUTICALS AND PHARMACISTS

Prescription for Care

Americans and pharmaceuticals. It has become a stormy relationship. Miracle drugs developed in U.S. laboratories wiped out polio and smallpox and are the basis for long life expectancies of hundreds of millions of people around the world.

But with the cost of pharmaceuticals increasing much faster than inflation over the last 15 years, millions of Americans who can't afford life-prolonging drugs are going without. At the same time, millions of others are taking too many drugs or the wrong drugs or are taking potentially hazardous combinations of drugs. "Drug abuse" is not just about illegal substances. Another kind of drug abuse—the misuse of prescription drugs—is a serious national health problem.

The more you know about prescription drugs—what they do, how they're sold, their potential danger points—the better you will be able to afford the drugs you need and avoid harming your health with needless or improperly taken medications.

THE BASICS

Uninformed Is Unhealthy

Americans buy some $50 billion worth of prescription drugs each year—more drugs than ever and, often, pricier ones. But how much do we really know about what we're putting in our systems? Not much, according to a poll conducted for the U.S. Food and Drug Administration (FDA) of persons who had recently filled a prescription. Only a third of the polled patients remembered being told about possible side effects, only 2% to 4% said they had asked the doctor questions about their prescription, and only 3% asked their pharmacist any questions. A mere 6% said they had received written information about the prescription while in the doctor's office.

Compare these poll results with the fact that about half of prescription drugs don't work as intended because they are not used properly.

This can lead to tragic consequences: missed doses of heart drugs may lead to cardiac arrest; missed doses of antiglaucoma medications can lead to eye nerve damage and blindness. And the FDA estimates that extra health care costs from preventable drug-related illnesses add at least $20 billion to the nation's annual health care tab. More than 125,000 Americans die each year because of poor medication practices—they failed to comply with a doctor's orders, took the wrong or an inappropriate medication, or took two medications that shouldn't have been taken together. These data show the urgent need for Americans to become much better informed about what the doctor prescribes.

Need additional convincing that there's a serious problem? A total of 11,000 of the 61,000 calls received at the St. Louis Regional Poison Control Center in 1992 were questions about medications and their side effects. And according to Public Citizen Health Research Group's book, *Worst Pills, Best Pills II*, recent studies among older people have revealed that "59 percent of patients were prescribed a less-than-optimal drug or one not effective for their disease . . . 28 percent of patients were given doses which were too high . . . 48 percent of patients were given drugs with one or more harmful side interactions with other drugs."

A Prescription for Savings

Increasingly, Americans obtain their medications through their health maintenance organization (HMO) or by mail order. Both sources can produce big savings. Mail order can result in savings from 5% to 40% off the average retail price of a drug, and HMOs may sell drugs to you at slightly above wholesale.

But the 40% of insured Americans who do not have prescription drug benefits and those without insurance at all still use a pharmacy to fill prescriptions. And because they choose their pharmacy based on convenience or prompt service, they often pay too much. Surveys around the nation have found extreme price disparities among pharmacies in the same communities for the exact same medications; prices can even vary within the same chain. The pharmacy just down the block from your home could be 50% more ex-

Rx
FOR PROFITS

According to *Consumer Reports,* here's how the costs of developing and marketing new drugs are apportioned.

administrative expenses and taxes	*22%*
sales and marketing	*22%*
net profit	*14%*
research and development	*16%*
manufacturing and distribution	*26%*

pensive than one a few miles away. *The Tennessean* found in 1997 that a typical 30-day prescription of Prozac cost $66, $77, and $80 at three different pharmacies in and near Nashville.

An informal price survey of 15 drugs at 11 Seattle pharmacies, including those operated by major chains and mail-order houses, checked prices for several short-term antibiotics and for a month's supply of a dozen medications, including birth-control pills, an antihistamine, an arthritis medication, and insulin. The market basket price of all the drugs differed by 45% between the most expensive store and the least expensive.

Next-to-least expensive was the mail-order drug service of the American Association of Retired Persons (AARP), and in third place was another mail-order service, Costco Wholesale Corp. The price of 30 tablets of the hormone replacement therapy drug Premarin ranged from $9.90 from AARP to $14.95 at a Rexall drugstore. The *Seattle Times* found that small, independent pharmacies generally (but not always) had the higher prices.

A 1997 survey, this one conducted by the NYC Consumer Af-

> "**M**y doctor prescribed me a 10-day supply (50 bottles) of Proventil, which I picked up at Duane Reade, and paid $81, less 10% for senior citizens. I went to Pathmark . . . and they told me 75 bottles would cost $45. Another drugstore quoted me 50 bottles for $90."
>
> —BEA P.,
> a Manhattan senior citizen,
> in a letter to the author

fairs Department of 18 medications at 112 pharmacies, found even bigger price differences. On the same street, Third Avenue in Manhattan, the Department found that 30 pills of the blood-thinner Coumadin cost $21.88 at a large chain drugstore and $89.85 at an independent pharmacy across the street. A prescription for 125 milligrams of the antibiotic Amoxil cost $17.49 at a Rite Aid in the Bronx and just $4.66 at an independent drugstore a few blocks away.

Why such broad disparities? One reason is that drug retailers know that people rarely comparison shop for medications. Another is that large chain drugstores are able to charge less because they buy in bulk and get a discount from the manufacturer. As a result—and also because the lower prices charged to HMOs and nursing homes have to be made up elsewhere—many small, independent pharmacies are losing business and closing their doors.

Do you figure "Why bother?" because your insurance policy covers drugs? Check your co-payment. There's a chance it's now calculated as a *percentage* of the prescription price. The higher the drug price,

A VALIUM BY ANY OTHER NAME

Here are some of the most popular brand-name drugs and their generic equivalents.

Name Brand	Purpose	Generic
Amoxil	Antibiotic	Amoxicillin
Calan	High blood pressure	Verapamil
Cardizem	Heart medication	Diltiazem hydrochloride
Dyazid	High blood pressure	Hydrochlorothiazide triamterene
Darvon	Pain relief	Propoxyphene hydrochloride
Lanoxin	Heart medication	Digoxin
Premarin	Estrogen replacement	Conjugated estrogens
Procardia	Heart medication	Nifedipine
Tenormin	High blood pressure	Atenolol
Valium	Tranquilizer	Diazepam
Xanax	Antidepressant	Alprazolam
Zantac	Ulcers	Ranitidine hydrochloride

the more you pay out of pocket. Senior citizens have to be especially concerned about overpaying, since Medicare doesn't cover nonhospital drugs, and supplemental coverage may be unaffordable.

Pharmaceutical Payola

Think you're getting the drug your doctor prescribed? Think again. There's a good chance you are getting a substitute determined by a drug distributor influenced by your HMO and owned by a drug company. While there is increased scrutiny over the practices of HMOs and other managed-care organizations, there is virtually no oversight over the selection of prescription drugs.

Good-bye to the days when your doctor selected the most effective drug for your ailment and your pharmacist filled the prescription. With managed care, the health plan effectively dictates which drugs your doctor prescribes and your pharmacist dispenses. HMOs contract out this function to pharmaceutical benefits managers (PBMs), huge drug distributors that develop lists of drugs—called formularies—the HMO will cover. If the drug your doctor prescribes is on the formulary, you will get it; if not, you will very often be switched to a different drug the HMO does cover.

For instance, a 7½-year-old boy with cystic fibrosis wound up in the hospital after his insurance company mandated a drug switch from Creon to Encron. In another example, a doctor told the FDA that an insurer had pressured him into switching an 86-year-old woman from Norvasc, which had effectively controlled her high blood pressure, to Adalat, which led to "nausea, weakness, and shakiness." A Florida senior citizen who had been taking Proscar to treat an enlarged prostate gland switched health plans when he heard he would be forced to change drugs or pay $56 a month that he couldn't afford. His new plan covers Proscar.

The American Medical Association says that the "frequency and intensity" of HMO substitution interventions "pit the interest of patients against the economic interest of their health care providers" and have risen "to the level of harassment." The American College of Cardiology argues that heart medications are highly specific to particular patients and warns that substitutions represent "a real and present danger." Surveys of almost 400 New York physicians and pharmacists by the NYC Public Advocate's office found that three quarters believe substitutions are diminishing care, while almost all said plans routinely contact and urge them to make substitutions.

The initial rationale for turning over drug management to PBMs was cost containment (but costs have continued to rise anyway). PBMs pay incentives to pharmacists to get them to push doctors to switch prescriptions, and drop independent pharmacists who do not engineer switches often enough. PBM consultants call and visit doctors to discuss specific patients and urge the use of specific drugs. They impose rock-bottom prescription budgets on doctors, and review the prescribing records of recalcitrant physicians to ensure they make the favored drug selections. They even punish patients who do not accept switches by charging them higher co-payments. Yet PBMs are neither licensed as health care providers nor regulated by any oversight agency.

And PBM drug preferences are frequently of questionable independence. Since 1993, the three largest PBMs, serving fully 80 percent of covered enrollees, have been acquired by pharmaceutical manufacturers at a total cost of $12.8 billion. Other manufacturers have formed "strategic alliances" with major PBMs, paying millions of dollars in rebate payments for preferential treatment on a formulary. The overarching corporate purpose of these acquisitions and arrangements has clearly been to increase market share for certain widely used drugs. Studies have shown, for example, that the manufacturer-

COLD AND FLU REMEDIES: COUGH UP LESS

When the prestigious Johns Hopkins Medical School compared children with colds who took antihistamine-decongestants to children with colds who received placebos or no medication at all, parents told researchers that the children felt better in a day or two with or without medication. Conclusion: The longest-running medical mystery remains unsolved. Time is the only known cure for the common cold or flu, though, yes, chicken soup isn't a bad idea—it is a natural decongestant and expectorant.

Nonetheless, Americans spend over $3.2 billion a year on over-the-counter cold and flu medications. "These products can make you feel more comfortable while you suffer," says FDA scientist Debbie Lumpkins. If you keep in mind that they treat symptoms, not the underlying illness, you may be able to get some relief, or at least a good night's sleep. But it will cost you.

Most popular remedies attack two or more symptoms with a combination of ingredients. To avoid spending more than necessary, familiarize yourself with names of the active ingredients and treat only the symptoms you have. No sense paying to cure ills you haven't got.

Expectorants are supposed to loosen phlegm, but their effectiveness is disputed. Common expectorants are guaifenesin, glycerol guaiacolate, and terpin hydrate.

Antitussives suppress coughs. Dextromethorphan hydrobromide is the most common. But don't overdo it—coughing has the important function of removing phlegm.

owned PBMs are, not surprisingly, pushing the prime pills of their owner.

PCS, for example, is the largest PBM, covering 50 million people. It was acquired by Eli Lilly, the manufacturer of Prozac, in 1994. Lilly's chairman openly declared after the PCS merger that "this purchase will help us sell even more Prozac." Internal PCS memos revealed a plan to steer the company's managed care customers toward Prozac and another top Lilly drug, the ulcer medication Axid. Yet both drugs cost more than effective alternative drugs offered by competing companies.

Such drug policies influenced by commercial interests can have damaging effects on care. Patients are being switched to chemically dissimilar agents that are not rated as equivalent by the FDA, and usually have different side effects, dosages, and efficacy rates. Patients stabi-

Nasal decongestants shrink respiratory system blood vessels that have been dilated, opening nasal passages and making it easier to breathe. Common decongestants are phenylephrine hydrochloride, phenylpropanolamine (PPA), pseudoephedrine hydrochloride (found in Sudafed and Actifed), ephedrine, and desoxyephedrine. Nonpharmaceutical methods that may also work include breathing warm, moist air, such as the mist from a hot shower, or eating spicy food like jalapeño peppers, garlic, or horseradish.

Antihistamines ease runny noses and sneezing. A common one is clemastine fumarate.

Analgesics—aspirin, acetaminophen, ibuprofen—reduce fever and relieve pain.

Compare the amount of the active ingredient in each product and buy whatever is cheapest. Here are a few tips if you're in too much of a cold-induced fog to figure it out.

■ Buy the store brand or generic. It's cheaper than the heavily advertised brand name and contains the same active ingredients in the same strength: e.g., Tylenol costs 26¢ a gram, but Valu-Rite acetaminophen costs only 8¢ a gram, and an antihistamine-decongestant ranges from 2¢ (Genovese store brand) to 13¢ per hour of relief (Fedahist D).
■ Buy tablets. Caplets, capsules, and especially liquids cost more: e.g., Comtrex Liquid costs two and a half times more than Comtrex Tablets but contains the same amounts of the same active ingredients.
■ Take an analgesic separately. Getting it built into cold remedies jacks up the price substantially.

lized on one medication are also being moved to another without any clinical cause, leading one doctor to label these switching strategies "massive unfunded human experimentation." With doctors constrained by preferred lists, the many differences between patients—age, ethnicity, multiple disease status—are not always factored into prescribing decisions.

Hurt most by these practices are the elderly and chronically ill because they often consume daily dosages of a variety of highly competitive medications. Take the example of 65-year-old Clara D., a retired grocery store manager from Bolivar, Tennessee. She lost a third of her stomach after her ulcer medication was switched. Her physician tried to persuade her plan not to force the substitution but it insisted. While recovering from the operation she suffered a paralyzing stroke.

FIND OUT WHAT'S WHAT

When your doctor hands you a prescription, ask these questions and write down the answers.

- What is the exact name of the drug? What is it supposed to do? What dosage am I taking?
- How and when do I take it? When do I stop?
- What foods, drinks, or activities should be avoided while taking the drug?
- What are the side effects? What do I do if I feel them?
- Will this new prescription work safely with the other prescription and nonprescription medicines I am taking?

You might also want to ask about those mysterious abbreviations doctors write on prescriptions. A few sample translations: QID means four times daily, TID means three times daily, PC means before meals, and HS means at bedtime.

Many seniors have enrolled in Medicare HMOs in the last few years—in large part because of the prescription drug benefit, which Medicare doesn't offer. Before enrolling in an HMO, seniors should discuss the list of covered medications with their doctors and whether a drug switch could be necessary and advisable given their medical history.

Save More with Generics

A new drug is first introduced to the market under a brand name by the company that researched and developed it. After a given period (usually 17 years), the company's patent expires and other companies are permitted to start making the same drug as a "generic," sold under a different name. The FDA says generics are as safe and effective as brand-name equivalents. Even though they may be a different color or shape, generics are required to have the same active ingredients and in the same amounts.

Although generic and brand-name drugs need not be *exactly* the same, most doctors believe that the only practical difference between them is price and that it is entirely safe to substitute them in the vast majority of cases. Generic drugs generally cost about half as much as their brand-name equivalents. A 1993 Minneapolis-St. Paul survey found some generics costing 70% to 80% less than their brand-name equivalents. Not surprisingly, given the pressure from American health insurers to reduce costs, generics have gone from about 5% of U.S. prescriptions 15 years ago to 43% today.

Generics cost less because all of the safety and effectiveness testing has already been done; the generic manufacturer need only prove to the FDA that its product is "bio-equivalent" to the brand-name counterpart, meaning that your body will absorb the generic at the same speed and to the same extent. Generic manufacturers also spend comparatively little on marketing, since the low price sells the drug without advertising.

To help resolve any remaining concerns about the safety and efficacy of generics, an FDA commission studied the differences and concluded that there was an overall effectiveness differential of only about 3.5% between brand-name and generic drug—not enough to make a significant difference.

Unfortunately, generics occasionally disappear from the market. One example: Warfarin is the generic version of DuPont's blood-thinner Coumadin. When the two manufacturers of generic Warfarin stopped making it, the price of Coumadin tripled.

Your Pharmacist Shouldn't Just Count Pills

Pharmacists receive years of specialized training, yet many pharmacists act merely as pill dispensers. You hand over a prescription and the pharmacist puts pills in a bottle, types a label, hands it back to you, and takes your money. Seldom do pharmacists take the time to strut their stuff.

Fortunately, this is changing. A new federal law requires pharmacists to offer counseling services and to keep records for all Medicaid prescriptions. All but a handful of states have extended this law to cover all prescriptions, not just Medicaid ones. The pharmacist

must record not only basic personal statistics like name and age, but also known allergies, drug reactions, chronic diseases, and a comprehensive list of all your medications. Most pharmacies have computer systems that enable them to easily record and retrieve all this data.

In addition, the new law requires pharmacists to conduct a "prospective drug review" before filling a prescription, which includes a review for possible harmful drug interactions, incorrect dosages, and serious interactions with over-the-counter drugs. Their computers are programmed to alert them to dangerous combinations.

In about half the states, the pharmacist must personally offer counseling each time you fill a prescription; in other states an assistant may make the counseling offer. You can always refuse the advice, but if you do want it, the pharmacist should tell you about dosage, form, at what times you are to take the medication, duration of therapy, any special precautions or storage requirements, common side effects, prescription refill information, and what to do if you miss or accidentally double a dose. Mail-order pharmacies may provide counseling over toll-free phone lines. The federal agency that wrote the initial counseling legislation estimates that counseling should take two to four minutes per patient.

This new approach is a cost-effective proconsumer breakthrough —why not utilize an expert who's already at the point of purchase to educate customers about their prescriptions and their health?

Some stores are embracing the new law; the large Walgreen and Eckerd chains have added waiting rooms or counseling areas in their new or remodeled stores. But too many high-volume, deep-discount chain drugstores are dragging their feet in complying; they make money by moving customers in and out of the store quickly, and providing a customer direct contact with a pharmacist slows things down.

In a 1996 Georgetown University Medical School study, testers presented prescriptions for both Seldane (an antihistamine) and erythromycin (a common antibiotic) to 50 Washington, DC, drugstores. About a third of the pharmacists filled the prescriptions without comment—even though this is a potentially deadly mixture. When Channel 10 in Miami repeated the study, the results were worse: 40% of the pharmacists raised no question.

If your drugstore is not complying, report it to your state pharmacy board. (Look under the government listings in the phone book.) In Iowa, two pharmacists at a discount chain drugstore formally complained to the state's pharmacy board that understaffing kept them from counseling patients as required by law. The store was fined $25,000 and its license was put on probation for three years.

WHAT TO WATCH OUT FOR

Inappropriate medication. Physicians are bombarded with misleading pharmaceutical advertising in medical journals; 92% of advertisements in one government survey potentially violated at least one FDA regulation. *Health Letter,* published by Public Citizen Health Research Group, reported that many ads promote the use of powerful drugs for trivial maladies, cite irrelevant or weak scientific studies, or do not appropriately highlight side effects. Yet the FDA has taken almost no disciplinary action against the offending manufacturers.

How can you protect yourself? Learn as much as you can about the prescription drugs you take. Consult the Health Research Group's guide, *Worst Pills, Best Pills II* (see **HELP** at the end of this chapter) and closely question your doctor and your pharmacist about their choice of medication.

OTC and prescription drugs that don't mix. Certain over-the-counter drugs shouldn't be taken with prescription drugs. One pharmacy owner says he sometimes sees customers, who he knows are taking high blood pressure drugs, buying over-the-counter cough medications. The two are dangerous together. If you're on a maintenance medication, ask your doctor or pharmacist before you take an OTC product for the first time.

Pharmacists who don't know you. Try to use one pharmacy, and give your pharmacist the whole picture. If you fill prescriptions at different pharmacies, tell each pharmacist all the drugs you take. Under the new counseling laws, pharmacists are required to keep track of your medications and warn you if there are two or more medications you should not be taking at the same time.

Busy pharmacies. An additional side effect of drugstore competition, managed care, and counseling laws is the increased workload at many pharmacies. To free up the pharmacist and cut costs, many pharmacies rely on technicians to do the things pharmacists used to do—and are trained to do—such as count out pills, mix medications, type labels, and enter prescription data into computers.

But 60% of pharmacists surveyed expressed worry that this could increase errors, as a Maryland mother found out when she picked up an antibiotic to treat her son's strep throat. Even after she had given her son the medicine for the prescribed week, the bottle was still half full. When she asked the pharmacist about it, she was told the syrup had been over-diluted by a technician. The mistake caused no harm, but, as the mother told *The Washington Post,* it was "really scary" that someone other than the pharmacist was preparing medication.

Expired medication. Although you'll rarely see an expiration date on the bottle, most medicines lose potency after a while. Liquids may partially evaporate, making the remaining medicine too concentrated to use safely. Eye drops can become contaminated with bacteria after a month. Unfortunately, most states do not require expiration dates to be placed on prescription medication packaging.

Ask your pharmacist to double-check how long you can keep using your supply of a drug. Surveys by the NYC Department of Consumer Affairs found that 78% of 200 New York pharmacists gave bad advice when called over the telephone about medicine shelf life. For example, estimates of how long a supply of propranolol (a common medication) would last varied from six months to four years. The wrong answers stemmed in part from the druggists' failure to check the lot number to see how old the medication in question was.

Drugs from south of the border. It's tempting. Down Mexico way drugs can cost a quarter of what they do in the U.S. One survey found that 60 Zantac pills, an ulcer medication, cost $105.58 in an El Paso drugstore but only $22.02 just across the border in Juarez. Inhalers with the drug Vanceril cost $31.92 each in Iowa; in Mexico you can get three for $17. But drugs bought outside the U.S. do not necessarily meet U.S. quality and safety standards. While some may indeed be the same brand-name drugs sold here, others may be generics made in factories without FDA quality controls. So be very careful about what you buy in Mexico or other foreign countries.

While it is unlawful to bring drugs into the U.S. without a prescription, the FDA says it practices "enforcement discretion." Translation: U.S. Customs can seize any drugs for which you do not have a prescription, but in practice they don't if you're bringing them back for personal use.

THE $MARTER CONSUMER

Use buying services and mail order. Your savings, when compared to drugstore prices, could be significant. For example, Consumer Reports found that if you purchase a 90-day supply of Glyburide, the generic version of the diabetes control medication Diabeta, it costs $8.09 per month through Medi-Mail. A month's supply of Diabeta itself from a pharmacy in the New York City suburbs cost $26.95 per month. You could save $226 a year. But you'll have to take the initiative to call the mail-order company's toll-free "800" phone number for counseling if you have questions or need advice.

Store your prescription drugs correctly. Most drugs do best in a cool, dry place, but follow any special storing instructions carefully.

Follow your doctor's orders. While it's a good idea to question the initial choice of a particular drug, once it's finally settled on, *take it as directed.* Numerous studies have shown that a third to half of all drugs are not taken correctly. Typically, patients don't take the medication for the complete course, or they take it at the wrong times or with the wrong foods. Their negligence could make the drug therapy ineffective, which may lead the doctor to needlessly prescribe a stronger drug—one that may be more expensive to boot.

Get what you pay for—the patient profile, the full counseling. Remember, if you're a senior citizen or a resident of one of the states requiring counseling for everyone buying prescription drugs, you're paying for that counseling; its cost has been passed to you through higher prescription prices.

Go generic, if appropriate. Ask your physician or pharmacist whether there is a suitable (and cheaper) substitute, such as a generic or a different drug that accomplishes the same therapeutic mission.

Take advantage of discounts. Many drugstores give senior citizens 10% off. Ask: It may not be posted.

Keep medication records. It's smart to keep an individual medication profile for each family member. Record every prescription medication taken, how long it was taken, the dosage, and any side effects. Include the manufacturer of the medication. Don't rely on the new pharmacist counseling laws to make your pharmacist keep all this information for you. And give the list to your family doctor periodically to review for potential problems.

H E L P

■ **The basic drug ref**erence book is the *Physician's Desk Reference*—the "PDR"—available at most public libraries.

■ **Want to know more about pre**scription drugs? For that, we suggest consulting the 690-page book *Worst Pills, Best Pills II*, published by the Public Citizen Health Research Group. It includes information on hundreds of commonly prescribed drugs and is available at bookstores.

■ **The American Association of Re**tired Persons (AARP) drug mail-order program can be reached by calling (800) 456-2277. You need not be a member to use it.

■ **Other mail-order houses from** which anyone can order: Medi-Mail,

(800) 922-3444, DPD Action Pharmacy, (800) 452-1976.

■ **The American Academy of** Otolaryngology–Head and Neck Surgery publishes a leaflet, "Antihistamines, Decongestants and Cold Remedies." They'll send you one if you send them a self-addressed, stamped envelope to 1 Prince Street, Alexandria, VA 22314, (703) 836-4444.

■ **The Public Citizen Health Research** Group, a not-for-profit investigative and advocacy organization, publishes a very informative monthly *Health Letter.* Among the regular features are medical device recalls, safety alerts, and the "Outrage of the Month." A one-year subscription is $18. Send check or money order made out to Health Letter, 1600 20th Street NW, Washington, DC, 20009.

CHAPTER 6

DOCTORS AND HOSPITALS

How to Keep Your Health and Wealth

American health care is the best in the world. Ailing people from around the world seek cancer treatment at New York City's renowned Memorial Sloan-Kettering Cancer Center and open-heart surgery at the Cleveland Clinic and Boston's Massachusetts General Hospital. Foreigners flock to our unsurpassed medical schools. American medical researchers almost routinely win Nobel prizes. New wonder drugs and amazing diagnostic tools like MRIs, ultrasound, and laser surgery have been developed and perfected here.

But another, darker side to the American health care success story is emerging. To curb the growth in health care spending, insurers and government are putting hospitals and doctors on severe reducing diets. Some hospitals are laying off staff in droves. Congress and the president had to step in to outlaw money-saving "drive by" baby deliveries. Doctors increasingly see their medical judgment second-

guessed by managed-care company utilization reviewers. And millions of Americans are being switched to outpatient instead of inpatient surgery, which isn't always in the best interest of the patient.

In most areas of consumer concern, arming yourself with information can save you money. In the increasingly austere health care environment, when it comes to doctors and hospitals, it could also save you your health and maybe your life.

THE BASICS

Doctors

She greets you wearing an immaculate white coat, a stethoscope hanging around her neck. You deferentially address her as "Doctor," and she has the special power to give "doctor's orders" and write prescriptions.

Don't be intimidated. Yes, the doctor had many years of schooling, followed by internships and hospital residencies. And yes, she kept you waiting for an hour. But don't forget, she's working for *you*. You hired her to provide a service for you, not the other way around.

Finding one. If you're one of those people who brags about not having a doctor because you are so healthy, you'd better change your tune. If you have no regular doctor and you need medical attention, the doctor you see may have to run more tests because she is unfamiliar with you and wants to protect herself from being sued. In fact, most doctors prefer not to see new patients who need emergency care.

Start your search for a doctor by asking relatives and friends for referrals. You might also call your local medical society, where you can also ask about credentials, although such societies don't screen doctors for any other qualities.

You can read up on doctors' basic credentials in *The American Medical Directory* and the *Directory of Medical Specialists,* available in many public libraries. Many HMOs will give you the necessary basic information about their participating doctors over the telephone.

> "**M**edical negligence kills more than 100,000 Americans every year and injures more than half a million. Yet only about 2,000 physicians are disciplined each year by state medical boards. The vast majority get a slap on the wrist— or a warning short of probation. . . ."
>
> —DR. HARVEY F. WACHSMAN, a lawyer and neurosurgeon in Great Neck, N.Y.

The medical school attended doesn't make all that much difference if it is in the U.S. or Canada, but standards vary widely for foreign medical schools. One indication is that foreign med school grads are somewhat less likely to pass important parts of the U.S. national licensing exam.

A residency is a tough three-year stint (even longer for specialists) working in a hospital right after graduating from medical school. Residency in a prestigious teaching hospital may be preferred.

It is important to note whether the doctor is board-certified. Board certification means that the doctor has passed rigorous exams in a particular field— everything from family practice and internal medicine to cardiology and neurology. Many HMOs now require their doctors to be board-certified or become so within a few years. A claim that a doctor is "board eligible" is meaningless.

Find out with which hospital(s) the doctor is affiliated. If you need to be hospitalized someday, that's where you will probably be admitted.

If you are looking for a specialist, start by asking a primary care doctor you trust. A specialist who also teaches the subject is best; they may have the title "clinical professor."

Most states collect at least some data on individual physicians. Massachusetts gives its citizens access to complete physician profiles through a toll-free hot line, including malpractice case history, hospital and medical board disciplinary actions, criminal convictions, hospital and health plan affiliations, medical school attended, and board certifications. In Florida, officials are working on the state's first doctor guide, identifying doctors with disciplinary and malpractice problems.

Private groups also are getting into the act. In 1997, the Pacific Business Group on Health published a ranking of 50 major California physician practice groups. The report card is based on preventive care records and patient surveys.

A new source of information about doctors became available in 1998. The American Medical Accreditation Association, a data system created by the American Medical Association, was rolled out in Idaho, Maryland, Montana, New Jersey, and Washington, DC, with the rest of the country to follow. Doctors will have to pay a small application fee to be listed. Education, licenses, disciplinary actions by a hospital or board of medical examiners, peer review of clinical performance, and participation in continuing medical education are some of the information that will be revealed at no cost to the public. But, at least for now, the new system won't reveal anything about malpractice suits or patient outcomes or satisfaction.

New York State's Health Department began releasing heart bypass operation mortality rates by surgeon and hospital in 1991. Twenty-one different risk factors are applied to the raw mortality rates, including the patient's age and severity of illness, to reach a risk-adjusted mortality rate for surgeons performing at least 200 such operations during a three-year period. The statewide average mortality for 1984 was 2.32%, although the death rate was less than 1.25% for a handful of physicians and exceeded 5% for some others. Pennsylvania began releasing physician bypass mortality rates in 1992.

Before the visit. How many times have you come home from the doctor only to realize that you forgot to ask an important question? This won't happen if you write down all your symptoms and questions beforehand, ranked in order of priority.

If this is a first visit, assemble any medical records you have or can get, and bring them with you. Ask how often the doctor is away or otherwise unavailable. Also ask whether the doctor accepts phone calls at any particular time of the week to answer questions. The doctor may attend numerous medical conferences, take long vacations, or split her practice among locations— in which case you'll definitely want to ask about the credentials of the doctor who covers for her.

During the visit. Take notes when you see the doctor. And ask lots of questions about alternatives to prescribed courses of treatment and tests. Don't be bashful.

Despite a new emphasis in medical schools on developing rapport with patients, too many doctors still lack a good "bedside manner." They can be terse and dismiss your questions. Some doctors speak to patients the way they talk to colleagues—in "medicalese" laced with clinical terminology and abbreviations.

Ask about any medication prescribed for you. How long will it be before it takes effect? What can (or can't) you eat while medicated? What are the potential side effects? How will it interact with other medications or over-the-counter drugs?

Physician penmanship is notoriously undecipherable. Combine this with medical abbreviations such as "q4h" (take the medicine every four hours) and the prescription your doctor hands you will probably make about as much sense as ancient Mayan glyphs. Ask the doctor to decode it.

If you need surgery, ask the surgeon how many times she has performed the operation in the last year. In this case, practice *does* make perfect.

Doctor billing. Billing can be a very sensitive subject. Most doctors prefer not to present themselves to patients as businesspeople. And they won't mention fees unless you ask.

Do check carefully and question any charges you don't understand. In one case reported in *The New York Times,* a doctor's hospital bill for a maternity patient included a code number next to a $4,225 fee. It turned out she had been charged for total obstetric care when, in re-ality, the doctor provided only pre-delivery care, which cost $98.

Many a billing dispute could be avoided if doctors only disclosed to each patient the cost for standardized procedures before treatment, just as haircutters, home improvement contractors, and mechanics do.

Physician oversight—or, perhaps we should say, undersight. While most physicians are competent and some are superlative, many should try some other line of work or be put out to pasture. Trouble is, in most areas of the country, you can't rely on state authorities to weed out the problem doctors.

The nonprofit and independent Public Citizen Health Research Group has been closely monitoring state disciplinary activities. Their conclusion: Most medical review boards are slipshod, take far too long to process complaints, and are very hesitant to mete out serious discipline. Public Citizen found that among states with the lowest ratios of disciplinary actions in 1995 were such major population centers as Massachusetts (ranked 40th), Pennsylvania (43rd), Illinois (45th), and Wisconsin (47th).

Here are three examples of how the current system has hurt people:

■ Dr. David Benjamin had been brought up on disciplinary charges in 1990 and 1991. In 1993, he allegedly killed a woman as a result of a botched abortion. His license was ultimately suspended and he has been indicted for murder.
■ A young girl went to the hospital for a routine tonsillectomy. While she was comatose, doctors argued

for 25 minutes over whose responsibility it was to administer cardiopulmonary resuscitation (CPR). The girl died.

■ Then there's the story of 8-year-old Gussie, as told by Laura Wittkin of the Center for Patients' Rights. The Illinois child had developed an aneurysm as a result of a car accident. It went undiagnosed and mistreated for four years; doctors said the child's odd behavior was mere acting out because he was jealous of his siblings. One New Year's Eve the aneurysm burst and Gussie underwent ten hours of brain surgery—and then died. Gussie had been "acting out" because he had been in such intense pain. He would have had a 95% chance of complete recovery had the easily detected aneurysm been treated in time. Yet according to Wittkin, ten years have passed and the responsible doctors are still practicing.

Unfortunately, the National Practitioner Data Bank—which is supposed to help keep problem doctors from restarting their practices in a new state—lets cases slip through the cracks. A few years ago, a Maine woman who had broken her nose underwent what she thought would be a simple surgical procedure to reopen an air passage. Instead, the surgeon did a radical nose job, which dramatically altered her appearance—without altering her breathing. She later learned that the doctor had been sued in Maine five times and had settled all of the cases out of court. Later, he moved to Kentucky, where he was sued twice again.

How can you protect yourself? Follow our previous advice on how to research a doctor's credentials before being treated. And lobby to make sure your state's regulatory authorities have the funds and incentive to discipline incompetent doctors.

Hospitals

Hospitals make many people so uncomfortable that they avoid visiting sick relatives. Being a hospitalized patient is an even more unsettling and disorienting experience. Yet if you find yourself about to be hospitalized, you or your loved ones will need to be alert, knowledgeable, and assertive if you are to get the best care possible.

This section is not a comprehensive consumer guide to hospitals. For that you should read *Take This Book to the Hospital With You*, by Charles B. Inlander and Ed Weiner of the People's Medical Society (see **HELP** at the end of this chapter). It tells you how to change your room, your doctor, or your nurse; how to lower your chance of becoming a malpractice victim; how to avoid signing away important rights; and includes a wealth of other practical advice. Since doctors, nurses, and hospital administrators both respect and fear this volume, just setting it on your hospital bedside table might improve your treatment.

Staying out of them. It's a good idea to avoid a hospital stay if at all possible. Hospitals expose you to interrupted sleep and more television-watching than you ever thought you could stand. More seriously, they expose you to infection. Between 5% and 10% of hospitalized patients pick up an infection they didn't have before entering the hospital, according to the U.S. Centers for Disease Control and Prevention. These include somewhat benign urinary tract infections but also potentially fatal pneumonias and infections of wounds and of the bloodstream. It has been estimated that hospital-based infections are implicated in as many as 150,000 deaths each year.

A Harvard Medical School study of New York State hospitals, released in 1990—and still cited as definitive—also disclosed just how unhealthy hospitals can be. Looking at the year 1984, they estimated that 27,000 patients—3.7% of those hospitalized—were injured as a result of an "adverse event" in their medical care. In about 1% of patients, medical negligence caused the injury, which sometimes led to permanent disability or death. The Harvard report also found that "eight times as many patients suffered an injury from negligence as filed a malpractice claim in New York State."

And it's not just New York. Sidney Wolfe, M.D., director of the Public Citizen Health Research Group, has written that 50% of hospitals around the country did not adequately monitor patients in intensive care units, 40% had safety standard deficiencies, and 51% did not adequately monitor whether unnecessary surgery was being done or was being done safely.

Hospitals also make numerous medication errors. The warning on a patient chart about a drug allergy might not be heeded, or the wrong dosage given, or the wrong drug administered. A study at one major hospital published in the *Journal of the American Medical Association* in 1997 concluded that "adverse drug reactions" complicated 2.43 of every 100 admissions to the hospital. The medication errors that caused these reactions led to longer hospital stays, a higher death rate, and increased costs.

Comparing hospitals. There is a regrettable absence of good statistical information with which to compare hospitals on issues like prices, infection rates, the ratio of nurses to patients, and average lengths of stay for specified diagnoses.

Fortunately, under pressure from major employers and consumer advocates, the walls of secrecy are starting to come down. Pennsylvania led the way in 1988 by creating the Pennsylvania Health Care Cost Containment Council. The Council monitors the cost as well as the out-

> "*I saw a male patient's hospital bill listing a hysterectomy and an entry for crutches on the bill of a patient who was admitted for chest pains.*"
>
> —JOANNE FRITSCH, a former registered nurse, now with a major national business consultancy

comes of 59 different procedures at each hospital in the state and publishes this information in periodic *Hospital Effectiveness Reports.* In Cleveland, 31 hospitals, 2,500 doctors, 50 corporations, and 8,000 small businesses have collaborated to collect information from hospitals on mortality rates and length of stay for a wide range of procedures. In 1996, Florida's Agency for Health Care Administration issued its first *Guide to Hospitals in Florida.* This 418-page book compares 15 of the most common hospital services according to average length-of-stay, average total charges, and mortality rates. The state's health chief is said to think of it as "a *Consumer Reports* for hospitals."

Regardless of the increasing availability of such information, it's a good idea to carefully check out a hospital before you are admitted if you have a chance to do so. Start by paying a visit. Does the place look and smell clean? For how long have the trays been left in patients' rooms after meals?

Also call the information line of the Joint Commission on the Accreditation of Healthcare Organizations (JCAHO; see **HELP** at the end of this chapter) to check on the hospital's accreditation status. About 6% of hospitals are accredited with "commendation," another 2% with no recommendations for improvement, and approximately 90% with specific improvement recommendations. Another 2% of hospitals receive "conditional" accreditation, meaning that they were performing only marginally. Every year only a small handful are not accredited.

Accreditation status is good for three years.

To learn your hospital's actual accreditation score (on a scale of 100), how it compares with other hospitals, and the specific areas where accreditors found your hospital needed improvement, you have to ask the JCAHO operator to send you a copy of the hospital's Performance Report. Reports for up to ten hospitals are free. They take a few weeks to arrive.

The JCAHO has been criticized by patient advocacy groups for going too easy on the hospital industry; critics point out that 80% of the revenues of this private group come from the surveyed hospitals and that the industry effectively controls the organization. Their accreditation scores are still useful, though, because if your hospital performs *comparatively poorly,* you should be concerned about the quality of the care you might receive.

If there is time, additional questions you should ask before admission include:

■ *Does the hospital have all the specialized services and equipment you might need?* Let's say you are being admitted for a cardiac condition. Does the hospital have a coronary intensive care unit separate from the regular medical-surgical intensive care unit? Does it have cardiac rehab beds so that you can stay in the same facility after your initial recovery if necessary? What if your child is being admitted? Some hospitals have designated pediatric units or floors, others don't. Or if your elderly parent is being admitted, does it have specialized geriatric-psychiatric services?

Some of the specialized equipment you might want to check for, depending on your diagnosis, includes: CT scanner (used for whole-body or head scans), extracorporeal shockwave lithotripter (used to noninvasively disintegrate kidney stones), MRI machine (if the hospital has none, you might have to be transported to another location if you require an MRI scan), positron emission tomography scanner (PET scans are done of the brain or heart), and single photon emission computerized tomography (combines gamma camera imaging and computed tomographic imaging).

You can also learn about services and equipment by consulting the American Hospital Association's annual hospital guide, available in many public libraries.

■ *Is it a major medical center?* If you are undergoing a complex or relatively risky procedure, a large medical center is probably preferable. It is more likely to have the most advanced equipment and the most (and most varied) experience, and all the labs are on the premises. Major medical centers are also more likely to be teaching (doctor-training) hospitals, which attracts top doctors who double as medical school professors. If it is a teaching hospital, you might want to check further to see if it is a member of the selective Council of Teaching Hospitals (COTH) and also ask about the areas where it has "residency" (training) programs. For instance, if you are to undergo a quadruple heart bypass operation, a hospital that has a cardiology residency program is likely to have top cardiac experts who also teach and conduct research.

■ *How many times has your procedure been performed in the hospital during the previous year?* Practice does make perfect. For instance, if you are undergoing open-heart surgery, the American Heart Association has recommended that you choose a hospital that performs at least 200 open-heart operations a year. A study reported in the *New England Journal of Medicine* in 1994 concluded that hospitals that perform at least 200 angioplasties a year do significantly better than those that perform fewer—the result is fewer mortalities and major complications. A hospital should be able to tell you these numbers. (Also find out how many procedures your doctor has performed compared to colleagues. A different study found that for doctors who perform at least 50 angioplasties a year, the mortality rates are lower.)

■ *What is the physician board-certification rate?* As explained on page 69, board-certification means that the doctor has passed rigorous exams in a chosen field. The top hospitals attract the top—usually board-certified—doctors. And many of the best HMOs now require that their doctors be board-certified or leave. So be a bit wary about a hospital in which fewer than 65% of the attending and staff doctors are board-certified. Be extra careful if the rate is less than 55%.

If you are pregnant, find out about your local hospitals' obstetric facilities well before your due date. There are big differences. Chief among them is the level of neonatal care. Some hospitals are authorized to offer only the most basic care and handle uncomplicated emergencies. Others can deal with higher-risk cases, and the highest-level hospitals take referrals from other hospitals. Also ask:

■ *Does the hospital offer educational programs in childbirth, caring for newborns, breast-feeding, pre- and postnatal exercises?*
■ *Does the hospital arrange physician interviews for prospective parents? Tours of the facilities?*

Many hospitals are opening special "birthing centers" with all the comforts of home—designer-decorated rooms, a full-size bed, a rocking chair, and a bassinet. A family room may also be provided.

About emergency rooms. In less-urgent emergencies, ambulance drivers in most localities will honor your emergency room preference if it doesn't lengthen the trip too much. So it makes sense to find out about your local emergency rooms ("ERs") now, before you need one. They aren't all the same.

Some of the smaller ERs can basically just stabilize a seriously ill patient for transfer to a larger institution. Others are certified as trauma centers and still others are regional trauma centers. Trauma centers have additional equipment and must have surgeons always on the premises or immediately available in the hospital. The highest-level trauma centers must also have various specialists on standby. Some ERs are designated as burn care units.

There are hospitals that hire moonlighters—doctors (sometimes postgrad residents) who make extra cash by working part-time or per diem in emergency rooms. You should be wary of a hospital that uses mostly moonlighting ER doctors.

Best is an ER where many of the doctors are board-certified in the specialty of emergency medicine—they're specialists in emergency medicine, much like a neurologist is a specialist in the nervous system. Board certification in emergency medicine shows a special commitment to the field and a desire to work in emergency rooms. Some ERs have no emergency medicine board-certified doctors, while at other hospitals half or more of the ER doctors have achieved this preferred status.

Your best bet: an ER certified as a trauma center in a hospital that has a doctor-training (residency) program in emergency medicine.

Outpatient vs. inpatient. Around the nation, hospitals are cutting back on inpatient beds—and opening ambulatory surgery centers—because an overnight stay is no longer being ordered for many kinds of surgery. Hospital stays are shorter, too, as managed-care insurers aggressively press doctors to reduce costs. (See pages 44–46 in the HMO section for more on this topic.) The use of less-invasive surgical procedures such as laparoscopy and laser surgery, and the rapid growth of the home health care industry and home infusion of medication have helped spur the outpatient trend.

Outpatient surgery has undeniable advantages besides saving the health care system money. You need not be away from your family and friends overnight. You avoid exposure to hospital-based infections.

But there are some big potential downsides. Your family might be pressed into caring for you—not just bringing you breakfast in bed, but helping dress your wounds and administering medications. You might not be mentally ready to go home immediately after a serious procedure, especially one so emotion-charged as a partial mastectomy or hysterectomy. And only at the hospital can you be injected with some of the more powerful narcotic painkillers. Among the procedures seeing a big rise in outpatient surgery—and where surgical complications could most easily arise—are removal of fallopian tubes and ovaries, extended simple mastectomies, abdominal hernia repair, and vaginal hysterectomy.

There has been a public backlash against some outpatient excesses. A new federal law mandates coverage for a minimum of 48 hours after a normal delivery if the doctor requests it. In 1997, New York State passed a law prohibiting outpatient radical mastectomies. But lawmakers can't legislate limb by limb or organ by organ.

So if you are being recommended for outpatient surgery for even a mildly complicated procedure, ask your doctor these questions:

- Exactly how comfortable is your doctor with taking the outpatient route? Is there a lot of pressure from your insurer? Ask your doctor, "If I was fabulously wealthy and paying out of my own pocket, would this procedure still be done on an outpatient basis?"
- How good is the follow-up care? Will nurses make home visits? Is there a 24-hour phone line staffed by competent professionals for you to call with questions? What is the procedure in case there is an after-hours emergency?
- If the surgery is in a freestanding, non-hospital-based ambulatory surgery center, is it affiliated with a hospital? Which hospital? What is the transfer plan in case of an emergency? Do the center's physicians practice at the hospital?
- Some of the freestanding surgery centers may not be accredited by any of the accrediting organizations, such as the Joint Commission on Accreditation of Health Care Organizations, even though a group of doctors runs them. And has your state certified or licensed the center (and not just the doctors in it)?

Do you need every hospital test? Probably not. Doctors trying to avoid malpractice suits sometimes practice "defensive medicine." That is, they order tests for every conceivable diagnosis so that they can prove they covered all the bases if you sue them. Sometimes, consulting physicians and "house" (hospital-based) physicians will order tests for their own use without realizing you just had the same tests done by another doctor.

Excess tests are also sometimes ordered by inexperienced student residents lacking confidence.

Most tests come with at least a bit of risk, from developing a minor infection after having blood drawn to potentially serious hazards such as excessive radiation exposure (if nuclear medicine tests keep being repeated) or injury from invasive procedures like spinal taps and catheterization. Keep X rays to a minimum because of the possible harmful long-term effects of accumulated radiation. Since a CAT (computerized axial tomography) scan consists of many X-ray pictures, it, too, should be used sparingly. On the other hand, CAT scans are often used in place of even riskier invasive diagnostic procedures such as angiography. Ultrasound tests, which bombard the body with ultrafast sonic waves, are entirely safe. MRI (magnetic resonance imaging) is also safe (unless you have a pacemaker), since the equipment merely records the body's electromagnetic waves.

Question carefully the purpose and necessity of each and every test, starting with preadmission testing; if you were just tested by your own doctor, you may not need a full battery of the hospital's preadmission tests.

> "*I magine a supermarket with no price tags, no lists of ingredients or nutritional information to judge value, and where prices increase 15% to 20% a year. That's the situation most of us find ourselves in when we need health care.*"
>
> —SEAN SULLIVAN,
> National Business Coalition
> on Health

Going under the knife. Despite the rise of managed care, some surgery is still unnecessary. Ask for a plain-English explanation of the need for and alternatives to any surgery. Surgery always involves some risk. According to the nonprofit People's Medical Society, 10% to 15% of the patients in a hospital at any one time will be the victims of surgical errors—some of very little consequence, but others causing some serious problems.

Women should be particularly alert if any of the following procedures are recommended:

■ *Hysterectomies.* In general, the reason for most hysterectomies is to resolve symptoms related to benign uterine fibroids. But studies are showing that if they aren't causing any serious and immediate symptoms, surgery is not necessary.

■ *Cesarian sections.* Many C-sections are not necessary. According to the New York State Health Department, the percentage of deliveries done by C-section in New York City in 1995 varied from 8.8% at one hospital to 23.9% at another—and the rest of the city's hospitals were spread out in between.

■ *Mastectomies.* The vast majority of women who have operable breast cancer are treated by mastectomy. Yet numerous studies have concluded that, for early-stage cancers, lumpectomy—removal of just the cancerous lump and the immediate surrounding tissue—is as effective as mastectomy when combined with radiation treatment.

Informed consent. The law requires that you give "informed consent" before undergoing surgery. You're supposed to be told in plain English exactly what is about to be done, the risks involved, the chances of failure, and the alternatives. You need not be informed of remote risks. You'll then be handed an informed-consent form to sign. Read every line carefully, and make sure you understand it completely. If you have a question or disagree, discuss it with your doctor; maybe a wording change can be worked out. Informed-consent forms are often the basis of lawsuits in which patients charge they weren't adequately informed of risks or alternatives.

Hospital billing. The better health insurance policies still cover your entire basic hospital bill, but some policies now make you pay some out-of-pocket, either as a deductible or co-pay or by not paying for the first few days in the hospital. Given the possibility that you may have to pay a portion of your bill, you can't afford to blithely ignore a hospital bill with the rationalization that "the insurance will cover it."

The Wall Street Journal in 1997 reported on the case of a woman who rushed to Columbia Florence Hospital with severe stomach pains.

As she got out of the car, she slammed her right finger in the door. She turned down a technician's offer to X ray her finger. But the hospital billed her $170.91 for the X ray anyway. She was also charged "hundreds of dollars for intravenous fluids that were administered a day or two after she was discharged," the *Journal* reported.

A survey a number of years ago by Congress's General Accounting Office found that over 90% of the bills reviewed had errors. The extraordinary error rate raises questions about hospitals' motivation to detect and correct mistakes in their favor. After all, they need to raise cash to cover the cost of treating poor and uninsured people, not to mention the debt for that newly installed state-of-the-art billing system. And financial pressures on hospitals are increasing as Medicaid and Medicare payments get cut and managed-care insurers continue to pressure hospitals to accept lower reimbursements.

The complexity of hospital bills leads to inadvertent mistakes. One part of the bill is your daily room rate, which includes nursing care and meals. But everything else is billed separately, from aspirins to oxygen, echocardiograms to crutches. So an itemized bill might have 20 or 30 entries for an overnight stay, and a hospital bill for a major operation could have hundreds of daily billing entries and go on for many pages. Mistakes are made more likely because five-digit computer codes have been substituted for the names of actual medical procedures. Transposing a digit or two could result in billing for a very different—and differently priced—procedure.

What are the most common mistakes? You could be charged for more days than you stayed. There may be charges for services you never received or double charges for services you did receive. JoAnne Fritsch, a former registered nurse who now works for a national benefits consulting firm, gave this example: Double-billing commonly occurs when a blood specimen is dropped, is inadvertently contaminated, or isn't tested soon enough and begins to clot, requiring the specimen to be drawn again. The patient shouldn't be charged for the second test but is anyway. "It's not so serious if it's just a $75 blood test. But if it's a spinal tap, it's really expensive," she told us.

Instead of a bill for an entire procedure, you may be billed separately for every aspect of the procedure, with, for example, separate bills for drawing blood, transporting the blood, and analyzing the results of a blood test. Added up, the individual charges total more than a single "bundled bill" for an entire procedure. This could add up to real money when a doctor who performed a hysterectomy charges separately for removal of the uterus and each ovary.

Fortunately, many hospitals are now trying to streamline billing and to better explain it to patients. For example, the Cleveland Clinic has produced a brochure explaining billing and how to deal with third-party payers. And at least one state is trying to help citizens avoid recourse to lawsuits for seemingly unresolv-able hospital billing disputes: In 1992, Nevada created a Commission for Hospital Patients in response to the extraordinarily high volume of billing complaints legislators were receiving. Commission staff explain bills to callers and mediate disputes.

WHAT TO WATCH OUT FOR

Doctors

Unnecessary tests. Excess tests might be ordered if the testing laboratory is owned in part by the doctor ordering the test because the doctor possibly could benefit financially from them. Fortunately, this practice is in decline since being banned by Medicare, but you still might want to check whether your doctor is sending you to a facility she has ownership in.

A study published in the *American Journal of Medicine* by a team of doctors from the famous Mayo Clinic concluded that several of the most common tests—complete blood count, urinalysis, thyroid studies, and a blood chemistry panel—aren't all that worthwile when used for routine exams. Money spent on these tests might be better applied to screening tests for various cancers.

Hospitals

Extra charges. You may know that you have to pay extra for a television set in your room. But be careful about asking for anything else special—those extra pillows could get added to your bill. There's a chance that your insurance company won't cover your special requests.

Truth-in-labeling lapses. Hospitals are increasingly joining together in networks in order to cut costs and wield greater bargaining power when negotiating how much insurance companies will pay. Often, a prestigious teaching hospital will buy or sign an affiliation agreement with a smaller community hospital. But just because the name of the big-league teaching hospital is now over the smaller hospital's front door does not mean that the quality of care has improved or in any way matches the big hospital's.

Recent major staff cutbacks. If you've read in your town's newspaper that a local hospital has significantly downsized, you should be on guard if you have to use it: Unless there has been a major restructuring, you might have to wait longer to receive pain medication, to have tests conducted and interpreted, and to get your questions answered.

Premature discharge and transfer to a transitional unit. In order to save money, some hospitals are transferring patients from intensive care units to floors of transitional units, where there are fewer specialized staff.

Unlicensed employees performing nursing. Many hospitals are saving money by replacing registered nurses with less-expensive and much-less-trained licensed practical nurses and unlicensed technical workers. But it's much better for you, as a patient, if an *RN* checks your vital signs and gives you your pills. Registered nurses have had years of training in how to note negative changes in your condition and what to do when there's a problem. The American Nurses Association cites well over a dozen reliable studies documenting that hospitals with a higher nurse-to-patients ratio have lower mortality rates.

So if you have a chance before being admitted, ask and compare among hospitals the answers to these questions: Will an RN—and only an RN—give you your medications and treatments? What other workers will be involved in your care? What tasks will they do? What are their qualifications? Will an RN prepare you for discharge? What's the RN-to-occupied-bed ratio? If it's less than one-to-one, you should be extra sure to ask the previous questions. And a low ratio could be a sign that the RNs are overworked.

Once you are admitted, you and your family should press for RN attention. You should be skeptical if you are predominantly being cared for by employees with titles like Patient Care Technician, Patient Care Associate, Medical Assistant, and Critical Care Partner. All of these are common terms for unlicensed persons who were once simply called nurse's aides. Some of them have had only minimal training.

Nurses' associations around the country are reporting cases where job descriptions for such individuals are including not just taking vital signs, but more complex and risky work such as taking blood from arteries, inserting or removing catheters from bladders, and obtaining urine by a suprapubic tap (a needle inserted through the abdomen into the bladder). There are reports of some hospitals even giving their housekeepers and orderlies a few weeks of "cross-training" and turning them loose on patients.

Some of the results have been disturbing. In testimony before a New York State Assembly hearing in 1997, the New York State Nurses Association cited such instances as a technician forcing normal saline through a catheter in a major blood vessel that was clotted and pushing the clot into the bloodstream; the patient could have died from a pulmonary embolism. In another hospital a technician used another patient's filter when starting up a dialysis machine. Filters can be reused, but only on the same patient. The affected patient could have contracted any number of blood-related infections. Elsewhere in the country hundreds of cases have been documented in recent years, such as the RN in a Cincinnati hospital who noticed that a cross-trained housekeeper was giving a blanket to a patient receiving blood platelets. The RN interceded because she noticed the patient shivering, an indication of an adverse reaction to a blood product.

Private, for-profit hospital. The percentage of hospitals run on a for-profit basis is rising. And that's worrisome. Although many for-profit hospitals deliver high-quality care, there are others that often deliver care in an assembly-line fashion.

In order to make money and compete with not-for-profit hospitals—which don't pay taxes—the for-profits have to save money somehow. A study reported in the *New England Journal of Medicine* in 1997 concluded that for-profit hospitals spend less on patient care than not-for-profit ones. Some of the difference goes to profits. Much of it is spent on administration; the clinical personnel to administrative costs and profit ratio in not-for-profit hospitals is 1.51, but in for-profit hospitals it's 0.90.

Be especially careful of any private hospital that allows doctors to become investors. Critics of these arrangements say that doctors' fi-

BEST TIMES WORST TIMES

Schedule elective surgery at teaching hospitals for any time but July. That's when a new crop of interns and residents start—and they have little experience. Also, try to avoid having your surgery performed on Friday since there is a reduced staff when you are recovering on the weekend.

Emergencies aren't so easily scheduled, but try to avoid the emergency room between 4 P.M. and 8 P.M., the only time doctors and nurses operate something like the fictional *E.R.* The confluence of happy hour, rush hour, and the end of doctors' office hours may create a traffic jam at the triage station.

nancial interests in a hospital could lead them to approve unnecessary tests and admissions.

Sleep-deprived interns and residents. Physically exhausted hospital interns and residents continue to be a safety concern, despite efforts to limit their hours. Young doctors undergoing hospital training go through a sort of baptism by fire, working 100-hour weeks and maybe catching a few winks in an unused patient bed. This system of servitude saves hospitals lots of money. But in a 1989 survey by the University of California, one-third of 114 residents said exhaustion had caused them to make a mistake that contributed to a death.

So before a hospital resident begins sticking you with needles, ask when he or she last had eight straight hours of sleep. If the answer is something like, "Oh, a few days ago," maybe the procedure can be delayed or a better-rested intern found.

A hospital resident might be poorly supervised as well as poorly rested. Major studies by the NYC Public Advocate's office in 1994 and 1998 revealed that at many teaching hospitals the residents were virtually unsupervised by attending (supervising) doctors. Patients were harmed when residents made medication mistakes.

Perhaps the most extreme example of residents working without supervision was reported by the *New York Observer* in 1997 at New York City's Columbia-Presbyterian Medical Center. Several plastic surgery residents were discovered running their own cash-only, after hours, plastic surgery business out of the faculty practice building. The facilities were inadequate—no nurses on hand, no extra blood in case of a surgery emergency. The budding entrepreneurs came to the newspaper's attention when several of their customers developed infections. The medical center ultimately paid a stiff state fine for failing to take action against the residents.

THE $MARTER CONSUMER

Doctors

If the fee seems steep, try negotiating. If you have a limited income or recently lost your job, many doctors will give you a break.

Know where to complain. Every state has a medical board that licenses doctors and acts on complaints. But since many of these boards are ineffective, don't stop there. Also complain about a problem doctor to your insurance company, the hospital(s) where he has admitting privileges, the administrators of your HMO, and/or the local medical society.

Question all tests. Are there one or two comprehensive tests that would cover the numerous individual tests being prescribed? Are results from a test you underwent, say, six months earlier still valid? In no event should you pay for tests you did not know about. Make sure you have a complete list and update it as necessary.

Consider home-testing. Why pay a big lab fee when, for less money, you can go to a nearby drugstore and buy a home pregnancy test, a blood pressure testing kit, a urinary tract infection test kit, a blood glucose monitor for diabetics, or a fecal occult blood test?

Get free advice over the phone for minor ailments. If you have the flu, talk to the doctor over the telephone. You'll probably be told just to drink fluids and rest. That way, you'll avoid the strain of traveling to the doctor's office, as well as the strain on your wallet.

Hospitals

Check for someone else with your name. If there is another patient in the hospital with your last name or a name that is close to yours, be on the lookout for potentially hazardous medical data mix-ups.

Read the Patient's Bill of Rights (most hospitals publish one) and make use of the hospital's patient representative, sometimes called a patient advocate or liaison. Most hospitals have such a person on staff full-time. Complain if you can't get answers about medical tests that seem unnecessary, if you're left on gurneys in hallways for long stretches, or even if your roommate insists on watching *Married With Children* reruns at high volume.

Ask for an itemized hospital bill. You will probably have to ask the billing office to explain the many abbreviations and codes in it. Examples: PT-PTT is a blood test for coagulation, and CBC (complete

blood count) is a blood test usually done by machine. Also request elaboration on anything appearing under the all-purpose heading "miscellaneous." Remember, you have a right to know exactly what you are being charged for. Don't pay until you have had ample time to fully review and understand the itemized bill.

Challenge overcharging even if you think your insurance will pay the entire bill. One reason medical bills are so high is that everyone figures the insurance company will pay. The reality is, needless claims payments are passed on to everyone through higher premiums.

Compare the itemized bill with your hospital medical records. If they don't match, find out why. An investigation into the former Humana hospital chain several years ago uncovered one family that had been charged for three hours of recovery-room time after their mother had already died. They were also charged for an "O.R. implant," dated after the body had been removed for funeral preparations. Most states require hospitals to turn your records over to you. (See **HELP** at the end of this chapter for a guide published by Public Citizen Health Research Group explaining how to obtain your medical records.)

Keep a notebook in which you write down the dates and times of all consultations, blood tests, electrocardiograms (EKGs), sonograms, etc., assuming you are well enough. Later on, compare your records with the itemized hospital bill.

Provide your own supplies. This is one way to cut your bills for incidentals, such as mouthwash. You might also try bringing your own prescription medications, although many hospitals strongly discourage patients from doing this because they are unsure of how old the medication is or of whether it has been properly stored.

You do not have to sign the informed-consent forms and patient-admission registration exactly as they are written. If you find a clause that you disagree with, suggest a change.

Be especially careful of any clause that says your surgeon *or his or her associates* can perform the operation. Since you might never have laid eyes on the associates, and you may not want some totally unknown doctor getting near you with a scalpel, you might want to cross out the words "or his or her associates."

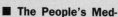

HELP

■ **The People's Med-** ical Society's publications *Take This Book to the Hospital With You* and *150 Ways to Be a Savvy Medical Consumer* have numerous helpful tips. $14.95 for the former, $5.95 for the latter, plus $4.00 for shipping and handling. Send a check or money order to 462 Walnut Street, Allentown, PA 18102. Call (610) 770-1670 to pay with MasterCard or Visa.

■ **To learn the status of a hospital's** accreditation, call the Joint Commission on the Accreditation of Healthcare Organization hot line, (630) 916-5800 or check the Web site, www.jcaho.org.

■ **To double-check your physician's** schooling, residencies, licensing, and certification status, write to the American Medical Association's Department of Data Services at 515 North State Street, Chicago, IL 60610, call (312) 464-5199, or check their Web site, www.ama-affn.org. You can also check the AMA's *American Medical Directory,* probably in your local library, which lists every doctor in the country.

At the library, you can check the American Board of Medical Specialties' *Directory of Certified Medical Specialists* to find out if your doctor is board-certified, or call the American Board of Medical Specialties at (800) 776-CERT during normal business hours. The American College of Surgeons at (312) 664-4050 will tell you if a surgeon is a member, which means they've passed a peer-review evaluation.

■ **The Public Citizen Health Re-** search Group has published a 66-page $10 guide called *Medical Records: Getting Yours.* Order from Public Citizen, 1600 20th St. NW, Washington, DC 20009.

■ **To learn more about patients'** rights, read the American Civil Liberties Union's 300-page handbook, *The Rights of Patients.* Send a check or money order for $9.95 plus $3.00 shipping and handling to: ACLU, PO Box 186, Wye Mills, MD 21679.

■ **The book 13,012 *Questionable*** *Doctors* by the Public Citizen Health Research Group lists doctors who are still practicing despite bad records.

■ **A new book, *How to Get Out of the*** *Hospital Alive: A Guide to Patient Power* by Dr. Sheldon Blau and Elaine Famtil Shemberg, might be a bit alarmist, but is nonetheless helpful.

CHAPTER 7

LONG-TERM CARE

Planning for Aging

The good news is that Americans are living longer. The bad news? Almost half of everyone older than 65 will need help with basic daily activities such as eating, bathing, and walking. That means that when the first baby-boomers reach their golden years, several million people will require some kind of long-term care. A one-year stay in a nursing home cost $38,000 in 1996; because of spiraling health care costs and inflation, by the year 2010 it's likely to cost upwards of $80,000 a year. Skilled home care may cost $100 per hour.

Many seniors who need care—some experts estimate that as many as two thirds—move in with their adult children, other relatives, or friends. But the added stress of caring for the disabled elderly at home can break the financial and emotional backs of families already struggling to make ends meet or to handle other domestic pressures. Families pay over a third of the long-term care bill out of pocket— and much more out of love.

> **"I** *f you need long-term care insurance now, you probably can't afford it. And if you can easily afford it, you may not need it."*
>
> —Kiplinger's Personal Finance Magazine

Take Ms. C. Her husband's sudden stroke in 1981 ended their life as they knew it. Since she could neither afford nursing home care nor qualify for state aid, Ms. C.'s life, as she described it on the CNN special "Caring Choices: Prohibitive Costs of Nursing Home Care," has turned "into a stressful routine, centered solely around her husband." Their relationship has become more like that of parent and child than that of husband and wife.

To avoid burdening their children or entering a nursing home, a growing number of seniors who own their own homes trade their home equity for home care. However, this trade has worked poorly for some seniors, including Jane R. of Lincoln, Massachusetts. Unable to afford $72,000 per year for a full-time nurse, Ms. R. agreed to sell her home to Linda Douglass in exchange for care and the right to live in her home until she died. But instead of providing care, Ms. Douglass ran a real-estate brokerage out of the house and neglected Ms. R.

Fortunately, Ms. R. was rescued before it was too late, and Ms. Douglass was charged with elder abuse.

Many seniors think that long-term care insurance will protect them in old age, but like Ms. O., a widow from Oregon, they can end up with hefty insurance premiums and no care when they need it. Despite having paid thousands of dollars in premiums for nearly ten years for two different long-term care policies, Ms. O. died penniless because her nursing home did not meet the definition of "skilled" care described in her policies' fine print.

THE BASICS

Making the Choice to Plan Ahead

While 60% of Americans worry that they or their spouse will one day need long-term care, they haven't done much about it. Just 13% carry a long-term care insurance policy, according to a 1996 survey sponsored by the National Council on the Aging and John Hancock Mutual Life Insurance Company.

As difficult as it may be to confront the possibility of long-term disability, the only way to avoid long-term tragedy is to plan ahead. Too often, consumers make decisions based on the government programs they qualify for, rather than on the medical care they need or the living arrangements they desire. You'll feel more in control of both your health and your finances, and be a better advocate for your loved one, if you know the parlance of long-term care and can participate in the decision on whether and how to purchase it.

What Are the Different Long-Term Care Options?

Typically, long-term care does not involve constant high-tech medical intervention but rather

THE MANY FACES OF CARE

There are three levels of long-term care. **Skilled care**, sometimes called **acute care**, is medical care provided by registered or licensed nurses and physicians, usually for specific curable illnesses or recoverable accidents. Skilled care also includes various "high-tech" procedures, such as dialysis and respiratory therapies. **Custodial care** is day-in, day-out assistance with such basic activities as bathing, dressing, eating, and moving around. Custodial care also includes constant supervision of those with mental disorders and dementia, such as Alzheimer's disease. More than half of all long-term care patients need custodial care, which Medicaid covers but most other government programs do not. **Intermediate care**, as the name suggests, lies between skilled and custodial care.

consistent basic assistance or supervision. You can opt to live in a nursing home, which is generally categorized according to the level of care it provides, receive care in your own home, or move to an assisted living center, which blends both. There are several different "titles" of home care providers that do not neatly correspond to levels of care.

Generally, home care workers are divided into "hands on" and "hands off" workers. Only "hands on" workers can administer medications, bathe, dress, feed, or physically touch the patient. "Hands off" workers generally maintain household finances, cook, and clean. Many states follow the federal Medicaid guidelines specifying what particular home care titles allow workers to do.

Registered nurses/licensed practical nurses/therapists. These professionals provide skilled care and "high-tech" therapies. They are professional home care workers and can charge from $25 to over $80 per hour.

Home health aides (often generically called home care workers). They can perform some "hands on" work, including such minor medical tasks as taking blood pressure and administering oral medications. Home health aides charge from $25 to $35 per hour.

Personal care aides. They, too, can perform such "hands on" work as bathing and feeding, but usually cannot perform any medical tasks. Personal care aides charge from $15 to $25 per hour.

Homemakers. These workers can perform the same "hands on" tasks as personal care aides as well as provide assistance and instruction in managing and maintaining household finances. Homemakers are the only home care workers who can provide such instruction; they can charge as much as home health aides.

Housekeepers. These aides do only "hands off" work, such as cooking, cleaning, and shopping. Housekeepers are often hired at or slightly above minimum wage.

Companions. These workers offer protection by "keeping company," with patients suffering from mental dementia. Several nonprofit agencies offer free companion services, and many employment agencies refer companions for wages comparable to those earned by housekeepers.

BEST TIMES WORST TIMES

Long-term care insurance options change rapidly, and there's no guarantee that the policy you buy 30 to 40 years early, when it's cheap, will cover the kind of care you'll need or want decades later. You'll pay more, it's true, but the optimal time to buy long-term care insurance is in the decade leading up to your retirement.

Which Government Programs Pay for Long-Term Care?

There are three major sources of federal funds for long-term care: Medicare, Medicaid, and Title III funds from the Older Americans' Act, which together pay for barely 40% of all long-term care costs. All three programs have economic criteria that disqualify many middle-class consumers.

Medicare. This entitlement program for all people over 65 with an illness or injury and certain disabled people under 65 pays only for skilled care—not custodial care—in a nursing home or at the patient's home, and only after at least a three-day hospital stay. More than half of those who need long-term care do not need skilled care and so do not qualify for Medicare's long-term care coverage. Even those who do qualify are not covered for 100% of the costs for as long as they need care. The biggest gaps in Medicare's long-term care coverage are:

- No coverage for custodial care in a nursing facility.
- No coverage for homemaker and personal care services at home.
- No coverage without prior hospitalization.
- No coverage for nursing home care after 100 days.
- Consumers must use Medicare-approved facilities.

Medicare supplement insurance (often called Medigap). This private insurance picks up where Medicare leaves off. Medigap policies still do not cover custodial care, but four of the ten policies recently standardized by the federal government will pay up to $1,600 per year for care at home if you are recovering from an illness, injury, or surgery.

Medicaid. This program provides health insurance, including coverage for all levels of long-term care, for people living at or somewhat above the poverty line. States set their own programs and qualification requirements. Since Medicaid is the only government program that pays for the custodial care most long-term care patients need, many consumers "divest" or "spend down" their assets in order to qualify. Medicaid will not help you until virtually all of your assets are used up. While Medicaid does not require the impoverishment of a spouse, *Consumer Reports* warns, "The husband or wife of a Medicaid resident may not necessarily retain enough in insurance or assets to live as he or she was accustomed to living."

How to Choose a Nursing Home

No one wants to live in a nursing home, but choosing the right home can turn a bad situation into a beneficial arrangement. If Medicaid is paying the bill, you must use a Medicaid-approved facility. If you're paying your own way, you can choose anything from a luxury resort to a grim motel. But while stories of filthy conditions and neglect abound, if you shop around, you can find both the medical care you need with a lifestyle and a price tag you can live with.

HOME HEALTH AGENCIES

PROS	CONS
■ You are not responsible for paying the home care worker's salary, taxes, and benefits. ■ The agency will probably intercede if you have a problem with your worker. ■ You can more easily change your worker as your needs change. ■ Most insurance and government programs cover home health services if provided by a home health agency.	■ You may not get the same caregiver every day or every week. ■ Home health agencies are expensive, and the home care worker receives only a small fraction of the hourly fee you pay to the agency. ■ Many home health agencies are impersonal, and if you have a problem you may have to take a number and wait in line.

Know what kind of care you need. Since 1990, most skilled care and intermediate facilities have merged, and many custodial facilities have diversified to include "assisted living centers" (which tend to be smaller, decentralized, apartment-like units that offer meals, health care, and supportive services, depending on the changing needs of the individual) and special homes for people with Alzheimer's disease, AIDS, cancer, and other specific diseases. Particularly if you need only custodial care, you may be able to find a facility attuned to your needs—if you know what they are.

Visit. Look for two things: Is the building comfortable and in good condition, and is the staff competent and cooperative? Specifically, inspect the bedrooms, bathrooms, dining rooms, recreation and therapy rooms, and all other common areas. Be suspicious if you are told that any part of the home is "off limits." Ask specific questions about the medical staff: Who are they and what are their qualifications? How many of them are on the premises or on call and how often? Also, find out if there is a social worker available to help a resident adjust to the new lifestyle.

Consider the subjective. If everything seems in order but you just don't feel "right" about a home, go somewhere else. Observe the residents: Do they seem happy? Are they dressed? Do they use the recreation areas or do they mostly stay in their rooms? Remember, you're not only looking for long-term care; you're looking for a place to live.

Consider moving to a cheaper area. Care in such states as Arizona, South Carolina, and Oregon can cost

---

NURSE REGISTRIES AND
DOMESTIC EMPLOYMENT AGENCIES

PROS	CONS
■ You can get the continuity of care that you often cannot get with a home health agency. ■ Direct contracts with workers can cost from 30% to 50% less than agency services. ■ You have more control over your home care worker than if he or she is supervised by an agency. ■ Medigap policies will cover direct contract home care arrangements.	■ You have all of the financial responsibilities of an employer, including supervision, which can be difficult for someone receiving care. ■ You have no one to help mediate problems between you and your caregiver. ■ Most states provide little protection for employers who have problems with employment agencies.

as little as one-third what you would pay for the same care in Florida or California. Unfortunately, there is no national clearinghouse for nursing home information. The cost of long-term care, however, generally mirrors the local cost of living as indicated by census statistics and the consumer price index.

How to Get Good Home Care

Most people would rather stay at home than live in a nursing home, but good home care is hard to find. You have four options:

Licensed and/or certified home health agencies provide a variety of services for an hourly fee. The agency recruits, trains, and supervises workers and technically is the workers' "employer," paying their salary, taxes, and benefits.

Nurse registries and domestic employment agencies refer home care workers for a referral fee ranging from a few hundred to a few thousand dollars. You contract directly with the worker and are responsible for wages, taxes, benefits, and, most important, supervision.

The want ads are often full of people looking for work as home health aides, homemakers, housekeepers, and even registered nurses and therapists. You take your chances but eliminate the expense and bureaucracy of agencies.

Volunteer agencies can usually provide only companion or non-health related services for a few hours of care per week. If that is all you need, these agencies may be your best bet.

How to Supervise Your Home Care Provider

Even if your worker is referred by a home health agency, you're still the boss in your own home. Most reported incidents of elder abuse are by family members and not by hired home care workers, but you should take precautions to make sure your relationship with your home care worker is appropriate.

Know what you need *and* what you, your friends, and relatives can take care of; know how many hours a day/a week you need help and whether you want a companion as well as a caregiver or a purely professional relationship. Make these decisions *before* you start interviewing applicants.

Always interview your home care worker and check references. Whether you are going through a home health agency or an employment agency, make sure you meet and feel comfortable with your caregiver and that he or she is qualified.

Put everything in writing. Write a specific job description, including the hours, salary, vacation time, use of the phone and car, and other household rules and procedures.

Treat your caregiver like a professional. Give your caregiver periodic written evaluations and have established grievance procedures.

Long-Term Care Insurance

Given the likely odds of needing costly long-term care and the dismal odds of qualifying for government funding, it's no wonder that long-term care insurance is the fastest-growing type of health insurance. (Even so, insurance covered only 0.2% of the nation's long-term care bill in 1993—though the ratio is sure to rise.)

Long-term care insurance amounts to a classic Catch-22. If you want to buy it when you are likeliest to need it, you may not be able to afford it—a policy will likely cost twice as much when you are 70 as when you are 60. Conversely, if you buy coverage earlier in life, when it's affordable, you

NURSING HOME NUMBERS

Length of Stay	Men's Odds	Women's Odds
Enter at some time in your life	33%	52%
Stay three months or more	22%	41%
Stay one year or more	14%	31%
Stay more than five years	4%	13%

Source: New England Journal of Medicine.

THE PITFALLS OF PUBLIC-PRIVATE PARTNERSHIPS

Neither consumers nor the government has the money it will take to pay for the baby boomers' long-term care needs. Four States—California, Connecticut, Indiana, and New York—are attempting to split the difference with "public-private partnership plans" that basically promise that Medicaid will pay your long-term care tab regardless of your income and assets if you purchase a private insurance policy and exhaust its benefits. If you pick your policy well, this can be a good deal, but beware:

■ Private insurance benefits won't cover all your costs; your out-of-pocket expenses may drain your assets to Medicaid levels anyway.

■ Since the average nursing home stay is two and a half years and most private policies provide coverage for three years, many consumers won't take advantage of the partnership benefit.

■ Partnership policies are not portable. If you move to another state, you won't be able to tap into Medicaid if your insurance dollars run dry.

■ Finally, partnership policies have the same loopholes—and potential premium hikes—as regular policies.

won't know whether you will live long enough to need it. More than half of all 65-year-olds will never enter a nursing home, and only 21% will stay in a nursing home more than a year, according to the Brookings Institution. Women, with their longer life expectancies, are far more likely to enter a nursing home than men. (See chart on the previous page.)

Policies available now have fewer restrictions and include more types of care than previous versions—home care, adult day care, assisted living in senior housing. But while the quality and comprehensiveness of policies have improved markedly over the earliest generation of policies sold in the 1980s and early 1990s, the quality of the salesmanship has not—and significant shortcomings in coverage remain. Long-term care insurance agents often promise financial security and "whatever medical care you need." But watch out—what you hear may not be what you get.

Undercover investigations by the U.S. House Select Committee on Aging (June 1991), the NYC Department of Consumer Affairs (April 1993), and *Consumer Reports* (October 1997) all found that long-term care insurance agents interviewed misled consumers about their policies. While *Consumer Reports* found fewer high-pressure sales tactics than in the past, the magazine reported that "many agents appeared clueless about the policies they were selling. They imparted misinformation, misleading information, or no information." One agent told an undercover *Consumer Reports* reporter, "All policies are virtually identical. It's not real important to compare benefits." In fact, the conditions that trigger benefits and the definition of assisted living (or coverage of it at all) vary widely from one policy to another, and comparing benefits is essential. Other agents disparaged inflation protection, another essential element. Look at the chart on page 96, and you'll see how quickly benefits and actual costs diverge without inflation protection.

Furthermore, most of the agents assured investigators (posing as consumers) that insurance premiums would never go up, even though industry experts all agree that premium increases are highly likely. The agent for First Unum Life Insurance Company told an undercover investigator:

> "[The rate at] the age at which you take it out is the rate at which it will continue. It will never go any higher. The only way it can possibly go higher is on a class basis, if they [the insurance company] apply to the State, which has never happened in the past with any company."

"With any company?" asked the incredulous investigator. "With any company," the agent replied. "Whatever you go in at—that's what the premium will be.... It will never happen. It will not happen." According to a 1997 *Consumer Reports* analy-

sis, increases of 25% were not uncommon in the decade between the late 1980s and late 1990s. And a few policies' multiple increases added up to 100% or more.

The lesson for consumers is clear: Do not trust insurance agents selling long-term care insurance. Even if the agent is honest, the policies themselves are complex and riddled with problems. First, they are expensive—from $500 to over $5,000 annually, depending on your age and the benefits you choose. Even at this price, no policy is guaranteed to pay 100% of your long-term care costs, and some policies that don't keep pace with inflation can pay as little as 30%. Having to foot 60% of the bill in addition to hefty policy premiums can quickly erode the nest egg you bought the insurance to protect.

And that's *if* you can qualify for benefits; many policies have big loopholes hidden in the fine print that make it so hard to qualify for benefits that you may never get a dime.

As bad, many policyholders don't keep their policies until they need long-term care, because they can't keep up with the premiums. Based on estimates by the National Association of Insurance Commissioners, of every 100 60-year-olds who take out long-term care insurance policies, only five still have coverage at age 80, when they are most likely to need it. A U.S. General Accounting Office survey of insurers concurs with these estimates: On average, the insurers they reviewed "expected that 60% or more of their original policyholders would allow their policies to lapse within 10 years."

In an article published in October 1997, *Consumer Reports* found some companies "low-balling" their premiums, or charging less in premiums than they will likely have to pay out in claims, to attract policyholders. To pay future claims, companies will have no choice but to raise premiums substantially. Be sure you can pay your policy's future premium hikes—*Consumer Reports* suggests that you prepare for an increase of 50% to be safe—or you're out of luck.

WHAT TO WATCH OUT FOR

If, after reading this section, you decide to buy long-term care insurance, consider the following:

Too little coverage. Buy a daily benefit that will cover all anticipated costs—including extra charges for drugs, supplies, and other add-ons to a nursing home's daily rate—or that leaves you with manageable out-of-pocket expenses that will not drain your assets. Contrary to what some sales agents will suggest, some insurance is not necessarily better than no insurance.

Inflation eroding your coverage. Between 1985 and 1995, nursing home prices increased by almost 10% a year, and the U.S. Congressional Study on Aging projects a rise of about 7% a year in the future. Inflation protection is a must unless you buy a high daily benefit and expect to need care within a few years. Inflation protection automatically increases your daily benefit amount without increasing your premium. Look for 5% compounded inflation coverage.

The length of the elimination period. The elimination period, similar to a deductible, is the number of days of care *you* have to pay for before your insurance kicks in. The longer the elimination period, the lower the premium. Don't let a low premium lure you into committing to a longer elimination period than you can afford. For instance, a 60-day elimination period with a policy that allows $150 a day adds up to a $9,000 deductible.

Also find out if every stay, however brief, counts toward the elimination period. If the clock resets each time you leave a nursing home, you will have to eliminate the first few days over and over again before the insurance begins paying. Also, ask if home care days count toward the nursing home elimination period and vice versa.

The inclusion of nonforfeiture benefits. These promise to pay reduced benefits if you qualify for care but let your policy lapse. It will cost about 20% more, but it's worth it.

Too short or too little benefit duration. Benefit duration is either how much money your policy pays or for how long it will pay benefits. A majority of people who enter nursing homes (75%) stay less than a year, and many never enter at all. But you won't know how long you will need long-term care until it's

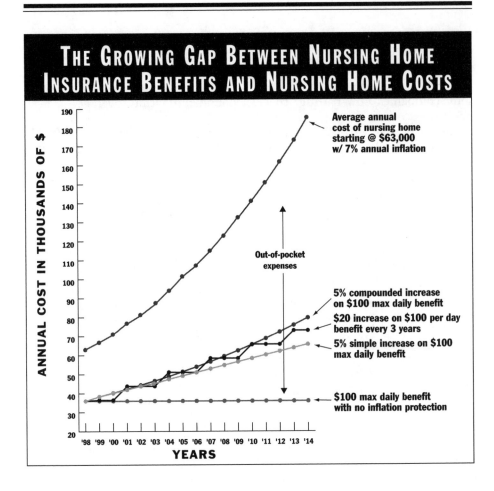

THE GROWING GAP BETWEEN NURSING HOME INSURANCE BENEFITS AND NURSING HOME COSTS

ANNUAL COST IN THOUSANDS OF $

YEARS

'98 '99 '00 '01 '02 '03 '04 '05 '06 '07 '08 '09 '10 '11 '12 '13 '14

Average annual cost of nursing home starting @ $63,000 w/ 7% annual inflation

Out-of-pocket expenses

5% compounded increase on $100 max daily benefit

$20 increase on $100 per day benefit every 3 years

5% simple increase on $100 max daily benefit

$100 max daily benefit with no inflation protection

too late to plan for it. You have no choice but to wager—a three- or four-year policy is a safe bet.

Old policies. Keep what you have, but keep in mind that the policy you bought in the early 1990s is probably out of date—many older policies don't cover home care, assisted living facilities, and other options in this evolving field. And a policy you buy today probably won't stay current with innovations over the decade or two or three before you need it. Review the policy periodically and ask your insurance company if you can update the coverage. Flexibility on features will allow you to maintain as much independence as you can handle and to stay out of institutions.

THE $MARTER CONSUMER

Get satisfactory answers to these ten questions before buying long-term care insurance.

■ *Do I need it?* Ask yourself whether you have enough assets to warrant insurance. As a very general rule, it's worth considering if you will have annual retirement income over $30,000 and if you have assets, not including your home, of $100,000 to $500,000. If you have less, you already or will very quickly qualify for Medicaid. Conversely, if your retirement plans and investments throw off enough income that you won't have to tap assets to pay for a nursing home, you don't need insurance. *Consumer Reports'* 1997 special report includes a worksheet to help you figure out whether your assets make long-term care insurance necessary for you.

■ *Can I afford it?* A recent Families U.S.A. study reported that only one out of five Americans age 55 to 79 can afford *both* the high premiums *and* high co-payments of most policies. If you can afford it, you might be able to afford long-term care without buying insurance. Financial advisors suggest that you spend no more than 5% to 6% of your annual income on premiums. And remember that you will be retired during some of the years you are paying premiums—so if your income will drop in those years, pick a plan accordingly.

■ *When should I buy it?* Good for you, if you're thinking about long-term care in your 40s—but it makes sense to wait. The younger you are, the lower your premiums will be, but the longer you're likely to wait before you need care, allowing more time for premiums to increase and inflation to erode your benefits. But if you wait too long to buy it, you won't be able to afford it. Financial advisors and consumer advocates suggest buying when you are in your 50s to 60s—young enough to be healthy but old enough to have a good sense of your retirement plans.

Exception: If your employer offers a low-cost or free long-term care plan as part of your benefits package, take a close look, even if you're years away from prime buying time. If the plan is flexible, comprehensive, and cheap, it may make sense to lock in a low premium early. Just be sure that you can and will keep up with the premiums over the very long haul you're about to sign up for.

■ *Will the policy cover anticipated costs?* Compare your policy's daily benefit and inflation adjustments with estimated nursing home costs (figure on 7% annual increases) when you will be 80 years old, the age at which people are most likely to need nursing home care. You'll have to pay the difference yourself—which can eat up the savings the insurance is supposed to protect.

Currently, no policy is indexed to the actual increases in long-term care costs, so no policy that pays a daily benefit can guarantee to cover 100% of the costs. The best you're likely to get is a 5% increase compounded annually, which is a lot better than nothing. Stan Hinden, a columnist at the *Washington Post,* didn't do a lot of research when he bought policies offered by the paper for himself and his wife. Turns out there's no inflation protection.

"Without it, we will still be getting $100 a day benefit when nursing home costs have gone up to $200 or $250 a day," he wrote. "That could be rough."

■ *Will I be able to qualify for the policy's benefits?* Look at the policy's fine print and avoid policies that require "continual one-on-one assistance to perform activities of daily living." You'd have to "be at death's door in order to meet a standard of 'continual assistance,'" according to Bill Dombi at the Center for Health Care Law. Also, avoid policies that have performance criteria for cognitive impairments. People with cognitive dementia, such as those with Alzheimer's disease, can usually perform basic physical tasks despite their memory loss, and so would not qualify for benefits. Finally, be wary of such vaguely defined criteria as "needs assistance" or "cannot perform," which makes it easier for a company to deny your claim.

■ *Does the policy provide the benefits I want at the facilities of my choice?* Most policies restrict the services and facilities they will pay for. Check whether there are facilities that meet your policy's specifications wherever you expect to live. And think hard about coverage for home care. When the time comes, most people prefer to remain at home as long as feasible.

■ *Will I be able to keep up with the premiums?* Beware of sales agents who say that their policy's premiums will never go up. As noted above, they can and do. Strongly consider nonforfeiture benefits to hedge your bet.

■ *Is the insurance company sound?* If your insurance company goes bankrupt—and hundreds have in the last couple of decades—you can lose your coverage, or at best, pay higher premiums to a new company that takes over your policy. Ask about your company's financial ratings by calling one of the insurance company ratings services. (See **HELP** in "Life Insurance: Betting on Your Life," page 453, for phone numbers.) Only do business with "A+" or "A" rated companies, but be aware that a high rating does not *guarantee* the company's solvency.

■ *Do I know and understand all of the policy's options?* Most policies give consumers five options: daily benefit amount, benefit duration, inflation protection, elimination period, and nonforfeiture benefits.

■ *Have I carefully reviewed the policy contract?* Do not purchase a policy without reading the fine print. Getting a second opinion from a lawyer or other expert is obviously best, but a trusted friend or family member can also ask guiding questions, like "Can you afford the premiums?" and "What will you get for your money?"

In most states, you get a 30-day free look after you buy long-term care insurance. Don't hesitate to ask for a refund if you don't like what you see.

HELP

■ **National Associa-** tion of Area Agencies on Aging is a Washington group with an "Eldercare Locator" to direct you to the appropriate government agency or service provider in your area; call (800) 677-1116, 9 A.M. to 8 P.M. EST, or go to www.n4a.org.

■ **Children of Aging Parents is a clear-** inghouse of information about caring for the elderly. It provides support and referrals to adult children who are caring for elderly parents; call (215) 345-5104.

■ **The National Association of Insur-** ance Commissioners (NAIC), 120 West 12th Street, Suite 1100, Kansas City, MO 64105, (816) 842-3600, www.naic.org, offers a *Shopper's Guide to Long-Term Care Insurance.* They can also tell you whether your state has adopted the NAIC model long-term care insurance law, which sets a minimum standard for consumer protection. You can also call your state Insurance Department, many of which have state-specific buying guides and can tell you if your insurance agent has been disciplined recently.

■ *Long Term Care Planning: A Dollars and Sense Guide,* a 100-page book published by United Seniors Health Cooperative, tells you what questions to ask and what resources are available. It costs $15 and can be ordered by phone if you pay with a credit card or by mail if you send a check to USHC, 1331 H Street NW, Suite 500, Washington, DC 20005; (202) 393-6222.

■ **The National Academy of Elder Law** Attorneys can help you with legal issues referrals. Call (602) 881-4005.

■ *Consumer Reports'* **special report** on long-term care insurance, including ratings of specific policies, appeared in October 1997. It's available at the library or from Consumers Union for $3. Write CU Reprints, 101 Truman Avenue, Yonkers, NY 10703-1057.

CHAPTER 8

NUTRITIONAL SUPPLEMENTS

No Magic Pills

From 1994 to 1997, the nutritional supplement industry nearly doubled in sales, from $6 billion to $11 billion. More than 100 million Americans take dietary supplements daily, but unfortunately they are more likely to ingest hype than elixir.

"Develop muscles while you sleep." "Improve your memory." "Grow healthier, more vibrant hair." "Experience an amazing energy burst." These are some of the preposterous advertising and labeling claims made by manufacturers of nutritional supplements—vitamins, minerals, and assorted muscle pills. The virtual withdrawal of government oversight of the supplements industry during the 1980s allowed a whole new industry of purported cure purveyors to establish itself, no more honest than the infamous snake oil salesmen of the 19th century. No pill or potion will develop your muscles. Nothing you can eat will improve your memory or transform a man into a Don Juan. But Americans spend tens of millions of dollars a year anyway on nutritional

supplements with names like Hot Sauce and Metabolol that promise to help make them into muscle men (or women) in short order.

This is certainly not to say that vitamin and mineral supplements have no health benefits. On the contrary, prolonged failure to obtain sufficient quantities of key vitamins and minerals definitely can lead to serious health problems. But the muscle pill industry is perpetrating an incredible hoax on those who wish to become an incredible hulk.

THE BASICS

Vitamins and Minerals: To Take Them or Not?

Vitamins are organic molecules that are essential to life. Some vitamins are fat-soluble, which means they are stored in the body and accumulate for long periods of time until needed. Among the fat-soluble vitamins are A, D, E, and K. Water-soluble vitamins do not build up in the system. They include the B vitamins and vitamin C.

Minerals are inorganic substances that are also essential to life. Among them are iron, calcium, zinc, manganese, iodine, and copper. According to the Council for Responsible Nutrition, an industry trade group, the most commonly ingested supplements are vitamins A, B1 (thiamin), B2 (riboflavin), B3 (niacin), B6 (pyridoxine), B12, folic acid, C (ascorbic acid), E, calcium, and iron.

For centuries, people have known that certain foods, later discovered to be loaded with vitamins and minerals, ward off disease. Citrus fruits, which are laden with vitamin C, prevented scurvy in sailors who ate little else but hardtack and salt pork. (British sailors used to eat limes for this reason; thus their moniker, "limey.") Other vitamin-rich foods have been used to prevent beriberi and pellagra.

More recently, people have been taking vitamins because they believe they will impart special health benefits, such as preventing cancer, augmenting the immune system to fend off colds and flu, and even forestalling heart disease. The late Nobel prize-winner Dr. Linus Pauling was a great promoter of vitamin C as a cure for the common cold and even as a human immune deficiency virus (HIV) inhibitor.

While it is clearly established that a lack of one or more vitamins or minerals can lead to illness, the scientific community does not agree that taking additional vitamins and minerals above what the body normally consumes will make you healthier. Many nutritionists say that the U.S. recommended daily allowance (RDA) is all or even more than most people need. You can get your RDA from a diet with a variety of foods. Stanley Gershoff, PhD, dean of the Tufts University School of Nutrition, writes in *The Tufts University Guide to Total Nutrition*, "Most people in the United States get all the nutrients they need from the abundant food supply." On the other hand, some nutritionists point out that many Americans do not eat a mixed diet with plenty of vegetables, grains, and fruits.

Still, most people consume more nutrients than they may be aware of. Milk is fortified with vitamins A and D. Iodine is added to salt. Even hamburger buns provide significant nutrition; most are fortified with extra B vitamins. While you don't need to get the full RDA for every nutrient every day, some people—especially chronic dieters—eat too little and don't get enough over time. For them, a basic multivitamin/mineral pill may be in order. People with unusual ab-

> "**M**ost dietary supplements, including ginseng, garlic, fish oils, psyllium, even shark cartilage, make claims that range from ambiguous to outrageous."
>
> —DOUG PUDOLSKY,
> *U.S. News & World Report*

THE ANTI-OXIDANT CONUNDRUM

Vitamins said to act as anti-oxidants—vitamins A, C, and E—have been generating much interest lately, and many people are taking special supplements of them. They may be on to something. Normal cell metabolism as well as exposure to smog, X-rays, and certain other environmental hazards create oxygen free radicals, which can attack cell membranes or even damage DNA and lead to illness. Certain vitamins—beta-carotene (A), E, and C—apparently neutralize these free radicals. Vitamin E is thought to be especially helpful with preventing free-radical-caused damage to the heart; one major study found that women who took at

least 100 international units (IU) a day for two years halved their risk of cardiovascular disease. And beta-carotene supplementation has been shown to reduce the incidence of heart attack and stroke.

But some experts are still skeptical. According to Dr. Stephen Barrett, author of the *Consumer Reports* book *Health Schemes, Scams and Frauds*, anti-oxidants can also *release* free radicals, and the latest research found that smokers who take beta-carotene actually have a higher rate of cancer. "Studies that support taking anti-oxidants are merely epidemiological and do not establish cause and effect," Barrett says.

sorption difficulties and pregnant and lactating women may also benefit from special supplementation.

Unfortunately, much of the "scientific" evidence cited to back up the health benefit claims for taking any other nutrient-specific pills each day is not well-grounded. "Studies" referred to in product promotions often don't meet rigorous scientific standards, nor do they report whether the subjects in such studies got the vitamins from pills or from vitamin-rich foods—the latter indicating a generally healthier diet and a healthier subject. Even if a credible study finds some benefit, another may disagree—but

the manufacturer cites only the study that takes its side.

Some claims are complete folderol. Don't believe anything that promises to:

Make men more virile. Men have been trying since the dawn of time to find a true aphrodisiac. Our advice: Keep looking.

Provide an energy burst, as advertisements for Nature's Bounty Ener-B (a vitamin B_{12} nasal gel) suggest. While a severe shortage of vitamin B_{12} can make you feel weak, giving yourself extra does nothing.

Make your hair healthier, fuller, thicker, and make your skin supple and healthy. The ingredients in popular hair and skin formulas include a range of vitamins and minerals, such as niacin, iron, biotin, beta-carotene, and inositol. Typical of these products are the Nature's Plus lineup, including "Ultra Hair," "Ultra Skin," and "Ultra Nails." It is impossible to target vitamins or minerals to certain parts of the body. Of course, extreme nutritional deficiency could lead to visibly unhealthy skin or hair, but this is very rare.

Improve your memory. The claims for products making this promise are based on a study that found that taking high doses of purified phosphatidylcholine (choline) helped a few patients with Alzheimer's disease. From this, manufacturers make an extraordinary leap to assert that taking choline will help people without Alzheimer's think better. Among other ingredients that may be found in so-called memory formulas are lecithin, vitamin B6, and L-glutamine.

Help your body cope with stress. One of the most prevalent claims on vitamin shelves is that you need special supplementation if you are heavily stressed. In this frenetic society, who isn't? But you don't need to take special vitamins or minerals for it. You might need such supplementation if you have experienced severe physical stress (such as surgery), but not for the emotional stresses of everyday life.

> "**P**eople get all the amino acids they require by eating an adequate diet."
>
> —DR. DOUGLAS ARCHER,
> of the U.S. Food and Drug
> Administration

In the 1980s, Lederle Labs, the makers of Stresstabs, was cited by the New York State Attorney General for deceptively claiming that this product helps the body deal with stress. Lederle agreed to stop making the claims and paid $25,000 in costs to the state. Although the company never admitted the claims were false, it agreed not to say or imply that emotional distress causes depletion of water-soluble vitamins and to start saying that people with ordinary stress can get all the nutrients they need from a balanced diet. Nonetheless, Stresstabs are still on the market, and the package and advertising as of 1997 still featured an image of a candle burning at both ends, although Lederle is now careful to write on the package—in small print—that the pills are for people who have had a long illness, who drink or smoke excessively, or who follow fad diets.

Dr. Victor Herbert, a professor at New York's Mt. Sinai School of Medicine and recipient of several national awards for nutrition research, advises patients not to believe anyone who says that most disease is due to a faulty diet and can be treated with such "nutritional methods" as vitamins. According to Dr. Herbert, common symptoms like malaise, tiredness, lack of energy, aches or pains, and insomnia are usually the body's reaction to emotional stress.

There is considerable doubt as to the efficacy of supplements that claim to help relieve premenstrual syndrome (PMS) symptoms. PMS formulas contain a lot of B vitamins, and some doctors do prescribe high B6 doses to alleviate PMS. But the *Mount Sinai Medical School Complete Book of Nutrition* says, "PMS has been erroneously represented as being 'cured' by B6, when in fact the same 80 percent 'cured' by B6 are in fact 'cured' by a placebo."

Controversies over claims and inquiries led to major legislation in 1994. A barrage of letters and lobbying by ardent vitamin and supplement enthusiasts stopped Congress from requiring the same kind of pre-market testing of supplements as is now required of drugs. Instead, the 1994 Dietary Supplement Health Education Act (DSHEA) prohibits supplement products from making specific medical claims but allows amorphous promises. Assertions about disease prevention or treatment will now require FDA approval. Unfortunately, the law does not prohibit the much more common (yet still suspect) "structure and function" claims.

So a manufacturer can still imply that, since a severe lack of Vitamin A could theoretically be harmful to your eyesight, a product with Vitamin A will help your vision. And a product can say that it helps you get a good night's sleep but not that it cures insomnia; a manufacturer of liver pills can boast about their ability to "tonify the liver" but not claim to "prevent liver cancer"; and Crystal Springs' "For Gentlemen Only" doesn't claim to actually improve sexual performance, only to renew a man's "stamina and endurance."

Still, the law is starting to better protect consumers from phony claims. First, between 1995 and 1997, the Federal Trade Commission settled cases against 24 dietary supplement manufacturers and marketers for making deceptive claims; for one example, it stopped three California firms from making unsupported claims that chromium, a trace metal, can reduce weight, increase muscle mass, and prevent diabetes. Second, the FDA advised makers of 41 supplements that their claims appeared to be unsupported by scientific evidence; in response, at least 25 of them either dropped or modified their claims. Most prominently, the FDA began to crack down on the marketing of popular ephedrine-laced pills, which promise drastic weight reduction, because 800 injuries and at least 17 deaths have been linked to this herbal stimulant. It proposed prohibiting supplements that provide 8mg or more of ephedrine per dose and requiring labels that warned pregnant women and individuals with hypertension, heart conditions, and neuralgic disorders to avoid ephedrine.

"I'm Not Going to Pay a Lot for These Vitamins!"

If you are among the estimated 40% of Americans who have taken a vitamin or mineral supplement in the past month, you probably paid too much. A 1997 survey in a two-block area of Manhattan found that the price of 100 tablets of 1,000 mg of vitamin C was $5.49 at one pharmacy chain, $8.39 at another, and $11.30 at a third. Natural vitamin E (100 tablets of 400 IU) ranged from $4.59 to $11.59.

Comparing prices can be difficult because the number of pills in bottles and their potencies are not standardized. If you're unable to compare exactly the same products, just remember that vitamins purchased in health food chain stores are usually more expensive than those purchased in drugstores.

Nutritional Supplements: What's in Them for You?

"**A** New Advanced Cell Growth Formula That Stimulates Muscle Growth Even While You Sleep!!!"

"Nothing is more powerful at adding muscle without fat."

"An Anabolic Inferno . . . the most efficient muscle building supplement. [You will] watch . . . muscles explode with incredible strength, massive size and pure energy."

What's in these products? Typical ingredient lists include choline, inositol, potassium, smilax (an extract of the Mexican sarsaparilla root), chromium picolinate, dibencozide, ginseng (it's supposed to increase stamina), sterols (made from vegetables and marketed as an alternative to animal steroids), growth hormones, and various amino acids.

LEAD IN CALCIUM

We've all heard that getting enough calcium is important, particularly for preventing osteoporosis and keeping our bones strong. But what you might not know is that many calcium supplements contain high levels of lead, which is highly toxic. The Natural Resources Defense Council, together with a number of other advocacy groups, had 26 calcium supplements tested by the University of California at Santa Cruz in 1997. Only two met the standards of California's Proposition 65, under which lead levels cannot exceed 0.5 micrograms per day, and many had ten times that much. One type, Source Naturals Calcium Night, manufactured by Source Naturals Inc., had more than 40 times as much—20.75 micrograms of lead per maximum dose. The two that met Proposition 65 standards were Posture-D High Potency Calcium with Vitamin D, manufactured by Whitehall Laboratories, with 0.46 micrograms of lead per maximum dose, and Tums 500 Chewable Calcium Supplements, manufactured by Smith Kline Beecham, with 0.44 micrograms of lead per maximum dose.

WHY PAY MORE?

Nationally advertised vita-min brands almost always cost more. Take the One-a-Day brand of multivit-amins, for example. You could pay $7.29 for 100 tablets or, for the same ingredients, buy the store brand at a drugstore chain for only $1.99—a price differential of more than 300%. One hundred tablets of Centrum, a nationally advertised vitamin and mineral supplement, sell for as much as $9.99; a store brand with a bit less silicon costs only $2.99.

There is no reliable evidence that any of these substances come anywhere near to living up to their claims. Inositol seems to have no use in the human body. The body makes more than enough choline on its own. There is no evidence that smilax does anything; in fact, it acts as a laxative, which is unde-sirable in athletes. Ginseng also hasn't been shown to do anything special. Nonetheless, nutritional supplement manufacturers argue that body builders and others need *more* of these ingredients than can readily be obtained from food. Nonsense.

Amino acids and growth hor-mones may even prove harmful. Amino acids are the building blocks of protein. Americans get more than enough protein in their regular diets, and ingesting yet more amino acids may put an extra burden on the kidneys. Moreover, amino acids are not meant to be taken free-standing, which is how they are often presented in supple-ments. Taking too much of a single amino acid might interfere in the absorption of another. And an ex-cess of growth hormone can lead to acromegaly, in which the muscles grow in mass but become weaker and lose functionality.

In trying to escape government attacks on efficacy claims, manufac-turers sometimes respond that the supplements are only part of an overall fitness program—that the products alone do not produce the benefit but work in conjunction with regular workouts. There is no credible evidence that taking sup-plements imparts any extra body-building benefit that isn't obtained from workouts and a good diet.

In 1992, the NYC Department of Consumer Affairs asked manufac-turers to provide scientific backup for their advertising claims. Some of the companies ignored the re-quest, and others sent information consisting primarily of ingredient lists and generalized claims about effectiveness. Notably, none sup-plied published reports from recog-nized or peer-reviewed journals.

The Department charged some of the companies with deceptive trade practices. In the fall of 1993, one of the firms, L&S Research (Cy-bergenics), settled by agreeing to place a disclaimer on certain ads reading, "Supplement component will not promote faster or greater muscular gains."

WHAT TO WATCH OUT FOR

Vitamins

Overdosing. Hundreds of people overdose on vitamin and mineral supplements each year, with consequences serious enough to be reported to the federal government. The point at which harm may be sustained is generally set at ten times the U.S. RDA for water-soluble vitamins, five times the RDA for fat-solubles, and three times the RDA for minerals.

What might actually occur?

Too much vitamin A (sustained by overdosing by more than 20,000 IU) can cause headaches, vomiting, and liver damage.

Too much vitamin B3 (niacin) can result in hot flashes, ulcers, and liver disorders, and excesses of vitamin B6, sometimes administered as a PMS remedy, can lead to neurological damage.

Excessive intake of vitamin C can lead to urinary tract problems. Several people with AIDS have died from dehydration after taking massive doses of vitamin C, which had induced severe diarrhea.

Too much vitamin D can cause kidney stones.

A Finnish study found that very high iron intake can more than double the risk of heart attacks. And according to nutritionist and personal health columnist Jane Brody, chronic iron overdoses can result in methemochromatosis, which can damage the liver, pancreas, and heart.

Marketing gimmicks. Manufacturers often make distinctions without a difference. For example, the body can't differentiate between synthetic and natural vitamin C—it's all ascorbic acid—but natural costs more. "Time-release" C is also more expensive with no proven benefit.

Varying potencies and dissolution qualities. Unlike prescription pharmaceuticals, vitamin and mineral pills don't have to contain the *exact* quantity of ingredients stated on the label. Because these manufacturing processes are not as controlled as they are for prescription drugs, one B complex pill may contain only 90 mg of active B complex vitamin while another has 110 mg.

Variances in manufacturing and a lack of testing means that not all vitamin and mineral pills will dissolve at the same speed in the body. The United States Pharmacopeia (not a government group) is trying to resolve this problem by issuing recommended dissolution standards. For example, they propose that water-soluble vitamins be at least 75% dissolved in an hour. But these are merely recommended standards. Products that meet the standards for potency, dissolution, disintegration, and purity will be able to display the letters "USP" on the label next to the product name.

Health food store salespeople. Their job is to sell you more vitamins and minerals, not to provide sound advice. In fact, they are prohibited by law from diagnosing medical conditions or suggesting remedies.

Eating a poorer diet because you are taking supplements. Fruits, grains, and vegetables are still the preferred sources of nutrients, and they impart other health benefits as well, such as better digestion.

Taking vitamins for "insurance." Don't take a pill unless you analyze your diet and determine if it is deficient. "In that case," nutritionist Dr. Stephen Barrett advises, "the best course of action is to fix your diet." He adds: "If you can't correct your diet, then purchase an inexpensive multivitamin that contains no more than 100% U.S. RDA for any ingredient."

Nutritional Supplements

Hyperbolic claims. When you see the following words used on a product or in an advertisement for a nutritional supplement, remember, it just ain't so: energy enhancer, fat burner, rapid muscle growth, converts fat into energy, anabolic activator, increases lean muscle mass, lipotropic, metabolic optimizer.

"True-life" testimonials. More often than not, the testimonials come from body-builders who are paid a fee by the manufacturers or are on their regular payroll.

THE $MARTER CONSUMER

Try to buy vitamins with expiration dates on the bottles. Vitamin and mineral pills don't last forever. There is no government mandate to state an expiration date, but some manufacturers do so anyway.

As regards nutritional supplements, the smartest thing you can do is eat a healthy diet and skip them.

Look for new nutrition labels. As of March 1999, the FDA will require all vitamins, minerals, herbal products, and other dietary supplements to carry "Supplement Facts." Like the "Nutrition Facts" on packaged foods, the "Supplements Facts" chart will make it easier for consumers to read labels and compare brands. Nutrients will be listed in a standard order, along with the percent of the daily value they deliver. Products will be allowed to make vague health claims, such as "promotes prostate health," but such a claim must come with a disclaimer that "this product has not been evaluated by the Food and Drug Administration."

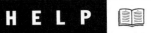

HELP

■ *Total Nutrition: The Only Guide You'll Ever Need,* Victor Herbert, MD, F.A.C.P., and Genell J. Subak-Sharpe, M.S., eds., St. Martin's Press, 1995, $16.95.

■ Read *The Health Robbers* (Prometheus Books, 1993), by Stephen Barrett, MD, a prize-winning author of 23 books. His book exposes all sorts of nutritional quackery and scientific mumbo-jumbo. Price: $26.95.

■ The United States Pharmacopeia *Guide to Vitamins and Minerals* is available from Avon Books, P.O. Box 767, Dresden, TN 38225; $6.99 plus $1.50 for shipping and handling. Allow 6 to 8 weeks for delivery.

CHAPTER 9

WEIGHT-LOSS PRODUCTS AND PROGRAMS

The Skinny on Dieting Deceptions and Dangers

Are you a waist-watcher? If so, your private battle of the bulge puts you roundly in the middle of a public obsession. At any given time, about 58 million Americans are dieting (50% of all women and 25% of all men), and an equal number claim they are struggling to maintain their weight.

A $33 billion industry has grown up to feed this all-American appetite for appetite control. About $6 billion of that is spent on fraudulent diet products. Fly-by-night inventors hawk gut-busting nutritional supplements that supposedly take off the pounds while you sleep or insoles for your shoes that melt fat away as you walk. Herbalists advertise miracle concoctions, purportedly from the Far East. Major

U.S. corporations hire such well-knowns as former royal Sarah Ferguson (Duchess of York) to star in slick commercials on network television. Franchised weight-loss centers dress their staff in doctors' coats. Reputable book publishers and booksellers brazenly promote the latest fat-fighting fad.

With all this calorie counting and liquid lunching, you naturally might assume Americans were getting thinner. But if you did, you'd be wrong. Americans are fatter than ever. A majority of the U.S. population is now overweight; about a quarter to a third of all adults are considered obese, usually defined as 20% to 30% or more over their ideal body weight. And the numbers have been increasing steadily over the last 20 years.

So Americans are dieting more, *and* getting heavier. What's behind this contradiction?

THE BASICS

Fat Facts

Losing weight is as simple, or complicated, as eating less, exercising more, or a combination of both. Any diet that includes fewer calories than you burn off will cause you to lose weight. Since about 3,500 calories make up a pound of body weight, you would need to reduce your caloric intake by 500 calories a day to lose one pound per week, assuming your weight is stable.

For this reason, virtually any diet, if followed closely, will result in temporary weight loss—purely because of reduced calorie intake, not because of any complementary combination of foods, miracle dietary supplements, or wonder gadgets.

Trouble is, the odds are slim that you'll keep the weight off. The best studies have shown a failure rate of 95%—that is, only 5% of the dieters managed to keep all or most of their weight off for five or more years. When *Consumer Reports* surveyed 95,000 of its readers who had recently tried to lose weight, it found that only 25% managed to keep off two-thirds of what they lost for over two years.

The human body physiologically adapts to eating fewer calories, and research has shown that this may account for the temporariness of the disappearing act. Dr. C. Wayne Callaway, associate clinical professor of medicine at George Washington University and co-author of the federal *Dietary Guidelines for Americans,* testified before two congressional committees that reducing on a very low calorie diet is a form of semi-starvation that signals the body to slow down metabolism to protect against actual starvation. Thus, for example, a person who switches from a 2,000-calorie daily diet to a 1,000-calorie daily diet will most often *gain* weight when they increase their daily caloric intake even slightly, because the body is now geared to burn calories at a slower rate. Furthermore, the body compensates for under-eating by over-eating. Human and animal studies show that food can both suppress and stimulate the appetite. People and animals who have been adequately fed feel satisfied and stop eating; people and animals who've been underfed overcompensate and binge. In other words, each of us has something close to a "natural weight" that is, alas, hard to beat over time.

> "**W**hen it comes to losing weight, nearly all of the people who try commercial programs are being fooled nearly all of the time."
>
> —JANE BRODY,
> health writer for
> *The New York Times*

Wasteful Waist-Watching and Dangerous Diets

Fad diets. Callaway's summary of the scientific literature explains why the temporary effects of fad diets don't usually last. Whether you cut way back on carbohydrates or protein, put yourself on a fruit fast, or whatever the latest pop wisdom suggests, you'll probably lose weight simply because you're shedding water and eating fewer calories. These radical diets are hard to sustain over time, and many people never complete them because they get too hungry or too bored. Even those who get to the end find the weight creeps back once they start eating normally.

Pill mills. Because of side effects and lack of success, diet pills have gone in and out of favor for the last several decades. The latest crazes—the phentermine-fenfluramine combination (phen-fen) and Redux—ended abruptly in September 1997 when fenfluramine and Redux were yanked from the market because an alarming 32% of patients in sample groups had developed potentially fatal heart valve abnormalities.

Dieters are understandably spooked, but the promise of new diet drugs keeps what critics call "pill mills" in business. The rather disturbing American dream to be thin—or thinner—without working at it has created a tempting opportunity for diet clinics to cash in. Doctors, and sometimes simply staff, spend a few minutes with patients, play down the risks of rare but devastating side effects associated with the drugs, play up promises of permanent weight loss, and provide the purported miracle diet pills. Doctors applying for jobs at an Atlanta weight-loss center, for example, reported being pressured to churn out prescriptions and allot just three to five minutes per patient.

The new generation of diet pills is not as addictive as the amphetamines doctors prescribed in the 1960s, but all the new pills come with the potential for side effects. Sibutramine, known as Meridia, fools the body into feeling full but may also cause constipation, insomnia, headaches, and almost always increases a patient's blood pressure. Orlistat, which will be marketed as Xenical, prevents the body from absorbing as much as 30% of the fat it takes in; its side effects include loose stools, oily intestinal leakage (we'll leave the specifics to your imagination), and difficulty absorbing vital food nutrients such as vitamins D and E and beta carotene. Unexpected side effects—both minor and serious—could arise when these drugs hit the market, just as they did with Redux and fenfluramine.

That's why the new diet drugs should never be used for "cosmetic weight loss." They are intended only for what the FDA classifies as the "morbidly obese." These people, who are 20% to 30% or more over their ideal weight, may be better off risking serious side effects than living with the risks of obesity itself.

Even so, supercharged claims and liberal prescription policies at diet centers appeal to the merely plump, even the barely pudgy, who are willing to sacrifice their health to improve their appearance—sometimes with deadly results. Mary J. Linnen, of West Quincy, Massachusetts, was a healthy, athletic bride-to-be who wanted to lose five pounds before her wedding when she started taking phen-fen. Several months later she was dead, allegedly from primary pulmonary hypertension caused by taking the popular drug combo. Her family has filed suit against the makers of the two drugs.

In addition to safety, you might want to think about effectiveness. Many patients who have tried appetite suppressants quit when they couldn't have their cake and eat it too. Seems these miracle drugs don't work that well without, you guessed it, watching what you eat plus exercise. And the only way to *keep* the weight off is to maintain healthy eating and exercise habits.

Old-fashioned diet pills. Some other pills have shown some effectiveness at curbing the appetite, but they also come with undesirable side effects. Amphetamines' appetite-suppressing effect is temporary; they are also highly addictive and can be dangerous to the central nervous system and heart. For this reason, using amphetamines as a diet aid is no longer recommended for the treatment of obesity and requires a doctor's conscientious supervision. And when the patient discontinues use, his or her appetite will return and weight is easily regained.

Over-the-counter diet pills such as Acutrim and Dexatrim contain phenylpropanolamine, a mild stimulant that's chemically similar to amphetamines and that many decongestant products also contain. While it is somewhat effective at decreasing appetite and may help you shed a few pounds, you'll probably gain the weight right back as soon as you stop taking the pills and your appetite returns to normal. In his book *The Health Robbers,* Dr. Stephen Barrett, a nationally known opponent of quackery and fraud in medicine, says this drug may be dangerous to people with heart disease, high blood pressure, diabetes, or hyperthyroidism.

In a *Consumer Reports* survey, fewer than 5% of the people who had taken non-prescription diet pills said they were very or completely satisfied with how well the pills helped them lose weight and keep it off, and half were very or completely dissatisfied. Furthermore, people didn't like how the pills made them feel. Over 30% said they were always hungry, and over 20% at times felt dizzy or nauseated.

Commercial weight-loss programs. Every year, about 8 million Americans enroll in one of these structured programs that range from private local clinics to massive national chains, and they all offer their own "exclusive" programs. These can include individual counseling or group meetings, specially prepared food you must buy from them, meal replacement liquids or nutritional supplements, exercise regimens, and medical and psychological exams. In general, they can be broken down into two kinds of programs: medically supervised,

FIRST, GET SOME ANSWERS

The U.S. FDA, FTC, and National Association of Attorneys General suggest you ask the following questions before you sign up for a commercial weight-loss program:

- What are the health risks?
- What data can you show me that prove your program actually works?
- Do customers keep the weight off after they leave the program?
- What are the costs for membership, weekly fees, food, supplements, maintenance, and counseling? What's the payment schedule? Are any costs covered by health insurance? Do you give refunds if I drop out?
- Do you have a maintenance program? Is it part of the package or does it cost extra?
- What kind of supervision do you provide? What are the credentials of your professionals?
- What are the program's requirements? Are there special menus or foods, counseling visits, or exercise plans?

very low-calorie liquid fasts, in which flavored liquid formulas replace all solid food, usually for a period of months (such as Optifast, Medifast, and Health Management Resources); and non-medically supervised low-calorie regimens, in which dieters eat solid foods within a regimented meal plan (such as Jenny Craig, Nutri/System, and Diet Center). Prices vary from a few hundred to a few thousand dollars.

Generally, people who sign up with a weight-loss program believe they will receive a health-care service. But in such a commercially driven atmosphere, a pound of fat is worth a pound of profit—all too often at the expense of the dieter's health, emotional well-being, and pocketbook. Indeed, one Nutri/System Inc. franchisee said in the company's franchise brochure: "Money is the reason I became a Nutri/System franchisee. And now I have more money than I ever dreamed I could make in a lifetime."

Emphasizing sales rather than health has led these programs to overprice and overpromise, even though their plans often underestimate the risks and fail to meet the expectations they set up. An undercover investigation, by the NYC Department of Consumer Affairs, into the sales tactics of New York City weight-loss programs, revealed that nine out of ten failed to warn potential customers of serious health risks and instead claimed "absolute" safety, even when investigators asked directly whether health problems could arise. In fact, there is evidence that rapid weight loss (more than three to five pounds per week) can cause gallstones and cardiac problems. Rapid weight loss can even lead to death, particularly in people who are not overweight to begin with.

After a several-year investigation into the promises of lasting weight loss made by commercial weight-loss programs, the Federal Trade Commission (FTC) in 1997 settled charges that several of the nation's largest commercial diet-program companies—Jenny Craig Inc., Diet Center Inc., Physicians Weight Loss Centers, Nutri/System, and Weight Watchers International—deceptively advertised unsubstantiated weight-loss claims and consumer testimonials without proof that the examples represented the typical experience of dieters in the programs.

One ad for the Diet Center practically admits as much: "Temporary weight loss is usually followed by weight gain. The only effective weight-loss program is one that produces a safe and permanent result." But then it resorts to hyperbole and implies—falsely—that the Diet Center is somehow different: "The Diet Center Program provides the perfect solution."

Unsupervised meal-replacement drinks. These powdered drink mixes, such as Slim-Fast and Dyna-Trim, contain protein, sugar, fiber, vitamins, and minerals and were designed to replace one or two meals a day. While many users in the *Consumer Reports* survey managed to lose weight, albeit small amounts, 20% *gained* five pounds or more. And a third said they gained back the weight they had lost as soon as they went back to solid food. Tommy Lasorda's testimonial to the contrary, you might as well eat real food.

Gimmicks. Too good to be true? You bet. Most are simply a waste of money. The effects of cellulite reducing cream, for example, are purely cosmetic and only temporary. In 1997, AmeriFit Inc. refunded $100,000 to unhappy consumers of its "Fat Burners" line of dietary supplement tablets and drinks. The FTC charged that the only thing they burn is a hole in the wallet. Some gadgets are even dangerous. The Food and Drug Administration has forced a number of electrical muscle stimulators off the market. They were promoted for weight loss but when used incorrectly, they caused electrical shocks and burns.

WEIGHT-LOSS WASHOUT

According to a *Consumer Reports* survey, the average dieter who used one of the commercial diet programs regained half what he or she had lost within six months of ending the diet and two thirds of it within two years. In one study published in *The International Journal of Obesity*, one fourth of the 4,026 obese patients who went on the Optifast program dropped out within the first three weeks, and only 5% to 10% of the Optifast dieters who achieved significant weight loss were still at their reduced weights after 18 months.

A POUND OF FLESH = $100

An NYC Consumer Affairs investigation found that one diet center in Manhattan would have charged a potential dieter $100 per pound to lose seven pounds and maintain the weight loss. "Worse, I was only one pound away from being *underweight* to start with," said the undercover investigator.

Weight Loss = Health Gain?

The question of whether dieting itself is hazardous to your health has bedeviled health researchers and dieters since a 1991 article published in the *New England Journal of Medicine* linked repeated changes in weight, no matter what the person's initial weight, with a generally increased death rate and twice the chance of dying of heart disease specifically. But a 1994 study by the National Task Force on the Prevention and Treatment of Obesity found no convincing evidence that so-called yo-yo dieting induced health risks, *caused* weight gain, or affected later attempts to lose weight. The report discouraged people who are not overweight from dieting obsessively but said, "Obese individuals should not allow concerns about hazards of weight cycling to deter them from efforts to control their body weight."

While the benefits of losing weight are generally indisputable for truly obese people, who are at greater risk of stroke, heart disease, diabetes, and gallstones, definitive advice for others is less clear. Some evidence suggests that if weight cycling does have any negative health effects, they are seen primarily in people of low or normal weight.

Recent research has shown that the number of pounds is less important than where the pounds collect in determining the health effects of excess weight. Obesity does not automatically result in high blood pressure, high cholesterol, diabetes, and the other unhealthy conditions associated with being overweight. "Apple-shaped" people, whose fat collects in the abdomen and above the waist, are more at risk of heart disease than "pear-shaped" people, who carry excess fat around the hips, rear end, and thighs. Men tend to be "apples" and women tend to be "pears." Thus, not all overweight people are at the same risk. But for those who are at risk and want to lose weight, the National Task Force Report concluded that losses of as little as five to ten pounds can improve conditions such as diabetes, high blood pressure, and high cholesterol.

If you are determined to do something about how you feel and look, there are two things that nobody has anything but good things to say about: increasing the amount of exercise you get and lowering the amount of fat in your diet.

You don't have to fit two-hour workouts into your hectic schedule to lose weight. Instead, adjust your routines and take exercise where you can get it: Use the stairs instead of the elevator; walk your dog instead of just letting him out the back door; park your car at the far end of the lot; allow a little extra time to walk to meetings rather than grabbing a cab.

Just lowering the fat in your diet may help you shed a few pounds, since fatty foods tend to be high in calories.

WHAT TO WATCH OUT FOR

Claims based on tantalizing words or concepts: effortless, easy, guaranteed, breakthrough, natural, burns fat away, blocks fat, blocks starch, amazing, and miraculous. It would indeed be a miracle if products pitched this way lived up to their promises, for the only "amazing results" are likely to be the promoters' amazing profits.

The claim game. Don't be swayed by testimonials or anecdotal evidence, such as startling "before and after" pictures of people who've dropped 50 pounds or four dress sizes. They skirt the fact that few studies back up short-term claims of success. Virtually no evidence supports the long-term effectiveness of commercial weight-loss programs and products, according to a 1992 report of the National Institutes of Health.

Jenny Craig, for instance, ran ads that said things like "I lost 95 pounds in just over six months. And, I've kept the weight off for nearly one year!" or "I used to dream that one day I'd wake up and be slim. Thanks to Jenny Craig, it happened. I tried other programs, but the second I'd go off, I'd gain everything back, and then some. While they helped me lose weight, they never taught me how to eat in the real world and keep it off." After the Federal Trade Commission asked Jenny Craig to substantiate the implication that its customers typically are successful in reaching their weight goals and maintaining their weight loss permanently, the company agreed in 1997 to stop using such testimonials and to add the following caveat to advertising for its programs: "For many dieters, weight loss is temporary."

Dangerous drugs. Don't let the fantasy of a better-looking body outweigh your better judgment. Prescription diet pills should be used only by people who are truly obese. And if you take these drugs, call your doctor the minute you experience any symptoms like shortness of breath, chest pain, faintness, or swelling of the lower legs and ankles.

Is there a doctor in the house? Although many commercial weight-loss centers claim their programs are "doctor-supervised," doctors may be on site only rarely, if ever. Take Physicians Weight Loss Centers, which said things like this in ads: "Our physicians, nurses, and counselors supervise your complete program. They show you how to eat for healthy weight loss, oversee your progress and well-being, and teach you new eating habits for staying slim." In fact, the FTC charged that the center physicians do not supervise participants.

Mumbo-jumbo that sounds scientific. Guildwood Direct Limited and Body Well Inc. actually advertised and sold "Slimming Soles," insoles worn in each shoe that purportedly caused weight loss through the principle of "reflexology." Every time the user took a step, the insoles were said to massage certain reflex zones that are connected to the digestive system. By stimulating the digestive system, the insoles were supposed to trigger the body to burn stored fat. Guess what! The companies could not satisfy the FTC's request for proof of this magic effect.

Deceptively low prices. Nutri/System, for example, ran various price promotions. One promised, "Lose all the weight you can for only $79." Another said, "Pay only $1 per pound." However, an FTC investigation found that there are "substantial additional mandatory expenses associated with participation in the program that far exceed the advertised price."

High-pressure sales tactics used by center-based programs. These can include limited-time deals, discounts when you balk at the price, psychological manipulation ("you'll feel better if you just get started"), money-back guarantees, and follow-up phone calls that verge on harassment.

Fat-fighting frauds. Diet candies, artificial bulk-producers, starch blockers, fat blockers, and fat flushers are bogus. Some of them are even dangerous. People who have used starch blockers have complained of nausea, vomiting, diarrhea, and stomach pains. Guar gum, a bulk producer, can cause obstructions of the intestines, stomach, or esophagus, which prompted the Food and Drug Administration to take legal action against companies marketing products containing this ingredient.

All-natural products. Natural isn't necessarily better, or safe. Herbal diet pills sold by mail and in health food stores have exotic ingredient lists that give few clues as to their contents. For instance, *ma huang* or *ephedra,* the primary ingredient in many herbal diet supplements, is ephedrine, a nervous system stimulant that acts like amphetamines and caffeine to stimulate the heart and central nervous system.

Ephedrine is a powerful stimulant extracted from a Chinese herb included in lots of health food store and supermarket products that promise victory over bulging waistlines and increased energy. Since 1993, the FDA has recorded more than 800 reports of "adverse reactions" to ephedra-based products—everything from strokes to high blood pressure to heart palpitations to seizures and heart attacks. Dietary supplements containing ephedra have been linked to three dozen deaths. Since there is little evidence that ephedra-based products actually do trigger weight loss, taking them hardly seems worth the risk.

Expensive vitamin or protein supplements. If you are eating a balanced low-calorie diet, you don't need them. If you will be eating fewer than 1,200 calories a day for a prolonged period of time, a vitamin supplement would be advisable, according to Dr. Stephen Barrett.

THE $MARTER CONSUMER

Pill power is no substitute for will-power. It may sound too sensible, and like hard work, but if you switch to a low-fat, reduced-calorie, nutritionally balanced diet and combine it with moderate exercise, you'll probably lose weight. Most doctors and registered dietitians recommend losing no more than one pound per week. While crash diets may work faster, at least at first, they often lack essential nutrients, can harm your health, and their results probably won't last. Furthermore, they do nothing to change for the long-term any unhealthy lifestyle eating habits you may have. Check with your doctor before you embark on any drastic change—this goes equally for changes in your diet and exercise routines.

Before you sign up with a commercial weight-loss program, check the company's reputation with the local Better Business Bureau. And before you sign a contract, make sure the costs and fees for all services, foods, supplements, and maintenance have been clearly spelled out.

HELP

■ **Read "Top-Selling Diets:** Lots of Gimmicks, Little Solid Advice," *Consumer Reports*, January 1998.

■ *The Skinny on Dieting* **is one of** several brochures on weight loss programs and products published by the Federal Trade Commission. Write to Public Reference Branch, Room 130, 6th and Pennsylvania Avenue NW, Washington, D.C. 20580, or visit the FTC Internet site at http://www.ftc.gov.

■ **The Weight-Control Information** Network (WIN) of the National Institute of Diabetes and Digestive and Kidney Diseases assembles and disseminates information on weight control, obesity, and nutritional disorders. Visit their Internet site at http://niddk.nih.gov/NutritionDocs.html, or call (800) 946-8098. You'll find guides to subjects like "Prescription Medications for the Treatment of Obesity" and "Weight Cycling."

■ **Read "Weight Control: Facts, Fads** and Frauds," in *The Health Robbers,* edited by Stephen Barrett, MD, and William T. Jarvis, PhD (Prometheus Books, 1993).

■ **To complain about a weight-loss** program or product, contact your state's attorney general, the Food and Drug Administration, the Federal Trade Commission, or the local Better Business Bureau.

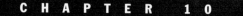

CHAPTER 10

HEALTH CLUBS

Exercise . . . Your Judgment

We all know the benefits of physical exercise, and the dangers of not doing any. C. Everett Koop, the former surgeon general, has argued that a sedentary lifestyle is equivalent to smoking a full pack of cigarettes every day. Yet despite all the evidence, Dr. David Satake, director of the U.S. Centers for Disease Control and Prevention, estimates that two-thirds of American adults are not getting recommended levels of physical activity, and 30% are completely sedentary. The problem is even worse among the elderly, Hispanics, and Southerners. The result: More than 250,000 deaths per year in the United States may be due to lack of regular physical activity. Many members of the health care community consider physical inactivity "the biggest health challenge of the 21st century."

In fact, every week seems to bring another reason to exercise. Gallup surveys indicate that those who exercise regularly feel more relaxed, experience improvements in creativity, have better social lives, exhibit more self-confidence, are more willing and able to change other health habits (like smoking and diet), feel a stronger sense of control over their health and their lives, and are even more attractive.

And these people don't just feel better—they actually *are* healthier. The 1996 Surgeon General's Report on Physical Activity and Health concludes that regular exercise helps prolong your life and reduce the risks of cardiovascular disease, high blood pressure, colon cancer, non-insulin-dependent diabetes mellitus, obesity, and osteoarthritis and that it is associated with improved mood, decreased anxiety, relief from symptoms of depression, and an enhanced sense of well-being. As much as 50% of the body's decline between ages 30 and 70 can be attributed to a sedentary lifestyle, according to data from the Canadian Fitness and Lifestyle Research Institute.

Exercising, in short, makes a lot of sense—dollars and cents, too. A study by an association of health clubs shows benefits not just to athletes but to their employers in reduced health care costs, increased productivity, and reduced absenteeism. After one year, for instance, participants in Johnson & Johnson's "wellness program" saw their sick leave go *down* 9% while it went *up* 13% for a control group. Large companies like IBM, Microsoft, and the

John Hancock Insurance Company now subsidize health club memberships for all employees; insurance groups offer rebates to subscribers who join. The Prudential Insurance Co. estimates that for every $1 spent on its fitness program, it saved 93 cents in health-care costs per employee who participated.

Fueled by such evidence and the aesthetic standards of Hollywood and fashion magazines, the past decade has seen an explosion in fitness facilities where young professionals could chisel their bodies, shave off a few pounds, or simply get a little aerobic exercise. The statistics are impressive: The number of health club members doubled from 1987 to 1995. Long the preserve of young single males, membership has gained popularity among women, married couples, and even the elderly. The International Health, Racquet & Sportsclub Association estimates that one in ten members is age 65 or older. Fitness has grown into an $8.5 billion industry. The development of the industry, however, was not without growing pains. In response to a spate of well-publicized club closings and pervasive abuses in the late '80s and early '90s, most states now have laws on the books placing limits on the number of years for which memberships can be sold, requiring health clubs to post bonds or to put membership money collected pre-opening in escrow accounts, or requiring refunds to members who move to a new part of the country. These measures have helped bring down the number of complaints filed with the Council of Better Business Bureaus from 3,270 in 1989 to 2,403 in 1994. But they have not eliminated aggressive sales tactics by the clubs or overambitious New Year's resolutions by short-lived athletes. So to make sure you lose the weight under your skin and not the shirt over it, some consumer warming-up is in order.

THE BASICS

To Join or Not to Join

A sedentary lifestyle ranks with high cholesterol, cigarette smoking, high blood pressure, and obesity as a major risk factor in heart disease and a variety of other life-threatening conditions. Government health experts now recommend that "[e]very American adult should accumulate 30 minutes or more of moderate intensity physical activity over the course of most days of the week." And the Surgeon General has made it clear that you can't hide behind the excuse that you can't afford an expensive health club membership or a trekking expedition to the Himalayas. Any number of daily activities—mowing the lawn, using the stairs instead of the elevator, washing and waxing your car, or a brisk walk home from the office—will do the job, so long as they are of at least moderate intensity. (However, walking down the aisles of your video store selecting tonight's movie and snacks probably won't fit the bill.)

The only real question, then, should be what type of exercise is best for you. Many find membership in a health club a necessary

PERSONAL TRAINERS

Personal trainers were once the exclusive province of the privileged few—moguls, movie stars and Madonna. But an increasing number of Americans are now willing to pay $20 to $100 an hour for a trainer's services. Why? For those who lack the motivation to stick with an exercise program, a trainer can act as a "professional nag," a Jiminy Cricket of steel muscles who will whisper in your ear—or scream in your face—to stick with it. As one believer explains, "I was always postponing exercising. Tomorrow, next week. There was no accountability. But now, when the personal trainer arrives, I have no choice. You get it done." Even if you trust your determination, you may not trust your judgment: a trainer may help you design a program that meets your needs and suits your abilities and limitations.

How to find the right match? As always, get recommendations from those around you. Once you have some promising candidates, ask for a free consultation to make sure your personalities —and exercising philosophies— match. Before you hire anyone, verify that they are certified from one of the major institutions, like the American Council on Exercise, the American College of Sports Medicine, the Association for Fitness Professionals, or the Aerobics and Fitness Association of America. Make sure that they have personal liability insurance; get their billing policy in writing; and don't sign anything waiving your right to sue if you get injured during a workout. You should generally expect to meet with your trainer with some frequency for a few weeks while you develop the right exercise regimen for you. You can then meet more sporadically, mostly to fine-tune your program as you progress.

Finally, a few tips to save a few bucks: if you belong to a health club, hire someone from the club; visit the trainer rather than have them visit you; and, if the trainer is willing, share him or her with a friend.

incentive to get their juices flowing—they like the setting, they want to get their money's worth, or they need the motivating force of a trained professional. Hence, 20.8 million Americans regularly exercise in health clubs.

Finding the Right Health Club

Let your fingertips get some exercise first: Try to narrow your choices by calling a few places and visiting the ones that seem to match your budget and your interests.

Once you're there, tour the premises, ask the staff questions, and ask to be set loose on the premises so you can talk with club members to get a sense of the place. In particular, pay attention to the following:

Convenience. Location and operating hours are probably the number-one consideration. Especially if you find it hard to get motivated, why make exercising even more of a challenge by joining a health club 40 minutes away?

Cost. The price depends on a number of factors, inluding the equipment and services offered, the size of the membership, and the staff-to-member ratio. Payment plans vary, from a membership fee up-front or in installments, to an initiation fee plus monthly dues, to a pay-per-use plan. (Some clubs charge extra for specific hours or features.)

If you're going to the gym for the first time, consider initially a one-month membership. You'll probably be paying more, possibly a lot more, on an annual basis, but you'll cut your losses if you are part of the majority who rediscover the pleasures of being a couch potato—and stop exercising—within 6 months of their first ride on the stationary bike. (But don't get confused with an annual membership payable in monthly installments, which requires you to keep making payments for the whole twelve months even if you decide to go back to your TV set after a few weeks.)

In addition, you may be playing into the hands of a greedy operator who'll take the money and run. That's what happened in 1991 to some 5,000 members at four Apple Health & Sports club branches in New York City when the spas shut their doors—after some members had recently paid fees of $1,000. Stay clear, in particular, of so-called "life memberships." They are illegal in most states and, as one academic notes, "For every club that opens, another one closes. A club with a large up-front fee offering a lifetime membership is a likely candidate for bankruptcy in three years."

If you go for a membership payable in installments, find out if there is a finance charge involved. Consumer investigators calculated that membership at Bally's Pacific in Bellevue, Washington, went up 17% when paid in monthy installments—more than the finance charge for most credit cards at the time.

Equipment and services. Figure out what you're interested in. Standard exercise features include aerobic equipment—such as treadmills, stationary bicycles, Stairmasters, or rowing machines—to burn calories and fat and improve circulation—

> " *I f a club attempts to sell you a long-term contract on your first visit by offering you a discount, turn around and walk out.* "
>
> —Dr. William Jarvis,
> President, National Council
> Against Health Fraud

SIGNING UP

Before you write your chosen health club a check, check with your local Better Business Bureau or consumer agency for any history of complaints. Find out what protection you have if the club shuts down. More than 30 states, for instance, require health clubs to post bonds for this purpose. Still, since many clubs fail to do so, call your state's attorney general's office or secretary of state to verify that your club is actually "bonded" and that it carries liability insurance. If you buy a pre-opening membership, make sure your fee is placed in escrow.

If there is an opportunity for a try-out period, take advantage of it. Make sure, however, that the try-out fee is applicable to your long-term membership fee.

Before signing the contract, take it home and read it carefully for any hidden costs. And remember, oral promises from a sales rep are legally worthless.

The contract should include all services listed. New York State law, for example, enables you to cancel your contract if "the services cease to be offered as stated in the contract." The more specific the contract, the stronger your case. The contract should also spell out your cancellation rights and compensation provisions if the club, or some of its facilities, shuts down temporarily.

Most states give health club members a right of cancellation if they move, if they are physically incapacitated for a period of time—or if the consumer dies. Some states also enable you to get out of a long-term membership short of such drastic events. Washington state law, for instance, enables you to cancel your membership if your contract runs for more than a year, by giving 30 days' written notice. Some clubs also allow you to resell your membership when you leave, but they generally will charge a fee—typically paid by the purchaser.

Do not sign a contract enabling the owner to change rules, hours of operation, location, or services at his or her discretion. Try to stay away from installment contracts under which the club can withdraw payments directly from your bank account—you'll have an easier time recovering your money in case of dispute if you make them charge your credit card account instead. For the same reason, be careful about contracts that the club can sell—or "assign"—to a finance company.

Finally, many states require a "cooling off" period enabling you to cancel within a few days (generally, three) of signing up.

and anaerobic equipment—such as Nautilus machines or free weights —that help you strengthen, tone, define, and build muscles. Other options include saunas, steamrooms, pools, whirlpools, juice bars, massage, racquet sports, tanning rooms, specialized exercise classes, private training, and nutritional counseling.

Overcrowding. Visit the club at the time you'll be using it. Ask what the number of members is and if there is a limit on membership. Experts suggest a ratio of square footage to total number of members of 10:1 to 15:1.

Maintenance and cleanliness. Visit both the exercise floor and the locker room, and inspect closely the condition of the various machines. Each piece of equipment should bear how-to-use instructions.

Staff. Find out about their qualifications—whether they hold degrees in physical education, exercise physiology, or in kinesiology; whether they are certified by a reputable organization, such as the American College of Sports Medicine or the Aerobics and Fitness Association of America, and whether they have cardiopulmonary resuscitation (CPR) training. A good instructor can help you develop the right exercise plan and motivate you to stick with your routine.

You may have other, specialized considerations. Does the club accept children or offer child care?

MORE THAN MUSCLES AT STAKE

Getting the right contract with a cancellation provision ensuring full or prorated refunds is only part of the battle. In April 1994, Bally's Health & Tennis Corp.—now called Bally Total Fitness, the largest chain of health clubs in the country—agreed to pay the Federal Trade Commission (FTC) $120,000 in civil penalties and to provide refunds believed to be in the hundreds of thousands of dollars to thousands of customers. The company, which operates 300 health clubs under the names Jack LaLanne and The Vertical Club, among others, and counts 4 million customers was charged with overbilling, harassing, and ruining the credit rating of customers, refusing to cancel memberships as provided in its contract, and billing charge accounts or debiting bank accounts without the permission of the purchasers. When the FTC set up a 16-line hot line to receive customer complaints, the volume of calls was such that the telephone system crashed. Bally's also settled similar complaints in various states, agreeing to pay $63,000 in civil penalties and costs in Washington State and $138,000 in civil penalties to the Los Angeles County District Attorney's office.

THE HOME TONE

If a ten-minute ride to the gym is more than you can bear—and if you have a few thousand dollars and a medium-size room to spare—you may a prime candidate for the latest trend in health and fitness: the home gym. More and more Americans exercise at home, and do so with more and more sophisticated equipment. Gone are the days of what one journalist describes as "some squeaky, dusty stationary bike that barely moves or doubles as a coat rack." A home gym means you have two or more pieces of health-club-quality equipment. At least one machine is geared for cardiovascular work, such as a treadmill or Stairmaster. At least one other machine, such as a small Universal multi-station unit, is designed for increasing strength through resistance training.

The benefit for baby-boomers torn between two jobs, two kids, and the dog is obvious: convenience. As one Massachusetts entrepreneur explains, "I can wake up, have my coffee, do my workout for an hour, take a shower, and get on with my day." But there are some downsides as well: your home gym is unlikely to match the quality and diversity of the equipment you find at the real thing; as a result, you're more likely to grow bored more quickly. You may need the structure of a professional gym—and distance from the distractions of home, the kids, the computer—to motivate yourself. And the home gym is not for everyone. You'll need an average of $5,000—and the room to store your new toys. But for couples facing high-priced health club memberships, it may represent a savvy investment.

Before you join the home gym set, make sure your sloth days are over. It's easy to spend $10,000 on a full panoply of fitness machines while you're recovering from the Thanksgiving stuffing only to see the equipment gather dust by Valentine's Day. If you're resolute, make sure to avoid what the International Association of Fitness Professionals calls the five cardinal sins of buying home exercise equipment:

- Don't buy machines that aren't designed to produce the results you desire—i.e., don't buy a Stairmaster if you want to develop your upper-body strength.
- Figure out which exercise activities you enjoy—and think you'll stick with.
- Don't buy equipment by mail or from an infomercial without having first tested it.
- Ask about warranties and repairs, maintenance and return policies.
- And don't buy a machine that's too big or too noisy for your home—avoid the humming, 1,200-pound steel monster if you're sharing a 600-square-foot studio with a newborn.

And if you travel often, you may want to join a club that belongs to a national chain or one with reciprocal membership arrangements with other clubs—as do members of the International Physical Fitness Association. Still, be wary of such representations.

Consider Sarah Z. Three months after she had paid for a two-year basic membership at a well-known health club in her Brooklyn neighborhood, she accepted a new job in San Francisco. Her club told her that she could transfer her membership to an affiliated club in California for $50. But in San Francisco, she found out that the ten local health clubs supposedly available for her use had either closed down or disavowed their affiliation with the Brooklyn club. Her calls to the corporate headquarters of the club were, of course, repeatedly ignored. Worse, she had never been told that, under New York law, she was entitled to a prorated refund if she moved more than 25 miles away.

Finally, run a "gut check." Do you feel good about, and comfortable with, the club? If everyone in the club looks like a cast member from *Baywatch* and your body type is closer to Seinfeld's friend George, you may find the presence of your well-toned peers a great motivator—or a reason to flee and look for a more suitable place. Notes fitness industry columnist John Sheehan, "People will not continue to do anything, *no matter how good it is for them,* unless it is pleasurable, unless it is enjoyable, unless it is social, unless it is entertaining."

WHAT TO WATCH OUT FOR

Blockbuster ads promising world-class facilities at bargain-basement prices. Example: A Jack LaLanne print ad promised in bold letters "80% off dues at Liberty Memberships," bringing down the usual $30 per month membership to a remarkably inexpensive $6 per month. The ad, however, failed to mention an "initiation fee" of $25 to $55, "depending on the program."

Watch out for high-pressure sales tactics. Stay away from pre-opening "specials" or "discounts" that may yield surprises down the road. If the club is a legitimate operation, you'll be able to snatch a good deal when it opens up. Similarly, your scam radar should perk up if the club refuses to provide you with any information over the phone, won't let you go over the contract at home, or offers you a discount "if you sign today only." Explains Collot Guerand, an attorney at the Federal Trade Commission, "If the company's not willing to give you a copy of that contract in advance, don't join the club."

THE $MARTER CONSUMER

If you haven't been exercising regularly, here are a couple of important health tips:

■ Start exercising slowly—for 20 minutes, three days a week, at 60% of your respiratory capacity, suggests the American College of Sports Medicine.

■ If you are over 40 or overweight, consult your physician before beginning a program of regular exercise.

Don't get discouraged if you don't look like the Terminator after two weeks of workouts. In fact, don't even try—be patient. As Laurie Patten, a Dallas trainer, explains, "You should ease into an exercise program and have a professional help design a program you can grow with. The 'no pain, no gain' philosophy is old hat. It doesn't work anymore."

Don't forget the "Y"—YMCAs and the like. You'll probably pay a lot less at a Y-run health club, but the facilities and equipment may not be of the level you can get in a commercial club. Other such nonprofit organizations as hospital-based fitness centers, park district programs, or university facilities may offer low-budget memberships.

Clubs affiliated with IHRSA, the Association of Quality Clubs, a self-regulating trade group representing more than 4,500 clubs, must abide by its membership pledge and code of conduct. Requirements include a ban on the sale of lifetime memberships, a three-year ceiling on pre-paid memberships, placement of pre-opening membership fees in escrow, and a ban on "deceptive, high-pressure sales tactics."

HELP

■ **To find out if a club is a member** of International Health, Racquet and Sports Association of Fitness Professionals (IHRSA), a self-regulating trade group representing more than 4,500 clubs worldwide, write: 263 Summer Street, Boston, MA 02210; or call (800) 228-4772, or go to www.ihrsa.org.

■ **You'll find useful tips on select-**ing a health club and staying with your exercise program in *Your Guide to Choosing a Quality Health and Sports Club*, a brochure published by IHRSA. Send a self-addressed, stamped envelope to the address above for a free copy or read the material on the Web site.

■ **For a free brochure, with a useful** and comprehensive checklist, write for: *ACSM Health Fitness Facility Standards and Guidelines*, from the American College of Sports Medicine, (800) 486-5643, or visit its Web site at www.acsm.org-sportsmed.

■ **For a free brochure about how** to buy home equipment, send a self-addressed business-size stamped envelope to: "Gearing Up," c/o the International Association of Fitness Professionals, 6190 Cornerstone Court East, Suite 204, San Diego, CA 92121-4701.

CHAPTER 11

INFERTILITY SERVICES

Deception in Conception

Every year, tens of thousands of people walk into the offices of fertility doctors and face a barrage of adorable baby pictures tacked up around the waiting rooms and offices. The implication: The high-tech techniques that are for sale have produced all those babies.

There's no question that such reproductive techniques as *in vitro* fertilization (IVF) have brought amazing advances. Couples who might have given up the dream of having their own children now have reason to keep hoping because of "assisted reproductive technologies" (ARTs). The key word is *hope*. For although it would be hard to discern from the sales seminars, promotional materials, and money-back guarantees, advanced infertility treatments fail far more often than they succeed. And the costs to the couples who try their luck are high—financially, emotionally, and physically.

THE BASICS

Nudging Nature

Doctors consider couples infertile if they have not conceived after a year of having unprotected sex. Estimates of how many such couples there are in America vary widely—from 2 million to 6 million, or roughly 1 in 6 couples of child-bearing age. In about 40% of the cases, infertility can be attributed to the woman; in about 40% of the cases, the problem lies with the man; and in about 20% of the cases, doctors cannot find the source of infertility. Doctors performed 42,000 advanced fertility procedures in 1996.

Couples who seem not to be able to conceive and who seek advice undergo examinations to determine the cause of their infertility. If doctors can identify problems, they will recommend procedures like laparoscopic surgery to clear blocked fallopian tubes, drug therapy to coax ovulation, artificial insemination of the woman's womb with her partner's sperm, or some combination of these treatments. Couples whose problems cannot be identified may be told simply to keep trying or to take drugs to increase the woman's production of eggs. In fact, most infertility cases, 85% to 90%, are treated with conventional medical therapies, such as medication or surgery.

THE JARGON

Assisted reproductive technology (ART) is the umbrella term for a group of the most advanced treatments for infertility, including *in vitro* fertilization and its variations.

Reprotech, short for reproductive technology, is another term for ART.

***In vitro* fertilization (IVF)** is the process by which eggs are taken from a woman's body, fertilized with a man's sperm in a dish, and then returned to the woman's body. In detail, it consists of drug stimulation of the ovaries to produce eggs, ultrasound monitoring of the eggs' development in the woman's ovaries, retrieval of the eggs from the woman's body, combining the eggs with sperm in a dish, waiting for fertilization, and return of the fertilized eggs to the woman's womb.

Male factor is used to describe infertility that can be attributed, at least in part, to problems with the male partner's reproductive functions.

Gamete intrafallopian transfer (GIFT) is a variation of IVF; eggs are taken from a woman's body and put in her fallopian tubes with sperm to attempt fertilization in the tubes, where it would naturally occur.

Stimulation is the process of coaxing a woman's ovaries to produce eggs by injecting the woman with hormones.

Retrieval or egg retrieval refers to the surgical procedure in which eggs are removed from a woman's body for external fertilization; sometimes called harvesting.

Embryo transfer (ET) is the surgical procedure in which fertilized eggs are returned to the woman's body.

Pregnancy can mean two different things. A "clinical pregnancy" is a real pregnancy in which fetal heart activity has been detected. Elevated levels of various hormones indicate a "chemical pregnancy," which often can be detected shortly after embryo transfer. (A chemical pregnancy does not always result in a clinical pregnancy.)

Success rate. There is no standard definition of "success." As noted, many programs define success as a comparison between the number of clinical pregnancies or deliveries of live babies and the number of embryo transfers attempted. This overstates the true rate of success because it does not take into account all the couples who began treatment but did not make it to the transfer stage. This definition has the additional drawback of being based on the number of procedures attempted and not the number of patients involved. (See the discussion of success rates on page 130 for additional information.)

Assisted reproductive technologies—such as IVF or GIFT—should be the treatment of last resort for people who have tried every other measure that might help them, although in certain instances it may make sense for people, especially older women, to waste no time and to go directly to the most advanced procedures.

Only 15% to 18% of the couples who try to conceive using the most advanced procedures end up with a baby when it's all over. This reality contradicts the so-called success-rate statistics doctors commonly toss off about how your chances might be one in two. For instance, a 1996 radio and newspaper ad campaign for the aggressive West Coast program Pacific Fertility Center hailed its advanced techniques and urged potential patients to "find out how improved technology with egg donation gives you nearly a 50% chance of having a baby after only one try." Unless consumers delved pretty deep, they would never know that Pacific rounded up to 50% from 45% and that the 45% figure is a true success rate only for a subset of patients with the best chances of success. Overall, Pacific's success at achieving live births out of egg retrievals using donor and nondonor eggs, as it reported to the National Registry, is 24%.

Mt. Sinai Hospital in New York, one of the finest in the country, distributed a promotional brochure for several years claiming that the "take-home baby rate for IVF is 20%." Thousands of people reading the brochure were led to believe that their chance of having a baby would be one in five after a single use of Mt. Sinai's advanced fertility services. But based on a New York City Department of Consumer Affairs investigation and legal charges, it turned out that the true success rate was about half the advertised rate.

The Failure of Success Rates

Because ART procedures involve so many steps, it's easy to fudge success rates. To illustrate, take the example of IVF. One cycle comprises four steps: (1) stimulation of the woman's ovaries to produce mature eggs; (2) retrieval of the eggs (rarely is there just one) and fertilization of the eggs in the lab; (3) transfer of the embryos; and (4) a pregnancy that results in the delivery of a live baby. Each of these steps can be said to have its own success or failure rate. However, successful completion of one step does not necessarily lead to achievement of the desired goal—a child.

So let's look again at Mt. Sinai's hyped-up claim of a 20% success rate. Mt. Sinai can claim a 20% success rate only if it excludes some patients from the statistical calculation: A comparison of the number of women who gave birth to live babies (step 4) to the number of women of all ages whose ovaries were stimulated (step 1) shows that Mt. Sinai's success rate in 1990 couldn't have been more than 10%. Most likely, Mt. Sinai used a subset of all its patients to generate the 20% figure: the number of successful deliveries (step 4) compared to the number of women 39 or younger who made it to the embryo transfer stage of IVF (step 3). Since then, in acknowledgment that its numbers were inflated, Mt. Sinai has overhauled its advertising.

Most programs prefer to focus on the ratio of egg retrievals or embryo transfers to pregnancies or births rather than the ratio of stimulations to pregnancies or births because the former creates a rosier scenario than the latter. These percentages are higher because many infertile couples never even get to the egg retrieval or embryo transfer stage in the process—even when chemically "primed," the woman does not ovulate, she produces too few viable eggs, or the eggs fail to fertilize. Whatever the case, even though the couples have attempted pregnancy with ART, their experience is not accounted for in the pool from which success rates are calculated.

These faked numbers have not gone unnoticed by federal regulators. The Federal Trade Commission (FTC) has taken legal action against IVF Australia (now called IVF America), the Fertility Institute of Boca Raton, the Fertility Institute of Western Massachusetts, Reproductive Genetics In Vitro of Denver, and Arizona Institute of Reproductive Medicine—all for fudging their facts. Because desperate couples are so easily misled about success rates, laboratory standards, and credentials, Congress passed the Fertility Clinic Success Rate and Certification Act in 1992. The law establishes standard formats for success rates and requires all fertility clinics to report their rates to the federal government annually. (Because of budget concerns, the government has not funded this program.)

> "*You don't open your newspaper and see, 'We have a 21% success rate with transplanted hearts.' This is the only branch of medicine doing success rate advertising on this scale. It succeeds because of the desperation and emotional vulnerability of the patients.*"
>
> —MICHAEL KATZ, federal medical investigator

Is ART Worth the Price?

Since the ART process can be so costly, it's important to do your homework before you decide whether it's worth a try. Including all the medical procedures, tests, lab fees, and drugs, one cycle of treatment can cost as much as $14,000, including drugs and lab fees. Since it usually takes several attempts to conceive, many couples spend as much as $50,000 before they have a baby or give up trying. In all, Americans spend about $500 million a year on advanced fertility treatments.

The physical and emotional costs are also formidable. Treatment for women involves daily injections with hormones and frequent trips to the doctor's office for blood tests and ultrasound monitoring. During a single IVF cycle, there are many dif-

A Baby or Your Money Back

Several fertility clinics have begun offering money-back guarantees to prospective repro-tech consumers. The packages generally include three tries at sustaining a pregnancy and a sort of insurance policy for patients who do not become pregnant.

Guarantee programs are virtually unheard of in other forms of medicine—and are controversial among doctors and the medical establishment, who say it's unethical to charge based on the outcome of a medical procedure. Plus there is a built-in incentive for doctors to do things that may be medically inadvisable—such as over-prescribe fertility drugs that increase the risk of cancer or transfer too many fertilized eggs into older women—to increase success rates and avoid having to return patients' money.

The promise of rebates may also give false hope to people desperate to have children. Plus the guarantees give insurance to a select group of medically qualified patients who have the best chances of success and deny it to those who will probably have a hard time getting pregnant. An American Medical Association task force concluded: "Such publicized guarantees manipulate and unfairly attract patients."

To wager or not to wager? Being selected for the money-back guarantee is a strong indication that you might be better off, financially speaking, if you turn down the offer and pay as you go. Clinics offer the rebate program only to those patients with the greatest likelihood of success—usually younger women or older women who agree to use donor eggs (from a younger woman). Thus, an offer of the rebate indicates you probably have a pretty good chance of getting pregnant on your first try. And even if it takes you two tries, it would probably be a wash financially. It's only if you had to try a third time that the package deal puts you in the better financial position.

Don't be fooled by the rebate offers. You'll still be paying plenty for *à la carte* items like drugs and lab fees. Plus, if you are lucky enough to have health insurance that covers infertility treatments, the package bill you get from the infertility program may not pass muster with your insurance company. One last thing super-stitious people may not want to think about: these programs guarantee pregnancy, not a baby. If you lose the baby late in the pregnancy, you can't collect your refund.

RATING FERTILITY CLINICS

You can compare one program to another with data compiled by the Society for Assisted Reproductive Technology (SART), a self-regulatory subgroup of the American Society of Reproductive Medicine. Ask for the *Annual Clinic-Specific Report* for your region of the U.S. (see **HELP** at the end of this chapter). The SART data are not perfect—annual reports come out a few years after the fact, the 300 member clinics supply their own information, and the data are not generally audited. However, programs are forced to report their data in a uniform way, which helps consumers strip away the puffery from promotional claims and materials.

The Annual Clinic-Specific Report gives success rates for individual infertility programs around the country by breaking down success rates into four categories: women younger than 40 whose partners' sperm is fine; women under 40 whose partners' sperm is abnormal ("male factor" infertility); women 40 and older whose partners' sperm is fine; and women 40 and older with male factor infertility involved. Statistics are given for egg retrievals and embryo transfers but not for stimulations.

ferent checkpoints at which to feel cheered or cheated—at the retrieval of eggs, fertilization, embryo evaluation, embryo transfer, and pregnancy test, to name just a few. Couples who have been through the process describe wild swings between hopefulness and depression—which are only exacerbated by the side effects of the hormone treatments—and the terrible strains on their marriages.

Beyond all that, the long-term risk to women who use the massive quantities of hormones necessary to undergo ART is not fully known. Although there is no definitive evidence that the drugs are dangerous, there is no evidence that they are not. A small, preliminary study published in the *American Journal of Epidemiology* in 1993 suggested that the use of fertility drugs may increase the risk of developing ovarian cancer. In 1993, the Food and Drug Administration began requiring Ares-Serono SA, the maker of Pergonal and Sero-phene, and Marion Merrell Dow Inc., the maker of Clomiphene citrate, to warn users of a possible link between these drugs and ovarian cancer.

WHAT TO WATCH OUT FOR

Keep in mind that for every success rate doctors tout, the flip side is a failure rate. If a program boasts a 15% success rate, it also has an 85% failure rate. It's not that it's inaccurate or deceptive of the program to show its statistics in the best light, but remember that "success rates" deflect attention from most people's experience.

Inflated success rates. Based on the Mt. Sinai story, you may be wondering whether to believe the statistics you hear. Yes and no. ART success statistics are a perfect demonstration of the way the straightest facts can be bent to create a skewed view. Be sure you clearly understand exactly what the statistics represent.

Misleading claims. For example, success does not necessarily mean babies, even though one program uses the headline "success means babies" in its brochure. The number of clinical *pregnancies,* where fetal heart activity has been confirmed, and the number of *deliveries* of live babies are both commonly used to describe success. The two are not interchangeable; not all pregnancies lead to successful deliveries. In fact, many doctors counsel patients that the risk of miscarriage is higher with ART pregnancies than with normally conceived pregnancies.

The incredible disappearing patients. To judge the usefulness of the success statistic, you also need to know to what group of patients were compared. Ask which procedures are included or omitted in the success rates. The most telling percentage is the number of successful deliveries compared with the number of ovary stimulations performed. This includes all the

attempts at pregnancy that failed (most programs won't volunteer the number). Also ask how old the women were whose experience the success rates reflect. Success rates drop precipitously for women 40 and older, and some programs may pad their numbers by excluding these women from their statistics.

THE $MARTER CONSUMER

Assisted reproductive technologies should be treatments of last resort because they are the most invasive and the most expensive. Investigate and try the many other treatments for infertility first, including drugs to coax ovulation, surgery to clear blocked fallopian tubes, and artificial insemination.

Only after close consultations with your physician, fertility specialists, and the staff of advanced fertility programs can you decide whether to try reprotech. The situation of every couple is different, and it's important to investigate all the alternatives for your specific case.

If doctors tell you about their "success rates," make sure you understand exactly how the rates were calculated and whether you can expect to have a similar chance at successfully undergoing treatment. The most useful statistic is live birth rate per egg stimulation attemped for couples within your age range with a similar diagnosis. Compare the results from several programs.

Look beyond the success rates when you're comparing one clinic with another. Since the success of ART procedures varies with the cause of infertility and the age of the woman, lower pregnancy success rates reported by a program do not necessarily suggest less effective care. Clinics that serve patients who are less likely to become pregnant to begin with will understandably have lower overall rates than clinics that only accept couples with better prospects.

Be sure you understand what you will spend. Infertility treatment expenses mount quickly, and insurance coverage is scanty. Ask not only what the fees are for the procedure(s), but also how much drugs and lab fees will add to the bill. These ancillary bills can be hefty, and they are not included in the money-back guarantee programs offered by several fertility clinics.

Check with your insurance plan to see whether and which infertility treatments will be covered. The degree of coverage depends on your insurance carrier's policies and where you live. Thirteen states have laws requiring insurers to cover or offer to cover varying forms of infertility diagnosis and treatment: Arkansas, California, Connecticut, Hawaii, Illinois, Maryland, Massachusetts, Montana, New York, Ohio, Rhode Island, Texas, and West Virginia. However, don't expect much. The laws vary, and insurance companies tend to be stingy when it comes to infertility treatments. Aetna's USHealthcare plan eliminated coverage for advanced fertility treatments in 1998.

HELP

■ **The American Soci**ety for Reproductive Medicine (ASRM) offers general information about infertility and also distributes the *Annual Clinic-Specific Report*, which gives success rates for ART programs around the country. Copies of the full report cost $90; partial copies covering the East, West, and Central regions of the U.S. cost $35 each or $65 for two regions. Write to the American Society for Reproductive Medicine, 1209 Montgomery Highway, Birmingham, AL 35216-2809, or call (205) 978-5000. Information is also available on ASRM's Web site: http://www.asrm.com.

■ **Resolve is a nonprofit support and** information organization for people struggling with infertility. The national office supplies information and can direct you to a local affiliate. Resolve publishes a newsletter, recommends reading material, and can help you get in touch with other couples who have had experience with the ART programs in your area. Resolve also publishes a booklet called *Infertility Insurance Advisor* ($5) that is an excellent source of insurance information. Write to Resolve, 1310 Broadway, Somerville, MA 02144-1731, or call (617) 623-0744, E-mail resolveinc@aol.com, or visit their Web site at http://www.resolve.org.

■ **The Federal Trade Commission** published a fact sheet on infertility services. Write to the FTC Office of Consumer/Business Education, Washington, DC 20580, or call (202) 326-3650 or visit the FTC Internet site at http://www.ftc.gov.

CHAPTER 12

EYEGLASSES AND CONTACT LENSES

For Your Eyes Only

If you are one of the 145 million Americans who need glasses or contact lenses to see well, put them on (or in) and read this chapter before you need to replace them.

And get out your magnifying glass, too, to read the fine print at the bottom of the eyewear ads in the newspaper. As chain stores like Pearle Vision Center and Lens-Crafter—as well as "optical centers" in retail chains like Wal-Mart and Shopko—have proliferated, so have discount deals, rebates, and two-for-one coupons and promotions. But the ads often gloss over additional charges that can send the price out of the bargain range.

LensCrafters in Minneapolis advertised: "Save up to $75." Only in a footnote do you learn you must spend at least $190 to qualify for the deal.

In a full-page ad in the *New York Post*, Cohen's Fashion Optical offers a free eye exam (no purchase necessary). But if you want a contact lens exam, that will cost extra, says the tiny type at the bottom of the coupon. In the same ad, Cohen's of-fers one pair of daily-wear, colored contact lenses for $79. A minuscule footnote discloses "professional fee and kit additional."

So much for eye-popping special prices.

THE BASICS

See Your Way Clear

You know a product is hot when Donna Karan, Ralph Lauren, Giorgio Armani, and Calvin Klein get in on the action. And so it is with eyeglasses—once a functional tool, now a fashion statement. The availability of single-use, colored, and even bifocal contact lenses has driven lens sales up as well. And advances in corrective eye surgery stand to redefine vision correction options.

Americans spend about $17.5 billion a year caring for their eyes. About three quarters of that is spent on eyeglasses and contact lenses and most of the rest on eye exams. And as baby boomers and

WHO'S WHO AMONG EYE CARE PROFESSIONALS

You'll have to decide for yourself whether you need to see an ophthalmologist or optometrist. But since 45% of the American public, according to a Gallup poll, doesn't know the difference between them, here's what each eye care professional does:

Ophthalmologists are physicians who specialize in eyes. They can prescribe corrective lenses and drugs, treat eye disease, and perform surgery. Some also sell eyeglasses.

Optometrists have degrees in eye care from four-year colleges of optometry, but they are not physicians. They have been trained to examine eyes, detect eye disease, and prescribe eyeglasses and contact lenses. The limits of their practice vary from state to state, but in all but one state (Massachusetts) they can use drugs to treat certain diseases; for example, they can administer prescription eye drops and prescribe medication. They sell eyeglasses.

Opticians make the corrective lenses prescribed by ophthalmologists and optometrists. They cannot perform eye examinations or prescribe corrective lenses. They need licenses to operate in about half the states.

Gen-Xers continue to move into middle age, those numbers will only rise: 90% of people need glasses by the time they reach their mid-40s. Are you one of them?

The Eye Exam

The only way to know if you need glasses is to have your eyes tested. A thorough eye exam should include collection or updating of your medical history and tests for eye health, visual acuity, eye coordination, focusing ability, and such common vision conditions as nearsightedness, farsightedness, and astigmatism.

The American Optometric Association suggests that babies have their first eye exam by 6 months of age and that children have their eyes examined at ages 3 and 5; that people 6 to 61 have exams every one to two years; and that people 62 and older go back to annual eye exams. However, diabetics and people who have a high risk of getting glaucoma (African-Americans 40 and older and everybody older than 60) should be especially careful to have their eyes examined annually. The doctor should dilate their pupils to get the best possible view of the retina and any damage, according to the U.S. Public Health Service.

If all you need is a routine exam, an optometrist will probably be your best bet. Two studies by the

State University of New York Center for Vision Care Policy found that ophthalmologists charge an average of $20 more than optometrists for the same routine eye exams and diagnostic tests. But don't let price be the only determining factor, especially if you think there's a problem.

You have the right to get your eyeglasses prescription from the doctor who examines your eyes. A 1978 Federal Trade Commission (FTC) rule requires eye doctors to give patients their prescriptions immediately after an eye examination, at no additional cost. This enables you to shop around for higher quality, better selection, lower prices, or plain old peace of mind before buying glasses. Before the rule took effect, eye care professionals often held on to prescriptions, which forced patients to buy glasses from the examiner.

Contact Lenses

The rules governing contact lens prescriptions aren't so simple. As of January 1, 1998, 23 states had guidelines that effectively required eye doctors to release prescriptions, but only after the patient has completed a "fitting period" usually set by the doctor. This means that once you've been examined and have a prescription, your doctor will provide your first pair of lenses. You'll wear these until a follow-up appointment, when your doctor will check to be sure that contacts are appropriate for you. After that, you're free to fill your prescription

PUZZLED ABOUT LENS CARE SOLUTIONS?

Get explicit instructions about what products to use, and how often, from your eye care practitioner. Not all solutions can be used in conjunction with others, some solutions have more than one function, and not all solutions are safe for all types of lenses. If you want to save some money, many generic solutions are available. Here's what the various solutions do:

- *Cleaning solution* removes dirt, mucus, and other debris that lenses pick up during wear.

- *Disinfectant solution* kills bacteria and germs on the lenses, preventing serious eye infections.
- *Rinsing solution* removes other solutions from lenses and prepares the lenses for wear.
- *Enzyme solution* removes deposits of protein and other things that build up on lenses over time.
- *Rewetting solution* lubricates the lenses while you're wearing them to make them more comfortable.
- *Multi-purpose solution* enables you to clean, rinse, and store your lenses with one solution.

EYE ON CONTACT LENSES

Lense type	Initial price	Average annual cost	Pros	Cons
RIGID, GAS-PERMEABLE LENSES	$200–$300	$60–$100	▪ *Sharp vision* ▪ *Correct serious astigmatism and other problems* ▪ *Last 2 to 4 years* ▪ *Easy care*	▪ *Take longer to adapt to* ▪ *May dislodge during sports*
SOFT LENSES	$175–$275	$100–$300	▪ *Easy to adapt to* ▪ *Comfort almost from start* ▪ *Least likely to dislodge* ▪ *Easy care*	▪ *Correct fewer problems* ▪ *May not provide sharp vision* ▪ *Less durable (6 months to a year)* ▪ *Need more daily care*
EXTENDED-WEAR LENSES	$225–$375	$70–$150	▪ *Comfortable to wear continuously up to 7 days* ▪ *Available as soft and gas-permeable with same advantages*	▪ *Increased risk of eye infection*
DISPOSABLE LENSES	— —	$450–$650	▪ *Soft lenses that can be worn continuously for up to 7 days and then thrown away* ▪ *No cleaning*	▪ *Less sharp vision* ▪ *Correct fewer problems* ▪ *Increased risk of eye infection if used improperly*

(for replacement lenses or your next batch of disposables) anywhere you like.

But even with your prescription in hand, it's hard to know whether you're getting the best lens deal. In 1996, Ciba Vision, the country's number two lens producer, settled charges that it had conspired with opticians and other lens companies to keep contact prices high by refusing to sell lenses to discount distributors. If you think you may not want to buy lenses from the doctor who examines your eyes, ask about the doctor's policy *before* the exam. Because of their more temporary nature, lenses generally cost more to buy and maintain than glasses.

Only you and your doctor can decide which kind of lenses will work best for you. Hard lenses, once the only contact lens option, are now worn by only about 1% of lens wearers and are generally no longer prescribed. Rigid gas-permeable lenses have replaced the traditional hard lens. These are often prescribed for people with high degrees of astigmatism. Consider which lens will most comfortably correct your vision problem, best suit your lifestyle, and meet your financial needs. For instance, think about whether you play active sports—soft lenses are less likely than rigid lenses to dislodge. Are you cost-conscious? Rigid gas-permeable lenses cost a bit more but last longer than soft lenses and are less troublesome and cheaper to maintain (e.g., they don't usually tear). There is also some evidence that rigid lenses slow myopia's development. Do you want to be able to see as soon as you wake up? Extended-wear lenses can be worn for up to seven days without being removed. Studies have shown, however, that extended-wear users are four to five times more likely to develop corneal ulcers than daily wear users. Smokers' risk is even greater.

Several companies now offer lenses you wear for a single day, then throw away. No cleaning solution to mess with means less chance of infection from wearing disposable lenses too long. The cost is the catch: about $1.75 a pair, which adds up to about $635 per year.

> "**A**s the industry is now, prices depend upon loading on extra bells and whistles, like special coatings, that most people probably don't need. If the eye exam that takes an hour is 'free,' the consumer's going to pay for it somewhere else."
>
> —MONTE BELOTE, executive director of Florida Consumer Action Network

WHAT TO WATCH OUT FOR

There's no such thing as list price for eyeglasses frames—or at least there's no list you'll ever get your eyes on. Just about every optician marks up prices by at least two or three times what he or she pays for the frames. For instance, a Giorgio Armani frame that sells for over $200 in L.A. (without lenses) costs the store about $70.

Even the markup on stock lenses alone —those used for common prescriptions that are filled often—can run as high as 1,000%.

As part of an investigation of Pearle Vision Center, the National Advertising Division of the Council of Better Business Bureaus pointed out the "special features" of the industry—"complex pricing systems, confidential price lists, limited information of comparative pricing, and consumers' reliance on the professional advice of the opticians." This can make it very difficult to know whether you are getting a good deal or an optical delusion.

Be wary of package deals and low-price offers as they may not be the bargains they seem at first sight.

SUNGLASSES SENSE

Ignore the hype. While many sunglasses (and many prescription eyeglasses) provide plenty of protection against harmful ultraviolet (UV) radiation, many do not. Prevent Blindness America, the American Optometry Association, and the American Academy of Ophthalmology all recommend sunglasses that absorb 99 to 100% of UVA and UVB radiation. Although there is currently no federally regulated labeling requirement, a voluntary labeling system, devised by the Sunglass Association of America and the Food and Drug Administration, tells you how much radiation sunglasses block. Sunglasses called "cosmetic" must block at least 20% of the longer wavelength UVA radiation and 70% of the shorter wavelength UVB. (The shorter waves are the most dangerous to your eyes.) Even the cheapest sunglasses you can buy generally meet the "cosmetic" standard. "General purpose" means they block 60% of UVA and 95% of UVB. Sunglasses labeled "special purpose" must block 60% of UVA and 99% of UVB.

Your choices may be limited to a small group of frame styles, and you most often will have to pay extra for frames outside the designated group, for the oversize, bifocal, or high-powered lenses that may work best for you, or for the various tints and coatings you may be persuaded to buy (more on coatings later in this chapter).

The Better Business Bureaus of Minnesota and Houston challenged a Pearle Vision Center program a few years back for failing to disclose the limitations of a buy-one-get-one-free promotion. Instead of getting a duplicate or similar pair of glasses, consumers were limited in the frames they could choose from, and there was an undisclosed $60 cap on the value of the "free" second pair. You might also be lured in by the promise of a free eye exam, but if the "free" exam can only be had by buying an overpriced pair of glasses from the same store, then it's not "free" at all.

Unprofessional help. Just because the people behind the counter wear white coats doesn't mean they're licensed doctors. More than half the states don't license opticians. In some stores, you might even be dealing with someone whose only expertise is telling you how good you look in those $200 Armani frames. American Eyework, an optometry chain in the Pacific Northwest, was charged in 1996 not only with false advertising, but also with allowing unlicensed (and unpracticed) employees to conduct eye exams and prescribe lenses.

LASER VISION

By now, you've probably heard one of the thousands of stories about "near-blind" people who've undergone "miracle" eye surgery and come away with the vision of a hawk. News reports of the surgery —radial keratotomy (RK), photorefractive keratectomy (PRK), and laser-assisted in situ keratomileusis (LASIK)—tend toward the hyperbolic. "I'm like someone who's been in a wheelchair her whole life and now walks," read one account. The push for the surgery has been called the "most widely marketed medical procedure in history," and some doctors say it will become a correction as common as orthodontia.

For $1,000 to $2,500 per eye—which will most likely come out of your pocket, as most insurance deems laser eye surgery cosmetic and won't cover it—what exactly are you getting? In RK, practiced in the U.S. since the late 1970s, the doctor cuts spoke-like slits around the cornea to flatten it. In PRK and LASIK, the doctor uses an excimer laser—a device invented to etch tiny computer chips—to reshape the cornea. PRK was approved by the FDA in 1995, and at this writing, LASIK is still under review by the FDA, although some 25,000 people have had the surgery in clinical trials.

RK and PRK are generally used on people with moderate myopia—20/100 or better. More advanced myopia demands PRK. And LASIK—the most exact and the most surgically demanding of the three—is currently used for people with severe nearsightedness, even as great as 20/1,200. All three can correct moderate astigmatism. Vision tends to stabilize between the ages of 20 and 40, and it's recommended that prospective patients wait until then before having the surgery.

These surgeries do not stop

Misleading pricing schemes. You would think that special-purpose contact lenses would have special characteristics. Not necessarily. In 1996 and 1997, Bausch & Lomb settled charges brought by 17 states that the company sold identical contacts under different brand names, each for a different price. The lenses—SeeQuence2, Medalist, and OptimaFW—ranged in price from $2.50 to $23 per lens and were marketed separately as disposable one-week, three-month, or daily wear lenses. In the settlement, B & L promised to cough up nearly $70 million in rebates, reimbursements, and free products. But while the lenses' packaging was changed to read only "OptimaFW," the com-

deterioration of vision. Rather they provide a (clear) window until people begin the unavoidable slide into the natural hardening of the lenses (presbyopia) that forces many into reading glasses in their mid-40s. A side effect of the surgery: you may need reading glasses sooner.

Although the success rate is good—more than 90% of PRK patients achieve 20/40 vision or better—5% to 10% of PRK patients return for "enhancement" operations because of under-correction, and 15% still use glasses occasionally. Badly performed PRK or LASIK can also result in a wrinkled cornea, which requires rigid contact lenses to correct. Because of all these risks, many doctors are telling patients to hold off. "It's best to wait until the surgery has been perfected," says one New Mexico ophthalmologist. "You have only one set of eyes."

As you investigate the surgery, keep in mind that many of the doctors who push it are also those with the most to gain. The equipment costs upwards of $500,000, and yearly maintenance rings up another $60,000. The more surgeries they perform, the closer doctors come to clearing their high overhead. Your optometrist may have a stake as well—some get kickbacks of up to $1,700 for every referral they make. Read the informed consent forms carefully—many let the doctor off the hook for bad results. And check to be sure your surgeon uses licensed equipment. The FDA recently seized $3 million worth of unapproved lasers in Florida after an investigation prompted by numerous reports of permanent eye damage from unapproved lasers. For listings of qualified ophthalmologists, call the only two companies that supply licensed equipment: VISX (800-246-8479) and Summit Technology (800-880-4582).

pany still sells the different models—which the investigators called identical "in design, composition, and quality"—for different prices.

Be skeptical of claims about UV-absorptive coatings. A glasses salesperson may ask if you work at a computer. If you say yes, he or she may tell you about the alleged risk of exposure to ultraviolet radiation and push you to pay $10 to $20 for UV coating. But the reality is that the risk is nonexistent. While it's bad for eyes to stare at anything for too long (heavy readers typically have higher rates of nearsightedness), there is no danger to your eyes from UV radiation emitted by your computer or TV screen.

Anti-glare or anti-reflective coating is often overhyped. You may be told that for another $10 to $20 you can reduce glare, say from computer screens, but in fact this coating does nothing to enhance vision. It simply reduces the amount of light that bounces off the lenses, which will reduce the reflection in flash photographs or create the cosmetic effect of making thick glasses less noticeable. Tinted glasses also serve no corrective purpose.

THE $MARTER CONSUMER

Eyeglasses

If your eye doctor does not give you your eyeglasses prescription, ask for it. It's yours to take with you, whether or not you buy glasses from that doctor.

Don't be myopic. Many stores will try to draw you in with one-stop shopping. They offer exams and a huge selection of frame styles, and they can make glasses in an in-store laboratory within as little as an hour. It's tempting to walk in and have everything taken care of before you can bat an eye. But convenience has its price. While one-stop chain stores may offer cheap deals and quick prescription turn-around, they might not be as thorough as a private doctor in examining your eyes or ensuring a good glasses fit. *Consumer Reports* found glasses bought from private

doctors to cost on average only $11 more than those bought at large chains. When *Consumer Reports* also sent three staffers to price glasses at five chains, prices differed as much as 75% from store to store for the same prescription and similar frames. As with any other purchase, you'll probably do best if you shop around.

Eyeglass retailers today are selling style, not just vision correction. Ever notice how they put the cheap frames in the back of the store? Remember what your glasses are for, and choose a frame for comfort first, then style. Different prescriptions demand different frames—some small frames can't fit bifocal lenses, and stronger prescriptions need larger lenses. Don't let sales tactics lead you to a frame that can't handle your prescription.

Beware of cheap package deals that supposedly include everything. The small print may say the price covers only simple prescriptions. If your prescription is more complicated (bifocals, for instance), you may not get what you need—or you may have to pay a lot more for it than you would elsewhere.

Make sure you get what you pay for. If you pay extra for impact-resistant polycarbonate plastic lenses, which are great for athletes and children, double-check to see that you haven't been given cheaper plastic lenses.

All polycarbonate lenses come with scratch-resistant coating, so don't be persuaded into paying extra for the protection. Some stores will charge you extra for the right to exchange the lenses if they get scratched within a certain period. Make sure that this is what you're paying for and not the built-in coating.

Contact Lenses

The basic fee for contact lenses usually covers the lenses, a lesson on wear, handling and care, and follow-up visits to check the fit and how well your eyes are adjusting to wearing lenses. But to be sure, ask your practitioner the following questions:

What tests are included in the price for the exam, and are there any additional fees you will incur? If you buy lenses from the eye doctor, ask if fitting is included in the price.

If you plan to buy lenses from the person who examines your eyes, make sure he or she offers a large selection of types and brands. The larger the selection, the more likely you are to find something comfortable you like.

Some independent retailers now offer contacts online. A quick Internet search for "contact lenses" and "prescription"—plus the brand name you use, if you know it—will land you at one or more of these sites.

Is there a refund policy? This is especially important for first-time contact lens buyers. Some eye care specialists will refund all or part of your money if you still find the lenses uncomfortable after 60 days of trying to adapt to them.

Is an insurance agreement (also called a service agreement) included in the price? If not, can you buy one separately? Such an agreement would enable you to replace a lost or ripped lens for a reduced fee. It might also lower the price of your next exam (and updated pair of lenses) when the time comes to replace your prescription.

Even if you've passed your optometrist's "fitting period" and are ordering your lenses online or from a discount warehouse, make sure you return to your doctor for regular exams.

HELP

- **Read the *Consumer Reports* July** 1997 story called "The Specs on Specs: Who Offers the Best Value on Eyeglasses?"

- **"Facts for Consumers on Eye** Care," is a free pamphlet distributed by the Federal Trade Commission. Write to Public Reference, FTC, Washington, DC 20580 or look at the Web site: www.ftc.gov.

- ***Contact Lenses: The Better the*** *Care, the Safer the Wear* is available free from the FDA. Call (800) 532-4440 or go to www.fda.gov.

PART 3

Home

CHAPTER 13

HOUSES, CONDOS, AND CO-OPS

Buying and Selling the American Dream

Charles V., who spends his weekdays in the hurly-burly of Manhattan, thought he had bought his dream getaway house when he moved into a cozy, knotty pine-paneled lakefront retreat in northern New Jersey, just an hour's drive from his office. And when the engineer he hired to inspect the property discovered that the septic system was outmoded, the owner knocked $10,000 off the selling price to pay for a replacement. But it was only after Charles had moved in that he discovered the defunct fuel oil tank buried under the front yard. Local regulations required that he dig down to the tank, test the surrounding soil for oil seepage, and fill the tank with gravel.

Charles was lucky; the bill came to "only" $1,000. The company that filled the tank with gravel said it could have cost more than ten times that much had the oil seeped.

When it comes to buying a home, there's always something else—be it a buried fuel tank, an underground stream, rotted timbers, or worse. The same goes for selling. Will the buyers turn around and sue you because the roof leaks? Will you waste a month dickering with a buyer who backs out at the last minute?

Here's how to accentuate the positive and avoid many of the negatives when buying or selling what is probably your most valuable asset, and your most valued possession—your home.

THE BASICS

Where to Buy

What makes one location more desirable than another? Whether or not you have school-age children, the quality of the local school system should be one of your top concerns. It is probably the single most important factor determining the true value of your home. And if you have school-age children, the reputation of the local schools is obviously paramount. You might even consider attending a meeting of the local Parent-Teacher Association or taking a school tour to find out more about the local school system. You might also want to be sure that the schools offer extra-curricular opportunities to develop the talents of your budding Midori or Pete Sampras.

If the schools aren't your primary consideration, then perhaps the local tax burden will weigh heavily on your decision. How well protected the property is by zoning laws and the quality of the police and fire departments are also near the top of many buyers' lists.

Before settling on a neighborhood, be sure to spend time there. If you drive to work every day, test the rush hour commute. Walk around to get a sense of the community and to ask residents what they think of living there. Local newspapers and meetings of the town planning board, the school board, and the city council can give you a pretty good idea of local concerns, and may clue you in to a major proposed development that could (adversely or positively) affect property values, if you decide to buy.

Of course, if you are moving to a new location because you or your spouse just landed a great new job or were transferred, you might not have time to interview dog walkers or attend community meetings. So it might be better to rent before taking the big plunge into home ownership. You will move twice, but you will get to know your new

community well before you make an expensive or hard-to-reverse decision that could lead to a second move anyway.

In other words, if you're about to make the largest consumer purchase of your life and one you'll live with (and in) for years to come, it's worth several days or weeks of investigation.

Zeroing In

Once you've found the right neighborhood, how do you find the right house? Scan house-for-sale ads in the local newspaper; drive around looking for for-sale signs on front lawns; the easiest way is to let a real estate agent (see below) steer you.

When you inspect a house, look at more than the physical structure. Get a sense of the sellers, too. Why are they selling? If there was a layoff or a divorce, perhaps they are eager to sell sooner rather than later; a seller under pressure will more readily reduce the asking price. Or, if the house is empty, it could mean that the owner had to move before selling, giving you an even stronger bargaining position.

Ask the agent how long the house has been on the market and how many times the asking price has been reduced. If it's been on the market a long time at the same price, the owners might not be very serious about unloading it or about reducing their asking price.

Bring a camera on your forays. Take careful notes and photographs of the exterior and, if the seller permits it, take interior pictures, too.

WHO'S WHO AMONG AGENTS

Before you start a relationship, ask an agent or broker to clarify what type of agent he or she is and to whom fiduciary responsibility is owed.

Broker. Often used interchangeably with agent. Both need state real estate licenses. Brokers, however, must take an additional exam. Agents—also called associates or salespersons—work in offices that are managed and run by brokers. A broker will not necessarily get you better results than an agent.

Seller's agent. Retained by the seller and owes fiduciary responsibility to the seller. Usual commission is 6% of the selling price and is paid by the seller— but may be reflected in a higher price for the property.

Dual agent. Represents both buyer and seller, with fiduciary responsibility to both. The seller pays the commission.

Buyer's agent. Works for buyers only. A buyer's agent is supposed to get the buyer the lowest price the seller will accept. Buyer's agents are paid by

sharing in the seller's agent's commission or may receive an hourly, flat, or percentage fee from the buyer.

Subagents. Agents working for other agencies who produce a buyer but who are legally responsible to the seller; the listing firm splits its commission with the subagent.

Facilitator. Represents neither side but acts as an intermediary and furnishes advice about real estate procedures. Paid either a percentage of sales price or a flat fee. Since facilitators have no fiduciary responsibility to anyone, there can arise no conflicts of interest such as those that may occur when agents for the same firm represent both parties.

Splitting commissions. In a typical transaction, it is quite possible that the 6% commission *the seller* pays will be split among several agents: the broker who sold the house, the salesperson who did the legwork, the broker who initially listed the house, and the salesperson at that agency who listed it.

Dealing With Real Estate Agents

First and foremost, your agent should have plenty of experience in the neighborhoods under

consideration. Before an agent starts showing you houses, ask how many properties he or she sold in the last six months. If the answer is "none," get another agent. In any event, since most homes are listed with the local Multiple Listing Service (MLS)—a computer database of houses for sale available to most real estate agents in a community—make sure your agent has full access to MLS listings.

The friendly real estate agent who has been bending-over-backwards-helpful really doesn't work for the buyer. Most people don't understand that, since most real estate agents dealing with buyers are subagents of the sellers or of a "listing" agent, their actual legal responsibility is to the *seller*. Practically speaking, this means that "your" real estate agent won't tell you, as a buyer, the lowest price the seller will accept. This is why you should not reveal confidential information to an agent, *especially* not the maximum you are willing to pay; if you do, that is probably what you *will* pay—the agent is obligated to pass this information on to the seller.

To obtain less biased help, you might consider using a "buyer's agent," an agent who has no fiduciary responsibility to the seller. Buyer's agents usually negotiate harder for a lower selling price, and they have become increasingly common as most states have enacted laws requiring real estate agents to tell potential buyers exactly whom they represent. The one big downside: Listing agents sometimes discriminate against them. And Steven Brobeck, executive director of the Consumer Federation of America, says that while consumers are better served by buyer agents than seller agents, you still have to be careful of a buyer agent promoting his firm's own listings; he may not be an aggressive negotiator when the property is also listed with his agency, which stands to profit from both ends of the deal.

What must a real estate agent tell you about a house you're considering? In most states, it's the agent's duty to tell you about anything that affects the *physical* condition of the property. So the agent need not disclose that someone recently died in the house or that a six-lane expressway is to be built through adjacent property.

Whichever kind of agent you use, stop dealing with one who isn't willing to spend ample time with you or who keeps showing you homes $50,000 more expensive than your explicitly stated target.

Agreeing on the Price, Negotiating the Sales Contract

How much should you offer? Start to compute an appropriate bid by checking actual selling prices in the neighborhood with a real estate agent, at the local town hall, or at the county clerk's office. Be sure to take into account the cost of repairs and remodeling before you make your written or verbal purchase offer. Factor in the anticipated property tax bill and annual heating and air conditioning costs. Find out from the sellers which fixtures are staying and which ones are going. Whatever you do, don't ask the agent how much to offer. Because agents get their commission only if the house sells, they will naturally recommend that you offer enough to make sure the seller says "yes."

Within a specific neighborhood, there may be small subneighborhoods that are deemed more desirable and are therefore more expensive. Corner-lot houses cost more than houses with other houses on both sides.

If you are really stumped, you might consider getting a limited appraisal of the property. A full-blown appraisal will take longer than you have—a week or so—and cost $200–$350, but there are a few outfits offering quicker turnarounds for cheaper but more limited research. Consumer Reports Home Price Service, (800) 775-1212, gives you information on an individual property, all sales on a given street, or all properties within a given price range. The call will cost $10 for a 10-minute search. (The service covers approximately 80% of the U.S.)

Another option is an outfit like Premier Appraisals, which covers Atlanta and Jacksonville. For about $75, you'll know within three hours whether the asking price is in the ballpark. The service taps into public and private valuation databases to tell buyers how much substantially similar homes sold for recently. Imagine how much stronger a position you will be in if the seller is asking $185,000, but you know that no home like the seller's has sold for anything more than $165,000. And that one had an extra half-bath.

Agents are required to present all offers to the owner, no matter how low. It's their fiduciary responsibility. And there's no rule against talking with the owner directly.

Reaching agreement. You'll have to agree on the price, the amount of deposit, the down payment, which fixtures are included, and on contingency clauses.

One way to resolve a negotiating deadlock is to agree to split the price difference. Negotiations can also be moved off the dime if you agree to close quickly—or to wait to close—depending on the seller's preference. Once you've decided to make an offer, the real estate agent may ask you to sign a binder. This document authorizes the agent to tell the seller your bid and, if the bid is acceptable, that a contract of sale will be executed. Since there is not yet a contract, you can still change your mind. But watch out! A binder may be a legally-enforceable contract unless it specifically states that a contract is to be signed later on.

About the contract. The sales contract (or "purchase and sale agreement") is the culmination of your home search. Among its basic elements are a legal description of the property, the price and down payment, date of occupancy, financing terms, escrow account terms, a statement of the condition of the property, what personal property and fixtures are included or excluded, the seller's warranties, an inspection clause, and who is responsible for any damage before the closing. If not written with extreme care—preferably with help from a good real estate lawyer—you could end up in financial hot water. (See page 567 to find out how to find a lawyer.)

Contracts should contain as many escape hatches (contingency clauses) as possible to allow you not only to cancel the deal but also to get your deposit back. Common are clauses that require the house to be repainted, the floors refinished, or the furnace to be replaced prior to the closing. A very important contingency clause requires that a professional inspector give the house a seal of approval before a closing can take place. To give you peace of mind, you might also make it a condition of sale that the seller disclose in writing all material defects, if such disclosure is not already required by law in your state.

One very helpful contingency clause says that the deal goes through only if you are able to sell your current home for a stated price, prior to a stated deadline. Another clause could provide that the deal is canceled unless you secure financing within 60 or 90 days of signing; you can even try to specify that you must get financing below a stated interest rate. Don't be pressured by the seller's real estate agent into dropping any reasonable clause you wish to include: remember, time is money and the agent wants to make the sale and go on to the next customer with as little delay as possible. On the other hand, if you press too hard, you may kill the deal.

If the seller fails to comply with the entire sales contract, then you may have a good case for cancellation and the right to get your deposit back. But you have to be very careful here—if the failure to comply was *your* fault, or if you fail to perform your end of the bargain, you could not only lose your deposit, but you might be sued by the seller for spe-

cific performance—that is, you could be forced to buy the house anyway (or pay money damages).

Check It Out—Very Carefully

Although you may have only limited time between the signing of the sales contract and the scheduled closing date, never buy a house without having a professional home inspector or engineer scrutinize each square foot. (An inspection should cost between $200 and $400.) Some localities actually require a report by an inspector before a sale can take place.

The basic things to look for are the structural integrity, watertightness, and the solidity of the land the house sits on; if it's built on a former landfill, beware—it could settle. Go with the inspector on his or her rounds.

Some of the major items on the inspector's checklist should be:

Grounds. How good is the drainage? Are the grounds mucky for a long time after a heavy rain?

Basement. Is there any sign of seepage or dampness? Are the walls beginning to bulge?

Roof. Include drainage systems, flashing, chimneys, and skylights. Is there evidence of water penetration? Bubbling or shingle-curling?

Walls, windows, and doors. Are they straight and true? The caulking and weather-stripping should also be checked.

Heating and hot water system. How old is the furnace and hot water tank? How frequently has either been repaired during the last five years? What is the capacity of the hot water tank?

Water supply. Does the domestic water come from a well? What's the flow rate? Does the well water require filtration? You might also consider testing the well for bacteria.

Plumbing. How old is it? What is the recent repair history of the plumbing system? How good is the water pressure?

Floors. What's underneath the wall-to-wall carpeting?

Electrical system. Is it adequate? Can it support the profusion of home electronics common in so many households?

Energy efficiency. Are there storm windows? How much insulation is in the walls and the top-floor ceiling under the attic?

The inspector should be able to provide you with a general estimate of the cost of necessary repairs and renovations.

You don't think you need an inspection because you're buying new construction? Don't implicitly trust a builder, especially if you didn't get a chance to inspect the house during construction. Builders often cut corners to make bigger profits. The *Orlando Sentinel Tribune* reported on a Florida town house whose walls started to crack only four years after construction. The builder made some repairs, but the cracks only worsened. The buyer moved to California and is still unable to rent her old unit.

You can't rely on an inspection by your lender to find many of the faults and defects that could cost you a lot of money to repair. The main purpose of lender inspections is to appraise the property's value, not to determine if you'll have to repair the roof.

Increasing numbers of states now require sellers to fill out a form revealing any defects in their property. The idea, of course, is to protect buyers from hidden surprises. These forms can be very detailed. California sellers even have to disclose if there are noise problems in the neighborhood. And in the 26 states where the law does not require such forms, real estate agents may require them anyway.

Buyers should also check for a wide range of environmental hazards that have the potential to endanger both physical and fiscal health—they can make your new home immediately worth a lot less than you paid for it. Watch out for asbestos (used in many houses built before the mid-1970s), lead paint (used widely before 1978), lead in solder (used in plumbing in older homes), formaldehyde (used in various building materials), buried oil tanks (removing one could cost thousands of dollars if the oil leaks and contaminates the soil), and especially radon, an odorless, naturally occurring radioactive gas that can come up through the soil and rocks below and around your house.

The Environmental Protection Agency and National Cancer Institute estimate that radon contamination leads to 15,000 cases of lung cancer a year. Radon exceeds safe levels in up to 10,000,000 American homes. The average level for radon in homes is 1.3 pCi/L. If you have 4 pCi/L, the EPA suggests that you take action, and it notes that homeowners with over 2 pCi/L might want to consider taking action to lower their radon levels. Levels as high as 3,500 pCi/L have been found in some homes. Certain geological deposits are likely to contain more radon, than others. Your state radon office (you can get the phone number by visiting the EPA's Radon home page on the web at www.epa.gov/radonpro/contacts.html) should be able to tell you where higher levels of radon are likely to occur in your state. However, there is no particular pattern within communities. One house may have high levels of radon and a house several hundred feet away might register hardly any. Smokers who live in radon-contaminated homes greatly compound the health risk.

The only way to guard against radon is to hire a firm to run a test before buying. To determine if there is a radon problem, the firm will install charcoal canisters or some other sensing equipment, such as an alpha track detector in the home, usually in the basement. After several days,

ENVIRONMENT CHECK

If you want to avoid buying into the next Woburn, Massachusetts, the leukemia-plagued town that led to the lawsuit chronicled in the best-selling book *A Civil Action,* you'll want to find out whether there are any environmental hazards near that dream house you are about to close on.

Do-it-yourselfers can probably find the information they need by calling the state environmental agency and/or county health department, and by looking at the Environmental Protection Agency's Internet site at http://www.epa.gov. They might also want to call the Citizens Clearinghouse for Hazardous Waste, (703) 237-2249, which may know about local issues or can recommend a local group that does. If you'd rather pay someone else to do the legwork, call Environmental Risk Information and Imaging Services of Herndon, Virginia, (800) 989-0402. (See Help for additional contact information.) ERIIS can give you an annotated map of the Superfund sites, abandoned industrial sites, and dumps in the area surrounding your home. But the reports are not infallible; you might want to make a few phone calls on your own just to be sure they're up to date.

Whichever way you investigate, you'll be protecting both your investment and your family.

RADON RISK		
LIfetime Radon Exposure (pCi/L)	**If 1,000 people who had never smoked were exposed to this level:**	**The risk of dying from lung cancer compares to:**
100	*About 35 people may die from radon-related lung cancer*	*Having 10,000 chest X-rays each year*
40	*About 17 people may die from radon-related lung cancer*	*Smoking two packs of cigarettes a day*
20	*About 9 people may die from radon-related lung cancer*	*Smoking one pack of cigarettes a day*
10	*About 5 people may die from radon-related lung cancer*	*Having 1,000 chest X-rays each year*
4	*About 2 people may die from radon-related lung cancer*	*Smoking at least five cigarettes a day*

canisters are taken to a lab for analysis; alpha track detectors must remain in place for two to four weeks. (Since canisters usually cost no more than $20 and can be purchased at hardware stores, you can easily use them to do an initial screening.) More accurate measurements require leaving equipment on the premises for up to a year. It costs $500–$2,500 to clean up radon in an average home.

If your written contract with the seller doesn't allow you to fully inspect the property for such dangers, don't walk—*run* away from the deal. If you have a special reason to think the locality has potential environmental problems, you might want to hire a special environmental engineer to run tests for you.

Consider what happened to the residents of Colonial Square, a town house development built in the New York City borough of Staten Island in the 1980s. Only after they purchased their homes and had been living there awhile did they learn that the abandoned landfill on an adjacent property was in actuality an inactive toxic waste dump. Their property values plummeted.

One potential environmental danger doesn't take a test to detect —high-tension power lines. While scientists debate the effect of electromagnetic fields (EMF) on the human body, the effect of nearby high-tension lines on a home's resale value is clearly harmful.

Condominium and Co-Op Considerations

Much of the previous advice also applies to co-ops, condos, or town houses. However, there are important special considerations.

The differences between condominiums and co-ops. With a condominium, you get a deed and you pay property taxes on your unit. Cooperatives are different. You buy shares in a corporation, which owns the property and which likely has an underlying mortgage on it. The corporation gives you a proprietary lease, which allows you to reside in a particular unit.

In both cases, the association or corporation maintains and sets rules for using common areas, such as hallways, elevators, and grounds. Individual owners are responsible for everything on their side of the walls. So if a toilet doesn't work, for example, and the problem isn't the plumbing inside the wall or floor, the owner foots the plumber's bill.

Co-op corporations and condo associations (sometimes called a "homeowners association") are run by boards of directors comprised of shareholders or owners elected at an annual meeting under legally prescribed voting procedures. There are usually between three and nine directors; they, in turn, select officers from among them. Officers' terms can range from one to several years. Many boards with longer terms have the terms overlap, ensuring that there are always some experienced hands on board. One downside of co-operative and condo living is that these elections can become quite nasty and personal, yet the opposing sides are stuck living together after the election is over. So before you buy, you might want to ask several residents how everyone gets along. You want to avoid a complex that is so strife-riven that important decisions keep being deferred or, at the least, is an unpleasant place to live in.

Most co-ops and condos hire an outside management company to take care of the day-to-day running of the building: collecting maintenance, paying bills, supervising staff. Still, the management company needs to be closely supervised by the owners to make sure money isn't being wasted and that services are being efficiently provided. In a series of scandals in New York City in 1994, officials of many of the city's most prominent real estate management firms were indicted for taking kickbacks from contractors and suppliers.

Once you're a member of a co-op, you might be expected to volunteer for a committee, such as a grounds or a finance committee, or one that reviews the applications of prospective purchasers.

One advantage of a co-operative is that it can be easier to finance capital improvements and repairs; the corporation can get a mortgage to pay for a new roof or furnace. In a condo, each owner may have to pay a potentially large special assess-

> "*I liked it better in the old days when there was a landlord to complain to. Now the landlord is us.*"
>
> — A DISGRUNTLED APARTMENT DWELLER whose landlord converted his rental building into a co-operative

ment over a short period for such capital work.

Another difference between the two—either a disadvantage or an advantage, depending on your point of view—is that co-operative boards can more carefully screen new purchasers. Co-operative boards can reject an applicant for any reason, as long as it is not on the basis of race, color, creed, or national origin. Condo residents have very little control over who buys a unit, although condo associations usually have a right of first refusal.

Condo and co-op finances. Before you buy, go over the condo or co-op's finances with a fine-tooth comb, including:

■ Annual audited financial statements for the last three years, the current operating budget, and the number of units in maintenance arrears. You will also want to check how much money the complex has in a reserve account to pay for future emergencies or capital projects.
■ Copies of the minutes of the last year's Board of Directors meetings. These could reveal a lot about the inner workings of the condo or co-operative corporation that you should know before you buy.
■ The prospectus, offering plan, or offering statement. In a condo, this may be called the declaration; master deed; or covenants, conditions, and restrictions (CCR). For both condos and co-ops, be sure to see the bylaws and the house rules.

Also, try to get a copy of an engineer's report, either one by an en-

BEST TIMES WORST TIMES

Get your Christmas shopping done early so you can spend December househunting. While there are fewer homes for sale, there are so few buyers that desperate sellers will be happy to oblige you. So happy, that you could be decking the halls of a very sweet deal.

The worst time to call a realtor is Saturday or Sunday. They are likely to be out showing houses. And the last week of the month isn't great either—if your realtor is any good at her job, she will be busy with closings.

gineer you specially hire yourself or a recent report by an independent engineer who the complex may have hired. This is similar to a report by a professional house inspector except that an engineer will know about the more complex systems found in larger structures. Realize that if the engineer identifies pressing deficiencies and you buy anyway, a maintenance increase or special assessment to pay for repairs could be down the road. If it is a new apartment complex, it is important to check the reliability and reputation of the developer. Talk to residents of other complexes the developer has built. If anything about the developer appears the least bit shady, don't buy.

IF YOU'RE SELLING YOUR HOME . . .

Much of what you should know if you are selling a house is explained in the previous section. Just switch roles: Pretend you are considering *buying* your present house, and you'll understand what a potential buyer might look for and ask about. Here are some considerations especially for sellers:

Dealing With Real Estate Agents

Do you really need one? After all, why should an agent pocket that 6% commission? Well, selling a house is not nearly as easy as it looks. A real estate agent probably knows much more about how to price your home than you do. Agents have access to the MLS. And agents perform an important screening operation, keeping parties who are just curious or nosy away from your doorstep.

However, increasing interest in discount brokers and Internet real estate listings is remaking the U.S. real estate market—and making traditional real estate brokers very nervous. They are losing their exclusive access to the MLS, and more and more buyers are using online services to go around MLS altogether. In 1996, 15% of homes sold were sold without a traditional broker, and the pace of these sales is increasing.

Get the right one. Try to hook up with an agent who knows your neighborhood and who sells houses like yours. If you live in a modest Cape Cod, an agent who sells only luxury estates will not help you much.

Find out how many houses your agent has sold in the last six months, and ask how successful your agent was at obtaining close to the asking prices. Some real estate offices give out awards to the agents selling the most homes, and in some communities the most successful agents receive awards from the local board of realtors. You want an agent who wins these awards, who is hungry, not one for whom real estate is a second job or a supplement to a pension.

How long should you list your house? Try to keep it to 90 days or less, unless your listing has an unconditional cancellation clause, which gives you the flexibility to switch to another agent. If you agree to an "exclusive agency," only that one agency is allowed to sell the property, unless you sell it yourself. With an "exclusive right to sell," the agent gets a commission even if you are the one who ends up actually finding the buyer. An "open listing" means numerous agents list your house and only the agent making the sale gets the commission. Be wary of provisions in the listing contracts that give the agent a commission as long as he or she delivers a bona fide purchaser, no matter if the deal falls through.

The main advantage of an "exclusive right to sell" is that the agent is likely to work harder for you than with an "open listing."

The vast majority of listings are exclusive.

Is there any advantage to signing up with one of the large franchised real estate agencies, such as Century 21? No. Since the vast majority of homes are listed with the Multiple Listing Service, all agents have access to the same listings. How quickly your house sells depends to a very large degree on the abilities and initiative of the individual agent. A good selling agent will put real effort into it—not just organize an open house or place a few newspaper ads.

You can pay less and keep more. There's no law that says you must pay an agent at least a 6% commission. Some sellers negotiate a commission of only 5%. Or you can use a discount broker who charges as little as 4%; in exchange for the smaller commission, however, it could take longer to sell your house (discount brokers may lack access to the MLS).

Get the House in Shape

Many sellers neglect the basics of presentation. Be sure to:

Clean up the place. There's no excuse for unmade beds and crumbs on the kitchen counter. Personal sloppiness sends a signal that the home isn't very well cared for, and real estate agents are less willing to show sloppy houses. It should be immaculate, even if you have to hire someone to clean. Vases of fresh cut flowers and a wall of family photos are good touches.

Make minor improvements. Walls that could stand a coat of paint, countertops with burn marks, and shrubbery that needs trimming are real turn-offs. On the other hand, some sellers go overboard with expensive improvements, remodeling kitchens or adding a finished basement or a deck. General rule: When the cost of renovations are added in, the market value of your house shouldn't exceed that of the more expensive homes in your neighborhood by more than 20%.

The Art of Setting the Price

Pricing a home is a very touchy subject. Emotional attachment to a home you've lived in for 20 years might lead you to overprice, which in turn might cause agents to avoid showing your beloved home, sweet home.

When setting an asking price, ask your real estate agent to prepare a written comparative market analysis. It starts with the recent sale prices of nearby houses and adds or subtracts for the special pluses (and minuses) of your house.

Learning the sale prices of these houses will give you a good idea of the strength of the local real estate market and whether your prospective asking price is high or low. (If the sellers had to reduce their prices a lot, then the market may be weak.) You should also factor in how long it took the houses to sell. If it commonly took longer than six months, then the market is weak or the sellers priced unrealistically.

You might consider hiring a professional registered appraiser. An appraiser's imprimatur on your asking price might help you get the price you want—and more than cover the appraiser's fee.

WHAT TO WATCH OUT FOR

Buyers

An overbuilt home. A massive Georgian Colonial in a neighborhood of modest ranch homes looks impressive by comparison, but the Colonial could be a white elephant. Unless you get an extraordinary price break, it's not worth buying such a house; some day, you'll have a hard time selling it.

Tampered radon tests. In a 1992 hearing, a Congressional subcommittee was told that between 30% and 40% of all home real estate transaction radon tests are intentionally or accidentally tampered with. How? Sellers or real estate agents secretly remove radon detectors from the premises for a while, cover them with plastic bags, or purposely ventilate the test area.

Sad to say, some testing firms have had to resort to building motion detectors, barometers, and thermometers into their test equipment in order to measure changes produced by windows being opened or devices being moved. Tests using this equipment are more expensive than tests with basic charcoal canisters. Another

way to guard against tampering is to conduct a surprise follow-up test; if the results vary significantly from the first test, then you can suspect tampering.

Cooperatives or condos filled with renters. If most residents rent, it's doubtful that you'll want to join a minority of shareholders or owners who are *de facto* landlords to most of their neighbors. And it can be very hard or even impossible to secure financing in such buildings for yourself or for a co-op corporation. In addition, owners who are outside investors may not be as interested in keeping the place up. And when such owners fall behind in maintenance payments, all of the other owners in a condo or co-op could end up financially responsible because the complex's full monthly bills still have to be paid.

Your real estate agent's recommendations. Take suggestions of a title insurance company, an escrow agent, and a mortgage lender with a grain of salt; the agent may have a financial arrangement with the recommended provider, although experts recommend complete disclosure of any such relationship. Compare prices and rates of recommended providers with those you know are independent.

Buyer's agents who work in a dual agency. You've decided you want to hire a buyer's agent. Good idea. Just be careful if he or she works in an agency that also has seller's agents, since the buyer's agent you hire could very well end up dealing with his or her own office—a potential conflict, even if this situation is fully disclosed. It's called a "dual agency" when both sides' agents work in the same agency. You might do better with an exclusive buyer's broker, ideally one who charges a flat fee instead of a commission based on the price of the house.

Sellers

Not disclosing a defect in your home. The buyer may hold you legally liable if you fail to mention a latent defect—a defect that may not readily be apparent to the buyer but that a non-expert could discover. You might be held liable for undisclosed defects even if the sales contract said that your home is being purchased "as is." Minor defects that would not have affected the buyer's decision to buy your home don't count. On the other hand, obvious defects, such as a roof that is visibly collapsing, need not be specially disclosed.

Agents who misrepresent themselves. Make sure to screen potential agents carefully. Ask for a list of references, and ask those references if they would hire the agent again.

Mispricing your house. Get the opinions of at least three agents as to the market value of your house. It would be a financial tragedy if you impatiently acted on the advice of an agent who said your house was worth around $200,000 when opinions from two more agents would have priced it at $250,000.

THE $MARTER CONSUMER

Buyers

Buy or rent? When the real estate market is hot, value appreciation quickly offsets closing costs and agents' commissions. But in times when the housing market is in the doldrums, renting could make better sense, unless you plan to stay in a house for a long time. Closing costs usually amount to about 5% of the purchase price. As a rule of thumb, you have to stay at least five years to recoup these costs.

Use a buyer's agent. You'll know your agent is on your side and has no hidden obligations to the seller. They advertise in the phone book and in local newspapers. Even if you have to pay the commission yourself, which you most often won't, you could save so much on the purchase price that you come out well ahead anyway.

Negotiate, negotiate, negotiate. If something looks like it needs to be repaired—or even just painted—ask for it to be taken care of before the closing or for the selling price to be knocked down to compensate. Do you like the hallway chandelier? Ask if it can be included in the price. And how about the seller resurfacing the driveway before the closing?

Inspect the inspector. Most professional house inspectors are on the up and up. Still, keep in mind that an inspector who does the job *too* well—who finds and reports every little defect—will probably not be recommended by real estate agents for long and could end up out of work. Fortunately, some states now license home inspectors. In the meantime, make sure your inspector is a member of the American Society of Home Inspectors.

Get your lender to pre-qualify you. To get an idea of how much house you can afford, get a lender to pre-qualify you for a mortgage. This can be done informally, in a short meeting at the lender's office. Once you know how much you will likely be able to borrow, you'll know the limits of your house price.

This can also be done more formally, through a written application, which can produce a loan approval letter. You'll have to pay something—usually, the cost of the credit report—but sellers will know you are a truly serious shopper who can buy quickly, which ought to strengthen your bargaining position. Of course, only that particular lender has pre-approved you. You still might get less expensive financing for your deal from another lender.

Ask to see your lender's appraisal. According to federal law, you have the right to see your lender's property appraisal—if you ask for it in writing within 90 days after the lender has informed you of its decision on your loan or within 90 days after you withdraw your application. A copy of an appraisal has to be furnished within 30 days.

A lender's appraisal can be very useful. If the appraisal comes in low, you may be able to renegotiate the price downward before the closing. If you are purchasing property in a predominantly minority neighborhood, a low appraisal could indicate that the lender is illegally discriminating—called "redlining"—against borrowers purchasing houses in that area.

Check into government and builder-sponsored auctions. Less frequent lately than during the late 1980s and early 1990s, and not for the run-of-the mill home buyer, real estate auctions can still be a good source for a below-market-price home. Generally you have to deposit 5% to 10% of the purchase price in cash or cashier's check. *Don't* get swept away at the auction. Know your maximum bid on a property and stick to it.

To find out about government auctions and foreclosures, check your local newspaper's real estate ads or call banks directly and ask if they have a list of properties. Some of the best deals can be obtained through foreclosures; lenders just want to get their money back and aren't so interested in making a profit.

Sellers

Providing seller financing might help move your house. And, if it's feasible, it could prove a good long-term investment.

Go it alone. While conventional wisdom suggests that you shouldn't try to sell your home without a broker—most people end up signing with an agent later anyway—it's easier than it used to be and you can save yourself thousands of dollars.

Take a $150,000 house. To use a discount real estate broker to get your house listed on MLS, you'd pay about $600. On the standard commission of 3%, you'd save almost $4,000. The key to going "fizbo" (for sale by owner) is knowing how to price your home. Getting a professional appraisal, which will cost $200 to $350, is invaluable. Appraisers can tell you what similar homes have sold for recently, what other people are asking for similar homes, and how to factor in current market conditions and any untraditional characteristics of your property. Discount brokers say the most common problems owners who sell for themselves face is asking too high a price and giving up too soon. So don't be impatient. And make sure you have a good lawyer lined up to draft a solid contract and advise you on all that you have to disclose to the buyer.

Consider renting, if worse comes to worse and you can't unload your house. This turns it into a business investment and allows you to deduct expenses and depreciation. You might even "gain" a tax loss.

Don't even *think* about tampering with a radon detector placed by a prospective buyer. Not only is it reprehensible, but you also could be sued for all you've got if the buyer finds out about it after the closing and it turns out that radon on your former property exceeds safe levels.

H E L P

■ **For basic informa-**tion, order the free booklet from the U.S. Department of Housing and Urban Development (HUD), *A Home of Your Own: The Home Buying Guide,* by calling (800) 767-7468. Or look at HUD's Internet site at http://www.hud.gov.

■ **To find a qualified appraiser, ask at a** local bank or contact the Appraisal Institute, (312) 335-4100 or http://www.appraisalinstitute.org. Those with MAI (American Institute of Real Estate Appraisers) or SREA (Society of Real Estate Appraisers) designations have usually been extensively trained in appraising.

■ **To learn all you'll need to know** about home inspection, borrow (at your local library) or buy *The Complete Book of Home Inspection* by Norman Becker; $16.95 from McGraw-Hill Publishing Company, (800) 722-4726.

■ **The Fair Housing Act of 1968 makes** it illegal to discriminate in selling or renting housing on the basis of race, religion, national origin, sex, familial status or handicap. If you believe you have been discriminated against in buying housing, complain to the U.S. Department of Housing and Urban Development, 451 Seventh Street SW, Room 5100, Washington, DC 20410. You can also call them at (800) 669-9777, option #2.

■ **To order information about environ-**mental hazards, contact the U.S. Environmental Protection Agency (EPA), (202) 260-5922 or check http://www.epa.gov.

■ **To find out more about radon, order** the U.S. EPA's booklet, *The Home Buyer's and Seller's Guide to Radon.* Call (800) SOS-RADON or check http://www.epa.gov.

■ **Is the property you're considering** buying located near a hazardous waste dump? Find out from Environmental Risk Information and Imaging Services in Alexandria, VA. For $75, they'll find out. Call (800) 989-0403 to order a report.

CHAPTER 14

HOME IMPROVEMENT CONTRACTORS

Don't Get Hammered

As baby-boomers evolve into middle age, they appear to be increasingly repairing and/or expanding their homes rather than moving into newer ones. The result: 40% of homeowners spent a record $120 billion in 1997 on home improvements. (The top three improvements: kitchens, roofs, energy efficiency.)

But while we laugh at Tim Allen's bravado and know-how on the TV show *Home Improvement,* all too often we're not amused by months of overruns and underperformance by contractors—as anyone who saw the movies *Tin Men* and *The Money Pit* can attest.

Here, art imitates life. Stories abound of cost overruns, substandard work, missed deadlines, un-

> *"Home remodeling can cost from a few hundred to tens of thousands of dollars. With so much money at stake, you would think that homeowners would select a contractor with more care than picking out a steak for dinner, but they don't."*
>
> —CHRISTIE COSTANZO,
> home design expert

paid subcontractors and suppliers, incomplete jobs, and outright fraud. According to an annual survey by the National Association of Consumer Agency Administrators and the Consumer Federation of America, home improvement contractors (HICs) are, along with cars, the largest source of consumer complaints; and they were the second largest complaint category for the Council of Better Business Bureaus, accounting for 10% of all complaints filed.

The victims are often among the most vulnerable consumers. Says Bill Richards, a consumer protection official in Florida, "[t]he elderly are the major victims of home improvement fraud."

Consider two stories from two cities. Peg in Washington, DC, was in her late 80s, living alone, and always promptly paid every bill sent her. When door-to-door handymen noticed this trait, like metal filings to a magnet they began flocking to her home—and bilking her. For example, $13,278 for putting concrete in a maple tree cavity that was no bigger than a man's fist. "Then the men began charging her without bothering to work at all," reported *The Washington Post* in August 1997, "sunning themselves on her roof, for instance, while occasionally banging on shingles to make it look and sound as if they were fixing something." By the end of the scam, Peg was out $300,000.

Then there's Mattie, an elderly woman living on Social Security in a low-income New York neighborhood. When a contractor visited her and promised to fix her porches, doors, and windows, she signed a blank contract on the spot for what she was told was $3,700, but was in fact $37,000. Sky-high interest charges tripled the cost to $119,000, or $650 a month for 15 years—payments she could not meet. Having unknowingly put her house up for collateral, Mattie faced foreclosure and homelessness. (NYC's Department of Consumer Affairs eventually got the contract rescinded.)

And it's not only the elderly who end up in battles with contractors. Producer Aaron Spelling hired contractor Robert LaMar to work on his 56,000-square-foot Los Angeles mansion. Suits and countersuits flew back and forth on everything from the positioning of a toilet to slates on the roof. In the end, Mr. LaMar's insurance company forked over $1.2 million to the Spellings. And on the opposite coast, Caroline Hirsch, the owner of Caroline's comedy club in New York City, refused to make a final payment to her contractor until problems including cockeyed windows and leaky terraces were fixed, reported the *Wall Street Journal* in 1997. Then one evening, she heard two thuds on her door and found a pair of arrows, one with the note, "Pay your bills. The natives are restless."

Whether elderly or prominent, consumer losses from home improvements can be *both* costly and invasive. Consider the anguish of Sally A. of Queens, New York, for example, who sobbed as she said, "I paid $10,000 down to re-do my kitchen. They tore up most of it but haven't come back for ten months. Where can I go to cook my meals?" Sally wound up like so many others having to lay out even more money to hire a second contractor to come in and get the job done.

THE BASICS

Remodeling your home can be a double benefit—enhancing both your quality of life and the value of your primary asset. But getting there from here can also be a true roller-coaster ride, interfering with your daily life and jeopardizing your savings. The process of remodeling involves turning over your home, or parts of it, to strangers for an uncertain period of time. Fortunately, picking the right contractor doesn't have to be like buying a lottery ticket; a few precautions can help.

The help you need varies, depending on whether your project is a big production or a one-person show. If you're just contracting for a specific job—recovering the roof, repaving the driveway, or repainting the house—you should look for a professional in that field. If you're undertaking a more ambitious project, you should turn to a general building contractor to oversee the entire process—from helping you define the project and securing the proper permits to hiring a crew and any necessary subcontractors and seeing the project through to completion.

Choosing the Right Contractor

Finding a contractor isn't very complex: just flip through the Yellow Pages or write down a name on a flyer pinned on a supermarket bulletin board. As an industry insider notes, "Basically all you need is a business card and a contract, and you're in the home-contracting business." The challenge is to find a contractor who'll do a good job in a timely fashion for a competitive price. While price is a key consideration, other factors—reputation, references, and quality of work—are just as important.

Get recommendations. Ask family, friends, colleagues, or trustworthy people in the construction industry for recommendations of local contractors who have handled jobs comparable to the one you're planning. A study by New York State's Consumer Protection Board found that consumers who relied on recommendations reported fewer problems than those who relied on radio, television, the Yellow Pages, or door-to-door sales pitches (more on those later).

Comparison shop. Get written, detailed estimates from at least three contractors after they've had a chance to visit the premises. (Find out if fees for such estimates are illegal in your jurisdiction by calling the Better Business Bureau [BBB], local consumer agency, or the attorney general's office.) Make sure that the various bids are based on the same specifics and that you're not comparing apples and oranges—or aluminum and steel. Do not automatically go to the lowest bidders; they may be low-balling their estimate to get the job or planning to use lower grade materials.

Check the contractors' references, background, and training. Check with your local consumer agency and BBB for records of prior complaints and to find out how long the contractor has been in business. Ask the contractor about reputable professional affiliations or certifications and for references (previous clients and suppliers).

You can also get a lot of information by interviewing the contractor. A conscientious builder should ask you plenty of questions and offer suggestions. And you'll get a sense of how well the two of you would work together.

Verify legal compliance. Prodded by the avalanche of complaints, state and local governments have taken various measures to regulate the industry and help consumers help themselves. Take advantage of the chits already on your side of the table. The main areas the regulations address are:

■ *Licensing.* Thirty-two states and the District of Columbia require some form of contracting license. These states are Alabama, Alaska, Arizona, Arkansas, California, Connecticut, Delaware, Florida, Georgia, Hawaii, Iowa, Louisiana, Maryland, Maine, Michigan, Minnesota, Mississippi Montana, Nebraska, Nevada, New Jersey, New Mexico, North Carolina, North Dakota, Oregon, Rhode Island, South Carolina, Tennessee, Utah, Virginia, Washington, and West Virginia. In addition, numerous counties, cities, and other local jurisdictions also require licenses. Licensing requirements vary greatly from state to state. California has a rigorous testing program that licenses contractors by specialty (roofing, windows, etc.) after they pass an examination. But in Iowa the only license requirement is payment of a fee.

Call the local licensing board to verify that the license is current and valid or you may end up like Michele K. of California, who hired a contractor after he gave her his business card with a contractor's license number. The contractor pocketed $2,600 to install a sprinkler system, replant the lawn, and remove a tree, but did such a shoddy job that Michele had to have the work redone by another contractor. When she contacted the board to complain about the first contractor, she was told his license number was someone else's: She was out $2,600.

A license is usually *not* a certification of professional competence or moral standing. In fact, disreputable contractors may go out of their way to get licensed precisely because it provides an air of legitimacy and tells the consumer, "See, I'm licensed. If you have any problem with me, I'll get into big trouble with the government." But it does indicate a minimum degree of accountability if you are later defrauded. For instance, New York City consumers who hire a *licensed* contractor can get back up to $20,000 from a city-run trust fund if their contractor does a shoddy job; the city awarded almost $2 million to defrauded consumers in restitution between 1990 and 1992.

■ *Posting bonds.* Many states require that contractors post a bond to compensate consumers who are defrauded. Again, this requirement is a help but no panacea: The bond may be too small to cover a large number of complaints.

■ *Cooling-off periods.* Federal law enables you to cancel your contract within three business days—except for emergency repairs and contracts solicited at "the contractor's place of business or appropriate trade premises."

Check that your contractor is insured. Unless your contractor has personal liability, property damage, and workman's compensation insurance (including coverage for sub-contractors), you may be sued if someone gets injured on the job. Ask for a copy of your contractor's certificate of insurance.

Still, none of these precautions are foolproof: Con artists learn to refine their schemes just as consumers learn the tricks of the trade. In 1993, several chimney sweeps in the New York region bent over backward to develop an aura of legitimacy, flaunting their registration or license, working by appointment only, providing customers with an "800" complaint number, and offering their cleaning services at cut-rate prices. The trick: Once on the roof, they would pry a few bricks loose and convince their customer that the chimney needed immediate repair—for several hundred dollars. They were especially hard to catch because they defrauded only selected consumers.

The Contract

Always ask for a contract, even for a small project. Once the job gets started, the contract will become your first line of defense—as long as it is carefully prepared. It should note the parties to the contract, including the contractor's name, address, telephone, and license number (if applicable), and the provisions that you and the contractor agreed upon orally—what is to be done, how long it will take, and how much it will cost. In particular, the contract should specify the following:

■ A detailed description of the work to be done, including materials. Es-

---

LOWBALL GAMES

"A good remodeler doesn't like to get into bidding wars, because there's always going to be someone lower," says Paul Deffenbaugh, editor-in-chief of *Remodeling*. "The reasons often are that he's paying his insurance and his workers' compensation and his employees, and he's running a good business. The lowball guys aren't covered by insurance and workers' compensation, so the consumer is getting a lower-priced job but running a risk. What the consumer wants, and should have, is a well-managed project with a contractor who has been around forever and everybody loves."

---

pecially when contractors are paid a flat fee, they may try to squeeze a greater profit by using low-grade or inadequate materials. Make sure that the contract spells out the types, grades, and brands of materials to be used. If you expect solid oak cabinets instead of laminated something, you'd better say so. In writing.

■ A schedule. The contract should include the estimated start and completion dates for the project as well as completion targets of intermediate parts.

■ Financial arrangements. You can contract based on either a *flat fee* or *cost-plus* basis. The former has the great advantage of (relative) certainty. The latter, "cost-plus," means that the contractor is paid a percentage of the expenses. It is more flexible but gives the contractor no incentive to keep costs down. Most experts recommend that you avoid contractor charges based on time and materials, since overruns could send the cost skyrocketing.

The total price should be broken down by individual subcontractors and materials. A hard and fast rule: Don't pay too much in advance. One computer programmer in Brooklyn hired a contractor to do a $65,000 renovation job on his 90-year-old brownstone after he was told the house had dangerous structural problems. The contractor insisted on being paid the $65,000 cash on Monday and—guess what? —never showed up the next day to start the job.

Instead, work out a payment schedule, don't pay cash, and hold tight to your money until the job is completed. Never pay more than a tenth to a third up front, half to one third midway, and the rest upon completion: that is, save the final 20% of a bill until the project is entirely concluded and final inspections passed. This is dispute time and you should hold up final payments to maintain some leverage.

■ **Compliance with the law.** Your home may be your castle, but you can't always do with your property as you wish. Construction projects must comply with local *building codes*, meaning that you'll need building permits for a lot of projects. The contract should assign responsibility to the contractor for complying with all applicable codes and obtaining all required permits, and those permits should be in the contractor's name. The National Association of the Remodeling Industry, a leading trade group, warns, "Do not obtain your own building permit— in most jurisdictions, the individual obtaining the permit is considered to be the contractor and is, therefore, liable if the work does not comply with local building codes."

Working without a permit isn't just illegal—it can be unsafe. Joan W. of Queens, New York, who had hired a contractor to redo her basement, called her consumer agency after the work started falling apart. It turned out that the contractor had obtained none of the required permits. Electrical wires were sparking and the toilet was "dangerous and illegal," with a possibility of sewer gas infiltration. The inspector's conclusion: The contractor's work reflected "a callous disregard for human life."

■ **Proof of payment for suppliers and subcontractors.** If the contractor leaves workers or suppliers unpaid, they may be able to place a *mechanic's lien* on your property, a nasty legal maneuver that could jeopardize your ownership title if the bills aren't paid. A clause in the contract should enable you to withhold final payment until you have received proof of payment to subcontractors and suppliers.

■ **Guarantees and warranties.** The contractor should guarantee labor and materials against defects or poor workmanship for a minimum of one year—agreeing to correct any

FINESSING FINANCING

Home improvements don't come cheap. The bill can quickly reach tens of thousands of dollars. Odds are therefore good that you will need financing. But can you get it?

People who moved into their home several years ago, and have seen the value of their home rise, usually find it relatively easy to get an equity line of credit or a second mortgage. But for those who've moved into their home more recently, and whose equity and value probably haven't risen much, financing is more difficult or expensive.

Shop around to find the best loan, taking into consideration the repayment schedule, interest rates, finance charges, and penalties for late or early payment.

If you're unsuccessful with conventional loan sources, you may be eligible for a Federal Housing Administration Title I loan of up to $25,000—but the interest rate for such loans can be nearly double the market rate.

Finally, a growing number of HICs and suppliers offer their own financing plans. Exercise great caution, however, because such financing has been the source of egregious consumer abuse. Look closely at the terms of the financing—the interest rate, the collateral (it could be your house!), and the financial institution that will actually be advancing the money.

Many contractors work hand-in-glove with unscrupulous finance companies to perpetrate all sorts of predatory lending practices. A smooth-talking HIC salesman shows up at the door and offers to do some remodeling—"no money down." The salesman (who is also an agent for a finance company) asks the homeowner to "okay a few forms"—in fact, a contract for the work and a blank mortgage agreement. The specifics—such as interest rate and cost of the work—are often sky-high and included *after* the consumer has signed the documents. The finance company then pays the contractor, who performs poor or no work. The homeowner is saddled with high monthly payments and, when she or he falls behind, faces eviction by a "legitimate" bank, which bought the mortgage from the finance company.

One reason why such schemes are able to proliferate is that redlining remains pervasive in the lending industry, making it very difficult for low-income or minority consumers to obtain loans from mainstream financial institutions. (See Chapter 62, "Selling Minorities Short in the Marketplace," page 667.)

shortcomings at no charge—and should give you the warranty cards for any items installed.

■ Financing. Finally, if you need financing, you should include a clause allowing you to pull out if you cannot secure financing under favorable conditions.

Don't sign the contract if any spaces are left blank and the contractor promises to fill them in "back at the office." Read it closely and in its entirety before signing. Estelle S. didn't: The contractor kept telling her, "Just read the top here to understand the job and I'll fill the rest in." The result: She signed a second mortgage on her house with high finance charges when she thought she was signing a work order to repair her leaky roof. The contractor botched the job and disappeared.

Any adjustments made to the original contract—known as *change orders*—should be put in writing, signed, and attached to the contract. You can often save yourself a good deal of money by *not* changing the project once it's started. On the other hand, *you* (not the contractor or anyone else) will have to live with the results—literally. If there must be changes, make sure you and the contractor have a clear agreement over any added costs.

Signing Off

At the end of the project, the contractor will ask you to sign a *completion certificate*—your acknowledgment that the work was completed as agreed to in the contract. Do not sign this document—

and do not make a final payment —until you've assured yourself that the work was properly done and that all subcontractors and suppliers have been paid.

Before signing the certificate, request that the contractor provide and sign an *affidavit of final release* that will protect you from liability for non-payment of suppliers or subcontractors.

WHAT TO WATCH OUT FOR

Fly-by-night operators. After the flood of the Mississippi receded from the Midwest in the summer of 1993, another kind of flood swept the region: out-of-state scam artists looking to make a quick buck out of someone else's misery. The construction union in Iowa even bought half-page ads in state newspapers warning residents against "fly-by-night contractors from Florida, Texas, and California."

One scenario: A "contractor" drives around a poor neighborhood searching for prospective victims, finds an elderly couple sitting on their porch, and offers to clean their gutters for a reasonable $35 and to inspect their roof "while he's at it." Once on the roof, he pulls out a (formerly concealed) hatchet, chops a hole in the roof, and empties a canteen of water into the hole he created. Mr. Contractor then comes back down, warns the couple that they have a hole in their roof and that "if they went upstairs they'd probably see water on the floor"— which, of course, they do. Mr. Contractor then generously offers to cover the roof with a "miraculous substance" (some whitish liquid) for a mere $6,500—payable in cash. He does the work, drives the homeowners to the bank to get the cash, and takes off. In the next rain, the "miracle substance" washes away, forcing the couple to spend another $9,000 for a whole new roof.

Tip-offs for a savvy consumer: an unmarked van, a post-office box address, or an answering service instead of an office. You may want to pay a visit to your contractor's address to see whether they're working out of the back of a truck (bad) or an office (good).

Hard-sell tactics. Be wary of anyone knocking at your door who "just happens to be in the neighborhood" and offers to clean your chimney or repave your driveway, or who threatens that your house will collapse unless you get the job done right away.

And stay away from contractors who call you with unbelievable "this week only" bargains or offer you a "special low price" for use of your home as a "model home." Your house might become a model, all right—of a typical consumer scam.

Do-it-yourself? You may be able to handle small projects yourself—things between changing a light bulb and changing your roof—by consulting how-to books and videos. Similarly, if you have experience in supervising large projects, you may do away with a general building contractor and act as your own owner/builder. But unless you know what you're doing, don't try this at home.

The big guns. For such major projects as renovations and additions, hire an architect to draw up plans.

Investment tips. Remember that a home renovation is also a major investment. How does the added value created by the improvement compare with the cost? Be cautious about remodeling just to increase the value of your house: According to the BBB, "When it comes time to sell, home improvements often do not pay back what they cost."

Don't overimprove. Don't turn your shack into the Taj Mahal before putting it on the market thinking you'll sell it at Taj Mahal value; you'll be sorely disappointed. Before any major investment, check with an experienced real estate agent about its potential payback.

Smart improvements are functional ones that add to the home's practicality, or low-cost cosmetic improvements that enhance your house's visual appeal.

Homeowner's insurance. Make sure to adjust your homeowner's insurance policy if the work done added substantially to the value of your house.

Complaints. You'll be able to avoid a lot of problems if you stay in constant touch with your contractor and supervise the project every step of the way. It's a good idea, for instance, to examine the materials and fixtures *before* they are installed. Don't be shy about asking questions or complaining if you find the work deficient.

If you need to complain, you'll be in much better shape if you have a solid paper trail—contract, proof of payment (such as canceled checks), written communications with your contractor, pictures of shoddy work, and agreements with subcontractors.

First, try to resolve your disagreement directly with the contractor. If you can't work things out, you have several options: You can file a complaint with the appropriate state or local agency. Or you can go to arbitration (if both parties agree) or file a lawsuit. Including a binding arbitration clause in the contract can save you from costly litigation if a disagreement occurs. Finally, you can fire the contractor—but be ready for a fight if he or she wants the balance of payment.

Emergency? The time may come when your house needs fixin' in a hurry and you don't have the chance to go through the orderly process outlined above. That's when you're at your most vulnerable, as Mr. and Mrs. C., in Seattle, Washington, found out. Their washing machine broke down—a true crisis when you have three children. They called a repairman who advertised same-day service in the Yellow Pages, who came and fixed the washer for $142—well, sort of. In fact, he

rewired the electrical connections in reverse order, so the machine would spin on the wash cycle and agitate on the spin cycle. They were unable to recontact the repairman until they got his home number, when they were given another run-around. Eventually, they stopped payment on the check and got another repairman to fix the machine in 10 minutes for $50.

Before calling some name plucked out of the Yellow Pages, verify at least that the contractor is licensed. Ask the contractor about minimum charges, and before repairs begin, get a written estimate and a right of veto over added expenses. After the ordeal is over, ask your contractor to provide you with an itemized invoice. Finally, be aware that, for obvious reasons, the cooling-off period does not apply to emergency repairs.

Health alert. If the house you live in was built before 1977 and your household includes children under 6 or anyone who is pregnant, find out if the house contains lead-based paint before remodeling. Lead ingestion by children or pregnant women can cause permanent brain damage to the child or fetus.

Easy money. If your construction project will promote energy efficiency or structural renovation, you may qualify for a government grant or low-interest loan assistance. For more information, consult the catalogue of federal public assistance at your local public library or your local building department and utility companies.

HELP

■ **To obtain a list of** contractors certified by the National Association of Home Builders: Contact your state or local chapter (there are 800 in the country). You can find out how to contact your chapter by calling the national association, (800) 368-5242. The list of chapters is also available on the Web; go to www.nahb.com/slass.html.

■ **The National Association of the** Remodeling Industry also offers examinations for both a general *certified remodeler* and *certified remodeler associate* designations. For a list of members in your area, to find out about NARI's arbitration program, or for a free brochure, "Masterplan for Professional Remodeling," call the national association, (800) 440-NARI.

■ **Under the Title I program, eligible** homeowners can obtain a HUD-insured loan of up to $25,000. For approved lenders in your area, call: (800) 767-7468.

■ *How to Get It Built*, by architect Werner R. Hashagen, is a treasure-trove of tips and techniques on how to build or repair your home. To order, send $24 to Werner R. Hashagen & Associates, 7480 La Jolla Boulevard, La Jolla, CA 92037; (619) 459-0122.

CHAPTER 15

THE ENERGY EFFICIENT HOME

Help Your Wallet and the Planet

As Dan D. began paying $450 electric bills during the summer months for his new 3,200-square-foot home in 1995, he knew they were excessive. After all, he was a supervisor of residential services for Houston Lighting & Power Co. So he quickly upgraded the 20-year-old home's central cooling and heating system, added new insulation, and replaced aging duct work. The cost was $7,000 and the savings were monthly summer utility bills falling to an average of $120. He figures to recoup his investment in less than three years.

Using energy efficiently is perhaps the most important aspect of being a smart, environmentally conscious consumer. Efficient energy use means we will burn less environment-harming fossil fuels, like the oil and coal used to fuel electric power plants. Conserving energy means less dependence on foreign oil. And, of course, it will save you money.

This ethic is understood and spreading. Because of the growing popularity of environmentalism in general—and the 1987 federal energy efficiency standards for home appliances and heating/cooling equipment in particular—consumers are reducing their energy use. Compared to the mid-1970s, for example, today's refrigerators use 70% less energy; washing machines and dishwashers, 40% less; and furnaces, 20% less. U.S. homes are one-third more energy efficient.

> "**M**any energy-conserving technologies can pay for themselves in short order, saving money while reducing the U.S. contribution to global warming."
>
> —HOWARD GELLER,
> executive director of the
> American Council for an Energy
> Efficient Economy

Still, beyond studying the yellow-and-black EnergyGuide labels on new household appliances, consumers can become Dan D. and save significant sums, year after year after year. Many people think that using energy efficiently is inconvenient, time-consuming, or complicated. Not true. A few simple measures can help clear the air—and lower your fuel bills.

THE BASICS

Home Heating

Home heating and cooling together account for 60% of the energy consumed in a home. But keeping our homes cozy and warm is not without consequence.

The Worldwatch Institute, an environmental group, estimates that home heating is responsible for spewing 350 million tons of carbon into the atmosphere each year—resulting in over a billion tons of carbon dioxide, the most prevalent greenhouse gas. And about an eighth of the nation's emissions of sulfur and nitrogen oxides (the leading cause of acid rain) comes from heating our homes.

Depending on where you live, heating with natural gas could save you money and make the air cleaner. Natural gas burns much, much cleaner, releasing none of the soot that comes from oil combustion. (It does, however, release some carbon dioxide.) Also, natural gas causes a lot less wear and tear on a furnace and so will reduce your maintenance expenses.

WHAT TO WATCH OUT FOR

If you choose to investigate natural gas heat, you should know you're about to walk into an advertising minefield. The oil and gas industries have been battling each other in the media like latter-day Hatfields and McCoys. The gas industry pushes the cleanliness of its product; the oil industry responds with a very hard-hitting "use safe oil" advertising campaign that plays on some consumers' fears about natural gas. For example, the New York oil industry ran aggressive ads in early 1993 that came very close to deception. One commercial included the male voiceover, "Take a chance? Yeah, maybe on a lottery ticket. But gas in my house? OK, so odds are, nothing would go wrong—but I'd rather not bet on it."

By all accounts, natural gas is a clean, safe, convenient, and cheaper alternative to oil. Don't be fooled by the oil industry's not-so-subtle disinformation campaign.

THE $MARTER CONSUMER

Since 40% of the energy we use at home goes for heat, you can reduce your energy demand by implementing a home heating energy conservation program.

Treat your furnace to a tune-up. An energy tune-up costs about $50 and will increase your furnace's effi-

BUYING GREEN: DO THE RIGHT—AND THE SMART—THING

Of course, buying energy-efficient appliances is the *right* thing to do. But so is eating your spinach when you're a kid. Does that mean you'll do it? Well, you should. As the *Consumer Guide to Home Energy Savings* explains, the "wonderful thing about saving energy is that, in addition to helping the environment, you save money. It's like contributing to a good cause and ending up with more money in your pocket."

How much money? At least $100 to $500 a year.

For $7.95, this little book by Alex Wilson and John Morrill contains all you need to know on the subject, including the top-rated "green" appliances by type and size and tips on how to make your whole living environment—from your house to your coffee-pot—environment-friendly. Among the gems included:

■ If you plan to buy a major appliance like a refrigerator, heating pump, or air conditioner soon, ask your utility company if it will give you a rebate if you buy a more efficient model. Many utility companies will, realizing that it costs less money to conserve energy than to build new power plants.

■ Front-loading (horizontal-axis) washing machines use one-third less water (and energy) than standard top-loading (vertical-axis) machines.

■ You can save up to 15% in the cost of running your dryer if you buy a model that senses dryness and automatically shuts off rather than one that's controlled by a timer.

Look for the book at your bookstore or send $10 (postage included; California residents add 8.25% sales tax) to the American Council for an Energy-Efficient Economy, 2140 Shattuck Avenue, Suite 202, Berkeley, CA 94704, or call (510) 549-9914.

---

ciency by about 5%. If you use oil to heat your home, ask the company that delivers it to make a service call to check your furnace. If you're paying for a service contract, you should take advantage of it; if not, you might as well take advantage of your oil company's expertise.

Keep your fireplace flue closed when you're not using the fireplace. About 8% of your heat can escape up an open damper.

Turn it down. Every degree you turn down your thermostat will cut your heating bill by 2%. By

SPECS FOR CHOOSING EFFICIENT BULBS

Use this chart to convert your regular incandescent bulbs to compact fluorescent (CF) bulbs, which last 13 times as long. For maximum efficiency, install them in fixtures that are on for an average of four or more hours a day (but *don't* use CF bulbs on circuits with dimmer switches).

If you have this regular bulb...	Replace it with this CF bulb.
25 watts	7 watts
40	11
60	15
75	18-20
90	23
100	27

Source: New York Public Interest Research Group

the same token, every degree you *raise* your thermostat during air conditioner days saves 5% in energy costs. Indeed, if all Americans raised the temperature settings of their air conditioners by 6 degrees, we'd save 200,000 barrels of oil a day.

Insulate, insulate, insulate. Nearly half of all the energy used to heat and cool our homes is wasted. It goes out through the attic, the window, the walls, you name it. "I've personally poked my head into attics from Massachusetts to California," said John Morrill of the American Council for an Energy-Efficient Economy, "and although the country has been more energy aware over the past 25 years, there are still millions of homes with pathetic levels of insulation."

A few simple insulation steps can greatly reduce your home energy consumption. For example, you may want to add another 6 inches of fiberglass insulation if your attic floor now has only a few inches of it and install double-paned, insulated glass windows.

The key to selecting insulation is its "R-value"—the higher the R-value, the better it insulates. Experts recommend insulating an attic to at least R-30 standards; exterior walls should be insulated to R-15 standards.

Electric and Gas Bills

Use compact fluorescent (CF) bulbs where possible. These lightbulbs are a real breakthrough and only now are aggressively being brought on the market. CF bulbs last for 10,000 hours (as opposed to 750 hours for conventional incandescent bulbs). Super-efficient CF lightbulbs cost more but burn just as brightly, and they significantly reduce the electricity we use. Less electricity means less air pollution and less oil we must import.

GETTING TECHNICAL ABOUT OIL BURNER TESTING

A combustion efficiency test can help you save energy from your furnace (a hot tip: have your furnace tested in the fall, before the fuel season heats up). The terms can be confusing, but here's what you need to know to converse with your mechanic.

1. *Flue gas composition* indicates how well the oil and air are mixing and how well the oil is being combusted. Carbon dioxide below the 9% to 12% range and oxygen levels above the 4% to 10% range indicate a problem.

2. *Flue gas temperature* also tells how well the oil is burning. Exhaust air above the 400- to 500-degree range indicates excessive heat loss.

3. *Draft measurement* rates the suction produced by combustion gases rising. A rating of .02 to .04 is ideal; any higher or lower is inefficient.

4. *A smoke test* shows how thoroughly the fuel is being burned. Smoke comes from incompletely burned fuel and stains a filter paper. The darker the paper, the worse the combustion.

Your furnace mechanic will measure combustion efficiency using a combination of factors. Above 80% efficiency is excellent, 70% to 80% is average, and below 70% means you're wasting too much oil and need a furnace tune-up. Tuning up the furnace can save fuel—and money!

By using a CF bulb instead of a traditional bulb, you'll prevent 1,000 pounds of carbon dioxide from entering the atmosphere. And you'll save a little money.

During its life span, the CF bulb uses about $10 worth of electricity. During the same period, you'd use about 13 regular lightbulbs, which would use about $40 worth of electricity.

CF bulbs have one other advantage: Since they give off less heat and more light, they reduce the cost of air conditioning. Consumers often don't realize how much of their air conditioning is required to overcome the heat produced by or-dinary lightbulbs. Substituting three 27-watt CF bulbs for three 100-watt incandescent bulbs will keep your room just as bright but will reduce a typical room air conditioner's workload by 12%.

Do an energy audit. "Any house built more than 15 years ago and never upgraded could benefit from an energy audit," according to Alex Wilson, editor of an environmental building trade journal in Vermont. Professional energy auditors, he adds, use special tools—such as infrared cameras and smoke pencils—to provide detailed assessments and recommendations.

But if you want to avoid the expense, consider a do-it-yourself home energy audit where *you* find the trouble spots in your house where energy is being wasted. To perform one, pick a cold, windy day, take a candle, and tour the corners of your house. By watching the flame, you'll be able to tell where the drafts are and where you ought to apply weather stripping. You'll probably discover that the windows and doors are the worst offenders. Weather stripping is fairly easy to apply, and the eventual energy savings, while modest, will more than cover the cost of supplies.

Keep the filter and coils of your air conditioner clean. The air conditioner will work more efficiently if it is clean. A clogged filter uses 5% more energy than a clean one.

Use your air conditioner efficiently. Keep it in the shade. An air conditioner exposed to direct sunlight will use up to 5% more energy than one that is shaded.

Set the air-conditioner on "low cool" rather than on "high cool"; you'll use a lot less power, and you probably won't notice the difference. At night, set the air conditioner to run the fan only. The air circulation makes the room feel cooler and lets you save energy. Try cooling your house to an even 76 degrees rather than to an icy 68 in the summer for environmental (and economic) conservation.

Make your refrigerator more energy efficient. If all households in the U.S. had the most efficient refrigerators available, the electrical savings—since this appliance alone accounts for 7% of the nation's total electricity consumption—would eliminate the need for 10 large power plants. Until that distant day, be sure the seals on the door of your refrigerator are airtight. To check, close the door over a dollar bill with half of it in the refrigerator and half of it outside; if you can pull it out easily, your seal may need replacing. Don't let frost build up in your freezer—it increases the amount of energy needed to keep the engine running. Clean the condenser coils on the back or bottom of your refrigerator at least once a year—a brush or a vacuum will do the job. (*Don't* use a knife or sharp implement, since you risk rupturing, and ruining, the coils.) You might also try adjusting the "feet" of your refrigerator to make sure the fridge is level and that the door shuts quickly and securely. (If a refrigerator leans forward a little, the door might not shut tightly.)

If your gas oven or stove has a pilot light, make sure the flame is blue, and cone-shaped. A yellow, "jumping" flame is burning inefficiently. Your local gas utility will usually check or adjust your gas stove for free.

Give your utility company a call. Its phone number is printed on your monthly bill. Many utilities nationwide are making extra efforts to conserve energy—witness Con Ed's monthly "Customer News" in every billing packet, with its June 1997 version full of summer air conditioner energy-saving tips. Some will even provide energy-efficient CF light bulbs at a discount or provide subsidies if you trade in an old refrigerator for a more efficient model. Call your utility and ask if it has an energy-saving program that you can "utilize" for big economic savings.

Check the seal on your oven door. Even a small gap lets a lot of heat escape. And know that every time you open the door to check on the progress of your roast, the temperature will fall 25°!

Set your washing machine to a cold water rinse. Cold water rinses just as well as warm and saves a whole lot of energy.

Cover vents and exhaust fans when they're not in use to keep cold air from getting in.

HELP

■ **For free energy-**saving tips, write or call the New York Public Interest Research Group, 9 Murray Street, New York, NY 10007, (212) 349-6460. Attn.: Director, Fuel Buyers Group.

■ **For more information on energy-**saving appliances, order these booklets ($3 each) from the American Council for an Energy-Efficient Economy, 1001 Connecticut Avenue NW, Suite 801, Washington, DC 20036, (202) 429-0063, or look at their Web site at www.crest.org/aceee: "Consumer Guide to Home Energy Savings" ($7.95, plus $5.00 for shipping and handling),

"The Most Energy-Efficient Appliances" and "Saving Energy and Money with Home Appliances."

■ **To learn how to weatherize your** home, get these booklets from the Massachusetts Audubon Society's Energy Saver's Series: "Saving Energy and Money with Home Appliances," "How to Weatherize Your Home or Apartment," "All About Insulation," and "Oil and Gas Heating Systems." Each guide costs $3.75 plus $1.00 for shipping and handling from Massachusetts Audubon Society, Educational Resources Office, 208 South Great Road, Lincoln, MA 01773, www.massaudubon.org.

CHAPTER 16

HOME SECURITY SYSTEMS

Case Your Place

Aaaaaaaaaaaaaaaaaaaaaaaaaaaaah! You just can't get a better security system than the perfect screech of Macauley Culkin in *Home Alone*!

But if you'd prefer not to leave any of your children behind when you leave the house, you can still make relatively certain your possessions are safe. "Nine out of ten household burglaries are preventable," according to the Insurance Information Institute. You simply have to take a few precautions. And they may not be as expensive as you'd think—things like keeping hedges trimmed low, replacing dim lightbulbs with photosensitive floodlights, and getting a noisy dog all make a difference.

If you're in the market for a sophisticated alarm system, burglar need beware—but so should buyer. Professional burglars, people who have made illicit but comfortable livings for years, told investigators from ABC News' *20/20* that even the best, highest-priced electronic surveillance systems are a "joke."

Whether that observation is self-serving or sincere, an alarm may be worth it just for peace of mind. Besides, national crime statistics show that more and more burglaries are committed by less-hardened criminals, who probably aren't as adept at slipping past motion sensors or alarms undetected. You can save money by buying wireless sensors, which you can probably install yourself and will do many of the same jobs as a more expensive professionally installed security system.

THE BASICS

The FBI says a burglary occurs every 10 seconds. That added up to more than 1.7 million homes being burglarized in 1996, with losses of more than $3 billion. (And burglary rates that year were the lowest they'd been since 1975.) These statistics are fueling a steady 15% annual increase in sales of locks, alarms, and other security devices.

Sensible Security
Is Simple

Start with deterrence. Experienced burglars can make it in and out of your house in less than two minutes, usually a lot less time than it takes for police to respond to your alarm. Your best bet is to take a few simple steps. They might be enough to send a burglar to somebody else's house.

Trim the trees and shrubs near your doors and windows, and think twice before you build a high wall or fence around your property. Hedges and high fences add not only to your privacy but also, unfortunately, to the privacy of a potential intruder—a fence is one of the first things burglars look for (along with the darkness that so comforted the cat burglar in Alfred Hitchcock's *To Catch a Thief*).

Burglars are also on the lookout for loot. Keep yours out of sight. Even if it means rearranging the furniture, it's probably worth it to move the Van Gogh—or the VCR —out of view.

No matter how good the lock is on your front door, it's worthless if you leave your windows open or unlatched, or if the back door is unlocked. You might as well send out engraved invitations. This all may sound obvious, but a Temple University study found that nearly half of all burglars in three suburban Philadelphia communities "broke in" to houses by walking through unlocked doors.

"Most people know these things, but they get careless," according to Detective Captain Raymond Nagel of the White Plains, New York, police department.

Fortify the door and locks. Dead bolts work best at deterring the 50% of break-ins that happen through the front or rear door. Unfortunately, many contractors build houses with esthetics and cost in mind rather than your security. Trading up from a simple key-in-lock knob to a substantial auxiliary lock will run you from $20 to $220, depending on the lock you choose. "But even the most rugged-looking locks could be defeated by a swift kick or two unless some reinforcement was added to the door or the doorjamb," according to *Consumer Reports*. The piece that's most vulnerable is the strike plate, which attaches to the doorjamb to receive the lock's latch. You can strengthen it by replacing two-inch screws with three-inch screws, or by buying a heavy-duty strike plate or door reinforcer.

Secure sliding glass doors with a wooden pole in the inside track to keep potential intruders from forcing the door open. If your garage is attached to the house, lock the inside door. Burglars may pry open the garage door or fool your automatic opener with a remote of their own.

Do the windows. *Consumer Reports* has found that most window locks available at hardware stores can be foiled with a crowbar or knife. Fear not: Secure your windows simply and cheaply by "pinning" the upper and lower sashes together. Just drill a hole through the sashes where they overlap, and insert a strong nail or eyebolt from the inside. If you want to feel secure while your windows are ajar, drill a second set of holes when the window is open (not so wide that there's no point in locking it), and insert a nail or eyebolt there.

The Alarming Reality

A burglar alarm can reduce the likelihood that your house will be robbed, perhaps by as much as 80%, according to *Consumer Reports,* if you choose a reliable system and use it scrupulously. However, alarms have their downsides: Most cost a bundle; they are not always reliable; they generate false alarms that try your neighbors' patience and waste law-enforcement time; and, more than likely, they are inconvenient to those they're meant to protect. People may also develop a false sense of security once a system's installed. Don't forget: No alarm is burglar-proof.

Professionally installed systems for a mid-sized home can cost anywhere from $800 to $2,000 and beyond. When Michael G. and his family (of Phoenix, Arizona) looked into replacing the security system that came with their new home, they invited four salespeople (and *20/20*'s hidden camera) into their home to assess how safe they were and how much it would cost to tighten up the house's security. The assessments ranged from "It's just a cheap little system" to "You've got

> "**T**he golden rule of private security companies is to make a profit."
>
> —HELEN MAXWELL,
> author of *Home Safe Home*

a good working system." The estimates ranged from $99 to $3,065.

What do all those bucks buy? The basic system usually includes some combination of the following: alarms on outside doors and windows, motion sensors in key areas (like the main stairway), a blaring horn and/or bright lights, and a connection to a central station, where tripped alarms ring so that they can be routed to police. Most systems also include a "call-back" function in which the company calls you before calling the cops in case of a false alarm. If you answer the phone and give a preset password or code, the police aren't notified. Many companies now offer a radio wave or cellular connection to their monitoring stations as a basic service—so that the clever thief who cuts your phone line is foiled and the call still goes through. Many communities require alarm licenses or registration with the police.

Selecting a Security System

Home security is a $13 billion industry, and the more "advanced" security they can push on you, the higher their profit. A reputable company, however, will offer what's best for *your* home, not Bill Gates'. Check various companies out with the Better Business Bureau, with friends who have used them, or with the National Burglar and Fire Alarm Association (see

MAN'S BEST FRIEND

For a trusty, low-tech security system, get a noisy dog. Burglars don't worry about getting bitten; they worry about getting caught. A barking dog may grab your attention if you are home, or your neighbors' if you aren't. "Home alarms really do work," says one New Jersey police chief. "But so does a dog with a real loud yapper." To burglars, the dog's bark is literally worse than the bite.

HELP at the end of this chapter). They can give you guidance on which companies to avoid.

Ask several companies for itemized, written estimates. When determining the best price, take into account not only the initial investment but also any monthly service charges or routine maintenance charges. Become familiar with equipment terms, and don't be afraid to ask questions. Compare warranties. And before you choose a system, ask friends or the company for references. Ask previous customers whether they are satisfied with the system and the service.

Helen Maxwell, author of *Home Safe Home,* for one, is certainly not satisfied. She relied on a high-priced, high-tech system. A robber slipped by it and held a gun to her temple as he forced her to walk around her home, pointing out where she kept her engagement ring, her wedding ring, and various other valuables.

WHAT TO WATCH OUT FOR

The Shortest Distance Between Two Points?

Although there are something like 14,000 home security companies in the country, there are far fewer dispatching centers.

So, if something sets off the alarm in your house in Pittsburgh, the alarm may very well be routed through Kansas or Louisiana on its way to the police precinct down the block. "Not a problem," says Dan S., a Washington, DC, lawyer whose alarm is set to summon the local police, after they hear about it from a central dispatching center rather than directly. "The one time we've needed them, they were here within 10 minutes."

Sounds fine, as long as you know this is the arrangement. Many salespeople will tell you about the relay method of delivering an emergency message only if you ask explicitly. One salesman told Michael G. of Phoenix that an emergency box labeled "local monitor" meant the signal went directly to the local police, when in fact it didn't.

Leasing vs. Buying

Some companies sell leased systems. You pay for installation and a monthly usage charge to borrow use of the system for a set period of time. You may pay extra if you want a hookup to a central monitoring station. Some companies offer "free" installation when you lease the basic package but they often make up for the discount with higher monthly fees. Your house might also require more alarm coverage then the basic package provides.

Be sure to compare *total* costs of different systems, not just month-by-month fees or free installation claims. One Long Island, New York, company offers to install its basic package for free when you sign up for five years of service and pay around $23 per month in monitoring fees—a total cost of $1,380, if you don't buy any extras. Another company in the area offers the same package, but for $780 less if you pay for it up front.

"While a free alarm system sounds wonderful, by the time you get done, it can become quite costly," says Janice Grossi of the Long Island Better Business Bureau. It may make sense to lease if you don't plan to stay put for long. However, if you plan to live in the house for more than two or three years, leasing most often costs more than buying.

False Alarm Fines

You know the neighbor whose alarm seems to never keep quiet? The one that always sets the block's dogs barking just when you're dropping off to sleep? About 90% of all alarms are false, according to the NBFAA, and police departments don't have the resources to answer every one. "Call-backs" from monitoring stations help to keep po-lice off unnecessary investigations, but many communities have taken deterring false alarms one step further—by fining or punishing repeat offenders.

In Nassau County, New York, if police are called by your alarm three times within three months you get a warning; after five times they suspend your alarm license for 90 days. In Fairfield, New Jersey, two's the limit. At three you're charged $50; at four, $100; five or more cost you $150 each. Chronic alarm abusers might find their alarms go unanswered by the monitoring station. (Police, of course, will still respond to a 911 call no matter how many false alarms you've had.) Alarms that are canceled by call-backs don't count as false and won't be held against you.

Double-Cylinder Dead Bolts

These locks require a key to open them whether you're inside or out. Security experts often recommend them for doors that have windows in or around them that may tempt an intruder to smash the glass, reach in, and flick the single cylinder lock open.

But think twice. You may just as easily find yourself locked in as intruders find themselves locked out; in a fire or another emergency, this can mean losing vital time. You can avoid this problem by choosing a double-cylinder dead bolt that only allows you to remove the inside key if the lock is unlocked. Better yet, since a burglar won't necessarily recognize that smashing the window is futile, use the double dead bolt and keep the inside key far enough away

GOING ON VACATION?

Going on vacation means you have to be extra careful about home security, and that means more than just setting the alarm. Let your neighbors know how long you'll be gone so they can keep an eye on your house. Cancel mail and newspaper delivery. Better yet, have someone reliable stop by and collect them for you.

Install timers to turn your lights on and off. If you're going on vacation and not taking Fluffy or Rex, consider using a sitter. The best pet-sitting services will not only feed and walk your animal but also bring in mail and newspapers, turn on lights, and make it known to prowlers that someone is around. Check your answering machine or voice mail by remote—a full voice mailbox is an obvious clue that you may be gone for long.

Hire someone to mow your lawn in summer or shovel your drive in winter. If you have particularly friendly neighbors, ask them to park their car once or twice in your driveway. Anything that gives the appearance of comings and goings will help keep burglars away and make sure you aren't called home from your vacation early.

---

from the door so that a burglar can't reach it, but close enough for you to get it quickly in an emergency. And make sure everyone in the house knows where to find it.

THE $MARTER CONSUMER

Call the police before a burglar calls on you. Most police departments have crime-prevention units that will come to your house to do a free security audit. They'll tell you where your house is vulnerable and how to improve security. The police can also give you an idea of how common crime is in your neighborhood and when it's most likely to occur.

See the light. For inside lights, buy timers that turn lamps on and off. While you're at it, put the radio on a timer to create some noise that will suggest activity even when you're not at home. For outside lights, get photosensitive floodlights that turn themselves on and off in response to dusk and dawn.

Post plastic security system signs in your yard and decals on your windows. Even if you don't have the system to back them up, these lend the appearance of high-tech security and are a great deterrent. The idea is that burglars will see them, decide it's not worth taking the risk of an alarm going off, and move on.

Check the contract. If you lease a system, make sure the contract period—usually two or three years—is appropriate for you. If you have a lease for longer than you plan to live in your house, you may be required to pay the remaining balance. Most companies will allow you to transfer the lease to the people moving in, and some will remove and reinstall the system for you if you're moving to an area they serve.

Go wireless. Wireless alarm systems offer many of the same advantages as hard-wired systems, but at a quarter—or even a tenth—of the price. With such a wireless system, you mount battery-operated sensors on door and window frames. Then you mount the central control console someplace convenient. No wires are needed: Radio transmitters embedded in the sensors communicate with the control console. You just need to be sure the console is close enough to pick up the sensors' signals. You program the console, usually, with a tool as simple as a bent paper clip.

Another advantage of wireless systems: They are portable, which means you can take them with you if and when you move, remount them, and use them again. Drawbacks: their batteries will run out, and most do not give you the option of hooking into a network that will alert the police or a dispatching center in the event something—or somebody—trips the alarm.

Security upgrades can equal savings. Ask your insurance company if you can get a discount on your homeowner's policy by upgrading your home's security. Installation of dead bolts or local or monitored burglar alarms could save you 2% to 25% off your premiums.

Check local ordinances to see if you must register your system and to find out about false alarm limits. Some communities require alarms that will shut off after a brief period. (In this event, look for systems that reset after shutting off.) If you're plagued by false alarms, demand that the security company check all connections.

H E L P

- **Read Home Safe Home,** by Helen Maxwell (New Horizon Publishing, 1992). $13.95. To order, call (800) 462-6420.

- **Read Safe Homes, Safe Neighborhoods:** Stopping Crime Where You Live, $14.95 (Nolo Press, 1993). To order, call (510) 549-1976.

- **For more information on reputable** home security companies, contact the National Burglar and Fire Alarm Association, 7101 Wisconsin Avenue, Suite 901, Bethesda, MD 20814. NBFAA also has a useful brochure: "Safe and Sound," and a helpful Web site: www.alarm.org.

- **Write for the free brochure Home** Security Basics, distributed by the Insurance Information Institute, 110 William Street, New York, NY 10038 (212) 669-9200. It describes all the things you can do to make your home more secure, short of buying an alarm system.

FURNITURE AND MATTRESSES

Don't Take Abuse Lying Down

N eil D. went to See Ltd. in New York City and picked out a glass table. See Ltd. told him the table was in stock and available for delivery anytime; he just had to let the store know two weeks in advance. He paid $1,700 in full, plus $100 for delivery.

When Neil called See Ltd. two months later to say he was ready for the table, the vendor said the table was no longer available and had to be reordered from the manufacturer in Italy. See Ltd. offered delivery in about six weeks. Neil said this was unacceptable and asked for a refund. The vendor persuaded him to take a loaner table and wait out the shipment. Six weeks later, Neil called to ask where the table was and was assured, "The table is definitely on the boat." He could expect it in three weeks. When the time came, he called again and this time was told the table had not yet left Italy and possibly was no longer being manufactured.

Nearly five months after full payment, Neil didn't have his table, and he demanded a refund. The vendor refused. When Neil complained to the NYC Department of Consumer Affairs, the vendor quickly delivered the table—and threw in an extra table base.

THE BASICS

N eil's experience is all too typical of the problems you might encounter buying furniture, carpets, and mattresses. It's hard to know what's a fair price, and the brands are not generally fixtures of daily American life, like Levi's or Coca-Cola. Plus, once you've made up your mind, you'll often have to wait weeks before you can begin to enjoy your new purchase. And that's if everything works out right.

It's best to get comfortable with your rights in order to avoid finding yourself uncomfortable with your purchase. Federal Trade Commission (FTC) Rules and Guides for the Household Furniture Industry require prominent, affirmative disclosure of various "material facts which, if known to prospective purchasers, would influence their decision of whether or not to purchase." These facts include the use of veneer construction, plastic with simulated wood appearance, simulated finish or grain design, imitation leather, and the national origin and style of furniture.

For instance, all wood or wood-like furniture and ads promoting it must be clearly labeled with a description of the true composition of the piece or a statement that the material is not what it appears to be. Acceptable (if factually correct): "maple solids and veneers" or "cherry-grained maple." Unacceptable: "molded components" or "walnut finish." Similar guidelines apply to leather and imitation leather, upholstery content, and national origin and style of furniture. "Danish" and "Italian" cannot be used without qualification unless the furniture was manufactured in Denmark or Italy. (These rules do not apply to mattresses or rugs.)

The basic problem with buying any furniture or mattress: because these are such infrequent purchases, unlike milk or steak, consumers are far less able to discern value. And as the following tricks-of-the-trade show, retailers know it.

WHAT TO WATCH OUT FOR

The Furniture Game

Lourdes G. bought a white lacquer bedroom set from Seaman's Furniture for $3,000. But after only seven months, the finish began peeling off. The manufacturer at first blamed Pledge, which Ms. G. used to dust her furniture, but eventually exchanged the shoddy set for a new one.

Besides endless waits for delivery and furniture that falls apart soon after delivery, typical problems include delivery of damaged furniture, delivery of the wrong furniture or carpet, and flat-out non-delivery. Is it any wonder, then, that surveys show people hate to shop for furniture, or that year after year furniture stores rank as one of the top five complaint categories, according to the Federal Trade Association and consumer affairs offices around the country?

Look beyond the surface. While problems are most likely to occur at high-volume stores that sell less expensive merchandise, "furniture games" exist throughout the industry. Don't make choices based only on style and color. Inspect the joints on the underside of tables, chairs, and dressers. Look for quality: Furniture constructed with screws will be more durable than furniture constructed with nails. Look for smooth joints, with no glue or fasteners sticking out. Try all moving parts, such as drawers and table leaves, to be sure they operate properly and smoothly.

The torture of waiting. Once you've made your selection, it's the nature of the business that you'll most often have to wait; usually the retailer must order the piece from the manufacturer. A wait of four to eight weeks is customary. The vendor should give you a realis-

CARPETING CAVEATS

When buying a carpet or a rug, many people neglect to factor in how much foot traffic it will have to bear. Carpet on the stairs will clearly get more wear than carpet in a guest room. Buy accordingly. For dens and other areas that get a lot of use, it pays to spend more on durable carpets made of high-quality fibers. (However, stick with dense pile of medium or short height, which holds up better than high-pile carpet, which tends to get matted down.) You can probably get away with slightly lower quality in bedrooms. When judging quality, the Better Business Bureau suggests keeping an eye out for the following characteristics:

Density. The denser the carpet, the higher the quality, generally. Compare carpet samples of the same fiber type by bending the carpet and noting how close the individual tufts are to one another and how much of the backing is exposed. Press on the carpet to see how easy it is to make contact with the backing.

Twist. In higher-quality carpets, the individual yarn will have "neat, tight, and well-defined" cut ends.

Heat-setting. Read the label or ask the salesperson whether the yarn has been heat-set, which locks the twist into yarns and helps carpet stand up to use and cleaning.

---

tic idea of when you can expect your furniture and keep you posted about any delays. It's not sufficient for you to be told "next week" week in and week out. One couple complained to local consumer officials after *five months* of the retailer telling them repeatedly that their dinette set would arrive "next week." (Given the prevalence of delays, it makes sense to hang on to your old furniture until the new stuff has arrived.)

In New York City, for instance, retailers are obliged by law to give you a delivery date (or a reasonable range of dates). If a delay arises, you must be notified in writing and given a new delivery date. If the date passes without explanation and you have not received your furniture, you can ask to get your money back, choose replacement merchandise, or agree to a new delivery date. The retailer must accommodate you on whichever option you choose.

Return policies vary from one store to another and even from one consumer to another. Retailers allow regular customers more leeway. But to be safe, you should inquire as to the return—or exchange—policy before you buy. What happens if the item arrives damaged? What happens if you hate the upholstery after all? What happens when your furniture shows up and it cannot fit into the elevator or through the doorways of your home? In this last instance, you may very well be responsible: Prudence calls for measuring stairways, doorways, and elevators *before* you buy, or arranging for the item to be assembled in your home.

Think twice about "rent-to-own" offers. If money is tight and you want instant comfort, you may be tempted. However, just remember Irene M. She told the House Banking Committee in 1993 that she paid $34.98 a week to rent a couch, chair, dining table, and four chairs. When she finally said enough was enough, she had paid $2,500 for merchandise that would have cost $1,000 to buy outright. And according to the rental company, she owed still more.

There are laws in 31 states—including Iowa, Maryland, Michigan, Minnesota, Nebraska, New York, Ohio, Pennsylvania, South Carolina, and Virginia—that protect rent-to-own consumers to varying degrees from such outrageous practices. But the laws aren't enough. An investigation of rent-to-own businesses in Pennsylvania found that the effective annual interest rate ranged from 82% to 265%, in gross violation of the state's interest

rate ceiling of 18%. Most contracts do not even specify a retail price or "principal" against which to determine how much interest you will pay, making it nearly impossible to test the interest rate against a ceiling that may exist in your state. (See "Lay-Away and Rent-to-Own," page 630, for more information.)

Permanent Sales

The final scam to watch out for is one of the all-time oxymorons—the "permanent sale." In an investigation of Levitz Furniture Corp., the nation's largest specialty furniture chain, an investigator in Missouri walked through Levitz stores a few times a month and found that "sale" prices never changed. Investigator Bennett Rushkoff, for example, found an advertised Glen Burn sofa in August 1994 for $699.99—$300 off the "regular" price of $999.99—and the "sale" price stayed that way through March 1995!

Because it clearly misleads consumers to believe that a regular price is a sale price, Levitz was forced to pay a $1.12 million fine to eight states. (Also, Levitz was no longer allowed to falsely advertise that consumers must hurriedly act within a specified time period to take advantage of sales prices, and it must disclose the beginning and ending date of a sale.)

> "**E**xpect a delay—don't get rid of your old bed before your new one arrives or you may find yourself sleeping on the floor."
>
> —BESS MYERSON,
> former Consumer Affairs
> Commissioner
> of New York City

In response to the Levitz case, some states began defining what constitutes a "regular" price: in Wisconsin, for example, it's a real sale if the higher, regular price was actually offered within that "trade area" for at least four weeks.

Mattress Mania

Mattress manufacturers and retailers are in bed together, and it's quite a cozy relationship. With hundreds of permutations of mattress coils, ticking (cover material), padding, and brand names, the potential for consumer confusion is a retailer's sweet dream—and a consumer's nightmare.

One retailer may sell scores of models made by the same manufacturer that are available nowhere else, each with subtle and often meaningless differences in specifications—370 coils instead of 380, or ticking of blue clouds instead of pink flowers, for example. Take one firm called Hillside Bedding: You can buy a Sealy Posturepedic Comfort, Posturepedic Deluxe, Posturepedic Extra Plush, Posturepedic Luxury Firm, Posturepedic Firm Premium, Posturepedic Premium Firm, Posturepedic Royal Firm, Posturepedic Super Plush, Posturepedic Premium Collection I, and on and on. These are just some of the 65 different Sealy mattress models—23 with the word "posturepedic" in their name—for sale at *one* store. It's difficult to comparison-shop within one store, and since only Hillside stocks these models, it's impossible to comparison-shop among stores.

It's a little unfair to pick on Sealy and Hillside, since the same kind of mind-bending model proliferation afflicts their major competitors—the network includes manufacturers like Simmons, Serta, Stearns and Foster, and major national department stores ranging from Macy's to your regional chain. One salesman openly admitted to an undercover investigator posing as a mattress shopper that the purpose of the maddening multitude of mattress models is "to stop people from shopping for price."

To add to the confusion, salespeople routinely daze consumers with conflicting claims about the superiority of one model or one type of mattress construction over another. They can get positively nasty when consumers try to write down prices and specifications in an attempt to compare one product to another. In fact, the differences among many mattresses may be more cosmetic than real. Generally speaking, the more coils the better, but a mattress's coils are only as good as the steel from which they are made. If the 380-coil mattress uses 10-gauge instead of 12-gauge steel (lower gauges are stiffer and provide more support), it could very well be better than a 400-coil mattress made with 12-gauge steel coils. The retailer selling the 400-coil mattress says it's better; the retailer selling the 380-coil mattress naturally disagrees. Who is to be believed?

In any event, mattress tastes have been shifting. "Ten years ago, 90% of those sold were hard as rock," according to David Wachendorfer, a general manager of Mattress Giant

No Magic Carpet Ride

Beware of carpet cleaning scams. Ads and promotional flyers may hawk unbelievably low prices—any two rooms for $24.95, for example—and, in fact, you can't believe the ads. Limitations, such as that the "any" two rooms measure less than 200 square feet per room, (10 x 20 feet), can effectively cancel the "bargain."

Stores in St. Louis. "Today, there are more than 50 models in our stores and of those, 19 are hard. The rest have pillow and plush tops with lots of padding." The most popular type of mattress now is the innerspring, with springs and coils sandwiched between layers of cushioning in a fabric case. Springless mattresses, which are replacing the waterbeds of the '60s and '70s, are either air mattresses with adjustable air chambers or solid, latex rubber mattresses, which are soft but more than double the price of standard bedding.

None of these practices or taste shifts would matter so much if comparable mattresses cost about the same everywhere. But in a series of shopping expeditions undertaken by NYC Department of Consumer Affairs investigators, the price for what was claimed to be the top-of-the-line, queen-size Simmons mattress set ranged from $900 at one store to nearly $2,100 at another. Similarly, the top-of-the-line Stearns and Foster set ranged from $730 to $2,020. Is the top-of-the-line mattress at one store comparable to that at another store? There's no clear answer, since information is so hard to come by.

THE $MARTER CONSUMER

Furniture and Carpets

Know what you want. Before you go shopping, make a list of what you're looking for, measure existing furniture or the space into which new furniture will go, and measure the access routes and entry points in your home, to be sure that what you pick can fit inside. Decide how much you can spend, and set priorities in case you can't afford everything. When you go shopping, take your list, a tape measure, and samples of any carpeting, wallpaper, paint, and upholstery you already have or chose earlier.

To avoid having the rug pulled out from under you in the store, measure the room(s) you wish to cover *before* you shop. If you're buying broadloom or stair runners, you'll probably have to buy a little more carpeting than you think to allow for installation and fitting.

Check the store's reputation before you buy. The NYC Consumer Affairs Department took legal action against one Queens store after 20 people complained it failed to deliver merchandise, kept consumers waiting unnecessarily when it failed to cancel delivery appointments, and delivered damaged or incomplete sets of furniture. It turned out that the NYC Better Business Bureau had heard from another two dozen irate consumers.

Be fire smart. Ask if the item is flame-retardant. The Consumer Product Safety Commission (CPSC) has a mandatory standard for floor coverings; the CPSC "standard" for furniture is voluntary but may soon become mandatory, given recent National Association of State Fire Marshals petitions.

Before you buy furniture, check the fabric label. It should give you cleaning instructions and information about any anti-stain treatments the manufacturer has already applied. Even though the retailer may try to sell you a fabric treatment to resist stains, don't buy any additional treatment unless you need it—and if the retailer offers a warranty on the finish, make sure you understand exactly what it covers and what it doesn't.

Get an itemized receipt that breaks down every detail, no matter how small: for furniture, make and model number (be sure it's the same model you saw on the showroom floor); number of chairs or end tables; a detailed description, giving the exact dimensions, color, pattern, style, materials (wood, plastic, leather, vinyl), finish, upholstery, and any optional details; total price, including delivery, credit terms, and any additional charges; and a delivery date as close to an actual date as

possible ("as soon as it comes in" is unacceptable; "four to six weeks" is okay; a specific date is best).

For carpets, make sure your receipt includes exact dimensions and price per yard for the carpet and any padding; the installation fee; the color (with code number); the type of weave and fiber by weight; a statement that the carpet passes federal flammability standards; and a guarantee of durability, resistance to shrinkage, and that dyes will not run.

The receipt will help prevent the merchant from substituting lower-quality merchandise, and will protect you if she tries to do so anyway.

Give as small a deposit as you can, with the balance payable on delivery. Do not pay in full unless you walk out with (or take delivery of) the goods.

Everything looks different in the store. If possible, bring a sample of the carpet or upholstery home with you. Don't throw the sample out until your carpet or sofa has been delivered and you have compared the sample to your new purchase to be sure you got what you wanted— and what you paid for.

Stay away from rent-to-own. Until disclosure requirements improve or rent-to-own transactions are regulated as installment purchases and are therefore subject to the interest rate ceilings on such transactions, it's probably best to find another way to get what you need. Just about any other payment scheme works out to be cheaper, unless you need to rent the item for a very short time.

Be firm about delivery dates. Don't let the vendor string you along with the "next week" excuse. If the estimated delivery date passes, check into the situation. If you get the runaround, complain to your local consumer office or BBB.

Double-check your delivery. Before you sign anything and show the movers out, carefully inspect your new rug or furniture. Look for defects, scratches, missing items, or missing parts. Compare fabric or rug swatches. If you aren't satisfied, have the delivery person take it back; if he or she refuses, do not sign the bill until the person writes on the bill that the item is damaged—and have him or her sign the bill, too. Then contact the store immediately. If the delivery person has to leave before you've had a chance to look at the furniture, write "subject to inspection" on the bill of sale before you sign.

Do it yourself. Stores like Ikea and Sears sell affordable furniture that you assemble yourself. Industry analysts estimate that you can save 25% to 50% by putting the pieces together themselves. Buying unassembled furniture means immediate gratification, too—usually you can walk out of the store with your purchase, rather than having to wait weeks for delivery.

Mattresses

Try the mattress out in the store. Since nearly every mattress sold is "firm," "ultra firm," "extra firm," or some other version of firm, these names and claims are meaningless.

Bring your mate. If you share your bed with someone else, shop together. Don't be shy about lying on the bed in your regular sleep position. Considering that you'll be spending a fourth of your life on this product, what's a little humiliation? So ask yourself—is it comfortable? Is it roomy enough?

The skinny on thickness. The thicker the mattress, the more comfortable it will be. Anything less than 7 inches between the top and bottom seams will provide less support. Keep in mind, though, that it can be harder to find sheets for extra-thick (9- and 10-inch) mattresses than for standard mattress sizes.

Reputation counts. Buy your bed in a reputable shop—one that's been around awhile—and get a written guarantee that the mattress is exchangeable if you find it uncomfortable or if it loses its shape too quickly.

HELP

- **Report complaints to your local** Better Business Bureau or local consumer official. You can also consult your local BBB to check the reliability of furniture stores before you buy.

- **For a guide to buying mattresses** and specific brands, see the March 1997 issue of *Consumer Reports*.

- **For information on how to tell** good furniture from bad, visit the Web site Home Furnishing Netquarters at www.homefurnish.com and go to the Information Center's Buyers Guide.

CHAPTER 18

PETS

Pet Peeves

Americans have a love–hate relationship with domestic animals. On the one hand, there are more pets per family in the United States than anywhere else in the world, and more than 60% of American households include at least one pet. Americans own 62 million cats, 53 million dogs, 15 million birds, 10.5 million other small animals, and 95 million fish. The pet-service industry has grown into a $32-billion-a-year business. Each year, we spend $9 billion on pet food alone (50% more than we spend on baby food) and over $1 billion on drugs and vaccines for cats and dogs. Little pets are big business.

Yet we often treat animals as mere commodities that can be produced factory-style in so-called "puppy mills" and discarded when we need to move on with our lives. Too many Americans go through pets the way Italy goes through governments. The Humane Society of the United States (HSUS) estimates that 12 million cats and dogs are left in shelters each year, of which more than 8 million are euthanized. According to the *St. Petersburg Times,* "each year an estimated 20 million to 30 million dogs and cats are killed because their owners have lost them, don't want them, or cannot afford their upkeep."

You may be tempted to run into a pet store and take home a cute and lovable furry, feathered, or finny friend. But adopting a pet means taking on important responsibilities and making a long-term commitment. Before you take the plunge, take the time to think it through—both for your sake and that of your future companion.

THE BASICS

Should You Adopt a Pet?

A successful human/animal relationship offers tremendous rewards. Pets make wonderful companions; they bring fun, joy, comfort, and unqualified love. Recent studies show, for instance, that pets actually can bring down blood pressure, reduce heart disease, and provide stimulation for the old and the young that friends and family cannot.

But pets require daily attention and care. So avoid impulse buying and surprises. (The American Society for the Prevention of Cruelty to Animals [ASPCA] maintains a "no surprises" adoption policy.) After the

CAN YOU AFFORD FIDO?

Keep in mind that raising an animal costs real money. It's not as much as a car or college tuition for the kids, but caring for a dog during an average 11-year lifespan costs in the range of $12,000 to $13,000, according to the American Kennel Club, while the cost of caring for a cat over a 15-year lifespan averages $9,000.

release of Disney's remake of the movie *101 Dalmatians* in late 1996, countless children successfully lobbied Santa Claus to drop off the real thing under the Christmas tree, despite warnings from animal activists. Many families quickly discovered, however, that while Dalmatians are cute and fun in the movie, they can be quite aggressive in real life, especially with children. As a result, some shelters report that in the ensuing months, the number of abandoned dogs more than doubled.

Before bringing home some cuddly critter, talk it through with your family and figure out who'll be responsible—who will feed, walk, and play with the pet, and ensure that the pet receives proper veterinary care for the next *decade*. If it's a pet for a young child, make sure a willing adult can step up to the plate if the child can't swing it. If you're on the road often, maybe you shouldn't have a pet at all.

After deciding that you're ready to bring home an animal, figure out what pet is right for you. One way is to do as actress Ann Miller did in *Easter Parade*—get the right puppy to match your outfit. We don't recommend it. Instead, get a companion that's compatible with your lifestyle. If you live in a 300-square-foot studio apartment, don't get a 100-pound German Shepherd who needs a lot of exercise. If you have young children, avoid puppies or kittens who may snap or bite at a curious toddler's advances. If you live with a frail older person, stay away from large, energetic, demonstrative dogs.

Can You Adopt a Pet?

There is a growing battle between pet-owner and anti-pet people in co-ops and condominiums that is becoming the modern equivalent of the rancher-farmer battles of a century ago.

Many senior citizens who urgently need the companionship of pets are being told by the governing boards of their buildings that pet ownership violates the rules of their co-op or condominium. In a recent case, a widow named Natare N. bought a unit in the garden apartment complex of Lakeside Village in Culver City, California. Six months later, she was told to get rid of her three cats because she was violating the association's rules limiting pet ownership to two domestic fish in a bowl or two birds in a cage. She claimed that the rules were unreasonable, since her indoor cats weren't bothering anybody.

The State Court of Appeals agreed, saying that the association had to demonstrate that the pets really did injure the living conditions or property values of other owners for the regulation to be reasonable. But in September 1994, the California Supreme Court ruled 6 to 1 that homeowner groups *can* flatly ban cats and other pets. Ms. N., having spent $50,000 in legal fees, put her pets and principles above her residence. She left Lakeside Village rather than leave her cats. "They are like my children," she explained. "They give me unconditional love, and I would rather have them than a husband or boyfriend at this point."

Where Should You Get Your Pet?

Pets come in all species, shapes, sizes, personalities—and prices. Dogs, for instance, can range from "free" to $5,000. Your first stop should be the pound—the Humane Society, the ASPCA, etc. Look in the Yellow Pages under "Animal Shelters." Other than a giveaway, it's the cheapest alternative and, except in shelters that can't afford it, the animals come neutered, with shots, fit for adoption, and healthy, even if they're a little scruffy. The ASPCA, for instance, charges a $55 processing fee for dogs and $45 for cats, which covers spaying or neutering, rabies and other shots, as well as a future visit to an ASPCA veterinarian.

If you're looking for a purebred or pedigreed pet, the American Kennel Club (AKC) and Cat Fanciers' Association are good sources of information. The AKC in particular can suggest which breeds are best for small children or small spaces, and direct you to a reputable breeder. (To contact either group, see the **HELP** section at the end of the chapter.)

Some pet stores and variety stores sell animals as well, but for cats and dogs, pet stores are likely to be expensive—two to three times higher than a reputable breeder—and not always reliable. Many get their animals from puppy mills, where purebred dogs are raised in horrendous conditions and are often inbred and genetically defective. When the California legislature looked at the problem some years ago, it found that over one-half of puppies from out-of-state sold in California pet stores were diseased or incubating a disease.

Doctor's Bills

Here's the mean amount that a pet-owning household spends on trips to the vet each year.

Dogs	$131.84
Cats	$79.75
Birds	$34.24
Horses	$163.23
Other pets	$9.05

Source: *Journal of American Veterinary Medical Association*

What If There's Something Wrong With Your Pet?

In 1987, Eugene A. Migliaro Jr., a Connecticut legislator, bought a

Miniature Schnauzer puppy for his granddaughter. Within days, the puppy fell deathly sick, much to the little girl's distress. Migliaro did not just get mad—he got even, with a vengeance. He took the puppy to a vet, who was able to restore her good health. Then he sued the pet store that had sold him the sick puppy and won $535 in damages. And he pushed through the state legislature one of the first "pet lemon laws" in the country.

You should have no such problem if you adopt from a shelter. Most screen their animals for health and temperament problems and offer only animals they deem fit for adoption. If you run into a problem, the shelter will probably try to cure the animal (if it has a clinic on location), give you a refund, or allow you to adopt another pet.

Things get trickier if you got your animal from a breeder or a pet store. In recent years, Connecticut has been joined by a growing number of states—including Florida, Massachusetts, Minnesota, New Jersey, New York, Pennsylvania, and Virginia—in enacting various "pet lemon laws" that offer some degree of protection if the pet you bought turns out to be sick or deformed. These laws typically cover only cats and dogs, and vary in their details, though not in their general terms. In New York, for instance, a consumer can bring a new pet to a vet-

erinarian within 14 days of purchase. If the vet finds the animal ill or deformed, the dealer is required to do any of three things, at the consumer's choice:

- Take back the animal and refund the cost of the pet and veterinary expenses;
- Exchange the pet and cover veterinary expenses; or
- Reimburse the consumer for veterinary expenses. (Reimbursement is generally limited to the purchase price of the animal.)

In New Jersey, the discovery period is six months. Contact your state's department of agriculture, attorney general, local consumer office, or ASPCA for a copy of the law.

If your state does not offer such protection (and even if it does), you should make sure to sign a written contract with the dealer laying out some key provisions:

- *Health history.* The contract should describe any health problems that the pet has had and guarantee that the problems have been cured and that the pet is now in good health. The seller's warranty on that last point should bring you not only peace of mind but also precious ammunition if things turn litigious down the road. If you're acquiring a cat, find out if he or she has had a feline leukemia test.

> "*The problem is that the person who pays the bill and makes the decisions is not the customer.*"
>
> —JIM KRACK,
> Executive Director, American
> Boarding Kennels Association

■ *Vaccinations.* The contract should list all the vaccinations the pet has received and when. You may also want similar documentation from the vet who administered the vaccinations—you may not be able to get your animals licensed, or take them traveling with you, without such records.

Other information may need to be included, depending on the circumstances. If you are getting your pet from a pet store, make sure the contract states where it came from. If it's from the Midwest, it may well be coming from a puppy mill. If the pet requires a certain type of training—most frequently obedience—the contract should disclose whether such training was provided. If you're buying a purebred, get the animal's pedigree. Finally, if you're getting any explicit promise from the seller—for instance, that your dog has a certain lineage or certain attributes, or that it has been specifically trained to bring the owner breakfast in bed on the weekend—any such "express warranty," as such promises are known in legalese—should be spelled out in the contract. As always, when you sign a contract before buying a pet, make sure you're not signing your rights away.

Also, under standard contract law, merchants in every state must sell goods that are "fit and merchantable"—whether parrots, poodles, or parkas—and most states have strong, general consumer laws that apply to pets. If you can't obtain satisfaction from the merchant, write or call your local consumer agency, state licensing agency, at-torney general, ASPCA, or Better Business Bureau for help. If all else fails, you may have to take the store to court.

Caring for Your Pet

The best health care for pets, as for humans, is prevention. Ask your veterinarian for advice about diet and other pet health information. In addition, both the ASPCA and the HSUS put out helpful literature regarding animal care. Take Fifi or Felix to the vet once a year for a check-up and required shots.

A few tips about selecting the right vet: Get recommendations from friends, neighbors, or local humane societies; check the vet's record with the state licensing agency; visit the premises; ask for an AVMA accreditation; and ask about services, hours, and fees.

Millions of cats and dogs are killed each year due to overpopulation. To be part of the solution, not the problem, and for your pets' health, get them spayed or neutered, usually shortly after their seventh month. If Malthusian concerns don't move you, consider the following: according to John Berg, a veterinarian at Tufts University, female cats spayed before their first or second heat cycle face a dramatically reduced risk of mammary cancer and are less vulnerable to a range of serious uterine infections.

License your dog in accordance with local laws (cats may also require a license) and make sure your pet wears a collar and ID tag at all times. Always keep your dog leashed when outdoors in an unfenced area.

WHAT WILL THEY THINK OF NEXT?

There has been an explosion of services in the pet industry in recent years. As Atlanta reporter Alan Paterneau noted in 1993, "Furry companions from purebreds to scruffy mutts are reveling in a plush lifestyle unknown to their ancestors." The reason, many experts believe, is that many Americans, living alone or without children, now consider their animal companion a full-fledged family member.

You can now send Rover to a luxury pet hotel in Bedford, Texas, with $21.95-a-night suites and a kitchen preparing hot meals for its furry guests. Kamer Canine College in North Hollywood, California, offers an eight-week acting class for Lassie wannabes, and Animal Behavior Consultants in Brooklyn offers therapy for dog phobia. And to make sure they're suitably dressed for the occasion, you may want to make a stop at Lick Your Chops, a pet accessory shop in Branford, Connecticut, that can outfit your pet with the appropriate item, be it a wedding gown or required bridesmaid dress, a bomber jacket or a fake fur. The Pet Set, a beauty salon in Atlanta, offers soothing oatmeal baths, whirlpool treatment, organic dip with citrus oil, and a full groom and cut. Here again, a healthy dose of skepticism may be warranted.

If You're Traveling . . .

The federal Animal Welfare Act sets requirements for the transportation of animals. For instance: Do not ship puppies or kittens under eight weeks old; provide a sturdy, well-ventilated container; ensure that your pet will be handled safely prior to departure; and, if you're planning to send Spot flying on an unusually long trip, don't assume that he too will get a cold drink and bag of peanuts on board—provide instructions and supplies for food and water.

In addition to these legal requirements, be aware that all airlines require a recent health certificate for your pet, and some ground carriers, like Amtrak, won't accept pets, even in a cage. Book your pet's flight well in advance and find out under what conditions he'll be traveling. Not all airplane cargo holds, for instance, are pressurized, properly ventilated, or temperature-controlled. It's a good idea to take your pet's vaccination records along for the trip—they may come in handy in an emergency. If you'll be staying in a hotel, find out the hotel's pet policy in advance. Many chains—including the Marriott, Holiday Inn, Days Inn, Howard Johnson, Residence Inn, Four Seasons,

Hilton, and Westin now accommodate four-legged "guests." At the Four Seasons in Washington, DC, the general manager writes a personal welcome note to each arriving animal. Room service then sends up a silver tray decorated with flowers and bearing dog or cat toys, Evian water, a porcelain bowl, and a selection of gourmet pet treats.

If you leave your animal at home when you travel, your best bet is to leave her with an experienced friend, neighbor, or relative. Your other options: a pet sitter or a kennel. On the plus side for pet sitters: Your pet will probably prefer staying at home with an animal lover than in a narrow kennel cage with no air-conditioning and little human contact. In addition, dogs in kennels may contract "kennel cough," a form of bronchitis that requires medical treatment. For referrals, contact the National Association of Pet Sitters or Pet Sitters International, two associations that offer accreditation, insurance, and animal educational conventions for members—and, hopefully, some measure of reliability for you. Good pet sitters should visit you (and their charge-to-be) and pester you with questions about your pet's special likes, dislikes, and needs (e.g., who's the vet). They should carry some form of insurance or a bond. And check their references.

But if your critter is more Cujo than Benji, or in need of constant medical care, you may opt for a kennel. Kennels run the gamut from detention camp to summer camp. A few tips: Visit several ahead of time (look for the exercise, confinement,

and food preparation areas); ask about health care arrangements and supervision; and inquire about possible add-on costs. The kennel *should* require proof of immunization. Call the Better Business Bureau for a background check. The American Boarding Kennel Association, the American Pet Boarding Association, your vet, or a friend are good sources for referrals.

To Insure or Not to Insure

We've come a long way since the days of *They Shoot Horses, Don't They,* when medical treatment for animals was practically non-existent and the only solution to an animal's illness or injury was to put the poor beast out of its misery—forever.

Animal health care has reached a level of sophistication and technological advance comparable to that available to humans, from computed tomography scans to chemotherapy. The bad news for pet owners is that costs, too, are comparable. As John Kelly, a veterinarian at Elliott Bay Animal Hospital in Seattle, explains, "Veterinary medicine, like human medicine, is becoming more expensive, with more diagnosis, ultrasound, special surgery, fiber-optic endoscopes, root canals, and orthodontic implants." A 1998 article in *The New York Times* mentioned a $4,000 experimental bone graft operation for a Great Dane with cancer; bills can exceed $10,000 for certain complicated procedures.

The market has responded to the quandary with a familiar solution:

health insurance. Veterinary Pet Insurance, based in Anaheim, California, and the leader in the field with 75,000 policyholders, offers policies ranging from the bare bones—Major Medical Plan 40, which provides up to $5,000 a year in coverage—to the top-of-the-line, VPI Advantage Plus, which provides up to $12,000 a year in coverage. As of this writing, it is available in 43 states and the District of Columbia.

Whether such policies are worth the premiums is open to debate. First of all, in addition to the overall annual cap, these policies also contain additional caps per incident—which are "generally so low that in effect you're paying for a discount on medical services rather than insurance coverage"—and, typically, deductibles and relatively high co-payments. Second, most policies do not cover routine care, such as vaccinations or dental cleanings, or pre-existing conditions. Additional limitations apply to recurring conditions. Finally, as Tina Kelley, a *New York Times* financial reporter, explains, "Because most pets cost less than most pet insurance deductibles, the financially minded person—heartless as it sounds to many pet lovers—might refuse heroic treatment if Rover gets run over."

For these reasons, the Consumer Federation of America and other consumer organizations discourage such policies. At the same time, Bob Hunter, director of insurance for CFA, acknowledges that "for some very limited number of people, because of the incredible attachment that occurs, pet insurance might make some sense." Indeed, Ms. Kelley's cost-benefit analysis must seem of little relevance to the 70% of pet owners who think of their animals as children, or to the 47% of pet owners who, when asked whom they depend upon most for affection, identify their animal companion. (By way of comparison, 49% chose their spouse!) For these people, Leslie Sinclair, a veterinarian with the Humane Society of the United States, offers the following suggestion: "You can put a few dollars out of every paycheck in a can in the freezer, or open a savings account with Fluffy's name on it."

Fido's Final Send-off

What happens when your pet dies? There are a number of options, depending on state regulations and local ordinances. The simplest: The city can collect the animal and bury it in the city dump. Or you can take your animal to an animal shelter or a veterinarian, who'll dispose of him or her for a small fee. You may be able to arrange a cremation by calling a crematory directly or with your vet's help. If you have a garden, some localities still permit you to bury your pet on your property.

Finally, Stephen King's book and film notwithstanding, from 1% to 2% of pets are now buried in pet cemeteries, and the number of such cemeteries has shot up from 400 in 1990 to over 650 in 1993, according to the International Association of Pet Cemeteries (IAPC). A pet burial can cost hundreds of dollars, but the cemetery will let you organize the ceremony of your choice, from a simple cremation to an elaborate funeral, including viewing, gravesite service, and a marker. Members of the IAPC are supposed to adhere to a strict code of ethics, but scandals occasionally occur. A Long Island, New York, couple was awarded $1.2 million in damages after they discovered that their beloved sheepdog had been buried in a mass grave instead of in a private plot.

Such departures aside, a pet cemetery may turn out to be less than an eternal resting place: unlike human cemeteries, pet cemeteries do not have to be protected from future development. The IAPC or a local ASPCA or Humane Society should be able to help you locate a pet cemetery in your area.

If you're having more difficulty disposing of your grief than of your furry friend's remains, the University of Florida's College of Veterinary Medicine offers a hotline for pet owners with mourning pains: (352) 392-4700, extension 4080.

WHAT TO WATCH OUT FOR

Vets who won't let you inspect surgery or kennel areas. As Donna Marsden of the Humane Society warns, "If vets will not let you in their back rooms, do not use them. Their operating areas should be as clean as hospitals, and without odor."

Dogs and cats from pet stores. Unless the store has a cooperative arrangement with a shelter, chances are the pet is from a mill. Animal mills are notorious for horrible breeding conditions, and inbred animals are prone to genetic defects.

Dog trainers with no credentials. Anyone can call himself—or herself—a dog trainer. Ask for qualifications and recommendations from a shelter or an AKC affiliation.

THE $MARTER CONSUMER

Affordable dignity. To bury your animal without the expenses of a cemetery, but with more dignity than the landfill or the vet, consider having his or her remains cremated—it costs as little as $30.

Short-term pet cemeteries. Will your animal's burial truly provide him or her eternal rest? Twenty-two years after burying her Collie Laurie, Doreen T. of Sunnyvale, California, got a letter from the graveyard requesting an additional $300 for the next 20 years—or the late Laurie would be dug up and reburied in a common grave.

Co-ops vs. pets. Especially since the *Narstedt* decision, be sure to check your co-op's or condominium's bylaws on pets *before* moving in. But if it's too late and the rules ban your pet, check with a lawyer whether you can claim that you'd be disabled under the Americans with Disabilities Act without kitty because of your therapeutic reliance on her. "We're getting a lot more pet owners claiming disability," said Karl Scheuerman, a chief attorney with Florida's Department of Business and Professional Regulation, to *The New York Times*.

HELP

■ **If you're bringing** an animal into a household with small children, the Humane Society of the U.S. recommends *Dogs, Cats and Kids,* by Donald Manelli & Associates, to teach children 5 to 12 how to be safe with pets and stray animals.

■ **For an animal shelter near you,** check your Yellow Pages under "Animal Shelters" or contact the Humane Society of the U.S., 2100 L Street NW, Washington, DC 20037, (202) 452-1100, www.hsns.org.

■ **Various insurance companies** offer pet health insurance. For information about the Animal Health Insurance Agency/Medipet, (800) 528-4961; DVM/Veterinary Pet Insurance Co., (800) 872-7387; American Pet Association, (888) 272-3686.

■ **If you're leaving Toto behind on your** next trip and can't arrange for a friend, neighbor, or relative to take him in, you can hire a professional pet sitter or send him to pet camp—the kennel. For pet-sitting referrals, contact the National Association of Pet Sitters, 1200 G Street NW, Suite 760, Washington, DC 20005, (800) 296-PETS, www.petsitters.org, or Pet Sitters International, 418 East King Street, King, NC 27021; www.petsit.com. For kennels, contact the American Boarding Kennel Association, 4575 Galley Road, Suite 400A, Colorado Springs, CO 80915, (719) 591-1113.

■ **For more information about pet** cemeteries, call the International Association of Pet Cemeteries, (800) 952-5541, www.iaopc.com.

■ **If you plan to travel with your pet,** you may want to consult *Take Your Pet USA* ($11.95), which lists lodgings where pets are allowed and veterinarians in all 50 states; to order, call (800) 255-8038, or *Pets-R-Permitted* ($16.95), which lists hotels, motels, kennels, pet sitters, and useful travel tips; to order, call (800) 274-7297.

■ **If the pet of your dreams is pedi-**greed or a purebred, the AKC and the Cat Fanciers' Association are good sources. The AKC, the principal registry of purebred dogs in the country, can be reached at 5580 Centerview Drive, Suite 200, Raleigh, NC 27606-3390, (919) 233-9767, www.akc.org. The Cat Fanciers' Association is the largest registry of pedigreed cats in the world. To contact the Association, write to P.O. Box 1005, Manasquam, NJ 08736-0805, (908) 528-9797, www. cfainc.org/cfa. In addition, your local shelter may occasionally have purebred animals available for adoption.

■ **To help you organize your animal's** next flight, write for the Air Transport Association of America's brochure, *Air Travel for Your Dog or Cat*, at 1301 Pennsylvania Avenue NW, Suite 1100, Washington, DC 20004. You may also want to consult "Traveling with Your Companion Animal," a free brochure of the Humane Society of the U.S. Send a S.A.S.E. to 2100 L Street NW, Washington, DC 20037.

■ **The American Veterinary Medical** Association (AVMA) puts out a useful brochure to help you figure out the right pet for you. To obtain *The Veterinarian's Way of Selecting a Proper Pet,* write to the AVMA, 1931 North Meacham Road, Suite 100, Schaumburg, IL 60173.

CHAPTER 19

LAWN AND GARDEN CARE

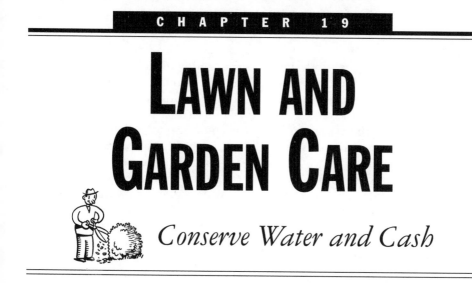

Conserve Water and Cash

"Gardening has become so much more to many of us than just a vegetable patch or a flower border," gushes the diva of domestic arts, Martha Stewart, in her eponymous magazine. More than keeping up with the Joneses' expectations. More than maintaining the manse's resale value. More than a few tomatoes—and basil to serve them with.

How much more to how many? There are now 23 million lawn and garden customers, up from 18 million in 1995, and they spent about $22 billion on their yards, twice what they spent a decade ago. About two thirds of that is lavished on the lawn; grass is America's biggest crop, carpeting an estimated 25 million acres. The balance goes for trees, shrubs, flowers, landscaping services, and, increasingly, toys for grown-ups—rubber garden clogs, specially designed pruning sheers for women, $1,000 teak benches, statues of geese and fawns to inhabit the flora.

All this exterior decorating consumes not only prodigious amounts of time and money, but also water. In some arid counties of the country, up to 60% of precious municipal water slakes the thirst of plants, rather than people. With a little planning, you can cut down on expenses and water use—not to mention wasted time with hose in hand. It will be easier on both your bank account and the environment.

THE BASICS

Hardy Times

The U.S. Department of Agriculture has broken the continental U.S. up into 10 hardiness zones—with zone 1 being the coldest and zone 10 the warmest. You need to know your hardiness zone in order to determine which plants will grow well in your area. If you fall for a plant that's hardy to zone 8 and you live in zone 3, you're out of luck. That lovely bougainvillea won't be able to stand the winter.

Within each zone, indeed each garden, there may be warmer or colder "microclimates" created by water, reflected light and heat, wind, and topography. (For example, Phoenix, Arizona, and Portland, Oregon, are in the same zone.) Thus, gardens by the water tend to be cooler, as do gardens in the mountains. That goes for you city-dwellers, too: it gets colder as the view gets better, and a terrace higher than the 9th floor will drop you down one full zone—unless your garden in the sky is bathed in light reflected off the windows or walls of your building.

Check with your county extension agent or state cooperative extension service (see **HELP** for contact information) for help figuring out what zone you garden in.

Poor Dirt

Soil is the other thing to assess. Even if you buy plants that will weather your storms, they won't all necessarily work. Some plants and trees require acidic soil; others like it alkaline. Some feast on a rich recipe of nitrogen, phosphorus, and potassium; others prefer to fast. Low-cost soil-testing programs run by the extension services' scientists are a cheap way to find out what's missing from your soil and which cocktails your favorite plants favor.

Going Shopping

In spring, you can buy plants virtually anywhere at a wide range of prices—on your way into the supermarket, or on your way out of the home building center, at roadside farm stands and flea markets, from the convenience of your couch via catalogue and computer and, of course, at nurseries and garden centers. You might find high-quality plants that thrive and bloom forever at any of these outlets, but there is no guarantee. "Azaleas and roses standing outside next to the shopping carts may or may not be hardy in your region," says Barbara Damrosch, author of *The Garden Primer.* "And no one [on staff] is likely to know whether they are or aren't."

Your best—though more expensive—bet is almost always a well-established nursery. They are likely to grow most of their own stock and know whether it will work in your yard and how to care for it. Plus, their plants are more likely to be free of disease. They'll probably even guarantee their plants and replace those that don't make it.

As you shop, look for compact, bushy plants with many stems. Steer clear of plants with yellowed or wilted leaves; tall, spindly plants; pots with lots of roots escaping out of the drainage holes; balled plants and trees when the root ball is dry or damaged; plants with signs of bugs or disease on the foliage, such as insect bodies, stickiness, distorted leaves, blackened areas, spots, blotches, streaks, or jagged bites.

Lawn Economy, Ecology, and Safety

Watering. With the price of municipal water rising and supplies dwindling, we can't afford to waste it. Established lawns require only about an inch of water a week (about an inch and a half if your soil is sandy). Since Mother Nature provides this amount of water in much of the country, you probably don't need to begin watering until about two weeks have passed with no substantial rainfall. Then, water infrequently, but regularly. Water enough to make sure the soil is thoroughly wet, not just the grass; too much water is a waste and just encourages the weeds, but too little encourages shallow roots, which can't reach water that lurks deeper during dry spells.

The best time to water is in the morning; about 30% of water applied later in the day merely evaporates, and morning watering gives the surface of the lawn all day to dry. Next-best is early-evening watering.

If you're conscious about water use, don't worry too much about moderate browning in the heat of the summer. The lawn is merely dormant and it'll come back. You might also invest in a drip-irrigation system, which delivers just the right amount of droplets directly to root systems. If you're putting in a new lawn, choose with an eye on water consumption. New varieties of grass have been developed that require much less water.

Mowing. Most people cut their grass to about 1 to 1½ inches. But taller grass keeps soil cool, which slows evaporation and reduces water use. A Smithsonian Institution test found that a 3-inch lawn looked "acceptable" and that a 2-inch lawn didn't look much different than a 1-inch one. Higher grass also helps smother weeds. A rule of thumb: Never cut off more than a third of the blade. But don't let the grass grow *too* high; grass higher than 4 inches tends to lean over and block essential sunlight.

Leaving the clippings on your lawn not only saves you the hassle of removing them, but their presence as a kind of mulch helps retain moisture and reduces the need for fertilizer. Of course, if you neglected mowing for a long time and you've got what could pass for hay, remove the clippings.

Thatch is a thick interwoven mass of roots, stems, blades, rhizomes, and other accumulations that builds up above the soil. Too much of it can prevent water, air, and necessary fertilizer from penetrating, and it can harbor insects. Prevent excessive thatch buildup by raking, clearing away excessive clippings, and aerating the lawn at least once a year.

If you can minimize the size of your lawn or mow less frequently, you'll help the environment considerably. Lawn mowers emit a lot of pollution. According to the Califor-

> "*You can have a beautiful lawn without using a lot of water. For example, there are some tall fescues—good in the Northeast and Midwest—that stay green during dry summers.*"
>
> —MARIA CINQUE,
> Cornell Cooperative Extension
> Agent, Plainview, New York

nia Air Resources Board, annual pollution emissions from such lawn power equipment as mowers and edgers in that state are equivalent to the emissions of 3.5 million late-model cars driven 16,000 miles each. That's why California implemented regulations in 1994 to limit lawn-equipment emissions, to be toughened in 1999.

Fertilizing. Your lawn probably doesn't need as much fertilizer as you think, especially if you leave the clippings. Grass makes its own food, in its blades (another reason not to mow it too short).

Still, your lawn could probably stand a moderate fertilization in late spring, about the time that the spring growth spurt has started to slow down, and, even more important, in early fall, to strengthen the lawn for its long winter dormancy. Early-spring fertilizing might also be considered if your lawn comes through the winter very weak and stunted. In the South, fertilization in midspring and midsummer is recommended.

It Ain't Necessarily So

Every year, more than 100,000 people in the U.S. are poisoned by pesticides, according to John P. Wargo, director of the Center for Children's Environmental Policy at Yale University. Those most susceptible are fetuses and children. Just because pesticides are registered with the U.S. Environmental Protection Agency (EPA) doesn't mean they're safe for humans and other living things. Note that:

■ The EPA studies only the active ingredients that kill weeds and pests, not inert ingredients, which might also be harmful.
■ The EPA registration is a "balancing act, a cost-benefit analysis," according to Phyllis Spaeth, an assistant attorney general in New York State. If a particular pesticide is deemed necessary for agriculture, that factor weighs heavily in the registration process.
■ The EPA is currently considering 18 major lawn chemicals for reregistration, and it takes years to analyze tests of environment and health effects. In 1994, the U.S. General Accounting Office concluded, "Until re-registration is completed, the safety of the 18 pesticides will be questionable, while the approximately 2,100 lawn-care products containing them will continue in widespread use."
■ The test data the EPA relies on are produced by labs hired by the manufacturer, which are more likely to be biased.

Nonetheless, pesticide makers trumpet EPA registration and imply that it means their pesticide is safe.

Remember, if you overfertilize, much of it will run off and could pollute nearby streams and ponds. If your lawn looks good and you've used alternatives, you might try skipping commercial fertilizers altogether.

What's the difference between organic and synthetic fertilizer? Synthetic works through chemical reactions that give your lawn a quick nutrition fix. Organic fertilizer, made of non-chemically processed minerals or animal or plant matter, works slower and usually costs more, but its "time-release" feature means you might have to apply it only once a year. There are also "bridge" fertilizers that incorporate both.

Weed and insect fighting. Perfect lawns aren't the traditional American way. It wasn't until after World War II, with the increase in the use of weedkillers and pesticides, that the "monoculture" lawn—lawns with just one kind of plant—became the ideal. Now, to meet our heightened expectations for a flawless lawn, we pour on the chemicals.

But no one really knows how safe these chemicals are. Very few have been fully evaluated. Yet there's plenty of anecdotal evidence that lawn chemicals can make you ill.

U.S. Senate hearings on the issue of residential pesticide safety heard from several witnesses who got very sick from lawn chemicals. Christina Locek, a concert pianist, was sunning herself in her back yard when a lawn care company began spraying the neighbor's yard. Wind blew the spray onto her, and she immediately got very ill and collapsed; she is now blind in one eye. Her cat died in only a few minutes, and her dog died later in the day.

The National Cancer Institute reports that dogs whose owners use the broadleaf weed killer 2,4-D, developed by the military, have an increased rate of immune system cancer. And the insecticide diazinon was banned for golf courses because it kills birds. It is still available, however, in 1,500 weed-killing products sold for residential lawns.

Avoid using lots of chemicals by adopting integrated pest management (IPM) techniques for your lawn, shrubs, and trees. IPM involves careful year-round monitoring of the yard, shrubs, and trees for pests. When needed, chemicals are applied on the affected spot rather than broadcast over an entire area, which means that fewer chemicals are used overall.

After chemicals have been applied to the lawn, keep kids, pets, and yourself away until the lawn is thoroughly dry. About half the states in the U.S. require lawn care services to notify you when applying pesticides. Usually they tell you directly or post warning signs on the lawn. In Connecticut, the lawn care company must also tell your neighbors. Unfortunately, most notification laws do not require the lawn service to say *what* is being sprayed.

WHAT TO WATCH OUT FOR

Lawn care services. The basic service is fertilizing and controlling weeds. Add mowing, reseeding, and soil aeration—for more money.

Lawn care services are worth the cost if you don't have the time or inclination to do the work yourself. But they can be unreliable. Lawn care companies have been known to skip promised treatments, to fail to show up when they're supposed to (and show up when they weren't expected—perhaps when you had planned an outdoor party), and to overbill. The biggest complaint against lawn-care services? The grass didn't grow. Other things to beware of: billing snafus and annual contracts that lock you in for years to come, unless *you* go to the trouble to opt out. Protect yourself by checking references and getting written bids and contracts before you hire. The bid and the contract should specify in detail exactly what services will be provided and how often, where the clippings will be taken if they are re-moved (preferably off the premises), and exactly what products will be spread around. Most states require companies that apply pesticides commercially to be licensed. They should carry a card proving their license is up to date. Check to see if the service is a member of the Professional Lawn Care Association of America. And, of course, make sure the service carries personal liability insurance.

Weed killer and pesticide safety claims. According to draft charges by the Federal Trade Commission, the Orkin Exterminating Company falsely claimed that its lawn products are "practically nontoxic" or have lower toxicity than many common household products like suntan lotion or shaving cream. Orkin went so far as to claim, "We'll keep weeds and harmful bugs out, using environmentally safe, biodegradable products that are neither harmful to you nor your soil." Not true. In March 1993, Orkin agreed to stop making such claims, and the FTC issued new rules requiring that "these claims should not be used for such products if they pose a significant risk" to humans or the environment.

Mowing injuries. The U.S. Consumer Product Safety Commission reports that thousands of people each year are injured seriously enough in lawn mower mishaps that they visit hospital emergency rooms. Avoid becoming one of these statistics by never mowing a wet lawn (you might slip and hurt yourself) and by clearing the lawn of sticks and stones before you start.

BEST TIMES WORST TIMES

It's tempting to buy trees and plants in spring, when all kinds of stores—from the local nursery to the home center to the supermarket—display lush plants with showy blooms. But the best time to buy trees, shrubs and perennial plants is the fall. It's generally just as good a time as spring to plant, and since the alluring flowers have fallen, so have the prices.

Carefully consider the safety of any lawn mower you buy. The June 1997 issue of *Consumer Reports* includes a comparison of lawn tractors and riding mowers. With such mowers costing $1,000 to $4,000 each, *CR* is worth a read. The testers found that four of the tested tractors had a worrisome tendency toward unintended "wheelies" when climbing a hill. The May 1998 issue rated 26 push (non–self-propelled) mowers for ability to mulch, bag, and discharge. With push mower prices ranging from $100 to a hefty $650, it makes money sense to read *Consumer Reports* before you buy.

Hardiness zones. Just because a plant is on sale at the local farm stand or supermarket doesn't mean it's necessarily right for your yard. Check with a knowledgeable salesperson or a gardening guide before you make your purchase.

Sticker shock. Don't be surprised when you look at sacks of natural fertilizers and find they cost two to three times more than synthetics. While it will hurt at first, over time it may end up costing you about the same or, over a very long time, even less—because you won't have to apply them as often.

Potent pesticides. It can be very difficult to translate the technical language on a pesticide label into everyday argot you understand, even assuming the type is big enough to read. If your 4-year-old just swallowed pesticide, would you know you should get medical instructions from the "Statement of Practical Treatment"? Would you like to try to pronounce, let alone guess what the following substance is: "1-((6-chloro-3-pyridinyl)methyl)-N-nitro-2-imidazolidinimine"? We thought not.

The EPA is working with the industry to make labels easier to read and understand. By the 1998 gardening season, many products had new labels that made translations like the following: Instead of "Merit 0.5G Insecticide for systemic insect control in turbograss and landscapes ornaments," the new label for Merit will read, "Merit Granular is a highly effective insecticide designed to kill white grubs and mole crickets in lawns, ground covers, flower gardens, around shrubs and trees." The old "Statement of Practical Treatment" will become "First Aid." Chemical names will be simplified. Labels will contain a toll-free number to call for help. And the labels will clarify what is meant by "inert" ingredients.

Even the industry welcomes the change. "Over 50% of the people who go into a store with a problem with their lawn or flowers and start looking at labels walk away confused without buying," said a top executive at a leading pesticide company. When in doubt, find a knowledgeable salesperson and ask her to steer you to the right product for the job you need to do.

The grass will be greener. Grasses with deeper roots require less watering. A heavy soaking less often is better than frequent sprinkles. That way, you'll coax the grass to grow deep roots, which will help it weather a drought. Buy grass seed with no more than 8% inert matter. The lower the inert matter, the better.

To protect your lawn against grass diseases naturally, sow a variety of grass types. This way, if a disease attacks one kind of grass, the others may still survive.

Take these basic safety precautions when hiring a lawn-care company: Get copies of labels for any pesticide mixture they are using. Be sure to find out how long you should wait after they are applied and what you should do if it rains right after an application. Make sure you know about any pesticide application well in advance so that you can take precautions—e.g., remove a wading pool or toys, or cover your vegetable garden before the lawn is sprayed.

Keep your mower blades sharp. Dull blades rip the grass, exposing it to diseases and insect damage. In addition, sharply cut grass looks better. And change your mowing pattern each time you mow. Constant mowing in one direction discourages grass from standing upright.

Free food. Ask if your town has a composting program. Many towns compost leaves and offer the dark, nutrient-rich mix free to residents.

Always read and follow the label instructions. You'll find answers to crucial questions like, is this pesticide safe to apply to my prize-winning tomatoes that I plan to serve at a barbeque this weekend; how long after application before children and pets can play on the lawn.

Go organic. Organic methods of lawn and garden maintenance mean healthier gardens and lawns that require less maintenance, but it takes longer to get there. But at least you can find the fixings: Mainstream stores like Home Depot, Wal-Mart, and the local garden center now carry organic fertilizer and pesticides that consumers used to have to hunt down at specialty stores and in mail order catalogs—for example, hot pepper wax to repel insects, insecticidal soap made from chrysanthemum flowers.

Know your hardiness zone and stick with plants appropriate to it. One of the biggest mistakes consumers make is falling for plants and trees that cannot thrive where they live. Even if a tree flowers and does fine for the summer, it may not be hardy enough to survive a harsh winter.

Gardening through the mail. Over 14.6 million households spent $2 billion ordering gardening products by mail in 1996. Most of that was for bulbs and seeds. But keep the same things in mind you would for any other catalog purchase: seeing is not believing. Just because a peony looks picture-perfect (and the adjacent ad copy confirms that this is the case) doesn't mean the plant is perfect for your garden's growing conditions. Furthermore, it can take years of care and coddling for the seedlings you order to turn into the bounteous beauties in the pictures. For further informa-

tion about your mail order rights, refer to the chapter on "Home Shopping," page 612.

H E L P

■ **The U.S. EPA's free** 54-page booklet, *Citizen's Guide to Pest Control and Pesticide Safety*, tells how to properly choose and use pesticides and how to handle an emergency. Write to Environmental Protection Agency, Office of Pesticide Programs H7502C, 401 M Street SW, Washington, DC 20460 or go to www.epa.gov for the EPA's "In the Garden" page on the Internet, which provides information and links on pesticides and a guide to landscaping with native plants. To order EPA publications on pesticides by phone, call the National Pesticide Telecommunications Network, (800) 858-7378. The NPTN's Web site is located at ace.orst.edu/info/nptn.

■ **Take care of your** lawn the organic way. Order these two brochures from the National Coalition Against the Misuse of Pesticides: *Least Toxic Control of Lawn Pests* and *Organic Gardening: Sowing the Seeds of Safety*. $2 each. Send a check to NCAMP, 701 E Street SE, Suite 200, Washington, DC 20003.

■ **Find out the real** story about your weed killer. Call the National Pesticide Telecommunications Network at (800) 858-7378; hours: 9:30–7:30 EST, 7 days a week. Operators can also advise you in case a pet appears to be poisoned. Another good information source is the National Coalition Against the Misuse of Pesticides, at (202) 543-5450 or www.csn.net/ncamp.

■ *Rodale's Chemical-Free Yard & Garden* (Rodale Press, $26.95) explains natural insect, disease, and weed control.

■ **To find the state cooperative** extension program in your area, check your phone book or go to www.gardenweb.com/vl/ces.html.

■ **You'll find lots of general and very** specific gardening resources on the Internet—everything from camellia societies to tree selection guides to garden designs. Use one of the Internet search engines to tailor your research to your gardening needs.

MOVING COMPANIES

A Moving Experience

Psychiatrists list moving as one of the top trauma-creating circumstances, right after death and divorce. Indeed, the words "moving experience" too often take an unfortunate dual meaning. But they don't have to. In fact, with advance planning, some consumer savvy, and a bit of luck, you just may be able to beat the odds and have your next move be— well, if not quite a pleasant experience, at least a successful one.

Americans are a people on the move. One in five families—or 41.6 million people—relocate each year, according to the U.S. Census Bureau. One third of people in their 20s change their addresses every year. Studies show that you and I will move an average of eleven times in our lifetime. Thus, it's not surprising that the moving industry generates $7 billion a year in revenues.

This constant coming and going doesn't come cheap. Transporting 10,000 pounds (the typical weight of goods from a three-bedroom house) from Los Angeles to New York costs about $5,000. And it doesn't come easy either: Complaints against the industry in New York more than quadrupled from 1989 to 1996, the result of what

one state investigation called "a law-of-the-jungle competition."

Movers operating across state borders are regulated by the Federal Highway Administration (FHA) of the Department of Transportation (which took over from the Interstate Commerce Commission in January 1996). In 1980, the federal Household Goods and Transportation Act partially deregulated the industry, increasing competition and, in many cases, lowering prices for consumers. Interstate movers are still required to obtain a license from and file their tariffs with the FHA, but they can now offer discounts, additional insurance, and binding estimates that guarantee a fixed price. However, when responsibility for regulating interstate movers got kicked over to the FHA from the ICC, the consumer watchdog lost the few teeth it had. The laws and rules governing moving companies still exist, and an additional requirement that interstate movers offer arbitration for damage or loss claims of $1,000 or less was added, but FHA did not get any staff or money to enforce the rules. FHA officials acknowledged that they hadn't acted on a single 1996 or 1997 complaint because they had no budget to do so. Then again, the

ICC acted on only nine complaints in 1994.

Movers operating within a state are regulated by that state—typically the department of transportation or public utility commission. Because rules vary greatly from state to state, this chapter deals primarily with *interstate* moving.

Even Bill Clinton, hours after his inauguration, was heard greeting the movers from United Van Lines driving up to the White House with a relieved "Y'all made it, huh?" While you can't eliminate the trauma of dislocation and relocation, you can save yourself a lot of grief and money by planning early and doing your homework.

THE BASICS

Picking the Right Company

To do the job well, plan early—*Consumer Reports* suggests getting started eight weeks before your anticipated moving day. When selecting a mover, the two key factors are reliability and price.

Reliability. First of all, make sure the company is licensed by the FHA (if you're moving interstate) or by your state for intrastate moves. If your state does not require a license, make sure the company is adequately insured. (Ask for a copy of the policy to ensure that it covers *your* losses, not just the mover's.)

The FHA requires every interstate moving company to compile and make available to consumers an "Annual Performance Report" that includes information about the number of claims they received for loss or damages, how often they delivered late, and how often they *incorrectly* estimated the final cost of shipment. In addition, ask family, friends, coworkers, or a reputable real-estate agent for recommendations, and check with your consumer agency or Better Business Bureau.

Price. The American Movers Conference (AMC) recommends that you get written price estimates from three different movers. Don't accept phone estimates. Otto G. had a textbook experience of everything that can go wrong when moving: His first inkling that he was in for trouble came when the foreman, before unloading the truck after the long trip from New York to Boca Raton, Florida, told him his bill was $3,600, when he'd been given a phone estimate of $2,200. Unfortunately, there's little you can do when your furniture is in their possession. Reflecting on his experience, Otto told the Fort Lauderdale *Sun Sentinel,* "Moving companies think they are God and they can do anything they want to the poor people who move."

Don't reflexively go to the cheapest company. As George Bennett of the AMC notes, "Be leery of the lowest one . . . the cheapest company could have old equipment, people who aren't trained movers, inadequate insurance, whatever." If one company vastly outbids the others, find out why. And remember that interstate rates—and intrastate rates in half of the country—are fully negotiable.

219

The FHA and most states enable you to ask for a binding or nonbinding estimate.

- Binding estimates are guaranteed final prices. Companies may charge you for this option. Make sure to tell the mover about special conditions—walk-ups, narrow doorways that require heavy lifting through the windows, etc.; appreciate that new arrangements may void the binding estimate. At your request, some movers will weigh your shipment even under a binding estimate option and, if the weight-based rate is less than the binding estimate, charge you the lower amount.

- Nonbinding estimates are just that —the mover's best guess. The final cost will be determined primarily by the actual weight of the shipment multiplied by the distance traveled. Interstate companies are required to post their rates with the FHA but can offer discounts of up to 50%. (For short-distance intrastate moves, costs may be determined by handling time and required personnel.)

Consumer Reports recommends binding estimates, "even though they can run slightly higher than nonbinding ones." Nonbinding estimates, on the other hand, give you the flexibility to alter your plans at the last minute. In either case, show the mover everything you're planning to take, including long-forgotten relics in the garage, under the bed, or in the attic. Ask about any potential extra charges. Some movers, for instance, may charge you an extra $55 to move Aunt Rosie's Steinway, and another $45 to get it to your fifth-floor apartment. There may be extra charges for additional stops, parking far from the front door, or a non-elevator apartment building.

For an interstate move, the company you selected should give you an "Order for Service" detailing the estimated charge, terms and method of payment, all special services ordered, and agreed-upon pickup and delivery dates (or spreads of dates). Don't accept a promise that they'll move you "as soon as possible." The company should also give you a pamphlet describing its procedures for handling complaints and questions as well as a brochure the FHA requires that it distribute to customers, *Your Rights and Responsibilities When You Move* (see **HELP** at the end of this chapter). Know that

> "**Y**ou have people wanting to move all their earthly possessions, and they just look in the Yellow Pages and call somebody. It's amazing. The truck pulls over; they take everything and drive away. That's fantastic faith in your fellow human beings. A lot of people just don't do enough checking."
>
> —GEORGE E. BENNETT,
> American Movers Conference

you can cancel the order without penalty at *any* time, up to the day of the move.

Packing Up

You can save hundreds of dollars by doing your own packing and unpacking . . . and a few extra bucks by getting your own boxes. (The mover will charge you premium rates for *their* boxes.) Consider at least packing non-breakable items—books, linen, clothing. Better yet, leave soft items like clothes inside drawers and tape the drawers shut. Pack heavy items (books) in small boxes. But you may want to let the movers pack the breakable stuff—dishware, electronic equipment, etc. Then *they'll* be responsi-

ble if anything happens. (Although not an FHA requirement, some companies accept responsibility for items you packed as long as you did so carefully.) But be aware that 55% of those who paid their mover to pack for them in a *Consumer Reports* survey reported damage, against 32% of those who did their own packing.

The movers must keep an inventory describing the nature and condition of the goods they pack. If you packed, they should still do an inventory of boxes and goods. Check it carefully before signing: It will prove an invaluable document down the road if you need to file a claim for items lost or damaged. Make sure it is specific—if you're moving your favorite Rembrandt or

Stashing It Away: Mini Storage Warehouses

If you're moving overseas or to a smaller or already-furnished home, you may want to consider sending some of your belongings on a trip to mini-storage land. Two pointers:

■ Inspect the premises before you arrive with all your possessions. Check that the security is good and the place seems well run. "If the place is unkempt with trash all over you might not want to rent space there," suggests a senior executive from one of the largest companies in the field.

■ You're probably aware of all the calamities that can happen to your goods while in storage: theft, fire, heat, rats, to name a few. In a perfect world, each of these could be dealt with through security systems, sprinklers, and pest and climate control. And it's a good idea to find out about these various options when you visit the premises. But in the world of mini-storage warehouses, these things do happen. If you go to the trouble of getting a storage space for your possessions, you may want to go the extra mile and get insurance as well.

a first-edition King James Bible, it shouldn't just say "painting" or "book." If you disagree with a description, ask the movers to change it. If they refuse, photograph the item in dispute and make your own notation on the inventory.

Carry with you irreplaceable items like fine art, jewelry, and family photos. Also, it's a good idea to have one box of essentials—bed linens, coffee pot, towels, favorite toys, a phone—set aside to get you through the first few chaotic hours.

Weighing the Merchandise

If you are moving interstate, you will usually be charged based on distance and weight (more rarely on volume) plus packing and other services. The mover may require a minimum weight—usually 500 pounds or more—and should inform you if your shipment falls below that. You should be given a "weigh ticket" identifying the "tare weight" of the vehicle without shipment (including necessary moving equipment) and the "gross weight" (with shipment), so you can figure out the "net weight" of your shipment. You can ask to—and should—be present at the weighing. If weight is measured prior to the trip ("origin weighing"), you can ask that the truck be reweighed at destination at no extra charge; but if the second weighing is higher, you pay the higher price. A rule of thumb from the FHA: If the average weight per article ranges between 35 and 45 pounds, don't bother reweighing—it's probably on the mark.

If no scale or certified weighmaster is available, the trucker will compute the bill based on an assumed weight of 7 pounds per cubic foot of van space used.

Loading Up

Before loading up, the mover must give you a copy of the "bill of lading," the contract of transportation. It should include much of the same information as the Order for Service—price estimate and method of payment, special services ordered, time and place of delivery—plus the tare weight and where you can be reached in case of delay.

Again, read the contract carefully before signing and work out all disagreements before the movers load up, or you might fall prey to what *New York* magazine calls "a basic law of consumer physics: Once somebody has all your worldly possessions on his truck, you must give him whatever he wants."

The bill of lading should also include the company's liability policy. Companies usually offer the following three options: released value liability, added value protection, and full value protection (see the chart on the next page for details).

Before selecting added or full-value protection, check that your homeowner's insurance does not already provide you with coverage, or that your insurance company does not offer such coverage for less than the moving company does. If you do select either option, make sure to note on the shipping papers items of extraordinary value

LIABILITY OPTIONS	
RELEASED VALUE LIABILITY	*Interstate movers are responsible for damages or losses up to 60 cents per pound, regardless of the item's value. To get this cheaper option, you must ask for it. Otherwise, you'll automatically receive—and be billed for—added value coverage.*
ADDED VALUE PROTECTION	*This plan enables you to recover the actual value of the lost or damaged item: replacement cost minus depreciation. If the value of your shipment exceeds the mover's maximum liability, you can obtain additional liability protection—at an extra cost, of course—by declaring your shipment at its real value.*
FULL VALUE PROTECTION	*Companies may offer alternative protection plans for the full current cost of replacement or repair. Such plans usually cost about 90 cents for every $100 of coverage with no deductible. (The higher the deductible, the lower the cost.) As always, read the fine print carefully for any restrictions or deductibles.*

(over $100 per pound). Otherwise, the mover may be able to elude liability.

Delivery and Payment

Delivery date. The mover is contractually bound to pick up and deliver your shipment on the terms set in the bill of lading. Usually movers provide a range of dates within which they'll deliver your things. (You may have to purchase a "liquidated damages" policy to arrange a specific date.) But a 1990 *Consumer Reports* survey found that 12% of respondents received their goods after the last promised delivery date. The mover is required to notify you by telephone, telegram, or in person if pickup or delivery will not be on schedule. Make sure you can be reached at all times, lest your goods be put in storage—at your expense.

If you incur any expenses as a result of the delay (e.g., hotel stay or restaurant meals), you should be able to recover them, unless the mover can present a "defense of *force majeure*," circumstances that are both unforeseeable and beyond its control—say, a hurricane. Some companies will be receptive to your "inconvenience" or "delay" claim; others will force you to litigate. And some may require that you purchase a "guaranteed service" option obliging them to pay you a fixed per diem fee if they miss the promised date. Such per diem fees often preclude a separate inconvenience claim. Find out your moving company's policy. In either case, save all receipts of expenses.

LEAST REGULATED STATES

	Limited or no regulation for household carriers	No intrastate license requirement
ALASKA	X	X
ARIZONA	X	X
COLORADO	X	X
DELAWARE	X	X
HAWAII		X
IDAHO	X	X
MAINE	X	X
MARYLAND	X	X
NEW MEXICO		X
VERMONT	X	X
WISCONSIN	X	
WYOMING	X	

Source: American Movers Conference

Payment. The bill of lading will specify the terms of payment. Most movers require payment before unloading and accept cash, certified checks, money orders, travelers checks—and, sometimes, credit cards—but *not* personal checks. If you opted for a nonbinding estimate and the mover asks for more than the estimate, you are responsible for paying only the estimate plus 10% before unloading, and the balance within 30 days. You are also responsible for any services not included in the estimate. (If you refuse to pay because you disagree with the final bill, the mover may lock your goods in storage and stick you with an extra bill for storage and redelivery fees.)

Receipt. You will generally be asked to sign a receipt or delivery paper. Before you do so, make sure all your goods have arrived safely. At a minimum, open up boxes with breakable items or boxes that look damaged and inspect fragile items —e.g., look for rips on your leather sofa. If you find any damage, write it down on both sets of delivery papers (yours and the mover's) before signing. If you discover damage after the driver has left, leave the item in its packaging and contact the moving company.

Claims

Nearly half of all people who move report some damage. If something goes wrong with your move, ask for a company claim form, complete it ASAP (the law gives you nine months from delivery to file), and return it to the mover via return-receipt-requested mail. Try to get independent estimates of the goods—the company may do so as well—but don't overreach. In addition, you are entitled to recover transportation charges proportional to the portion of the shipment that was lost or destroyed.

The company must acknowledge your claim within 30 days, and either deny it or offer a settlement within 120 days. (Most claims are settled within 30 days.)

BEST TIMES WORST TIMES

Avoid moving during the summer. More than half of all moves in the United States are completed from May to September. Service may therefore be slower—and prices higher. You'll also do well to avoid the last four or five days of the month. And remember to start your move early in the day to avoid over-time costs that some movers charge for working after 5 PM.

If all else fails, you may have to take the mover to court (within two years of the company's response or lack thereof) or request that your case go to arbitration (within 60 days): the American Movers Conference offers binding arbitration for interstate disputed loss and damage claims. Written arbitration by mail is free, but in-person proceedings cost $300, which you and the mover split.

Moving Intrastate

Moving intrastate is a lot cheaper and a lot less complicated. But it is not regulated by the FHA; regulations vary from state to state, and 10 states have no regulations at all. Most rate regulations are based on time, weight, or distance. To find out regulations in your state, contact your state public utilities commission, depart-ment of transportation, or attorney general's office, or the American Movers Conference.

An unregulated field is fertile ground for what one exposé described as "estimate-lowballing, tip-extorting, chandelier-dropping, wedding-album-losing scam art-ists." This provides all the more reason for asking family, friends, and colleagues for recommenda-tions, discussing bids from several movers, and going over the contract with a fine-tooth comb to catch all the tangles.

WHAT TO WATCH OUT FOR

"Moving companies are not looking for repeat busi-ness," said James E. Miller, who was one of the people who handled mov-ing complaints for the defunct ICC in the eastern part of the country. "The average person moves every five to seven years, and the movers figure that's long enough for you to forget how traumatic it was." It's probably been awhile since you last moved, so here are some reminders:

A telephone estimate is a flat-out guess. Once the mover liberally ap-plies packing tape and muscles your belongings onto a truck, you will very likely find the bill inflated to twice or three times the estimate. Instead, have several movers come look at your belongings, or you could end up as unhappy as Gale A. She got a telephone estimate of $272 from MIFA Moving to haul her belongings 15 blocks. The final bill was more than three times the estimate, $988, after the company insisted on repacking her things in its own boxes and demanded an enormous tip.

Beware New York and Florida moves. Lots of moving activity and lax enforcement combine to make these states tops in consumer complaints.

Low-ball estimates. A low price snags your business, but your belongings may, effectively, be held hostage on the truck or in a storage bin until you pay a much higher price.

Movers are required to carry minimal insurance. And minimal it is. If the mover drops your 20-pound television during a move from Manhattan to Montana, you could be owed as little as $12 (60 cents per pound). And you'd get the same $12 for a 20-pound Ming vase.

THE $MARTER CONSUMER

Look closely at the moving companies' annual performance reports. Track records (on giving out nonbinding estimates, for instance) can vary greatly. North American Van Lines low-balled its estimates 50% of the time one year; Mayflower Transit, 33%; United Van Lines, 30%. In contrast, Atlas, Bekins, and Global Van Lines ended up charging customers at or below the estimate in 95% to 99% of cases.

If you sign a guaranteed service agreement binding the mover to a specific pickup or delivery date, read the penalty provisions carefully. The mover may offer you a per diem compensation that precludes other compensations, such as costly hotel accommodations.

If you choose a full-value protection plan, read the fine print very closely. Many plans cover only inventoried items that are either lost or not delivered.

Travel light. Go through your belongings and figure out what you need and what you can sell, offer at a garage sale, give to charity, or throw away. (Remember to get receipts: Charity donations are deductible from your federal income tax.) Think of your new space and what's not going to fit in.

Do your own packing and save up to one third of moving expenses. But unless you know what you're doing, it's often best to let the movers pack fragile items—like your great-aunt's china. Ask about the company's policy on liability for self-packed cartons.

If you have the energy, time, and person-power, you may save up to 50% by doing your own move. Jonathan Elias, a TV news reporter who landed a job in Minneapolis, decided to do just that after receiving bids of $3,500 and up to move him from Sacramento, California. Total cost of the do-it-yourself operation: $2,000, including dinner for a "crew" of four friends.

But consider carefully whether it's worth it. Factor in all expenses involved (rental and insurance for the truck, pizza, chips and gallons of soda for your friends helping out)—and the effort. If you do go ahead, Ryder, U-Haul, and other truck rental companies have booklets suggesting the furniture capacity of their various trucks. U-Haul will even give you a free video detailing packing and loading procedures if you buy your moving boxes from them.

Keep records of all moving expenses—they may be tax-deductible. Call the IRS and ask for Publication 521 on tax deductions for job-related moves.

If you are moving at your employer's request, find out what portions of your expenses the company will pick up.

■ **The Federal High-** way Administration requires interstate movers to distribute a detailed booklet, *Your Rights and Responsibilities When You Move.* The FHA will answer very basic questions about interstate moving companies. The recent dismantling of the Interstate Commerce Commission has left consumers with less government oversight of movers than in the past. The phone number for the FHA is (202) 358-7027.

■ **The American Movers Conference** publishes various useful brochures to help consumers prepare their moving arrangements: *Guide to a Satisfying Move; Moving and Children; Moving With Pets and Plants.* For free copies, send a self-addressed, stamped envelope to 1611 Duke Street, Alexandria, VA 22314.

■ *Consumer Reports'* most recent comprehensive article on moving and the industry came out in August 1990, replete with company rankings, consumer surveys, and useful tips and schedules.

■ **For information regarding the** American Movers Conference arbitration program, write to Dispute Settlement Program, 1611 Duke Street, Alexandria, VA 22314.

CHAPTER 21

PRODUCT SAFETY

The Hidden Hazards in Everyday Products

In the summer of 1994, the Consumer Product Safety Commission (CPSC) required the makers of disposable lighters to make them child-resistant. Sounds like a major victory for the health and welfare of the nation, right? After all, children under five playing with lighters caused more than 5,000 fires in homes every year, which resulted in approximately 150 deaths and more than 1,000 injuries annually. Obviously, child-resistant lighters are an important advance for consumer safety. But what's troubling is that it took more than eight years to repair a safety defect the nation had known about for so long.

The lesson is that although a product safety apparatus exists in the United States, you cannot count on it to protect you or your family from every hazard, even known hazards. For example, baby walkers caused 25,000 injuries a year. Many

> "*Annually, more than 940,000 preventable deaths and millions of illnesses and injuries occur, at a cost to the American people of more than $400 billion.*"
>
> — THE COALITION FOR CONSUMER HEALTH AND SAFETY

consumer groups think baby walkers should be banned; Canada allows only baby walkers that cannot fit through doorways. Here's why: In April 1992, eight-month-old Chase W. fell down a flight of stairs in his baby walker and suffered a serious brain injury. Although his parents always kept the door to the stairway shut, relatives were visiting that day and the stairway door was mistakenly left open. Chase was cruising around in the low-slung frame on wheels and rolled through the doorway and down the stairs. Most injuries are not this serious, but 71% of them involve falls down stairs, 21% are simple tipovers, 5% result in burns, and 3% result in falls from the porch, according to a 1994 study published in *Pediatrics*.

In all, 21,000 product-related deaths and 29 million product-related injuries befall American consumers each year—at a cost to the nation in excess of $200 billion a year. Risks lurk around every corner, occurring where you'd least expect them nearly as often as where you'd most expect them. Toys, lawn mowers, household cleaning solutions, furniture, and pull cords on window blinds and shades, to name a few, all pose hazards.

For instance, about 50 children under age two drown in 5-gallon buckets every year. In the summer of 1991, Tina E. was using a 5-gallon bucket to wash her children's car seat covers on the lawn outside her home. Tina took the covers out of the bucket and walked around the side of her house to hang them on the clothesline. About 3 inches of soapy water remained in the bucket. She returned after less than a minute and found her 12-month-old daughter, Alora, missing. Tina called neighbors to help with the search for Alora. After several minutes, they found that Alora had toppled head first into the bucket and had drowned.

If you live or work with children or the elderly, it pays to be especially careful. Since young children cannot always recognize or avoid hazardous situations, they are especially vulnerable to household dangers. Likewise the elderly, who may recognize danger but cannot always respond as quickly as necessary. That's why the CPSC must issue strong industry-wide safety standards for hazardous products. The CPSC's pace not-withstanding, the standards work. In the decade following the establishment of the CPSC, accidental household injuries declined by 28%, as compared to the decade preceding the existence of the CPSC, when accidental injuries declined only 11%. Post-CPSC, accidental deaths declined by 27%; pre-CPSC, they declined only 13%. And since 1980, annual deaths and injuries related to consumer products have declined by an additional 20%.

THE BASICS

It's a Jungle Out There

The concept of consumer product safety dates back to the outrage and stir created in 1906 by the publication of Upton Sinclair's novel *The Jungle,* which depicted the unsanitary and gruesome conditions under which America's meat was processed at the time. Enactment of the Food and Drug Act and the Meat Inspection Act followed shortly after.

Since then, Congress has given four federal agencies or departments responsibility for overseeing the safety of the products you buy: The Food and Drug Administration (FDA) oversees the safety of drugs, cosmetics, medical devices, and all food except meat, poultry, and produce; the Department of Agriculture ensures the safety of meat, poultry, and produce; the National Highway Traffic Safety Administration (NHTSA) regulates automobile, truck, and tire safety; and the CPSC looks out for the safety of virtually everything else.

Created in 1970 at the suggestion of Senate Commerce Committee Chair Warren Magnuson

(D-WA), the National Commission on Product Safety found that "the exposure of consumers to unreasonable product hazards is excessive by any standard of measurement." This set the stage for the creation of the CPSC. The new agency opened in May 1973, at the end of the so-called Consumer Decade (1965 to 1975), during which Congress established or strengthened a number of federal agencies. The CPSC mandate: To "protect the public against unreasonable risks of injuries and deaths associated with consumer products" by developing voluntary industry-wide safety standards, issuing mandatory safety standards if voluntary standards were not established, conducting research, investigating the causes and volume of injuries, recalling and banning hazardous products, educating the public, and working with industry to create safer products.

To get an idea of the agency's reach, former CPSC commissioner David Pittle and Consumers Union board member Robert Adler suggest visualizing everything you'd find in a large shopping mall. "Except for guns, drugs, tobacco, food, and boats, the safety of virtually everything in the mall falls within CPSC jurisdiction." In all, that's about 15,000 product categories, and the businesses producing, distributing, or importing these products number well over a million.

One of its main functions is collecting data about injuries and deaths caused by consumer products through the National Electronic Injury Surveillance System (NEISS). Approximately 100 hospi-

tals around the country report the incidence of emergency room visits that are related to a range of consumer products. The data allow CPSC to track broad trends and take action on some dangerous products—such as drawstrings on children's clothing, which garment manufacturers agreed to remove from kids' clothes after 17 deaths and 42 non-fatal accidents caused by drawstrings that got tangled up with kids. Nobody else collects these data, and they support the work not only of the CPSC but also of activists and injury prevention researchers in and out of government and industry.

However, the CPSC's reach too often exceeds its grasp. Although the CPSC has nominal authority for ensuring the safety of a vast array of products, it lacks the clout—or the economic resources—to carry out its mission. For instance, in 1981 Congress required the CPSC to defer to voluntary industry-created, industry-wide standards of safe products rather than impose federally mandated standards, unless adequate voluntary standards were not forthcoming. This move essentially *required* the corporate foxes to guard the chicken coop—not to mention legitimized the idea. After evaluating this policy six years later, the Consumer Federation of America (CFA) concluded:

"There were excessive time delays in developing voluntary standards, there was deferral to inadequate standards, there was reliance on non-existing voluntary standards, and there was inadequate monitoring of voluntary standards."

The NEISS data pose another hurdle. Since relatively few of the nation's hospitals are included in the sample, the data are incomplete and lack specificity. Mary Ellen Fise of CFA suggests that "to further understand and prevent childhood poisonings, CPSC could collect more specific information from hospitals that have emergency poisoning admissions—asking what type of containers held the substance and what type of closure was used."

Even worse, the CPSC is the only health and safety agency that restricts the release of reports of potential hazards. Under section 6(b) of the Consumer Product Safety Act (CPSA), before the agency releases information from which the identity of a manufacturer could be ascertained, it must first notify the manufacturer that the information may be released, permit the manufacturer to comment, and take steps to assure that disclosure is fair.

These cumbersome requirements allow manufacturers to intimidate the agency into withholding news of serious hazards with the threat of drawn-out, expensive lawsuits—during which time the hazard is still on the market. For instance, the CPSC began to suspect that a popular portable heater might pose a fire hazard in early 1988. In November of 1989, it issued a preliminary determination that the heaters might be risky, but it was not until August 1991, after negotiations with the manufacturer, that the public was alerted. In the 21 months between the CPSC determination and the public alert, eight people died in two fires that might have been caused by the heaters, according to the lawyer who represented some of the plaintiffs in the cases.

Another part of the CPSA requires manufacturers to notify the Commission if they receive information about defects in their products that could create a substantial hazard. This is similar to requirements of the automobile industry and the medical device industry that they report potential hazards to the NHTSA and the FDA, respectively.

Companies must report potential hazards to the CPSC if:

- They receive information suggesting that a product fails to meet a consumer product safety standard or regulation.
- A product has a defect or otherwise could create substantial risk of injury.
- A product is the subject of at least three federal or state civil actions that allege the involvement of that product in death or grievous injury cases and that result in settlements or judgments which favor the victim.

These reporting rules apply to both domestic manufacturers and importers.

Although the public has immediate access to these reports as soon as they are filed with NHTSA or the FDA, access to CPSC reports is severely limited. Within the legally mandated CPSC operations, the public can see these reports only in relatively narrow circumstances, such as when the agency brings an imminent hazard lawsuit in court.

The CPSC has the power to ban and recall hazardous products. Most often, the Commission acts in cooperation with the manufacturer, who agrees to recall the product voluntarily. To pick a typical example, late in the summer of 1997, the CPSC recalled 40 million torchère-style halogen floor lamps. This kind of lamp had caused 189 fires and 11 deaths since 1992, including the widely reported fire that landed jazz great Lionel Hampton in the hospital. The action called for consumers to pick up free halogen bulb guards at one of 12 major retailers, including Home Depot, Kmart, and Wal-Mart. The guards shield bulbs, which get much hotter than regular light bulbs, from draperies, bedding, and other flammables that may fall on the lamp or that the lamp may topple onto.

WHAT TO WATCH OUT FOR

Drowning

Drowning is the third leading cause of accidental death in the country, and children under the age of five are especially susceptible. Beware of buckets, even if only partially full of water or other liquids—especially the 15-inch-high, 5-gallon buckets familiar at construction sites and in institutional kitchens. After their original contents—spackle, canned peaches, or whatever—have been used up, many people reuse the handy 5-gallon containers for household chores.

If you have young children, don't leave any filled bucket unattended. In the short time it takes to answer the phone or to find a mop, a toddler can fall in, as was the case with Alora E. (described earlier). The bucket openings are large enough to permit easy entry, and the sides are not quite tall enough to prevent it. And even if the bucket is only partially full, the liquid makes it extremely stable and unlikely to readily tip over—which is great for mopping the deck, but could be deadly for a child.

The CPSC also issued a public warning about the dangers of leaving infants unattended in bathtub seats. Forty-five young children have drowned in these seats since 1983; in more than 90% of the cases, children were left without supervision by a parent or caregiver for anywhere from one to 35 minutes. The seats may tempt you to leave the child while you make a quick trip to find clean clothes or answer another child's call, but when you aren't looking, children may be able to tip the seats over or unlatch them.

Riding Mower Mishaps

The risk of an accident with a riding mower is almost twice that of a rotary push mower. Accidents have several common patterns: The machine tips over, the victim falls under or is run over by the machine, or the victim is thrown from or falls from the mower. Read and follow all the safety precautions that come with the equipment. If you've misplaced the literature, write to the CPSC to get a Product Safety Fact Sheet

(Publication No. 588, Riding Lawnmowers).

Small Electronics

About $2.6 billion-worth of small electrical goods are imported from East Asia each year—everything from electrical cords to ceiling fans to night lights. Many jof these items are safe, but with imports you have to be especially careful to look for a genuine UL mark. This seal of approval from the Underwriters Laboratories assures you that the product has passed a safety test and won't injure you or your loved ones.

Unfortunately, not all UL marks are created equal. There has been a rash of phony UL marks on cheap electronics imported from abroad, mainly from China. But also be careful with products from Korea and Taiwan. Government investigators have found surge protectors that not only wouldn't protect your equipment from electrical surges, but also had wiring so shoddy that plugging in a computer, printer, and lamp all at the same time would overload the strip.

To be sure your electronic goods are safe, call the Underwriters Laboratories' toll-free number: (888) 854-6275.

Product Recalls

Deaths and injuries from dangerous products often continue for months or even years after warnings or recalls are issued. Did you know that certain cribs can collapse and trap children in a cage of rails or that some bean bag chairs are easily unzippable and may create a suffocation hazard if the kids inhale the stuffing? Likely not, and you've probably missed numerous other product recalls or warnings. Think twice before you use or lend

ANNUAL INJURIES ASSOCIATED WITH SELECTED PRODUCTS	
Product	**Injuries**
BICYCLES	549,988
PLAYGROUND EQUIPMENT	241,319
TOYS	138,154
ALL-TERRAIN VEHICLES	62,400
BUNK BEDS	42,599
SKATEBOARDS	30,353

Source: Consumer Product Safety Commission, 1995

old stuff stowed in your attic or bought at a yard sale or second-hand store. To get information about old items, call the CPSC's Recall Roundup or check for listings on its web site. Contact information is in the **HELP** section at the end of the chapter.

THE $MARTER CONSUMER

Whether you're thinking about buying a car or a child's car seat, taking something for your cold, slathering on cosmetics, or cooking a chicken, safety should always be a primary consideration—before price, before appearance, before keeping up with the Joneses.

Don't Toy Around

You cannot assume a toy is safe just because you see it for sale at the toy store. Thousands of children are injured seriously enough playing with unsafe toys each year to be hurried to the emergency room, and about 20 die. Choking on small parts is the leading cause of toy-related deaths.

There simply are not enough safety experts in the toy store aisles —or the warehouses of manufacturers, distributors, and importers. Recalls of hazardous playthings can take months, and it's rare that every purchaser can or will be notified. And no number of inspectors can stop or detect dangerous imported

toys that are sold by street vendors without any federal review.

When recalls finally do take effect, they are usually so poorly publicized that it's prudent for you to check up periodically on your own to be sure that the toys your child plays with are considered safe. To find out about toy safety recalls, look for the Recall Notice Board at your toy store or periodically call the CPSC at (800) 638-CPSC.

Do your own legwork: Be on the lookout especially for small parts, sharp points and edges, cords and strings, loud noises, and potential electric shocks. (For more detailed information, read "Toys" on page 519.)

Wear a Helmet

Over 60,000 children suffer head injuries while bike riding or in-line skating every year; another 250 under age 14 die from bike-related head trauma. And tens of thousands of teenagers and adults suffer serious bike- and skate-related head injuries each year. Bradley M., a 6½-year-old from Washington, DC, fractured his skull and suffered an epidural hematoma while riding his bike without a helmet. Another child playfully pulled on the back wheel of his bike and Bradley tumbled over the handlebars onto his head. He was in a coma for a week and then underwent surgery to drain the hematoma. After months of rehabilitation, doctors expect Bradley to fully recover.

Wearing a helmet can reduce your risk of head injury by as much as 85%, yet fewer than 15% of chil-

CRIB SAFETY

The most dangerous item in the nursery is a child's crib. Each year, 50 children die in crib accidents. Over the years, the CPSC has ensured that new cribs are vastly safer than those of yore. But that won't protect your child from cribs that were manufactured before the CPSC's safety standards went into effect.

Watch out for bargain cribs you might pick up at a garage sale or have handed down to you. They may not meet current safety standards. And when your child is 36 inches tall, replace the crib with a bed.

For more information on crib safety, contact the Danny Foundation, which was named for a child who tumbled out of a crib, caught his undershirt on a post, and hung himself. Its number is (800) 83-DANNY.

---

dren or adolescents wear helmets regularly. When shopping for helmets, look for ones that meet standards set by American National Standards Institute (ANSI) or the Snell Foundation (noted on the helmet itself and its packaging). Adults in the household should wear helmets, too—for safety, and as a good example to children.

Wear Your Seat Belt

The federal government requires car manufacturers to equip all cars with "automatic crash protection," which means air bags or automatic safety belt systems, but there is no federal law requiring people to actually use them. Most of the states have passed laws requiring people to wear safety belts, however, the laws are relatively weak and almost uniformly unenforced. Even if your car has been equipped with automatic shoulder harnesses and air bags, buckle up. The shoulder harnesses were not designed to work without the lap belt. And in all but a few car models air bags will only pop out in a head-on collision of sufficient speed. In accidents involving slower speeds or side collisions, air bags provide no protection whatsoever. Your seat belt could save your life.

Equip Your Home With a Smoke Detector

The risk of dying in a fire is twice as high in a home without a detector as in a home with one. For this reason, many states have laws requiring smoke detectors, which can increase the time you have to escape, as well as the time the fire department has to save your property. Although the devices have become ubiquitous, *Consumer Reports* estimates that one in three would not respond properly to a fire—primarily because of dead or missing batteries.

The U.S. Fire Administration suggests the following:

- At a minimum, install a smoke detector outside each bedroom or sleeping area in your house, and keep bedroom doors closed when you sleep. It's also wise to have at least one detector on every level of the home. Be sure to install detectors away from air vents, windows, and other places where drafts may interfere with smoke detection.
- Don't forget to maintain your smoke detectors. Test them at least once a month. Clean the dust that collects with the vacuum cleaner at least once a year. Change the batteries every year, and use only the type of batteries recommended on the detector.
- If smoke from cooking causes the alarm to go off, do not remove the batteries or disconnect the power source. Simply fan the smoke away from the detector until the alarm stops. If this happens often, you might want to relocate the detector or install a different type.
- Develop a fire escape plan and review it with all members of your household. Don't forget to include a plan for children and elderly people who need special assistance.

While more than 90% of all homes are equipped with smoke detectors, only 30% have at least one fire extinguisher—even though both cost as little as $10. Since where there's smoke there's usually fire, your household should have at least one multipurpose extinguisher. Look for an A:B:C label,

after classifications of the three types of materials that burn—A) ordinary combustibles, like paper and wood; B) flammable liquids, like cooking grease, gasoline, and paint solvents; and C) electrical fires, in wiring or television sets. In addition, you may want to invest in a B:C extinguisher for the kitchen, which will be much more effective on a grease fire than the multipurpose A:B:C: extinguisher.

To find out what kind of fire protection is required in your area, or to get further tips, check with your local fire department or your state's fire marshal. You might also want to contact the CPSC.

Report Hazardous Products

Reporting dangerous products will save others from your misadventures or worse. Here's how:

Safety hazards associated with cars and tires should be reported to the NHTSA Auto Safety Hotline, (800) 424-9393. Through this number you can also get useful safety information on new and used cars, child safety seats, tires you may be considering, and the results of government crash tests.

Problems and questions related to food, drug, and cosmetics safety should be addressed to the FDA. If you experience food poisoning, an allergic reaction, product tampering, or other suspicious effects from drugs, medical devices, cosmetics, or foods other than meat and produce, write the FDA at 5600 Fishers Lane, Rockville, MD 20857.

Problems with meat, poultry, and produce should be reported to the Department of Agriculture. The USDA Meat and Poultry Hot Line operates Monday through Friday from 10 AM to 4 PM EST, with extended hours in the days before Thanksgiving; call (800) 535-4555.

For most other products, call the CPSC hotline at (800) 638-CPSC and be prepared to give the following information:

- A description of the product.
- The company's name, address, and, if you know, whether the company is a manufacturer, distributor, importer, or retailer of the product.
- The nature and severity of the hazard and of the injuries that can result from using the product.
- Your name, address, and telephone number.

H E L P

- **To report an unsafe** consumer product or a product-related injury, or to request information, call the U.S. Consumer Product Safety Commission's toll-free hot line: (800) 638-2772. There's also a teletypewriter for the hearing-impaired: (800) 638-8270 (everywhere but Maryland); (800) 492-8104 (TTY, Maryland only). You can also find CPSC information on the Web: www.cpsc.gov.

- **To find out about product recalls,** read *Consumer Reports'* monthly feature, local papers, the Product Recall Notices at toy stores, call the CPSC Hotline or check its Web site.

- **For information on keeping babies** and children safe, contact the National Safe Kids Campaign at (202) 662-0600.

- **For more specific information on** fire safety, smoke detectors, and fire extinguishers, read the May 1994 issue of *Consumer Reports* or contact your state fire marshal or the U.S. Fire Administration, 16825 South Seton Avenue, Emmitsburg, MD 21727; (301) 447-1080.

- **Consumer Federation** of America is a national non-profit consumer advocacy organization that has worked extensively on product safety issues. For their materials, write them at 1424 16th Street NW, Washington, DC 20036; or call (202) 387-6121.

- **National consumer, health, and insurer** groups work together in the Coalition for Consumer Health and Safety to educate the public, identify and promote federal policy solutions to health and safety threats relating to motor vehicle safety, home and product safety, indoor air quality, food safety and nutrition, tobacco use, alcohol consumption and AIDS. For more information, write to the Coalition for Consumer Health and Safety, 1424 16th Street NW, Suite 604, Washington, DC 20036.

- **For more safety information, see** the following chapters in this book: "Groceries," "Water," "Houses, Condos, and Co-ops," "Airlines and Airfares," "Cosmetics," "Lawn and Garden Care," "Pharmaceuticals and Pharmacists," and "Weight Loss Products and Programs."

Technology

COMPUTERS

A User-Friendly Guide to Powering Up

Writing about computers may be as vexing as shopping for them. Practically as soon as the author commits words to paper—or the shopper commits dollars to retailer—what was once state-of-the-art turns white elephant. The 100 MHZ Pentium chip, the far cutting edge in 1995, wasn't even available in 1998 on entry-level desktops. Call it Grove's Law, a corollary of Murphy's Law named in honor of chip-maker Intel's CEO Andy Grove: Anything you buy today will be obsolete in a year—and on sale for about half of what you paid for it.

Ditto advice that gets too specific about product specifications. That's why we've limited this chapter to offering broad advice on how much computer is enough, shopping strategies, and common consumer pitfalls. To get an idea about the most up-to-date product specifications and what they cost, you'll be better off shopping around in stores or on-line than reading any book.

So relax. Get used to the possibility that no matter how hard you try (or how much you spend), your computer could be out of date by the time you figure out how to hook it up.

THE BASICS

If you aren't already familiar with computers, you'll want to know something about the basic components of today's computer systems.

The processor. This is the computer's engine or brain and is most commonly identified by the speed of its chip, which ranges from 120 to 400 megahertz. The higher the number, the faster the processor can execute the instructions you give it—and the more it costs. Assuming that other components are properly matched to the processor, speed is a good indicator of how fast the system will perform. But you can't judge a computer's performance by megahertz (MHz) alone. When *Consumer Reports* tested 200 MHz models against some far less expensive, supposedly slower processors, the tortoise sometimes tied the hare.

Deciding which speed of processor is right for you is a classic trade-off between price and performance.

Most computer users who just want to write letters, send e-mail, and use the Internet to help their kids with their homework will be fine for a couple of years with a 233 MHz processor (or its equivalent). But if you want to pit your machine against chess grandmaster Gary Kasparov, play arcade-equivalent games, or use heavy-duty desktop publishing and number-crunching programs, you'll be happier buying as much power as you can afford.

Memory. The amount of random access memory (RAM) in your computer determines its capacity to juggle information. The more RAM you have, measured in megabytes, the more programs you can run at once and the easier it will be for your computer to digest large database programs or programs with lots of graphics.

These days, you need a minimum of 16 megabytes of RAM to run Windows 95 and Windows 98 smoothly and connect to the Internet, but you'll probably be happier with more. If you are choosing between buying a faster processor or more RAM, go for the memory. Memory is more likely to improve performance than chip speed.

Hard drive. The amount of space the computer has to store programs and the data and text files you produce is measured in megabytes or gigabytes (one GB equals 1,000 MB). The bigger your hard drive, the more software and data you can file away for future use—and the better your system will be able to take on software upgrades, which tend to bloat up rather than slim down as new features are added.

Modem. This is your telecommunications link to other computer systems and data bases. Even the cheapest PCs now come with a speedy 56K modem as standard equipment. Make sure it meets the new international standards for these modems, known as V.90, or can be upgraded to do so. Many modems can also be used for faxing from your computer. If you want this capability, be sure you get a "faxmodem."

Video memory. You probably don't need to fully understand all the mumbo jumbo, but be sure to get at least 2 megabytes of video memory, VRAM for short.

Monitor. Most computer monitors look like small television screens. They accept signals from the processor and translate them into images on the screen. Screen size is measured on the diagonal, ranging from 14 inches to 21 inches. The ubiquitous workstations you see usually have 15-inch monitors, but 17-inch models (with 28% more viewing area) are in-

> "*There's no other major item most of us own that is as confusing, unpredictable and unreliable as our personal computers.*"
>
> — WALTER MOSSBERG, computer columnist for *The Wall Street Journal*

242

creasingly popular. The first thing to decide is how big a monitor you want. This is easier said than done: the actual viewing area varies even among models that are supposedly the same size. For instance, the viewing area on so-called 15-inch monitors ranges from 13.7 to 14 inches.

Another monitor concern is dot pitch, the size of the space between the dots that make up the images on your screen. The smaller the space, the sharper the image will be. Look for dot pitch of 0.28 mm or less.

Now you need to figure out the optimal combination of these components. You need enough computer to suit your current needs, and some room to grow. But how much is enough? Experts advise that you work backwards from the software you want to be able to use. If word processing, surfing the Web, sending e-mail, and tracking family finances will be the main uses of your new machine, one of the cheaper machines for the masses is probably more than adequate. But if you want to play cutting-edge games or create huge Web sites, you're better off spending the extra money for the cutting-edge machine.

WHAT TO WATCH OUT FOR

"Monitor not included." You'll find this caveat buried in many computer ads, even those for "complete" systems. Why? Because the deals seem better: Including a monitor jacks up the price 20% to 50%. Under other circumstances, this would qualify as a consummate consumer deception—e.g., selling a camera with "lens not included." But the quality of monitors varies so much that you may be better off choosing your own rather than ending up with whatever the store throws in.

Price promotions. Color printer, $199*. Virus-detecting software, $39*. Don't gloss over the asterisks, or you'll get a surprise at the checkout counter. That color printer actually costs $249 and the software $59. The tiny asterisks it's so easy to ignore lead to tiny print telling you of mail-in rebates that bring the printer price down $50 and the software price down $20. This kind of advertising is perfectly legal, but it takes a good eye to figure out what you will pay up-front. Then, it takes divulging all kinds of personal and demographic information, along with a copy of your sales receipt—and the product's serial number and waiting a few months to collect your rebate. If you don't want to end up on the manufacturer's mailing list, or the mailing list of anyone to whom your name is sold, be sure to inform the manufacturer of your desire to be left off all mailing lists.

Extended warranties. It's hard to get out of a store with a new computer without a salesman pressing you to buy an extended warranty that'll cost anywhere from $100 to $400. And it might be tempting, since manufacturers' warranties have gotten shorter. However, the retailer's profit margin on an extended warranty is enormous, unlike on the item they are insuring, where the margins are razor-thin. And it's probably not worth the money. The ratio of contracts used to those sold is 2 or 3 out of 10, according to *Smart Money* magazine. Plus, computer experts say that if anything is going to go wrong, it is most likely to go wrong while the machine is still under the manufacturer's original warranty (generally one year). If you pay for the computer with a credit card, you can probably extend the manufacturer's warranty even further. Check with your credit card company.

SOS. These days, computers and software come with minimal written instructions—with the expectation that you will find all the documentation you need in the hard drive or on the Internet. But neither of those options does you much good if you can't get your computer up and running or if it has taken it upon itself to shut down.

When you call technical support telephone lines, get ready for more frustration. Home computer vendors receive an estimated 28.5 million calls for technical support every year. Is it any wonder you couldn't get through to a human being the last time your computer crashed? And once you get through, it can be difficult to get answers, even to simple questions. When the market research firm Service Intelligence used mystery shoppers to survey technical support lines at six major software companies in 1997, in a quarter of the 90 calls that got through, technicians either provided the wrong answer to a problem or said the problem couldn't be solved. Thing was, all the questions had been taken from the companies' own lists of frequently asked questions posted on the Internet, where there are also answers.

PC or Mac?

Before you decide anything else, you'll have to choose between computers that run the Windows operating system and those that run Mac OS—a decision akin to the old days of choosing between Betamax and VHS video players. Connoisseurs will tell how much more elegant a Mac is—it's easier to set up, use, and add to. But Windows systems have long dominated the home and office market, and they are getting easier to use. Cachet will cost you—Macs tend to be more expensive than their Windows equivalents, and you'll find less and less software and peripheral equipment designed for Macs. However, you no longer have to worry that files created on one system will be irretrievable on the other. The latest chips and special software make switching between the two possible, if not always simple.

On-site or in-home service warranties. You might naturally infer that having such a warranty means that a handy person will be dispatched to help you shortly after you call the help line with a complaint. Nope. Actual on-site service is the exception rather than the rule. More often than not, you'll spend a long time trying to get through to the help line, then you'll spend a long time on hold, and finally a support technician will talk you through a battery of fixes. If you've still got a snafu, a new part may be shipped to you (so you can make your own "on-site" repair) or you may be asked to ship the computer to a repair center. It's very rare that you'll get a house call.

Restocking fees. Even if you return a piece of equipment or software within the allowable money-back guarantee period, you may get slapped with a re-stocking fee. These fees are designed to dissuade people who do not intend to keep the equipment from taking it home temporarily. But the fees can sting anybody. Say you buy a new computer system and after several days you still can't get it working properly. Even though you are entitled to a new machine or a free repair, you are so frustrated that you just want your money back. You could get your whole payment back, or you could get your payment back minus a 15%–25% restocking fee. That's a steep $500 on a $2,000 non-functioning computer system. And if you'd opened any of the software that came with the system—likely, since you were trying to get everything working properly—you could owe a restocking fee on the software that came bundled with the machine, even if the store doesn't take a slice of the computer's price.

Needless to say, it's smart to ask about restocking fees before you buy. When you hear a vendor's policy, you may want to take your business elsewhere. Just in case.

Shopping at home. Computer equipment is the biggest seller on the Internet, and mail order merchants like Dell and Gateway 2000, as well as catalogues, offer competitive or lower prices than many retail stores. Don't let good prices (and no sales tax) grab you, if you're a novice and need hand-holding through the purchase and a helping hand afterward. First-time buyers will likely be more comfortable—and confident—buying from a store they can return to for help and repairs. If you want to buy through the mail or the Web, it's worth checking potential vendors or on-line auctions with the Better Business Bureau beforehand. For more information on the rights of mail order shoppers, see our "Home Shopping" chapter on page 612.

THE $MARTER CONSUMER

Insist on upgrade-ability. Stan Davis and Christopher Meyer, authors of *Blur: The Speed of Change in the Connected Economy,* rightly point out that "it would be nice if we could stay current by tweaking, rather than trashing, our worldly goods." More and more computers offer this worthy option in the form of open slots for accommodating additional RAM memory or expansion bays so you can add another hard drive or a special graphics accelerator. However, some of the cheaper models that have become popular are designed for obsolescence rather than upgrading; they contain very little undeveloped real estate. And laptops are notoriously difficult to upgrade.

Prices can drop from one week to the next. Even if you saw an ad just a week ago, ask for a specific system rather than the system selling for "X" price. This week's $2,600 laptop could be next week's $2,400 laptop.

Bait and switch. Salespeople will almost certainly try to sell you more computer than you came into the store thinking you needed or wanted. Listen, but don't give in unless you are getting something you actually want or need.

Check boxes. Be sure they are sealed closed and that the manufacturer's name is on the box. Serial numbers on components should match serial numbers on the packaging. You are looking for a system that is new and covered by a warranty.

Always pay with a credit card rather than cash or check. That way you will have some leverage if something goes wrong before you've paid the bill in full and you don't get a satisfactory response

---

SIZE DOESN'T MATTER

You can get virtually all the power and features of a regular desktop computer in a notebook computer that's smaller than your average dictionary and designed to be portable. So for people who need to compute when they travel—or want to get their work out of sight—laptops are the way to go. Of course, you'll pay a premium for the miniaturized components, and the systems come prepackaged and, for the most part, are not customizable. Plus, laptops are harder (and sometimes impossible) to upgrade with expanded memory and the latest chips.

---

from the retailer or manufacturer. Under the Fair Credit Billing Act, you have 60 days from the onset of the problem to report to your credit card company your refusal to pay the bill for the product in dispute. If you are right, you'll never have to pay the bill. But beware: if the vendor turns out to be right, you'll owe not only the bill but any finance charges that accrued during the period you refused to pay.

Better to buy than lease. Computer leasing promotions make it seem as though leasing will keep your computer current. Perhaps, but it will cost you. With leasing, you don't own the computer—you agree to make monthly payments and return it or buy it at the end of a fixed term. The benefits: low initial cash outlay, affordable monthly payments, and the chance to trade the machine for a current model when the lease ends. The catch: over the long run, finance charges bloat the total cost even above what you'd pay if you financed the purchase on a credit card charging 19% interest.

Student discounts. If you are buying a computer for your child to take to college, ask the university about any hardware and software discounts students might qualify for. One student told of a deal that allowed him to buy the Microsoft Office suite of software for $199, less than half what his parents would have paid at going retail prices.

Insure it. Make sure your new equipment is protected against theft or loss. And don't assume it will simply be covered by existing homeowners or renters insurance. *Computer Shopper* magazine suggests checking the following aspects of your policy.

■ Do you have an "all risk" or "named perils" policy? Named perils will only cover losses from things like fire and flood. Under all risk, much more common mishaps like Diet Coke spilled on the keyboard would be covered.
■ Are your belongings valued at "replacement cost" or "cash value"? Since computers depreciate so fast, cash value approaches zero just as

fast. The difference between what the insurance company would pay and what you would have to spend to get a new machine could be thousands.
■ What will the computer be used for, and do you plan to deduct its purchase price as a business expense? Even if your computer is destined for a mix of firm and family use, your insurance probably will cover it only if you buy it out of family funds and take no business deduction.

Buying a reconditioned computer. Any appliance that has been reconditioned should be clearly marked as such. Shop with care; even reputable companies such as Packard Bell have sold computers as new that actually contained parts from previously sold computers. Plus, with entry-level computer prices so low these days, you could very well get more for your money buying one of the cheap new machines. But if money is tight, or you want extra features for less money, you might find a bargain.

If you go this route, you'll want to investigate which components are new and whether they are reliable brands, what happens if the machine fails, and who if anyone warranties it. If a well-known store or a manufacturer with a decent return policy stands behind the machine, you could be getting a real bargain. Even so, insist on the same warranty period that you'd get if you bought new equipment. One last thing: find out whether the reconditioned machine can be further upgraded. If it's maxed out, you might be better off paying more now and giving yourself some room to grow into.

Used but not used up. This isn't for everyone—there's no hand-holding, probably very little, if any, service, and warranties are likely to be short. But a handful of companies sell used equipment and discontinued models for a fraction of the price you'd pay for new models. For example, a Boston stockbroker bought a discontinued Toshiba laptop (new) from the Boston Computer Exchange for $1,250. The same computer had sold at retail for $1,900 just a month earlier, before it was made obsolete by a new model. Since he traded in his old laptop for $500, he got a decent laptop that was only one generation behind current technology for only $750. Not a bad deal. Used and closeout items, available from various Web vendors, are usually covered by a warranty that can range anywhere from 90 days to a year.

Upgrading the old rather than buying new. Before you commit to buying a new computer, it may be worth considering upgrading your existing computer's memory, modem or hard drive. Especially if your current machine runs on a 166 MHz or faster Pentium processor, upgrading could give you more bang for your buck. According to *Consumer Reports,* "Even a new $1,000 machine will cost you more than a thorough upgrade and probably won't offer much of an edge in performance." Installing RAM is a snap. An internal modem or hard drive is more complicated. And

transferring your files from the old hard drive to the new one is additional work. If you are nervous about staring into the guts of your computer, you can probably find a local shop or computer nerd to install new components for you. The price for consulting services can vary a lot, so ask around.

■ **If you want to buy a computer** via the Internet, click on www.bbonline.org to check the vendor's complaint history.

■ **Good sources of purchasing** information for both computer novices and nerds can be found on the Web. Click on C-Net's www.computers.com, compreviews.miningco.com/, and www.maven.businessweek.com, *Business Week's* on-line computer resource. All these sites give you access to general buying advice and specific product reviews.

■ **For ratings of computer systems,** look at the June 1998 issue of *Consumer Reports,* or click on www.ConsumerReports.org (for site subscribers only).

■ **The Better Business Bureau can** advise you on buying a used computer. Contact your local BBB for a free brochure on "How to Find a Reputable Computer Reseller," or go to www.bbb.org.

■ **To complain about deceptive** sales tactics—selling used goods as new, bait and switch, and the like—find your local consumer office or state Attorney General's office in the Appendix in the back of this book.

CHAPTER 23

THE INTERNET

Click Here for Help

You've seen the ads of people zooming through cyberspace. You've heard people who couldn't fit in a wet suit talk about "surfing." People give you their e-mail address along with their phone number. And you've seen those funny "http://" addresses everywhere from billboards to bus stops to boxes of cereal.

Welcome to the Information Age. The Internet is no longer the private domain of the *Revenge of the Nerds* set, as more and more of the mainstream is going online to buy and sell, to research term papers, or play around in "The Dilbert Zone." Families with Net access are replacing TV time with online time, using easy e-mail programs to replace expensive long-distance calls, and touring "virtual" museums and libraries.

But "getting on" for the first time can be confusing—the computer-speak, the funny acronyms and "dot-coms." Don't be frightened; the Internet is getting easier and easier to use, and there is plenty of straightforward, useful information online where you can learn to better utilize the Net (or learn all the geek-speak your heart desires). Just explore and have fun.

THE BASICS

The Internet—the network formed by linked computer systems around the world—has been around in some form since the late 1960s but has only recently become popular with the general public. The World Wide Web—that portion of the Internet that incorporates graphics and sound and allows users to hop from one "site" to another with the click of a button—is just a baby by comparison, making its debut in 1992. But that baby hit a tremendous growth spurt: By the end of 1998, 26 million households had online access, and everyone from NASA to *Baywatch* to the kid down the block has their own site on the Web. And by the year 2000, Boston-based Forrester Research projects that "netizens" will number close to a billion.

The World Wide Web is just one branch of the wide-reaching Internet. You can sound off on anything from Aleutian folklore to Zen meditation in online discussion groups called Usenet news groups, and read what other like-minded folks have to say. You can "chat" with people in "real-time" (i.e., you read what they type as they type it) in special networks called Internet Relay Chats (IRCs) or "chat rooms." And don't forget e-mail, which accounts for the most traffic on the Internet highway.

Getting On

Hardware. If you've bought a new computer in the last few years, it's almost certainly Internet-ready. If you've got an older machine, you need at least a 486 processing chip (or faster than 80 megahertz), and you should be running a graphical operating system like Windows 3.0 (or higher) or Mac OS with at least 32 megabytes of RAM. (If none of this makes sense to you, turn to "Computers," page 241.) If you have an older machine, you may want to install a graphics card and a sound card to better exploit the Web. Adding extra RAM will help speed downloads and other information transfers.

You'll also need a modem, the piece of equipment that connects your computer to an Internet service provider (or ISP) via telephone or cable. There are both external and internal modems; many new computers come with an internal modem already installed. External modems are generally a little more expensive, but don't need to be installed. Also, you can turn an external modem off when something goes wrong; to reset an internal modem, you must shut down all your software and restart your computer. Another convenient piece of equipment: a line splitter that turns one phone jack into two—so you

won't have to keep unplugging and replugging in your phone.

Today's standard modems transfer information at 28.8 or 33.6 kilobits (a "bit" is a tiny piece of information, and a "kilobit" is 1,000 bits) per second. There are modems that run faster, like 56 kbps models, although many ISPs —certainly not all—have limits on how fast they can send data to you. And your modem can work only as fast as theirs do.

The higher your modem's speed, the more you'll pay for it. 28.8 kbps models can cost as little as $25; a 56 kbps can cost more than six times as much. (You'll also pay more for modems that double as fax machines, allowing you to send and receive faxes directly on your computer.) Digital, or ISDN, lines offered by some phone companies have top speeds of 128 kbps but cost nearly $200 to install—plus a monthly service fee and additional charges from your ISP. But if you plan to use the Net a lot, or to transfer lots of information, a faster modem may be a useful investment. Remember, though, that phone modems will tie up your phone line while you browse.

In some areas, cable companies have started offering modems that use cable television wires to connect you to the Internet. These relatively new devices can download in a few seconds what takes many minutes over phone lines, but they aren't yet widely available—only about 10% of America's cable systems are properly equipped. You can expect to pay at least $30 for a cable modem, but installation can run as high as

ACCESS ALTERNATIVES

A computer isn't the only way to access the Web. New services like NetChannel and Microsoft's WebTV pair a traditional television set and a special set-top box to give you access to the Web. The box—manufactured by the likes of Sony, RCA, and Philips—can cost anywhere from $99 to more than $350, while connecting will cost you $20 per month for unlimited access. Like computer modems, the one hooked to your TV set will busy your phone line while you're connected to the Net. You browse using a remote control device rather than a mouse, and you can also "bookmark" sites, which means you can readily access the site again. (The services include proprietary browsers.) For e-mail you must use an on-screen keyboard (on which you "type" by clicking letters with your remote) or kick in another $50–$70 for an optional wireless keyboard; or you can use any PC-compatible keyboard, which you hook into the set-top box. You can also hook up a printer. As of mid 1998, you could not yet browse the Web and watch TV at the same time—you have to switch between the two—but WebTV and NetChannel were both promoting this capability as "coming soon." Such a feature will allow television shows to be embedded in Web pages and surrounded by links related to the show: You might click over to an *X-Files* trivia page while Agent Mulder investigates the latest odd occurrence.

The lower initial investment—a $300 set-box versus a $2,000 computer—may sway non-computer users to this Net alternative. One plus: no reports of TVs "crashing"—yet.

$150 (usually discounted if you're already a cable subscriber).

Internet providers connect your computer, via a modem that has dialed in to their service, to the worldwide network that is the Internet. When you're ready to make the jump to cyberspace, there are two ways to get there: online services and Internet service providers. Both give you access to the Internet—e-mail, news groups, chat rooms, the Web—but in different environments.

The four major online services—America Online (AOL), Microsoft Network (MSN), Prodigy, and CompuServe—are all-in-one setups that offer Web and e-mail access as well as members-only chat rooms, like "Love@AOL," and other proprietary publications and services.

These providers are very popular, and it shows—just try hooking up to AOL in the early evening, when millions of others are doing the very same thing. Busy signals and slow service are two of AOL's biggest complaints; in January 1996, users failed to get through to their accounts 80% of the time. AOL has added capacity and things have improved since then, but it can still be difficult or slow to connect during peak hours.

Many people start out with online services but move to one of the nation's 1,000-plus Internet service providers. There are both local and national ISPs, offering a wide range of choices, from barebones connections where you provide all the software to full-service digital hook-ups where you can host your own Web site. In do-it-yourself style, they don't offer proprietary content like online services, but most offer online guides to the Internet from their home pages. (A "home page" is the main page of a Web site. For example, the *New York Times'* home page is www.nytimes.com; from there you can jump to the paper's different sections and articles.)

Software. You don't just pop into the Web once you dial one of these services. Each aspect of the Internet—dialing in, reading e-mail, surfing the Web—needs special software. While AOL and others will give you and walk you through all the software you need to make full use of its services, an ISP may offer only the very basics. (You may

want to pay an expert to come to your computer to set everything up, but all ISPs provide a rudimentary set-up guide, and many have programs called "wizards" that either guide you through the set-up process or do it for you.)

Mac OS and Windows 95 users already have software that will maintain your modem connection; those with Windows 3.0 will probably have to install new software. Good ISPs will either provide such tools or recommend where to find what you'll need.

A Web "browser" translates digitized information into pictures, words, and sounds and is most often included free with your Internet service. Two browsers currently corner the market: Netscape Navigator and Microsoft Internet Explorer. Although specialists will talk your ears off about the superiority of one or the other, these two differ little, and both are surprisingly easy to use. Once you're online, you can "download" (i.e., transfer from the Net to your computer) a copy of either browser for a trial period. If you don't like one, you can try the other.

Both Netscape and Explorer allow you to receive, read, organize, and send e-mail—electronic messages that can be sent over the Net from one computer to another. Your ISP assigns you an e-mail address, usually your name or a nickname

> "*Cyberspace is like a giant yard sale. There is a lot to buy, but consumers don't always get what they bargained for.*"
>
> —SUSAN GRANT, Director of Internet Fraud Watch

and the ISP's Internet location—like joepublic@aol.com. Your mail is sent to an "in-box," where you can read it and then store it in a specific file, or trash it. Your e-mail address is usually tied to your ISP, so if you switch services, you'll have to switch addresses. "Stand alone" (i.e., separate, non-browser) e-mail programs such as Eudora allow you more options with your mail, like automatic sorting of incoming messages, spell checking, and archiving old mail.

You can also send attachments with e-mail, such as lengthy documents, pictures, even entire programs. But the person you're mailing must have the same program you used to create whatever you're sending—or the ability to translate it with another program—or the attachment can't be read. (Simple messages between two different brands of e-mail applications—say, Eudora and Lotus cc:Mail—are no trouble, however. Mail programs all adhere to certain universal standards.)

Although there are "news reader" applications available as well, news groups can also be read off Netscape or Explorer without additional software.

Again, there may or may not be significant differences between programs that matter to you, so experiment with a few kinds if you can, or ask friends or software dealers for advice.

Choosing an Internet provider. Ask friends who are online or a computer dealer about their experiences with various Internet providers. You'll want a firsthand account of how many busy signals or disconnects they've experienced, what kind of help they received, and how much hand-holding each service offers. You can also call the ISP and ask them a few questions yourself (many are listed in the Yellow Pages), like how fast their dial-up connections are; do they meet or exceed your modem's speed? Ask them about their modem-per-customer ratio. If there are 24 users dialing in for every one modem, your chances of connecting aren't so hot. Ten users per modem is a good standard to go by. Is there technical support available 24 hours a day? The last thing you need is a connection problem on late-night last-minute Internet research. What, if any, are their set-up or activation fees? What software and user guides are included? Can you pay for service month-by-month or will you be locked in to a longer contract? You may want to start out with a shorter service period to try out an ISP.

Most ISPs and online services offer two types of payment plans: by the hour and all-you-can-eat. If you don't see yourself doing much more than checking e-mail and maybe reading an online newspaper, opt for an hourly plan. You will get a set number of hours per month for a set amount, and you'll pay a fee for every hour over the limit. America Online has a $4.95 per month fee for three hours, plus $2.50 each extra hour; in a similar deal, MindSpring, a national ISP, offers five hours for $6.95, plus $2 each extra hour.

The all-you-can-eat plans do not vary much among providers. Most, including AOL, MindSpring, and AT&T's WorldNet, offer unlimited usage for around $20–$22 per month. What you should look for in these plans is not the cheapest rate, but what kinds of services they offer that fit your needs. Some, like AOL and IBM's Internet Connection, allow you to divide your e-mail account between five or six users at no extra charge, which is good for families or small businesses; others, like MindSpring, charge for these so-called child accounts. If you plan to use your access on the road, some offer toll-free service for an additional fee; many national ISPs have local access numbers you can call when you're in another city they serve. Are you the type who will need a lot of help? National providers may have more customer service reps, but they also have more customers; local providers can offer more personalized help, but they may not offer all the services you want.

More advanced users might want to explore Web site hosting services. Ask how much space is available under the flat rates. Mind-Spring and another national ISP, Concentric Network, offer 5 megabytes of space with their all-you-can-eat plans; Concentric also offers a "wizard" to help you set up your own site. AOL also offers site space with its plans. Check what limits there are on the amount of traffic your site can handle. ISPs suffer gridlock when sites get too many visitors.

If you can get online at your public library or from a friend's account, you can get a list of ISPs from The List (www.thelist.com), which provides an interactive ISP database. Fill in a form describing your online needs, and they'll reply with a list of ISPs that answer those demands. ISP Finder provides the same service on the Internet (www.ispfinder.com) and over the phone, at (888) ISP FIND. CNet.com offers its "Ultimate Guide to ISPs," based on customer reviews, at www.cnet.com/Content/Reviews/Compare/ISP.

Getting Around

Learning the Net *on* the Net is the best way to discover all it has to offer. Plenty of sites exist to teach "newbies" (those new to the Net) everything from browsing basics to designing your own Web site to "tweaking" your modem. Three of the most helpful: Paradesa Media's Learn the Net (www.learnthenet.com), *Wired* magazine's Webmonkey (www.webmonkey.com), and Web 101 (www.hotwired.com/web101).

Searching. Once you're online, you'll need help sifting through the 100 million (and counting) Web pages out there. Search "engines" use words and phrases that you submit to hunt for the information you're after. Different engines use different methods. Infoseek (www.infoseek.com), Alta Vista (www.altavista.com), and Lycos (www.lycos.com) search Web sites for words that you've entered and then display on your screen a list of sites, ranked by the number of times those "keywords" appear in them. The more you know about

ONLINE KIDS

The Internet can be a great place for kids to learn. An estimated 2.6 million kids are online, reading newspapers from around the world, investigating colleges, and talking to new pen pals on the other side of the planet. But we've all heard about the other side of the Web, with ads for beer or cigarettes, dirty pictures, and all-too-frank adult discussions.

There are several ways to protect your kids. Filtering software—either included with your ISP package or downloadable from the Web at a cost of around $35—can block access to inappropriate Web sites, chat rooms, and news groups by recognizing prohibited addresses and keywords from special lists. Some programs, such as CYBERsitter and Cyber Patrol, can also restrict the kinds of information that can be given out online—say, your child's age or address in a chat room. The time of day or amount of time a given user can go online can be controlled as well. (AOL, MSN, Prodigy, and CompuServe all offer some kind of parental controls.) You can also opt for a browser that supports the Platform for Internet Content Selection (PICS), which allows site operators to rate themselves, and removes or restricts access to sites with an "adult" rating.

The downside to such methods was perhaps best expressed by Solicitor General Seth P. Waxman during an oral argument before the Supreme Court over the Communications Decency Act, which among other things sought to control obscene content on the Internet. He said, "With hundreds of thousands of Web sites and tens of millions of pages that can be discreetly accessed, and with the number of sites increasing so rapidly, there is simply no way that parents can keep up with what can and can't be screened out."

The best way to help your children have a healthy Web experience is to spend time with them online. Talk to them about your concerns and guide them to sites you feel are appropriate. Tell them never to give out personal information to anyone they've encountered online, and never to respond to e-mail or chat-room discussions that make them—or you—feel uncomfortable.

the subject you're looking for, and the more keywords you enter about that subject, the narrower a search engine's list will be. If you're looking for information about Internet fraud, for instance, and you simply enter "consumer," you're bound to get millions of sites simply because they mention consumers. But enter "consumer," "fraud," and "Internet," and you'll shave the results to a more manageable (and relevant) list. After your first keyword search, the Excite search engine (www.excite.com) returns a list of words that may help narrow your search. Type in "consumer," and Excite search offers "affairs," "overcharged," and "scams" as well.

Search directories like Yahoo! (www.yahoo.com) allow you to search under different subjects, from the general ("Recreation & Sports") to the specific ("Table Tennis"). You can search under any subject heading; whatever category you choose, after you enter key words Yahoo! returns a site list just as the above engines do. At each stop along the way, Yahoo! also offers a list of sites it's chosen that might contain what you're looking for within that subject.

There are also multi-engines like MetaCrawler that use several different search engines—Yahoo!, Excite, Infoseek, Lycos, and others —at once to conduct simultaneous searches, trimming the number of matches to your query.

Just because information turns up in a search result doesn't mean it's accurate, however. Anyone can post a Web page, and search engines can only search for words or information, not for accuracy. Consult second and third sources before you decide what's a good resource and what's just plain hooey.

Online shopping. You can order almost anything on the Internet these days: airplane tickets, rental cars, computers, clothes, cigars, kayaks, champagne flutes . . . the list goes on. Countless big-name retailers have gone online to peddle their goods, like Barnes & Noble, Ticketmaster, and JC Penney. Yet in 1997, *Business Week* magazine found that only 1% of consumers with online access frequently shopped via the Internet. The reason? Most people don't feel comfortable typing their credit card number into a system that works by bouncing information over a series of computer systems.

As you become familiar with the Net, you'll find that there are bargains (and convenience) to be had. Just as you wouldn't do business in a store you didn't trust—or buy a "genuine Rolex" from a vendor in Times Square—you shouldn't buy online except from reputable, recognizable companies. A flashy, high-tech site doesn't guarantee the business behind it is legitimate, but the Better Business Bureau does. The BBB (www.bbbonline.org) certifies Web retailers that meet its standards. These feature a special BBB seal on their sites that you can click on; if the seal is genuine, you'll be transferred to BBBOnline, where you can investigate the company's profile. You can also check for any consumer alerts about the company at the Federal Trade Commission's site, www.ftc.gov, or check for news stories about the company by searching with one of the engines described above.

Shop only on "secure" sites that use some kind of encryption—the scrambling and descrambling of information. Anything you send to the site, like your credit card number and other personal information, is scrambled automatically before you send it, making it unreadable to any prying eyes. At the other end of the transaction, the details are descrambled by the retailer using special programs that only they have access to. Secure sites are marked by an "s" after the "http" in the Web address, like this: "https://www.amazon.com". (Amazon.com is an online bookseller that uses encryption technology.) On Netscape, the small key symbol in the bottom left corner of the window, usually broken, will be whole when you're using secure sites. A small, locked padlock appears in the bottom right corner of Internet Explorer's window.

If it still sounds risky, call the vendor. Any retail site worth its salt will also have a toll-free number that you can call to place orders. While Internet commerce has become safer in recent years, it's not so safe that hackers couldn't break into the online sites of ESPN Sportszone and *Outside* magazine in 1997 and find the credit card numbers of 2,400 customers who had purchased goods from those sites. Luckily, the intruders claimed they were trying to make a point about online security, and there were no reports of wrongful use of the card numbers.

There are also the thousands and thousands of "classified ad"-like advertisements found in news groups and unsolicited e-mail messages offering used computers, used cars, even used sporting equipment. It's easy to spot a sound deal from a major store, such as Barnes & Noble offering 20% off a hardcover book advertised on its Web site, but what about that news group post by a "company" offering a used $1,200 notebook computer for $500?

That's just what one Indiana man wondered after he replied to a similar posting. He jumped at the chance and overnight mailed a $70 check as a down payment to the vendor in Florida. The check cleared, but he received neither a computer nor further mail from the vendor. When the man threatened to report the vendor, he admitted to ripping him off and promised to return his money, but no check ever came. Eventually, the vendor stopped replying to the man's e-mail messages, and since he was unable to find a phone number for the vendor he was out of luck.

Privacy

Sitting alone in your living room in your bathrobe, browsing the Web, you may imagine your time online is private, but don't be fooled. As you click from site to site, download software, or e-mail friends, information can be gathered about you—which sites you frequent, what sort of advertising you respond to, even your name and phone number. A 1998 study by the Federal Trade commission found that more than 85% of 1,400 commercial Web sites it surveyd collect sensitive personal information from Web surfers, but only 14% explained how that information would be used. And only 2% had policies protecting consumer privacy.

There are many ways to inadvertently give out such personal information, but even information given in good faith will sometimes end up in places you wouldn't want it to. Like any other commercial service, online providers maintain subscription lists, and some will share your name, address, e-mail address, and phone number with telemarketing and other direct sales firms. The idea isn't popular with consumers: In 1997, America Online had to abandon plans to sell subscribers' phone numbers to telemarketers after a flurry of angry e-mail and news group postings alerted subscribers to the impending plan.

While much on the Net is free, some sites, like *The New York Times,* require you to register to access their Web pages. Usually they ask for your name, address, and e-mail address, but some will also ask "just a few short questions" about your interests and habits. Sound familiar? Telemarketing firms use the same technique to discover what kind of advertising will catch your attention. The banner ads that spread across commercial Web pages change according to who's seeing them. Answer a site's questionnaire that you enjoy mountain biking and traveling, and that banner will likely feature something like *Outside* magazine's Web site or an airline's online travel guide.

Most Internet providers and some registration-requiring Web sites have privacy policies that detail to whom, if anyone, your personal information will be given—ask about these before signing up. An ideal policy will allow you to "opt out" of having your personal information shared. If your Net access is through work or school, you'll probably be asked to sign an "agreement of use" or "code of conduct" policy that deals with privacy issues.

Any news group post you make—which may be read by thousands of people—will contain your e-mail address, allowing anyone who reads your post to send you a message. Online directories such as Who Where? (www.whowhere.com) and Four11 Directory (www.four11.com), compiled from phone books and other sources, can be used by anyone to find your real name (and possibly other information) just by entering your e-mail address. (These services let you delete your name from their directories if you choose.)

Even if you guard against giving out your personal profile, information on you can be gathered without your consent. Small bits of software called "cookies" install themselves on your hard drive when you visit certain sites. Cookies track your online habits as you browse within a site or even as you hop from site to site; they monitor, for example, which stories you read while at an online magazine or which products you're checking out in a Web store. They also record any other information they can about you—like where you work or what type of computer you're using.

Site producers use this digital footprint you leave to manage a site's ads, directing ads to people in a particular occupation or in specific companies. While cookies can recognize you as a particular individual, they can't collect personal information, unless you've already provided it somewhere else on the site, like on a registration form. (You can check if anyone's handed you a cookie by searching your hard drive for files containing the word "cookie.")

WHAT TO WATCH OUT FOR

E-mail is not private. Sending e-mail isn't like sending a letter in a sealed envelope— it's more like sending a postcard. People aren't supposed to read it, but they're able to. Even after you delete a message from your reader, your ISP usually retains a copy for at least a few days. If you get the address wrong, and your message is "bounced"—sent back to you and to the ISP's system administrator— it will be stored in a part of the system where all messages with bad coding go, where it can be easily read by the system administrator. A nosy system administrator at your ISP can also access any sent or received e-mail. E-mail can also be subpoenaed.

If your Net access is through school or work, in most cases your e-mail is technically their property, and they have a legal right to monitor your correspondence.

"Spam." If you get e-mail, you've probably seen plenty of messages in your mailbox that read "Make $$$ Now!" or "Easy Grant Money—Guaranteed!" These junk e-mailings are known as "spam,"

and Internet arteries are getting more and more clogged with them—AOL says as much as 30% of its daily e-mail traffic is spam. "Spammers" use special means to send the same message to millions of e-mail addresses, often for illicit reasons. One Texas offender claimed he could match big-money grants with customers for a $19.95 "application fee." Everyone who took the offer received the same generic, photocopied list of grant foundations. Even those who don't respond suffer: All that spam causes online traffic jams and slows download times.

Online investment fraud. Internet fraud tripled from 1996 to 1997, reports the National Fraud Information Center, and most of the scams are familiar: pyramid and "multilevel marketing" schemes, bogus investment opportunities, and fake sweepstakes.

In one multilevel scam, an Arizona college student posted Web ads for "GMG Global Marketing Group" that offered any takers a credit card issued by a foreign bank and a monthly newsletter about offshore investing, all for a low $100 charge up-front and a $25 monthly fee thereafter. Sign up another person, and GMG would pay you $25 plus a portion of that person's fees, and of the fees of anyone brought in by that person. All "tax-free," of course. But customers never received any credit card, although many got a few small checks for signing others up. Once federal investigators started asking questions, the student—who claimed by this time to have made over $300,000—had moved to the Cayman Islands.

Unsolicited stock advice, usually in the form of spam or other unfamiliar e-mail, is the mark of another online scam. The U.S. Securities and Exchange Commission calls it the "pump and dump," where a message writer claims to have "inside" information about the sudden surge or drop of a stock and urges you to quickly buy or sell. The hand behind the message is probably that of someone who stands to gain by selling shares if the stock price is pumped by gullible investors, or can buy up shares of the suddenly low-priced stock.

Hidden charges. Much on the net is largely free, but not everything. If a Web site asks for your credit card number, they're going to use it. Don't fall for sites that need the number "for tracking purposes." Also beware of "Trojan horse" scams like the one the FTC halted in 1997. Consumers visiting www.beavisbutthead.com, www.1adult.com and www.sexygirls.com thought they were downloading a free picture-viewing program, but they had unwittingly installed a program that disconnected the user from his or her ISP and reconnected them to the Net through a phone number in Moldova, resulting in huge international phone bills.

"Free" e-mail service, from companies like RocketMail or Hotmail, is available via the Web and can be used without a stand-alone e-mail reader. Like TV, it's "free" because

you will be forced to view ads every time you log on to the site to get or send e-mail. As you read a message from Mom, a banner at the bottom might read "Click here for more catalogs than you can handle!" Still, if your only Internet connection is somewhere public, like the library, you can get an e-mail account for nothing.

THE $MARTER CONSUMER

Use trial periods. Not sure if all this hype is worth it? Try the Internet out for a month. Many ISPs and other providers offer trial periods. It seems you can't flip through a magazine these days that doesn't have pasted somewhere inside a disk or CD-ROM from America Online offering 50 hours of free service. Take advantage and use AOL to check it all out. Some ISPs, like New York City's bway.net, offer the first week or even month free. (Avoid any that require a set-up fee for trial periods.) You can use the free time to investigate other service providers by checking out The List or ISP Finder.

But be careful: With these tryouts, you may have to give a credit card number as a "deposit." Don't forget to cancel service at the end of the trial period, or the provider will automatically begin billing your credit card for monthly service.

Be realistic. The average American household with Internet access spends less than 4 hours per month online, which may be plenty for you. So why pay $20 or so for all-you-can-eat service? At $6 for five hours, you'd come out way ahead with a less generous package. That said, if you—or your kids—find yourself spending more and more time online, opt for a flat rate that allows unlimited access.

Mark E. of Port Washington, New York, signed up for four hours of Net service per month for about $5, with each additional hour costing $2.50. His first bill was a little more then $10. His second was a little more than $25. His third was more than twice that. No, he wasn't being swindled, at least not by his service provider; his three daughters had discovered chat rooms, and were spending hours and hours online making new friends and mooning over the pop-band Hanson's fan pages. He switched to a $22 per month flat rate and made a bargain with his girls that for each hour they spent goofing off online, they had to spend another hour hitting the books.

Speeding up the "World Wide Wait." The "information superhighway" can be painfully slow sometimes—just ask the guy who researched this chapter. You can speed up download times by turning off your browser's ability to read images. This option is in the "Preferences" or "Options" menu on the toolbar. You'll miss a few things when you visit sites that depend heavily on graphics to provide information, but it's easy to turn the graphics back on when you need them. Some sites give you the option of switching to text only, where they display everything you'd get otherwise *sans* graphics.

You can also speed up response times by logging on at night or early in the morning. A lot of people only have connections at the office, and Net traffic can be less busy after 7 P.M. or before 9 A.M.

Faster modems also help, but as mentioned above, you can only go as fast as your server provides, and even the fastest modems are useless weapons against a busy signal.

Guard your password. When you sign up for Internet service, you're asked to choose a "log in" name (which also doubles as your e-mail address) and a password. Your stand-alone e-mail program will require one, and you'll usually need one to gain access to online services, like electronic magazines or personalized stock quote sites. Pick different passwords for each different service. Use difficult passwords; don't use your birth date, your name, or recognizable words that can be found in a dictionary. Mix letters and numbers, and make your passwords at least six characters long. Never give your password out to anyone online, even for "identification purposes." Giving out a password is like giving out your bank card's PIN number.

Throw away stale cookies. Search your hard drive for any file with the word "cookies" in it. If you're using Netscape Navigator 3.0 or above, or Internet Explorer 3.0 or above, you can delete your cookies file. (Keep in mind that you will probably lose some settings, like passwords into registration-required Web sites, when you do this.) Under the "Preferences" or "Options" menu in your browser, you can choose to be notified each time a site tries to install a cookie. Newer (4.0 and above) versions of the two major browsers have more specific options, like being able to control what type of cookie, if any, you're willing to accept.

You can also download software that blocks your cookies file altogether. Mac OS users can download Cookie Cutter at www.shareware.com for free. Windows users can check out PGPcookie.cutter at www.pgp.com.

Don't believe everything you read. Nobody owns the Internet, and there are no real controls over what gets published there. You may find yourself reading that eating a pound of squid every week reduces the risk of brain cancer, but that doesn't make it so. Anybody can post pretty much anything.

Take the case of Kurt Vonnegut. Copies of the famous author's 1997 commencement speech to graduating M.I.T students were forwarded from e-mail box to e-mail box, posted to news groups, and put up on Web sites as a model of sage advice like, "Do one thing every day that scares you." Only Vonnegut didn't write the speech—he wasn't even anywhere near M.I.T. during graduation. The "speech" was a humor column written by *Chicago Tribune* writer Mary Schmich that was picked up from her Web site and incorrectly (perhaps mischievously) attributed to Vonnegut.

(Connoisseurs of other Internet hoaxes and myths will delight in www.urbanlegends.com.)

Avoiding online fraud. Internet Fraud Watch, sponsored by the National Fraud Information Center, receives over 100 complaints every month about online scams and fraudulent sites. To keep yourself from falling into an online trap, here are a few commonsense tips.

- Don't do business with a person or company you're unfamiliar with, especially if the offer came by unsolicited e-mail.
- Get all the details—the name of the person or company, their phone number, and all terms of the sale—before making a purchase.
- Find out if anyone else has done business with the vendor, or ask the Better Business Bureau of the state in which they're located.
- Don't give out any information until you know the company is legitimate. Web sites can be put up and taken down in a matter of hours. High-pressure tactics are a sure sign of fraud. Sites urging you to "Act now!" may well disappear as soon as you do act.

Reject spam. If you've been spammed, send a compaint to the spammer's server, including a copy of the e-mail message. Usually you mail complaints to "postmaster" at the spammer's address. (Simply replace the user name before the @ symbol with "postmaster." So "spammy@service.com" would become "postmaster@service.com".) Leave the subject-line intact, and be sure to include all the headers (not just From, To, Date, and Subject, which is the default in most mail programs) in your reply, just in case the e-mail was cleverly forged. That way, the postmaster can trace it back to its source if necessary. If the server has an anti-spam policy—as

many do—the offender's service will be dropped if there are enough complaints. If the spam continues, most stand-alone mail programs have a "block sender" function to keep a specific sender's e-mail out of your box.

H E L P

■ **For reviews of 11** major Internet providers, read *PC Magazine*'s September 9, 1997 issue.

■ **For more about children and the** Internet, read the May 1997 issue of *Consumer Reports*.

■ **A list of the 100 most popular Web** sites, compiled daily by Alta Vista, is available at www.100hot.com. (The list excludes those of browser companies, ISPs, colleges, and "adult" sites.)

■ **The Better Business Bureau pro-**vides instant access to business and consumer alerts and other helpful resources, which you can access at www.bbb.org. Or write Council of Better Business Bureaus, Inc., 4200 Wilson Boulevard, Suite 800, Arlington, VA 22203-1804. Phone: (703) 276-0100.

■ **The U.S. Securities and Ex-**change Commission provides "Investor Alerts" about risky financial investments at www.sec.gov. You can also complain about online investment fraud by e-mailing help@sec.gov., sending a letter to the Office of Investor Education and Assistance, U.S. SEC, Mail

Stop 11-2, 450 5th Street NW, Washington, DC 20549, or calling (202) 942-7090.

■ **If you've been the victim of fraud,** complain to the National Fraud Information Center, sponsored by the National Consumers League. Call (800) 876-7060. Online, you can read daily reports of fraud investigations or complain via e-mail at www.fraud.org. If you want to send a letter, the address is 1701 K Street NW, Suite 1200, Washington, DC 20006.

■ **For more information about online** privacy, go to the Electronic Privacy Information Center (www.epic.org) and the Center for Democracy and Technology (www.cdt.org). Both provide their own information and extensive links to relevant news reports, legislation, and other resources. The CDT site also has a privacy demonstration about the kinds of information a Web site is able to gather when you visit.

■ **For more about cookies and other** electronic "junk," visit Junkbusters at www.junkbusters.com.

CHAPTER 24

CABLE TELEVISION

What You Get When You Get Wired

We are living in a time of technological wizardry (and chaos) that makes it hard to watch TV without two or three remote control devices—and from all indications, this is just the beginning. You think programming your VCR or ordering a pay-per-view movie is hard? Just wait until you have to choose among hundreds of channels—and have several companies knocking on your door eager to provide those channels. Wireless and satellite programming services have arrived. Telephone, cable, and Internet companies are merging. And by the time you bring home a new VCR, the cable company's next generation of gizmos may have made it obsolete.

All the promises of the cable companies—more channels, hundreds of movies-on-demand, interactive TV—amount to one thing for consumers: higher prices. Federal regulations allow cable operators to pass along most cost increases to subscribers, regardless of who benefits. For instance, when Cablevision spent $1 billion to upgrade its New York area system, it passed that cost on to subscribers. The upgrade was made to prepare the system for, among other things, cable modems for Internet service—but what if you couldn't care less about the Net? Even if all you want to do is catch a Bulls game, you'll pay for the upgrade.

And despite all the hoopla surrounding the 1996 Telecommunications Act—Congress' attempt to promote cable competition—the 73 million Americans who just want their MTV, CNN and ESPN have little choice but to hook up with one of the 11,000 local cable companies. Since most cable companies

> "**A**lthough Congress has tried to promote competition to local cable monopolies, consumers continue to face excessive and abusive rate increases for cable services."
>
> —GENE KIMMELMAN,
> co-director of Consumers Union
> Washington office

DAVID VS. THE CABLE GOLIATHS

Fed up with slow service and soaring rates, some small towns are building their own cable systems to compete with cable giants like Tele-Communications Inc. (TCI) and Comcast. In 1997, the citizens of places like Harlan, Iowa, and Newnan, Georgia, decided by public referendum to start municipal telecommunications networks. Incumbent cable providers spent a bundle campaigning against the idea —TCI ran ads in Alta, Iowa, calling it "creeping socialism" —but voters decided by overwhelming majorities to compete with the industry Goliaths. Municipal systems garnered hundreds of subscribers in their first year, offering lower rates and local control of programming.

operate as de facto monopolies and are usually the only game in town, they can charge whatever they like (within certain broad guidelines), foist equipment on you that hobbles your existing equipment, and treat you rudely.

THE BASICS

For years, the phone company seemed to be the most hated company in town. Now, it's the cable company. So-called "customer service" representatives too often serve up only surliness when there's a problem—"your arrogance and lack of common decency (i.e., a return phone call or acknowledgment of your error in any way)," as one irate consumer wrote. Another unhappy consumer told of having no luck correcting a billing error after four phone calls, a cumulative total of over three hours on "hold," and a letter; the only response he got was a series of threatening phone calls from a bill collection agency. Installers or repair people never showed up—"no one ever came [to pick up the converter box], although I'd made sure someone was there all day. Two weeks later I received in the mail a bill for the amount of $667.90 for 'unreturned equipment.' "

And to add salt to the wound, prices just keep going up. Between the deregulation of prices in 1986 and 1992, cable rates rose at more than twice the rate of inflation. After the FCC relaxed regulation in 1996, rates increased almost three times faster than inflation. According to the FCC, cable operators with no competition in their markets charged about 25% more per channel than those with competitors. And that's just the difference in bills; no doubt there is also a sizeable service disparity. And current price guidelines are scheduled to go out the window in 1999—

thanks to the 1996 Telecommunications Act—which will allow rates to shoot even higher.

WHAT TO WATCH OUT FOR

Equipment Equivocations

Since every cable system differs to some extent from another, you will no doubt discover incredibly annoying quirks for yourself, but here are some common ones:

The most infuriating problem is the incompatibility of the equipment provided by the cable company with your own video equipment. Many cable companies distribute converter boxes to customers through which the cable signal must pass on its way to the television set. This wouldn't be so bad except the boxes have set home technology back a decade or so. Many consumers have found they need multiple remote controls just to change channels, adjust the volume, or turn on a videocassette recorder. Still others find that they cannot record one show while watching another or use their split-screen televisions without renting additional equipment—for a hefty fee, of course.

Cable companies counter these complaints by saying they need the boxes to provide additional services to customers and to keep non-customers from stealing cable service. However, the boxes also enable you to buy pay-per-view programs, cable products that have the potential to provide huge profits to the cable companies.

Since all televisions sold these days are "cable-ready," don't let an electronics salesperson lead you to think this feature is anything special. Furthermore, the term "cable-ready" is virtually meaningless for people who need a converter box to receive cable service.

Reception Misperception

One of the original promises of cable television was perfect reception. In practice, however, even Diane Sawyer doesn't always come in loud and clear. Sometimes the problem can be traced back to the origination of the signal at the cable company; other times, the equipment that moves the sig-

ADVERTISING OR ENTERTAINMENT?

Infomercials step way over the already blurred line between commercials and the shows they sponsor: Infomercials are both. Thousands of these program-length commercials have run at odd hours during the day and night, the most successful of which rake in more than $30 million a year. No wonder Ross Perot figured the best way to "sell" his vision of America was to go direct to the consumer via half-hour infomercials.

Infomercials often use stars at varying heights in their careers—from Dick Van Patten (of *Eight Is Enough* fame) to former Olympian Bruce Jenner to Dionne Warwick—in mock talk show or news formats with cheery average "Joes" and "Janes" who unanimously attest to the product's wonders. Viewers are frequently reminded that operators are standing by at the other end of 800-numbers. The top-selling infomercial merchandise includes exercise equipment, beauty potions, self-improvement programs, diet aids, kitchen accessories, and real estate and money-making opportunities. And it's a huge market: In 1996, infomercial shoppers spent more than $1.6 billion on Abflexers, CardioSliders, "psychic" advice, spray-on hair, and other infomercialized gewgaws and services.

"The great infomercial gives a great solution to a perceived problem, and sometimes you don't even realize you have the problem," says Tim O'Leary of infomercial producer Tyree Productions in Portland, Oregon.

Anybody smell snake oil? The claims made about the products are those of the advertisers, not objective or independent evaluations. And they are not always true. The Federal Trade Commission (FTC) has challenged the accuracy of more than a dozen infomercials.

As a result, voluntary industry guidelines require program-length commercials to be clearly identified as paid advertisements at the beginning and any time ordering instructions are given. The sponsor's name must be disclosed, false claims or deception through omission are not allowed, the product must be available in sufficient quantity, and there must be a reasonable basis for the claims.

nal interferes with its clarity; in other instances, your receiver (either the TV or the cable box) renders *Seinfeld*'s Kramer more shaky than usual. If it's a problem with the cable company's equipment, they should adjust your bill to reflect any missed service.

IS SATELLITE THE SOLUTION?

Hate the cable company? Satellite providers are cable's biggest competitors. While there are only 5 million satellite customers—to cable's 64 million—their numbers are growing. As the battle for your remote heats up, here's how to choose what's right for you.

Satellite TV services, a.k.a. direct broadcasting services (DBS)—PrimeStar, DirectTV, USSB, and DISH Network are the big ones—claim to offer everything but the moon and stars. Mutltiplex movie channels, thousands of football, baseball, and even rugby games per month, remote-controlled shopping . . . all at "incredibly low prices" and discounts compared to cable. Reality check: Satellite services don't carry the big four broadcasters' affiliates, ABC, CBS, Fox and NBC, so you'll need a regular antenna to watch first-run *ER* and *The Simpsons*.

As for being cheaper than cable, once you add the initial investment in equipment and installation to the monthly service charges, it's a wash.

To go satellite, you'll need to purchase or lease a small, portable satellite dish that grabs the service's signal and a converter box that translates the signal into pictures on your TV. (But don't buy equipment until you've talked to DBS providers; each has its own equipment requirements.) You buy the equipment from an electronics store or through a DBS provider. Cost: $199 to $400. Monthly "access" fees start at $20 for the most basic service. (Leasing a system tacks $10 to $15 on to this monthly payment.) The dish goes outside your house, where it must have a clear shot of the south with no trees or buildings

THE $MARTER CONSUMER

Because cable companies are essentially government-sanctioned monopolies, you're pretty much stuck with the indignities and inferior service.

You could always cancel your service—if you don't mind parting with it. If you aren't willing to go that far, here are a few suggestions:

What's your loyalty worth? If you live in one of the few areas with more than one cable provider, see how far each company will go to keep or win your business. Your current provider may kick in free services to keep you from going to the new guys.

Review your bill carefully. Are you getting everything you pay for? Are you paying the price you were promised?

in the way. Installation can be done by a technician—for a hefty fee—or some companies offer how-to videos that help you set everything up yourself.

As with cable, you subscribe to packages of channels ranging from "basic" (CNN, MTV, ESPN) to "premium-gold" (many movie and sports channels). But before you give in to temptation, ask yourself if you're really going to watch a hundred or so channels more than you've already got. Of course, if you live in a rural area where cable's lines don't stretch, satellite TV may be your only choice.

If you are choosing between satellite and cable TV, here are a few things to consider: Your monthly satellite bill will be less than a cable bill for comparable service. But don't forget that's only after you've coughed up a few hundred dollars for equipment—especially if you are outfitting several TVs in your home

for DBS. Unlike cable, DBS works with only one TV at a time; you have to buy another converter, usually at about two thirds the original's cost, for each additional set. DBS offers more channels than cable, but cable is fast catching up. The programming varies little between satellite and cable—with DBS you simply get more start times for the same old movies and obscure sporting events played by teams you've probably never heard of. Both cable and satellite can be affected by bad weather, and both offer digital pictures, so the reception (and the potential for reception problems) is about the same. If you want to use your television to connect to the Internet, satellite won't help much—you can get information from the Internet, but you can't send information back—i.e., no e-mail and only very limited interactivity. Cable, however, allows full Internet give and take.

Assess your viewing habits. Do you really need to pay extra for a movie channel when you rent movies all the time? Both cable and satellite dealers brag about "hundreds of movies a month," but how many of them will be good, and how many will you want (or be able) to watch? Are you going to watch the thousands of games the expanded sports channels offer when you can get highlights from one channel? Do you watch enough of

the channels in the expanded service tier to justify paying extra for them?

Companies may try to lure you with promises of six or seven versions of the same movie channel—say, six channels of HBO. But these channels play mostly the same movies (with the exeption of HBO Family, which broadcasts only G- and PG-rated movies), just at different times. You can get the same effect from just one channel by taping those movies you miss.

Buy your own equipment. Your cable company may have foisted a converter box and remote control device on you for which you pay monthly usage fees. Check to see if you can buy the box outright—either from the cable company or from a retailer—and if that would save you money in the long run. Shop for a "universal" remote control device, which will work with many different brands of equipment and enable you to retire some of the remotes you now use to operate all your equipment. They cost about $35, but the convenience might be worth it.

Address complaints first to the cable company. If you don't get satisfaction, complain to your local franchising authority or consumer affairs office, whichever has jurisdiction over complaints about signal quality, billing errors or questionable billing practices, inadequate handling of complaints, disconnections in service, or damage to personal property. However, be forewarned that the power of local government to regulate cable companies is extremely limited. At best, the weight of documented problems might influence a municipal decision about whether to renew the franchise and under what terms. Before their franchises were renewed in 1990, several New York City cable companies were forced to meet minimum customer service standards regarding leaving people on hold when they telephoned and setting up service appointments.

Don't get boxed in when it's time to move. Have the cable box picked up before you move. Even if you have called the company to cancel your service and a representative failed to come get the box, do not assume your responsibility ends. You probably paid a deposit for the cable equipment; if you fail to return it, you could be out not only the deposit but the hundreds of dollars the cable company says the equipment is worth. At that price, it's not worth taking the risk of entrusting this job to your landlord or the next occupant.

HELP

■ **The Federal Communications Commission's Cable Information Line operates around the clock,** giving consumers information about filing complaints about rates and service: (202) 418-2225; in Spanish, (202) 632-0100; TTY, (202) 632-6999. You can also write to FCC, General Cable Inquiries, P.O. Box 18698, Washington, DC 20036. The information is also on their Web site at www.fcc.gov.

■ **If you're concerned** about cable rates in your area, call the FCC Cable Information Line at (202) 418-2225.

■ **To complain about dishonest or** ill-identified infomercials, contact the FTC, Division of Advertising Practices, Washington, DC 20580; or call (202) 326-3131.

CHAPTER 25

ELECTRONIC GOODS AND APPLIANCES

Just the Fax, Ma'am

Buying electronic goods intelligently is one of the greater challenges of the late 20th century. There is a phenomenal array of products, brands, technologies and other specifics that the average consumer—and many salespeople—simply cannot master. Take that most ubiquitous of home appliances, the TV set. Should you buy a new set now or wait for digital sets, whatever those are? Is stereo sound worth it? Do you need picture-in-picture? Multi-language programming? In addition, new technologies constantly render our "toys" out-of-date, and it's hard to keep up. Technological aficionados who shelved their VCRs when laser disks were introduced are now debating whether to jump aboard the DVD bandwagon.

As if the technical hurdles weren't enough, you can count on unscrupulous merchants to ply a few tricks of their own. Some of it is just the rough-and-tumble of the free market: In midtown Manhattan, stores within a few blocks of each other have sold the same camera for $69 or $169. But a lot of merchant mischief is unethical or illegal, like using bait-and-switch techniques on unwary consumers or selling them refurbished goods as new: Electronics stores regularly rank in the top tier in complaints received by the NYC Department of Consumer Affairs. As one expert concludes, "There's no way I know of that the average guy can work this out."

THE BASICS

Whether you're shopping for a dishwasher or a new PC, the process is in many ways the same. Here's some basic advice.

Look before you leap. It's a good idea to do some research *before* you step into a store, to get an idea of what you want—and what you're likely to get. For one thing, you'll be better able to figure out what features are important for your purpose and to resist being pushed into buying features you don't need.

There's no such thing as a standard price. A *New York Times* reporter shopping for a pair of portable Sony stereo speakers in Manhattan found the same items priced from $49.49 to $259.95—a range of more than 500%. In particular, don't be taken in by the "list price" or Manufacturer's Suggested Retail Price (MSRP)—a price that is often inflated far beyond what most people ever actually pay.

Beware of decoys. Sometimes an advertised item may not be the same as the item sold. So be careful the thing you see in the store is the same as the one you read about: Check the model number.

Stores' return policies vary widely. Many states require the return policy to be posted prominently or in writing on the receipt. If the item is defective, basic contract law entitles you to a refund or replacement, regardless of the return policy. In any case, keep your receipt—it'll make future exchanges or claims go a lot smoother.

Use your plastic. Unless you already have high-interest debt, consider using your credit card to make electronic purchases. Under federal law, you don't have to pay a charge made on your credit card if you have a legitimate dispute with the merchant. If you believe you've been cheated, call the credit card company and stop payment.

Measure those doorways. Before buying a major home appliance—refrigerator, washing machine, etc.—make sure you can get it inside your home and fit it in a convenient and adequate space.

Extended Warranties

We've all either experienced or heard a story like this: The day after the manufacturer's warranty expires, the answering machine eats the message tape and stops functioning. When you take it to the appliance doctor, you discover that repairing it will cost just as much as replacing it with a new one. Well, the industry has come up with a solution: extended warranties.

As the hottest trend in electronics marketing for the past few years, "extended warranty" is a fancy name to describe what is essentially a service contract. They are sold either by the manufacturer, the retailer, or, increasingly, a third party called an administrator. (Such administrators now account for 50% to 70% of the business for appliances and consumer electronics.) The contracts vary in countless ways, but there are six basic plans: date-of-purchase plans; extension plans; major component programs (on the wane); comprehensive programs; replacement programs (mostly on low-priced items); and deductibles.

Extended warranties have become increasingly elaborate in recent years. While they used to deal in straightforward parts-and-labor coverage, they now run the gamut, from maintenance (VCR head-cleaning, annual "spec checks" for audio equipment) and theft protection to insurance against freakish occurrences like lightning damage, and food spoilage insurance (for refrigerators and freezers).

The very idea of an extended warranty is somewhat paradoxical: It makes you wonder how good the product that the salesperson just gushed about really is. "If you push extended warranties, you're all but telling [customers] that the product you just told them was the best product isn't going to last," acknowledges Lee Schoenfeld, who is a senior vice-president of marketing for Best Buy.

But the industry justifies this seeming paradox by arguing that modern-day electronic gadgets have grown so sophisticated and complex that, well, nobody and nothing's perfect. Apparently, a lot of consumers are buying both the rationale and the warranties. Droves of consumers are purchasing extended warranties because it brings them peace of mind, quality service, and convenience: An extended warranty means they won't have to frantically search around for a repair store when technological tragedy strikes.

Electronics stores sell them for the same reason Willie Sutton robbed banks: That's where the money is. Says one department store executive, "One clear reason why we must sell service contracts lies in the competitive pricing structure of consumer electronics products. These contracts give us the necessary margin to keep our electronics departments in business." In other words, merchants are now dependent on extended warranties and the high profit margins they generate.

How high? Retailers generally admit to 40% to 65% profit, although Schoenfeld estimates that his legitimate cost on a $200 extended warranty is $50—a 300% profit margin. And the Financial Accounting Standards Board in Norwalk, Connecticut, estimates that large retailers spend only four to fifteen cents on actual service for every dollar collected in service-contract premiums. Needless to say, the pressure is intense to sign up customers: Industry experts estimate that salespeople receive commissions as high as 15% to 20% on the sale of extended warranties.

In short, there's no question that extended warranties are a good deal for the seller. The question is, are they such a good deal for consumers? Dennis Garrett, associate professor of marketing at Marquette University in Milwaukee, pretty

> "**B**uying an extended warranty is like making two bets: that the appliance will break down after the manufacturer's warranty expires (and before the extended warranty does) and that the cost of the repairs will exceed the cost of the contract."
>
> —*Consumer Reports*

EXTENDED WARRANTIES: THE BASIC PLANS

DATE-OF-PURCHASE PLAN	*Runs from the time of purchase of the item, but takes effect only after the original manufacturer's warranty expires*
EXTENSION PLAN	*Begins at the expiration of the original manufacturer's warranty*
MAJOR COMPONENT PROGRAM	*Insures only the product's major component*
COMPREHENSIVE PROGRAM	*Covers all parts and labor for a specified period of time*
REPLACEMENT PROGRAM	*Guarantees product replacement if the product fails during the plan's period of coverage*
DEDUCTIBLE	*Customer is responsible for an initial amount ("deductible") for the repair, after which the coverage kicks in*

well sums up the consensus among consumer experts: "Just say no. Avoid them like the plague."

First, watch for the bad apples—companies that sell long-term warranties and go under. The Manhattan-based electronics emporium Crazy Eddie, for instance, went into bankruptcy in 1989, defaulting on an estimated $6 million in extended-service contracts. In 1991, EWC, Inc., an Oklahoma City–based company that carried 3.2 million service contracts through retailers across the country, filed for bankruptcy protection amid allegations of financial fraud.

In response to these stories and others, the Financial Accounting Standards Board established accounting regulations for the industry that should help sellers of extended warranties operate in a more fiscally responsible fashion. And several state insurance boards have started regulating the service contract market. In Florida, for instance, sellers of extended warranties are required to meet a certain minimum of reserves, post a bond, or obtain insurance coverage for the policies. But when extended warranties are not subject to state insurance regulations, consumers have little recourse if the business extending the warranty folds. All policyholders can do: line up in bankruptcy court.

Therefore, it's always a good idea to find out if the firm selling you the warranty is backed by a solid insurance company and if it is easy to file claims if the need arises. In addition, to protect yourself against a third-party administrator going out of business, ask the retailer selling you the product if it will assume responsibility if the administrator folds. Either way, if the administrator goes out of business, check with the retailer, who may still assume the warranty or refer you to another party that will.

Ask yourself whether the extra protection is worth the expense, even if you're dealing with a reputable company. The answer: probably not, with the possible exception of delicate, big-ticket electronic items. Although as many as 40% of people who buy at electronics and appliance chain stores purchase warranties, only 12% to 20% of people who buy extended warranties ever use them.

One reason has to do with the fact that most defects in electronic goods show up within a few weeks of purchase (when the item is still covered by the original warranty) or after several years (when the average extended warranty has expired). Engineers call this phenomenon the "bathtub curve," to reflect the curve you would obtain by charting these early and late breakdowns over time. Extended warranties, in short, are expensive insurance policies to protect your goods against defects and disruptions at a time when those are least likely to occur. With the downward trend in the price of electronic goods, you may be better off pocketing the money and, if the worst-case scenario materializes, going to the electronics store and buying a brand-new appliance.

Finally, an extended warranty is certainly a bad deal if it is disproportionately expensive compared with the item it is supposed to insure. The threshold amount is arguable, of course; one expert suggests that the cost of the warranty should not exceed 10% to 15% of the total value of the product. And there are alternative ways of planning for a breakdown that don't require the purchase of a costly policy. For instance, you may be better off setting money aside in an appliance-repair fund.

Digital Television

The Next Big Thing in the world of electronic goods—an industry built on Next Big Things designed to render your existing equipment, state-of-the art just yesterday, hopelessly out of date tomorrow—is digital television.

According to the industry, it doesn't get much bigger than digital TV. Those who have caught a glimpse of it describe it as the biggest leap in television technology since the advent of color. Jim Barney, a spokesman for the Consumer Electronics Manufacturers Association, even suggests that "it's much more dramatic than going from black and white to color. It's more like going from a telegraph to color TV." Hype aside, digital TV promises to bring more channels, movie-screen-like images—including a rectangular screen, extra-sharp picture (twice the resolutions of your existing set), and lifelike sound—into the home, along with as-yet-undefined interactive possibilities, including high-speed Internet access.

If you are one of the 24 million Americans who would normally buy a new set in the coming twelve months, however, digital TV promises a list of headaches and difficult decisions. Should you buy a regular TV or go for the first-generation digital sets, currently expected to be available in the fall of 1998?

The good news is, you don't need to master all the technical intricacies of "analog" vs. "digital" transmission to decide. The bad news: there is still a list of unknowns about the what, when, how—and how much—of digital television. A lot of money is at stake and a lot of agendas are in play, so that no one—not Congress or the Federal Communications Commission, who call the policy shots; not the manufacturers, who are waiting to learn what the broadcasters will do; and not the broadcasters, who send conflicting signals on a weekly basis—really knows what's going on. But there is enough information available about what may become available, and at what price, that consumers don't need to decide wearing a blindfold.

First, the technology. Starting in 1998, the networks are required by law to start offering digital programming. Until 2006, they will broadcast in both analog and digital, after which they will switch off analog transmission and broadcast exclusively in digital.

But that's only the beginning of the story. Much of the promise of digital TV centers around HDTV ("high definition"), a form of digital transmission that delivers the movie-screen-like image. The problem is that HDTV takes up a lot of bandwidth, the "pipeline" through which television signals are transmitted. Instead of one channel in HDTV, the networks can, using the same bandwidth, transmit the signals for six channels in basic digital transmission—which means lesser image quality but more programming and potentially more revenue. And the networks are under no obligation to broadcast in HDTV. In October 1997, HBO promised to start an HDTV feed for the summer of 1998. CBS and NBC seem likely to offer at least some HDTV programming early on as well. But ABC and the Sinclair Broadcasting Group, which owns or provides programming for 29 stations nationwide, have suggested that, for the short term at least, they may take a pass on HDTV in favor of more channels—including lucrative pay-per-view programs. To complicate matters further, the law requiring the networks to offer digital programming does not apply to cable providers, who bring the networks to your cable box (if you are a cable subscriber). As a result, they, too, may skip HDTV, even if it is available from the broadcasters, and opt for more programming instead. (Satellite transmissions, on the other hand, are already digitized, though satellite providers, too, are unwilling to commit to HDTV.) So what will be available when is still up in the air.

The second big question for potential buyers is how much all this will cost. As of October 1997, Mitsubishi announced that its first models would range between $7,000 and $8,000. Zenith, which initially promised 60-inch sets for a starting price of $5,000, is now floating figures comparable to Mitsubishi's. But these announcements must be taken with a grain of salt. The rate of growth for high-end televisions (big-screen or projection) has slowed dramatically in recent months as consumers decide to wait for digital sets.

But manufacturers are eager to sell their sets now on the market. To do that, they need to convince potential buyers that they won't be able to afford the early digital sets and that, accordingly, there is no reason not to buy a TV now. And so it comes as no surprise that they have had little encouraging to say on the pricing front. Bruce Allan, a senior executive at Thomson Consumer Electronics, the nation's largest maker of televisions (under brands RCA, G.E., and Proscan), dismisses his competitors' projections as "just ridiculous." He expects Thomson's initial models to start at $4,500. And regardless of how high prices start initially, they will inevitably come down quickly. Thomson's direct-broadcast satellite receivers, introduced on the market in 1994, sold for one-third of their original price in 1998, a price curve that a Panasonic executive describes as "quite typical for our business."

What to make of all of this? Ultimately, it depends on your financial situation and how much of a gadget junkie you are. If you're in the market now for a medium-range to low-end television, it probably is not worth waiting for its digital equivalent. Even if digital catches on with programmers

and providers a lot faster than current indications suggest, you'll still be able to use your analog set. Remember, programs will still be available in analog until 2006. In addition, you will be able to acquire a converter for your regular set to receive digital signals, though not with the same quality as a digital set; and you won't be able to receive HDTV pictures. It's too early to tell what these converter boxes will cost; estimates range from minimal sums to several hundred dollars.

If you're looking to invest a substantial amount for a TV that you'll use for many years—if you're thinking of buying a projection TV, for instance—it may be worth waiting a few years for the second wave of digital TVs. As Dale Cripps, who publishes an HDTV newsletter, explains, "I think if you are planning to spend $2,000 to $3,000 for an entertainment system, you may want to make the investment after the conversion."

If you decide that you can't wait, look for special offers like trade-in guarantees (enabling you to switch your set for a digital set) or free or discounted converter boxes for your analog TV. Zenith was the first to announce such a plan for purchases of large-screen TVs between August 1 and December 1, 1997. As always, get it in writing!

WHAT TO WATCH OUT FOR

Bait-and-switch. It's the oldest trick in the world, but it still works. Cheap Tricks Electronics advertises

Item A (in print, on the air, or in the store window) at an unbeatable price. Mr. Consumer, lured by the ad, goes to buy Item A but Ms. Slick Vendor pressures him to switch to Item B which, just coincidentally, has a greater profit margin, by disparaging Item A or simply claiming that it is no longer in stock. Many electronics stores play this scheme with gusto, despite laws prohibiting the practice.

Refurbished goods. These are used goods that have been "souped up" and returned to the market. There's nothing wrong with buying or selling these items—as long as the customer realizes the goods are used. But some unscrupulous merchants have figured out they can make a quick buck by removing the "reconditioned" label from the box or the goods themselves and selling them as new. In one instance, the New York City Department of Consumer Affairs sent lawyers to serve papers on one electronics store that allegedly engaged in this practice and found employees there scissoring the word "refurbished" off of manufacturers' boxes. In fact, consumer inspectors estimate that nine out of ten stores in low-income areas sell some refurbished goods as new. Not only do you get a used item instead of the real McCoy, but most likely you won't get a manufacturer's warranty.

How can you tell the item is refurbished? Usually, you can't. But you can make sure there is a manufacturer's warranty; verify that the model number on the equipment matches that on the box; check that the product comes in a new, sealed, brand-specific box; and examine the product, front and back, for scratches or other signs of use. An "R," "B," or "X" burned onto the back of an Emerson VCR or television, for instance, is that company's code to show it's been overhauled.

Gray-market goods. Also called "parallel imports," these are name-brand products intended for sale outside the country and brought into the country by an unauthorized importer. Again, there's nothing illegal per se about selling these items, and the goods you're getting may be perfectly fine. But then again, they may not. For instance, they may not operate on U.S. voltage levels or the instructions may not be in English. Some jurisdictions require stores that sell such goods to post a sign saying that "gray" goods are on sale and that they are not covered by an authorized manufacturer's warranty. Here, *caveat emptor*—let the buyer beware—is the name of the game. (For more information, see "Counterfeit and Gray-Market Goods," page 635.)

THE $MARTER CONSUMER

***When* you shop can be as important as *where* you shop.** It's often smart to buy big-ticket items out of season—e.g., an air conditioner in November. Unless you're a gadget junkie (with disposable income),

July or August may be a good time to buy certain appliances—televisions, for instance—before companies unveil their new designs with all the latest features.

Shop in "superstores" that offer huge selections at rock-bottom prices.

Comparison shop. Look for ads. Remember that products can vary by margins of 500%! Bargain with stores and hold them to their "nobody beats our prices" ads. (Be careful of restrictions, though, some of which may be of the "not applicable to items purchased between Monday and Sunday" variety.)

Your best warranty is a superior product. Buy products with proven histories of problem-free, long service. It may be worth a trip to the library to look at past issues of *Consumer Reports* for performance reports, which include breakdown rates. Generally, electronic goods have a breakdown rate of 12% to 14%, while "white goods"—refrigerators, washing machines and other major household appliances—have a breakdown rate of 8%.

Make sure your purchase comes with a warranty. Compare the warranties offered by various dealers or manufacturers—they come in all shapes and sizes: "Full" warranties provide comprehensive coverage, while "limited" warranties may require you to pay for diagnosis and labor costs. It may be a good idea to test all the features and controls of an appliance while it is under warranty; most defects show up during the first few uses.

Pay by credit card as often as possible, and always keep the receipt to protect yourself.

American Express and many MasterCards and Visas double the original manufacturer's warranty for up to a year if you buy an item with one of their credit cards. Citibank offers its own "Lifetime Warranty" —free warranty protection up to $1,000 per item or $2,500 a year on most major household appliances, consumer electronics, and small outdoor appliances for the "expected" life of the product—from 12 years for a washing machine to three years for an answering machine.

When a product needs repair, look for a reputable company by asking for recommendations from friends or by looking for membership in professional groups, such as the National Electronics Service Dealers Association (NESDA) or the Professional Service Association (PSA). (Contact information for both the NESDA and the PSA is listed in **HELP** at the end of the chapter.) Ask about the qualifications of the store's employees, such as whether the business employs a certified electronics technician. Make sure the company carries liability insurance to protect your goods.

If your unit is covered by a warranty, make sure that the business will honor it. If not, before you commit to a repair or even an appliance service call, ask for an estimated service charge, the expected range of anticipated costs (in writing), and whether a minimum fee is required and what it will cover.

Don't neglect to ask about the warranty on completed repairs. Ask for (and save) detailed receipts whenever repairs are made on an appliance, even if no charge is involved, and ask how the repairer guarantees the services performed. If the problem recurs, you are more likely to convince the manufacturer or retailer to service the appliance again at no extra charge if you can document their earlier work.

H E L P

■ **To complain about** a service/repair company or a contract/extended warranty company: Contact the company first. If you do not obtain satisfaction, contact your state attorney general or the Better Business Bureau.

■ **The Major Appliance Consumer** Action Panel, sponsored and funded by the home appliance industry, offers mediation services for any complaint regarding your major appliances; contact 20 North Wacker Drive, Suite 1231, Chicago, IL 60606; www.aham.org.

■ **The Electronics Industries Associ-** ation Consumer Electronics Manufacturers Association (CEMA) issues numerous publications regarding the purchase, use, and care of consumer electronic products, including computers. For more information, contact CEMA, 2500 Wilson Blvd., Arlington, VA 22201, (703) 907-7500, www.eia.org.

■ **The Professional Service Associa-** tion puts out a *Consumer Guide to Finding Reputable Service Companies.* For a copy, contact the Association at 71 Columbia Street, Cohoes, NY 12047, (518) 237-7777; www.psaworld.com.

■ **The National Electronics Service** Dealers Association (NESDA) publishes very informative brochures regarding repair work and service dealers: *"Extended Warranty" Service Contracts: Good or Bad?; Getting Good Service for Electronic Equipment; Consumer Complaint Checklist for Electronic Equipment Repair.* To order, send a self-addressed, stamped business-size envelope to NESDA, 2708 West Berry Street, Fort Worth, TX 76109 or call (817) 921-9061; www.nesda.com.

■ **The Consumer Guide to Home** *Energy Savings* contains all you need to know about purchasing energy-efficient appliances, including the top-rated appliances by type and size. To order, send $7.95 (D.C. residents add sales tax) to The American Council for an Energy-Efficient Economy, 1001 Connecticut Avenue NW, Suite 801, Washington, DC 20036 (202) 429-0063; www.crest.org/aceee.

■ **Write for** *Service Contracts* and *Warranties,* two brochures from the Federal Trade Commission. Its address: Public Reference Branch, Sixth Street and Pennsylvania Avenue #130, Washington, DC 20580. (202) 326-2000; www.ftc.gov.

■ **For additional information on digi-** tal television and HDTV, consult the following sources: Federal Communications Commission Web site at www.fcc.gov; Consumer Electronics Manufacturing Association, (703) 907-7674; www.cemacity.org; HDTV newsletter hotline, 800-LOV-HDTV.

CHAPTER 26

TELEPHONES

The High Cost of High Technology

Telephone technology is changing at warp speed, as they would say in *Star Trek,* and in ways that inventor Alexander Graham Bell couldn't possibly have foreseen. You can immediately learn the number of a caller, trace phone calls, forward your calls to anywhere in the world, and even be assigned a phone number for life. And recent deregulation of the phone market has made it possible to have one company handle your calls across town, another your calls across the state, and yet another your calls across the country. You may also have your local or long-distance carrier connecting you to cellular or Internet service.

Each of these companies—and their competitors—spend millions developing and advertising new "convenient" services to attract your dialing dollars. But these amazing conveniences don't come cheap. And if time is money, then you can spend a lot of "money" just trying to figure out the new services.

THE BASICS

Let's look first at the hardware—phones—before tackling the profusion of telephone line services

—the "software." You can either buy your telephone or lease it from the phone company. The only advantage of leasing is that if the phone breaks, the phone company delivers another one. But decent phones cost about $30; just buy another and it'll likely be cheaper than leasing charges in the long run.

When buying a phone, beware of $10 to $20 models, since they probably won't last long and sound tinny. A built-in speakerphone will add another $10, and multi-line features add about $15 more.

Over half the phones now sold are cordless models. Cordless phones work better than they used to, but wired phones often still have superior sound quality. Cordless phones can't be used if the electricity fails (they plug into an electrical outlet), and they stop working when the battery loses its charge. Consider whether buying a longer cord for your existing telephone will give you enough roaming room before you plunk down $100 or more on a cordless.

Line Services

Phone services are like car options—the vendor makes the big profit on the extras, not on the basic product. So the cost of service options promoted in advertising inserts with your monthly statement can really add up.

The fact is that you could pay up to an extra $135 a year if you order just three services—touch tone, call waiting, and call forwarding—and initial hook-up fees may be additional. The annual cost of "the works" could be $400 or more.

Still, while most people probably don't need very many of these services, they may be handy for a few. This guide will help you decide whether to order one. If a service is not yet offered in your area, it probably will be available soon. (The fees cited below don't include one-time hook-up charges.)

Touch-tone service. There are two basic types of telephone service, pulse (which includes rotary phones) and touch tone. A clicking sound is heard when you make a call on a rotary phone, a tone pitch when you make a touch-tone call.

Touch-tone calling is faster than pulse calling, and it is required for certain computerized phone company services like call answering. (You will likely also need it to access your voice mail and answering machine.) Touch-tone phones also allow you to access electronic answering systems ("Press 1 for the accounting department, 2 for customer service . . ."), although you'll still be connected to an operator if you have a rotary phone.

Call waiting. Phone companies report that this is the most popular of the special line services. You avoid missed calls by taking a second call while you're already on the phone. The fee comes to around $50 to $60 a year. Pressing *70 (or dialing 1170 on rotary phones) before you make a call will disable call waiting for that call.

Call forwarding. For about $50 a year, your phone calls will follow you wherever you go. You can also order that only selected callers be forwarded.

Speed dialing. Is it worth paying between $45 and $75 a year to be able to press just one or two numbers for frequent calls? Only you can decide. But remember that many push-button phones allow you to program ten or more numbers into their memory; you can call these numbers by pressing just one or two buttons.

Call answering. This works much like an answering machine, but with two advantages: calls can be answered while you are on another line (similar to call waiting), and it doesn't break down. On the negative side, call answering services cost from $40 to $50 a year plus a hook-up fee of about $20; a decent answering machine costs only about $60 and ought to last far longer than a year.

Call connection. In many localities, after the directory assistance voice tells you the number, it asks if you would like to have the number called; you then just say "yes" or press 1. Not just a courtesy—the connection fee in New York and Chicago is 35 cents in addition to the 35-plus cents you pay for assistance in the first place.

LOWER LOCAL RATES—HOW SOON?

Perhaps the biggest promise of the 1996 Telecommunications Act was that it would create competition in the $100 billion local phone market—long a monopoly of the Baby Bell companies. Greater competition is supposed to lower local phone rates, as it did for long-distance service in the years after the Ma Bell breakup. But sixteen months after the act was passed, fewer than one-half of one percent of the nation's 97 million residential phone customers were served by a company other than the incumbent carrier, according to a study by the Yankee Group, a Boston-based research service. The long-distance giant AT&T offered local service in only 15 cities by 1997's end.

And it's more likely your rates have gone up than down. Many local providers raised rates within ten months of the Telecom Act's passage; for example, Great Plains Communications in Nebraska bumped rates up 30% in the first half of 1997. And genuine competition seems far off, as phone companies squabble with federal and state regulators over the new law's details.

But competition will come, however leisurely, to the local market. As it does, keep in mind that savings on local service are pretty minor. In New York, for example, switching from Bell Atlantic to MCI for basic local service might save you three or four dollars —per year. And the new contenders might not yet offer all the conveniences you're used to, like voice mail or paging. As one rather candid MCI sales representative told us after listing the services MCI could *not* provide: "Bell Atlantic's service is better than ours, but that's because we're just beginning."

Extra line. If you've got talkative teenagers or a fax or Internet connection at home, you may want another phone line. An extra line—and any special services you order for it—will cost as much as your first line, except there is an additional $1.50 monthly access fee. You'll also pay an installation fee of around $200.

Priority ringing. You can also add one or two new incoming lines electronically, without new wiring. Each number produces its own distinctive ring. You could give one number to, say, your kids and keep the other for your own calls. Or, if you work at home, you could have a business line and a personal one. In New York, one extra number costs

$5.14 a month and two cost $7.22. The drawbacks: You'll only have one *outgoing* line, and if you have call waiting, you can't tell by the beep which line was ringing.

Automatic call-back. You can return the last call you received, whether you answered it or not, by pressing *69 (or dialing 1169 on rotary phones). This service is also called "call return." Fees could be up to 75 cents per use.

Repeat dialing. Can't get through to the box office to order tickets because the line is busy? Pressing *66 (1166 on rotary phones) will automatically repeat the last number you called for up to half an hour and complete it once the line is free. Cost: 75 cents per use or $35 to $60 a year. While many phones are equipped to repeat-dial a number if you press the pound (#) button, with the repeat-dialing service offered by the phone company you leave the phone while the repeat dialing continues—or you can make and receive calls in the meantime. It rings you back when it has made the connection.

Three-way (conference) calling. Being able to talk to two parties at once can cost $40 to $50 a year.

Caller ID. For $85 to $100 a year, this service displays on a special monitor next to your phone the number of the party calling you (only for local calls). This way, you'll know exactly who is calling and can decide whether to answer. Of course, the call-screening feature on most answering machines accomplishes much the same goal, although it doesn't reveal the identity of callers who choose to remain anonymous by not leaving a message.

Privacy advocates are concerned that caller ID could lead to an invasion of privacy. How would you like to have *your* phone number displayed on a monitor whenever you place a call? Fortunately, many states have required phone companies to offer a free blocking service in which you can prevent anyone with caller ID from learning your number. You can order either total blocking or per-call blocking. Caller ID rejects "anonymous" calls, those from numbers that cannot be identified because they are blocked.

Call screen. This service blocks calls from certain numbers in your service area that you program into the phone. A loophole is that someone who really wants to bother you, such as a bill collector, can simply call from a different number. The cost is around $40 a year.

Call trace. At your request, the phone company will trace the number of the last call and notify the police. The cost ranges from $2 to $5 per trace. Obviously, this service is of limited value if the harasser calls from pay phones. And it works only on calls that originate within your local service area. An alternative would be to change your phone number; the phone company may waive its usual fee if the reason is to avoid a harassing caller.

Lifetime phone number. You keep the same Social Security number for life. How about keeping your phone number too? You can with

"500" number service. For $5 a month AT&T will assign you a new lifetime ten-digit phone number including a "500" prefix. You use this number in addition to your regular phone number.

Callers dial the "500" number; it's directed to your home phone or forwarded to a number you punched in on your phone. It's like call forwarding, except that you keep the same number forever, even if you move several times. You can also arrange for people to call you toll-free when they dial a code.

Voice dialing. No need to remember or look up numbers. You can program up to 50 phone numbers, then say the name of the person you're calling into the receiver, and the phone company does the rest. Works from any home phone. Bell Atlantic in New York charges $4.50 a month for 30 different numbers, $5.50 for 50 numbers.

Calling Rates

Phone companies usually offer two kinds of billing: flat rate billing and measured billing. With flat rate billing, you pay one set fee each month and make all the local calls you like. Calls outside your local calling area (sometimes called the "home region"), which are handled either by your local phone company or another carrier you choose, cost extra. Some companies restrict flat rate billing to "life-line" services reserved for eligible fixed- or lower-income customers.

With measured service, your basic monthly service charge is probably about half of what it is for flat rate service. But a flat charge is also imposed for each call within your local calling area.

You may know that evening and night long-distance rates are lower, but did you know that some local service also has time differentials? If you're a penny pincher, you might want to wait until 11 PM to call Aunt Maude, even if she's on the next block. Check with your local company for the details. A typical rate discount schedule for local calls (Ameritech/Illinois) is: Weekday (full price) 8 AM to 5 PM. Evening (discount) 5 PM to 11 PM. Nights/weekends (bigger discount) 11 PM to 8 AM.

Schedules and discounts vary considerably around the country. New York's Bell Atlantic, for one, charges the full weekday rate between 8 AM and 9 PM and the evening rate from 9 PM to 11 PM. Consult the instruction pages at the beginning of your local phone directory for the rate schedule in your area.

The percentage discount also varies. Bell Atlantic offers one of the steeper discounts: a 40% reduction in regular rates during evening hours and 65% for night/weekend calling. In Los Angeles, Pacific Bell's discounts are 30% and 60%. Southwestern Bell, in Houston, gives no discount at all. Some companies offer automatic volume discounts. For example, Ameritech provides residential customers with volume discounts of up to 33% when the total local bill exceeds a certain amount.

Measured and flat-rate service is also offered for calls outside your local calling area but within the "Local Access and Transport Area" (LATA). With measured service, such calls are timed and billed in one-minute increments; the rate for the first minute may be substantially higher than for each additional minute. Time-of-day and volume discounts also apply.

If you can't wait until the monthly bill comes to learn how much a call costs, you can always ask the operator for "time and charges," that is, to tell you how long you talked and how much it will cost. You must dial the operator first to ask that this be done and the operator will stay on the line until the end of your call. Of course, there's an additional charge for this operator-assisted call.

Billing

Telephone industry deregulation has made phone bills infinitely more complicated. Your local telephone bill is separated into these sections:

The local carrier. This covers the basic cost of regular monthly service, which may include the FCC line charge (covers the cost to connect your phone to the network), the exchange access line, special line services like touch tone, and state and local taxes.

Included in the local portion of your phone bill are calls within your local calling area, which means your town or city and maybe some areas a mile or two beyond the limits. Usually listed separately is a call break-down if you have measured service. How many minutes you

called and whether you called during day, evening, or night/weekend hours are reported here. Also listed are calls made with your local company's calling card, directory information request charges, and service order charges.

Regional toll call providers. You're now able to choose who carries your regional calls—those calls past the local calling area but still included in the LATA, which could be 40 or 50 miles from your local calling area. Most states have at least two LATAs; New York has six and California, with 11, has the most. When you sign up for phone service, you may be asked to select a regional call provider, depending on where you live. If you don't choose one on your own, your calls will be automatically routed to your local service provider or to one of its competitors, depending on state regulations. (In Connecticut, if you don't choose one yourself, your calls are assigned to one of 21 companies at random.)

Many of the major long-distance companies like AT&T and MCI now offer regional service. Within most LATAs, non-local calling area calls are automatically routed to your regional call provider when you dial "1" plus an area code and phone number, a method called "one-plus dialing." In some states, however, you must still dial a five-digit access code before the phone number.

Your primary long-distance carrier. If your primary long-distance carrier doesn't bill you separately, then this page itemizes your long-distance calls. All of this information is provided by your primary long-distance carrier. (We tackle the ins and outs of long distance in the next chapter.)

Other providers. Local telephone companies are required to provide a billing service to long-distance carriers and other telephone service providers. There may be a separate page with the trademark of another long-distance carrier if you used one and had calls charged to your home phone, such as with a calling card. Additional pages may be for operator service providers and for "900" calls placed from your phone.

Cellular Phones: Talk Isn't Cheap

Cellular phones aren't just essential equipment for Maxwell Smart, or simply status symbols for the power-suit set. Lured by ubiquitous ads promising convenience, low costs, and cool, everyone from grandmothers to soccer moms to teeny-boppers is carrying a bleeping flip phone. There are more than 50 million cell phone subscribers nationally, in a booming $25 billion industry that didn't even exist until the 1980's. Lures of "free" phones and "free" air time pick up 30,000 new subscribers every day.

So many consumers are going cellular that the question *Should I buy one?* has quickly been replaced by *Where do I sign up?* But don't ditch your home phone just yet. Talking on a cell phone just 42 minutes a month—as the average customer does—will blow about

$600 of your annual budget. And with all the choices—analog or digital, bare-bones service for a low monthly fee or feature-laden service at a higher price—comes understandable consumer confusion.

A book can't make the choice for you. Products, prices and packages vary too much from one city to another and from one dealer to another. But we will give you basic information about your options— the upsides and the down—so that you will be in a strong position to make a smart choice.

Digital or analog service? This is the first thing to think about. Digital service is quickly supplanting analog service, and eventually there will be no choice but digital. So if you buy an analog phone today (and there are still good reasons to do so), you will probably have to replace it in a few years. The digital or "PCS" (personal communications service) phones pushed by major carriers like AT&T and Sprint as the cutting edge of technology— with clearer signals and features like e-mail and call-waiting—aren't all they are cracked up to be. For one thing, digital networks don't extend very far. In 1998, about two-thirds of Americans lived within reach of digital service, whereas over 90% could get analog service.

Once you get out of the city, your digital phone may die. John Bethke, a Seattle mortgage banker who uses a phone on the road in and around the city, told *The New York Times* that he needs to carry both a digital and an analog phone: "Most people go into it not knowing that with PCS, the coverage may drop when you go over a [mountain] pass." Another thing: the digital telephone itself typically costs twice the price of analog. Ask yourself whether your mobile phone is really going to be called upon to send e-mail or, more likely, to order pizza on the way home from picking up the kids at piano lessons.

Rural customers will have no choice but to go analog. And urbanites who want tons of fancy features will want digital service. But price-conscious city folk should think twice before signing up for digital cellular service; analog may be cheaper in the end.

Phone models. Cellular phones range from standard models that come "free" with certain service plans to $500 cigarette-lighter-sized wonders. But most people can get by without a souped-up, compact phone. Look for useful features like call timers that keep track of how long you talk; phones that you can set to vibrate instead of ring to keep from disturbing others; spare batteries that you can switch while you're talking; and phones that let you answer a call by flipping open the mouthpiece.

Analog carriers tend to offer cheap phones, or give them away, and lock you into long-term contracts. Before you take the "free phone," figure in that whatever service providers lose handing out phones, they gain in long-term contracts and high charges. For every $150 to $300 phone they "give" away, cellular companies earn at least $500 a year in subscribers'

fees, estimates *Consumer Reports*. A digital phone will cost substantially more, but you may not be locked into a service contract. Many analog and digital phones work with only one service—so you can give your phone to your kids to play with if you decide to switch providers.

Rate plans. Here's where it gets really confusing. With a half-dozen or so carriers competing in most cities, and each of them offering an array of service plans, you're excused for feeling befuddled.

Generally, your monthly bill will be based on a monthly fee plus a per-minute "air time" charge for each of your calls, whether you place calls or receive them. You will also be charged a 5-cent to 12-cent per minute "land line" fee for any call you make to non-cellular phones (like your home phone). If you are like most cellular customers, land line calls will probably account for most of your phone time.

If you use the phone outside a predetermined service area, you will likely be charged extra for "roaming." Roaming can cost you an extra $1 per minute, and there might be an additional $4 or $5 monthly fee just for the ability to roam. (Although at this writing, AT&T and Nextel had dropped their roaming fees in some areas, and clamorous competition was expected to push other companies to do the same.) Advanced features like paging, voice mail, Caller ID, call forwarding, call waiting, and e-mail cost extra. These basic rates and features are bundled in various ways into calling plans.

The main thing to consider before you choose a rate plan is what you think you'll use the phone for. Then consider what you may actually end up using it for. Cellular companies count on the fact that most people get a cell phone for special reasons—for roadside emergencies, say—but find themselves using it to check their voice mail and other non-emergencies that increase their usage beyond the free minutes that come with the low introductory rates. Take the national average cell phone usage—42 minutes per month, 17 during peak times, 23 off-peak, and 2 while roaming—and adjust it to your own needs and compare what various plans would cost. Look beyond the low monthly rate in advertisements; that charge may not include the air time you'll need.

And offers of low introductory rates and loads of "free" minutes are designed to hook you before the introductory offer runs out a few months later and your rate jumps—when you will typically find yourself stuck paying higher rates for the duration of a one- to three-year contract. If you can, choose a plan that lets you change your service terms within the first 30 days. That way you can switch plans if you find yourself needing more or less air time, and you don't pay for service you don't use.

Generally speaking, people who use the phone primarily for ordering take-out on the way home from the gym are better off paying the lowest possible monthly fee and a moderate charge for extra minutes. Heavy users and those who leave the service area frequently are better off paying more monthly in return for a few free hours of calling a month, with low charges for additional minutes. And if you are going to use the phone exclusively from the car, you'll save money by installing a mobile car phone rather than carrying a portable with you. Plus, the batteries last longer and the signal is stronger.

Safety. There is no evidence to back the claim of a man who said that his wife's cell phone gave her brain cancer, but there are some dangers in using them. People with pacemakers should keep active phones away from their chest areas, as the phone's signal can confuse the pacemaker's signal to the heart and cause palpitations. (There is no such danger when phones are held to the ear.) And don't chat while you drive. According to a 1997 University of Toronto study, drivers using cell phones were four times more likely to get in an accident than

> "*With credit cards, at least you are limited to $50 in liability if you report unauthorized use in time. Not so with calling cards. . . . People don't appreciate that calling cards are really money.*"
>
> —FRANCES FELD,
> Executive Director,
> Communication Fraud Control
> Association, Washington, DC

those who kept all their attention on the road.

For more on cellular phones, see **HELP** at the end of this chapter.

Calling Cards

Calling cards, which are issued by both local phone companies and long-distance carriers, are cards you use to charge local and long-distance calls to your home phone.

You can use your local phone company calling card for local and long-distance calls. A service charge of about 40 cents is imposed on each direct call charged (some are as low as 25 cents); it may be higher for longer distances. You use a local company's calling card by dialing "0" before the number called, which is different than for long-distance calling cards; service can also be accessed by dialing a special five-digit code or toll-free number (explained in the next chapter).

Alternative Pay Phones

Have you ever placed a calling card call from a pay phone, only to be billed several times the amount you expected? If so, you've got lots of company. Such charges are not out of the ordinary. A four-minute collect call to a phone only four blocks away billed through a national company named "Integretel" cost one caller an incredible $6.21. A *one*-minute credit card call to a phone only a few miles away cost another caller $5.36.

The problem here is not with "Bell" company phones operated by your local telephone company

(local companies are called "local exchange carriers"). At issue is independent pay phones, called a COCOT—for Customer-Owned, Coin-Operated Telephone—that can look just like a regular pay phone but sure doesn't charge like one. Tens of thousands of COCOTs have sprung up in places like hospitals, hotels, beauty salons, airports, and convenience stores since the divestiture of AT&T in 1984.

A COCOT-providing company is essentially a reseller of telephone services provided by the local exchange carrier and by long-distance companies. The local exchange carrier supplies the phone line, and a merchant, such as a restaurant owner or hospital, contracts with one of the COCOT providers to have a phone installed. Merchants like them—COCOT phones yield commissions to the merchant, which can be much higher from each call than with a pay phone provided by the local phone company.

For long-distance services, COCOTs presubscribe with an Operator Service Provider (OSP) company, much as you might subscribe with Sprint or MCI for home long-distance service. These OSPs perform switching functions, verify credit and calling cards, and perform all the other functions of a long-distance carrier. They might surcharge you $1 or more if you use a calling card, and the total charges for a call placed through an OSP could be a few times more than through AT&T, Sprint, or MCI. (See the next chapter for more about OSPs.)

Responding to out-of-control "Wild West" conditions in the new

COCOT industry, a 1990 federal law required COCOT companies to file rate information with the Federal Communications Commission. But the law didn't limit how much a COCOT can charge.

Many states have also enacted COCOT restrictions and information disclosure requirements. Generally, these require signs to be posted on or next to the COCOT disclosing the name of the owner, the phone numbers for refunds, repairs and directory assistance, and the name of the alternative operator service the phone uses.

Despite the new laws, there is still a long way to go before you can let your guard down when using one of these phones. A survey by the Pennsylvania Public Utility Commission found that 87% of the COCOTs surveyed at rest areas on a major toll highway had inadequacies, such as price gouging, unreachable COCOT providers, and inadequate informational postings.

The COCOT industry defends its surcharges and high rates by blaming what they call the excessive fees they have to pay the local exchange carriers for the "dial tone." And they complain that every time you use a calling card, the local exchange carrier gets a big cut of their surcharge.

WHAT TO WATCH OUT FOR

Push-button phones that are really pulse models. Just because it has push buttons doesn't mean that it's not a pulse phone—in effect, a dial phone with push buttons that takes almost as long to use. To find out for sure, inspect the FCC registration number imprinted on the phone. If it ends in "T", it's a tone phone. "E" means it can be both pulse and tone.

Cordless phone interference. Since they have only one or two channels, the cheaper cordless phones can be subject to interference from a nearby neighbor's cordless phone. To avoid this, purchase a 10- or 25-channel model on which you can switch channels or that automatically switches your call to a clear channel. 900-MHz phones—those that operate on a higher radio bandwidth—have 25 to 100 channels and a much wider "roaming" range of up to 800 feet from the phone base.

Wire maintenance fees. For about $30 to $35 a year, you can sign up for wire maintenance service. This means that you won't have to pay the company's expensive repair fees if the phone company has to fix the lines within your house. The repair fees generally are at least $35 just to show up and another $15 to $20 for each additional 15 minutes the repairers are at your home.

Still, wire maintenance service is probably not a good deal. How often does a wire break? You can probably fix it yourself if it does. Wire maintenance fees are a big phone company profit generator.

Deposits. You may have to pay a deposit to get your phone turned on if it has been shut off because of non-payment. A deposit might also be required if you failed to pay at least half the amount due in two consecutive bills. The deposit is usually for the cost of two months estimated usage. Terms may be easier for senior citizens.

Non-published number fee. You might reasonably think this would be free, but it can cost up to $2 a month *not* to have your number listed in the phone directory and/or given out by directory assistance.

Busy signal verification fee. You could be charged up to $1 when you ask an operator to verify that a line is busy. There is an additional fee if you then ask for a call to be interrupted.

COCOTs in disguise. COCOTs usually look like any old pay phone. Some even adopt the same color scheme and graphics as the local exchange carrier pay phones. You can tell the difference by looking carefully for the name of the servicer on the phone. If the name of your local exchange carrier, like Pacific Bell or Ameritech, isn't on the phone, then it's a COCOT.

Higher-priced operator service providers. If you require operator assistance to call from a COCOT, you'll be hooked up with an OSP rather than an operator from your local phone company. OSPs generally charge more for their operator assistance services—sometimes a great deal more.

Difficulties getting refunds. Ivan Kotcher, who handles complaints about California COCOTs for the Tele-Consumer Hotline, says that the overwhelming majority of the complaints he receives are about refunds. Rather than an operator offering an immediate refund or credit, COCOT callers sometimes are asked to leave a message on an answering machine or they must contend with an automatic complaint-handling system. He suggests that callers test the refund number posted on the phone before placing a potentially expensive call.

Higher coin call charges. When the price ceiling on initial pay phone charges was lifted in 1997, pay phone companies lost no time in raising the cost of a call an extra dime. Bell Atlantic, Southwestern Bell, and Pacific Bell, which together own almost all the pay phones in America, all now charge 35 cents (except in New York). And if all you've got is two quarters, it's too bad. Pay phones can't make change.

Cellular pitfalls. A few things to watch out for: Don't be surprised if the "included minutes" you get each month are still subject to land line and roaming fees. The same goes for the "free" minutes carriers advertise. Cellular service also has time differentials: "Peak" hours are typically from 7 AM to 8 or 9 PM; all others are "off-peak." The difference between the two can be enormous. AT&T's basic cellular plan charges 49¢ per minute during peak times, but only 10¢ off-peak. "Free" minutes are usually only good off-peak. Mark A. of New York got a shock when his 40 "free" minutes had disappeared into a $39 bill: Those minutes were only good at night, but his calls had all been made during peak hours at 25 cents per minute. Land line fees added another $5 to the tab.

And before you sign a long-term contract, scan the fine print for hefty penalty fees you will owe if you break the contract early. And about that bill: you may have to ask for a call-by-call bill. The standard bill offers so little detail about where you called and when that it's enough to make a Rothko painting look rococo.

THE $MARTER CONSUMER

Ask your local phone company for a free customer service record. It will tell you exactly what services you are paying for and how much they cost. You may see a service listed that you don't remember ordering or use rarely and could easily cancel.

Check into economy and low-cost "life line" service plans. Your local phone company probably offers "economy" or "basic" service plans. For example, customers of C & P Telephone in Washington, DC, can order a bare-bones service for which they may receive unlimited calls but pay for each outgoing call; touchtone and special line services are unavailable. C & P's senior-citizen plan is even cheaper—it allows for 60 outgoing calls a month, after which a per-call charge is imposed.

If you receive Supplemental Security Income (SSI), a Veterans Disability Pension or Surviving Spouse Pension, or local public assistance, your local company may also offer a reduced rate "life line" plan.

Subscribe to "bundled" services —local, regional, and long distance—*only* if it will save you money on *your* calling habits. AT&T, for one, offers significant discounts on its regional service in Connecticut, but only if you're already an AT&T long-distance customer.

Know where your local calling area is. If you have measured local service, be sure to know the boundaries of your local calling area, which is where a flat, untimed rate is charged per call. If you call just over the border, you'll pay by the minute and the total charge will be much higher.

Get a credit for wrong numbers or poor connections. After you hang up, immediately dial the three-digit credits number (it's listed in your local phone book).

Don't immediately say "yes" to phone solicitations for special line services. What's the rush? Read all the fine print in the phone company's brochure. Compute just how much the new service will cost for an entire year and ask yourself if it is worth it.

Avoid becoming a victim of calling card fraud. Imagine opening your phone bill and seeing hundreds of dollars' worth of calls to Pakistan, Hong Kong, or France. It could happen to you if you aren't careful when placing a calling card call at a public phone. Snoops with amazing eyesight and hearing abilities may learn and memorize your identification number as you dial or recite your number to an operator. Then they sell the number on the street. There are public pay phones in New York City where queues of alien residents line up to call home for a discounted flat rate with a calling card number provided by a numbers thief standing nearby.

Services for the deaf. Most local phone carriers provide discounts for users of Telecommunications Devices for the Deaf (TDD). There are also relay calls, in which TDD users can reach non-TDD users by a telephone company Communications Assistant, who will complete the call, relay the conversation, and type a response on your TDD.

Install an inexpensive network interface, which allows you to determine if a phone problem is due to the wiring inside or outside the house. The interface is installed at the point where the outside wiring (the phone company's responsibility) meets the inside wiring (your responsibility if you aren't paying a wire maintenance fee). If you plug a phone into the interface and it still doesn't work, the problem is outside the house. Why would you want to know? Because if the phone company comes to fix your phone and the problem is in the line inside your home or with your phone—rather than with the outside line, which the phone company must fix—you'll have to pay a visit charge of at least $35 anyway. You can buy interface parts for less than

$25 at most electronics stores. Included should be instructions for how to mount it near where the phone line enters your house or apartment. Lucent (formerly part of AT&T) will provide free installation instructions if you call them at 800-222-3111.

Call the COCOT's information number to learn how much a call will cost *before* placing it. The 1990 Federal law requires phone companies to post on or near the phone their name, address, and a toll-free number consumers can call for information, along with the address of the Federal Communications Commission informal complaints office, which is where consumers can take grievances. On top of this, many states have passed even stricter information posting requirements.

If you call for a rate, be sure to ask the operator about surcharges imposed on top of the regular timed rate; ask how much the call will cost with *all* of the fees included.

Make long distance calls on COCOTs through your regular carrier. It is now against the law for a COCOT/OSP to prevent you from dialing your preferred carrier's access code. (See page 299 in the next chapter for a list of these codes.)

Margaret S. learned this the hard way when she used her calling card for a two-minute daytime call from New York City to Santa Monica, California. A month later her phone bill had a $9.90 Oncor Communications, Inc. charge for the call. Why so much? She hadn't initially accessed her preferred long-distance carrier. The calling card surcharge was $5.33 and the operator surcharge was $2.50. The per minute rate was 69 cents. Fortunately, Oncor offered to drop all but the per-minute charge when she called its customer service line.

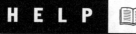

H E L P

■ The Tele-Consumer
Hotline is a toll-free number you can call for answers from trained counselors to questions about telephone concerns and to receive publications on those issues. Information is available on a wide variety of subjects, from calling cards and bill dispute handling to telephone fraud and phone features for disabled people. Call (800) 332-1124. Information is also online at www.teleconsumer.org.

■ For ratings of 15 leading cellular
phones, see *Consumer Reports'* November 1997 issue. *CR*'s February 1997 issue has ratings and advice on different cellular service providers.

■ Want to complain?
Check the government listings section of your phone directory for your state's public utilities commission. They handle complaints about local residential service and pay phones.

■ Complaints about cellular service
can be directed to the FCC's Wireless Telecommunications Bureau, 1919 M Street NW, Room 644, Washington, DC 20554. You can also call (202) 418-0569 or e-mail wtbweb@fcc.gov.

■ For tips on choosing cellular phone
service, go to www.wow-com.com, the Internet site of the Cellular Telecommunications Industry Association.

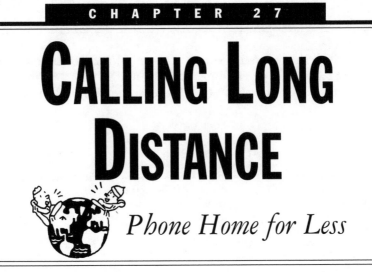

CHAPTER 27

CALLING LONG DISTANCE

Phone Home for Less

Few consumers gave much thought to their long-distance carrier before a federal judge in 1984 ordered the break-up of the AT&T-regulated telephone monopoly. Now there are several major carriers, and together they spend billions of dollars a year on advertising to get you to think a lot about long distance.

The ads—soft-focus "feel-good" appeals and hard-hitting criticisms of competitors' service, quality and rates—have one major goal: to get you to switch carriers. And to lure you, carriers have introduced a long list of complicated special discount plans.

Trouble is, the ads and the discount plans have led to a profusion of confusion. Sprint says it offers only two different calling plans, while AT&T has over 20. New discount plan variations, each with its own special rules and prices, seem to be introduced weekly. Add to that the new services offered by pre-paid phone cards and "dial around" numbers (both discussed below), and the mix gets more confusing.

Our major conclusion: Unless you spend at least $10 a month on long distance, it makes very little difference which carrier you select. It's a matter of nickels. Even long-distance bills of about $25 a month don't present much opportunity for real savings; a 15% reduction would amount to $45 a year, which may not be worth the effort required to compare the many rates and arcane calling plan rules. Still, don't skip this chapter if you aren't a heavy caller, because you probably *can* save substantially by taking advantage of your current carrier's discount plans, which we discuss here.

THE BASICS

How to Pay Less for Domestic Long Distance

When it comes right down to it, no one can say which firm among the six major nationwide carriers—AT&T, LCI, Matrix, MCI, Sprint, or WorldCom—is the cheapest. The cheapest carrier is the one that costs the least for *your* particular calling pattern. This is the conclusion of the consumer group Telecommunications Research & Action Center, which regularly publishes comparisons of long-distance carriers' rates. Callers who talk only 53 minutes a month would do just as well with LCI as with MCI.

If you want to see if you can find cheaper service, start by gathering your last four months' long-distance bills and assess how many minutes you call during a typical month, the time of day you usually call (day, evening, or night hours), and whether there are certain parties or areas you call especially often (you might get a lower rate). Next Step: dial each of the major long-distance carriers' toll-free information numbers (provided below) and have them analyze your typical bill against all their discount plans. You might have to be insistent to be sure you find out about all the calling plans and not just the plan *du jour.* You might also check the Yellow Pages directory for names of regional long-distance carriers.

Also ask for rate charts, which provide per-minute rates (initial and additional minutes) broken down by "mileage band" for all the carrier's various calling plans.

You might have to wait. We were on hold with AT&T for ten minutes when we called one weekday morning. MCI put us on hold for eight minutes shortly thereafter. We were disconnected from WorldCom three times before establishing a connection with a human being—which didn't make us feel too good

HOW TO REACH THEM	
AT&T	*(800) 222-0300*
LCI	*(800) 860-2255*
Matrix	*(800) 282-0242*
MCI	*(800) 444-3333*
US Sprint	*(800) 877-4646*
WorldCom	*(800) 275-0100*

about their service or their customer responsiveness.

Discount programs are generally worth looking into if you spend at least $10 a month calling long distance, although they might require you to make your calls during specified hours to benefit.

Described here are some basic examples of discount programs:

Volume discount. As of mid 1998, AT&T's True Reach Savings plan, for example, offered a 10% discount on any type of domestic call for customers who spend between $10 and $24.99 a month, and a 25% discount if customers spend more than $25. MCI's One Rate offers a 20% discount if your monthly bill is more than $25. Sprint's "Most II" program offers discounts to customers spending $30 or more per month—20% off for $30–$75 spent, 30% for $75–$150 spent, and 35% for bills over $150.

Flat rate plans with multiple time periods. Depending on the time of day, you're charged for calls at a flat rate per minute, regardless of the distance of the call; rates are higher during daytime "peak" hours and lower for evening, weekend, and nighttime calls. With Sprint Sense, for example, you pay 25 cents per minute on calls made between 7 AM and 7 PM during the week, and 10 cents per minute all other times. MCI offers a similar plan, but Sunday rates are just 5 cents per minute. These plans are good deals for people who chat most in the evening or on weekends.

Flat rate anytime. These plans offer one per-minute rate no matter when you call. Sprint offers a 24-hour rate of 15 cents per minute with Sprint Sense Day, as does AT&T's One Rate plan and Matrix's Flat-Rate I. With AT&T One Rate Plus, you pay a monthly fee of $4.95 to get a 10-cent-per-minute rate, a fee that easily pays for itself if you're a heavy caller. Flat rates are higher than off-peak rates, but lower than peak rates, which makes sense for people who make a lot of daytime calls.

Discounts based on consumer calling patterns. You get rewards for things like heavy use or for calls to other customers on the same carrier. AT&T's True Rewards customers earn points (much like frequent flier miles) that can be redeemed for free phone time.

Term commitment plans. Loyal customers get discounts or cash back. Once you've been with the service one year, Sprint Sense, for example, gives you 10% cash back from each of that year's bills if

you've spent a minimum of $250 on long distance.

As you can see—if you hadn't already noticed—discount programs *are* complicated. It seems to us that the carriers could do everyone a favor by simply reducing basic rates and vastly simplifying the discount programs. But it increasingly makes sense to sign up for one. In June 1997, AT&T announced it was lowering basic evening rates by 5% to 15%—after it had raised those rates by 5.9% in November 1996.

Working Assets long distance. Working Assets donates 1% of your charges to such progressive groups as Greenpeace and the Children's Defense Fund, and every month they send you information on some current topic, such as welfare reform. This actually doesn't amount to much—a $2 contribution if you charge $200 all year. Working Assets also offers discounts and dime-a-minute rates that are competitive with the majors.

There's one unique benefit, though. Working Assets allows one free call a month to a designated Senator or corporate executive regarding the issue discussed in the monthly newsletter.

"Casual calling" and "dial arounds." The company you designate becomes your "primary carrier." But you don't always have to use your primary carrier. The 1984 decree ending AT&T's long-distance monopoly mandates "equal access," meaning that you must be afforded full opportunity to use any long-distance company that serves your area.

It's referred to as "casual calling" when you use a company other than your primary carrier. Why would you want to "casual call"? Perhaps to test the quality of a carrier's service before you sign them on as your primary carrier. Or you may "casual call" if your primary carrier is experiencing technical difficulties—or if its circuits are loaded on Mother's Day. Be sure to request the carrier's rate charts first, and check the casual calling rates before you dial, since they are often the company's highest.

You need not set up an account with a carrier to place a casual call. These "dial around" codes allow you to circumvent your designated long-distance carrier on a per-call basis.

AT&T	10 + 288
LCI	10 + 432
Matrix	10 + 780
MCI	10 + 222
US Sprint	10 + 333

Any dial-around charges you incur will appear on a separate page in your monthly phone bill.

Finally, when settling on a carrier, decide if you want to have your bills mailed separately or included with your local telephone company bill. Some carriers offer separate billing.

Collect Calling

A mazing technological advances allow long-distance carriers to offer services no one imagined just a few decades ago. One of these is residential toll-free 800 service. Anyone can call you toll-free, rather than collect. But there could be a monthly fee no matter how many or how few calls you get. Although LCI, MCI, and Matrix give this service away free with certain services, Sprint charges $3 a month, as does WorldCom. Both waive the fee if you spend more than $15 or $20. Most per-minute rates are 25 cents, though Sprint has a 10 cents off-peak rate.

Of course, anyone can call *you* collect without talking to an operator by dialing an 800 number: for MCI, (800) COLLECT; for AT&T, (800) CALLATT; and for Sprint, (800) ONEDIME. It is generally cheaper, however, to use a calling card. For instance, AT&T's calling card surcharge is 89 cents per call, compared with the (800) CALLATT surcharge of $2.25. Still, calling collect via an 800 number is probably your best bet when using an off-brand pay phone not provided by the dominant local carrier. You'll always be routed to your long-distance company, bypassing the potentially very expensive intermediary that the pay-phone company might be connected to.

Long-Distance Calling Cards

L ocal calling cards were briefly discussed in the previous chapter. But long-distance calling cards actually started back in the 1950s. There are now about 15 different kinds—even a card in Braille.

To use a calling card, you dial an access code, the number you're call-

JUST SAY NO

Thieves are constantly developing new *modus operandi* to get your calling card number. According to Frances Feld, Executive Director of the Communications Fraud Control Association, thieves have lately been telephoning calling card holders and, posing as phone company employees, they ask for personal identification numbers, "just to verify it is you." Many naive consumers gladly comply, especially college students.

ing, and your calling card number. Charges show up on your phone bill. The Sprint Sense FONCARD, for instance, offers a 24-hour, 30-cent-per-minute rate on domestic long-distance calls, plus a 30-cent connection fee. Calling cards are essential if you don't want to pump buckets of coins into a pay phone. They are very useful for travelers, who can use the card to avoid hotels' high direct-call surcharges.

Calling card providers offer many frills, like teleconferencing and speed-dialing. They also offer special message-forwarding services. If you make an AT&T calling card or Universal Card call and the line is busy, you can dial a few digits and leave a message with a service. For $1.75 ($2.50 if person-to-person) the service will automatically keep dialing the number for up to ten

hours. If there is an answer, your message is played.

It probably makes sense to get basic calling cards from each of the major carriers—they're free and you might get a special discount just for signing up. To order, call AT&T at (800) 225-5288, MCI at (800) 456-6712, Sprint at (800) 366-1044.

WHAT TO WATCH OUT FOR

Switchover fees. Your local telephone company will charge a service fee, probably $5, to switch your long-distance carrier. Sprint credits you for it. Before you sign up, ask the others if they will, too.

Unfamiliar 411s. It used to be that when someone in Denver wanted a number in New York City, he would call directory assistance in New York. NYNEX (now Bell Atlantic) was constantly updating its directories for the territory. (Besides, they had New Yorkers working for them, who could be expected to know a bit about how to find a number in their own city on less than complete information.)

Now, however, AT&T has taken over national directory assistance for about half the country. Since many of the Baby Bells (like the old NYNEX) won't sell up-to-date directories of their service areas, AT&T relies on old phone books, Internet searches, and motor vehicle records. No only that, but AT&T hands off many of their requests to

PREPAID PHONE CARDS

Prepaid phone cards have fast become a big business, generating revenues of over $1 billion in 1997. Just as fast they have become a source of consumer complaints about high rates and hidden charges, bad connections, and cards that just don't work.

Prepaid phone cards work like this: You buy the cards in increments of $5 to $100 at convenience stores, newsstands, Wal-Marts, even video stores. You don't need any coins; you just dial a toll-free number and enter a special code printed on the phone card. The card's value drains as the minutes slide by. And the minutes slide pretty fast: Calls to United States numbers can run as high as 45 cents per minute. Make sure you understand the rate structure, which should be printed on the card or its package so you can read it *before* you buy the card. The New York Phone Card's packaging simply reads "Local or Regional Phone Company Charges May Apply."

Card companies that aren't long-distance carriers in the first place buy telephone time from a carrier and resell that time to you. When cards go partially or totally unused, it's the carriers and card companies that keep the change—you've already bought the time, even if you don't use it all. Let's say you've got 37 cents left on a card and you need to call Aunt Enid in Alabama. Are you really going to make a minute-and-a-half call, hang up, and call her back on a new card? Doubtful. (Although some cards, like those offered by American Express and the U.S. Postal Service, are rechargeable.)

Be careful which card you buy. Several service resellers have gone bust, leaving their bills to the long-distance carrier unpaid—and leaving card holders with some useless plastic. A super-low rate can signify a poor connection. Test out a card's quality by first buying one in a small denomination, say $10.

contractors located in Florida, Arizona, and Virginia.

The result? When an out-of-towner asked AT&T directory assistance for the New York Stock Exchange's number, the operator asked, "Where's that?" Needless to say, callers frequently end up with the wrong numbers—at a charge of 60 to 95 cents per request.

The "round-up." AT&T, Sprint, and Matrix charge you for a full minute, even if you spoke for only three seconds of it. (MCI and LCI charge in six-second intervals, and

WorldCom does either, depending on your service plan.)

Higher charges for calling cards. Long-distance calling cards are a great convenience. But for Sprint, MCI, and AT&T card customers, there is a surcharge on domestic interstate calls of 60 or 75 cents, although most carriers will provide you with a special discount if they are your primary carrier and you also use their calling card. For example, for $2 a month, AT&T Reach Out America customers can apply their calling card calls to the plan, and the 80-cent calling card fee is waived during non-peak hours.

Dial-arounds. The major long-distance companies aren't the only ones in the dial-around business. By now you've probably seen the ads or received mail solicitations that promise dialing one of these codes will save you heaps over your regular carrier. Many small start-up carriers are offering dial-arounds to win your phone dollar. But as with many marketing campaigns, the large print giveth and the small print taketh away.

Telecom USA claims that dialing its 10+321 code will save you 50% over AT&T on calls over 20 minutes. A big savings, but that's

only over AT&T's most expensive basic rate. VarTec's "DimeLine" promises 10-cent-per-minute rates anytime—but you have to pay a $5 fee to get that rate, and there's a 3-minute minimum on each call. A quick "hi" on someone's answering machine would cost you $5.30.

Being switched via slamming. Mrs. Bowers didn't understand that "no" can sometimes mean "yes." She thought that AT&T handled all of her long-distance phone calls. But one day she opened her phone bill and noticed a $5 service charge from a different long-distance company. As it turned out, she had opened an account with a new long-distance carrier without realizing it during a call from a very persistent telephone salesman a few weeks before. She thought she had said "no" but the salesman interpreted what she said as "yes, connect me." In telephone industry parlance, she had been "slammed."

The practice of "slamming" was specifically outlawed in 1991 by the Federal Communications Commission. But even with newly required customer confirmations for carrier changes, many Americans still end up switching companies without completely understanding what

> "*One person had a small microphone hooked to the back of his watch that he was speaking into. . . . Another wrote the number down, and another person looked like he was mouthing the numbers to memorize them.*"
>
> —JAMES SNYDER,
> an MCI lawyer, describing how calling-card number thieves who hang out near public phones do their work

ROOM SERVICE COSTS

According to *The Wall Street Journal*, the lodging industry can collect close to $2 billion worth of phone fees in a single year. What kinds of fees? Potentially enormous surcharges if you dial long distance directly from your room. Some hotels fail to pass along the carrier's evening and night discounts. Others don't print the duration of the call on your bill, preventing you from checking the bill's accuracy and easily enabling overcharging. Some hotel chains charge a fee of a dollar or so if you try to bypass hotel surcharges by using your own calling card—and some hotels block card calls altogether. And most hotels charge fees of 50 cents or $1 for local calls. What to do? If in doubt about how much the hotel will tack on, use the pay phone in the lobby.

they're doing. This is because competition in the long-distance industry for new customers has become so cutthroat that sales representatives are sometimes less than clear about what they're asking people to do.

Some slammers aren't even that scrupulous. A New York man named Charlie, whose name is listed in the phone book as "Chas."—a name he never goes by—was slammed in 1996. The new carrier's bill was addressed to "Chas." Charlie's guess? The slammer lifted names from the public phone book and simply forged signatures on "consent" forms.

The FCC is considering proposals that would force companies making the unauthorized switches to be responsible for any costs or lost benefits—even frequent flier miles—that customers would have received from their authorized carrier.

High-priced operator service providers (OSPs). If you place a long-distance call on a phone other than your own and hear a voice identifying an unfamiliar carrier (i.e., one not among the major carriers), you'll know you're being serviced by an OSP—and that the sky's the limit on how much the call will cost. Examine pay phones before calling long distance to see if they are connected to your usual long-distance company; federal law requires pay phones to have a sign disclosing their long-distance company connection. Or you can find out from the long-distance operator by dialing "00" or by calling the switchboard (of a hotel or hospital, for example, if that is where you are calling from).

You can also ask the "00" operator for rates and surcharges for the call you are about to place. If you are calling from a pay phone or a residence, call (700) 555-4141 (toll-free) for a recording stating the name of the carrier the phone is connected to.

If you want to use your regular carrier from any phone, just dial your equal access code.

THE $MARTER CALLER	
DAY RATE	*Monday through Friday, 8 AM to 5 PM (7 AM to 7 PM for Sprint)*
EVENING RATE	*Sunday through Friday, 5 PM to 11 PM (7 PM to 7 AM for Sprint)*
NIGHT/WEEKEND RATE	*Sunday through Friday, 11 PM to 8 AM and all day Saturday*

Discount plan start-up fees. AT&T, for one, charges a $5 processing fee for its One-Rate plan.

Bribes. AT&T sent Nancy R. a $100 check. Depositing it would switch her to their One-Rate Plan —15 cents per minute for every call, no matter where or what time of day she called. Tempted, she called MCI, her current carrier, to see if they would do any better. MCI didn't counter the bribe, but they immediately pulled her last few bills to compare the AT&T plan to MCI plans. Using AT&T would have cost her $5–$10 extra per month, so her $100 would have disappeared within a year.

Limitations on low rates. It's hard to miss Candice Bergen advertising Sprint's dime-a-minute plan. "No matter how far away, it's just ten cents a minute with Sprint Sense." But if you can read the tiny type that flashes across the bottom of the screen, you'll see that the low rate applies only during "off-peak" hours.

Sales spiels and sniping. When you call carriers for information about their services, they launch into their sales pitch and may make disparaging remarks about the competition. An MCI representative informed us that AT&T charges a $30 hookup fee for its personal 800 number and MCI charges none. An AT&T representative responded that the charge was only $10 and it would be deducted from the bill if the service was kept for a year. When we called AT&T to ask for rate charts, a representative wanted to know the details of our personal calling patterns, since AT&T offers "17 or 18 different plans—one for every kind of caller"—and he clearly wanted to sell us one. He also knocked the quality of the competition's service. Representatives will go on and on about the plan their company spends millions to advertise, but they'll be reticent about unannounced—but still available— plans that may be better for you.

Before we could pose our first question, every carrier we called to inquire about savings plans, calling cards, or 800 numbers asked for our name and phone number. To avoid undesired solicitation calls, ignore these requests. We did, and we still got the necessary information.

THE $MARTER CONSUMER

Get the discount. Even if you hardly ever make long-distance calls, don't simply opt for your carrier's basic rate plan—it's like paying the full sticker price for a car. This may sound like obvious advice, but two-thirds of all residential customers pay full price for long distance, according to Boston-based telecom research firm the Yankee Group.

Call when it's cheapest. You can cut your bill by more than half if you wait until after 7 P.M. on week-days with Sprint Sense, or after 5 P.M. weekdays with WorldCom's Home Advantage Plan. If you call New York from San Francisco, even with AT&T's basic rate, you can save 38% by calling after 5 P.M. and 53% by calling on weekends. See the basic time chart for the six major carriers on the opposite page.

Watch out for rate changes and time-period changes. Some companies base the rate for an entire call on the rate when you placed it. This is preferable if you often start your calls at a cheaper time and end them in a more expensive time. On the other hand, if your calls often extend to lower rate hours, you would do better with a carrier that changes the rates when the time period changes.

Get credits for wrong numbers. Above, right, are the six major car-

CALL FOR CREDIT

AT&T	*Call the operator for immediate credit or (800) 222-0300 for bill adjustment*
LCI	*(800) 860-2255 for immediate credit*
MATRIX	*(800) 282-0242 for immediate credit*
MCI	*(800) 444-3333 for immediate credit*
US SPRINT	*Call the operator for immediate credit or (800) 877-4646 for bill adjustment*
WORLDCOM	*(800) 275-0100 for immediate credit*

riers' phone numbers for getting a credit. You can also dial "00."

Reassess annually. Rates and plans change constantly, so it makes sense to reconsider your long-distance carrier and your calling plan at least once a year.

Avoid calling-card fraud. There's a new illicit profession, "surfing." "Surfers" are people who use your card number to sell heavily discounted long-distance calls. They get your number by observing you punch it in or by listening to you recite it to an operator while using a public phone. To avoid being billed for thousands of dollars worth of calls to China, for example, try to punch in—rather than orally recite to the operator—your personal identification number. Use your free hand to cover or screen the hand that's punching in the numbers. Better yet, try to use phones that read the magnetic strip on your calling card. If you must recite the number, do so in a soft but clear voice. Always be alert to anyone lurking about while you are placing a calling card call.

Don't get "slammed." To stop unauthorized switching of your long-distance carrier, the Federal Communications Commission now prohibits local phone companies from honoring a request to switch your long-distance service unless you are provided written confirmation of the switch, you electronically authorized the change, you received a follow-up mailing saying that you will be switched within 14 days unless you cancel, or there was an independent third-party verification of the switch. If you're unhappy about being slammed, immediately ask your phone company to be switched back—for free.

Try call accounting. Who's making those three-hour late-night calls? If your kids won't 'fess up, consider getting Call Accounting. For a monthly fee of $5 or so (AT&T has no charge), each caller will have to punch in a short special code when calling. There will be a separate page in your monthly statement for each caller.

HELP

■ **The Telecommunications** Research & Action Center publishes periodic rate comparisons among the major carriers. For $5, they'll send you their *Tele-Tips Residential Long Distance Comparison Chart*. Send your payment with a 55-cent stamped, self-addressed #10 envelope to TRAC at P.O. Box 27279, Washington, DC 20005. You can compare major carriers' rates online at their Web site, www.trac.org.

■ **To complain about long distance,** calling cards, or international service, write to the Federal Communications Commission, Common Carrier Bureau, Consumer Complaints, Stop Code 1600A2, Washington, DC 20554. Include copies of disputed bills and other documents to help them understand your complaint. To receive a written explanation of how to complain, call the FCC at (202) 418-0200.

■ **For answers to nearly all your** long-distance questions, contact the experts at Tele-Consumer Hotline. Call (800) 332-1124, or visit their Web site at www.teleconsumer.org. They offer a series of free publications which you can get by writing to Tele-Consumer Hotline, P.O. Box 27207, Washington, DC 20005.

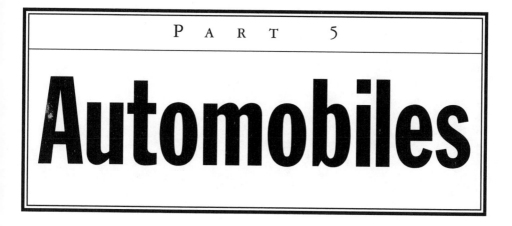

P A R T   5

Automobiles

NEW CARS

Don't Get Taken for an Expensive Ride

More and more of the 45 million Americans who buy cars each year are prepared to do battle on an equal footing with dealers who just a few years ago sat around waiting for suckers to walk in the door. With a little preparation, you can, too.

Log on to the Internet, hire a broker to dicker for you, or go to a modern automotive supermarket, where you'll find competitive brands lined up chassis to chassis like so many boxes of cereal. Touch screen computers, salaried sales associates straight out of Nordstrom's, even child care services and coffee bars are quickly replacing smarmy salespeople and arbitrary (and sometimes bigoted and chauvinistic) pricing. The result: wider selection, better and more pleasant service, and rock-bottom prices.

Take Alice H., a San Francisco graphic designer, who used CompuServe's Auto Net on-line guide to find out what dealers actually paid for the cars she was interested in buying. When she went shopping for a Honda del Sol, the salesman wanted to start the negotiation with the sticker price of $24,000.

Alice immediately cited the dealer invoice price of less than $13,000. The salesman was not happy, but he knew he'd lost the game. She paid $14,000. Says Alice: "It was fun. I can't wait to buy another car."

But don't breathe too heavy a sigh of relief. The revolution in car showrooms isn't yet complete. If you aren't careful, you could go through the more traditional torture endured by Richetta S. of Washington, D.C.: "I didn't want to fight with those people. I just wanted a [Toyota] 4Runner. I just wanted to take a look at it, make up my mind about it, and buy it. But I'd talk to one salesman, and then they'd have me talk to someone else, and then to someone else. When I thought everything was okay, they sent me to the finance people, who forced me to buy an extended warranty (for about $1,000) that I didn't want." Speaking for her fellow Americans, she told *The Washington Post:* "I'm telling you, if I never have to go into another dealership again to buy a car, I never will."

It doesn't have to be so bad. Do a little research ahead of time and be prepared to walk away from any dealer who won't give you the straight story.

THE BASICS

Safety First

All cars must meet the safety standards set by the U.S. government. Given that 41,000 people die in car accidents every year and millions more are injured, it makes no sense to buy anything less than the safest car you can afford.

Safety equipment and crash protection. It may seem like the safety of a widely heralded new safety device—the air bag—was called into question by the deaths of 80 people, including 44 children, between 1986 and 1997. But given the millions of crashes that occur each year, fatalities from air bags are extremely rare. And air bags remain one of the most important car safety innovations. Through January 1998, air bags had saved over 2,600 lives; an air bag on the driver's side reduces deaths from frontal collisions by 34%, according to the National Highway Traffic Safety Administration.

In response to concerns about air bag safety, the federal government worked with auto manufacturers to produce safer air bags, which pop out with explosive force designed to protect the driver and front seat passenger in a collision into a fixed barrier at 30 miles per hour. The force required to do that can put infants and smaller adults at risk; thus, standards have been relaxed to

allow manufacturers to use lower-powered air bags. These began appearing in 1999 model year cars.

However, the government declined to allow mechanics to disable air bags without special permission. With the 1998 model year, all new cars were required to have both driver and passenger air bags, and starting in model year 1999, all new light trucks were required to have air bags on both sides.

Whether you are driving or going along for the ride, you should always wear a seat belt, regardless of whether the car has air bags or where you sit. Air bags do no good in side and rear collisions in the majority of cars; they pop out only in front collisions, and they are designed to work in conjunction with seat belts. Indeed, most of the people killed by air bags were not wearing their seat belt or were not properly buckled in.

By automatically pumping the brakes, anti-lock braking systems (ABS) prevent you from skidding out of control when you stop short. Even if you are braking, you will still be able to steer. This safety feature, along with dual-side air bags, is strongly recommended by auto safety advocates, even though an Insurance Institute for Highway Safety study showed that the death rate from accidents between 1993 and 1995 involving ABS-equipped cars was slightly higher than for similar cars without ABS. Tests have shown over and over again that cars with ABS stop shorter and straighter than cars without.

For ABS to work properly, you need to keep firm pressure on the

AIR BAG SAFETY CHECKLIST

- Always wear a seat belt.
- Passengers who are too small to wear lap-and-shoulder belts properly should sit in the back seat.
- Front seat passengers should wear a safety belt and slide the seat as far back as it will go.
- Drivers should sit back 12 inches from the steering wheel, assuming they can still see and reach to drive safely. Those who can't reach the pedal sitting that far back might consider buying pedal extenders.
- Never put a child in a child-safety seat in the front seat of a car equipped with a functioning air bag.

Crash test performance. Since 1979, the U.S. DOT has been test-crashing cars to see how well they protect drivers and passengers who are wearing seat belts. DOT releases the data to the public through the National Highway Traffic Safety Administration (NHTSA). *The Car Book* analyzes the government data and presents the results, using a "Crash Test Index" number that makes it easy to compare the crash test results of cars of comparable size—the lower the number, the better the car protected its occupants. However, keep in mind that NHTSA does not regularly test for rear, or angled collisions, rollovers, or how a car would do in a collision with a bigger or smaller vehicle. However, in 1997 (when a new law took effect), auto makers were required to assure the safety of their vehicles in side collisions, and NHTSA began testing side impact crash performance.

Child safety seats. Every state requires them—for good reason—for kids up to a certain age or size (requirements vary from state to state). Once infants get beyond the first few weeks of life, car crashes are the leading cause of death and serious injury for children. The middle of the back seat is the safest place for children in car seats.

King of the road. These days, consumers seem to be saying that bigger is better—and fuel economy be damned. Sales of full-size pick-up trucks doubled between 1991 and 1996, and sales of large sport utility vehicles quintupled over the same five-year period. Consumers

brake; if, startled by the pulsing of the brake pedal or a noise that may sound like grinding, you take your foot off the brake too soon, the braking system will not continue working. To get used to how ABS will feel, try your brakes out in a parking lot on a rainy day. ABS will not activate at slow speeds; you'll have to drive at about 30 miles per hour and then hit the brakes hard.

ABS comes standard with many cars, but if you have to buy it as an option, be prepared to pay anywhere from $500 to $1,000.

think they are safer, like the feeling of riding higher than the rest of the traffic, or they want to intimidate or impress with a bigger and badder vehicle. Never mind that large vehicles go only about 14 miles per gallon, or less—or that the overall safety record of such vehicles is mixed. Their higher center of gravity leads them to roll over during tight, high-speed turns, and occupants of light trucks fare worse than occupants of cars in single-vehicle accidents like crashing into a tree.

However, consumers' newfound love for hulking sport utility vehicles and minivans poses a growing risk to drivers and passengers in smaller vehicles. Because the behemoths can weigh a ton more than, say, a Ford Taurus, and ride higher, accidents involving a mismatched pair are deadlier. According to government statistics, more people die in accidents involving a car and a light truck than in two cars, and that is true even though light trucks make up only one third of all vehicles on the road. And of the 5,426 people killed in these mismatched collisions in 1995, only 20% were in light trucks; 80% were in cars. This is because sport utility vehicles ride so much higher; a collision with a car isn't bumper to bumper, but bumper to some much less structurally sound part of the car. Most cars are designed to withstand a collision with a similarly shaped vehicle weighing within 500 pounds of its own weight and are reinforced with this in mind. "Continued growth in the number and weight of light trucks, unless offset by safety improvements, is likely to increase the hazard in collisions between the trucks and smaller road users," according to a report by the National Highway Traffic Safety Administration.

> ## "When I began my one-year stint selling cars, the first serious advice I got came from a veteran salesman who said, simply, 'Tell them what they want to hear.' Another pro described the typical car sale as a 'lying contest': 'The customer lies to you, you lie to the customer, the customer lies to you, you lie to the customer, and so on. . . . The better liar prevails.' "
>
> —DEBRA SHERMAN,
> former car dealer

Driving a Hard Bargain

Timing. If you can, shop for a car when the dealer is likely to need the sale. The biggest sales slump is in the weeks just before and after Christmas. (Exception: Do not let on that you are buying the car as a Christmas present or the salesperson is likely to hold out for a higher price with the knowledge that you need the car by December 25.) The end of any month is often a good time to buy because only a few days remain for the dealer and salespeople to meet their monthly quotas; any additional sales mean an extra bonus. Hungry for sales, they are likelier to sacrifice profit than their bonus.

Do your homework. Go into the showroom with as much information as can be had. You'll even the playing field with the salesperson if you know how much you can spend, have a promise of financing at a reasonable rate from a bank, and know how much the dealer paid the manufacturer for the car and options. Don't share all these thoughts with the salesperson, but keep them in mind as you shop.

To find out what the dealer paid for the car, consult *Consumer Reports* Auto Price Service (see **HELP** at the end of the chapter). It will tell you price information about any make, model, trim line, options, and factory rebates. If the dealer challenges your research, ask to see the manufacturer's invoice. If you're getting the straight story on what the car costs dealers, they have nothing to lose by proving it.

Be flexible. Don't get your heart set on only one car; it's too much like going to the grocery store when you are hungry. You probably don't need the exact make and model rated highest by *Consumer Reports*; you want one that scores near the top. Many cars have nearly identical twins or corporate cousins that go by different names but are essentially the same car. For instance, the Ford Explorer is similar to the Mercury Mountaineer, and the Geo

BEST TIMES WORST TIMES

You can get great prices on cars late in the model year (which varies from model to model). It's a time when dealers clear out their showrooms to make room for new models. Just keep in mind that as soon as you drive the car home, it will depreciate a whole year. If you plan to keep the car more than five years, buying late makes sense; but if you want to trade the car in sooner, you may lose out because your three-year-old car will have depreciated four years' worth. Also keep in mind that your insurance company will cover the car based on its model year, not based on when you bought it. If you wreck the car after two years, the insurance company will reimburse you for a three-year-old car.

Prizm is practically the same as the Toyota Corolla. Keep in mind that a twin with a higher price tag may also come with more standard options. If they are the options you want, you might get a better deal than if you outfitted the lower-priced car with the same extras.

Don't let high-pressure sales tactics get to you. Ads are designed to bring you into the showroom. Read them very carefully and be on the lookout for footnotes. Car dealers may be hiding information in small print that they would be just as happy to have you gloss over. A price that's good today ought to be good next week. Don't leave a deposit unless you've got a firm agreement; it will just pressure you into returning to buy the car. If you leave a deposit, make sure you get a written receipt that also says it's refundable.

Take the car for a spin. To test the car's performance, you'll want to tool around town, navigate through traffic, and cruise down the highway (within the speed limit, of course). Does the engine run smoothly? How does the car do going up steep hills or passing another car on the highway? Try stopping short and taking a variety of turns. And try it all again with the air conditioner on to make sure the car's engine can both keep you cool *and* meet your standards.

You'll spend many hours in your car, so get in and make sure you're comfortable. Is there enough headroom and legroom? Can you get in and out without bruises? Try the back seat, too. (Don't forget that your gangly teenager may one day be driving his basketball teammates home from practice: Will he and his tall friends fit comfortably?)

Comparison shop. More than one dealer sells the cars that you have decided best fit your needs, and each of them may offer you a different price. Don't be shy about reminding the dealer of this—and your willingness to drive down the road for the better deal you found last weekend. Remember, they know what their cost is and how low they'll go. The only way you can find out their bottom line is to negotiate in its direction.

WHAT TO WATCH OUT FOR

Stiff competition, consumers armed with dealer's invoice prices they pulled off the Internet, and car-buying services like CarBargains have cut into dealers' profits on cars. To make up for it, they may try to sell you extras like extended warranties or credit life insurance. Pass on them; the value of these items is dubious, at best. And stay alert through the discussion of financing and trade-in, or your hard-won good deal could go bad.

Extended Warranties or Service Contracts

The quality of cars has improved markedly, and consumer advocates are unanimous in their view that extended warranties generally aren't worth the one-time $350 to $2,000 they can cost. Even so, one in four Honda and Toyota buyers surveyed in 1996 bought the overpriced extended warranty—just what the dealer was hoping for. The company offering the contract is betting that making necessary repairs will cost them less than you paid for the contract; otherwise, they wouldn't be in business. Nationwide, about 2 million consumers are overcharged a whopping $300 million annually on service

SECRET WARRANTIES

Manufacturers deny they exist, but there has long been a quiet tradition of auto makers paying for repairs of problems resulting from design defects, even after the warranty has run out. Manufacturers prefer to call such repairs "policy adjustments." Sounds reasonable, except that since auto makers do not notify all car owners, the policy applies only to people who complain the loudest. In other words, squeaky wheels get free grease, and everybody else has to pay for their own. Because of past problems with secret warranties, Ford, General Motors, and Volkswagen are required to make bulletins public (see **HELP**).

Only California, Connecticut, Virginia, and Wisconsin require auto makers to notify consumers of post-warranty adjustments.

contracts. One Chrysler dealer charged $1,620 for a contract it paid only $125 for, according to an investigation by the New York State Attorney General.

Jack Gillis, author of *The Car Book,* says the typical buyer ends up using only $100 to $200 of the coverage. His suggestion: put $500 in a special savings account; let interest compound the nest egg; and draw on it to pay your repair bills. You will probably have money left over to buy something more useful, or fun, than breakdown insurance you'll hardly, if ever, use.

Add-ons for Gimmicks

Avoid buying rust-proofing, paint sealant, fabric protection, and other services. Not only is the price steep—$400 to $800 for treatments that cost the dealer $5 to $100 to add—but most cars don't need such treatments. These days, cars are made to be much more rustproof and paint jobs much sturdier. What's more, some of these processes can actually damage your car and void parts of your warranty.

Dealers often try to tack on additional charges for these services after you have agreed on a price. Take Olympia Z., who agreed to purchase a car for $11,411. After she signed a contract to buy the car, various salespeople tried to sell her options she wasn't interested in. She asked for information about some options, but never agreed to purchase any. Nevertheless, when she picked up the car, the invoice said she owed $14,140 for the car and options she did not want, nearly $3,000 more than she had authorized with her signature on the sales contract.

If you still want any of these treatments, you'll almost certainly pay less if you have the work done elsewhere. And you can buy a couple of cans of Scotchguard and apply fabric protection yourself.

315

Some dealers will say that available cars have an option or two you don't want—a cassette deck, for instance, or up-front door lock controls. If you want the car, be clear about your willingness to buy it—and equally clear that you won't pay for the extras you didn't request. You may be able to negotiate the purchase without paying an extra cost.

Skip the "credit life" insurance many dealers are pushing these days. They'll tell you it will pay off your loan if you die before you finish paying for the car. And it will. But they won't tell you how outrageously priced this coverage is. You'd be better off buying a term life insurance policy for far less, which would cover *all* your debts.

The No-Dicker Sticker

In recognition of consumers' distrust of car salespeople and dislike of the bazaar-like atmosphere in many showrooms, some dealers have abandoned bargaining in favor of a pre-set, take-it-or-leave-it price. This takes a lot of the pressure out of the process. Witness the success of General Motors' Saturn Corporation, which sells all its cars this way; a few years ago, it couldn't manufacture the cars fast enough to keep up with demand.

You can also avoid haggling by hiring a car-buying service like Auto-By-Tel, AutoVantage, or Car-Bargains to do it for you. Using the Internet or the companies' toll-free numbers, you pay a fee, tell them the make, model, and options you are looking for, and they will get guaranteed bids from several dealers

FUELING UP FOR LESS

How much difference does fuel economy make? Even among cars of similar size, fuel economy varies all over the lot. Say you pay $1.25 per gallon of gas. If you drive 15,000 miles a year in a car that gets 34 miles to the gallon, you'll pay $551.25 for gas. Compare that to the $937.50 you'd pay if you drove a gas guzzler that gets only 20 miles to the gallon.

The EPA tests and approximates new cars' gas mileage—the "22 mph city and 30 mph highway" familiar to TV commercial viewers. But as the car ads point out, "Your mileage may differ," and you should expect it to. Because fuel economy depends upon driving conditions and your car's condition, both of which are likely to be inferior to the EPA's test conditions, your mileage will probably be something less.

in your area. All you have to do is go and pick up the car. But keep in mind that dealers pay for their listing with some of these services, which probably inflates prices a bit. CarBargains does not accept payment from dealers.

However, pleasantness has its price. *Consumer Reports* tested both haggle-free and haggle-*sí* approaches and found that "people who are willing to do their home-work and bargain hard can save somewhere between $200 and $300 doing it the old-fashioned way."

Warranties

Government standards for "full" manufacturers' warranties require car makers to cover all aspects of the car's performance. For this reason, most manufacturers offer only "limited" warranties, which cover the costs of making repairs that are necessary to correct defective parts or assembly during the warranty period. Warranties do not cover problems resulting from routine wear and tear, nor do they cover the costs of routine maintenance. And they are void if problems result from misuse of the car, negligence, accidents, of if you fail to maintain the car as recommended in the owner's manual. If you have routine maintenance done somewhere other than the dealer's shop (which is a good idea, since alternatives will almost always be cheaper), keep records so that you can prove you've kept up with the manufacturer's prescribed maintenance schedule.

Dealer-added options can sometimes void your warranty. If you have any questions, contact the manufacturer before you have options installed.

Tricks of the Trade-in

Most people have no idea what their current car is worth and as a result get taken on their trade-in. It's more work, but you'll almost always get more for your old car if you sell it yourself.

Rule 1. Whether you want to trade it or sell it yourself, you need to know what your old car is worth. To find out, call the *Consumer Reports* Used Car Price Service or look it up in one of the price guides available at newsstands, the library, or on the Internet—such as the National Automobile Dealers Association *Official Used Car Price Guide* or in the *Kelley Blue Book*. With this information you should be able to negotiate a fair price for it with an individual or with a dealer.

Rule 2. If you're going to trade in the old car, keep the negotiation for the new car separate from the negotiation over the value of your old car. If you let on that you want to trade in your old car too early, the salesperson can shave a bit off the price of the new car and make up for it by giving you less than your old car is worth.

Financing the Car

Car dealers often try to entice buyers into the showroom with the promise of low monthly loan rates. Be on your guard. The favorable rates may apply only to cars the dealer wants to unload or to more expensive cars than you had in mind. Also, don't let the salesperson give with one hand and take away with the other by making up for a good deal on the purchase price with a bad deal on the financing, or vice versa.

If the price is right, by all means take it, but shop around. You might find a bank or credit union willing to give you a better deal. (For more information on installment credit, see the chapter "Installment Loans," page 620.)

Leasing

While leases are in some ways similar to installment credit purchases—both call for monthly payments over a fixed period—the monthly cost of leasing a car will be cheaper than financing. However, other long-term and hidden costs can sour the deal. And, keep in mind that you will own a car at the end of a finance period, whereas you will have nothing but a potential headache at the end of a lease. Even so, leasing makes sense for some people, especially those who couldn't otherwise afford to drive as nice a car as they'd like. (For more details, read the chapter later in this section, "Car Leasing: Look Before You Lease," page 330.)

Lemon Laws

State laws vary, but all have "lemon laws" that will help you get a refund or a new car if you buy a car that doesn't run right. For specific information on the law in your state, contact the Attorney General's Office. Generally speaking, a new vehicle is defined as a "lemon" if it has been in the shop at least four times for the same problem or has been out of service for a total of 30 days during the first year you own it. Attention, leasing customers: Lemon laws do not apply to leased vehicles in every state.

THE $MARTER CONSUMER

Get all agreements in writing. Oral promises are virtually impossible to prove should a dispute arise.

Pay as little as you can get away with over the dealer's cost. Most often this will mean a profit of 2% to 5% over the dealer's invoice, which is reasonable, except if the car is in unusually high demand. Shop around until you find a dealer who will go along with your terms.

Compare the sales contract to the invoice. Don't let the dealer add charges after you have agreed on a final price.

Inspect the car before you drive it off the lot. Do not settle for inspection of a similar car. Make sure your car has all the options you have paid for and no nicks or other visible damage. And by all means take it with you once you've inspected it. If you leave it overnight, you may find the AM/FM radio turns out to be AM only or some other mysterious transformation or disappearing act.

Think twice about extras. Don't buy anything but the car from the dealer. Extended warranties, security-alarm systems, and chemical treatments may not be necessary. If you decide they are, be aware that they certainly cost less at shops whose primary business is selling these items or services.

Shop around for financing. Arranging your own financing might be cheaper than the dealer's financing, and having a finance guarantee can give you leverage when you are negotiating a real price—the salesperson will know you are ready to buy, and you can just as easily take your business elsewhere if you aren't offered a fair price.

Buy a fuel-efficient car. It will be good not only for your wallet but also for the environment. The Environmental Protection Agency (EPA) suggests a manual transmission (it can save 6.5 miles per gallon over an automatic transmission), a smaller engine (which runs more efficiently and burns less fuel), radial tires (which can improve gas mileage 3% to 7% over bias-ply tires), and using the air conditioning wisely. Turn it off in traffic—you'll save three miles per gallon—but use it on the highway, where open windows create drag and make your engine work harder.

Pull over before you make that call. Using a telephone while driving quadruples the risk of having an accident. The combination of gabbing and driving is so dangerous—equal to driving drunk, according to the *New England Journal of Medicine*—that Australia, Brazil, and Israel have banned talking while driving.

H E L P

■ *The Car Book* by Jack Gillis. (Harper Perennial). This annual guide covers all aspects of car buying: safety, fuel economy, maintenance, warranties, show-room strategy, insurance, tires, and how to complain. Available in bookstores or from the Center for Auto Safety, 2001 S Street NW, Washington, DC 20009, or call (202) 328-7700. The Center receives a portion of the profit if you buy it from them.

■ *Consumer Reports* **Annual Auto** Issue, published in April of each year, available at the library year-round or for $5 from Consumers Union, 101 Truman Avenue, Yonkers, NY 10703; call (800) 234-1645 to order.

■ *Consumer Reports* **New Car Price** Service can tell you exactly what the dealer paid the manufacturer for any make, model, and trim line you are interested in. For $12 you will get a printout listing the standard equipment, list price, and dealer cost of the basic car, along with an itemized list of the dealer cost and list price of every individual option and options package, and current information about factory rebates. It costs $10 for each additional car; call (800) 458-0436.

■ **The National Highway Traffic** Safety Administration's Auto Safety Hotline, (800) 424-9393, provides useful information on cars, child safety seats, or tires you may be considering; the results of government crash tests, and uniform tire quality grades. You can also use the hot line to protect others by reporting any safety problems you discover. The same information is also on the Web at www/nhtsa.dot.gov.

Continued on next page

Continued from previous page

■ **The Lemon Book: Auto Rights** by Ralph Nader and Clarence Ditlow. (Moyer Bell Limited, 1990). Available for $15.95 from the Center for Auto Safety, 2001 S Street NW, Washington, DC 20009; (202) 328-7700.

■ **The *Gas Mileage Guide*, published** by the Environmental Protection Agency, lists estimated fuel economy by make and model. Available free from the U.S. Department of Energy's Conservation and Renewable Energy Inquiry and Referral Service; call (800) 523-2929 or go to www.eren.doc.gov.

■ **Insurance Institute for Highway** Safety publishes a booklet, *Shopping for a Safer Car,* which lists the safety features that come with many different car models. To get this free booklet, send a stamped, self-addressed envelope to the Insurance Institute for Highway Safety, P.O. Box 1420, Arlington, VA 22210; or call (703) 247-1500.

■ **To avoid negotiating for yourself,** call CarBargains, a service offered by the nonprofit Center for the Study of Services. For $165, you tell CarBargains which makes, models, and style of car you want to buy, and they will get firm price quotes from at least five dealers in your area who know they are competing against one another. You will receive the prices and additional information about the dealers' costs and options, and can choose from among them. Send a check to CarBargains, 733 15th St. NW, Suite 820, Washington, DC 20005. To use Visa or Mastercard, call (800) 475-7283. Internet: www.checkbook.org.

■ **For information on secret war-** ranties, contact the Center for Auto Safety, 2001 S Street NW, Washington, DC 20009. Ford's defect line is (800) 241-3673; GM's is (800) 551-4123; Volkswagen's is (800) 544-8021.

■ **The Internet offers many useful** sites for car buyers. For instance, you can find dealer invoice prices (note: without the valuable factory rebate information offered by *Consumer Reports* and CarBargains), compare makes and models and costs of ownership, calculate how much car you can afford, find out how much your trade-in is worth, and get a buying service to haggle for you. Go to CarBargains,www.consumer.checkbook.org/consumer/; Intellichoice, www.intellichoice.com; Microsoft Car-Point, carpoint.msn.com; *Kelley Blue Book,* www.kbb.com; or *Edmund's Automotive Buyer's Guides,* www.edmunds.com.

CHAPTER 29

USED CARS

Buy a Peach, Not a Lemon

If you saw Robin Williams trying to sell a used car to a grieving widow at her husband's funeral in *Cadillac Man*, you know why this chapter is necessary.

What's more, with so many two- and three-year-old vehicles flooding the used-car market after original car leases run out, there are plenty of good bargains to choose from. Nearly two out of three cars sold in 1995 were used. Cars have gotten so much more reliable over the last decade, consumers have realized that compared with a recent-model, high-quality used car, a new car at $20,000-plus is not necessarily a good investment. You can get more car for your money, and since features like air bags and anti-lock brakes have been around for a while, you don't have to sacrifice safety for price. Plus, insuring a used car generally costs less than insuring a new one. If you aren't convinced, the box on the next page illustrates how you can save almost $5,400 over three years if you buy a used car rather than a new one.

THE BASICS

Much of the advice about buying a new car applies when buying a used car (see the previous chapter), but there are even fewer objective standards of comparison and additional potential trouble spots.

Finding a Reliable Car

A wealth of sources exists to help you investigate worthwhile prospects. The *Consumer Reports* annual car-buying issue (published every April) can tell you which used cars to seek and which to avoid based on their repair records. And Jack Gillis's *Used Car Book* rates cars based on their relative complaint records and their government crash-test performance when they were new.

New-car dealers. You'll pay top dollar for a used car at a new-car dealership, but it might be worth it for the selection of late-model cars, service, and warranty. Following a long-standing Mercedes-Benz tradition, virtually every manufacturer now "certifies" its own used cars. "Certified" used cars have been inspected and refurbished according to the manufacturer's standards and come backed by manufacturer's warranties, which range from one to three years. Goodbye mysterious alarms or warning lights signifying

321

nothing. Every little thing, and large thing, gets checked and, if necessary, replaced—motor, brakes, transmission, tires, switches, hinges, cup holders, you name it.

There must be a catch, you say. How could everything old be as good as new again? You'll pay a lot less for a "certified" used car than for a new car, but you'll pay a premium over a similar used car—anywhere from $500 to $1,500 more (depending on the make), according to the National Automobile Dealers Association price guides. For the consumer who might otherwise be tempted by a new car, buying certified is a relatively anxiety-free way to save several thousand dollars over new. It's also a good way to buy something a little more luxurious

than your neighbor might think you could afford. And keep in mind that you are getting something for your money: peace of mind, a pleasant buying process, and service if you need it.

Used-car superstores, like Car Max and Auto Nation USA. The new customer-friendly car superstores are run more like a Home Depot than a Homer's Dealership. Compared to the old days, they make shopping for a used car easy. Touch-screen computers containing lists of their vast inventory help you winnow down the possibilities to cars that meet your needs within your price range. You can then print out each vehicle's vital statistics—make, model, year, mileage,

THE PRICE DIFFERENTIAL

	New Car	Used Car
Price	$21,000	$12,000
Sales tax (7%)	$1,470	$840
Finance charges (8% over 3 years, less $3,000 down payment)	$2,300	$1,150
Insurance (3 years)	$3,500	$2,900
Repairs	0	$1,000
Payments over 3 years	$28,270	$17,890
Trade-in value	$12,000	$7,000
Total cost (assumes sale of car after 3 years)	$16,270	$10,890

warranty information, and no-dicker sticker price—to take home with you or out to the lot to inspect the cars you have zeroed in on.

The superstores stock so many vehicles that you can check out a number of cars very efficiently without having to drive all over the country. The cars themselves tend to be mostly recent models of high quality, many of which recently came off lease. Some of them may even have part of the original manufacturer's warranty left. At some superstores, you can even leave your child to play with the nanny provided on-site while you shop. Since prices are fixed, you won't find many great bargains, but then again you won't get fleeced.

Independent used-car dealers. These smaller dealers, who sell only used cars, offer lower prices but have a smaller selection to choose from and are potentially riskier. Before you go, find out about the dealer's reputation from your local government consumer office or Better Business Bureau.

Auctions. Cars that have been abandoned by their owners or repossessed are often auctioned off. Look for ads in local papers. But exercise extreme caution. A NYC Department of Consumer Affairs investigation showed that consumer complaints, rather than cars, zoom off auto auction lots. For instance, one man paid $2,256 for an old Renault; it was only later that he discovered the car would not run in reverse. The auctioneer refused to give him a refund.

Other consumer abuses include cars sold without titles, cars that immediately break down or are in unsafe condition, cars with the odometers turned back, and salespeople who deny buyers the chance to thoroughly inspect car interiors and engines. Used-car lemon laws apply, but good luck collecting.

Individuals and service stations. The price may be right, but you have to choose carefully. If possible, buy from someone you know. Someone you're acquainted with is theoretically less likely to lie, and you may be able to double-check their version of the car's history. The mechanic who regularly services your car probably isn't going to steer you wrong. And he may know the car's history and quirks.

> "*Despite all the laws, your best warranty is a skilled, independent mechanic or an American Automobile Association diagnostic test center. . . . If the used-car dealer won't let the mechanic check out the car, don't buy it.*"
>
> —JANE BRYANT QUINN,
> consumer finance columnist

Is the Price Right?

Prices vary based on mileage, condition, and geography. Since every used car is unique, figuring out a fair price can be tricky. Good places to start are the various guides available at libraries, bookstores, and newsstands, such as the National Automobile Dealers Association *Official Used Car Guide*, *Kelley's Blue Book* (popular in California), and *Edmund's Used Car Prices*, which list prices you can expect to pay for various cars and optional equipment. Use the difference between the wholesale and retail prices as a range within which the price you pay should fall; clearly, you don't want to pay anything higher than the average retail price, and the dealer probably won't let you go any lower than the average wholesale price. One caveat: Since the mileage and condition of each car are unique, and market conditions vary from one area of the country to another, you might also want to compare prices in the guidebooks to prices advertised in your local paper. For up-to-date information on prices for specific used cars in your area, you can also call the *Consumer Reports* Used Car Price Service. (See the box below for more information.)

The new-car leasing boom of the early- and mid-1990s has resulted in a buyers' market for used cars. Whereas a million cars came off lease and into the used-car market in 1994, more than 3 million became available in 1997. Since so many two-, three-, and four-year-old cars will be on lots, prices should be very favorable—particularly for the cars most often leased, like the Ford Taurus and Toyota Camry.

WHAT'S A FAIR PRICE?

The *Consumer Reports* Used Car Price Service quotes prices, based on where you live, for all vehicles built since 1988. You'll get an idea of what you should pay and, in many instances, a reliability report on the cars you are considering. Have ready your ZIP code, the car's model name and year, mileage, major options, and approximate condition. Call (900) 988-3838; the charge for calls ($1.75 per minute) will appear on your phone bill. Expect the call to take at least five minutes.

Warranties and Used-Car Lemon Laws

The Federal Trade Commission's "Used Car Rule" requires anybody other than a private individual who's selling a used car to display a "Buyer's Guide" sticker in the window. The sticker will tell you if the car has a warranty, what it covers, and how long it lasts, and also lists any major problems the car might have. If a car is sold "as is," as are most used cars, there is no warranty, and you will be responsible for all repairs. Connecticut, Kansas, Maine, Maryland, Massachusetts, Minnesota, Mississippi, New York, Rhode Island, Vermont, West Virginia, and Washington, D.C., restrict or prohibit "as is" sales.

Six states have Used Car Lemon Laws—Connecticut, Massachusetts, Maryland, Minnesota, New York, and Rhode Island—which protect consumers in the event the used car they buy needs a major repair. The laws vary; the New York State Used Car Lemon Law requires the dealer to offer a 90-day/4,000-mile warranty (whichever comes first) for cars with up to 36,000 miles on them; 60 days/3,000 miles for cars with 36,001 to 79,999 miles; and 30 days/1,000 miles for cars with 80,000 to 100,000 miles. If the dealer cannot repair the defect after three attempts, or if the car's accumulated "down" time is more than 15 days (not necessarily consecutive), consumers have the right to request a refund or a replacement. In New York, it is illegal for a dealer to disclaim responsibility for major repairs. To get information about your state's law, call your State Attorney General's office. (Phone numbers and addresses appear in the Appendix at the end of this book.)

A Lemon Law won't save you from the hassle of dealing with a heap, but it could save you a lot of money. One woman bought a 1986 Buick from a used-car dealer for $3,500, plus the value of the 1975 Chevrolet she traded in. Shortly after she bought it, the car began shaking violently while she was driving. When she tried to stop the car engine, it wouldn't cut off immediately. The dealer, agreed to fix it. After four trips to the dealer, the car still wouldn't run smoothly. New York's Used Car Lemon Law allowed her to demand a replacement car, which the dealer gave her.

WHAT TO WATCH OUT FOR

When you're shopping around, never forget that since it's easy to just plain lie or temporarily camouflage a clunker by simply painting over rust or replacing the power-brake fluid, used cars will rarely appear used up—even if they are.

Missing and Misleading Prices

It's rare to see a price tag (even in states where they are mandatory). Leaving prices off the cars allows the salesperson to size you up and juggle the price accordingly. Don't give the salesperson too much information: For instance, if you say you can spend $5,000, you'll be shown cars that will cost $5,000, even if they are worth only $4,200.

And be wary when you see prices advertised or slapped on the window of the car. Dealers may try to lure you into their lot with insincere offers. When you get there, you find out the car has "already been sold." Remember that the price marked on the windshield or first quoted by the salesperson is always negotiable.

Odometer Fraud

Increased demand for used cars has sparked a revival of "clocking," scammers' parlance for turning back the odometer to make a used car seem less used. According to law enforcement officials, reported cases were at a 10-year high in 1996. Between 1994 and 1996 alone, consumer complaints about odometer fraud tripled. Sport utility vehicles and mid-size cars are popular targets. The Truth in Mileage Act, passed in 1986, makes tampering with the odometer a federal felony and requires automobile titles to include mileage counts, but it hasn't stopped unscrupulous middlemen and dealers from taking what the National Highway Traffic Safety Administration estimates to be $4 billion a year from motorists like Mark W., who was tricked into paying $3,000 to $4,000 more than he should.

Mark W. of Richmond, Virginia, bought a 1990 Cadillac Sedan de Ville for $22,000 in 1992 when the odometer read 27,000 miles. About 20,000 miles later, like an aging beauty queen whose cosmetic surgery and makeup can't patch over a weakened heart, the car gave in to age. The fuel pump broke, the transmission went, the air conditioner conked out twice. "I thought, 'this doesn't usually happen until 80,000 miles.'" How right he was. A mechanic later told him the actual mileage probably was around 80,000.

To avoid cars whose odometers have been turned back, check the condition of upholstery, pedals, and tires to see whether the wear they show correlates to the mileage. Since dealers keep repair and mileage logs, ask whether the dealer has the repair history on the car. Check the owner's manual to see if pages on which the owner noted mileage and maintenance have been torn out. Finally, have your own mechanic give the car a once-over.

Used Rental Cars

Used-car dealers often sell used rental cars, which might be called "program," "executive," "slightly used," or "manufacturers' auction" cars. Auto Nation, for instance, has a built-in supply of used rental cars; its owner also owns Alamo and National Car Rental Systems. You might be able to find a good deal on a used rental car, which salespeople will tell you was probably driven lightly by a stream of business travelers or families on vacation. They could be right, but they probably won't point out that it could just as easily have been driven hard by a series of people who mistreated it because they didn't own it.

Buy with care or you could end up like Donna S. In July 1992, Donna bought what she was told was a used 1991 Chevrolet Lumina with an odometer reading of 8,229 miles. She inspected the car when she got home and found a rental car agreement in the glove compartment, even though the salesman told her it had been used only as a "courtesy" car. What's worse, the rental agreement showed that the odometer had been turned back! The car had been rented in January 1992 with an odometer reading of 17,762. Donna was lucky the dealer was sloppy—she found the rental agreement and demanded her old car and all her money back, and got it. But we can't all expect to be so fortunate.

Because dealers have not been completely straight with consumers about their cars' backgrounds, two states (Missouri and New York) now require dealers to get signed statements from customers to show that they have been told the car was once owned by a rental company.

Lies and Misinformation

Everybody wants to buy a car with low mileage that has been driven little more than back and forth between home and the office 15 minutes away by a mild-mannered middle-aged bachelor. Hence, a used-car salesperson is likely to tell you that, *mirabile dictu,* this is just the background of any car you show interest in. In a 1997 sting investigation, the New York City Department of Consumer Affairs found four out of five used car dealers cheated undercover inspectors posing as consumers.

Know your rights. Frank S. of Brooklyn paid $2,723.25 cash for a 10-year-old Cadillac with 84,000 miles on it. The dealer claimed the car had been inspected and erroneously asserted that this made it ineligible for warranty coverage. Frank signed a form that absolved the dealer of any financial responsibility for car parts and labor used in the repair of the engine and brakes.

Within a week, the engine started smoking. "There is no way this car could have passed an emission inspection, much less a New York State safety inspection," Frank complained to the NYC Department of Consumer Affairs. Frank had a mechanic examine the car and was told the engine had been tinkered with and that the valves were shot. The dealer agreed that the engine was bad, but offered to pay only half of the cost of fixing it. Frank accepted the deal even though he had a right to more.

Lemon Laundering

A patchwork of state lemon resale laws makes it hard to know whether the cream puff you have your eye on was someone else's lemon. Since 1982, every state has adopted a lemon law. Generally speaking, these laws entitle car owners to a full refund on new vehicles if a defect is not corrected in four attempts or if the car is in the shop for 30 days for any combination of defects. However, how much of this information and in what form it is disclosed to subsequent buyers varies enormously from state to state. Delaware, Idaho, Kentucky, Michigan, Mississippi, Missouri, Nebraska, Nevada, New Hampshire, Oklahoma, Tennessee, and Wyoming do not require disclosure that a car is a lemon; California, Connecticut, Maryland, and Utah have among the strongest laws. But the strength of the law is meaningless if it isn't enforced: Florida discovered in 1995 that automakers had made the required disclosures in only 12% of vehicles sold between 1992 and 1994.

To avoid buying a laundered lemon, be wary of cars labeled "executive" or "program." Be alert to cars from out of state (to avoid a strong lemon law in one state, they may have found their way to your state). Try to get the car's repair history: the dealer may know it or have access to it; and Carfax will research the title history (not repair history) for you for $12.50. Call (800) 346-3846. For "lemon-aid," contact your state attorney general's office (see Appendix for phone numbers) or public interest groups, such as the Center for Auto Safety, Consumers Union, and Consumers for Auto Reliability and Safety (see **HELP** for phone numbers).

THE $MARTER CONSUMER

Don't buy from a car dealer who doesn't affix the mandatory Buyer's Guide to the window.

Keep a copy of the bill of sale. In many states, it must list the name, make, serial number, year of manufacture, and total price, including all finance charges.

No two cars are the same. Even if you've chosen a specific model, inspect the individual car carefully, inside and out, before buying. Do this in daylight. Look under the hood, inside the tailpipe, and under the body for stains, soot, dents, rust, and breaks in the frame. Hold a piece of paper behind the tailpipe and rev the engine. If it comes out sooty or splattered with oil, the car has costly problems. Check the inside of the tires (they may simply have been turned around). Look to see if the upholstery is worn, a sign of heavy wear and tear. Test every light, knob, and button to be sure they work.

Take the car for a spin over varied terrain, both on and off the highway. Listen for funny noises, be sensitive to odd vibrations or bad-bump performance, and watch the gauges. After the drive, recheck the power steering and power-brake fluid to make sure the short ride didn't deplete the supply.

Have a professional look it over, if the car passes your inspection. Don't buy a car if the dealer won't let an independent mechanic examine it. Use a mechanic you trust or one who participates in the American Automobile Association's diagnostic test center program. It will cost $50 to $100.

If you can, talk to the previous owner. Ask whether he or she had any trouble with the car, how it was used, what kind of gas mileage it got, whether it was ever in any major accidents, and whether it was maintained as suggested by the manufacturer.

Get written certification from the dealer that the car is in safe condition at the time of the sale.

Get the recall history for the make and model of any used car you may buy. It's available from the National Highway Traffic Safety Administration Auto Safety Hotline (see **HELP** on the next page).

Keep records of *everything*. Retain all receipts from repair shops, the dealer, the dealer's mechanic, the tow service, etc., as proof of the problems you've had with the car.

They will come in handy if you have to take advantage of your warranty or local Used Car Lemon Law.

Skip the lemonade. If a dealer or an individual sells you a lemon, take advantage of your state's Used Car Lemon Law.

HELP 📖

■ **The Used Car Book:** *The Definitive Guide to Buying a Safe, Reliable, and Economical Used Car,* by Jack Gillis (Harper Perennial). This annual $12.95 guide rates hundreds of used cars based on safety, maintenance, insurance costs, fuel economy, and price ranges. It also provides checklists, negotiating strategy, and maintenance tips.

■ **The Lemon Book: Auto Rights** by Ralph Nader and Clarence Ditlow. It is available for $15.95 from the Center for Auto Safety, 2001 S Street NW, Washington, DC 20009, (202) 328-7700.

■ **The National Highway Traffic** Safety Administration's Auto Safety Hotline, (800) 424-9393, provides useful information on the safety recall history of used cars. They also have a Web site at www.nhtsa.dot.gov.

■ **Buying or selling?** Several popular used-car price guides have Internet sites that will help you determine a fair price for a used car. The online version of the *Kelley Blue Book* can be found at www.kbb.com, and the online version of *Edmund's Automotive Buyer's Guides* can be found at www.edmunds.com.

■ **Looking to buy? You can also find** classified ads and buying services for used cars at Internet sites like Microsoft Network's CarPoint, carpoint.msn.com; Intellichoice, www.intellichoice.com; Auto-By-Tel, www. autobytel.com. Carfax can trace the title history for 1981 and newer vehicles, including whether a car has been "totaled," www.carfax.com (you need the car's Vehicle Identification Number; $12.50 per report.)

CAR LEASING

Look Before You Lease

A t first glance, car leases seem little different from finance contracts. Once a month, you write a check that enables you to drive a car you can't afford to buy outright. At some point, you don't have to write the checks anymore. But that's where the similarity ends. After you've paid off the loan on an installment contract, you own the car. Once you're paid up on a lease, which is more like a long-term rental arrangement, you have to return the car to its owner and start over again.

That's why car companies push leases on the public. The theory goes that if they keep you happy enough, you'll return the car and lease another one . . . and another one . . . and so on. In practice, the theory works pretty well. The number of people leasing vehicles each year has skyrocketed to more than 4.5 million, triple the number who leased in 1991, according to the Federal Trade Commission (FTC). In 1997, that was about one of every three car sales, and for luxury cars like Jaguars, three out of

> "**N**ever under any circumstance lease a car based on monthly payments. Know what the total purchase price is."
>
> — JIM MILLER
> automotive writer

four customers chose to lease. Leasing has gotten so popular that people are even leasing *used* cars.

The appeal is clear. Viewed purely in terms of monthly costs (which, by the way, is exactly how the leasing companies hope consumers look at it) leasing is cheaper than financing—and allows people to drive classier cars than they could afford to buy. And many people like the idea of getting a new car protected by a full manufacturer's warranty every two or three years. A good, honest lease can be competitive with buying on time, but when viewed over the longer term, it usually isn't.

Getting such a good, honest lease takes more work than most consumers care to take on—understanding the art and the finer points of the deal means cutting through unfamiliar terminology with the focus of a semiotician and crunching numbers using formulas few economists would understand. A trusting consumer could end up like Julie G., a San Francisco native who, without realizing it, paid

$2,300 over the already inflated *sticker price* for a Toyota RAV4. To avoid Julie's expensive predicament, you need to deconstruct the contract to figure out how much you will pay for the car and whether the price is fair, what the car is projected to be worth at the end of the lease, the effective interest rate you are asked to pay, and how much you would owe if you bailed out of the lease early. Uniform, national disclosure requirements that went into effect in January 1998 help, but there is no getting around it—car leases are extremely complicated financial documents.

THE BASICS

What Is Leasing Anyway?

Simply put, leasing is an arrangement that allows you to drive a car owned by someone else, the leasing company, for a predetermined period of time. You pay a finance charge for this convenience *plus* for the portion of the vehicle's original value that gets used up over the term of your lease. The price of the new vehicle and this "depreciation" in value determine how much you pay. For instance, a new car worth $21,000 may be worth only $12,000 after three years. The total you will pay is roughly the difference—$9,000— plus a finance charge. Your monthly payment is 1/36 of this total for a three-year lease or 1/24 for a two-year lease.

While you "buy" the car at an auto dealer, most often the dealer does not own the car. Your monthly payments go to a leasing company —a finance arm of one of the major car makers, a bank, or some other financial institution.

In a standard "closed end" lease deal—the only kind of lease you should take—you can return the car at the end of the lease term in reasonably good condition and walk away; the lease usually also allows you to buy the car outright at the end of the lease if you choose. Steer clear of "open end" lease deals, which would make you responsible for paying the difference between what the car is actually worth at the end of the lease and what it was projected to be worth.

Wheeling and Dealing

The ads, which imply that leasing is as easy as paying $250 a month, only confuse matters. The low monthly payments touted in most lease advertising in newspapers and TV commercials distract you from taking a close look at the financial underpinnings of the lease deal and are just bait to get you into the showroom.

Earlier in the decade, leasing companies took these tactics to confounding, and illegal, lengths. The boom in car leasing led to a boom in car leasing complaints reported to consumer officials around the country. To name just a few, the New York Attorney General's office charged a dozen car makers and dealers with misleading and deceptive advertising that promoted artificially low monthly payments in 1992. In Florida, the Attorney

General's office found some sort of deception or fraud in 10% of 15,000 leases it reviewed. And in 1994, a group of Washington State auto dealers paid several hundred thousand dollars to settle a civil complaint brought by the state. In 1996, the FTC curbed the widespread industry practice of burying key information in a blur of tiny type at the bottom of a print ad or in screens on TV commercials that go by so fast consumers don't have time to read them—forget about understanding what they say. One typical ad was Mazda Motor Corp.'s "penny down" lease promotion; rather than one cent, consumers actually had to pay $900 at the inception of the lease.

Said Robert Pitofsky, chairman of the FTC at the time: "I actually got down on my hands and knees in front of my TV set and tried to see if I could read what these [lease] disclosures were and find out what the payment was and how much money you had to put down, and I simply couldn't read those disclosures, even though I was waiting for them and looking for them."

In response to these sorts of problems, the Federal Reserve now requires simplified and clarified disclosures in lease transactions. Leasing companies must give you the key financial figures on which the deal is based that were previously nearly impossible to pry out of salespeople. You'll understand why this information is so important, and what it means, when you finish reading this chapter. Leasing companies must provide:

- an itemized accounting of the amount due by the time you pick up the car
- the negotiated price of the vehicle and any other additional items, such as license fees or a service contract
- what the car is projected to be worth at the end of the lease
- how much the car is expected to depreciate over the term of the lease
- the total charge for using the car over the life of the lease

Lease companies must also warn you about previously hidden charges, like how expensive it can be to end the lease early, how you will be charged for use of the car beyond the allowed number of miles, and what it will cost to buy the car at the end of the lease if you choose to do so. Unfortunately, they are not required to give you all this crucial information until you are about to sign the contract.

While much has changed since the early to mid-1990s, when there was no such thing as a standard leasing contract and few rules regulated the advertising and marketing practices of the exploding industry, you'll still find plenty of important details divulged only in the ads' footnotes, withheld by sales reps, or buried in the lease itself. And once you're drawn in, you're likely to find that it will cost an unexpected bundle to enter into the lease or to extricate yourself from the camouflaged traps.

Striking a Deal

Much of the same advice that applies when buying a car ap-

LEASING LINGO

Capitalized cost. Simply put, this is what you agree to pay for a car, less any down payment, including license, registration, fees, taxes, and insurance. This term is analogous to the "amount financed" if you purchase the car on an installment contract.

Capitalized cost reduction. Down payment, including cash and/or the value of your trade-in.

Deposits. Money you pay up front toward fees you may owe when the lease ends. (Deposits *do not* reduce the capitalized cost.)

Disposition fee. What you pay if you don't buy the car at the end of the lease.

Early termination charge. What you would have to pay to end the lease ahead of schedule.

Excess mileage and wear and tear charges. Money you owe at the end of the lease to repair damage to the car.

Gap insurance. Covers the cost of replacing the car if it is totaled or stolen. The "gap" is the difference between how much you would have to pay the leasing company to end the lease and how much the insurance company will pay to replace the car.

Lease charges or money factor. The money you pay to lease the car in addition to the capitalized cost. This fee is comparable to the "finance charge" you would pay in an installment contract.

MSRP. Manufacturer's Suggested Retail Price—i.e., the "list" price.

Purchase option. Gives you the right to buy the car from the leasing company when the lease ends and a price or formula for calculating the price.

Residual value. An estimate of the value of the car at the end of the lease, which you agree upon at the outset of the lease.

Subvent. Car manufacturer subsidy that lowers the price of the lease.

plies when leasing one. Thus, you will probably want to refer to "New Cars" (page 309). As you select a make and model, keep in mind that the best cars to lease are those that depreciate slowest. In addition, familiarize yourself with the arcane terminology and formulas underlying lease deals. Down payments are referred to as "capitalized cost reductions," begging the question of what "capitalized cost" means. Basically, it's the price of the car. There is a complete glossary above.

Capitalized cost. Shop for a car lease the same way you would for a purchase contract. Before the salesperson gets you talking about how great leasing and low monthly payments are, agree on the price of the car. Some dealers may refuse to negotiate the price of a lease; eight out of ten salespeople in a *Consumer Reports* investigation would reveal *only* the monthly payment. If you hit one of these, walk out and find another dealer who will. It's best to visit a few dealers and compare prices. Exactly as if you were buying, bargain up from the dealer's invoice price less any manufacturer's rebates or dealer discounts, which you can find on the Internet or from *Consumer Reports'* New Car Price Service (see the "New Cars" **HELP** box on page 319). The price you negotiate will become the basis for the "capitalized cost" of the lease. Keep in mind that all key financial terms in the lease, such as monthly payments, residual value, and early termination charges, will be set in direct proportion to the net capitalized cost. Thus, the more you agree to pay for the capitalized cost, the higher your monthly payment or penalty for ending the lease early.

With the price settled, you are ready to start the lease negotiation. Various items may be added to the capitalized cost—tax, service contract, and perhaps some of the upfront fees. Always insist on an itemized accounting of all the amounts included for fees and services above the cost of the vehicle. If you subtract the cost of these items, the capitalized cost should not be higher than the price you negotiated for the car.

Lease term. Decide how long you want the lease to run. Two- or three-year terms are common, and most consumers like them because it means the car will be covered by the manufacturer's warranty for the full term of the lease.

Residual value. Ask what the dealer expects the car to be worth at the end of the lease. Be sure it is stated as a specific dollar amount and not a vague valuation such as "market price." Be careful of inflated residual values. While a high residual value will lower the monthly payment, it will also increase what you would have to pay to end the lease early. And, if the used car will sell for substantially less than the lease estimated, the leasing company may try to make up for the loss by tacking on high end-of-lease charges for things like excess wear and tear, disposition fees, and excess mileage. Also, if you think you might want to buy the car at the end of the lease, an inflated estimate of residual value will make you pay a lot more for it than it's worth.

Lease charge. The lease charge is comparable to the finance charge you would pay in an installment credit arrangement. But while creditors disclose the finance charge as an interest rate, leasing companies use a "money factor." You can get an idea of the approximate interest rate you will pay by multiplying the money factor by 2,400. This probably won't be negotiable. If it's

SIMPLIFIED SAMPLE LEASE FORMULA

Capitalized Cost	$21,000
Capitalized Cost Reduction (down payment/trade-in)	$2,000
Net Capitalized Cost	$19,000
Lease Term	36 months
Residual Value (set by leasing company)	$12,000
Depreciation (net capitalized cost – residual value)	$7,000
Money Factor (set by leasing company)	0.00333
Effective Interest Rate (money factor × 2,400)	8%
Monthly Depreciation (depreciation/36)	$194
Monthly Lease Charge (capitalized cost + residual value × money factor)	$103
Monthly Payment	$297

a lot higher than the going interest rate for a car loan, find another dealer who will do better.

Monthly payment. Your monthly payment comprises the monthly lease charge and a monthly payoff for the depreciation of the vehicle over the term of the lease. The depreciation is determined by subtracting the residual value of the car from the capitalized cost. In the real world, salespeople will probably insist on beginning the negotiation with monthly payments (maybe they don't understand anything else themselves), but the example above will help you understand how they derive a monthly payment of $297. Be forewarned: this example is a simplification.

The formulas for computing lease payments are so complicated that Ford created special calculators *solely* for this purpose.

Back-end costs. As you consider the deal, look beyond the monthly payment for hidden fees and restrictions. High fees owed later could turn that sweet deal sour. Can you live within the mileage cap in the lease? Typical leases allow 12,000 or 15,000 miles a year, with a charge of 10 cents or so a mile for any mileage over the limit. You will have to pay for any wear and tear beyond what the leasing company considers normal. Can you and your family live up to this standard? Is there any chance you will have to give up the lease before the end of the term? Bill B.'s elderly grandparents are stuck paying off the lease on a car that never leaves its parking space. Bill's grandfather leased the car a year before he had a stroke and had to stop driving; Bill's grandmother stopped driving long ago. How high is the "disposition fee" for returning the car at the end of the lease if you don't buy it?

Car dealers probably won't make it easy to collect all this information, but the only way to strengthen your hand against the dealers' is to take each lease you are considering apart so that you understand the financial terms on which it is based. To help you, the FTC and Federal Reserve Board provide a handy worksheet that you can take with you when you shop. You may want to add a few lines for things like money factor, hypothetical early termination charges, and an itemization of the capitalized cost, but the worksheet is a good place to start. Fill one out for each deal and compare the terms. You can download it from www.ftc.gov.

WHAT TO WATCH OUT FOR

Early Termination Rights and Obligations

Before you sign a lease agreement, be sure you understand what happens if you need to end your lease early for any reason—the car could be stolen or wrecked, or you could no longer need it. Since as many as half of all lease contracts terminate prematurely, it's as likely as not that this clause in the contract will be critical later. You need to know about two things: if you have the *right* to terminate the lease early and how much it will *cost* you. What you might owe varies greatly from one lease to another.

The right. Most leases strongly discourage early termination, but avoid a lease that bans it. Shun a lease with language like: "You may not terminate this lease before the end of the term. This lease terminates early only upon default." Under this lease, you would be in default even if the lease had to be terminated early because of theft or destruction of the car.

Look instead for a lease that includes a clause specifically entitling you to terminate ahead of schedule without a penalty: for example, "Providing I am not in default, I have a right at any time to terminate this lease. . . ."

The cost. The early termination charge—the amount you would have to pay to end a lease ahead of schedule—is the costliest and usually best-concealed trap in a lease. And generally speaking, it's a bad financial move to terminate before you're two thirds to three quarters of the way through the lease term. Avoid any lease that would require you to pay all remaining monthly payments in a lump sum to get out of the agreement or you could be stuck in an expensive bind. For instance, one woman who unwittingly agreed to an unfavorable lease tried to terminate early after paying $9,240. She was told she owed an *additional* $16,000 for a car with a manufacturer's suggested retail price of only $14,927. Under the terms of the contract, the bill was legitimate—if wholly unscrupulous.

In most cases, a consumer's early termination obligation is determined by a formula stated in the lease. When comparing early termination terms, there are a few things to look for:

■ The cheapest and fairest method of computing liability for future lease payments is "the actuarial method." Steer clear of other computation methods such as "the rule of 78ths," "the sum of the digits," or "net present value." These methods will usually end up costing you much more.

■ How will the value of the car be determined? Look for a lease that gives you the option to use a professional appraiser or that gives you a role in determining the value of the vehicle before termination.

■ Are there any other fees or payments that would be owed at termination? How much would they cost?

■ To compare the early termination terms of one lease to another, ask the salesperson to compute how much you would owe if you terminated after making exactly half the monthly payments, before crediting the value of the vehicle. For instance, ask what you would owe if the lease ends after you have made 18 payments on a three-year lease.

Purchase Option and Price

About a quarter of consumers who lease end up buying the car. And it makes sense if the car ends up being worth more than the leasing company estimated—you'd be getting a bargain on a used car whose reliability and maintenance and service record you know inside and out. You could buy it and sell it at a profit or you could buy it and drive it.

The price at which you can buy the car should be stated clearly in the contract. The fairest price for the car is the estimated residual value or its price as determined by one of the well-known used car price guides, such as the *Kelley Blue Book* or National Automobile Dealer Association *Price Guide*. Don't sign a lease that gives a vague price, such as "fair market value." Your idea of what's fair is likely to be very different from the leasing company's.

Up-front Charges

You'll most often have to pay various fees to enter into the lease deal. Contrary to the ads warbling about "no money down," the sum can be substantial. You may be asked to cough up the first month's payment and fees for "lease acquisition," title, license, security deposit, and other things. Get an itemized list; some or all of these fees may be negotiable. And if they add up to more than your budget can bear, you may be able to get some of them added to the capitalized cost of the car so that you can pay them off over the course of the lease. Beware: adding up-front charges will up your monthly payments.

Tricks of the Trade-in

If you are trading in another car as part of the lease deal, be sure the leasing company subtracts the value of your old vehicle from the capitalized cost of the leased vehicle.

Dealers know that most consumers are pretty much only interested in a deal that fits their monthly budget and is free of the hassles of disposing of a used car and the depreciation risks that come with owning. Don't fall for a conversation that is about nothing more than the monthly payment. Because the formula for computing the monthly payment is so complicated, it's easy for the dealer to hide a high sales price for the vehicle, a ridiculous interest rate, the failure to account for your trade-in, or other expensive traps in a seemingly low monthly payment.

THE $MARTER CONSUMER

Manufacturer-subsidized leases can be good bargains. The manufacturer "subvents" the lease by allowing the dealer to inflate the vehicle's residual value; this narrows the difference between the car's selling price and what it's worth at the end of lease, which decreases what you pay. However, it probably means the car is not a good candidate for purchase at the end of the lease—you'd have to pay more for it than it's worth.

Not having to put money down is one of the benefits of leasing, but do it if you can afford it. Making a down payment will lower your monthly payments substantially. To see how much difference a down payment can make, ask the dealer to compute the financial terms using different down payment scenarios.

You'll pay dearly for excess mileage, anywhere from 10 cents to 25 cents a mile. Be realistic about your driving habits and don't take a lease with a lower annual mileage limit than you are likely to need.

"Excess wear and tear" is a vague term. Make sure you and the dealer agree on the definition. A *normal* dent probably won't be deemed *excess* damage, but check. It's standard that you will be responsible for mechanical malfunctions; keep the car in tip-top shape or you may have to foot the bill for costly repairs.

Also, if you return the car to lease another from the same dealer, they will probably be more lenient than if you return the car and walk away.

Gap insurance pays the difference between what you owed on the lease and what your automobile insurance company pays in the event that the car is totaled or stolen. Many dealers will throw it in for free. Read the policy carefully to be sure that it truly closes the gap.

Choose your car wisely. Cars that lose their value slowest make the best lease deals. Since the leasing company will be able to sell the car for a hefty price when you are finished with it, your monthly payments will be lower than with a car that quickly loses value. Also, go easy on the options. You'll pay a tidy sum up front for things like a fancy stereo system or a sun roof, but they add little to the residual value of the car at the end of the lease and thereby increase your monthly payments.

Keep deposits down. Security deposits do not lower the cost of the car or the size of monthly payments. Negotiate hard to get as low a security deposit as possible. Minimize the charges a lessor can auto-matically apply against the deposit; the easier it is for the company to eat into your deposit, the harder it will be for you to get any money back at the end of the lease.

At the end of the lease, put the residual value to work for you. If the car is in good shape with low mileage, it may be worth more than the residual value. You could buy it and sell it for a profit or you could use the equity to negotiate a good deal on your next lease. If the market value has eroded below the residual value, return the car to the dealer and let them take the loss. However, if the car isn't in such good condition at the end of the lease, you could avoid paying hefty lease end charges by buying the car.

Know what you are signing. Do not sign a lease until you understand every word. If you have any doubts, hold off. Do more reading (see **HELP**, below), talk to a knowledgeable friend or relative, and keep shopping for an agreement you *do* understand.

What can you do if you are already paying too much for a lease? You've signed the contract and are stuck with it. There is no remedy like refinancing your mortgage.

■ **Still daunted by** the process of getting a fair lease deal? The LeaseWise service of the not-for-profit Center for the Study of Services will do the work for you. For $290 you get a report that compares all the terms of several bids to each other, based on monthly costs. The report also points out the best deal for motorists who think they will want

Continued on next page

Continued from previous page

to buy the car at the end of the lease. Call (800) 475-7283, Monday to Friday, 9 to 5:30, EST, or look at their Internet site at www.consumer.checkbook.org/consumer/.

■ **To complain about a problem with** a car leasing company, write or call your state attorney general's office. Addresses and phone numbers are at the end of this book.

■ **Lease or Buy? The December 1997** issue of *Consumer Reports* compares 3-year lease deals with purchase deals on the 25 most commonly leased car models. You'll see that buying is usually, but not always, the better deal.

■ **If the leasing company is a finan-** cial institution, such as a bank or credit union, you can also complain to:

Office of the Comptroller of the
  Currency
250 E Street SW
Washington, DC 20219
(800) 613-6743
(National banks)

Board of Governors
  of the Federal Reserve System
  Consumer and Community Affairs
20th and C Streets NW
Washington, DC 20551
(202) 452-3693
*(State member banks of the Federal
  Reserve System)*

Federal Deposit Insurance
  Corporation
Office of Consumer Programs
550 17th Street NW
Washington, DC 20429
(800) 934-3342
(Non-member federally insured banks)

Office of Thrift Supervision
Consumer Affairs Program
1700 G Street NW
Washington, DC 20552
(800) 842-6929
*(Federally insured savings and loans and
  federally chartered state banks)*

National Credit Union
  Administration
1775 Duke Street
Alexandria, VA 22314
(703) 518-6308
(Federal credit unions)

CHAPTER 31

GASOLINE

Pay Less to Drive More

Americans enjoy some of the cheapest gasoline in the world. Fuel here is cheaper than bottled water: We pay a third or one fourth as much as folks in Europe or Asia do. Yet millions of American motorists still pay more than they have to. They buy premium gas when their car doesn't need it, or they get low-octane fuel from high-octane pumps. They don't get the maximum fuel efficiency from their cars, or they believe bogus claims about the advantages of expensive brands.

Getting every last mile out of every fuel dollar is more important than ever. New taxes and requirements for cleaner gasolines that cost extra have now kicked in, and more price increases are sure to come when even stricter clean air regulations take effect. Worldwide demand for petroleum is ever increasing and may soon eclipse supply. Regional pull-outs by major oil companies, industry consolidation, and a one-third decline in the number of service stations since 1980 are making price wars among neighboring gas stations a thing of the past. All the while average fuel efficiency for the nation's cars has been inching down every year since 1991.

THE BASICS

Is All Gas Created Equal?

Each of the major oil companies spends a fortune trying to convince you that its gasoline is superior, that you'll feel a new-found power surge as soon as you fill up, or that their brand will clean your engine better than the others.

In fact, different brands of gas are all about the same—they're even usually stored in the same jointly operated tanks before being distributed to different stations. The only possible difference may be in the ability of detergent (added just before distribution) to prevent deposits on engine intake valves. But when *Consumer Reports* asked oil companies if their gasolines could pass a rigorous 10,000-mile valve-cleansing test established by the auto maker BMW, most passed or would soon be reformulated to pass.

Claims that an advertised brand's cleaning power is superior to all other brands are therefore basically meaningless, since any of the many brands that passed the tough BMW test are perfectly acceptable for even the most discriminating engines. Unfortunately, you can't

BEST TIMES WORST TIMES

Tuesday is the best day to fill up the tank. With the weekend long gone and the work week already revved up, business is slower at service stations. You might even get the windows washed.

easily find out if the gas you regularly buy is one of them, since the law doesn't require pumps to disclose detergent abilities as it does octane levels.

One independent retailer of discount gasoline told us that when a refinery production problem caught one of the "majors" short of supply, it simply bought gasoline from his company for several weeks. He visited one of the major company's service stations after it had been selling his company's "cheap" gas for a while and asked motorists what they thought of its gas compared to gas from his company. He heard comments like, "Oh, I would never buy gas from [his company]" and "I only buy gas here."

How Much Octane Is Enough?

Octane is a measure of a gas's ability to prevent knocking, which occurs when a portion of the fuel detonates spontaneously and prematurely in the cylinder. Higher-octane gas better resists knocking.

The chart below shows the octane levels of gas sold in most American service stations. Federal law requires that the octane level appear on a yellow label on the pump.

Gasoline advertisements in recent years have claimed that premium gas provides more power, faster acceleration, and cleaner engines. These ads have been very effective: The market share of premium gasoline doubled during the 1980s and continues to enjoy high demand in the 1990s, even though premium costs an average of 18 cents a gallon more than regular and the vast majority of new-car owner manuals recommend using regular gas.

Contrary to the premise of the ads, most premium gas buying is unnecessary—it can't make an engine "more powerful," it doesn't burn more easily, and it won't improve mileage—unless your car's model specifically demands it. Public Citizen, a Washington, DC–based consumer advocacy organization, found that while 20% of gasoline sold is premium, only 5% of cars actually need it—cars

OCTANE LEVELS

REGULAR UNLEADED	87 octane
REGULAR LEADED	89 octane
MID-GRADE UNLEADED	89 octane
PREMIUM	91 to 94 octane

THE INCREDIBLE MAGIC GAS PUMPS!

Octane fraud is easy to perpetrate. A Congressional study described a gas station that had just one underground tank—but that tank somehow dispensed regular, plus, and premium gasoline. This type of highway robbery is especially common in localities that rely only on the Federal Trade Commission and the Environmental Protection Agency for consumer enforcement rather than on their own octane-accuracy testing programs. Forty states have their own testing programs.

such as Jaguars, Mercedes-Benzes, Ferraris, and Rolls Royces. For the remaining 95%, premium provides only premium profit for the oil industry. The Federal Trade Commission has ordered some companies —Exxon, Sunoco, and Unocal among them—to stop advertising high-octane gas as superior to lower-octane gas.

Public Citizen concluded that Americans waste $3 billion a year on premium gas—about $95 per vehicle. Of course, the oil industry disagreed. An industry spokesperson responded that while there are no advantages in "overbuying" octane, 25% of cars on the road, including cars that have traveled

more than 15,000 miles, need higher octane levels. But the oil industry is self-interested; premium gas produces bigger profits than regular gas does.

Are You Getting What You Pay for?

It's bad enough that many Americans needlessly buy premium gas. But too often the gasoline flowing out of the premium pump is less than premium grade, as retailers try to pass off lower-octane gas as higher, figuring the public will never know the difference.

How widespread is octane fraud? A Congressional study found that Americans are being overcharged a total of $600 million a year for octane they never receive. One Massachusetts state official says that even though complaints of octane fraud are low, actual incidents could be higher because most cars don't need premium gas, so most consumers wouldn't notice the difference if it was mislabeled. A cheating Wisconsin distributor was discovered only after a customer had engine trouble when he filled his boat motor with "premium"-labeled gas from a local station. (Many boats require high-octane fuel.) The boat owner's mechanic traced the trouble to the "premium" gas, prompting an investigation by the state's Bureau of Petroleum Inspection. The distributor—who was making an extra 10 cents a gallon on fraudulent sales to four unsuspecting stations—was fined $1,000 and placed on two years' probation.

Greener Gas—but Less Green Stuff in Your Wallet

You don't have to live in Southern California to know that gasoline produces smog. Finally, though, something is being done about it. In November 1992, in order to meet federal Clean Air Act rules, 39 cities started to require gasoline sold in winter to contain a new additive, either ethanol or methyl tertiary butyl ether (MTBE), which boosts gasoline's oxygen content, making it burn more completely and reducing carbon monoxide (CO) emissions. (Oxygenated gas is required only in winter weather because the atmosphere's inversion layer, which traps pollutants, is much lower.) A gas pump label is supposed to tell you the dates when it is pumping oxygenated gasoline. While oxygenated gas costs slightly more, this sacrifice is worth the health benefits oxygenated gas provides.

Since 1995, federal law and voter mandates have required gas stations in 15 metropolitan areas with severe summer ozone problems—Baltimore, Boston, Chicago, Hartford, Houston, Louisville (Kentucky), Milwaukee, New York, Philadelphia, San Diego, Portland (Maine), Norfolk (Virginia), Dallas-Ft. Worth, Washington, DC, and the smog capital of the nation, Los Angeles—to sell a specially reformulated anti-smog gasoline, which added another 5 cents to 8 cents per gallon to the pump price. California has its own special formula, which adds 15 cents to 25 cents per gallon to the pump price there.

Consumer Reports found acceleration and fuel economy in the "green" fuels to be no different from those in conventional gasoline. But only some of the new gasolines burned cleaner—producing fewer hydrocarbons and less carbon monoxide—than conventional gas from 1990. The special gas sold only in California, where pollution laws are among the nation's toughest, burned the cleanest. By 2000, the California gas will be sold in all areas with heavy pollution problems.

The debate rages, however, on whether some additives—MTBE in particular—are creating new health hazards at the same time that they reduce emissions. MTBE was blamed for health problems in Milwaukee and Alaska, where people complained of fatigue, headaches, shortness of breath, and seizures. The EPA is still gathering evidence on this additive's possible hazards.

> "**F**or the vast majority of cars, there's no reason to buy premium gasoline. None. Contrary to everything you learn from advertising, it will not make your car run better; it will not make your engine cleaner; and it will not provide more power."
>
> —JOAN CLAYBROOK,
> president, Public Citizen

CRYSTAL CLEAR NONSENSE

You might remember TV ads touting Amoco's clear Ultimate gasoline. "There's nothing like crystal clear Amoco Ultimate ... for unsurpassed performance and a cleaner environment," the narrator intones. Or how about commercials for Exxon Supreme 93 implying that it was a supreme engine cleaner?

Don't be fooled. Fact is, burning a gallon of gasoline produces plenty of carbon dioxide and other air pollutants, and *all* gasoline provides sufficient detergent power for all but the highest-performance engines. Not only did the Amoco ad garner a Harlan Page Hubbard Lemon Award from consumer advocacy groups (Hubbard was a notable snake-oil salesman in the late 19th century), it earned an FTC investigation, as did Exxon. Neither could provide the FTC with proof that their claims were not deceptive.

Alternative Fuels—When?

Remember the long lines at gas stations in the late 1970s after oil-exporting countries slapped us with an oil embargo? That crisis encouraged research into alternative fuels, which is just starting to bear fruit. Cars fueled by methanol or natural gas are coming on line.

As an inducement to buy alternative fuel vehicles, you can get a federal tax deduction of up to $2,000 for buying a car fueled by ethanol, methanol, natural gas, or propane, and a deduction of up to $4,000 for buying an electric car. California and Massachusetts offer additional tax breaks.

It's not so easy to find one of these cars, but that's changing. Ford, GM, and Chrysler all offer alternative fuel vehicles, including electric minivans and trucks, methanol sedans, and even a Ford Crown Victoria that runs on compressed natural gas. Filling stations for these cars have just started to appear, encouraged by the alternative fuel vehicles that will make up 75% of all federal and some state vehicle fleets by 1999.

But a practical electric car that can travel more than a few hundred miles before a lengthy battery recharge or one that can go faster than 70 miles per hour still hasn't been produced. A public–private effort, The U.S. Advanced Battery Consortium, has more work to do on developing affordable and usable batteries for electric cars. In the meantime, Saturn dealers in Arizona and California offer the GM EV1, an electric sports coupe designed for short commutes or quick trips of up to 90 miles. Existing cars work fine on gasohol, which is 10% ethanol, although there is a fierce debate on whether ethanol is, on balance, unfriendly to the environment.

WORTH ITS WEIGHT IN SAVINGS

Each year, the average car emits hundreds of pounds of carbon monoxide, hydrocarbons (which form smog), nitrogen oxides (lead to acid rain), particulate matter (better known as grime and soot), and carbon dioxide, a major contributor to global warming. About 30% of carbon dioxide emissions in the U.S. come from motor vehicles.

The federal government could require the average car to get 40 miles per gallon.

Energy-saving technologies, including the use of four valves per cylinder, low-friction rings and pistons, and overhead cams, now exist. But the push to lower fuel use isn't coming from environmentalists alone. A 1994 congressional report called the unchecked growth of U.S. automobile use a threat to national security because it increases U.S. dependence on foreign oil—a habit that is worse now than it was in the 1970s.

Despite these encouraging developments, gasoline is likely to remain the primary fuel for at least the next few decades. All of the other fuels have disadvantages: Methanol can blind or kill if swallowed and is highly corrosive; ethanol is expensive; natural gas refueling takes two to three times longer than gasoline refueling and the tanks are bulky; and, as mentioned, electric cars still have limited range and speed. Reformulated gasolines with additives that improve efficiency and reduce emissions may extend this old standbys' natural life span.

WHAT TO WATCH OUT FOR

Octane fraud. You can reasonably suspect octane fraud if you fill up with your usual octane and you hear knocking or pinging sounds. Other signs of too-low octane: a lack of power and the engine's continuing to run after you turn the car off.

Scrubbing bubbly claims. Oil companies entice consumers into buying higher-priced gas by putting more and supposedly special detergents into fuels, claiming more detergent equals a cleaner, better-performing, or lower-maintenance engine. But since the federal government requires all gasolines to meet minimum detergent standards, any reports of a "cleaner gas" for a "cleaner engine" are exaggerated.

Oxygenation drawbacks. Oxygenated gasoline can cause hard starts, stalling, and rough idling. This is a particular problem with poorly maintained cars.

Gas savers. According to Jack Gillis, author of *The Car Book*, out of the hundreds of "gas-saving" products tested by the federal government, only five actually saved gas, and then only a little. Among the worthless products were air-bleed devices, fuel line devices, fuel additives, ignition devices, engine modifications, mixture enhancers, oil additives, and vapor bleed devices. Those that do work somewhat were a gadget that shuts off your air-conditioner when you rapidly accelerate, a buzzer that alerts you if your car has been idling too long, and a device to circulate heat from the engine to the passenger compartment, which can keep you warm in cold weather after you've shut off the heater.

THE $MARTER CONSUMER

Don't buy more octane than necessary. To find out your car's optimum octane level, try this simple test recommended by Jack Gillis: When your tank is empty, fill up with your usual gasoline and drive ten or so miles. Stop. Now accelerate rapidly. If your engine knocks, then you should use a higher octane. If it sounds fine, the next time you fill up, switch to a lower octane and repeat the test.

Skip the gas-guzzling 4-wheel drive. Four in ten of the vehicles sold in 1996 were vans, sport utility vehicles (SUVs), or pickup trucks, up from one in ten in 1973. And these big boys can drink. While a Volkswagen Passat station wagon cruises the highway at 47 miles per gallon, a Toyota RAV4—the most fuel-efficient SUV—gulps 50% more to go the same distance.

Improve your car's fuel efficiency. As AAA and car manufacturers attest, simple steps like these are the real cost-cutters:

- *Tires.* Poor alignment and insufficient tire pressure can cost two miles per gallon. Radial tires are more fuel efficient than bias-ply because, even though the sidewalls in radial tires are quite flexible, their treads are very stiff and strong.
- *Air conditioning.* Uses up to three miles per gallon in city driving, but in highway driving at constant speed AC use doesn't matter.
- *Transmission.* Automatic transmissions generally are less fuel-efficient than properly used manual ones.
- *Engine condition.* A tune-up—still possible in older cars where ignition timing can be manually adjusted—can improve mileage up to 20%.
- *Driving practices.* Avoid sudden accelerations when possible. In a traffic jam, inch along instead of stopping and starting. Keeping to the speed limit—or even slower—keeps fuel costs down. Driving 75 mph instead of 55 knocks fuel efficiency down by 45%. Aggressive acceleration can kick fuel comsumption up by 20%.
- *Car weight.* Even simple extras like soundproofing or power steering add weight and reduce efficiency. Don't carry unnecessary cargo in your trunk. An extra 100

pounds of stuff can reduce your gasoline consumption by up to a mile per gallon.

Filling up. Don't let the tank slip below half-full on cold days. It can cause condensation, and if that water gets in your fuel line and freezes, you'll have trouble starting up. Also, stop filling on the first or second "click" of the pump handle. Overfilling is a fire hazard and can ruin your car's paint if the overflow isn't wiped off.

H E L P

■ **Jack Gillis's** *The Car Book* has the latest fuel economy ratings for the most popular vehicles and helpful hints for increasing your fuel economy.

■ **For performance tests of regular** vs. high-octane gas and regular-grade gasolines vs. clean-burning fuels, read *Consumer Reports'* November 1996 issue.

■ **The U.S. Department of Energy's** Energy Information Administration Web site (www.eia.doe. gov) offers a weekly assessment of retail gas prices, as well as links to other fuel-related sites. The EIA also has a gas-price hotline: (202) 586-6966.

■ **The Federal Trade Commision of-**fers a consumer guide to "Saving Money at the Pump." Go to www.ftz.gov or write to Public Reference Branch, Room 130, 6th & Pennsylvania Avenues, NW, Washington, DC 20580.

CHAPTER 32

AUTOMOBILE INSURANCE

Drive Down the Cost

The rising cost of automobile insurance has made and broken political careers. Two governors of New Jersey, first Jim Florio then Christine Todd Whitman, made slashing the highest auto insurance premiums in the nation central planks in their platforms. California, with the third-highest premiums, switched from an appointed to an elected insurance commissioner . . . who fast became one of that state's most visible politicians. Most recently, Congress has been talking about enacting a proposal known as "Auto Choice," which would supposedly help consumers who forfeit the right to sue and be sued for pain and suffering get lower auto insurance rates.

No wonder. Auto accidents take a $150 billion chunk out of the U.S. economy every year, an amount equal to 2% of the nation's gross domestic product. There are few places in America where you can get by without a car. And virtually every state in the union requires drivers to purchase automobile liability in-

surance. So if you drive, you have to deal with an insurance company.

And dealing with an insurance company may be enough to give you a migraine. You might find yourself surcharged for no apparent reason. You might not be able to renew your policy because of a few too many speeding tickets. Or the cost of replacing your totaled car may be a lot higher than the amount your insurance company will pay. The quality of customer service varies from prompt and courteous to a version of the creaking bureaucracy in the former Soviet Union.

Making the business even more complicated and frustrating are the wide and sometimes inexplicable differences in premiums among states and among communities within states, as well as among different car models, driver ages, and gender. The total annual payments for a 55-year-old driving a sedate sedan in Nebraska could be as low as a few hundred dollars a year, while a 23-year-young New Jerseyean who drives a sports car will probably pay at least $2,500 just for a bare-bones policy—if he or she can find a company willing to write a policy at all.

Still, no matter where you live or what you drive, it always pays to shop around for a lower premium and a better company. Otherwise, you could waste anywhere from a few hundred to a few thousand dollars a year—and that's before you've shelled out for headache remedies. To take just one example, the Arizona Department of Insurance's annual survey of auto insurance rates showed that depending on which insurer he chose, a 48-year-old married man with a clean driving record who lived in Phoenix and commuted 30 miles round-trip daily in a 1995 Ford Taurus would have paid $482, $690.50, or $2,020 for six months of coverage in 1997.

THE BASICS

Types of Coverage

First, learn the coverage terms in the declarations page (cover sheet) of your auto insurance policy. Each coverage category charges its own separate premium. Added up, they equal your total premium.

Bodily injury liability. If you're in an accident and someone else is hurt, this covers your legal liability to them. Typically, this coverage has "split limits," which means that there is a coverage maximum for an entire accident and separate maximums per individual in the accident. It's described in terms of tens

or hundreds of thousands of dollars. So, for example, "100/300" coverage would provide up to $100,000 coverage per person and a total of $300,000 for everyone injured in an accident.

Most states require minimum coverage, ranging from 10/20 to 25/50. These limits are absurdly low, of course, and rarely enough to protect a household with any assets. If you ever lose (or settle) a liability lawsuit, and it's your fault, you can be sure that you'll have to pay much more out of your own pocket. Coverage of at least 100/300 is recommended.

Property damage liability. If you're in an accident and someone else's property is damaged, like the plate glass of a store window you accidentally drove through, this is the part of your policy that covers you. It also covers the car that you hit when you tried to back out of the glass-covered storefront. Bodily injury and property damage liability are the two most expensive parts of your policy, probably about half your premium.

Uninsured motorist. This coverage pays for injuries, including pain and suffering, if you're in an accident with an uninsured motorist or with a hit-and-run driver. Your claim will be paid only if the other person was at fault.

Underinsured motorist coverage. This covers you when the other driver was at fault but didn't have very much coverage. Mandatory coverage levels of $10,000 to $25,000 don't go far these days.

Collision coverage. Covers the cost of car repairs or replacement. With body shops charging hundreds of dollars for minor fender benders, this coverage may account for as much as one third of your total premium. You'll certainly want it if your car is less than four years old or worth more than $4,000, suggests *Consumer Reports.* But you can lower the cost of collision coverage by increasing your deductible.

Collision claims are paid in one of two ways. Either you get the cash value of the car if the company determines it's not worth repairing, or you get the amount needed to repair or replace it. A lot of drivers get steamed when the company pays cash value because the market value of the car is usually a lot less than the cost of a suitable replacement vehicle, especially when the company considers how much your car depreciated and deducts an additional charge for unusually high mileage.

Comprehensive. This kind of coverage includes theft and vandalism, as well as forces of nature, such as hail and earthquakes.

Medical expense. The policy, also called "med pay," will pay medical expenses for accidental injuries to you and your passengers. It also covers funeral expenses. In these cases, fault doesn't matter.

Personal injury protection (PIP). This additional coverage is required by law in no-fault states. It pays for medical expenses and some earnings, regardless of who was at fault.

In New York, for example, such coverage must be in place for at least $50,000 per person.

Under no-fault, you get to sue only if a damage threshold has been passed. The threshold may be monetary or verbal. With monetary thresholds, you can sue if your medical costs exceed a base amount. Verbal thresholds allow you to sue if there are serious injuries or death. Property damage compensation is not included under the laws of most states with no-fault.

The states with some form of mandatory no-fault insurance are Colorado, Florida, Hawaii, Kansas, Kentucky, Massachusetts, Michigan, Minnesota, New Jersey, New York, North Dakota, Pennsylvania, and Utah.

Other possible coverages include towing and labor, glass breakage, umbrella coverage (which pays out when all of your other coverage is exhausted), and special endorsements, such as coverage for built-in camper equipment.

The Insuring Agreement

There is an insuring agreement attached to the declarations page. Read it carefully because it includes important definitions, such as exactly whom the policy covers and under what conditions a claim will be paid.

The people who are covered are known as the "insureds." They include the individuals specifically named on the declarations page, other residents of your household, and occasional users of your car (with your permission). Non-permitted

LOWERING RATES

While rate increases have stabilized in the last few years, auto insurance is still expensive, particularly in large cities like Chicago and New York that have experienced sharp drops in auto theft without commensurate decreases in insurance premiums. However, alternatives to the high-priced sue-and-be-sued system exist and have been getting renewed attention. "No-fault" car insurance, modified to eliminate problems that have plagued it in the past, is under consideration in several additional states and in Congress, variously called "Auto Choice" and "Consumer Choice."

Under the no-fault concept, blame is irrelevant. After an accident, motorists make claims against their own insurers, who promptly pay their medical bills, car repairs, and other economic losses. Because there are no lawsuits, except in the most serious cases, there are no legal fees, and premiums can be reduced. However, accident victims lose the right to sue for pain and suffering and, in effect, end up compensating the party at fault.

But poor no-fault systems have resulted in the worst of both worlds: premiums driven up by incentives to boost medical claims above the lawsuit threshold and less than adequate coverage for policyholders who have been seriously injured. No-fault can work only if it provides a significant benefit to consumers in exchange for forfeiting their right to sue. Consumer advocates point to Michigan's existing no-fault system as a good model; insurance rates are reasonable even though the state mandates high levels of coverage and generous benefits for seriously injured accident victims.

drivers—such as car thieves—are not covered if they, and your vehicle, are involved in an accident. But you are covered if you have an accident driving someone else's car, as long as it is with the person's permission.

The insuring agreement also lists any exclusions—that is, whatever is specifically not covered. Read these before you sign, not when you file your first claim.

The Factors That Determine Your Premium

Winston Churchill called Russia "a riddle wrapped in a mystery inside an enigma." The same might be said for the way insurance companies compute premiums.

Your premium is figured by multiplying a per-unit rate by the amount of insurance (the number of units of insurance) you wish to buy.

Your rate is computed by taking into account the factors described below. As explained later, surcharges or discounts may then be applied to your premium.

Your state of residence. No one can entirely figure out why, but some states, like New Jersey, Pennsylvania, and California, have much more expensive auto insurance than others. One reason may be that heavily urbanized states have more cars, more traffic congestion, and therefore more accidents, raising the cost of providing insurance; New Jersey is the most densely populated state in the union, and Southern California traffic is legendary.

Where you garage your car. If you live (and park) your car within the zip code of a heavily urbanized area, you can pay two or three times as much as your twin sister who happens to live (and park) in a rural area some miles away, even if you both have perfect records and drive the same model car. Suburban drivers' premiums tend to be somewhere between the premiums paid by urban and rural drivers. Premiums tend to be highest in lower-income, inner-city neighborhoods.

According to a 1996 *Consumer Reports* survey, the *best* rate available in Philadelphia for a married couple with two cars and a teenage driver is a whopping $6,238; a similar family living in suburban Levittown, Pennsylvania, would have paid $3,507, almost 60% less.

The insurance industry calls the system of figuring rates based on a car's home address "territorial rating." How fair is it? Not very. Premiums decline as you age, but you have to physically relocate to reduce a premium based on address. The poor pay more because low incomes and racial discrimination in housing keep many people from moving into areas with cheaper premiums. And territorial boundaries tend to be arbitrarily drawn. Besides, how fair is a system where your premium could be cut 25% just by moving a few blocks into a different "territory"?

The amount of coverage you buy and deductibles. In California, raising coverage from the minimal state-mandated level to, say, 50/100 will raise your premium an average of about 34%. A Florida couple who raised the deductible for their 1995 Volvo and 1993 Acura Legend from $500 to $1,000 cut their annual premiums from $3,200 to $2,800, a decrease of 12%.

Your age, how long you've been driving, your sex, and marital status. There's no denying it: Younger male drivers tend to have more accidents —*many* more accidents—than more mature drivers. So it's not unreason-

> **"I** *nsurance makes consumers both intimidated and bored at the same time. As a result, most don't shop well."*
>
> —ROBERT HUNTER,
> Director of Insurance at the
> Consumer Federation of
> America

353

CITY SLICKERS GET TAKEN

Urban drivers pay far more for the same coverage than rural, and even suburban, drivers do. In 1996, a Travelers Phoenix policy that cost $3,750 a year in densely populated Miami cost $1,570 in suburban Homestead, Florida, about 30 miles away. Even within a small state, the differences can be significant: in Delaware in 1991, Aetna Casualty and Surety Company charged a married female (25 to 49 years old) $340 in the city of Wilmington, $302 in New Castle County, and $248 in rural Kent and Sussex counties.

able for male drivers under 25 to pay 100% to 200% more because, unlike racial or gender discrimination, all young drivers can escape this classification by successfully aging. If you have been driving for only a few years, you'll pay a surcharge regardless of your age. Generally, you have to have been driving for five to ten years before this surcharge is entirely erased.

You'll probably pay less if you're married—insurance companies believe that married drivers have fewer accidents. But adding a teenage child to your policy could increase your premium by 50%; in Pennsylvania, a teenager could eas-

ily *double* your annual bill. Unfortunately, the use of marital status as a factor inherently discriminates against unmarried hetero- or homosexual couples, whose domestic partnerships the law doesn't recognize, and against lower-income drivers, who are statistically less likely to be married.

Your driving record. Logically enough, people with poor driving records pay surcharges. There may or may not be a small surcharge of about 5% for your first ticket if you are an otherwise good driver. If you have a small accident, though, you can expect at least a 25% increase in your premium. Your premium could double or your insurance might not be renewed at all if you get one or more drunk-driving tickets.

Your car model. If you drive an armored personnel carrier and a compact sedan runs smack into you at 30 mph, chances are that your vehicle will hardly be dented and you won't be filing a liability claim. The moral of the story? While it's illegal to drive an armored personnel carrier, you *can* save a lot of money if you buy the safest car possible—and you might just save your life.

A car that is costly to fix is costly to insure. A 12-cylinder Jaguar is a wonderful car, but insurance may cost a lot more than it would for a basic Dodge or Ford. Comprehensive coverage for cars that are both expensive to replace and popular with thieves, such as sport utility vehicles and luxury cars, is, of course, more expensive.

How you use your car. A car used for business costs more to insure because it is driven more and the chance of an accident is therefore greater. You'll also probably pay more if you commute a long distance or if your commute is entirely within a heavily urbanized area. But you'll enjoy a reduction if your car is used solely for "pleasure." "Farm use" is cheapest of all. Your agent may ask you how many miles you drive a year, and you could be surcharged if you drive a lot more than the annual average of 12,000 to 15,000 miles.

Besides using these factors to figure the premiums, the company will use them to decide whether to accept you in the first place. The process of making this determination is called *underwriting*. While the insurance agent makes the first cut by deciding whether to do business with you at all, it is the insurance company underwriter who reviews the application, makes the decision whether or not to insure you, and sets the premium. The underwriter determines if you are a preferred, standard, or nonstandard (i.e., high) risk driver. A standard-risk driver usually pays about 20% more than a preferred driver. A nonstandard-risk driver's application may be rejected or surcharged.

Underwriting is more art than science. While a computer could apply a formula to place you in any one of hundreds of possible insurance classifications based on the factors listed earlier (such as "female driver over 65 living in suburban territory driving a full-size sedan"), the underwriter tries to get a "feel"

for your riskiness, perhaps giving a little extra weight to one or another factor in a particular application. Among the subtle factors that might help determine if a company will accept you is your occupation. For example, insurance companies don't seem to favor police officers, firefighters, and bartenders.

Premium Discounts

Once your premium is figured, you may be eligible for a discount. Be sure to tell your insurance agent about any of the following factors if they apply. By one estimate, Americans are paying $300 million more than necessary per year simply because they aren't getting credits they qualify for. But don't let the number of discounts available decide which insurer you'll use; a company that offers only a few of the following discounts might charge a low basic premium.

More than one car. Most companies offer a discount for bringing them all your auto insurance business.

Safety equipment. If your car comes equipped with such passive restraints as air bags, you may be entitled to a large reduction on your medical coverage premium. Discounts for anti-lock brake systems (ABS) are not as common as they used to be because of mixed research on their effectiveness, but they still exist, so it may be worth shopping around.

Anti-theft devices. City dwellers trying to get a full night's sleep loathe car alarms, and their effectiveness in stopping theft is dubious. Still, car alarms can reduce comprehensive coverage premiums in some states, as can more neighbor-friendly devices like Chapman locks and other ignition cut-off devices.

Lots of driving experience. Mature drivers, usually drivers over 50, may enjoy a 10% discount. Insurers presume that older drivers drive less than they used to.

Good grades. Young people pay through the nose for auto insurance. But if your high school or college student gets good grades, usually a "B" average or better, a "good student discount" may be available. Some companies apparently assume that good students are more likely to be studying at home than out cruising for adventure.

Nonsmoker. People who smoke have more accidents. Perhaps the smoke gets in their eyes, or they take their hands off the wheel when lighting up. Or perhaps people who take fewer health risks also take fewer risks behind the wheel.

Driver safety course. Taking a defensive driving course may reduce your premium 5% to 15%.

Car pool. Presumably you're driving your own vehicle less and exposing yourelf to less risk if you car pool.

Shared Markets and Assigned Risk Pools

The basic concept of insurance is to spread risk. The driver who has never filed a claim subsidizes the hapless fellow who backed into the light post in the mall parking lot.

However, the insurance companies don't let you wreck cars and rack up claims indefinitely—it would jack up rates for everyone else. Drivers who are considered at "high risk" of future claims get put into categories called "shared markets" or "assigned risk pools" with sky-high insurance premiums. You can avoid this fate by driving defensively.

Cancellation and Non-Renewal

Nothing makes motorists angrier than being canceled or non-renewed without so much as an explanation.

Cancellation. Basically, after the first 60 days of coverage, insurers can cancel your coverage only if you don't pay your premium, your license is revoked, or if someone covered by the policy is convicted of driving while intoxicated. Before the first 60 days, they can cancel your policy pretty much at will.

Non-renewal. Much more frequent and problematical is the insurer's refusal to renew your policy. An insurance company can decide not to renew your policy for any reason, except for age, sex, occupation, or race in the states where non-renewal for such reasons is specifically prohibited. In many states, the insurer doesn't have to tell you why you were dropped.

WHAT TO WATCH OUT FOR

The wrong information from the agent. According to one survey, applicants who ask agents for premium comparisons get the wrong answer one third to one half of the time. To find the right information, first try your State Insurance Department; many, such as Texas and Arizona, issue guides with a comparison of premiums among companies for various driver classifications. You might also call or have a friend call an agent back later to double-check a premium quote. If you live in California, Florida, Illinois, New Jersey, New York, Ohio, Pennsylvania, or Washington, you can use the Consumer Reports Auto Insurance Price Service to get price quotes tailored to your specific insurance needs. (See **HELP** for more information.)

Sloppy service. Price isn't everything. The least expensive insurer may provide lousy service. So ask friends and relatives about an insurer's reputation before applying. Also, an insurance company operating on the edge of solvency isn't likely to offer very good service. Find out about their financial health through a research service (see **HELP** at the end of the chapter).

Inconsistency across rate classes. By all means, ask around for recommendations, but don't stop with that. A *Consumer Reports* investigation found few instances where the insurance company offering the most favorable rate to one category of drivers was also the best for another. Translation: the company that gave your parents a good deal isn't likely to be the cheapest for you.

A misleading or incorrect C.L.U.E. report. Most drivers haven't a clue about C.L.U.E., the Comprehensive Loss Underwriting Exchange. It's a national database run by Choice Point, formerly Equifax Inc., with up to five years' worth of claims histories on some 134 million drivers covered by liability insurance. C.L.U.E. is one of the things insurers use to decide whose premiums to raise, whose policies not to renew, and whose applications to reject.

Few motorists have checked the accuracy of what their C.L.U.E. file says about them. Yet there could be irrelevant or outdated claims. And entries could be misleading, since there are no facts describing the circumstances of any of the claims, other than the claim amount. Choice Point says less than 1% of complaints about inaccuracies result in changes in the data base. But it's the insurer's, not the consumer's, word that decides. Plus, if you are one of those 3,000 people a year, you are in for a nasty surprise. (See the chapter "Consumer Privacy" on page 640.)

One unwary consumer found out her auto insurance application was rejected by Allstate and she ended up in the assigned risk pool because of her C.L.U.E. report, even though she had never been in an accident and had never had a moving violation. A closer inspection revealed that two of the biggest claims in her file were for vandalism and theft and were no longer relevant; she had moved several years earlier from the neighborhood where the incidents occurred to a much safer area.

The woman says that another claim listed as an accident was a spurious accusation that she had knocked someone's mirror off in a parking lot. Since it was cheaper for the insurer to pay than to defend against a wrongful claim, the claim went into the database unexplained.

To get a copy of your report, call Choice Point at (800) 456-6004. You will need to have available your driver's license number, date of birth, Social Security number, and, if you can, a 14-digit reference number that appears on the notice from your insurance company, if that's what prompted your call.

Expensive subsidiaries of major insurance companies. One law school dean felt happy because he had State Farm as his insurer, until his neighbor told him that he also had State Farm and that he paid several hundred dollars less than the dean. The dean looked into it and found out that he was insured by State Farm Fire and Casualty, which as it turns out, is more expensive than his neighbor's insurer, State Farm Mutual. His agent had signed him up with the more expensive subsidiary to earn a higher commission. When the dean threatened to sue, he was switched to State Farm Mutual and got back his extra premium payments.

Such costlier subsidiaries are supposed to insure only higher-risk drivers. But you might not really be a higher-risk driver and still end up with the expensive subsidiary.

The Texas Insurance Department brought charges against Farmers Insurance Group for improperly placing 4,000 people into its high-risk subsidiary, leading them to overpay by an estimated $400,000.

Adequate uninsured and underinsured motorist coverage. It would be easy to "economize" by overlooking this area or buying less coverage than you need. Don't—it's penny wise but pound foolish. The California Department of Motor Vehicles estimates that one quarter to one third of the state's motorists have no insurance, and there are many uninsured drivers in other states. If you are in an accident with one of them, you will have to rely on your own insurance to cover you—or cover yourself out of pocket.

Uninsured motorist coverage is especially advisable if you live in a state without no-fault coverage. If you don't have it, you'll have to pay all of your expenses above your medical coverage if you are in a hit-and-run accident or if the other driver doesn't have insurance.

Shop around. In a survey by the insurance industry, a third of all drivers said it had been at least six years since they last shopped for a new policy; 20% said they never shopped at all. When Robert Hunter was Texas Insurance Commissioner in the mid-1990s, he had about 30 consumers come in with their car insurance policies. He gave them each a telephone, a copy of the state's insurance buyer's guide, and one hour and told them to shop around for a policy. When the hour was up, they had saved an average of $125. Asks Hunter: "How many jobs do you know that pay well over $100 for an hour's work?" Yes, it takes some work. But different insurance companies have very different premiums, even in the same zip code area.

Two examples from the Consumer Reports Auto Insurance Service database: In Chicago, the annual premium for the same female driver, coverage, and car varied from $728 at GEICO to $1,050 at Chicago Motor Club Preferred. A forty-something married couple living in the suburbs of San Francisco with a teenage son and two cars could pay an annual premium of $1,416 to Mercury Insurance Co. or $2,382 to GEICO, almost 70% more.

Just because a company has high premiums does not mean it offers good service. And a company with low premiums does not necessarily offer bad service. Some insurance companies have lower premiums because they specialize in insuring low-risk drivers. You might also find that an insurance company that sells directly, like State Farm and GEICO—rather than through an independent agent—is cheaper.

Drop unnecessary coverage. Examine your declarations page carefully for coverage that you can reasonably reduce or eliminate. The most promising area for saving money may be your collision and comprehensive coverage. You may

decide that this coverage is no longer worthwhile when your car is four or five years old. If you're in an accident, chances are that the company will "total" rather than repair your car—that is, give you what they calculate to be its cash value—which won't be much for an older car. The general rule is to drop collision coverage when the premium is 10% of the car's market value.

You might also reduce medical coverage, particularly if you have a good health insurance policy.

Reducing your liability coverage could be risky. Remember, if you are sued you'll want the company to defend you in court, and they're much more likely to put up a strong defense if they might have to shell out $1 million rather than $10,000.

Raise your deductibles. Consider this: You're probably not going to file a claim for a minor fender-bender, because if you do, your premium will most certainly go up, probably offsetting any amount the insurance company paid out to you. So if you're not going to file small claims, then why not raise your collision and comprehensive deductible to, say, $1,000 and put the premiums you save in the bank?

You could do as the experts do and, in effect, self-insure. Take high deductibles and put the premium savings in a separate bank account, which you can use to pay for any repair of fender-bender damage.

Report any changes in status that might reduce your premium. Say you start car-pooling or your teenage son goes off to college. Tell your insurer immediately.

Ask about a "first accident allowance." If you have an accident after many years of driving accident-free, some insurers will overlook it and not surcharge you.

Drive a safer car. Logically enough, larger and heavier cars tend to be safer and therefore less expensive to insure (though they are more expensive to drive).

Put your kids on your policy if they drive your car less than half the time. It's a lot cheaper than buying them separate insurance. If they have their own policies, then they are "principal," as opposed to "occasional," drivers. Occasional drivers are cheaper to cover. If they go to school more than 100 miles away (*without* your car), you'll also get a discount.

Buy your homeowners and auto insurance from the same company. You could get a discount of about 10% on your auto policy.

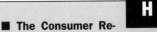

HELP

■ **The Consumer Reports** Auto Insurance Price Service will compare as many as 70 policies, taking into account factors like your cars, the drivers in your household, annual mileage, and how much coverage you want. The service covers California, Florida, Illinois, New Jersey, New York, Ohio, Pennsylvania, and Washington, but call to see if your state has recently been added: (800) 807-8050. It costs $12 for the first vehicle and $8 for each additional vehicle. They will fax or mail you a report that lists up to 25 of the lowest-priced policies for you.

■ **Where to complain?** Most states have a consumer services division in their insurance departments where you can report your insurer if you think you have been mistreated. Check the government listings in your local telephone directory.

■ **Are you driving a thief's favorite** model? Find out for free from the Highway Loss Data Institute, 1005 North Glebe Road, Arlington, VA 22201; (703) 247-1600; www.hwysafety.org. Surprisingly, some older models are favored because of demand for their parts.

■ **Should you maintain** collision coverage? Check the market value of your car with the National Automobile Dealers Association. Most public libraries have their price book. Or you can get price estimates on such Internet sites as Edmund's Automotive Buyer's Guides, www.edmunds.com or Kelley Blue Books, www.kbb.com.

■ **If you suspect insurance fraud, call** the National Insurance Crime Bureau hot line at 800-TEL-NICB. Remember that insurance fraud, like shoplifting, raises costs for everyone.

■ **For answers to your insurance** questions, try the National Insurance Consumer Helpline at (800) 942-4242. This service is paid for by the insurance industry, so take what they say with a grain of salt. Another industry organization that can answer basic questions is the Insurance Information Institute, 110 William Street, New York, NY 10038, www.iii.org; (800) 331-9146.

■ **Check out an insurer before applying.** Call your state insurance department to find out if a company has been the subject of government disciplinary actions.

CHAPTER 33

CAR REPAIR

Take Your Car in Without Getting Taken In

In 1941 and again in 1997, *Reader's Digest* reporters took a car that was in perfect working condition into repair shops around the country to see how many would make expensive, unneeded "repairs." The result: 63% of the shops did unnecessary work in 1941 and 56% in 1997. The 1997 survey also found big bills for unnecessary computerized diagnostic tests for problems that should have been easy to spot.

This worthless work costs you dearly. In 1979, the U.S. Department of Transportation found that American consumers paid $26.5 billion for unnecessary car repairs and related costs—about half of what they spent at the garage. And things haven't gotten much better: Out of the $100 billion Americans now spend annually on auto repair, Ralph Nader estimates that Americans shell out more than $40 billion unnecessarily.

One New Jersey woman, for example, was forced to pay $1,000 in cash to retrieve her car from the repair shop. As she drove away, she realized she'd paid a lot for nothing—the car had not been repaired.

In another example, thousands of Sears Auto Repair customers paid anywhere from a few dollars to $500 for unnecessary repairs before California's Bureau of Automotive Repair cracked down.

Don't let these stories or a phobia of car dealers and mechanics scare you into submission. You don't have to take it—if you take care when selecting a mechanic and overseeing repair jobs.

THE BASICS

Routine Maintenance

After plunking down thousands and thousands of dollars for a purring new car with a three-year warranty, it's natural to assume (or at least hope) that you won't have to pay it much mind for a few years. Simple upkeep can keep your car away from premature visits to the shop. A three-year Federal Trade Commission study of the auto repair industry found improper maintenance to be a major cause of many costly repairs: Following the maintenance guidelines for your car may mean paying for a $20 oil change now and then, but you'll likely steer clear of a $1,200 overhaul.

Easier said than done. In a sort of duel of the maintenance schedules, manufacturers suggest one thing and dealers another. An investigation by *U.S. News & World Report* found that 80% of auto dealers surveyed performed more services than the manufacturer recommended, and 63% of dealers replaced parts that manufacturers said had plenty of life left in them.

Various car experts and the American Automobile Association recommend changing the oil more frequently than the manufacturers suggest—every 3,000 to 5,000 miles—and following the manufacturers' guidelines for other services. To be really safe, the AAA recommends that car owners use the "frequent service" schedule recommended by manufacturers for the cars they produce.

Not only is regular service good for the car, it's also essential if you want your warranty to cover major repairs. Most manufacturers' warranties are void if you haven't kept up with the prescribed maintenance schedule.

> "*Consumers can— and should— seek a second opinion if they have doubts about the {car repair} advice they are receiving. . . . Some all-inclusive offers may include unnecessary service, while others may be too limiting for your particular needs.*"
>
> —JIM CONRAN,
> former director of the State of
> California Department of
> Consumer Affairs

Finding a Repair Shop

According to the FTC study, misdiagnosis rather than fraud causes 75% of unnecessary car repair. And with only one mechanic for every 142 cars—nearly a third fewer than in 1950—finding a mechanic who knows your vehicle model and can properly diagnose its problems can be difficult.

You have a number of options when choosing a repair shop. Here are some things to consider.

Car dealers. As the profit in selling cars has decreased, dealers have become more reliant on their service centers to be profit centers. Just 13% of dealer profits came from the service department in 1986, according to the National Automobile Dealers Association. Ten years later, only 7% of their profits *don't* come from repairs. While the prices for nonwarranty work will be high, the dealer's mechanics have been trained to understand thoroughly your car's quirks. Furthermore, dealers are often the only convenient supplier of the diagnostic equipment necessary to understand bugs in the complex computer systems that run today's cars.

Specialty shops, franchise shops, and department store auto centers. Service is usually fast and convenient and prices reasonable. Different chains specialize in particular services, such as muffler repair or tune-ups, and often know little about other systems in the car.

Independent service stations. Services and prices vary. The main attractions are convenience and customer satisfaction. There's a good chance you can have the same mechanic service your car time and again, and he or she will know your car, which can help you to feel more confident about diagnoses and price estimates.

Choose a shop based on the kind of repair you need. For work covered by the warranty, go straight to the dealer. For routine maintenance, the automotive center at the local department store will probably do just fine, as will one of the chains, such as Jiffy Lube, that specializes in what you need. For routine repairs and individualized attention, try your local mechanic.

WHAT TO WATCH OUT FOR

The problem? You may not know what kind of service you need. If this is the case, you need to find a full-service shop you can trust. As with most other things, the first thing to do is ask your friends, neighbors, and relatives whom they recommend. If that nets nothing, you're on your own. Here's what you should look for:

Credentials. Seek out repair shops endorsed by the American Automobile Association; the AAA holds them to rigorous standards and guarantees their work for AAA members. Shops in AAA's Approved Auto Repair Program must have at least a 90% customer satisfaction rating and offer a 6-month/ 6,000-mile service guarantee. AAA will also mediate disagreements between its members and repair shops it has endorsed.

Look for certification by the National Institute for Automotive Service Excellence (ASE). Certification is no guarantee of quality, nor is it legally required, but it is an assurance of experience. The institute certifies mechanics in eight repair areas, and mechanics who are certified can advertise this fact. Ask if the mechanic is certified to do the work your car needs. A shop can post an ASE sticker if only one mechanic has been certified, and a mechanic certified in, say, brake repairs isn't necessarily better than the garage down the block if your car needs a new transmission.

Poor service. Although Americans spend $100 billion a year on automobile parts and service, every third car repaired requires a return visit to the shop, according to automotive consultant J.D. Power and Associates. It's no wonder, then, that auto repair consistently rates as a top complaint category at local consumer affairs agencies and better business bureaus.

Unnecessary repairs. The examples are innumerable. When the NYC Department of Consumer Af-

REPAIR AD ABSURDUM

What would you do if your mechanic jacked up your car, with your wheelchair-bound wife in it, and tried to extort $1,000 from you before you could get your wife or your car back? Sounds like a *Saturday Night Live* skit, right? This is exactly what happened to Robert and Shirley A. of Canoga Park, California. They brought their RV into a dealer who had offered a free lubrication and oil change. What they got instead was a demand for $1,000 "ransom" before the dealer would take the mobile home off the jacks. Robert had no choice but to pay. When he got home, he stopped payment on the check. The RV dealer had to repay the couple $1,300 and eventually went to jail.

fairs took in test vehicles—rigged by expert mechanics with small problems that should have cost little to fix—more than half of the transmission shops wanted to do unnecessary work, ranging in price from $75 to $1,133; a third of the muffler shops wanted to charge $60 to $325 for superfluous service.

A 1997 sting operation by the Nassau County, New York, District Attorney's office found that one quarter of the auto repair shops they investigated made unnecessary repairs and overcharged customers. The shops were caught replacing alternators and batteries when only new fuses or hoses were needed. In one instance, an investigator was told his idle rate had been adjusted, but the car came back from the shop with the idle adjuster still sealed from the factory.

Mechanics in franchise stores frequently work on commission or have quotas to fill. The more work they do, the more money they make. That means they may be tempted to line their jumpsuits' pockets by performing unnecessary repairs on your car. Sixty percent of the mechanics interviewed by the FTC said sales-based incentives are one of the biggest reasons for unnecessary repairs or replacements.

After receiving a slew of complaints, the State of California's Bureau of Automotive Repair (BAR) went undercover and caught Sears Auto Stores selling unnecessary service and parts, overcharging by as much as $550 for unnecessary repairs, and pressuring employees to meet daily quotas for the sales of alignments, springs, shock absorbers, struts, and brake jobs. Once caught, Sears changed its compensation system to remove the incentive to do unnecessary work. While Sears has cleaned up its act, one-stop shops like Jiffy Lube and Zip Lube still give their mechanics bonuses based on sales.

Not-so-"new" equipment. Sears found more trouble in 1996 when an Alabama man sued for receiving a used DieHard battery when he had paid for a new one. A private investigator hired by the man's lawyers bought, used, and returned some of the company's batteries, then secretly videotaped employees putting them back on store shelves. He also found signs of usage on 78 of 100 batteries he bought from Sears stores in 32 states.

Sears officials denied company-wide scheming, but former employees serving as witnesses in the case said that they were acting under management's orders when they reshelved the batteries. One former manager said used DieHards accounted for 15% or more of "new" battery sales.

Charges for work that wasn't done. Lisa C. of New Jersey has a classic story. One rainy day, she couldn't get her car to start. The next day, the car started fine, but just to be safe she took it in to a repair shop for a check-up. She was told that necessary work would cost $1,000.

When she came back to pick up the car two days later, the mechanic asked her to pay in cash and would not let her test-drive the car first. Since she needed the car, she had no choice but to pay. She took the car to another mechanic, who told her that no work had been done and that the job should have cost only $50. The car had a cracked spark plug; when plugs get wet, they can keep a car from starting.

Trial-by-erroneous-replacement repair. A study by the National Association of Attorneys General found that "technical incompetence" of mechanics often results in "diagnosis through replacement." Parts are replaced one by one until,

voila! The problem is solved. The consumer ends up with some shiny, new, totally unnecessary replacement parts—and a big hole in the pocket.

Misleading ads. Beware of commercials promising unbelievably low prices for repairs. The low prices often do not include all the necessary parts and labor. Midas Muffler franchises in California were charged with deceptive advertising by the California Bureau of Automotive Repair several years ago for touting nonexistent brake pad replacement deals for $25 off when customers had to pay that, and more, to buy each part of a standard brake pad replacement package.

"Extraordinary deals." Three auto body shops in Brooklyn, New York, were charged with stealing cars, stripping them, and then dumping the cars where police would find them. The shops then sold the parts back to the original owners, enticing them with too-good-to-be-true deals. The criminals were caught when the owners noticed that some parts looked familiar.

The captive consumer. Some garages will try to strong-arm you into letting them repair your car. Don't let them; you have a right to choose your own mechanic. Take the case of John G. His van was stolen, recovered by the police, and—without his knowledge or approval—towed to a garage. When John went to the garage to claim the van, he was told he could not have it unless he authorized the garage to do the necessary repairs. The garage claimed that some work had already been done and that parts were on order. But because John had not authorized *any* work, he refused to pay. Until local consumer officials intervened, the garage refused to release the van.

In many states, by law, you can be charged for repairs only if you sign an authorization. Do not let yourself be coerced into paying for repairs that were performed without your consent.

Towing tricks. Tow services are another consistent source of consumer complaints. Once they've got your car, it can be difficult to get them to give it up. Some unscrupulous (and unlicensed) towers make careers and profits out of monitoring police scanners for accidents and then showing up within minutes to take advantage. The "chaser" may be the first to arrive, but that's hardly a convenience if he's going to rip you off. Even if you would prefer to have your regular mechanic make the necessary repairs, towers may try to strong-arm you into having their shop work on your car.

A tow truck was sitting across the street when a drunk driver crashed into Chandra B.'s car in Los Angeles, and the tower offered to tow her car for free to a repair shop nearby. Once there, Chandra was given a rental vehicle and told her car would be ready within the week. After 34 days and countless excuses from the garage, Chandra paid an unannounced visit and found her car in almost the same condition as when she left it—broken windows and all. The only change? It was now splotched with Bondo to cover paint scrapes.

William S.'s story is also typical of how towing companies pad their bills. He was driving home from work when his car broke down. When he asked the tow truck driver who responded to his call how much the tow would cost, he was told $130 for 27 miles, which he then authorized. The next day, William clocked the trip and found that it was only 19 miles. When he looked at the bill, he noticed charges for "motor trouble" and "wrecked vehicle" that did not apply to his case. He calculated that this modern-day highway robber overcharged him by $55—for a tow that should have cost only $75.

Warranty waivers. Many dealers insert clauses into their warranties stating that if something goes wrong as a result of repairs done by a facility other than the dealer's service center, the cost of fixing the problem will not be covered by the warranty. Don't let the dealer use this clause to persuade you that *all* routine work, such as oil changes or 10,000-mile check-ups, must be done by the dealer in order to keep your warranty. You can save money using independents or chains for routine services—or by doing simple maintenance yourself—and the dealer must still honor your warranty for bigger repairs.

"Service notices." Don't be fooled by mailings from your dealer that look like official service notices from the manufacturer. One local Mazda dealership mailed notices to 5,000 Mazda owners in Palm Beach County, Florida, telling them to bring their cars to the dealership to have the timing belt inspected and possibly replaced. The mailing referenced "Mazda and Service Notification TTB #46A, May 1992" and said, in part: "This is to notify you of a Special Vehicle Maintenance Inspection regarding timing belt replacement on most 1984–1989 Mazda models." As official as the letter sounded, the directive had not come from Mazda of America but from Mazda of Palm Beach County—it was just a sneaky promotion concocted to drum up repair business. Dealers across the country employ this tactic, and it may result in more than misspent money. One phony notice sent to Ford Explorer owners in 1996 in Connecticut recommended an oil treatment that their owner's manuals strongly cautioned against. The cost? $350, and possibly a damaged motor.

Choose the right shop for the job. Routine maintenance jobs are easily and inexpensively handled by franchised chains and department store repair shops. Dealers will charge top dollar. Be sure to use a shop that specializes in what you need. And once you've found a respectable shop, tell others about

it—that's how good businesses stay in business.

Know what your car requires. Car manuals are the best-selling books in America that nobody reads, according to an auto mechanics' trade group. Bring yours with you to tune-ups, and ask the mechanic to perform only those services the manual recommends. If the mechanic suggests more work, find out why.

Do your own maintenance. It's relatively simple and the cheapest by far. But keep receipts for oil or filters you buy so that you can prove you adhered to the manufacturer's maintenance schedule if you ever need to.

Get a second opinion, unless you're sure of the mechanic. This is particularly important if you've been towed to a shop you know nothing about. You may have to pay for another tow and a couple of estimates, but in the end you may save hundreds of dollars.

Talk directly to the person who will work on your car, whenever possible. If it's the only way to describe the symptoms, have the mechanic take a test drive with you.

Get an estimate and tell the garage not to begin repairing the car until you have approved the repairs at the estimated price.

Know what you're paying for. If work was performed without authorization or if you were charged for work that wasn't done, don't pay for it. Complain to the garage, and, if the matter is not resolved satisfactorily, complain to local consumer authorities.

Don't sign a service order until you know what will be involved. At the very least, the service order should describe your car's problems specifically; ideally, it should state exactly what work will be done. Tell the mechanic not to do any additional work without getting your explicit approval.

If you are in an accident, and you aren't hurt, try to keep your head. Don't play first-come, first-served with towers. If someone approaches you with an offer for a cheap tow, check out his credentials first and then *you* decide where to tow the car. In some cities, only the police can call a tow truck to the scene of an accident. Even so, don't let yourself be towed where you don't want to go.

Rebuilt parts are as good as new ones, and at as little as a quarter of the price, a better buy. Ask ahead of time—otherwise the mechanic will probably put in the more expensive new part. One catch: Rebuilt parts come with shorter guarantees than new parts.

Don't pay for work that was never done. If you had parts replaced, ask to see the old ones. Some states even require mechanics to give you the parts they remove from your car—in Maryland, for instance, consumers are not obligated to pay for repairs if key parts are not returned to them.

Keep a copy of any estimates, agreements, and invoices for your records. They may come in handy if you are the unlucky one out of three people who needs a follow-up visit to get things running right. You might also need them to prove to the dealer or manufacturer that you have been maintaining the car properly and qualify for the warranty.

Know your warranty. Before you take your car to an independent mechanic, check if the repair work would be covered by the warranty if you took the car to the dealer. Conversely, for routine maintenance or a repair, take your car to the dealer only if the warranty covers it.

Avoid garages that accept only cash. It may be a sign they won't stand behind their work. Taking this precaution would have protected Lisa C., the car owner we met earlier, whose car was released only after a $1,000 cash payment. If she had paid by check, she could have asked the bank to stop payment; if she had paid with a credit card, she could have asked the credit card company not to pay the charge until the dispute was resolved. The credit card company cannot charge you interest or penalties until the problem is settled or resolved in court. If you need to do this, write a letter to the credit card company and garage explaining the problem, and be sure to keep copies.

HELP

■ **If you have a prob-** lem with a garage that has been endorsed by AAA, report it to the organization. Garages can lose their standing with AAA if the problems are common or serious enough.

■ **The State of California Bureau of** Automotive Repair investigates every complaint it receives and mediates between mechanics and car owners when necessary: In California, call (800) 952-5210 (7 AM to 5 PM weekdays). Residents of other states, call your state department of transportation to see if anything similar is available where you live.

■ **For a list of the 1,800 tires rated** by the National Highway Traffic Safety Administration and a list of long-lasting tires, call the agency's Auto Safety Hotline (800) 424-9393 or look at their Web site: www.nhtsa.dot.gov.

■ **The Center for Auto** Safety can send you a list of lawyers in your area who specialize in helping consumers with car repair problems. Send a stamped, self-addressed envelope to 2001 S Street NW, Washington, DC 20009.

■ **For more advice, consult** *The Car Book* or *The Used Car Book*, by Jack Gillis, $12.95 (Harper Perennial). They come out yearly and are available in bookstores, but if you buy them from the Center for Auto Safety, this nonprofit group gets a portion of the profits. Write to 2001 S Street NW, Washington, DC 20009, or call (202) 328-7700.

■ **For car repair tips—and a laugh—** you can find Click and Clack of NPR's "Car Talk" radio program on the Internet at www.cartalk@cars.com. The site includes "Mechanics File," a list of mechanics recommended by listeners around the country.

PART 6

Finances

CHAPTER 34

CREDIT CARDS

Still Expensive After All These Years

Millions of Americans breathed a sigh of financial relief when credit card interest rates began to moderate in the early 1990s. For years, rates had remained stubbornly stuck at record highs of close to 21%, even as earnings on deposit accounts plummeted to their lowest levels since automobiles had tail fins.

But most cardholders continue to pay way too much. The national rate still averages around 17% to 18%, several times what issuers pay for the money they lend cardholders.

And most of what the issuers gave with one hand—the modestly-lowered interest rates and annual fee waivers—they have been quietly taking back with the other, through a profusion of new fees, shrunken grace periods, and costlier methods of computing finance charges.

If you have a decent payment history and are armed with some basic knowledge of the industry's tricks and traps, you should nonetheless be able to get a credit card with an annual interest rate at least several points below the national average and with a full 25-day grace period.

THE BASICS

Credit Card Jargon

Do credit cards have you confused yet hooked? If so, you're not alone. According to the Consumer Federation of America, the nearly 60 million American households with outstanding balances had an average of more than $7,000 of credit card debt.

Surveys have shown that many cardholders lack basic information about the plastic cards filling their wallets. Here are the definitions of the basic terms:

Credit cards and charge cards. They're not the same. With credit cards, you are borrowing money when you choose not to pay your entire outstanding balance. Most credit cards are sponsored by banks, although department stores, oil companies, and large corporations like General Motors and General Electric sponsor them, too. Charge cards (also called travel & entertainment cards) do not charge interest and require you to pay your entire balance each month. American Express, Diner's Club and Carte Blanche are charge cards.

Annual membership fee. This typically ranges from nothing to $25 for a regular card and $45 to $50 for a gold card.

APR. You are charged interest on your outstanding balance for the use of the card issuer's money. This rate is expressed as the APR, or annual percentage rate. The actual APR is usually higher than what the card issuer says it is because finance charges are added to your outstanding balance, so you pay interest on your interest as well as your balance. A 16.4% rate, for example, actually becomes 17.69% if you revolve a $100 balance for one year, make no other purchases, and interest is compounded monthly, as it is with most cards.

Grace period. The time the issuer gives you to pay off the new balance before assessing finance charges is called the grace period. It's often measured from the close of the billing cycle to the payment due date and is typically about 25 days long. You owe finance charges if your entire outstanding balance is not paid during the grace period.

Fixed-rate and variable-rate interest. With variable-rate cards, the interest rate is adjusted automatically (usually every quarter) and is keyed to an index, typically the prime interest rate. Fixed-rate cards maintain the same interest rate—unless, of course, the issuing bank decides to change it, which it's supposed to tell you about in advance.

How to Find the Cheapest Card

Compare interest rates and fees. If you are among the approximately 36% of cardholders who always pay the entire monthly bill, then you are what the industry calls a "convenience user." Technically, you shouldn't care if the interest rate is 100%, so long as the card has a sufficient grace period to give you plenty of time to pay without incurring a finance charge. What you do want is a card with a low or no annual fee.

If you usually have an outstanding balance, then the annual fee will not be nearly as important as finding the lowest possible interest rate. If you virtually never pay off your entire balance, opt for a card with no grace period; such cards usually impose the lowest interest rates of all.

What if you do both—pay it all off some months, revolve charges in other months? You might want to carry both a low-interest-rate credit card and a charge card. Reserve the credit card for major purchases you know you will have to pay for over a long period and use the charge card for purchases you plan to pay off right away.

You can save a lot by switching to a lower-rate card. Say you use a Visa card to buy a $1,000 refrigerator. If you make only minimum payments, in this case 2.8% of the monthly bill, and your card issuer charges 19.8% annual interest, the true cost will be $1,349 after two years. If you had charged it on a 12% card, you would have paid

EVERY LITTLE BIT COUNTS

Interest rate*	6 months	12 months	24 months	36 months	48 months
19.8%	$1,096	$1,186	$1,349	$1,490	$1,611
18%	$1,087	$1,168	$1,312	$1,434	$1,534
16%	$1,077	$1,148	$1,272	$1,375	$1,455
14%	$1,067	$1,128	$1,234	$1,319	$1,380
12%	$1,057	$1,109	$1,197	$1,265	$1,311

*On a loan of $1,000.

only $1,197. The $152 savings would be enough to stock that refrigerator with groceries. The chart above shows how much you'd spend on finance charges on $1,000 over varying periods of time for several different annual interest rates.

Switching cards isn't difficult. Most issuers offer free transfer checks. But be very wary of low "teaser" rates offered to card switchers. Mailed solicitations may proclaim annual rates as low as 4.9% in large headlines, but smaller print reveals that after only a few months, the rate jumps to the 16% to 19% range. And consider that if the teaser rate applies to balance transfers, and if you're transferring a sizable balance, you might not be able to pay off the entire balance before the rate rises. Other small print may further disclose that the introductory rate applies only to purchases, not to cash advances.

Issuers increasingly pick and choose among their applicants when setting interest rates, giving lower rates to applicants with better credit histories. This makes it hard to comparison shop for the lowest rate because you are kept in the dark about the most important credit card term—the interest rate. For instance, Wells Fargo Bank's application recently listed three possible rates ranging from 12.50% to 20.05%. There's no indication of what you need to do to get the 12.50%. The GE Rewards card has two possible rates, prime plus 8.9% or 12.4%. And some issuers reveal even less. When the "teaser" rate expires, Providian Bank will establish an APR of between 5.9% and 15.9% "that is lower than the lowest non-introductory APR you are currently paying."

If you already have a card with a top rate and think you deserve better treatment, and if your issuer has tiered rating, you might not need to switch. Try calling the customer service number and asking for a reduction. If your credit record is pretty good, threaten to switch to another issuer unless they give you a reduction.

Is a variable- or fixed-rate interest card better? Variable-rate cards, which typically have lower interest rates because you assume the interest rate risk, can make it harder to budget—with the rate changing periodically, you can never be sure just how much that refrigerator will end up costing. So, if you're not the gambling type, stick with a fixed-rate card. But choose carefully—the interest rates on many fixed-rate cards have remained just that, *fixed,* at high levels.

If you sometimes pay your bill late, be aware that with more and more issuers, if you are a certain number of days late, the rate automatically increases rather dramatically. For instance, Fleet Bank's Classic and Gold card APR rises to prime plus 12.0%—20.25% at this writing—if you "made late payments or exceeded the credit limit during the immediately preceding Account Review Period." Some issuers are much vaguer, with card agreements saying that your APR will remain the same "provided your account is in good standing."

Compare fees. When assessing which card will cost you less, be sure to take into account the various fees that may be charged. These may include:

■ *Over-the-credit-limit fee.* If you don't keep close tabs on your spending and accidentally exceed your credit limit, even by only a few dollars, most issuers will slap on a fee of $15 to $25, up from $10 or $15

when the last edition of this book was published in 1994.

■ *Late payment fee.* Most issuers now charge a late fee of $15 to $25 if your payment arrives after the payment due date (it's printed on your monthly statement). To add insult to injury, interest is usually also charged on fees. And ten-day late-payment grace periods have been shortened to one or two days. A 1997 study by Consumer Action, a national consumer advocacy organization, found an average 26% increase in this fee since 1995.

■ *Annual membership fee.* Most issuers have dropped the annual fee. The big exception is rebate cards. Some issuers waive the fee only for the first year or only if you use the card at least once a year.

■ *Transaction fees for writing a check against your credit card or for a cash advance.* These fees are usually 2% of the total, although a few issuers charge 2.5%. There is a $2 or $3 minimum and a $10 to $20 cap. So use your credit card to get cash only as a last resort. And watch out for the cash advance "convenience checks" some issuers will send you if you are a new cardholder. They're really just a convenience for the issuer to charge you fees and cash advance interest rates, which may be higher than interest rates for purchases.

■ *Other fees.* New fees are being invented every week. Advanta Bank, one of the biggest issuers, charges $25 if you close an account after an increase in the APR and $15 for every half-year period during which you failed to charge anything to your card. Bank of America charges $3 for each extra copy of a previous statement and $15 an hour for "research you request." If you hold a First Premier Bank card and ask "too frequently" for account information, you will be charged $1 a month.

Assess rebate offers. There has been an explosion in the number of cards that rebate a percentage of the value of your card purchases in the form of cash, airline tickets, or merchandise discounts. Back in 1986, the Discover Card was probably the first to offer rebates—you get back a small percentage of your charges as cash. More recent offerings are the AT&T Universal Card, the GM-Household Bank MasterCard, and the GE Rewards MasterCard. The GM card offers a 5% rebate on all card purchases, which is then deductible from the cost of GM products as well as a 10% rebate on purchases from GM "partners," such as Avis and MCI. The GE Rewards MasterCard has a 2% rebate applicable toward purchases at 27 different retailers, ranging from Macy's and Lens Crafters to K-Mart and Volvo. The Ameritech card offers higher rebates to customers who agree to forgo the grace period, lower rebates to all others.

Perhaps the most popular of the co-branded Visa and MasterCards cards—co-branded cards carry the name of an issuing bank and a sponsoring retailer—are those offered by the major airlines. Most of these cards pay holders one frequent flier mile for each dollar charged on the card.

Many more retailers have recently climbed on the co-branding, rebate bandwagon. Typical are the M&T Bank-Fisher Price card (offers points toward U.S. Savings Bonds), Wachovia Bank-BMG Entertainment card (holders earn points redeemable for concert tickets, award shows, compact discs, and other merchandise and perks), and the TJX-People's Bank card (gives rebates at TJ Maxx and Marshalls stores).

Cards offering rebates and discounts can be a good deal. Indeed, the Ford Motor Company thought their Ford-Citibank Visa and MasterCard was too good a deal and deep-sixed it in 1997. Ford's liability if all cardholders had redeemed their rebates had reached an astounding $4 billion. Additional issuers have canceled cards or reduced rebates. For example, in 1996 GM lowered its annual rebate cap from $1,000 to $500 for its Gold MasterCard.

Now for the downsides of rebate and co-branded cards. Since finance charges could quickly offset the value of the rebates, and APRs for these cards tend to be either average or above average, they make sense only if you usually charge a lot on them *and* don't accumulate a large outstanding balance. The United Airlines Mileage Plus Card is typical in charging 18.40% annual interest (prime plus 9.9%) at a time when good credit risks can snare cards for annual rates of 15% or less.

In addition, rebate and co-branded cards often charge an annual fee that could be as much as $50; most regular cards waive the annual fee. So if you have one of the co-branded airline cards, the value of a free ticket after charging $25,000 to the card (i.e., to earn the required 25,000 frequent flier miles for a domestic round-trip) may be nearly offset by the annual fee. (If it takes three years to accumulate the 25,000 miles, and the annual fee is $60, that's $180 right there.) Also consider that at many airlines, frequent flyer miles start to expire after a few years.

You may also have to buy merchandise at specified retailers. What if you've been charging everything on a GM Mastercard and when you go shopping for your new car your local Ford dealer makes you an offer you can't refuse. Finally, cash rebates may not be worth all that much in the long run. If you make $4,000 in annual purchases on a Discover card, you'll get only a $40 rebate; you might do better with a card whose APR is less than Discover's.

What to Do About . . .

Lost cards. If you lose your credit card, you are not liable for any charges—as long as you notify the issuer before any unauthorized charges are made. You also pay nothing if someone fraudulently used your card number and you still have the card.

So what do you do if you lose your card, then learn that the finder took it to Tiffany's for a spending spree? No problem. The most you're liable for is $50, as long as you report the loss by calling the customer service number on your statement. There's no time limit. It's not legally required, but it's a

good idea to follow up with a written notification to the issuer.

If you discover that someone else has used your credit card number, Bankcard Holders of America recommends that in your letter to the issuer, you say that an "unauthorized charge" was made; if you don't use these words, it may be treated as a billing error, and restrictive rules (explained below) will apply.

Most issuers try to persuade you to sign up for a credit card registry service when they send you new or replacement cards. For a fee of about $15, you make only one call to this service; it will cancel all your cards and order replacements. Since it should take only a few minutes to cancel a card yourself, this service is hardly worth it unless your wallet is chock-full of credit cards or you're too busy to take the time.

Billing mistakes. If you find an error on your bill—say, you did not get the promised credit for the $2,500 crystal chandelier you bought on a whim and returned—the law says you have 60 days from the date that the bill containing the error was mailed to dispute the charge *in writing* to your card issuer. It's a good idea to use certified mail, return receipt requested. You do not have to pay the disputed portion of your bill, and you can still use your card while the issuer investigates. The issuer has 30 days to acknowledge in writing receipt of your letter. Within two billing cycles (or a maximum of 90 days), the issuer must have conducted a reasonable investigation and either corrected any mistake or explained why *you* are mistaken. When writing, state your name, account number, the amount of the mistake, and the reason you think the bill is in error. The creditor cannot impose a finance charge on the disputed amount pending an investigation.

Defective merchandise. If your problem is with the *quality* of goods or services, and if the cost was at least $50 and they were bought in or within 100 miles of your home state, different rules apply. Depending on your state's law governing your right to withhold payment to a merchant, you might be able to withhold payment from the credit card issuer, as long as you made a good-faith attempt to resolve the problem with the merchant. In fact, the card issuer may very well have charged back the amount to the merchant, so your dispute will be directly with the merchant.

If you regularly pay off your entire balance, you should withhold the disputed portion and immediately raise your claim with the merchant and the card issuer. One of the advantages of revolving charges is that—since you haven't fully paid for the merchandise yet—you preserve the leverage to withhold payment from the card issuer.

Avoiding Fraud

Massachusetts' practice of imprinting Social Security numbers on drivers' licenses led to six months of bureaucratic misery for Susan P. after she used her license as identification for a check written at a store. A thief saw her Social Security number, memorized it, then used it to order a new MasterCard, giving her first name as Susan and attributing a different last name and a new address to a recent marriage. After charging several thousand dollars' worth of purchases, the pseudo-Susan figured the coast was clear and ordered credit cards from two department stores on which she racked up even more charges. Eventually, the impostor used Susan P.'s good credit to buy a new car—with a $14,000 loan from the General Motors Acceptance Corporation (GMAC).

Susan P. learned about the thefts only when she ordered a copy of her credit report to apply for a mortgage. All of the borrowings were in default, and it took Susan six months to clear her record. The credit bureau repeatedly ignored her letters and put her in what she called "voice mail hell" when she telephoned them directly. The Massachusetts Attorney General's office said they couldn't help; even the local police department said they could do nothing.

In desperation, Susan phoned "Call for Action" on Boston radio station WBZ. The Attorney General's office was suddenly much more accommodating when WBZ called on her behalf and put her in touch with the Cambridge Consumer Council and the Massachusetts Public Interest Research Group. They advised her to get in touch with the creditors and, through GMAC, Susan tracked down the impostor and eventually straightened it all out. She learned that the thief had been borrowing off her good name for three years.

Unfortunately, Susan P.'s story is not unusual. Fraud cost credit card companies more than $1.5 billion in the United States in 1992.

Retailer Credit Cards

There's one big exception to the recent trend in slightly lower credit card interest rates: cards issued by department stores and oil companies. Although they impose no annual fees, most such issuers still charge interest rates several percentage points above even the costlier Visa cards and MasterCards. For example, as this is being written, Sears still charges 21.07%, Kmart 21.47%, Bloomingdale's 21.6% and Office Max a phenomenal 21.96%. If you need to buy on credit and your department store or gas station accepts Visa, Master-Card, Discover, or Optima, use these cards and keep your store-brand card in your wallet, where it can't hurt you.

WHAT TO WATCH OUT FOR

The incredible shrinking grace period. A "full grace period" used to mean 28 to 30 days—that is, an entire month. A few years ago, card issuers started to redefine "month" as only 25 days. And 20-day grace periods may be on the way. Robert V. discovered this when he was paying his "Citibank AAdvantage" Visa bill and just happened to notice that the "Payment Due" date

was five days earlier than usual. In fact, his payment was due the next day. Knowing that a late payment would trigger hefty finance charges on his entire outstanding balance, which he fully paid each month, he called Citibank to complain. "Don't worry," he was told, the payment date would be moved back. He had merely been randomly selected for a "test" in which payment due dates were moved several days earlier.

Cardholders had not been specially notified of the change because the very fine, light print on the reverse side of the monthly statement disclosed that the grace period "is not less than 20 days"—although the bank had been allowing 25 days. So keep an eye out for shifting payment due dates on your monthly statement and read all the small "mouse type" in your contract and on your statements.

Some issuers effectively reduce grace periods simply by taking their time putting your bill in the mail. The end of the billing period might be, say, the 16th of the month, but when you check the postmark you might notice that your statement did not leave the issuer's office until the 23rd of the month. Before you realize it, your promised 25-day grace period has been reduced to a mere 18 days. Add the three or four days it may take the statement to reach you, and your effective grace period is now only 15 days. With normal postal delays, it's a good idea to mail your payment at least five days before the due date, further compressing your effective grace period into about a week.

Minimum and skipped payments. Card issuers love it when you charge up a storm and then send them only the minimum payment each month. That's how they make their money. And they make it exceedingly easy to pay very little, typically requiring that you send only a minuscule portion of the total monthly balance. In fact, the average minimum payment percentage has been reduced from 5% to less than 3% since the mid-1980s. But don't take the bait. You'll be paying for what seems like an eternity and forking over a lot more interest. For example, if you buy a $2,000 dining room set at a 15.9% interest rate and make only minimum monthly payments of 2.083%, it'll take you 207 months (more than 17 years) to pay it off, and you'll fork over $2,944 in interest. The dining room set will end up costing nearly $5,000.

The following chart, prepared for this book by Mark Eisenson, author of *The Banker's Secret*, shows what a major difference a slight difference in the minimum payment makes in your total payout. The chart assumes you borrowed $2,000.

You have to wonder how total interest or very similar costs for cards with the same annual interest rate differs so much. The answer is in the hidden aspect of credit card math: the minimum percentage payment.

Moral: *Always* pay more than the minimum because even a very small difference in your minimum payment makes a big difference in total interest cost and payoff period.

WHAT A DIFFERENCE THE MINIMUM PAYMENT MAKES*

Interest rate	Minimum payment	Total interest cost	Months to payoff
19.8%	2.000%	$7,636	502
19.8%	2.083%	$6,271	425
17.65%	2.000%	$4,479	353
17.15%	2.500%	$2,332	210
17.1%	2.083%	$3,636	298
12.25%	2.500%	$1,141	133
10.15%	3.500%	$589	106
10.15%	3.000%	$714	122

* On a loan of $2,000.

Around year-end holiday time, some issuers suggest that you skip your January and February card payments. Be careful! They're playing more Scrooge than Santa. Such "deferred payment" programs are a trap—you'll still accrue interest on your entire outstanding balance during the skipped months and end up with even more to pay off.

Instead, try to pay off as much principal as possible. *The Banker's Secret* explains that paying just $50 a month more than the minimum payment against $2,000 in credit card charges (at a 20% interest rate) would save more than $6,500 in interest and cut 30.5 years from the payment period. At the least, try to make your payment just after receiving your bill in order to lessen your average daily balance and the impact of compounding of finance charges.

What you see is not necessarily what you'll get. To encourage you to fill out an application, many card solicitations are now for ostensibly high-prestige Platinum Cards, often with high credit limits. But you still might be sent the plain old Classic card. A typical example is First USA's Real Jazz Platinum Visa solicitation, which says that the credit limit is $5,000 to $10,000. But an asterisk refers you to very fine small print at the bottom of the page, which very significantly discloses that "in certain instances, you may receive a Classic card with a credit line of up to $5,000."

Sometimes you might not get any card. Federal law has been revised to allow issuers to turn down someone who receives in the mail a "pre-approved" application.

Incentives to charge more. Every time you charge something, there's a greater chance that you will not pay your entire bill and that you will incur finance charges. Since issuers make most of their profit from the finance charges, many of them are adopting financial incentives to encourage you to carry a balance. Here are some examples: GE Rewards MasterCard charges some of its members a $25 annual fee for never carrying an outstanding balance and charges some of its other members a $20 "maintenance fee" for not having at least $25 in finance charges. A Chase Manhattan Bank Gold Card charges a lower APR if your balance exceeds $2,500. And while the BancOne TravelPlus Card offers one point toward specified travel benefits for each $3 charged on the card, the offer is sweetened to one point for each $1 charged if you have an outstanding balance.

Transfer tricks. If you're transferring an outstanding balance from your current high-interest-rate card to one with a lower rate, make sure the low interest rate on the transferred balance is the same as for new purchases, and not the higher rate sometimes charged for cash advances.

Card offers for travel accident insurance, lost luggage assistance, emergency roadside help, and extended warranties. You probably will never need these services or you have them already. There could be a lot of paperwork for you to fill out when you do use them.

Affinity cards are issued by a bank in conjunction typically with a museum, college, or charity. Each use of the card generates a donation to the organization. Usually it comes to very little, maybe 25 cents per transaction. If you regularly pay finance charges, you may very well qualify for a card elsewhere with a significantly lower interest rate; it might make more sense to write a check to the organization you wish to support than to pay needless interest charges on one of these cards.

THE $MARTER CONSUMER

Tear into small pieces every unwanted credit card application. Otherwise a thief—maybe one of the people the industry refers to as a "dumpster diver"—may find it in the garbage, fill it out with a supposedly "new" address, and get a card in your name. Organized dumpster-diver rings exist in many areas.

Be aware of the date your monthly statement usually arrives. If it doesn't show up within a few days of when it's supposed to, prevent "account takeover" by notifying the issuer immediately. Someone could have stolen the statement from the mail and used the information to order first-class plane tickets to some far-off locale.

Never disclose your account number in response to a call, postcard, or ad you receive. Give your number over the phone only to a reputable business that you call. For similar reasons, destroy anything that may have your credit card number on it, like travel ticket stubs and copies of charge slips. If you have to give your card number to make reservations, for example, try to get the name of the person asking.

Never write your address, phone number, or Social Security number on a credit card slip (or your credit card or social security number on a check), even if a merchant insists. There is no legal requirement to provide this information; your signature is enough.

Destroy your expired cards to prevent anyone from altering and using them.

Check the issuer's reputation before applying. Many cardholders are under the mistaken impression that Visa or MasterCard issue credit cards. They don't. And since it's the bank that actually issues and services the card, one Visa or MasterCard is not like another. The quality of service varies.

Judy H. learned this the hard way when she opened her monthly statement and noticed a charge for a rental car—in Hawaii. She called her card issuer, a medium-size bank, to complain that she had never set foot in the Aloha State. They agreed to drop the charge once she showed them that she had incurred charges in her hometown on the same date she was supposedly driving around Hawaii. She was told to deduct the rental charge from her bill and that everything would be fine.

But it wasn't. The bank didn't remove the car rental charge until three more billing cycles. And Judy—who scrupulously paid her entire balance every month—started to accumulate finance charges on everything she charged on the card, since she had not paid the bank her *entire* outstanding balance. When she called and wrote to the bank to complain about the finance charges, the bank deducted from her next bill only the finance charges pertaining to the car rental, but not the charges accrued on the rest of her outstanding balance. When more phone calls and letters still didn't resolve the problem, Judy threw up her hands and resignedly paid the remaining outstanding finance charges. Then she canceled the card.

The second lesson of this story: You will become a "revolver" and owe finance charges on your entire outstanding balance unless you pay off *every penny* of your balance by the due date.

Use your grace period. One good way to take full advantage of your grace period is to make major purchases at the very beginning of your billing cycle. This allows you to add the one-month billing period *and* the grace period and therefore effectively borrow money for up to 45 days interest-free. Of course, this works only if you paid off your previous balance in full and therefore don't incur finance charges.

If you want to cancel your card, the law provides that you do not have to pay an annual fee as long as you notify the issuer in writing within 40 days of receiving the statement containing the fee.

Collision damage waivers are a useful "perk." One credit card benefit that might actually save you real money if you travel and rent cars frequently: The card issuer picks up the cost of car rental companies' collision damage waivers. You may save $8 to $12 a day. (See page 558 for a full discussion.)

Pay down your highest-rate card first, not the one with the biggest balance.

Avoid a rejection complex. Since retailers' cards are often easier to get than a regular Visa or MasterCard, you might start to build a credit record by getting a card from a department store you regularly patronize. (Just don't take long to pay your balance; retailers' rates are very high.) If you have had a good payment record for a year or more, you might "graduate" to a Visa or MasterCard. But be sure not to apply for two or more cards within several months of each other; issuers have access to your credit records and may get nervous that you are overextending yourself and may not approve your application.

Another route to building your credit record is through a secured card. Secured cards look just like regular Visa or MasterCards, but they are secured by a bank account deposit equal to the amount of the card credit limit at the issuing institution. On the downside, you will not be able to draw on this account as long as you use the card. And interest rates may be higher than for regular cards.

Platinum isn't necessarily worth more than Gold. So many people now carry the once-prestigous Gold Card that issuers came up with the Platinum Card. Platinum Visa cards are supposed to offer a credit line of at least $5,000, 24-hour-a-day customer service, and other perks like travel accident insurance. But so do Gold cards. With the possible exception of the American Express Platinum Card (which comes with a $300 annual fee) there really isn't a difference. Platinum loses its luster when you consider that nearly half the credit card solicitations mailed in 1997 were for Platinum cards.

HELP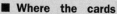

■ **Where the cards are.** Ask for CardTrak, a $5 monthly report on 500 low-rate, low-fee cards from Ram Research. Call 800-344-7714. Internet address: http://www.ramresearch.com. Ram also has a list of secured cards. Consumer Action, a national consumer advocacy organization, has issued a free survey of 73 cards from 48 issuers. Send a self-addressed stamped envelope to Consumer Action Credit Card Survey, 116 New Montgomery Street, Suite 233, San Francisco, CA 94105.

■ **Swimming (drowning?) in credit card debt?** Call 800-388-2227 for the name of your local consumer counseling service.

■ **To help you avoid** fraud, Visa USA will send you their "Credit Card Owner's Manual," a free booklet on card fraud and personal credit management; call (800) VISA-511 to order.

■ **Report merchants who impose a** minimum credit card purchase requirement to: Visa U.S.A., Minimum Purchase, P.O. Box 8999, San Francisco CA; MasterCard International, Customer Service, P.O. Box 28468-0968, St. Louis, MO 63146-0968; American Express, Executive Consumer Relations, 200 Vesey Street, New York, NY 10285-3130. Include name, address, and phone number of the merchant and a receipt for the purchase if possible.

BANKING ON BANKS

The Safety and Soundness of Your Accounts

Y ou've probably seen one of those newspaper or TV bank ads depicting cheerful consumers saving money and time because their bank is so convenient and the staff so helpful. Unfortunately, feel-good bank ads rarely reveal anything very useful, such as the monthly checking fee or the early withdrawal penalty on a certificate of deposit (CD). And their pricing claims can be misleading. "Low minimum balances" can be a lot higher than the competition's, "free" checking can turn out to be expensive, and a savings account can fast become a "losing" account once hidden fees are paid.

You can save quite a bit of money by shopping around for a bank as carefully as you would shop for a VCR. For example, a 1998 ranking of 50 local banks based on fees and interest rates by the NYC Public Advocate's Office determined that when interest earnings and fees were totted up, a hypothetical customer with a consistent yearlong balance of $2,600 would have *made* $105.79 at the cheapest bank and *lost* $110.32 at the most expensive one.

THE BASICS

Checking Accounts

L et's start with checking accounts. There are two basic kinds, regular and NOW (negotiable order of withdrawal).

You might have opened your first checking account in high school or college. If that was in the 1970s or earlier, chances are you weren't charged more than 10 cents for each check you wrote, plus a modest check-printing fee. Since then, however, checking account fees have increased dramatically. A certified check that cost only 25 cents in 1979 will now set you back $2 or $3.

Still, if you check around for checking, you needn't overpay. The minimum balance to avoid a fee on a regular checking account could be as little as $100 or as much as $3,000, and the monthly service fee could range from only $1 to as much as $12.

"Regular checking" is the best choice if you have only a few hundred dollars in the bank, because the minimum balances to avoid fees and the fees themselves tend to be lower than for NOW "interest on checking" accounts. NOW checking accounts have significantly higher fees because interest is paid—although the interest may not amount to much, since interest rates plummeted in the early 1990s.

Some banks offer what they call "relationship banking," which lets you add together all your account balances to reach the free-checking minimum.

How much can a NOW account cost? In 1998, New York's Citibank, a national price leader, required customers to have a hefty $6,000 in combined balances to avoid paying $12 a month and 50 cents per check or automatic teller machine (ATM) withdrawal.

Monthly and per-check charges aren't the whole fee story either. Increasingly, fees are charged for the use of ATMs. Because ATMs save banks money, they were free when the machines were introduced in the late 1970s. But by the mid-1980s, as banks felt the pressure to make up for both their huge real-estate and third-world loan losses, they began viewing ATMs as revenue-producers in their own right. Besides charging

up to 50 cents for a withdrawal or transfer if you fail to maintain a minimum balance, most banks now also charge special fees of up to $1.50 to use another bank's ATM in a shared network like NYCE or HONOR. A Study by the Consumer Federation of America in 1993 concluded that banks make 78 cents pure profit for each ATM fee dollar. With even greater ATM fees since then, this percentage may have increased.

One of these new fees is the double-dipping surcharge: you'll usually pay $1 to $1.50 to a bank where you don't have an account for the use of its ATM. This surcharge has been permitted ever since the Visa Plus and MasterCard Cirrus ATM networks lifted a surcharge ban in 1996. The double-dipping surcharge started tentatively, at only a few banks, but by 1997 the U.S. Public Interest Research group found that 45% of the nation's banks were imposing this surcharge. When you add this surcharge to your own bank's ATM fees—say, $1 for each withdrawal from another bank's ATM—you could end up shelling out $2.50 just to get your own money.

> "**B**anks have a four-part strategy to earn fee income by gouging consumers. First, they are raising fees. Second, they are coming up with new fees. Third, they are making more people pay fees by raising the balances necessary to avoid fees. And fourth, they are changing those balances from averages to minimums."
>
> —EDMUND MIERZWINSKI,
> Consumer Program Director, U.S.
> Public Interest Research Group

Some banks even charge $1 or $2 for the privilege of phoning to find out how much of your money they have.

Stop-payment-order fees also are often hefty, ranging from $5 to $20. Be sure to ask the bank how long the stop is effective for. Usually, but not always, it'll last six months. Also, most banks put stops into effect immediately, but some take up to 24 hours.

STEALING COOKIES FROM A BABY

In 1994, ten-year-old Ryan Lorraine Cobb told a panel of Congress members what happened to the $54.50 she had earned for selling 109 boxes of Girl Scout cookies. The State Department Federal Credit Union charged her $12 when a check someone had given her bounced. She was charged another $12 when it didn't clear a second time. And she was hit for another $15 for bouncing a $7 check she had written because she didn't know the deposited check had bounced. Word got around, and besides testifying before Congress, Ryan appeared on the *David Letterman Show.* The embarrassed credit union gave Ryan back her $39 in fees and donated an additional $100 to the Girl Scouts.

How do you find the checking account that will cost you the least? Look first at savings banks. Generally speaking, savings banks—especially smaller neighborhood banks—offer better deals than big commercial banks with many branches. The bigger banks used to be able to say that the convenience of having so many branches outweighed their higher costs, but now that even small savings banks have joined shared ATM networks, this argument is not as persuasive.

Next, calculate your average monthly balance and the number of checks you wrote each month for the last year or so and apply this experience to the different checking accounts at the banks you are considering. How often would you have fallen below the minimum balance for free checking? How much would you have paid in monthly, per-check, or ATM withdrawal fees? Use your final cost figures to compare competing banks. If two banks' costs are close and you're considering a NOW account, then include in your calculation how much you would earn on your money.

Debit cards. An increasingly popular way to access the money in your checking account that avoids checks altogether is the debit card. Debit cards look like credit cards, but they deduct the amount of your purchase directly from your checking account.

There are two kinds of debit cards: on-line and off-line. On-line debit cards work like an ATM card. Once you've punched your personal identification number (PIN) into a

YOUR MONEY...ALMOST

Item	Day funds are available	Day available for deposits over $5,000 and for new or problem accounts
LOCAL CHECKS	*2nd business day following day of deposit*	*7th business day following day of deposit*
NON-LOCAL CHECKS	*5th business day following day of deposit*	*11th business day following day of deposit*

terminal in the store and the bank's computer verifies that you have enough money to cover the purchase, the sum is deducted from your checking account immediately. And there's the rub. Immediate deduction means you lose the interest you would get during the several days it can take a check to clear (i.e., you lose the "float"). The "float" could be as long as 45 days if you pay with a credit card (billing period plus grace period).

Most banks' ATM cards now double as on-line debit cards. You might not even be aware that you are carrying a debit card in your wallet right now. In addition, Visa and MasterCard have rolled out on-line checking account debit services as add-ons to your bank ATM card.

Off-line debit cards, which are sponsored by Visa (Visa Check Card) and MasterCard (Master Money) are accepted in the same places as the corresponding credit cards. Your debit card goes in the same machines to process your payment. Since it usually takes several days to clear the charge, you still enjoy a brief "float."

Debit cards aren't free. Issuing banks may charge $1 or $1.50 a month for off-line debit cards. You might be charged as much as a dollar per transaction when you use an on-line card. You may also have a daily purchase limit of several hundred dollars.

Recently, both Visa and MasterCard changed their rules in order to clear up a serious security problem. The applicable law says that debit card users could be liable for a far bigger portion of unauthorized withdrawals than credit card users—up to $500 if they don't notify the issuer within two business days of learning that a debit card is missing, and sky is the limit for not reporting within 60 days. In 1997 MasterCard and Visa agreed to cap liability at $50 regardless of when the problem is reported and to limit liability to zero if it is reported within two business days.

How long to clear a check? Every bank should do the same thing when it comes to clearing a check. Because banks use your money for days without making it available to you, the federal Expedited Funds Availability Act now limits how long banks can take to make deposited funds available to you. What the law requires is outlined on page 389.

Cash, electronic payments, and certain low-risk checks (such as government checks) must be made available the first business day following the day of deposit.

Savings and Money Market Rate Accounts

There are two kinds of savings accounts: passbook accounts and statement savings accounts. With the former, you get a passbook in which your current balance and interest earnings are recorded. With the latter, you get a monthly or quarterly statement instead of a passbook, and you can access your money through an ATM; you may also be able to have your account status included on a monthly statement that presents the status of all your accounts at a bank.

The two most common methods of figuring how much interest you earn are "day-of-deposit to day-of-withdrawal" and "average daily balance." Day-of-deposit to day-of-withdrawal is better—you earn interest on every dollar every single day. The average daily balance method pays interest on the average daily balance for the month or quarter, depending on the bank. In addition, market rate accounts sometimes offer tiered interest rates; you earn at a lower rate if your balance goes below a minimum.

Money market rate accounts differ from savings accounts because they allow you to write checks, although usually no more than three a month. Banks introduced these accounts with interest rates higher than savings accounts to keep customers from defecting to money market funds. But these accounts still pay less than real money market funds, because they are insured by the Federal Deposit Insurance Corporation (FDIC).

Good news for all "deposit account" (savings, checking account, money market rate account, CD) customers: The federal Truth-in-Savings Law requires banks to adopt a uniform manner of disclosing how they figure your fees, interest rates, and yields, including minimum deposits and balances, and they must tell you this when you open your account and on periodic account statements after that. You can compare banks through their APYs—annual percentage yields.

Certificates of Deposit

CDs tie up your money for a set period of time in return for a higher rate. As a general rule, the longer the term, the more you earn.

Shop around for the highest possible yield. Many local newspapers publish CD rate charts comparing area banks. Since you cannot deposit into or withdraw from a CD once you open it without paying a penalty, how convenient the bank is to you should not be a major factor in your choice. In fact, it's not even necessary to visit the bank—in many cases, everything can be handled by mail.

When you compare one CD to another, compare the yield, not the rate. Interest on CDs is not necessarily compounded. Some CDs, such as those bought through brokers, pay only simple interest: For example, if the rate is 4% and you open a one-year CD for $1,000, you'll have $1,040 when it matures. CDs may also compound interest daily, weekly, quarterly, or even semiannually.

Don't worry about CD fees; there aren't any. But the penalty for early withdrawals is usually three months' interest on CDs of less than one year and six months' interest on others.

Banks have devised many clever new CD products to lure you away from other investments. These special CDs might promise to keep pace with increases in college costs or to double the average return of a stock index. Others offer variable rates—the rate could be indexed to U.S. Treasury bills and adjusted monthly, for example. Rule of thumb for these innovative CDs: No bank simply gives away money.

Credit Unions

Credit unions are financial institutions open to people who have a "common bond." No, a passion for blues music or bungee jumping does not qualify. You usually have to belong to a sponsoring labor union or work for a particular employer to join. Approximately 37 million Americans belong to federally chartered credit unions.

The rationale for credit unions is that people gain financially when they pool their money and lend directly to one another without shareholders to siphon off profits. A 1992 survey by the publication *Bank Rate Monitor* bore this out: Credit unions pay about one percentage point more on CDs, and their rates for auto loans, credit cards, and personal loans are, on average, below the national average.

To top it off, credit unions also typically charge lower fees *and* have ATMs. They managed to avoid the banking industry crisis of the 1980s because they made relatively few of the types of commercial loans that got banks into such deep trouble.

One indication that credit unions must be a pretty good deal is that the banking industry is accusing them of competing unfairly and wants Washington to regulate and tax credit unions more severely.

Bank Account Insurance

It used to be that each account at a bank was insured for up to $100,000. If the bank failed, you could have a million dollars in your name at one bank and you wouldn't lose a dime, as long as it was divided into at least ten different $100,000 accounts.

It's not so simple anymore. Now the FDIC adds up every dollar you have in the bank in a *separately titled account* in each *ownership category* and reimburses you only for a maximum $100,000 per title (i.e., owner name(s)) in an ownership category at each bank. The most common ownership categories are individual

COVERING YOUR ASSETS

Here's how "Bonnie" and "Clyde" can deposit $600,000 in the same bank and still be protected.

INDIVIDUAL ACCOUNTS

Bonnie $100,000
Clyde $100,000

JOINT ACCOUNTS

Bonnie and Clyde . . . $100,000

JOINT ACCOUNTS

Bonnie as trustee
for Clyde $100,000

RETIREMENT ACCOUNTS

Bonnie $100,000
Clyde $100,000

accounts, joint accounts, trust accounts, and retirement accounts such as individual retirement accounts (IRAs) and Keoghs. You still can hold several accounts and each will be covered, as long as each account is in a different ownership category or your name appears along with a different name on each account.

You also used to be able to count on the government to bail you out if your bank failed and your deposits exceeded the $100,000 ceiling. But in 1991, Congress passed a law making it harder for the government to reimburse depositors for amounts exceeding the $100,000 insurance cap. Besides slowing depletion of the Bank Insurance Fund, the idea behind the law was to get large depositors to pressure banks into operating more soundly—which seems an unfair expectation of the not untypical middle-class American family that just sold its house and is parking the proceeds at a bank for a while.

So you have to be careful. Over 8,500 depositors lost a total of $108 million when American Savings Bank of White Plains, New York, failed in the early 1990s. The *Wall Street Journal* reported on one depositor, Helen Patterson, who had saved more than $100,000 to buy her retirement home. The FDIC didn't fully reimburse her.

Unfortunately, there's no free phone number to call to learn if the bank holding your nest egg is about to fold. The FDIC keeps lists of problem banks, but they won't tell you if your bank is on it because that could start a bank run. But for $10 you can learn how your bank rates on a soundness scale. (See **HELP** at the end of this chapter.)

Bank Safety

Banks lose billions of dollars a year through fraud. Thieves with the right information can pilfer personal accounts—a Social Security number can be used to order new checks sent to a "changed" account address. Easy access to your credit reports (see "Consumer Privacy," page 640 for a full discussion) can provide thieves with even more information that's useful for impersonating you. Or, if thieves have your ATM card and somehow learn your PIN, they can go on a spending spree with your money.

IF YOU LOSE YOUR ATM CARD

When you report card loss to the bank	Monetary limit on your liability for unauthorized use
BEFORE FINDER OR THIEF USES IT	*Responsible for no charges*
WITHIN TWO BUSINESS DAYS AFTER YOU REALIZE IT IS MISSING	*$50*
AFTER TWO BUSINESS DAYS FROM WHEN YOU REALIZE IT IS MISSING	*$500*
MORE THAN 60 DAYS AFTER RECEIVING THE BANK STATEMENT WITH THE UNAUTHORIZED ACTIVITY	*The sky's the limit. (Don't forget that a thief with your ATM card might also be able to access your overdraft line of credit.)*

Should you become an ATM fraud victim, don't panic. The chart above shows how great a loss from your bank accounts you can be liable for. (If your state's law or your contract with the issuer provides for lower limits, those limits apply instead of the limits in this chart.)

Banks are reluctant to release figures on ATM crime, but it's clearly a problem. Crooks know you have money when you're leaving an ATM, and they can force you to withdraw up to the daily maximum. Almost any kind of card with a magnetic strip can open an ATM vestibule door.

In response, New York City enacted an ATM safety law that could become a model for the nation. ATMs are required to have surveillance cameras, rear-view mirrors, and door locks that only the bank's own ATM cards can open. Other localities are now considering similar laws. Also, Chicago and Los Angeles are pioneering a new concept: placing ATMs in higher-crime neighborhoods in or around police precinct buildings—locations that provide potential customers with greater security.

WHAT TO WATCH OUT FOR

Checking Accounts

New fees and tricky rules coming down the pike. Banks are thinking up new fees every day. A few have started charging a fee for each day your account is overdrawn. In 1994, 85% of banks charged a fee if you unwittingly deposited a check that bounced—up from 35% in 1991— and some banks charged for closing a checking account within six months of opening it. There may also be a "dormant fee" if the account is inactive for six months.

ChexSystem. Big Brother is watching you. When you open an account, most banks will check you out with ChexSystem, a national computer database, to see if you have previously bounced checks or engaged in some sort of financial shenanigans. Since about the only notice of this review that many banks give you is a small ChexSystem sign somewhere in the branch, you may be incorrectly or unfairly listed and not know it—and thus not know to challenge it. (See **HELP** at the end of this chapter for contact information.)

Many banks will automatically reject you if your name was added to the ChexSystem database during the last five years. Consider this story from San Francisco Consumer Action about Amy L.: She had a joint bank account with her husband, who had bounced $8,000 worth of checks. Although they were later divorced and she paid all the bounced check fines, she was turned down for a checking account because *her* name was listed with ChexSystem.

Non-return of canceled checks. Rising numbers of banks offer lower-cost "truncated accounts" that send you only an "image" of your check and only if you ask for it and pay a fee. Be sure to ask before opening the account if you get your canceled checks—or at least copies of them—back automatically.

Stopping payment on a check. Sure, you're angry that the VCR is still broken after you spent good money on a repair. But think twice before stopping payment on the check you gave the repair shop. It could then be treated as a bounced check, with potentially unpleasant legal and credit-rating consequences for you.

Stand-alone ATMs. Since 1996, when Visa Plus and MasterCard Cirrus dropped their ban on ATM owners surcharging, there has been a proliferation of stand-alone ATMs not owned or operated by banks. By 1997, the stand-alones accounted for nearly one-quarter of all ATMs.

But the convenience of an ATM in your local drug or convenience store doesn't come cheaply. The surcharges are usually at least $1.50 per withdrawal and can be as much as $2.50—surcharges in remote areas are higher. Part of the reason for high stand-alone fees is that the merchant hosting the machine gets a cut.

Be sure to find out the amount of the fee before you withdraw money. Fee disclosure on some machines is clearer than on others.

Higher fees after a merger. Seems like every week brings a new headline about another bank merger. If your bank is involved in a merger, it is more likely than not that whichever bank's fees are highest will apply to the merged institution. So keep an eye out for a fee hike.

Savings and Money Market Rate Accounts

Savings accounts were pretty basic in the '70s. You needed only $1 to open a passbook account, and if you were a kid and earned $200 for a summer of chasing toddlers or pushing mowers, you didn't have to worry about the bank whittling away most of it by the next summer. Now you have to be careful.

Balance minimums. If your savings account balance falls under a minimum level, you are likely to be charged monthly or quarterly penalty fees—and to forfeit interest. The fee itself could be as high as $5 a month.

Stiff check fees. Money market rate accounts may charge a stiff per-check fee if you write more than three checks a month.

Certificates of Deposit

Low interest rates. You can no longer rely on three- and six-month CDs to pay a significantly higher rate than savings accounts.

Bank takeovers. If another bank takes over your bank, the CD interest rate might be reduced. You'll be notified of this and given a period of time within which to withdraw your money without penalty.

Automatic rollovers. The bank will automatically roll over your CD for the same term if you ignore the maturity notice. You might not want this to happen if the new rate is lower or if you need the money.

Credit Unions

Few mortgage bargains. Mortgage interest rates tend to be the same as they are at banks in the same markets, since all mortgage originators (including credit unions) unload their mortgages on the same secondary market.

A limited number of offices. Unlike banks, most credit unions don't have a lot of branches, and their locations might not be convenient.

A credit union isn't *always* cheaper. Some savings banks are very competitive, and rates and fees vary among credit unions.

Bank Safety and Soundness

Warning! Don't come too close to $100,000 in one account. Interest earnings could propel you above the limit by the time a CD matures. (You can get around this by asking the bank to send you periodic interest checks.)

THE $MARTER CONSUMER

Checking Accounts

Check into check-printing fees. You'll probably pay less if you don't use the bank's designated check-printer. (See **HELP** at the end of this chapter for alternatives.)

Consider overdraft protection. You'll pay a high interest rate, but you only pay if you use it. As long as you are overdrawn for only a few days, an overdraft loan will probably still be significantly cheaper than the bank's bounced-check fee.

Ask about lower-cost accounts. "Lifeline," senior citizen, veterans, and student accounts may allow you to write from six to eight checks a month for one relatively reasonable flat monthly fee. But look for a potentially steep per-check charge if you exceed this limit. Under the 1994 New York lifeline account law, the bank can treat your account like a regular account for the months when this occurs.

Demand a waiver of unwarranted bounced-check fees. If you wrote several checks one day and every one bounced, the bank may have played a little game with you—clearing the largest one first and treating it as an overdraft, thereby ensuring that the others also bounce. This generates a separate bounced-check fee for each check. Demand to know which check cleared first and ask for fee waivers if it was the biggest. Banks engage in this tactic with increasing frequency. *American Banker,* an industry publication, reported one bank executive exclaiming, "Since we started clearing the largest first, our income in our small bank has gone up over $80,000 a year!" In 1998, Core State Bank settled for $12.2 million on class action law suit in a Philadelphia court for allegedly engaging in this practice.

Actually read the pamphlets banks stuff in your monthly checking statement, especially anything printed in small type and black and white—it's probably telling you about a fee increase or a money-costing rule change.

Use your debit card to avoid high ATM fees. Say you're on a shopping expedition and you need cash. If your bank charges for using another

bank's ATM and if you withdraw cash from an ATM not owned by your own bank, the total withdrawal fee could easily exceed $2. However, many banks charge no fee at all for use of their online debit card, or the fee may be only 25 cents. If you pay for your purchases with the debit card rather than from withdrawn cash, you can save a few dollars.

Savings Accounts

The fee/interest rate balance. Evaluate whether you are going to keep enough money in a savings or market-rate account to offset fees. You might find it makes more sense to keep all your money in an interest-bearing checking account—or even a regular checking account—if the fees and interest forfeiture would eat into your savings.

Certificates of Deposit

Analyze the yield. When CD-shopping, ask the bank how much money you will have at the end of the term instead of relying on the annual yield to compare offerings. Advertised yields are good only for one-year CDs. If you are buying, say, a six-month CD and you let it roll over when it matures, the rate could drop later in the year and the actual one-year yield could be a lot less than you had anticipated. Odd-length terms, like 11 months and 15 months, make it especially difficult to use the annual yield to compare banks' CD offerings.

Diversify your CD maturities. If you want to put a lot of your money into bank CDs, buy a mixture of short- and long-term ones. If rates decline, some of your CDs will still be earning excellent yields. If rates go up, you'll have funds to reinvest at the new yields.

Shop the nation for a higher yield. (See **HELP** at the end of this chapter to learn how.) Another way to earn more is with insured bank CDs bought through stockbrokers—although the broker takes a small fee and the market price of your investment may go down if CD rates rise. On the other hand, you avoid early-withdrawal penalties (there may be a small early-withdrawal service charge). If you go through a broker, ask for the name of the CD's bank(s) and check if they are financially sound by calling Veribanc (see **HELP** for contact information).

If you opt for a variable-rate CD, make sure it has a high minimum interest rate (i.e., "floor") and be sure to find out the index it is keyed to so you can follow it in the newspaper.

Credit Unions

Ensure that you're insured. Double-check that the credit union is insured by the National Credit Union Administration (NCUA). If it is among the 95% or so that are insured, you'll enjoy the same degree of deposit protection as if you were at a federally insured bank.

Bank Security and Safety

One reason to put money in a bank instead of under a mattress is to keep it safe. But if you aren't careful, the mattress could turn out to be the better depository.

Immediately report any unusual transactions that appear on your monthly statement.

Try to use ATMs during the day. If you must use an ATM at night, make sure it is well-lit—both inside and out—and in a well-traveled location. Stay clear of ATMs with people loitering about.

Opt for a unique PIN. Make sure your ATM PIN does not match any other numbers you carry, like your birth date or the first digits of your Social Security number. Don't write the PIN anywhere that someone might see it.

Don't leave your ATM receipts behind. Crooks can get useful information from them, like your account number and balance. If they also get your PIN, real damage can be done. PINs are sometimes obtained by sharp-eyed people hanging around ATMs and even by people using binoculars to watch your hand movements as you punch in your number.

HELP

■ If you get nowhere with the bank branch manager, take your complaints to a higher authority.

For *federally chartered commercial banks*, complain to the Director of Consumer Activities, Comptroller of the Currency, Department of the Treasury, 49 L'Enfant Plaza SW, Washington, DC 20219, (202) 287-4265.

For *state-chartered banks*, contact your state's banking department or commission. Complain about *federally chartered savings banks and savings and loan institutions* to the Office of Thrift Supervision, Consumer Affairs, 1700 G Street NW, Washington, DC 20552, (800) 842-6929.

Complain about *any bank that is a member of the Federal Reserve System* to the Consumer Affairs Division, Board of Governors, Federal Reserve System, Washington, DC 20551.

In addition to your own state's authorities, you may complain about *state banks that are not members of the Federal Reserve System* to the FDIC, 550 17th Street NW, Washington, DC 20429, (800) 424-5488.

■ Cheaper checks. Current Inc. sells 200 basic checks for $4.25 plus $1.95 handling; call (800) 533-3973 or www.currentchecks.com. Checks in the Mail also has low prices; call (800) 733-4443—you can get all the rainbow and scenery designs you want.

■ Certificates of deposit. To find the highest-paying CDs, check business sections of major national newspapers like *USA Today* and *The Wall Street Journal* or the weekly financial paper *Barron's*. Or subscribe to the newsletter *Highest Yields* by calling (800) 327-7717.

■ Bank soundness. To get a $10 safety rating of your bank, call Veribanc at (800) SAFETY-3 or (800) 44-BANKS. The ratings are updated every three months. If you know how to read financial statements, for $2.40 you can order your bank's quarterly balance sheet, called a "Call Report," from the federal government; call (800) 843-1669 to order.

■ For further explanation of how to figure out how safe your bank is, read the book *How to Keep Your Savings Safe*, by Walter L. Updegrave, an editor of *Money* magazine (Crown Publishers, 1992), $19.00

■ Need help finding a credit union? Call (800) 356-5710. (In New York State, it's (800) 342-5710.)

■ See if you are listed with ChexSystem, and why. You are entitled to a free report as well as to insert a 100-word rebuttal in it. Write to ChexSystems, Inc., Attn: Customer Relations, 1550 East 79th Street, Minneapolis, MN 55425.

CHAPTER 36

MUTUAL FUNDS

A Good Bank Alternative?

Millions of Americans have responded to low bank deposit rates and a raging bull market by voting with their feet—fleeing banks for alternative investments. Savers are not easily accepting a puny 3.0% return during the 1990s. And by 1997, 40% of all adult Americans had investments in the financial markets— mainly in mutual funds—double the proportion of a decade earlier.

No wonder increasing numbers of Americans have come to associate "Magellan" with a popular mutual fund rather than with a 16th-century explorer and, thanks to prime-time TV ads, the Dreyfus lion is practically as well-known as MGM's. Dazzling returns, baby boomers saving for retirement, and all of this marketing muscle help explain why mutual fund assets increased over 1,000% from $370 billion in 1984 to over $4 trillion in 1997.

> "**I** *don't care if a fund is named 'The Rock Solid Honestly Safe U.S. Government Guaranty Trust Savings Fund'—in any market investment, you stand a chance of losing your principal.*"
>
> —ARTHUR LEVITT,
> Chairman of the Securities and
> Exchange Commission

Of course, Americans have also been drawn to mutual funds by the promise of lucrative returns. According to Ibbotson Associates, which tracks financial trends, from 1926 to 1995 the total compounded annual rate of return from risk-free U.S. treasury bills was 3.7%; the return from slightly riskier corporate bonds was 5.6%; the return from blue chip stocks was 10.4%; and the return from small-company stocks was 12.4%. Doesn't sound like *that* much of a difference? Andrew Tobias, author of the perennial favorite *The Only Investment Guide You'll Ever Need,* points out that the compounded annual rate of inflation during that time was 3.1%; and forgetting taxes for a minute, $1,000 invested in Treasury bills over that time span would have netted $12,500; in corporate bonds you'd have ended up with $44,100; in large company stocks, $974,000;

and in small company stocks, $3.4 million. Each example assumes you reinvest dividends.

But past performance is no guarantee of how a fund will do in the future. Millions of investors learned this the hard way when some 93% of the mutual funds listed in *The Wall Street Journal*'s daily charts lost money in the first half of 1994. The dangers of "derivatives" contained in mutual funds—complex contracts that "derive" their value from underlying investments and whose value can fluctuate wildly—have also been in the news.

But if you are one of the 60% of people who aren't in the market (or you're in but are uncertain of your investment prowess), be cautious but don't be scared away—and don't let all the investment information swirling around you overwhelm or paralyze you. Whether the financial markets are booming or slumping, many mutual funds remain superior investments. The trick is knowing how to read prospectuses and ask questions of the fund's customer service representatives so that you'll understand exactly what a fund is investing in, how much it is costing you, and the true amount of risk you're taking on. Invest time before you invest money.

THE BASICS

What's a Mutual Fund?

Maybe you were always interested in playing the stock market but weren't confident enough to jump in. Well, mutual funds allow you to grab a share of the benefits of a bull market and leave the heavy thinking and worrying to the experts. Paul Samuelson, the highly respected economist, compared stock picking to mutual fund investing in one of his regular *Newsweek* columns: "What you lose is the daydream of that one big killing. What you gain is sleep."

This is possible because you pool your money with other investors by buying shares in a mutual fund corporation, not in individual investments. The fund managers then buy bonds, stocks, or money-market securities. A fund portfolio could include a few dozen or a few hundred different stocks, bonds, or other investments. So besides getting professional management, mutual funds may be advantageous because your portfolio, and therefore your risk, is diversified.

With one in three U.S. households invested in mutual funds, there now is more money in mutual funds than in FDIC-insured bank accounts. There are over 6,500 different mutual funds—more than the number of stocks listed on the New York Stock Exchange.

It's easy to buy into a mutual fund. (Maybe too easy: Surveys by the Investment Company Institute, the mutual fund industry's trade association, show that about half of mutual fund investors don't even open a prospectus before buying into a fund.) Just call a mutual fund company or broker's toll-free phone number to order a prospectus. You can also buy through a financial planner. Most funds require an initial investment of $500 to $3,000.

Increasing numbers of investors buy mutual funds at banks. It is estimated that banks sell as much as 30% of all mutual funds, up from virtually zero in the early 1980s. Why such growth? People trust banks, and it's easy to buy mutual funds at the same place you have your checking and savings accounts. A few of the big banks even sell mutual fund shares through their ATMs. And some banks have taken to posting bond yields next to the usual charts of CD rates. To make it even easier, banks are conveniently beginning to report the status of your mutual funds along with your other accounts in one monthly mailing.

Now for an issue of prime concern, especially to people thinking of investing in a mutual fund for the first time: risk. Like the securities they are comprised of, mutual fund values can go down as well as up. You own "shares" in a mutual fund corporation, not absolute dollars. If you must have complete safety and if you need to know exactly how much you'll have earned a few years hence, keep your money in a bank account.

But if you can take some volatility in the short term, mutual funds give you a better chance of realizing significant long-term gains.

Types of Mutual Funds

Money market funds invest in short-term debt securities in the money market, such as CDs and U.S. Treasury bills. Risk level is considered the lowest among mutual funds.

Bond funds, naturally, invest in corporate and government bonds. What's the risk in a bond fund? Bond fund values can tumble if interest rates jump, because investors earn better yields in new issues. The basic principle is that bond yield moves inversely to prices on the bond market. The risk is magnified by the effect of group psychology. If yields begin to climb strongly, many bond investors—especially neophytes who have been switching from bank CDs in large numbers—could get ice-cold feet and pull out of the bond market in a hurry, further depressing prices and scaring still more investors into leaving, creating a downward price spiral.

Of course, you get your entire principal back if you hold on to an individual bond until maturity as long as it doesn't default, but with a bond fund you might not if you bail out at a time of rising interest rates. Still, bond funds tend to be less volatile than equity, or stock, funds (see next page).

Municipal bond funds are popular in high-tax states because you don't have to pay state or local taxes on the earnings.

What are the chances of a bond defaulting? Pretty remote. And since bond funds are made up of lots of different bonds, you spread your default risk even wider.

Some bond funds are much riskier than others, which is why you should always understand exactly what is in the bond fund before you buy. Many people who bought into First Investors "Fund for Income" learned this the hard way. Some of the investors didn't understand they were actually buying junk bonds. Kenneth and Mary W. of Barkhamsted, Connecticut, lost most of their life savings, amounting to over $60,000. A sales representative had told them the fund was "very secure." When they expressed concern, the company representative assured them that the fluctuation would "correct itself." It didn't.

"Many investors are under the mistaken impression that bond funds are always less volatile and less risky than stock funds. In fact, bond funds can be every bit as risky, if not more so," warned Sue Anne Gilroy, Secretary of State in Indiana, in 1997 when the state settled its cases against First Investors, getting just 3 cents to 30 cents on the dollar for Indiana investors who got stung.

U.S. government securities are, of course, backed by Uncle Sam; if he defaults then we're *all* in deep trouble.

Equity (stock) funds tend to be more volatile than bond funds. Some stock funds emphasize providing "income" and so invest in high-dividend-paying equities, while others stress earning high market gains and so invest in stocks with high "growth" potential. Sector funds specialize in the stocks and bonds of particular industries; they are especially volatile. If you want more stability, think about buying an index fund. These buy the stocks of well-known stock indexes and seek to mirror their performance— say, the Standard & Poor's 500.

Balanced funds invest in a combination of stocks and bonds, and depending upon the mix and the investments themselves, may be more or less volatile than pure stock or bond funds.

International funds invest in foreign stocks and bonds. The level of risk depends on the type of investment. Generally, though, foreign funds are riskier. Some foreign markets are not as tightly regulated as ours, markets in some foreign countries tend to be more volatile, and currency fluctuations might erode fund value.

Gold and precious metal funds. If you're a pessimist and believe we're about to face a major war or a domestic uprising, you can always retreat to these investments—as well as to your fortified mountain redoubt. But risk is high when you put all your nest eggs in one basket. As with a sector fund concentrating on one industry, you've given up one of the stabilizing influences of mutual funds: diversification.

Stock funds are further distinguished by the size of the companies they invest in. There are three basic categories, divided according to "capitalization" (cap) or market value. Small-cap funds invest in companies with up to $1 billion in total market value; mid-cap funds buy stock of companies worth $1 billion to $5 billion; large-cap stocks are those worth more than $5 billion. Small-cap funds tend to be more volatile and hence risker; large cap funds are considered more stable. But keep in mind, the volatility assessments are just generalizations and actual volatility de-

WHAT YOU DON'T KNOW CAN HURT YOU

In November 1993, *American Banker*, an industry publication, spot-checked ten New York City bank branches for compliance with new mutual fund consumer disclosure rules. In only two of the branches did the staff volunteer that mutual funds, unlike bank deposits, are not federally insured. Mutual fund fees were seldom mentioned, and inappropriate investment recommendations were also heard.

pends upon market conditions and how each fund is managed.

The last important distinction among funds is "load" vs. "no-load." A "load" is a flat up-front sales commission of about 3% to 6%. Most of the funds sold at banks and through brokers are load funds. No-load funds charge no commissions and are usually purchased directly from the fund company, although some discount brokers also sell them. A "back-end load" fund charges fees (ranging from 0.5% to 6.0%) when you sell your shares. Often these fees decline the longer you hold the fund. Generally—and especially if you are investing short-term—you should favor no-load funds, because all of your money goes to work for you right away. And it pays off: On average no-load

funds have outperformed load funds, even before accounting for commissions and fees, which most load funds charge.

Performance

Several different indicators can be used to compare fund performance. You will often see fund ads touting the yield. This is computed by dividing total dividends for a time period by the current price per share. Yield is important, but a more comprehensive and potentially useful indicator is *total annual return*. It takes into account yield as well as changes in market value. A fund with a high yield may have shrinking asset values and, therefore, a reduced total return.

Some other indicator terms you may hear include *net investment income* (or loss), which is what the fund is earning in dividends and interest, after expenses, and *net realized and unrealized gains* (losses), which is a measurement of the fund's increase in value. *Net asset value* (NAV) is the price per fund share, which is the same as total fund assets divided by the number of shares, after distributions. Both the NAV and changes in NAV from the previous day are reported in daily newspaper quotations of mutual fund performance.

Choosing Funds

To decide which stock fund to buy, start by comparing the fund's performance (without dividends reinvested) over the last several years with one of the stock

FUND OBJECTIVES

Fund Objective	What It Invests In	Pros and Cons
AGGRESSIVE GROWTH	*Stocks of companies expected to have extra-high earning potential, including new and small companies.*	*High risk, more volatility, and low dividend payments, but high potential for excellent long-term growth.*
GROWTH	*Equities of companies expected to increase in value, especially larger and blue-chip companies.*	*Relatively high-risk; may have bigger "net realized and unrealized" gains—or losses—than with less growth-oriented funds. Dividend income is likely to be small.*
INCOME	*Income-producing securities that provide sizeable periodic payments; includes bonds as well as stocks that pay dividends.*	*Medium risk; when stock market drops, loss is cushioned by continued dividend payments.*
REASONABLE INCOME WITH MODERATE GROWTH– "BALANCED" FUNDS	*Stocks that have the potential for rapid increase in value and bonds, which provide a steady income stream and are not as volatile.*	*Income is reasonable—so is risk level—but growth potential is not as great as with riskier funds.*
SAFETY	*CDs, U.S. Treasury securities, commercial paper.*	*Low risk, but earnings are lower, too.*

indexes, such as the Standard & Poor's 500 and the Dow Jones Industrials. To compare bond fund returns, check against the well-known Shearson Lehman Government-Corporate Bond Index.

Be sure to find out about redemption fees of 1% to 2% of assets for early withdrawal, transaction or exchange fees, management or advisory fees of 0.2% to 1.6%, and ac-

count and administration fees of 0.2% to 1.0%. There also may be a Section 12b-1 fee (named after a section of the securities regulation) of as much as 0.75%, which is the percentage of the fund assets spent on marketing. Try to pick funds with 12b-1 fees below 0.25%.

When comparing funds, be sure to consider the expenses charged by the fund, as measured by the total expense ratio. Funds with low overhead put more money to work for you. Stock funds tend to have higher ratios, usually around 1.5%, because of the work involved in picking stocks. Basic bond funds should charge around 1%.

Remember that with the long-term effect of compounding, a slight difference in expenses and fees really mounts up over time. Take a hypothetical example. Let's say you have $1,000 to invest for 20 years. You are choosing between two funds, both of which will return 5% a year before expenses every year. If you choose the fund with a 1.5% expense ratio, you would have $1,990 after 20 years. If you choose the fund that spends just .5% on expenses, you would end up with $2,410. That 22% comes a lot more easily than chasing high annual returns from one fund to another.

One of the best ways to minimize the chunk of your investment

you lose to expenses: Buy index funds, which seek to mimic the performance of a given index by buying the securities that make up that index. Since the funds only buy and sell shares when the index's components change, management expenses are virtually nil, there are minimal tax effects, and an index fund tends to be broadly diversified.

Stock mutual funds specialize in a particular investment strategy. You choose among funds based on how well the fund matches your financial goals and your tolerance for risk. The chart on the opposite page summarizes the most basic major mutual fund objectives categories.

EXPERT ERRORS

In September 1992, *Money* magazine interviewed 32 of the practitioners listed under "Financial Planners" in the Santa Rosa, California, Yellow Pages. *Money* reporters asked a series of questions about professional practices and knowledge. More than half of the planners answered at least a third of the questions incorrectly.

WHAT TO WATCH OUT FOR

Tricky advertising. The Securities and Exchange Commission has fairly strict advertising rules, but due to understaffing, the rules are not enforced very well. So take mutual fund ads with several grains of salt.

That's what the New York City Department of Consumer Affairs did when in 1993 staff reviewed over 50 mutual fund advertisements that ran in daily newspapers and financial magazines. They found some very serious problems, including these gimmicks:

■ *Misuse of the words "guaranteed" and "insured."* An ad headline for Franklin's Valuemark II fund claimed, "Retirement Income Guaranteed for Life." The guarantee was provided by an insurance company, which promised that future payments would continue if the mutual fund went sour. But the "guarantee" in the ad was really only as solid as the insurance company that made it. A Franklin customer service representative admitted to the Department of Consumer Affairs that Valuemark II "has some risk."

■ *Exaggeration.* One Dreyfus ad trumpeted, "High Yields Without High Risk." Not exactly.

■ *Claims of "no fees."* The Vanguard Small Capitalization Stock Fund advertised, "The Portfolio does not pay investment advisory fees." But the prospectus said the fund pays 0.06% in "management expenses" and a charges $10 annual account maintenance fee. When it comes down to it, no fund generously provides the public with a free service.

Sales spiels. As confusing as the ads themselves are the claims you hear when you call a fund's toll-free number for information. A well-rehearsed representative may tell you your money will be safe because the fund has performed extremely well —which is no assurance at all of future performance. Or, if you ask about fees, they'll omit a few. Some will try to sell you investments that are inappropriate for your financial circumstances. Others cite high historical total returns; further checking might reveal that returns were extraordinarily high a decade earlier but that recent returns have been lackluster, although the average of all the years—the figure cited—still sounds impressive.

Brokers aren't necessarily any more straightforward. A broker might steer you to a fund with a higher commission—good for the broker but maybe not so good for you. And they get their commission no matter how the investment they sell you performs.

In defense of brokers, many do have real investment expertise and familiarity with a wide range of funds. If you're a novice, a broker might provide some comforting hand-holding, too.

Nonetheless, it's not all that difficult to choose a fund if you follow the advice in this chapter.

Believing the fund is government-insured. A 1993 survey for the American Association of Retired Persons and the North American Securities Dealers Association found that a disturbing 39% of consumers whose banks offer mutual funds incorrectly responded that the FDIC insures mutual funds —and another 43% said they did not know. Some banks are only sowing more confusion by attaching names to their funds that could make people believe the bank and the fund are insured as one. NationsBank sells *NationsFunds* and Boston's BayBanks has *BayFunds*, for example. If you buy a fund at a bank, remember that mutual funds are not insured by the government, despite the FDIC decal on the bank's door.

Banks call it "cross-selling" when they deploy their usual staff, accustomed to marketing CDs and checking accounts, to push alternative investments. Watch out! Cross-selling can get quite aggressive; staff earn commissions, and even the tellers might be awarded $10 bonuses for successfully referring you to a sales agent.

And if you are told the fund is insured by the SIPC—the Securities Investor Protection Corporation—know that this protects you only if the brokerage goes belly up, not if the investments themselves perform poorly. It's nothing at all like FDIC deposit insurance.

Believing a fund is "safer." Because of their broad diversification and low expenses, index funds are widely mistaken as safe. But their performance is wholly dependent on market conditions. Vanguard Group, to its credit, pointed this out in its January 1997 newsletter after a stunning 1996 performance of its S&P 500 index fund: Since index funds must be fully invested, shareholders participate fully in market run-ups, but they likewise feel the full effects of market tumbles. "And the declines can be terrifyingly steep," Vanguard reminded its investors.

Departure of a star manager. The fund manager who was responsible for the stellar returns that attracted you may leave for another fund. You might want your money to follow.

A wolf in sheep's clothing. Make sure what you are being sold is truly a mutual fund. Rosemarie Chaviano didn't, and she was sorry—and part of a class action suit against The Equitable Cos. alleging unlawful sales practices that led Chaviano and others to believe that the "Championship 2000 Contract" they bought was a mutual fund when in fact it was variable term life insurance. Chaviano says she was told that she could freely withdraw, without penalty, the $5,500 she invested. That turned out to be false, and to heap injury on injury, the policy

No Free Lunch at the Supermarket

Fund supermarkets like Charles Schwab's One Source or Fidelity Funds Network appeal to consumers because they consolidate paperwork and transactions. But investors pay for the convenience. A 1997 study by Morningstar Inc. showed that while investors are not directly charged for the costs of supermarket distribution, these additional costs may be built into the expense ratios of funds that participate. The average expense ratio of funds sold through Fidelity Funds Network was 1.37%; compare that to the average expense ratio of 1.08% for funds sold directly to consumers. And it's not just supermarket shoppers who pay. The higher expenses are paid by *all* investors, whether they shop at the funds supermarket or not.

levied substantial fees that drained her principal by $1,488 the first year she owned the policy.

Fee waivers. Be on the lookout to see if any part of a fund's fees or expenses have been waived. When the waiver period ends, fees and expenses may increase suddenly. By how much? The part of the prospectus after the fee table should tell you.

Funds of funds. These mutual funds made up of a mixture of *other* mutual funds haven't performed all that well: Merriman Capital Appreciation returned just 6.3% for the five years ended December 31, 1996. The S&P 500 over the same period returned 15.2%. Part of the problem is that you pay an additional fee to the manager who assembles the fund of funds. So you are, in effect, paying a second level of fees, which cuts into returns.

Performance measures. The raging bull market of the mid 1990s lifted fund performance into the stratosphere, which cannot continue indefinitely and which can distort your expectations of future performance. Be sure to look at a fund's record over the long haul. And if you are looking at 10-year figures, keep in mind that a fund's performance may appear to have improved substantially since several years ago— the market crash of October 1997 is no longer in the 10-year time frame.

The 1997 tax bill's capital gains tax changes could cut into your mutual fund returns, and mutual fund managers won't be paying much attention, since *you* pay the tax and it doesn't harm *their* records. The aver-

BEST TIMES WORST TIMES

Be careful not to buy shares just before a fund distributes realized capital gains. If you invest in a fund just before the capital gains distribution, you'll pay more than you have to for each share and you'll end up paying taxes on gains you didn't share in. This is because the share price is inflated by gains taken before you invested, and you will owe taxes on these gains. If you ask, funds will tell you the date they plan to distribute capital gains. It's typically sometime in December.

age stock fund turns over almost its entire holdings in a year—90% on average. In 1996, this meant that 29% of the capital gains distributed by U.S. stock funds were short term gains. This is bad news if you hold mutual funds in a taxable account. You pay taxes on realized capital gains. Under the new law, stock sold within a year could be subject to 39.6% capital gains tax. To avoid capital gains tax, keep your mutual funds in an IRA, 401K, or other qualified retirement account or buy index funds, which rarely sell their holdings.

Information overload. When it comes to mutual fund information, it can seem like there is *too much* of a good thing. A 1997 Merrill Lynch ad says it all: "With mutual funds, choice isn't the problem. It's choosing." Between personal finance magazines, Web sites, daily or hourly price quotes on financial news channels, books, and your cousin who got a hot lead from his mechanic, it's easy to become overwhelmed by all the investment information swirling around you. You need only enough information to make sound choices that meet your investment objectives and a small dose every once in a while to keep up with what is happening. Ignore the rest, and, as John Bogle, chairman of mutual fund giant Vanguard famously advises, "Stay the course."

Always read the prospectus before buying. Don't buy a fund based solely on an advertisement or on what a sales agent or broker said. Yes, these 15- to 20-page documents are more of a puzzle than a guide and often bury or obfuscate important information, such as whether the fund invests in derivatives, the degree of market risk, and the fees charged. Still, if you know what to look for and are patient, you'll find important information about the fund's past performance, objectives, and risk. And new model prospectuses written in plain English, required by the Securities and Exchange Commission, should make it easier to find key information and compare one fund to an-

other. For instanace, 12b-1 fees will now be called marketing fees. And there will be a bar chart to help you take into account risk and compare a fund's performance to that of a similar index. To summarize:

■ *The investment objectives* section says what the fund is primarily interested in—for example, growth or current income—and describes its principal investments.

■ *What the fund invests in* tells you about the kinds of bonds or stocks it buys. You'll find out here if it buys low-investment-grade bonds. It could take some digging, but you should also be able to discover if a fund invests in derivatives. Derivatives are very complex and possibly risky investments—usually traded over-the-counter—that derive their value from underlying assets, which could be anything from a stock index to a rate. And this value can change dramatically. Most major funds say somewhere, somehow that they can use derivatives. Among indications that it does: The prospectus says the fund "may invest" in other securities, such as "options, futures, forwards, swaps." Or derivatives could be disguised with terms like "income-enhancement opportunities" or "portfolio investment techniques."

Also look out for "asset-backed securities"; some funds were badly eroded in the first half of 1994 because their investments in mort-gage-backed securities went down when interest rates went up.

■ Under *the investment risk* section you'll find important statistics that indicate how volatile the fund has been over the years, how much it has paid out (dividends from net investment income), how much was earned from trading securities (distributions from net realized capital gains), and change in net asset value (the change in a share's purchase price).

■ *The summary of fees and expenses* is also very important; high expenses could turn a potentially good investment into a mediocre one. Or, as Ben Franklin noted, perhaps forecasting the mutual fund deluge: "Beware of little expenses; a small leak will sink a great ship."

■ *Description of managers' experience* is supposed to tell you the manager's name, how long he or she has been managing the fund, and business background. But funds managed by a committee need not disclose names. And, unfortunately, prospectuses tell you barely any more than the most basic information about managers, often omitting their academic degrees or their responsibilities at their previous jobs. Ignore boasts about the manager's guidance of a previous employer's fund. You aren't investing in *that* fund. Plus, while prospectuses are allowed to tout a manager's earlier successes, there is no requirement that they also disclose a manager's previous mediocre or lousy performance. And you can bet they won't.

Look for longer-term gain. Don't necessarily buy a fund based on one or two high-return years. Sure, fantastic performance in the last year or two may show that the fund managers have real savvy, and maybe they'll repeat their feat next year. Or it could have been luck.

Unless you really know what you're doing, it's best to go for funds with solid returns over several years—the longer the better.

Get more information. You might request a free Statement of Additional Information (SAI) and the fund's annual report before buying. You will find a detailed list of its investments and learn more about the fund's investment strategy, which is useful to know before you sink real money into any fund.

Don't put all your eggs in one basket. Protect yourself by diversifying as much as your investment objectives allow. You can do this by investing in one fund that in turn allocates its assets in a variety of areas that have different investment objectives. Or you can devise your own spread of mutual fund investments, perhaps with the help of personal finance software like Quicken or Microsoft Money or the advice of an independent financial planner.

Even the experts aren't so good at timing the market, and if you need to read this chapter, you shouldn't bother. You can only seize opportunities if you are savvy enough to recognize them and figure out how to capitalize on them. For proof how hard it is to pick the right moments to move your money in and out of the market, just look at how few managed funds beat the S&P 500 during the banner years of 1995 and 1996. Stick with your plan. If you had missed the best 40 days for the market in the 1980s, your portfolio would have been worth 25% less than if you had hung in there.

And don't chase high-flying funds. Funds often look best just before their investment strategy stops working—and if you aren't careful, you could arrive just in time for the slide. *Money* magazine figures investors trying to time the market or cashing in what looked like lagging funds to pile into hot funds missed out on gains of $44 billion in 1995 alone.

Wonders of the Web. Use fund family or discount broker Web sites to save time and money. But curb the impulse to play around with your portfolio just because it's cool and you can. The fees will probably outweigh any gains.

Don't be polite. Ask your broker about his or her credentials and dis-ciplinary history. You'd want to know about your doctor's, right? Too many people have lost their life savings because they were too polite to ask. Ask how much training and experience your broker has. Ask if he or she has ever been disciplined. And you can check your broker's disciplinary history yourself by calling your state securities regulator or the National Association of Securities Dealers, (800) 289-9999.

When you redeem mutual fund shares, tell the fund exactly which ones you want to sell. Selling the shares for which you paid the most will lower the capital gains tax you owe. Make sure you get written confirmation that says something like: "sell 50 shares purchased March 23, 1994, at $25 per share."

HELP

■ **There are many** ways to find out about a mutual fund's past performance. *BusinessWeek* magazine publishes an annual survey in February. *Forbes* publishes one in September. *Money* and *Smart Money* evaluate mutual funds throughout the year. An old standby is *Morningstar Mutual Funds,* a newsletter that costs hundreds of dollars a year but that you might be able to read for free at your local library. A cheaper, truncated *Morningstar Investor* newsletter that might be all you need is available for $79 a year; call (800) 735-0700.

■ **To get information about mutual** funds on-line, check out Mutual Fund World at www.mutualfundworld.com, the Morningstar Mutual Fund data bank at www.morningstar.net, and the Stock Smart web site at www.stock-smart.com. You can get performance history over various time periods for thousands of funds. And you can screen for a fund that fits your investment objectives and risk tolerance. But beware of information overload.

■ **If you want to know more about** mutual fund risk, perhaps the most comprehensive yet understandable explanation is found in a chart in Jane Bryant Quinn's book *Making the Most of Your Money* (Simon & Schuster, 1991).

■ **If you have a problem or question** about a mutual fund, the Securities and Exchange Commission may be able to help you; call its toll-free investor information service at (800) SEC-0330, or check the agency's Internet site at www.sec.gov.

CHAPTER 37

RETIREMENT NEST EGGS

IRAs, 401(k)s, and Annuities

Will Social Security benefits have to be scaled back when baby boomers retire *en masse*? Will the federal government insure your woefully underfunded pension? Will Social Security and a full pension together be adequate to maintain the lifestyle you've come to expect?

If questions like these keep you awake some nights, then you ought to think about creating a special nest egg. Three options for doing so are individual retirement accounts (IRAs), salary-reduction plans such as 401(k)s and 403(b)s, and annuities. And if you've already laid a nest egg, you may want to review your strategy in light of the tax law changes in 1997. There's a whole new IRA to consider, and the capital gains tax cut may take some of the appeal out of annuities.

Indeed, you may have no choice but to manage your own retirement fund, which could require learning about these investments. Increasing numbers of Americans are self-employed or work for companies that have abandoned the traditional

defined-benefit plans. In such a traditional plan, the employer contributes a fixed amount each year and you are entitled to a fixed pension for the rest of your life. Only 56% of employees of large and medium-size companies are covered by traditional defined-benefits plans, down from 70% as recently as 1988, according to the Employee Benefit Research Institute (EBRI) in Washington, DC. In many current plans, employers leave it up to the employees to determine how best to invest the company's contribution to the retirement program.

It's never too early to start planning for the "golden years." The earlier you start saving, the less you'll have to salt away each year in order to provide a secure retirement.

THE BASICS

Individual Retirement Accounts

Americans weren't saving enough. That was the premise

of the 1981 law that created IRAs. Congress believed that tax incentives would encourage Americans to save and invest more money.

It worked. And with the economy booming, the stock market roaring and many Americans feeling flush in 1997, Congress expanded the traditional tax-deductible IRA and created a new tax-free IRA. Here are the basic rules for traditional IRAs:

■ You and your spouse can each invest up to $2,000 a year from earnings in a range of investments, such as bank certificates of deposit, stocks, bonds, and mutual funds.

You've probably seen newspaper ads and TV commercials for IRAs just before April 15th every year. They tell you that you can still open an IRA with a lump sum up until April 15th and, if you're eligible, deduct your contribution from your previous year's tax return.

■ If you don't participate in a company pension plan, you can deduct the full amount you contributed to an IRA. If you do participate, you can still deduct the full amount if your adjusted gross income is no more than $50,000 in 1998 for joint filers (rising to $80,000 by 2007) and $30,000 (rising to $50,000) for single filers. You can deduct some of the IRA contribution if your income is under $50,000 (married) and $35,000 (single). Under the new plan, a non-working spouse whose partner is covered by a pension can make a fully deductible IRA contribution as long as household income is less than $150,000.

■ Whether you can deduct the contribution or not, you defer paying taxes on earnings until you start withdrawing money at age 59½.
■ You can move your IRA investments from one account to another, from one bank to another, or between bank accounts and other types of investments.
■ You can make penalty-free withdrawals to cover some college expenses and for up to $10,000 to buy a first home.

The downside of traditional IRAs: If you withdraw the money before age 59½, you pay a hefty 10% penalty and the taxes owed—although there are a few loopholes, such as if you become totally disabled or if you take "substantially equal periodic payments" over the course of your life.

In addition, you'll have to pay taxes if you don't start withdrawing by April 1st of the year after you reach 70½. Then you must withdraw enough each year to empty your account during your life expectancy, which is based on Internal Revenue Service (IRS) mortality tables. If you die before your predicted longevity and your surviving spouse is your beneficiary, she or he is allowed to roll over the entire amount into her or his own IRA with no adverse tax consequences. If you have already started taking required distributions because you are at least 70½, your surviving spouse can continue to take them. Since these are only the basics and the 1997 tax law changes are being phased in over a decade, ask your IRA custodian or your financial advisor for details.

BEST TIMES WORST TIMES

Make IRA contributions in January of the applicable tax year, not April of the next year. Thanks to compounding, you'll make easy money, $20,000 to be exact. Assuming 10% interest, that's how much more you would end up with if you contribute $2,000 to an IRA every year for 25 years, on January 2nd each time, rather than April 14th of the following year.

In the event you didn't start taking required minimum distributions, your surviving spouse can take distributions based on her or his life expectancy. Alternatively, she or he can take a full distribution by the end of the fifth year following your death. More special rules apply if the beneficiary is someone other than a spouse; again, follow up with your financial advisor or IRA custodian for details.

The IRA Plus, also known as the Roth IRA—named for its principal sponsor, Senator William V. Roth, Jr. of Delaware—will be a big hit with you if your income has been too high for you to benefit from the tax advantage of the traditional IRA. (And, no doubt you've noticed that it's also a big hit with banks and brokerages, which are feverishly marketing it.) As with the tra-

ditional IRA, you and your spouse can contribute up to $2,000 a year into an investment vehicle of your choice. Contributions are not tax-deductible, but income will not be subject to federal tax as long as the money is used for retirement or for the few other qualifying purposes. (At publication, it was not clear whether states and localities would also waive income tax on the Roth IRA.)

■ The income limits for full contributions to the Roth IRA are much higher than for the traditional IRA—$150,000 for joint filers and $95,000 for single filers. Contributions phase out as incomes rise to $160,000 for joint filers and $110,000 for individuals.

■ You can withdraw money tax-free starting when you are 59½, as long as the account has been open at least five years.

■ You can pull out an amount up to your original contribution at any time, penalty-free.

■ You can make penalty-free withdrawals for some college expenses and for up to $10,000 to buy a first home.

■ There is no requirement that distributions begin at age 70½.

■ You can move your account around as you wish.

For those people who qualify for both kinds of IRA, choosing between them comes down to predicting whether their income tax rate will be lower when they use the money than it is when they invest it. Preliminary projections suggest that the tax-free accumulation of gains means many people will come out ahead with the Roth IRA, as the chart below illustrates.

At this point you may be wondering whether you can convert your traditional IRA to a Roth IRA. You can. Tax is due on some or all of the money in your existing IRA (depending whether you funded it entirely with tax-deductible contributions). Anyone with adjusted gross income over $99,999 would get hit with a tax penalty. You would pay today for the promise never to pay taxes on the build-up in the Roth IRA. Whether you'll come out ahead with this maneuver is no simple calculation, but financial analysts say that for investors with non-deductible IRAs the switch may make sense since they've already paid tax on the money they contributed to their IRAs.

Individual retirement options got much more complicated in 1997. The basics are outlined above. Since each family's situation is unique, getting some personalized advice from your IRA custo-dian or a financial advisor is highly recommended.

401(k) and 403(b) Retirement Plans

Named after sections of the tax law, 401(k) and 403(b) employers plans are available to people whose companies establish them. Forty-two million Americans have invested in 401(k) and 403(b) plans.

Think of a 401(k) as a portable pension. Quite simply, your employer sends a certain amount of your paycheck to your 401(k) account. You invest it in one of several different investment plans your employer offers. You might be able to choose among a money fund, a guaranteed investment contract (in which insurance companies agree to pay a definite interest rate), a bond fund, a stock fund, a "balanced" fund containing both stocks and bonds, and, less commonly, an international fund and the company's own stock. The money fund and guaranteed investment contract

COMPOUNDING'S CONFOUNDING IRA CHOICES

Value of a $2,000 retirement investment after 10 years, assuming 8% annual return

Tax-deductible IRA		Roth IRA	
32% tax rate at contribution; 18% at withdrawal	32% tax rate at contribution; 32% at withdrawal	32% tax rate at contribution; 18% at withdrawal	32% tax rate at contribution; 32% at withdrawal
$4,640	$4,023	$4,318	$4,318

Source: Deloitte & Touche in *The New York Times*

present the least amount of investment risk; the international fund and the company's own stock, the most. And you can take the retirement fund with you when you change employers.

If you have a chance to join a 401(k) plan, grab it. To all of your company savings plans, including a 401(k), you and the company can together annually contribute either up to 25% of your net salary or $30,000, whichever is less. The maximum pre-tax 401(k) tax deduction increases slightly each year; it was a very substantial $9,500 in 1997. Earnings on additional contributions are tax-deferred.

As with IRAs, your 401(k) earnings are also tax-deferred. You can start making withdrawals when you reach 59½, and you must begin to withdraw by 70½ or pay a 10% federal tax penalty, with certain limited exceptions.

You direct this investment. You can change your investment allocations, usually quarterly. In addition:

■ When you leave the company, you can roll over your 401(k) savings into an IRA.
■ The majority of companies offering 401(k) plans match part or all of your contribution. This is free money. Andrew Tobias, in his bestselling *The Only Investment Guide You'll Ever Need*, presses the point: "If your employer offers a deal like this and you're not taking full advantage of it, you're an idiot. (Well, I'm sorry, but c'mon: if your local bank decided to give out free money to attract deposits—say, $500 for each new $1,000—there would be

riots in the streets, so eager would people be to get in on it.)"
■ Since your contributions are made through payroll deductions, you never see the money and you won't be tempted to spend it.
■ If you need cash, it is possible to borrow from your 401(k) fund under most plans.

Tax-Deferred Annuities

Tax-deferred annuities are investments sold by insurance companies that allow you to defer taxes on the income until later in life. They are like traditional IRAs with no limit on how much you can contribute (but you can't deduct your contribution). You pay one or a series of up-front lump sum payments to start, and taxes are completely deferred until you withdraw money, when regular income tax rates apply. The company puts your money in CDs, a mutual-fund-type account, or other investments.

During an "accumulation period," you pay no taxes on your earnings, which leaves you with even more money to reinvest. You pay taxes during the payout period, by which time you'll presumably be retired and the tax bite will be relatively modest on your reduced income. You can withdraw one lump sum or periodic payments.

You can invest in either a fixed-rate or variable-rate annuity. Fixed-rate means the rate is guaranteed for a period of years, usually from one to ten. After that, the company can adjust the rate at will, but most promise that it will remain competitive at a rate related to interest rates. There is a floor below which the rate can't drop, although it is always very low. Usually, the longer the commitment period, the higher the interest rate. The insurance company guarantees repayment of your principal. (Remember, though, this guarantee is only as sound as the insurance company itself.)

Variable-rate annuities are mutual funds in an insurance wrapper. You get to select the annuity's investments, which means that the rate of return depends upon the performance of those investments and can vary. *You*, not the insurance company, therefore assume all the rate risk. (See pages 401–402 in the previous chapter for a discussion of mutual fund investment risks, which are similar to the risks you would assume if you invest in a variable-rate annuity.) Your principal may also go up and down, although its return is assured in the guaranteed death benefit; even if the insurance company loses, say, half the principal, your beneficiary will still get everything that you had invested when you die. One of the nice things about variable-rate annuities is that you may be able to invest with your favorite mutual fund company.

Unlike investing in a mutual fund, though, you usually can't transfer money from a poorly managed family of funds to funds elsewhere. You're locked in, because, in return for the tax break, Uncle Sam imposes a 10% tax penalty on your interest earnings if you take money out of an annuity before you turn 59½. You'll pay an annual fee, typically around 1.4% of assets.

To compensate for the loss of future fees, you will also probably have to pay the annuity company a surrender charge when you begin withdrawing money. Usually, new surrender fees are imposed for each additional cash withdrawal. Most fixed-rate annuities allow withdrawal of up to 10% of the principal each year without charging surrender fees.

One advantage that annuities have over traditional IRAs is that you don't *have to* take your money out of an annuity at any particular time, while deductible IRAs require you to start withdrawals by age 70½. But annual fees and surrender charges take a big bite out of your gains. Thus, the performance of *your* annuity does not equal the performance of the mutual fund your annuity invests in.

Insurance companies, financial planners, stockbrokers, and increasingly, banks are only too eager to sell you annuities and grab fat fees. Before the tax changes of 1997, all of them talked up the tax-deferral feature to wealthy baby boomers nervous about the likelihood of retiring in the style they had come to appreciate. As a result, sales of variable annuities climbed tenfold in the decade between 1986 and 1996, with assets topping $400 billion, according to the Variable Annuity Research Data Service. But the capital gains tax cut made them somewhat less attractive. Pre-tax-change, financial advisors said it took 10–20 years for compounding and tax deferral to add up to enough to break even when compared to straight mutual funds. The

417

THEN, THERE'S SOCIAL SECURITY

In the early years of the Social Security program, there were 40 people working for every person receiving benefits. Now there are just three people working for every Social Security recipient. It's reasonable to wonder whether there will be anything left for your retirement. It's a good idea to send away for your free Social Security benefit record. You'll find out exactly how much you'll receive at a stated retirement age, as well as how much you'll get if you are disabled, and how much your beneficiaries will get if you die. You'll also see an historical accounting of your earnings subject to Social Security tax and the amount of Social Security taxes you paid each year. Your benefit record will also tell you if you've worked long enough to qualify for benefits. How to get one? Call (800) 772-1213.

Note: A law that took effect in 1995 requires the Social Security Administration to automatically mail a benefit statement to anyone who is about to turn 60.

Here's a tip: Hold off taking your social security benefit. If you begin taking benefits when you are 62, your monthly take will be about 20% less than if you waited until you were 65. In fact, the longer you wait, the more your benefit grows. For each year you delay after age 65 until age 70, your benefit will rise 3% to 8%, depending when you were born.

---

capital gains cut means the break-even point will probably be more like 20 to 25 years.

WHAT TO WATCH OUT FOR

Individual Retirement Accounts

Withdrawal penalties for certain kinds of IRAs. Banks usually charge an early-withdrawal penalty on CDs. Mutual funds may have minimum-withdrawal requirements. Before you get to the point of withdrawing, be sure to check early withdrawal penalties or restrictions.

And if your IRA is in a CD, avoid a bank penalty by withdrawing, transferring, or rolling over your money on the day the CD matures.

Before investing in an IRA, check the contract to see if there are any special fees for withdrawals; they could amount to $30 or so.

The 60-day reinvestment time limit. Your IRA can be paid to you if you choose to withdraw it, but to keep all the benefits, you must put it back into another IRA within 60 days. You also need to watch out for institutions that are slow to pay out; after all, you're no longer their customer—what do they care if they inconvenience you?

Other pitfalls. There are numerous tax traps aside from the 10% penalty for early withdrawal. Consult your tax advisor. (If you want to go it alone, IRS instructions booklet 590 explains IRA tax issues.)

401(k) and 403(b) Plans

Risk. Many companies have turned to 401(k)s because they don't want to be in the business of managing funds. And, under a U.S. Labor Department rule that took effect in January 1994, your employer no longer has any legal responsibilty for 401(k) losses you may incur, as long as they offer at least three broadly diversified investment options, provide ample information on the offerings, and allow you to shift your investments at least once a quarter. This rule should encourage employers with only one or two plans to beef up their offerings. But it also means that if you goof, you lose.

Don't overindulge on your company's stock. You are already dependent on your employer's fortunes for your job and your health insurance. If you have a choice, don't tie all of your retirement money to the same institution's performance, or you could end up sorry. Carter Hawley Hale invested the entirety of its employees' 401(k) money in company stock. When the company filed for bankruptcy in 1991, the stock, and the workers' retirement accounts, were worthless.

Get what you deserve. You can't take it for granted that your lump-sum payout or distribution is correct. You have six years from your first payment to double-check it. Ginny Burton got what seemed like a lot of money, $110,000, when she retired from Lord & Taylor in 1993. But a pension payout investigator found that she had been short-changed $60,000. She paid a third of that as a bounty to the investigator, National Center for Retirement Benefits Inc., but, as Burton pointed out in *Business Week:* "Most of something is better than zilch."

Management fees. The mutual fund you invest in will deduct management fees from your account. This usually amounts to about 1.5% of the fund assets each year.

Annuities

There's no free lunch. The insurance company sponsoring the annuity is not doing so out of goodwill. Management fees, mortality expenses, and administrative fees of up to $60 can add up to as much as 3% of your cash infusion. There may also be sales commissions. If such charges are high enough, you'll offset the benefits of tax deferral, meaning that your annuity must have a great rate of return to make it worthwhile. When the stock market does well, you may not notice the fees, but when the market turns down, a big fee will magnify the sting.

Alluring rates are often guaranteed for only a year. And the steady uphill graphs in the sales materials represent what *might* happen to your investment, not what necessarily will.

If you are in your 70s or 80s, annuities probably don't make sense for you. The money will not compound long enough for the returns to make up for fees and exceed the returns of regular mutual funds.

The guarantee is only as solid as the annuity company. Since fixed-rate annuities "guarantee" a rate, always look for insurance companies that will live up to the guarantee. Your best bets are those rated A or A+ by a rating service, such as A.M. Best or Standard & Poor's.

While annuity contributions are tax-deferred, they are not tax-deductible; contributions to an IRA or 401(k) plan may be.

Individual Retirement Accounts

Consolidate your accounts. Don't keep several small IRA accounts at different institutions. Avoid potential maintenance fees as well as the annoyance of keeping track of several accounts.

Need money from your regular IRA? You can get it without paying a tax penalty if you set up a schedule of "substantially equal periodic payments" for the rest of your life. You must withdraw on a fixed schedule *only* for at least five years and until you are 59½. Doesn't sound too practical for most people. But if you are in your 50s and need extra money for your child's college tuition, this may be the way to do it.

Another way to get at your IRA money, at least temporarily, is through a "tax-free rollover." You close down your IRA and maintain tax deferment by putting it in another IRA within 60 days. Meanwhile, you have 60 days to use your money. Before you try this, though, make sure you'll definitely reinvest the full sum on time.

401(k) Plans

Invest the maximum in a 401(k) plan, especially if your employer also contributes. They are a good deal—they combine large deductibility with tax-deferral. And you're contributing pre-tax money.

Avoid unnecessary switching from one investment to another. Many company retirement programs make it as easy as pushing a few buttons on the phone. Don't be tempted. For the 10 years between 1986 and 1995, Dalbar, a Boston investment research firm, found that investors who aggressively tried to time the market by moving money from one investment to another saw their portfolios grow about a third as much as investors who made their choices and then ignored their accounts.

Take your money with you. If you leave your job, roll your money over into an IRA or into your new employer's 401(k). When you switch, don't get a check made out to you. The IRS requires your former employer to withhold 20% of your money, on the assumption that you are cashing out. You would then have to come up with that money out of your own pocket to ensure that your entire account balance goes into your IRA or your new employer's plan. Instead, ask your employer to make a trustee to trustee transfer. Typically, you will get a check for the full amount made out to your rollover IRA trustee "FBO" (for the benefit of) your name. Be sure to get the check into your account within 60 days of its issue date or you'll be taxed on it.

Annuities

Ask about annuity surrender charges. If the surrender charge never disappears or is higher than that charged elsewhere and is not offset by a higher interest rate, go elsewhere—unless you're sure you'll never take the money out early.

When choosing a fixed-rate annuity, factor in the length of the guaranteed rate period and the interest rate offered. For variable-rate annuities, take a good look at their total returns for three years or more.

Good annuity alternatives can save you sales fees and insurance charges. The tax advantages are different, but they exist. Plus, there's no penalty for early withdrawal. Instead of a fixed-rate annuity, try tax-free bonds. And instead of variable rate annuities, look for a solid performing no-load stock fund that hangs on to its investments.

HELP

■ **For the ins and** outs of retirement investing, read *Making the Most of Your Money,* a very detailed book by Jane Bryant Quinn. (Simon & Schuster, 1991), $27.50.

■ **Want to know a lot more about annuities?** A weekly column on annuities appears on Mondays in *The Wall Street Journal.*

■ **Independent Advantage Financial** provides an annuity shopping service; call (800) 829-2887 for more info.

■ **Morningstar Variable Annuity/Life** Performance Reports tells you how most of the major funds have performed. $45 per issue; call (800) 735-0700 to order.

■ **IRS pamphlets and brochures may** be obtained by calling your local IRS office or (800) 829-1040; TDD consumers should call (800) 829-4059.

■ **The Variable Annuity** Research & Data Service tracks variable annuity performance data. Each thick issue is $49. Call to order.

■ **To do some retirement planning** on-line, check out the following helpful Web sites: Vanguard, www.vanguard.com; American Association of Retired Persons, www.aarp.org; and the Social Security Administration, www.ssa.gov.

■ **If you think your 401(k) short-**changed you, the National Center for Retirement Benefits Inc. will investigate—and keep 30% of any money it recovers. Call (800) 666-1000.

■ **To figure out which IRA is best for** you, try the computerized calculators provided by financial services companies via CD-ROM or their Web sites. You'll need to enter your age, income, and if you are considering converting to a Roth IRA, the value of your existing IRA.

MORTGAGES AND HOME EQUITY BORROWING

Financing Your American Dreams

I f you're like most Americans, you want to own your home—preferably a 14-bedroom mansion, but you'll most likely settle for a comfortable Cape Cod. And if you haven't inherited a small fortune, you will need to borrow a substantial amount of money to reach your goal.

So how do you (legally) get your hands on, say, $100,000? Are ads touting low interest rates and "no points" to be believed, despite the lengthy fine print disclaimers? How about the TV pitchman who "says yes" when your bank "says no"?

MORTGAGE BASICS

Different Kinds of Mortgages

S tated simply, a mortgage is an installment loan on your home. A lender gives you a large lump sum, which you add to your own money to buy a piece of property. Then over a period of years—called the term—you pay the lender back in monthly installments until you've repaid all the principal and the interest. Your monthly payments consist of the principal, interest, and extra money that sometimes is required to be deposited in an escrow account to cover property taxes and insurance.

In the early years of the mortgage, the lender makes sure it will profit from your loan by applying most of your monthly payment to interest charges. If you default after only a few years, you'll still owe practically the entire principal. Later in the term, most of your monthly payment will reduce the principal, as the chart on the facing page illustrates. It assumes a $75,000 mortgage, an annual interest rate of 10%, a 30-year term

(360 months), and a monthly payment of $658.18.

While mortgages come in a bewildering array of combinations of terms, rates, and special features—Norwest Mortgage Corp. of Des Moines, Iowa, alone offers 60 different loan packages—there are two basic types: fixed-rate and adjustable-rate.

Fixed-rate. The interest rate and the amount of the monthly payment is set for the entire term of the loan. The advantage is peace of mind—that you'll always know how much you owe. Also, if you're lucky at predicting the future course of interest rates, you might be able to lock in a low rate and pay less than you would if interest rates go up. Fixed-rate mortgages are always popular but have become more popular as home buyers and refinancers have taken advantage of the low interest rates of the 1990s.

With some fixed-rate mortgages, your payments increase slightly each month. The object of these "growing equity mortgages" is to pay off the principal sooner and thereby potentially save thousands of dollars in interest.

Another variation is the "graduated payment mortgage," designed to make it easier for you to qualify for a mortgage. You pay less than normal amortization for the first several years of the mortgage and more later on. The reduced payments are arranged by deferring interest. Of course, a big disadvantage of such a mortgage is that you may be too optimistic about your future earnings potential and be unable to afford the larger payments down the road. Another disadvantage is that graduated payment mortgages generally end up costing more over the entire term. Furthermore, they are not a wise choice if you are thinking of keeping your house for

360 MONTHS OF MORTGAGE PAYMENTS

$658.18 Payment	Interest Paid	Principal Paid	Remaining Balance
1ST	$625.00	$33.18	$74,966.82
2ND	$624.72	$33.46	$74,933.36
3RD	$624.44	$33.74	$74,899.62
358TH	$16.16	$642.02	$1,296.91
359TH	$10.81	$647.37	$649.54
360TH (last)	$5.41	$649.54	$0.00

only a few years because you will pay off too little interest; when you sell, you'll have to pay off *more* than what you borrowed.

Then there are "balloon mortgages" in which you still owe a substantial portion of the principal at the end of the payment period; it was not fully amortized. At the end of the term, you would presumably refinance or sell, if you can. The advantage to the borrower is that the monthly payments are lower than if it was a fully-amortizing mortgage, although the interest rate when you refinance years later could be high.

Adjustable-rate. In the early 1980s, banks began to transfer interest-rate risk to borrowers by introducing adjustable-rate mortgages. The rate changes at regular intervals, usually once a year, and is tied to a published index, such as the rate on U.S. Treasury securities. The margin is usually 1 to 4 percentage points above the index.

What's in it for you? The initial interest rate is lower than for fixed-rate loans. And, if national interest rates go down, so do yours. What's in it for the lender? If national interest rates go up, so do yours.

You won't know in advance exactly how much your monthly payment will go up, but adjustable-rate mortgages aren't completely unpredictable. Most include a "lifetime cap," typically 6 percentage points above the initial rate that the rate can never surpass and a "payment cap," which is the most the rate can increase in any adjustment period and is usually set at about 2 percent-

age points. Never get a mortgage without both caps.

A popular alternative to the straight adjustable-rate mortgage is known as a "hybrid" and gives a fixed rate for anywhere from 3 to 10 years that reverts to a variable rate when the specified term ends. As with a regular adjustable, the rate is tied to one of the indexes of benchmark rates. (If your mortgage broker quotes you a rate on a 3/1, you are discussing an adjustable mortgage with a three-year fixed rate that reverts to an adjusted rate that is determined each year.) Interest rates—and monthly payments—are lower than on a pure fixed-rate mortgage. This means you can qualify more easily. The catch? Once the fixed term is up, rates can swing as much as two percentage points in a year, and even if they don't swing that drastically, you still could get socked with more than you can handle. But if you don't plan to stay in your house longer than the fixed-rate period, these are good deals. However, if your plans change, you'll pay more over the long haul than you'll save in the early years of the loan.

How Much Will It Cost?

Borrowers are often shocked when they get their mortgage commitment letter and see for the first time how much the loan will end up costing when all the interest is paid. So compare carefully the interest annual percentage rate (APR). What is APR? It includes interest, "points" (explained later), and other mortgage closing costs

15 vs. 30 Years

Percentage*	Term	Monthly Payment	Total Interest Payment
8.5%	*15 years*	*$985*	*$77,300*
8.5%	*30 years*	*$769*	*$176,840*

*On a $100,000 loan

and presents them as if they were paid over a one-year period.

In addition to the APR, factors that affect how much the mortgage will ultimately cost include:

Term. The most common term is 30 years, although 15-year mortgages are becoming more popular. A longer-term mortgage may be appealing; by stretching out payments, each monthly installment is lower. But, because you are using the lender's money longer, you end up shelling out more for interest payments.

The chart above illustrates our point: Assume a $100,000 loan. The interest rates are the same, but when all is said and done, the 15-year mortgage will save you $99,540 in interest—no small change.

If you send the lender more money every month, you're reducing the outstanding loan balance on which 8.5% interest is due—and that's like putting the extra money in a tax-free 8.5% certificate of deposit. Also, you are increasing your equity in your home; if real estate values go up, that's a good investment, too. Another plus: Interest rates on 15-year mortgages are usu-ally slightly lower than on 30-year mortgages because the lender takes on less risk in the shorter-term loan.

However, several factors can offset much of the seemingly enormous gain in the chart above. First, if you take the 30-year mortgage instead of the 15-year one, you might be able to invest the difference between the $769 monthly payment and the $985 payment in something that pays better than 9%, especially if interest rates climb.

Second, tax write-offs partly offset the interest burden. However, Marc Eisenson, author of a book on the advantages of mortgage prepayment, *The Banker's Secret,* says that the tax benefit is often overstated because many homeowners opt for the standard deduction anyway. As New York City tax specialist Curtis Arluck put it, "In deciding between a shorter and longer term mortgage, tax implications are the tail and the amount of money you pay is the dog."

So selecting a term depends on your own psychological makeup (do you have such a strong aversion to debt that is it *important* to you to shed this obligation in only 15 years?), financial situation (a shorter

KEEP ON SHOPPING

A small reduction in the APR can produce enormous savings over the life of the loan. For example, after 30 years, a $100,000 mortgage will cost you a total of $245,584.80 in interest and principal if the annual interest rate is 7.25%, but only $239,511.60 if the rate is $7.00%. Decide for yourself if saving $6,073.20 is worth a few extra hours spent mortgage-shopping.

term locks you into making larger monthly payments no matter what happens to you financially), long-term plans (will the children you and your fiancée eventually plan to have hate you for making them share a room?) and alternative investment options. And remember, almost every 30-year mortgage allows you to send in larger-than-billed payments to reduce your principal and your total interest payments. So the best alternative in the chart above could be to take the 30-year mortgage and write a $985 check every month anyway, with the extra payment earmarked for principal reduction.

Fees. It's easy to overlook them when you are talking about spending thousands and thousands of dollars. But lenders charge for everything imaginable. The myriad fees add up quickly, and you have to be prepared to pay them. Plus, while the listed interest rates may appear similar from one bank to another, a comparison of all the various fees may make one lender's price significantly better, or worse, than another's. The lender is required to give you a ballpark estimate of all the up-front fees you will be asked to pay.

For openers, there's the application fee of anywhere from $50 to several hundred dollars and a property appraisal fee of $200 to $400. You may think your prospective dream home is perfect, but the lender will still want to have an engineer inspect it for structural problems and termite damage, and you'll foot the bill. (Of course, the engineer's report is very helpful for you, too.) You also may have to pay for your own credit report. These fees usually are not refunded if the loan application is rejected.

There's more: A recording fee of as much as $12 is charged for each document that has to be officially recorded. You have to pay your own attorney anywhere from $150 to $1,000 to represent you at the closing (discuss the fee ahead of time), plus you'll have to pay for the lender's attorney (ask if this is negotiable; it may be). Lenders also require title insurance, which protects both you and the lender by insuring that the seller is conveying clear title to you—that no other ownership claims, easements, liens, or judgments are filed against the property. Title insurance reimburses you in case the title searcher makes a mistake and overlooks something. The fee for it is based on the amount you borrowed; for a $50,000 loan, it can range from $150 to $300.

The biggest fee could be "points." One "point" equals 1% of the amount financed, so two points on a $150,000 loan comes to $3,000. While fees are generally not tax-deductible, points are, in essence, prepaid interest and are fully deductible as mortgage interest on an original home purchase. (Double-check with a tax advisor to be sure this remains true.) On a refinancing, points must be amortized over the life of the loan.

You'd think these levies (except for your own attorney's fees) would be included in your interest payments. After all, points were originally allowed in order to enable creditors to recover their costs and keep the interest rate below the legal usury ceiling—and loans rarely approach the usury ceiling these days.

Points allow the lender to discount the mortgage. The loan officer may tell you the interest rate is 7.5%, but if you are paying two points, the interest rate is closer to

MORTGAGE WORKSHEET

	Mortgage A	Mortgage B	Mortgage C
APR			
Points			
Total fees			
Term			
Loan-to-value ratio			
Index*			
Margin*			
Payment cap*			
Lifetime cap*			
Adjustment frequency*			
Adjustment period*			
Convertible?* When? Cost?			
Pre-payment penalties			

*For adjustable-rate mortgages.

8%, which is why it's so important to check the annual percentage rate. Why not just charge the higher interest rate and make the whole process a lot easier to understand? "That would be too simple and logical," says Robert Irwin, a real estate broker and author of the popular guide *Tips and Traps When Buying a Home*. "Lenders prefer to play games with mortgages and borrowers, sticking to an older and arcane system that uses discounts to make it appear that the interest rates are really lower than they are."

Taxes. Depending on where you live, the tax man may want to take a bite. Mortgage taxes won't vary from lender to lender, since they're set by the government. But keep in mind that they could total hundreds of dollars. For example, New York's mortgage tax is 1% to 2% of the amount borrowed.

How to Find a Mortgage

Start by gathering mortgage information from your local newspapers and by telephoning lenders. Organize the information into a worksheet. You can put several mortgages you wish to compare in separate columns on the same worksheet, as in the sample on the previous page.

For each mortgage, the worksheet should report the APR, points, fees (including application, credit check, appraisal, bank's attorney), term, and the loan-to-value ratio. For adjustable-rate mortgages, add the index, margin, payment cap, lifetime cap, adjustment frequency and period, whether the loan is convertible to a fixed rate,

and if there is a fee for doing so. For both kinds of loans you might also add pre-payment penalties and allowable debt-to-income ratio. For an adjustable-rate mortgage, also take into account the duration of any low introductory "teaser" rate—usually it's for just a year.

Now it's a matter of comparing the offerings for similar mortgages and answering such questions as:

■ Is an adjustable-rate loan with a lower APR a better deal than a fixed-rate loan with a slightly higher APR? The answer depends on how long you plan to keep the home, whether the adjustable-rate mortgage has a low enough lifetime rate cap, and what direction you predict interest rates will go.

If you expect to move in only a few years, an adjustable-rate loan is preferable: You'll benefit from the lower rate for a while, and if the rate goes up, you won't be stuck with it. If your loan adjusts once every three years, it's possible that you'll have sold the house before the adjustment.

Also consider the lifetime and payment caps of an adjustable-rate loan. Be a pessimist and calculate the monthly payment if the interest rate climbs to the capped rate. Could you afford it? For how long? On the other hand, if you have a mortgage that caps the monthly payments, and the rate goes high enough, you could end up negatively amortizing (explained in "What to Watch Out For," page 433).

■ Should you take a 30- or a 15-year loan? The answer may be decided for you if you can't make the higher monthly payments required with a 15-year mortgage and *have* to take a 30-year term. This might not be such a bad alternative if the 30-year mortgage has no pre-payment penalty, which would enable you to pay extra when you can and reduce principal.

Nonetheless, lenders charge more for long-term promises. Thus, a 15-year mortgage may be preferable because the interest rate is likely to be ¼ to ½ percentage point less. The choice all depends on your specific circumstances. If you don't need a long-term rate commitment, you can save a bundle. On a $100,000 loan, a difference of ½ percentage point costs about $35 per month. If you stay in your home only four years before moving on, you've paid an extra $1,680 for a long-term rate commitment that you didn't need anyway.

■ What's the best index for an adjustable-rate mortgage? Some indexes, such as the commonly used Treasury bill rate, are more volatile than others. Higher volatility means wider rate and payment swings.

■ How much of the cost of the loan do you want to pay up front? If you're planning on staying in your new home for quite a few years, it probably pays to pay for points, since you're spreading the cost over a long period. Generally, you need to stay put for six years to recoup points. But if you think you might keep the home for only a few years, you might consider paying a slightly higher interest rate in exchange for fewer fees and no points.

How to Apply for a Mortgage

You can apply for mortgages at commercial banks, thrift institutions (savings banks and savings and loan associations), mortgage bankers (they are licensed by your state, funded by private investors, and offer only mortgages), and credit unions. Nearly half of U.S. mortgages are arranged through brokers who will, for a fee, find a mortgage for you and help you qualify.

Start by getting copies of your credit reports. If there are errors, get them corrected *before* you apply for a mortgage. (See the **HELP** box, page 650, in "Consumer Privacy" to find out how.) Next, you'll want to get your down payment together (sell some mutual funds, borrow from Mom and Dad, etc.) and figure out how much you can afford to borrow. As a rule of thumb, lenders require that your payments not exceed 28% of your monthly gross income or 36% of your gross after considering monthly payments for other debts. As for your down payment, 20% is standard. If your down payment is less than 20%, you'll probably be required to buy private mortgage insurance to protect the lender, and the interest rate could be higher.

Your application must be as complete as you can make it. Lenders will not help you fill your information gaps. So to avoid mortgage application processing delays, have all your documents ready for submission with the application, including several months of bank statements (to show where your down payment and closing costs are coming from), all of your bank account numbers, at least two years' worth of W-2 tax forms, tax returns from the last two years, the name(s) of your stockbroker(s) and recent account statements, a list of all your debts with documentation, any alimony and child support payments, and a letter from a relative if they contributed some or all of your down payment.

Should you co-sign a mortgage with a relative? Generally this should be avoided in all but the closest families. If the buyer is unable to make the payments, the co-signer becomes fully responsible for every penny. By the way, parents who give (or loan) their kids money for a down payment may be subject to taxation according to IRS rules specifically covering such generous gestures.

The lender will want to know where any sudden cash infusions in your checking account came from to make sure it isn't laundered money or a temporary loan from a helpful friend. If you are buying a co-op, bring the corporation's recent financial reports, prospectus, and by-laws. For a house, supply a copy of your sales contract.

Should You Refinance?

Interest rates have stayed relatively low in the 1990s. If you were unlucky enough to get your mortgage when rates were high, you might consider refinancing. An old rule of thumb says you will benefit from refinancing if there is a difference of more than 2 percent-

age points between the interest rate on your current loan and a new one.

How much could you save? Say your current $100,000 30-year loan is financed at 11.25%. The monthly payment is $971.27. If you refinance for 30 years at 7.0%, the monthly payment would be only $665.31, giving you an extra $305.96 a month. Even if you refinanced into a 15-year mortgage, you'd pay $898.83 monthly, still a significant reduction. Better yet, you would pay only $161,789.40 in interest and principal over the term of the new, shorter loan, compared with $349,657.20 interest and principal paid over the term of the original loan.

The 2% rule on refinancing is not hard and fast. Be sure to consider how long it will take to recover closing costs such as points, as well as appraisals and application fees. Application fees for refinancings can be as high as 1.5% of the amount borrowed; this high fee is intended to discourage you from applying to several lenders simultaneously.

Refinancing probably makes no sense if you're planning to pull up stakes relatively soon, but if you're staying for more than a few years, refinancing might be worthwhile even if the reduction in the basic rate is only one percentage point. To find out if you'd come out better refinancing, compare the new loan's total up-front cost—title insurance, legal fees, document fees, appraisal fees, points and whatnot—with the amount you will save in monthly payments. Say the total costs of refinancing add up to $2,500. How many months of paying the lower interest rate would it take to break even? If you don't plan to stay in the house for as long as it takes to break even, it makes no sense to refinance. But if you will stay put at least that long, do it.

You should also consider the time and effort necessary to complete the paperwork. There's about as much of it as for a new mortgage, since your existing mortgage has probably been sold to another lender who doesn't know much about you or your property and has to find out. Finally, if the value of your home has declined, you may have to pay off a large chunk of your mortgage before refinancing. If you already have that money in a good investment, removing it could offset the benefits of refinancing.

Reverse Mortgages

Reverse mortgages, which give access to cash and deduct it from the value of the home, can be a godsend for seniors who have little cash but significant assets tied up in their home. You can tap into a line of credit anytime you want, take a lump sum or arrange periodic payments. In any case, you don't pay anything back until the home is sold, which means you can live in your own house for the rest of your life. The bank will get paid back, plus interest of course, out of the proceeds of the sale of your home after you die. If your heirs can pay the bank back, they can keep the house. Reverse mortgages are available in every state but Texas. For more information on the tricks and

traps, see Chapter 63, "Seniors as Consumers." If this chapter doesn't answer all your questions, contact the National Center for Home Equity Conversion, 7373 147 Street W, Apple Valley, Minnesota 55124.

HOME EQUITY BORROWING

Let's say you own a home and you're intrigued by ads urging you to tap the equity in your home to take a cruise or finance your kids' college bills—perhaps you're tempted by one of those ads picturing houses with U.S. currency bursting out of windows and the chimney. In this a good move?

Many Americans have used the equity in their homes to pay for home improvements or college tuitions they otherwise would have foregone. Interest is tax-deductible on up to $100,000 worth of borrowings, $50,000 each for married spouses filing separately, while deductibility has been phased out for credit cards. (See your tax adviser for more information.) And home equity interest rates are generally several percentage points lower than credit card rates.

Not surprisingly, lenders are more than willing to help get you into debt. They've made application forms simple. Turnaround is fast. And if you are approved for a home equity line of credit, you'll probably be given a checkbook—or even a credit card—to encourage you to spend. Not surprisingly, more than $400 billion worth of home equity loans are now outstanding.

But home equity borrowing has enormous disadvantages. Home, sweet home is the collateral. If you fall behind on payments, the bank could take it. And it's *always* a bad idea to finance immediate consumption or depreciating purchases like cars with a long-term loan such as a home equity loan. Nonetheless, a 1997 Consumer Bankers Association study found that home equity loan borrowings are used primarily to consolidate credit card debts, buy a car, or just for spending money.

Home equity vies with refinancing mortgages with larger ones as a way to get tax-deductible dollars to pay for tuition or a swimming pool. Still, home equity borrowing may have several advantages over refinancings. Application processing usually goes faster, closing costs may be less or nothing at all, and you can draw on a line of credit periodically and only as you need the money.

Types of Loans

The two basic types of home equity lending are *home equity loans* and *home equity lines of credit*.

With home equity loans (HELs), also known as closed-end, fixed-rate loans, you receive the entire amount you borrow at the loan closing. The term is generally up to 15 years. Fixed interest rates are usually a little higher than variable rates.

Home equity lines of credit, also known as open-end, variable-rate loans, typically allow you to draw on a credit line, usually by writing checks or using a credit card, during an "access period" of the first five to ten years. Then you have another five to fifteen years to pay it all back—with interest, of course. During the access period you are required to pay only the interest on whatever you've borrowed. Paying principal is optional during this time.

The interest on home equity lines of credit is typically indexed to banks' prime lending rate, as published in *The Wall Street Journal*. The law requires a lifetime interest rate cap but lets the lender set it.

A home equity line of credit is preferable to a HEL when you have periodic payments to make, such as college tuition, since you pay no interest until you actually write a check or use a linked credit card. You may prefer a HEL when you are making only a few big payments over a short time, such as to a home improvement contractor.

> " *S*ome people who have a home equity line available to them are using it like unemployment insurance. If they get thrown out of work, they borrow up to the hilt on their equity credit line to provide the money to see them over what they hope is a temporary embarrassment. "
>
> —JOHN P. LaWARE,
> Federal Reserve Board Governor,
> April 1992

How much are you allowed to borrow? The average approved home equity line of credit in 1996 was about $40,000 (fixed term borrowers averaged $25,000), according to the Consumer Bankers Association, a trade group in Arlington, Virginia. One of the hottest trends lets borrowers pocket more than their house is worth. These so-called "125" loans let you borrow up to a total of 125% of your home's value. How much you can borrow depends upon your credit history, the value of your home, and how much you owe on any existing mortgage—and how well you can sleep at night knowing your house is on the line.

What about fees? Home-equity loans involve many of the same fees as mortgages, including application fees, credit check fees, title insurance, and points. These fees may be negotiable, or they can mount up so high that several percentage points are added to the effective annual interest rate. Costs depend on market conditions: When this book was written, competition was so hot that many lenders were waiving some or all closing costs.

WHAT TO WATCH OUT FOR

Mortgages

Negative amortization. This occurs when your monthly payment does not cover the interest due. The interest that isn't paid is added to the unpaid principal balance. Negative amortization happens most frequently when monthly interest payments on adjustable-rate mortgages fail to keep up with the interest due—say, because you can't afford the increase or because there is a lag between an increase in the interest rate and the increase in your billed monthly payment. Even after making many payments, you end up owing more each month than the month before.

Lowballing and bait-and-switch. You're elated when your phone search uncovers a lender whose rate is a full point below its competitors. Be careful. The rate may be guaranteed for only ten days, which is obviously insufficient time to close on the property. Always ask how long a low rate is locked in. And make sure your lender would be willing to lower it if rates drop.

Also be on the lookout for bait-and-switch artists. After you've handed over hundreds of dollars in nonrefundable fees, you're told that a small problem has been found with your credit history and the lender requires only sterling credit records. Then you are offered a somewhat costlier loan. You might not even realize that you were baited and then switched.

Dishonest mortgage brokers. The vast majority of brokers are honest and hardworking. Mortgage brokers can save you a lot of time and effort. With their help, you fill out just one application, and the broker does the hard work of searching for the best mortgage. (Keep in mind the deal is only as good as the broker.)

But some consumers have run into problems with mortgage brokers. And only about half the states regulate them. Some of the less honest operators take a fee up front, produce nothing, and fail to give a refund. Another scam is to inflate your creditworthiness in order to get you the loan—and the broker his or her commission. But you may end up with a bigger loan than you can handle.

Still other brokers charge "junk" fees—$60 Federal Express bills, 200% markups on appraisals, and the like. A barrage of pending class action suits accuse mortgage brokers of pocketing the proceeds of jacked-up loan prices. In one case, a $100,000 mortgage cost an extra $8,000 in fees paid to the middleman. The only fees you should pay up front are for property appraisal, your credit check, and the basic application fee. Since mortgage brokers are paid by the lender, you shouldn't be charged any more than if you went directly to the lender.

Conversion fees. Some mortgages allow you to convert from an adjustable-rate to a fixed-rate mortgage without reapplying. Ask how much the fee will be for converting. But bear in mind that the fixed rate you convert to may be higher than the market rate for similar kinds of fixed-rate mortgages.

Mortgages provided through home improvement contractors. A scam has swept the nation, called "equity fraud." At a U.S. Senate hearing on the subject, experts testified that tens of thousands of homeowners—mostly in minority neighborhoods of big cities like Oakland and New York—have been victimized by dishonest contractors working hand-in-glove with home finance companies. The con men cruised lower-income neighborhoods looking for houses that needed work. They made house calls and charmed (usually) elderly owners with promises of easy credit. The homeowners often did not understand that when they contracted for a new roof or the creation of a basement apartment, they had agreed to a mortgage, and the work was rarely done properly. As loan payments ate into savings and fixed incomes, homeowners stopped paying and faced losing their homes.

Lesson: Don't sign any legal documents until you have had plenty of time to read them carefully, and be sure to request and receive copies of anything you sign. Alarms should sound if the documents include a retail installment obligation or mortgage application.

Home Equity Loans

Too much debt. If you overextend yourself when the economy is booming, you leave yourself little room to maneuver if or when the financial picture turns gloomy. A large home equity loan may make it harder to move up, and when you sell your home and pay off the loan, you have less money to reinvest.

Higher interest rates on no-fee loans. Choosing a bank loan can get pretty complicated: Some loans have no fees but a higher rate; others have moderate fees and mid-range rates; and still others have full fees but considerably lower rates. Compare carefully, remembering that thousands of dollars may depend on a few hours of research.

Teaser rates. Low interest rates may be in effect for only a short time. A 1989 law requires lenders that mention interest rates in their ads to also reveal other key costs and terms, such as how long the rate is in effect. Still, small-print disclosures can be confusing and easy to ignore.

THE $MARTER CONSUMER

Mortgages

Beware of ads for "guaranteed" mortgages. One scheme advertising mortgages with a "money-back guarantee" requires calling an "800" number for information. The caller is told to send in an advance fee of several hundred dollars, which will be "applied to the loan." The scamsters disappear once the mark sends the money.

Check out brokerages before paying them money. Find out how long a mortgage broker you may use has been in business and check its state licenses (most states license them) for administrative actions and consumer complaints. Learn if it is a member of the National Association of Mortgage Brokers. Try to patronize a broker with whom a friend or relative has had good results.

Ask how many lenders the mortgage broker represents—it should be more than a handful—and get a written breakdown of your broker's fees.

Once a broker has found you a lender, double-check the rate and terms with the lender directly to make sure the broker isn't overcharging you.

Ask if an escrow account is absolutely required. An escrow account is set up to guarantee the lender that property taxes and insurance will be paid. As a borrower, you pay into this account an extra amount on top of the regular monthly mortgage payment.

Avoid escrow if possible. Depending on the law in your state, you might not earn any interest on an escrow account. Even if you do, you could probably earn more on your money investing it elsewhere.

Tax escrow should be avoidable if your cash down payment was 30% or more of the selling price or if you have a low loan-to-value ratio. You might be able to get the insurance escrow dropped too.

Prepayment penalties. Sounds bad, right? But it might be a good deal for you. You can shave a few points off your loan if you agree not to refinance for a set period of time —three years is typical. It's not worth it for a break of only a quarter of a percentage point. And it's not smart if there is any chance you will move or that interest rates will drop significantly.

Cancel mortgage insurance as soon as you qualify. Private mortgage insurance (sometimes referred to as PMI) was designed to cover

TOO GOOD TO BE TRUE?

Think twice before you take a "no-equity" home loan, also known as a "125," since it lets you borrow up to 125% of the value of your home. You read that right. You can now borrow more than your home is worth to consolidate debt at a lower interest rate or for home improvements. (So much for the wag's observation that developing countries get more favorable loan terms than the average American!)

Here's how it works. Say your home is worth $120,000 and you still owe $105,000. If you have a good credit record and a stable job, you can probably find a lender to give you a second mortgage of $45,000. Then you would owe $150,000 on a house worth $120,000. Interest rates are usually 3 to 6 percentage points below the 17% many credit cards charge, but they are still higher than regular home-equity loans, which are about half what credit cards charge.

With personal bankruptcies at an all-time high, many experts say 125s should be a loan of last resort, and only for those with sterling credentials and rosy financial prospects. The problem is that it could take as long as ten years to pay off 25% of a home's value. And even after all that time, you won't have much, if any, equity. This gives you very little flexibility if you want to move—which Americans do on average every seven years—especially when you consider the $9,000 or so you'll pay a broker to sell your house. "No one has ever borrowed themselves out of debt," warns the Consumer Credit Counseling Service of Central Florida. To top it off, lenders charge a fee of as much as 10% of the loan amount up-front, and the Internal Revenue Service will not let you deduct any portion of the loan that exceeds the value of your home.

the difference between what is owed on a loan and the home's actual value if a lender is forced to foreclose. People who put down less than 20% usually have to buy it, and about 40% to 45% of loans today carry such insurance, which costs anything from $240 to $1,200 a year. "The problem is people are not told they can cancel," attorney Charles Zimmerman told *The Wall Street Journal.* "They keep paying this expensive, unnecessary insurance at a profit to the insurance company and profit to the mortgage company." Zimmerman's firm is suing several mortgage lenders to recover mortgage insurance overpayments. The rule is that borrowers can cancel once they have paid back principal worth 20% of the home's value. Borrowers usually must take the initiative and get (and pay for) a new appraisal, which will cost $200 to $500.

Check into Federal Housing Administration (FHA) and Veterans Administration (VA) mortgages that are available from participating lenders. The rates may be lower because the government insures repayment. FHA loans may require only 3% down, and you can finance your closing costs. You must have excellent credit to qualify, however, and the most you can borrow for an FHA loan is about $100,000 to $160,000, depending on the locality; these loans are meant for houses moderately priced for their communities. VA loans have somewhat higher borrowing limits and might even let you waive the down payment. But only veterans—which includes National Guard members and reservists —are eligible. The law requires an escrow account for taxes and insurance with both kinds of loans.

Choose your own insurance providers. You don't have to use the title insurance recommended by the lender. You might find a cheaper one if you ask around. The same goes for homeowners insurance.

Get a copy of your appraisal. A new federal regulation says that, if you request it in writing, the lender must show you the property appraisal it relies on in reviewing your mortgage application. If your application was rejected, you could use a mistakenly low appraisal as a reason to ask for a second review. In addi-

tion, a correct low appraisal could be used to bargain with the seller for a lower price.

Under a special new program, you can pay as little as 3% down with some lenders, including Chase, GE Capital and Norwest Mortgage. To be eligible, you must earn no more than the median income for your region, as determined by the federal government.

If You Already Have a Mortgage

Consider pre-paying your mortgage to save big on interest, especially in the mortgage's early years. In his book *The Banker's Secret*, Marc Eisenson, the apostle of loan prepayment, explains how small prepayments of only $25 a month toward principal can save more than $34,000 in interest on a 30-year, 10%-rate, $75,000 loan. Pre-paying doesn't reduce your monthly payment. Whatever extra you pay comes off the principal, so you never pay a penny of interest on the extra money you kick in. "Pre-paying your mortgage is like making a tax-free investment at the interest rate that your mortgage lender is charging you," says Eisenson. His book also answers tax questions about pre-payment.

Growing equity mortgages— in which monthly payments are increased annually, with the additional money going to principal— and biweekly payment mortgages have much the same interest-eliminating effect as pre-payment, but they are less flexible. With simple pre-payment, you can send in $100 extra one month and only $10 extra the next if you wish.

Beware of payment mistakes. Recent disclosures that lenders have made hundreds of millions of dollars' worth of errors in calculating mortgage payments should make you a bit wary if you have an adjustable-rate loan. If you are concerned that your outstanding principal doesn't seem to be declining fast enough when you've made principal pre-payments, that you are paying more than your latest adjustment would seem to warrant, or that you are paying too much into escrow, ask the lender for a complete payment history. If this doesn't help, consider paying a professional to check your payments with a computer. (See **HELP** at the end of this chapter for names of companies that will check your payment for mistakes.)

Don't be a mortgage payment scam victim. With mortgages bought and sold like scalped tickets to a hot concert, thieves have figured out how to cash in. There have been cases where official-looking letters were mailed from a "company" claiming to have purchased mortgages and directing the homeowner to send future payments to them. The letters gave an excuse for why a certified check or money order should be sent instead of a personal check. You can avoid becoming a victim if you send money to a new company only after the old lender sends you a letter saying the mortgage is being sold. And send only personal checks.

Online; off-price. You can avoid meeting a mortgage loan officer until the day you close on your new home. In addition to saving time and inconvenience, you might even save money. Countrywide Home Loans, Inc., one of the largest mortgage lenders in the country, charges on-line home buyers with impeccable credentials 1.25 points less than walk-in clients. That's a savings of $1,250 on a $100,000 loan. American Finance and Investment Inc., www.loanshop.com, doesn't even have an office to walk into. It accepts *only* online customers and says that what it saves on bricks and mortar pares about $1,500 off the cost of a loan.

Here are some other Web sites to have a look at to get started: the Department of Housing and Urban Development's Web site offers a home-buying guide and mortgage calculator at www.hud.gov; HSH Association will send you a list of mortgage rates, terms, and fees in your area, www.hsh.com; Bank Rate Monitor compiles interest rate surveys by city, www.bankrate.com. Once you've done some background research, many lenders accept applications on-line. You can find lots of links to lenders at Mortgage Market Information Services, www.interest.com, and many lenders have their own Web sites.

Home Equity Borrowing

Use home equity loans and credit lines judiciously. Obtain them for home improvements, education, and other capital investments with long-term benefits rather than for clothes, vacations, and eating out.

Home equity credit lines linked to credit cards. Danger! Such linked cards make it far too easy to overspend on eating out and vacations. Are the memories really worth the risk of losing your home? Even more common are banks that allow you to draw on your credit line through a cash machine—almost as much a temptation to go on a spending spree as a linked credit card.

If the disclosed terms of the loan change before it is finalized, you can refuse to take the money. You are also entitled by law to a complete refund of all fees.

H E L P

■ **Find the lowest rate.** For $20, HSH Associates will send you a list of rates, terms, and fees for 25 to 50 lenders that make loans in your area. HSH tools can also help you figure out if it makes sense to refinance. To order, call (800) 873-2837 9 A.M. to 5 P.M. EST or go to www.hsh.com on the Internet.

■ **Check your rate adjustment.** Mortgage Monitor will run a computer check to find out if your lender has correctly adjusted your mortgage payment. The charge is a third of your recovery; call (800) 283-4887.

■ ***The Banker's Secret* by Marc** Eisensen (Villard Books, 1990) explains principal pre-payment. To order, call (800) 255-0899.

■ **Looking for a mortgage broker?** The National Association of Mortgage Brokers will help you find a broker in your state. Write to them at 1735 North Lynn Street, Suite 950, Arlington, VA 22209.

CHAPTER 39

LIFE INSURANCE

Betting on Your Life

Throughout the 1990s, one scandal after another rocked the life insurance industry—as well as consumers' confidence that they can get a fair price. Between agents' tricks and having to think about dying, it's tempting to forget about buying life insurance. Don't dismiss it out of hand. When you buy insurance, you pay someone else to take a financial risk you don't want to take yourself, and depending on your situation it could be well worth it.

If you determine that you are indeed a candidate for life insurance then you'll have to figure out what kind of policy you need. Whom should you buy it from? How do you know if you're getting a good deal? And will the insurance company you choose be around in 20 or 30 or 40 years to pay off?

THE BASICS

Americans spent $78 billion on life insurance premiums in 1995. Unfortunately, they probably spent about $8 billion too much, according to industry experts. Most policyholders do not fully understand what they buy or realize that the price of the same insurance pro-

tection can vary by 100% among insurance carriers. Life insurance is usually sold rather than bought—an insurance agent comes calling, your discount broker entices you, or someone from your bank calls.

In all fairness to confused consumers, life insurance is very complicated. While there are only a few basic kinds of policies, there are literally hundreds of variations, hybrids, and permutations. If someone tries to sell you life insurance and you're considering buying it, use this chapter as a primer, but make sure you also investigate thoroughly any policies you're considering before you write a check. Buying with care is the only insurance that you're getting a good deal.

Do You Need Life Insurance?

Consider the purpose of life insurance: to protect the financial well-being of the people you name as beneficiaries in case you—the insured person—die. The basic rule of thumb is that a family of four should have coverage of at least five times the principal breadwinner's annual income. But if your survivors can easily handle the immediate funeral and postfuneral expenses and support themselves for an indefinite time without insurance, then you don't need it.

Senior citizens usually don't need life insurance to replace lost income. Nor do young, two-income couples with no dependents.

Factor in all the financial resources that will be available to your beneficiaries after you die. There may be Social Security; bank, credit union, stock brokerage, and mutual fund accounts including Individual Retirement Accounts, annuities, and Keogh accounts; saleable real estate other than your home; pension plan death benefits; wealthy (and generous) grandparents and so on. If you find that your beneficiaries will have ample resources to cope with the loss of income, you may not need coverage.

But think of *every* possibility. There may be uninsured medical expenses. You may want your survivors to be able to immediately pay off a mortgage or credit card balances. A spouse's domestic responsibilties are certainly worth plenty in monetary terms if the survivor has to hire domestic help. If you're supporting an elderly parent, life insurance could pay to hire helpers to look after them if you die. Factor in the cost of your children's college educations.

Consider talking to your tax or financial advisor about the tax benefits of life insurance. Some life insurance—the cash-value kind discussed later—is a tax-deferred investment. Any earnings on a cash value policy aren't taxed until withdrawn. And the proceeds payable when you die for any kind of insurance policy are not taxable income either. Spending a little on life insurance now can help offset substantial estate and other taxes later.

Term Insurance

Term insurance covers your beneficiaries for a particular period of time (or "term")—anywhere from one to 70 years—as long as you keep up with the premiums. Rates start low but go up every year, and rise rapidly when you hit 50–55. You buy a designated amount of coverage, and if you die during the term, the insurance company pays your beneficiaries that amount in a lump sum.

With "straight term" insurance, the policy ends at the end of the term. If you still want life insurance, you have to buy a new policy.

Renewable term insurance—either annual renewable or multi-year renewable—provides either that your renewal is automatic or that the company has a right to order a medical checkup at renewal time, called the "re-entry" feature. With automatic renewal, your premium will go up because you aged and your chances of dying are greater. A "re-entry" policy could be cheaper because, if the checkup concludes that you're still healthy, you get a special rate. If you're not in such great physical shape, though, your premium may climb dramatically. Robert D. Stuchiner, an industry analyst with the Ascott Alliance Group, calls the re-entry feature "a bad buy, since you're saving a few bucks today with the possibility of paying a horrendous amount more tomorrow."

Among variations on the term insurance theme are:

- *Decreasing term* insurance. This coverage is often linked to a mortgage. You designate the term, say 19 years, to correspond to the term of the mortgage. You pay the same premium throughout the term, but your coverage is reduced over time as your debt decreases. Decreasing term is often called family income, or mortgage, insurance.
- *Level term policies*. These are policies in which your premium is the same for five, 10, or 15 years and then suddenly shoots upward. The future premiums can be either projected or guaranteed.

The biggest advantage of term insurance over the cash-value policies (described later in this chapter) is that term insurance is much more affordable when you're young, during the first several years of the policy. A $100,000 term policy on a 35-year-old can be purchased from a reliable carrier for as little as $140 a year, while a cash-value policy will cost several times that. Another advantage of term insurance is that you can easily drop it when it's no longer needed.

A disadvantage is that annual premiums climb rapidly as you move into middle age—although by 60, you probably won't need life insurance as much anymore—your kids may be through college, your mortgage close to paid off. Generally speaking, term insurance is not a good buy for senior citizens. In fact, according to Stuchiner, in New York State "you can't even hold term insurance after age 70. It's

prohibited because it's not in the consumer's best interest."

Another disadvantage of term insurance is that you have to find new insurance at the end of the term, unless it is a guaranteed renewable policy or a convertible (into cash value insurance) policy. Your temporary insurance need could have become a longer-term need and you could be left out in the cold.

Most insurance agents won't try very hard to sell you term insurance; it pays them smaller commissions than other kinds of policies. Yet "the vast majority of people—95%—who need insurance should buy term insurance," says Bob Hunter, director of insurance for the Consumer Federation of America. "Cash value only makes sense when your tax advisor suggests it for estate planning."

To compare which term policy will cost less, look at more than just annual premiums. With inflation, premiums in the later years of a policy are paid for with cheaper dollars. So a policy with very low early-year premiums and very high later-year premiums could be preferable to one with more level premiums. The "interest-adjusted cost index" takes this time value of money into account. The law in 38 states requires insurers to make this index available—stated as a cost per $1,000 of insurance.

If you'd rather have someone else do the shopping, you might consider using a telephone or Internet quote service. After you've told them about your age, health, and the kind of policy you're looking for, a computer will spit out the names of the five best buys. (See **HELP** at the end of this chapter for quote service names.) Still, remember that this is a limited service and you won't learn much about the policies; plus, you have to know what you're looking for.

Cash-Value Policies

Whole life insurance is a whole lot more complicated. As long as the premiums are paid, a whole life insurance contract continues for the insured's "whole life" or until the age of 100. In addition to the protection of term insurance—if you die, they pay—you get a tax-deferred savings account.

Premiums are level year after year. This means you, the insured, pay more in your younger years than the actual cost of protection and less in your later years. The extra cash accumulates in the reserve fund and earns interest. The "cash surrender value" of the policy is the amount of money you would get back if you dropped your coverage.

To illustrate: Let's say you are "30-something" and you buy a $100,000 whole life policy. For the duration of the policy, the annual premium stays at $1,500. Right after you buy the policy its cash value is zero and the death benefit is $100,000. In the policy's sixth year the cash surrender value has gone up to $6,400—$6,400 is what you would get if you gave up the policy then. The death benefit remains at $100,000.

Most policies guarantee at least a minimum return, but you have to ask the insurer what the actual

interest rate is. Most whole life policies also pay dividends, sometimes referred to as "excess earnings." These can be paid out in cash, applied to help build up cash values, applied to premiums, or used to buy more insurance. Dividend-paying policies are called "participating" policies. Dividends are paid depending on the yield on the company's investments, how much it has paid out in death benefits, the company's expenses, and, naturally, on the particulars of your own coverage.

An insurance agent will probably show you charts illustrating "projected earnings" of a cash value policy over the years. These figures are typically exaggerated to convince you that a policy is a good investment. One enterprising agent testified before a U.S. Senate hearing that he personally checked the state insurance department filings of 20 major insurance companies and found that 80% admitted they could not meet the earnings assumptions used in their projection charts. They could not meet even the first two years of their cash-value policies.

This is a long-standing abuse—a scandal, really—and a testament to the weakness of insurance industry oversight. (For more on this, see **What to Watch Out For** on page 448.)

One reason some people consider buying a whole life policy is that the interest earned is tax-deferred until it's withdrawn. And at that time, taxes will be paid only on the portion of the amount withdrawn that exceeds the premiums

443

you paid plus dividends. Another positive feature is the ability to borrow against cash value—perhaps at a favorable interest rate—directly from the insurance company.

Universal life. Universal life is like whole life, except it is much more flexible; you decide how much to pay in premiums, whether to skip premiums, or whether to pay extra for a few months. You can structure the policy so that for, say, eight years, you pay large enough premiums to make sure that your cash value entirely covers premiums thereafter. You can also change the death benefit.

Your universal life premiums go into an "accumulation fund," on which you are paid interest. Periodically, "mortality charges" (the cost of insurance protection), administration expenses, and commissions are deducted. An annual statement breaks down how much has gone to mortality charges and expenses and how much is in your accumulation fund. You can stop contributing to the accumulation fund for a while or even make extra payments to your account. It's also possible to increase your coverage without incurring a new "load" (payments for expenses), although this may require some evidence of good health, perhaps a medical exam.

Some policies pay only the death benefit. Others, which cost more, pay the death benefit plus whatever is in the accumulation fund.

About surrender charges: If you have a "front-load" universal policy, administrative fees as well as the agent's commission will be subtracted from your premiums. However, most policies these days are "back-load," which means that the charges, fees, and commissions are together called "surrender charges" because they are deducted from the cash surrender value if you discontinue your policy. During the first few years of such a policy, most of your accumulation fund could (and probably would) be wiped out by surrender charges. The charges diminish later on and disappear altogether with some policies.

Most policyholders are told next to nothing about surrender charges. Jim Hunt, an actuary with Consumer Federation of America, said that one of his clients was sold an annual premium universal life policy as a substitute for an IRA. After two years—when he had invested $4,000 and wanted to take his money out—he discovered to his consternation that after paying surrender charges, his payout was only a few hundred dollars. To add insult to injury, since he was single and had no dependents, he didn't even need life insurance.

A common variation on universal life and whole life is single-premium insurance. With single-premium, you make one large up-front premium payment. Earnings on this single payment augment the cash value over time. The main reasons to buy such a policy are to defer taxes and to build collateral to borrow money.

Variable life. Variable life insurance is cash-value insurance that allows you—rather than the insurance company—to decide where to invest the savings component, called the "separate investment account," typically a mutual fund.

The most positive thing about variable life insurance is that you might do better than the insurance company would in choosing investments. This could be a downside, too, since you might make bad decisions and there is typically no minimum interest guarantee. Risk also extends to the value of the death benefit, although there is usually a minimum below which it can't fall.

As with universal life, variable life policies impose substantial surrender charges as well as mortality and administration charges. And because they are so investment-dependent, they can only be sold by agents who have registered with the National Association of Securities Dealers.

Your Premium

If an insurance company has reason to believe that you are a bigger risk, you'll pay more. Age is the initial determinant; inevitably, your chance of dying increases as you grow older.

Then comes health. Insurers find out how healthy you are from your medical records, which can be accessed from the Medical Information Bureau (MIB), an insurance-industry–sponsored national computer data base. (See page 648 for more about the MIB.) If you are asking for a substantial amount of coverage and/or are middle-aged or older—around 45—the insurance company will probably ask you to submit to a medical exam. If you have a chronic health problem like high blood pressure, you might still be able to buy a "guaranteed acceptance policy." But you'll pay through the nose for these heavily promoted policies; benefits may be limited and you might do just as well paying the higher rate for a regular insurance policy. Unfortunately, people who are seriously ill, such as people with AIDS, probably can't get any insurance at all.

Tobacco companies may claim that smoking isn't bad for your health, but insurance companies beg to disagree. Nonsmokers pay up to 50% less for life insurance than smokers. Don't lie about smoking on a life insurance application; the urine taken during your insurance physical will probably be tested for nicotine, among other chemicals. And if you die from lung cancer and lied about smoking on your application, your survivors may get a reduced benefit.

Another risk factor is alcohol consumption. For larger amounts of requested coverage, the company will probably check your driving record for driving-while-intoxicated (DWI) convictions. In addition, if you're in a hazardous occupation like lion-taming, fighting forest fires, or if you fly your own aircraft, you'll pay more. Potentially dangerous hobbies, such as scuba diving and rock or mountain climbing, could also cost you extra.

Gender is another consideration. Women live longer than men. Unless the company has unisex rates, men pay extra.

THE BEST POLICY IS NONE OF THESE POLICIES

You can insure against practically anything these days—dying in a taxi, veterinary bills, even missed theater outings. Save your money and beef up the coverage you really need: health, disability, life, homeowner's, and auto insurance. You can probably skip the following widely touted policies:

Credit life insurance pays off a specific debt if you die. Auto dealers, finance companies, credit cards, and others aggressively promote it. Stephen Brobeck, Executive Director of the Consumer Federation of America (CFA), calls credit life insurance "the nation's worst insurance rip-off." On average, in 1995 it paid out only 42 cents on each premium dollar, while consumer organizations recommend a ratio of at least 70 cents. (New York, Maine, Rhode Island, and Washington, DC, are exceptions.) CFA estimates the total overcharging at $400 million a year.

Flight insurance, tempting because it's cheap, rarely pays off because planes hardly ever crash. Your family should be adequately protected, no matter how you die.

Cancer insurance probably duplicates insurance you already have if you have adequate health insurance. Consumers generally pay out so much more in premiums than they receive in benefits that two states, New Jersey and Connecticut, have outlawed cancer coverage.

Wedding insurance coverage is limited to deaths in the family and other circumstances, but it won't pay if the happy couple gets cold feet. The kinds of postponements covered are so rare that it makes sense to say, "I don't."

Theater ticket insurance, at about $5 a ticket, would pay only if you cancel your theater party in writing and return the tickets two days before the show. In other words, you'd still be stuck if you caught a nasty flu or if your car broke down on the New Jersey Turnpike.

Once they've amassed all the information they need, if they agree to take you on, the company applies a complex scoring system to place you in one of three risk categories: preferred, standard, or substandard. The vast majority of policies are written at standard rates.

Insurance Company Soundness

"Like a good neighbor," will they really be there? Are you and your family truly "in good hands?" Is your insurer as solid as the Rock of Gibraltar?

These are important questions, as almost a million policyholders learned in 1991. Within a few months, six major life insurance companies were seized by regulators. Accounts were frozen. Some customers were not allowed to cash in their policies or borrow against them, except in cases of extreme hardship.

Many retirees on fixed incomes were hurt when one of these companies, Executive Life Insurance, began paying only 70% of benefits in group pension plans. The *Providence Journal-Bulletin* reported that at Landmark Medical Center in Woonsocket, Rhode Island, more than 400 nonunion and 50 union employees had annuities in a group pension plan with Executive Life, and the hospital had no plans to make up the 30% benefits shortfall.

The problem is that there's no FDIC to protect the policy-holding public. Consumers are protected by state insurance guaranty associations, and the amount of maximum guaranteed death penalty payment ranges from a low of $100,000 up to $500,000. However, the guaranty funds do not protect you at all from cash surrender and borrowing prohibitions that could be imposed if your company gets in trouble.

To protect yourself, do your own research. Check a company's financial soundness ratings with the five major rating companies: A.M. Best, Moody's, Standard & Poor's, Duff & Phelps, and Weiss Research (see **HELP** at the end of this chapter for contact information). The rating agencies look at the company's capital base and surplus, its reserves, its profit history, management record, and intangible factors, such as how well-run the company appears to be. Find out if the company you are considering has been downgraded in recent years. If it was rated triple-A for four years and in the fifth and most recent year it was only double-A, then there was a change in the company that triggered the downgrade. Generally, you should buy only from insurance companies with the highest ratings for the last five to ten years. And bear in mind that small firms may not be sufficiently diversified to withstand an economic downturn. Industry analyst Robert D. Stuchiner also suggests reading the report on which the rating is based. It'll say which way the company is likely to go. Be on guard if it says something like "downgrade implications." These reports, usually costing around $25, can be obtained through your agent or by calling the rating company.

Understand, though, that the ratings are carefully nuanced and that the rating agencies avoid giving a bad-sounding grade. So, for example, Duff and Phelps gives seven levels of "A" (AAA, AA+, AA, AA-, A+, A, and A-), and their worst grade is CCC.

Where Should You Buy Life Insurance?

The biggest disadvantage of buying life insurance from insurance agents is the large commissions they earn, especially for cash-value policies. Not only do commissions erode the funds you want to have working for you, they may affect the agents' choice of which policy to recommend, with the policy paying *them* the most urged on you, instead of the policy that pays *you* the most. Agents counter that they provide a valuable advisory service and that they would lose their customers if they didn't serve them well.

Many insurance policies have A and B versions, with the B version charging maybe 20% less. Agents have little incentive to offer the B version: *Money* magazine reports that discounted policies can cut the agent's commission in half.

You might save a lot of money by dealing with an insurance company directly—by phone, mail, Internet or through financial planners —and avoiding agents altogether. Insurance consultant Glenn Daily, author of *Low-Load Life Insurance*, says that with agent-purchased cash-value insurance, commissions, administration costs, and other fees typically run 100% of the premium in the first year, 10% to 15% for the next three or four years, and then about 5% until the tenth year. In contrast, you'd pay only 20% the first year and a few percent a year for ten years with policies charging lower-than-usual loads, called "low-load" policies.

Why doesn't everyone buy low-load? Because the projection charts used by agents to sell full-load policies so often exaggerate future return. Since low-load issuers don't normally use these tricks and subterfuges, their policies often don't look any better than load policies, and consumers figure they might as well buy from an agent. And, as

Daily puts it, "Most people don't affirmatively buy life insurance. They buy when approached by an agent, maybe a golf partner. People don't like to think about death, so they don't learn much about the subject."

The Consumer Federation of America recommends two direct-writing companies, USAA Life and Ameritas. Both operate over the phone, and can also serve as a benchmark to measure other companies against. (See **HELP** for phone numbers.)

You can also buy life insurance from financial institutions. Savings banks have been selling term insurance for decades, and commercial banks and discount brokers are now getting into the insurance sales act.

One of the better deals could be term insurance purchased through your employer. Group rates tend to be lower and, as part of an employee group, you might not have to undergo a medical exam.

Still, going through an agent has many advantages. A good agent can tell you the pros and cons of various policy options, review your insurance with you every few years to make sure you're keeping up with any changes in your family or financial situation, and identify companies that are more likely to accept you if you have a medical condition.

WHAT TO WATCH OUT FOR

Illusory illustrations. Benjamin Disraeli's aphorism, "There are three kinds of lies: lies, damned lies and statistics," applies perfectly to life insurance marketing. Americans are deceived in droves by insurance company computer-produced projection charts full of statistics of future earnings and death benefits of cash-value life insurance policies. Small-print disclaimers in these charts, like "projected earnings" and "based on current assumptions," are used to make cash-surrender values look better than they really are. In fact, it is virtually impossible to project what might happen 15, 20, or 30 years down the road.

"Illustrations may appear official, but they are merely guesses of future results based on the assumptions an agent feeds into the computer," says Morey Stettner, author of *Buyer Beware: An Industry Insider Shows You How to Win the Insurance Game.* "It's the old 'garbage in, garbage out' trick." Some illustrations fail to distinguish between guaranteed figures and best-case scenarios: the maximum premium you'll pay and the minimum payout you'll get back. Others assume, with no basis at all, that administrative expenses will be cut five years hence. Or they assume, again with no basis, that life expectancy will improve. And some insurance companies could just as well predict future interest rates by throwing darts.

When Consumer Federation of America reviewed more than 100 policy illustrations in 1997, they found that high commissions, especially in the early years, eat into returns. One universal policy from The Hartford had annual *losses* of 19.5% over the first five years, and after 10 years still hadn't gained a penny for the policyholder.

In other words, projection illustrations are utterly worthless for purposes of comparing policies.

In 1992 and 1993, former Senator Howard Metzenbaum (D-Ohio) held hearings of the Senate Judiciary Committee Subcommittee on Antitrust and Monopolies to highlight the deceptions. One witness described how he and his father were sold a policy with projections showing that the policy would be all paid up in five years. He called the company after five years and was horrified to learn that his father still owed thousands of dollars in premiums. Since his father was suffering from terminal cancer, he wouldn't be able to get insurance elsewhere. He had no choice—pay or go uncovered.

Jolted by the Metzenbaum hearings, the National Association of Insurance Commissioners (NAIC), the body that coordinates state insurance regulation, formed a working group to study the deception problem and issued a report that corroborated many of Metzenbaum's findings. The NAIC is considering prohibiting the use of projection illustrations, but the insurance industry is gearing up to fight any such move.

Vanishing premiums. An agent may tell you that premiums will disappear after a number of years. What he fails to communicate is that the disappearing act depends upon interest rates, and when the deadline passes, there is no guarantee that you won't still have to pay premiums. A lot of people who had bought "vanishing premium" policies during the 1980s when interest rates were high found this out the hard way when interest rates dropped in the 1990s.

Very low cash-surrender values in earlier years. Agents trying to sell you a cash-value policy will point to the generous cash surrender value in, say, the 21st year, and gloss over the extremely parsimonious cash surrender value in early years—one that may be eaten up by high surrender charges. Most people don't realize—and agents certainly never reveal—that agents earn a total 55% to 105% commission on premiums paid during the first few years of a cash-value policy. (Term insurance garners them much less, perhaps 35% of a much smaller premium.)

Insurance companies know that most customers let their policies lapse after only several years. This encourages insurance companies to "churn" policies; that is, to get you to replace your perfectly good policy after only a few years with something "new and better." But with a replacement policy, you pay big early-year commissions and fees all over again, accruing very little if any cash surrender value for several years. According to CFA's Jim Hunt, about half of all cash value policies are dropped in seven or eight years—causing a loss or only a small gain for these policyholders.

The difference between gross and net yields on cash-value insurance. Which policy would you choose? One policy has a 12% annual return. Another policy returns only 8%. Annual premiums on both are $1,000. You'd choose the

first policy, of course. But what if surrender charges on the first policy came to $600 and to only $300 on the second? The second policy may then become the better deal. It's a common deception to tell potential policyholders about only the *gross* and not the *net* yield.

Combination term and whole life. Such policies have a whole life component, say for $50,000, and a term component for, say, $200,000. The agent explains that over time the dividends from the whole life portion of the policy will pay for the term insurance, or that the dividends go for "paid-up additions" to your whole life component's death benefit, and, eventually, the term insurance is replaced by the whole life. The trouble is, future dividends are often exaggerated.

Paying insufficient premiums on a universal life policy. If the earnings assumptions are too rosy and don't pan out, you could easily pay too little to cover the premiums on the term insurance component without being aware of it. And you'll be left unprotected.

Riders that take you for a ride. According to CFA, insurance companies make big profits on certain riders, which is why they often are a poor value. Some examples:

■ *Premium waiver riders.* You can skip premiums if you are disabled and can't work, and your insurance will remain in force. Generally, if you can't work in your usual occupation, such waivers keep you covered for two years. After that, they apply only if you can't work in an occupation for which you are reasonably fitted. But check carefully how the policy defines this. And compare the cost of this rider with a good disability insurance policy.

■ *Double-indemnity riders.* Such riders provide for double benefits to be paid in case of accidental death. In the 1944 movie *Double Indemnity* Fred MacMurray is an insurance agent who falls in love with Barbara Stanwyck. Together they conspire to murder her husband and make it appear like an accident in order to collect on his double-indemnity rider. If you think you might be married to a Barbara Stanwyck type, think twice about purchasing such a rider. The other reason not to buy one is that the vast majority of deaths are not accidental, and this extra coverage is usually overpriced. Plus, if your survivors really need the cash, why limit the extra benefits to this one cause of death?

■ *Guaranteed insurability rider.* You can purchase additional cash-value insurance without undergoing a new medical exam. The premium is very high for this option; you're likely better off buying more insurance in the first place.

Insuring your children. Insurance companies promote buying insurance on your children. Unless your child is a prodigy who has been supporting you in a style to which you would like to stay accustomed, there is no good reason to buy it.

Meaningless names. Many policy names do not include the important descriptive words "whole life," "universal life," or "variable life." Instead, they go by such un-helpful names as "lifetime protector" or, "heritage extra." Be sure to ask exactly what kind of policy you are being sold.

Life insurance targeted at seniors. A bad deal. You give them $5 a month, they give you next to nothing—maybe only a few hundred dollars coverage as you get older. And there are exclusions, like you have to die in an accident during the first few years of the policy.

Life insurance policies sold as a retirement plan. Metropolitan Life got into hot water in 1993 when authorities learned that company agents were selling Florida nurses whole life insurance policies disguised as retirement plans; most takers thought they were getting some kind of tax-deferred annuity. Met Life is offering refunds to tens of thousands of people who were deceived and is paying millions of dollars in fines. Prudential got into similar trouble and is paying hundreds of millions in refunds and penalties for deceptive sales practices between 1982 and 1995. The best way to avoid becoming a victim is to understand the basic kinds of policies—and ask a lot of questions.

THE $MARTER CONSUMER

Keep up with the payments. If you buy level premium term insurance, try not to let the policy lapse before the end of the term. Such policies are structured so that the premium is a good deal only if you keep the policy in force for a long time.

Think twice before buying a cash-value policy. Consumers Union doesn't think very highly of cash-value policies, generally. IRAs and 401(k) plans could be preferable from an investment and retirement planning point of view. (See "Retirement Nest Eggs," page 412, for more information.) And before you go for a cash-value policy, make sure you have adequate health and disability insurance to cover truly catastrophic events and expenses. The odds of becoming disabled (and unable to work for an extended period of time) are a lot greater than the odds of dying.

Still, CFA's Jim Hunt believes that in light of their tax advantages, cash-value life insurance policies "can be a good investment, provided that you buy in a good company and you commit to keep the policy for 15 or 20 years in order to amortize the huge up-front costs over a longer period of time and to give the tax advantages and ability of companies to invest well to overcome those high front-end costs."

If you do buy cash-value insurance, at a minimum ask for:

■ All variables, including surrender charges, dividends, interest rates, mortality charges, and administrative fees.
■ An illustration that shows projected and guaranteed values of both cash and death benefits to at least the age of 90. It is most important to concentrate on the early years because all policies will show great numbers after 65.
■ The agent should sign the illustration when you are handed the policy, confirming that the illustration corresponds to the policy actually issued.
■ An internal rate-of-return analysis to age 85. This figure is computed from a formula used to determine your investment return at any given point in the policy. The analysis takes into account the premiums paid, the cash value accumulation, and the time value of money. It compares the amount of premiums paid against the ultimate death benefit promised or the cash value.
■ If buying from an agent, make sure he or she is well-qualified, licensed, and has not had the license suspended. At the least make sure the agent sells insurance full-time and is a "CLU" (Chartered Life Underwriter) or a "ChFC" (Chartered Financial Consultant).

And if you have a medical condition, make sure the agent has a good grounding in the medical science behind insurance underwriting. One of the consultants for this chapter suggests that you ask your prospective agent what elevated liver enzymes are. If he or she doesn't know, consider going to someone else.

The Internet is a great way to shop for insurance. You can have a policy about a week sooner than if you went through an agent. But if you buy via the Internet, check to be sure that the insurance agent, agency, and underwriter are licensed to sell insurance in your home state. If they aren't, you won't be covered by your state's reserve fund and if you and the insurance company disagree, your state won't have the jursidiction or power to come to your aid.

H E L P

■ **Rating agencies.** The major rater is A.M. Best & Company, which each year publishes two volumes of *Best's Insurance Reports*, one rating life insurance companies and the other rating property-liability companies. These volumes are probably available at your local library. Weiss Research, considered the toughest grader, will give you a rating over the phone for $15; (800) 289-9222. Standard & Poor's, (212) 208-1527; Moody's, (212) 553-0377; and Duff & Phelps (312) 368-3157 give out their ratings for free. A.M. Best charges $2.95 for the initial call, $4.95 for each rating (900) 555-2378, but call (908) 420-0400 to get the insurance company's identification number first.

■ **You should also call your state in-**surance department and ask if a company you're considering has faced any regulatory action. And ask if the company has had problems paying claims.

■ **Among the free term insurance com-**parison shopping services: Term Quote, (800) 444-TERM; SelectQuote (800) 343-1985; and Insurance Quote Services (800) 972-1104, www.iquote.com. A $50 fee is charged by Insurance Information, Inc., (800) 472-5800, since they don't earn anything by selling policies; the $50 is refunded if you don't save $50 through their service. Quotesmith charges $15; (800) 556-9393 or www.quotesmith.com.

■ **The Consumer Federation of Amer-**ica recommends buying your low-load universal life policies direct from two Texas companies, USAA Life, (800) 531-8000, Ameritas, (800) 552-3553. Geico, (800) 841-3000, and Amica Mutual, (800) 242-6422, are two others. A new, free, low-load quote service is offered by the Wholesale Insurance Network (WIN), except in Oregon, which requires only fee-paid advisors to sell insurance; call (800) 808-5810.

■ **Clear explanations of life insurance** can be found in *Buyer's Guide to Insurance,* available for $3 from Consumer Federation of America, 1424 16th St. NW, Suite 604, Washington, DC 20036, (202) 387-0037 and Joseph Belth's *Life Insurance: A Consumer Handbook* (University of Indiana, 1988). Belth is a nationally known and feared industry watchdog. In-depth explanations of the tricks of the trade can be found in *Life Insurance: How to Buy the Right Policy From the Right Company at the Right Price*, by the editors of Consumer Reports Books with Trudy Lieberman (1994, Consumers Union).

■ **For an analysis of a policy's rate-**of-return (after fees and expenses), contact the Consumer Federation of America at (202) 387-0087. CFA will compute the real rate of return on the cash value part of a policy—minus all the charges—and tell you if you could do better investing your money elsewhere. Price: $40 for one policy and $30 for additional policies.

■ **Answers, please. The American** Council of Life Insurers has a helpline, (800) 942-4242, but keep in mind that this is an industry group. They also distribute a free brochure, *What You Should Know About Buying Life Insurance,* and worksheets that will help you compute your insurance needs.

CHAPTER 40

HOMEOWNERS INSURANCE

Covering Your Castle

Private property. It's the American way. And to protect their private property from fire, hail, lightning, theft, burglary, vandalism, and floods, Americans spend over $17 billion a year on homeowners insurance premiums.

But gone are the days when you could grab a solid policy, write your premium check every year, and forget about it. Homeowners and insurers alike have gotten soaked mopping up after the natural disasters of the 1990s—Hurricane Andrew smacked Florida in 1992; the Northridge earthquake hit California in 1994; major floods deluged the Dakotas in 1997, to name just a few. And the huge payouts from those disasters have made insurers pickier about who and where they insure and have jacked up premiums. Don't be smug just because you don't live in California or Florida or a floodplain. You might be surprised to know that earthquakes threaten Memphis and southern Missouri because of the New Madrid fault; Denver and Dallas–Fort Worth make the risk

list because of hailstorms; Long Island, New York, is a hurricane risk. And to protect themselves further, home insurers now routinely weed out policyholders who file too many claims. As with auto insurance, you may find yourself in a *"don't* use it or lose it" bind.

With the closer scrutiny and significant disparities in premiums among insurance companies for the same coverage, it's easy to overpay. Yet comparison shopping for the least-expensive policy isn't very difficult; you just have to know what to look for.

THE BASICS

The Standard Policies

Wherever you live in the United States, you'll find these same basic policy categories:

■ HO-1 (Homeowners 1) is basic protection for the most common perils: damages from fire and lightning, smoke, hail/windstorm, explosion, vehicles, riot or civil disorder, vandalism, and for theft, burglary, and glass breakage. It covers your personal property as well as your home. This coverage is rarely enough.

- HO-2 adds additional coverage to HO-1 policies for falling object damage; roof collapse due to ice, sleet, or snow; collapse of your home generally; damage from an electrical surge or short circuit; and damage from frozen pipes or an air conditioning system malfunction. It doesn't cost much more than HO-1.

- HO-3 is even more comprehensive. All risks to your house, except for a few specific exclusions, like floods, earthquakes, and wars, are covered. You will also be reimbursed for damaged trees and shrubs and for debris removal. HO-3 is the most commonly purchased protection. Many companies have been writing an alternate form of HO-3 promising reimbursement at "guaranteed replacement cost." This new HO-3, which is preferable to previously standard "current market value" policies, would pay the full amount needed to replace your home and its contents even if you exceed the policy limit. However, these policies most often set a limit of 120% to 150% of the policy's face value.

- HO-4 is for renters. It covers personal property and liability.

- HO-6 is designed for condominium or co-operative apartment owners. It covers personal belongings, liability, and can also be written to cover physical improvements you made to your apartment,

like adding an expensive parquet floor.

- HO-8 is for valuable or unique older homes. Its coverage tends to be restricted because of the high cost of replicating the original.

While your homeowners insurance covers your personal property anywhere in the world you take it, unless the policy states otherwise, you will be reimbursed only for the *current market value* of the personal property, not what it would cost to replace, and for a maximum of 50% of the face value of the policy. That old TV destined for the dump will fetch next to nothing. And your three-year-old computer that worked fine won't get you much more. You can purchase additional "replacement-cost coverage" for an extra premium.

The typical policy also pays your additional expenses for alternative lodgings if damage to your house forces you out. These expenses must be "reasonable," so no resort living while your house is made habitable.

Homeowners insurance policies also cover you for liability—the chandelier falling on your boss at dinner, your dog taking a small chunk out of the newspaper girl's leg. The standard coverage is for $100,000, which is probably not enough; you can buy more for a small addition to your premium.

How Premiums Are Figured

How much you actually spend depends on the cost of replacing your home and personal property. The insurance company will do an appraisal for free. If you want an independent appraisal, you'll have to spend a few hundred dollars on your own appraiser.

The big bad wolf couldn't blow down the little pig's house made of brick, and insurance companies charge less for houses of brick or stone than for wooden ones. (Straw houses are probably uninsurable.)

Location is critical. Insurance companies compile loss statistics for neighborhoods, and you'll pay more if losses are high in your vicinity. They also assign your neighborhood to a fire protection class. You may pay extra if your neighborhood is served by a volunteer fire department or lacks hydrants.

Seemingly inconsequential qualities of your life can raise your rates or disqualify you—things like the trampoline your kids love so much, or the diving board in your swimming pool, or the quaint and cozy wood-burning stove. State Farm is finicky about dogs, specifically breeds with a penchant for biting. But State Farm is actually and actuarially on firm ground: the company got bit by $58.7 million in dog-bite claims in 1994, about a third of all bodily injury claims State Farm paid that year.

Extra liability coverage also adds to the premium bill. But raising the deductible to above the usual $250 will yield significant savings.

> "*The biggest challenge with insurance is trying to cover all possible situations with all kinds of people, and I've never seen anything designed by man to do it.*"
>
> —IRVING LEPELSTAT,
> Brooklyn, New York,
> insurance agent

There are numerous discounts to ask about. Since so many fires are traceable to lit cigarettes, many companies offer a nonsmoker discount. Smoke detectors and burglar alarms can earn you a discount, too. And you can save on your home and auto insurance if you buy from the same company.

How Much Insurance Do You Need?

Six months after Hurricane Andrew devastated parts of South Florida in 1992, a *Miami Herald* survey found that 17% of policyholders who had filed claims believed they should have had more coverage. And in the wake of the catastrophic floods in the Upper Midwest in the spring of 1997, it came out that only 10% of the buildings damaged by the floods had enough flood insurance to bring them back from the deluge.

An old general rule was that if you bought coverage for at least 80% of your home's replacement cost, you'd be fully reimbursed for claims other than for total rebuilding, such as for repairs to a fire-damaged kitchen. The problem is, what happens if the entire house burns to the ground? If rebuilding costs $200,000, the company will pay only $160,000; you'll have

STUPIDITY INSURANCE?

Coverage expectations can be pretty unreasonable. One broker related the story of a woman who once hung wet dungarees over a live fire in her fireplace to dry. When they started to smoulder, she extinguished them—by beating them against her new wall-to-wall carpeting, making a terrible mess. She asked if her homeowner's policy would reimburse her for the $3,000 cost of her carpet. The broker's answer: "Your policy doesn't cover stupidity."

to come up with the rest. This is exactly what happened to many homeowners after Hurricane Andrew and the 1994 Northridge, California, earthquake. So avoid the common mistake of buying only for 80% of replacement cost and get full coverage.

Better yet, buy a guaranteed replacement-cost provision—called an "endorsement"—for your policy. No matter how much it costs to rebuild your home, you're covered. The additional cost of this endorsement is usually minimal, yet its value was well learned by the people who lost their homes in the 1991 Oakland firestorm. But be very clear about exactly what "guaranteed replacement" means. In Oakland, insurance companies maintained that

"guaranteed replacement" did not mean that insurers had to pay to meet new, more stringent building codes prompted by recent California earthquakes. However, under pressure from the state—and from the many influential burned-out citizens who banded together as United Policyholders—34 insurance companies retroactively upgraded hundreds of policies. Great for them —but it's unlikely that you could garner such clout all by yourself.

Exclusions and Limitations

Before plunking down your first premium, read carefully the policy's sections on exclusions and limitations. Here is a partial list of what most homeowners policies will *not* pay for: earthquakes and floods; damage from a nuclear meltdown; damage from freezing or vandalism after the property has been vacant for several weeks; damage from an area-wide power failure; slow and constant water seepage; normal wear and tear; breakage of personal property; property belonging to a roommate (only your *personal* property is covered). Sorry, pet lovers, neither Fifi nor your piranhas are covered. And your liability coverage won't apply if you intentionally hurt someone in your home.

Typically, homeowners policies place dollar limits on reimbursement for such personal property as cash and securities, coins, bank notes, deeds, passports, bookkeeping records, tickets, jewelry, furs, watches, and the family silver. You have to buy extra protection to fully cover such items.

And in this era of telecommuting and starting a business in the garage, you can't assume that your home office and the equipment in it are covered—even if your number-crunching computer doubles as a family entertainment and homework center. Most policies provide only minimal coverage for business losses—like a computer that conks out when it's "rained" on after an upstairs bathroom springs a leak. For an additional payment of a few hundred dollars, you can probably modify your policy to cover a truly small business. For larger businesses, especially those that bring clients to your home, you'll probably need a separate policy altogether that will cost at least several hundred dollars.

A homeowners policy wouldn't have helped Noah; flood insurance has to be bought separately. Flood policies can be purchased through the National Flood Insurance Program (NFIP), which is available to an estimated 11 million homes in designated communities where flood risk is high. In return for NFIP coverage—the government guarantees that participating insurers' premiums will cover all losses—the community has to take flood prevention measures. Unfortunately, only 10% of eligible homeowners sign up for this subsidized coverage. Thousands of homeowners displaced by the 1993 Mississippi River floods sure wish they had bought it. Insured losses came to less than $300 million, compared to more than $15 *billion* for Hurricane Andrew in Florida a year earlier.

Earthquake coverage also has to be bought separately, or you can buy a special earthquake endorsement on your policy. When it comes to earthquake protection, the third little pig had it backward. Earthquake endorsements cost less for wood houses, which better withstand quake stresses, than for houses made of brick.

Unfortunately, those enormous Hurricane Andrew and Northridge, California, payouts have prompted many insurers to get out of the homeowners insurance business in certain high-loss geographic areas. Thousands of homeowners in affected communities are, in industry parlance, being "non-renewed," and others are facing astronomical rate hikes—87% in Florida since Andrew struck. In Florida, the insurer of last resort is the state-sponsored Resident Property and Casualty Joint Underwriting Association. It offers bare-bones coverage and costs about 25% more than the non-renewed coverage. It may not be much, but it's better than nothing.

And in 1996 California had to set up its own state-sponsored earthquake insurance plan after $12.5 billion in insurance losses from the Northridge temblor paralyzed the homeowners insurance market. Insurers all but stopped writing new policies to get around the requirement that they also offer earthquake protection. And as homeowners renewed, even those who never filed a claim had no choice but to accept 50% premium increases. Californians who buy from the state plan have to accept steep deductibles of as much as 15% of their home's insured value, and still pay Richter scale–breaking rates.

Condo Insurance

Your condominium apartment association has insurance on your apartment complex—or at least it's supposed to. But the coverage may be insufficient. In case of severe damage, the condo association might be forced to impose an assessment on all owners to cover an insurance shortfall. Your share could come to thousands of dollars.

So if you own a condo (or a co-op), it's wise to buy an individual policy to cover shortages in the condo association's coverage and your own special improvements, like your renovated kitchen. It will also cover you for liability, cover your personal possessions, as well as pay for a modest condo association damage repair assessment.

To avoid overpaying or underinsuring, get a copy of the condo association's policy and compare it to an individual policy you might buy. You can tailor your individual policy to coordinate benefits with those of the association's.

WHAT TO WATCH OUT FOR

Buying coverage based on the market value of your home and property rather than on the replacement cost of just the house. The cost of replacement, of course, has little to do with a home's market value: it keeps rising no matter what. Plus, what's the point of insuring the dirt your home is built on? Unless you live on the shoreline, it's not going anywhere. A guaranteed replacement-cost policy ensures that you always have enough coverage to rebuild.

Inflation creep. The cost of rebuilding keeps going up. If you don't have a guaranteed replacement-cost policy, then you could become underinsured over time. Automatic inflation protection is a second-choice alternative to guaranteed replacement cost. But don't assume that your policy has automatic inflation protection. It does not have it unless it says so. And even if you have inflation protection, it won't usually cover the expense of upgrading an older home to meet current building codes.

Overpriced insurance. Most lenders require home buyers to insure the property. Many borrowers simply buy the insurance from the company the lender recommends. But you might pay less for the same or more coverage by shopping around. You may also get a discount if you buy from the same agency that sold you your other insurance. You might also get better service when you file a claim if you are a "regular customer" who has more than one policy.

Insufficient insurance. Don't get caught covered only for the amount you owe on your mortgage. Especially if you've paid off a good part of it, you could be in a spot if your house burns to the ground. Your mortgage company will be paid off, but you'll be left with an empty lot.

Pay for the small stuff yourself. Multiple claims for the same thing raise a flag, and too many claims will not only raise your premium, but they could also keep you from having your policy renewed. That's what happened to Lori D. of Trenton, New Jersey. Over four years, she filed five claims. But when it came time to renew, she got the thumbs-down from her insurance company. After much shopping around, she finally found a new policy, but her premium more than tripled. "What are you paying for, protection? Why have it if you can't use it?" she asked *The New York Times*. After all, isn't the point of paying for insurance year after year that one day, when you need it, someone else will pay for repairs? Yup, and you are welcome to file every single claim. But it may not be wise to do so.

Too little liability coverage. Make sure your policy has enough liability coverage. Most experts recommend buying enough to cover as much of your net worth as possible. The standard coverage of $100,000 might not do it. Additional coverage up to $300,000 will probably cost less than $30 a year. You may have to buy a separate policy for coverage above $500,000. If someone comes to your home to care for your children, you'll need a separate worker's compensation policy.

"The check is in the mail." Don't buy homeowners insurance solely on the basis of price. Ask friends and neighbors about their experiences; especially about how long it took to pay a claim, and sign up only with a company with good references.

Before you renew your policy, shop around for lower premiums, as rates change frequently. But it may not be worth it to switch if all you'll save is a few bucks. Having a long claim-free relationship could work to your advantage if you finally have to file a claim.

Review your coverage every few years and renovate it when you remodel your home. That way your insurance coverage will increase with your quality of life. As insurers write more and more "guaranteed replacement-cost" policies for new customers, long-term customers have not necessarily been informed and converted. If you haven't reviewed your policy in a while, you could be undercovered. The house you figured would cost $125,000 to rebuild five years ago could cost $160,000 to rebuild today. If you've made any significant improvements—added an extra wing, redone the kitchen, bought grown-up furniture to replace the flea market finds you've been carting around since college—you could get caught short. And if your assets have grown substantially, you may want to up your liability coverage.

Be honest about what you use your computer and other home office equipment for. If you took a tax deduction for them as home office expenses, don't expect the insurance company to let you construe them as family property. They can legitimately refuse to pay a claim.

The Fair Access to Insurance Requirements (FAIR) plan provides protection against insurance red-lining. Red-lining is when an insurer figuratively or even literally draws a red line around a neighborhood where policies will not be written—often neighborhoods with predominantly minority residents. FAIR was created to ensure coverage for residents of areas insurance carriers have historically shunned. Ask your insurance agent about it; 30 states and the District of Columbia offer FAIR policies.

Homeowners policies usually cover you for up to $500 in unauthorized credit card purchases. If you lose your credit cards and the "finder" takes them on a spree, the law says you are liable for a maximum of only $50 per card if you report the loss promptly. If you carry a lot of plastic, you could be out several hundred dollars without homeowners insurance.

Keep a running inventory of valuable possessions. Record the date of purchase and how much you paid. It'll make filing a claim easier. Ask your insurance agent for an inventory form. When you're filling it out, record the serial numbers of appliances. Don't keep these documents or film, video, or photographic records in your house.

The higher the deductible, the lower the premium. You can reduce your premium by 12% or more by raising your deductible from $250 to $500; raising it to $1,000 saves about 25%.

HELP

■ **For information on** federal flood insurance, call the Federal Emergency Management Agency, Federal Insurance Administration, at (800) 638-6620, or write to them at P.O. Box 6464, Rockville, MD 20849-6464.

■ **Insurance questions? Call your** state insurance department or the National Insurance Consumer Helpline, (800) 942-4242.

■ **For help in finding a public ad**juster, call the National Association of Public Insurance Adjusters at (410) 539-4141, or write to them at 300 Water Street, Baltimore, MD 21202.

■ **Many states have internet sites** that let you compare the rates of the top insurance companies writing coverage for homes, autos, and apartments. For Florida, you can find this information and consumer guides at www.doi.state.fl.us; for Texas, similar information is www.tdi.state.tx.us.

■ *12 Ways to Lower Your Homeowners Insurance Costs,* published by the Insurance Information Institute, is available by mail or on the Internet. Call (800) 942-4242 or check its Web site at www.iii.org.

■ *How to Insure Your Home,* a book from Merritt Publishing, gives tips on how home insurance works and how to avoid problems when you make claims. It's available for $12.95 (plus shipping and handling) from the publisher, (800) 638-7597.

CHAPTER 41

DEBT COLLECTORS

What They Can and Can't Do

Intimidating phone calls at odd hours. Calls to your coworkers—and even your boss. Nasty and profane language. Threats of putting you behind bars. These are some of the hardball tactics used by a disturbingly large number of the nation's 6,000 debt collectors, despite the 1977 federal Fair Debt Collection Practices Act, which Congress enacted to stop such abuses.

Everybody should pay their bills promptly. But if you don't, there is still no reason to put up with abusive collection tactics. The 1977 federal Fair Debt Collection Practices Act (subsequently called "the Act") gives consumers potent weapons to turn the tables on any strong-arm collection agency that comes calling.

In addition, many innocent people who really don't owe money can get caught up in collection nightmares. The creditor or collection agency may have been in error, the merchandise might not have been sent or be in working order, or the purchaser may have been the victim of misleading advertising. The Act protects them, too.

While the law is tough, it isn't much help unless you are prepared to invoke it in confrontations with bill collectors. If you don't stand up for your rights, the collectors will know they have little to fear, and they will squeeze every possible penny out of you.

THE BASICS

The Fair Debt Collection Practices Act

Applicability. The Act generally covers debts arising from consumer transactions, such as goods or services bought on credit for personal, family, or household use (e.g., appliances or car repairs). Broadly speaking, it applies to anyone who regularly collects consumer debts for other creditors, like the Tightfist Collection Agency that tries to make you fork over money owed to the doctor, furniture store, or any other creditor.

The Act does not usually apply to the tactics of creditors, like department stores or banks, collecting their own credit card bills.

Who can be contacted, and how? A bill collector's stock-in-trade is making contacts to pressure debtors into paying. And earning 25%–35% of what they collect for businesses from "listings" of people behind in their payments can produce a powerful incentive to get really aggressive in recovering debts.

Bill collectors used to have a free hand to contact debtors or anyone else they believed could be used to coerce debtors. One collector actually parked a black hearse with the inscription "A deadbeat lives here" in front of a debtor's house.

But not anymore. The Act puts collectors on a short leash, allowing them to contact only a few persons about an individual's debt. These restrictions almost completely bar all contacts with "outsiders" that collectors could previously count on to pressure or embarrass you into paying, like relatives, friends, or employers.

When calling others in trying to locate you, bill collectors must identify only themselves (i.e., their names)—not who they are collecting for—unless specifically requested to do so. They must also call only to confirm or correct location information. This prohibits a collector from calling your office and saying, for example: "Hi, I'm Sam Jones, calling from the Acme Collection Agency. Could you tell me if Mary Jones still works there?" They cannot even print the agency's name or a phrase like "Open immediately. Overdue bill inside" on the envelope.

How can't a bill collector contact you? What can't they say or do? The Act gives collectors a fairly free hand in how they can contact you about a bill, such as by mail, telephone, telegram, or in person. But they cannot use a postcard. And they can't reveal in any way that they are trying to collect a debt when communicating by telegram or the mails.

In addition, they are not allowed to contact you at inconvenient times or places. This usually means before 8 AM and after 9 PM, unless, of course, the collector knows you work at night. If they know you are represented by an attorney, they cannot contact you directly, unless

---

FACING THE FACTS

Ogden Nash once wrote that he could "resist anything, except temptation." Apparently, millions of consumers have eyes bigger than their stomachs, financially speaking:

- Consumer installment debt in November 1996 was up 7% from the prior year—and at $1.2 trillion was the highest ever.
- In the '90s, according to the Federal Reserve, consumer debt grew at twice the rate of wages.
- In 1996, 1.1 million U.S. consumers filed for personal bankruptcy, up 25% from the prior year.
- In 1996, credit card delinquencies were running at their highest level since the American Bankers Association began keeping such records in 1974.

COLLECTION PROTECTION: WHAT THE ACT PROVIDES

The 1977 federal Fair Debt Collection Practices Act basically allows collectors to contact only the following persons about a bill:

- The debtor (including the debtor's spouse). Collectors cannot contact you in a way that would let someone else in on your financial troubles, such as by mailing a bill with the collection agency's name on the envelope to your place of employment.
- The debtor's attorney.
- A consumer reporting agency, as permitted by law.
- The bill collector's own attorney.

A collector can, however, contact "outsiders" in the following circumstances:

- The debtor specifically allows it. (The law doesn't require you to say "no"; you only have to avoid saying "yes.")
- The collector needs to locate a debtor. That's called "skip-tracing" in the trade, and the Act strictly limits how collectors can do it.
- A court specifically authorizes the contact.
- The contact is made to implement a post-judgment judicial remedy, like a wage garnishment.

your attorney fails to respond within a reasonable time—usually within 30 days. And they cannot contact you at work if the collector knows (or should know) that your employer disapproves. When they do contact you, they are supposed to identify themselves and make clear the purpose of their call—no anonymous, intimidating calls.

"Can you spell harass?" taunted one abusive debt collector when William P. of Queens, New York, asked him to stop harassing his wife about an overdue American Express bill. The collector then told William P. that his physical disability was just an excuse not to pay and that he was going to "have the sheriff come to [his] house and pick [his] wife up at her place of employ-

ment and arrest her." One of the most important prohibitions in the Act is against abuse or harassment. This bill collector's behavior egregiously violated the law.

Collectors are also not supposed to intimidate consumers, such as by threatening criminal acts or violence, publishing lists of debtors with your name included, or repeatedly telephoning you. Audrey S. told the NYC Consumer Affairs office that National Financial Services called her several times a day and told her she'd be sued not only for a $2,000 balance but also for legal fees as well, and that her name would be published in the newspaper—a no-no.

When they contact you, collectors are also prohibited from

such false or misleading representations as:

- Implying they represent a government agency, or that they are employed by a consumer reporting agency. Manuel A. complained to the NYC Department about collectors from International Collection Agency who claimed to be police officers. One of them had a gun, and the other held out handcuffs and threatened to take him to jail.
- Misrepresenting the character, the amount, or the legal status of a debt. For example, collectors can't claim that a creditor has obtained a judgment when she or he has not, or that the debt is secured by collateral the creditor will repossess, when in fact he or she has no collateral covering the debt.
- Making bogus claims about what they can or will do to collect the bill. They cannot, for example, threaten to garnish your wages unless it is actually legal to do so.
- Using misleading communications, such as official-looking documents, that make you think you are being sued.

They also can't use a wide range of unfair or misleading collection techniques. Examples of such practices include:

- Collecting any amounts or imposing charges that are not expressly authorized under the agreement involved or by law. For example, a collector cannot impose a collection charge unless the agreement you signed specifically permits it, which is extremely unlikely. Once a bill is past due, however, the creditor would usually be entitled to charge interest at the rate set by your state's law.
- Taking or threatening to take your property when there is no present legal right to do so, when they do not intend to do so, or when the property is legally exempt from repossession.

> "**H**e said he didn't care if he harassed me enough to give me another heart attack, he was going to get his money."
>
> —BOB D.
> of Morganton, North Carolina

What must collectors do to identify a debt? Unless a collector has already done so or you pay first, within five days after you are first contacted, a collector must send you a *written* notice stating:

- How much you owe and the name of the creditor.
- What you can do if you dispute the debt.
- How you can ask the collector to verify the debt.
- What the collector must do if you ask for verification.
- That the creditor will assume the debt is valid unless you dispute it within 30 days after receiving the written notice.

At the very least, this written notice identifies the debt and tells you about key steps to take to enforce important rights. These written particulars can help you confirm that the collector is really authorized to collect the bill for the original creditor.

Even if you owe the money, never discuss or agree to payment arrangements until you get this written notice. Waiting for this notice also gives you some breathing room to figure out how you can deal with the collector if you do owe the money.

What if you dispute the bill or can't identify the creditor? The Act helps you stop debt collectors in their tracks if they try to collect bills that you either dispute or can't identify. It entitles you to demand that a collector verify the identity of a creditor or the debt that you dispute. To make it count, you must send the collector a written notice within 30 days of receiving the notice that you dispute all or some portion of the debt or to ask the collector to identify the name and address of the original creditor if it is different from the current creditor.

The written request for verification is your way to tell collectors to get lost until they can show you who you owed the bill to or that you owe it.

You must make this demand in writing within the required 30-day period. One of the biggest mistakes consumers make is not putting this demand in writing. Consumers instead simply ask collectors verbally. This mistake telegraphs at least two things to collectors: First, the consumer does not know what the law requires. Second, the consumer may be too lazy or too afraid to stand up

for his or her rights as the law requires. In either case, it's a green light for the collector to ignore the law.

The Act does not spell out what counts as verification of a debt other than a judgment. It would, however, usually be at least a copy of the contract you signed or some other written documentation showing that you in fact owe the money.

Can you stop collectors from contacting you? You certainly can. The Act entitles you to tell a bill collector to stop all further contacts. This is your fail-safe in any confrontation with bill collectors.

You can use this defense any time. To make it count, you must notify a collector *in writing* and indicate either that you refuse to pay the bill or that the collector is to cease communicating with you. Since the notice is binding on the collector upon receipt, always send it by certified mail, return receipt requested. You then have proof of the exact date after which the collector must comply.

Once a collector receives your demand to stop communications, he or she can contact you one more time to tell you that all further communications will be stopped. Collectors can't use this communiqué to make idle threats, however. They can say they may sue, for example, but only if they usually do so in cases like yours and intend to do so.

Laura H. didn't mail any written notice at all. Like many recent college graduates contending with small salaries and large bills, Laura had trouble paying back her student loans. But she did make some payments over a period of years, demonstrating her intention and at least a limited ability to pay, and unfortunately encouraging two collection agencies, Windham Professionals and Superior Credit Services, to call her daily and sometimes several times a day with such threats as "this will not go away."

Of course, telling a creditor to stop communicating with you merely stops collectors from using nonlegal recourse to collect. It does not keep them from taking you to court.

Using the Act Against Abusive Collectors

The threshold question to answer before tackling any bill collector is: Do I owe the bill? Your answer will determine what parts of the law can help you the most and what parts you can use most forcefully against a collector. Here's how:

Bills you are unsure about. If you are unsure whether you owe a bill, immediately send the bill collector a written verification request. Make clear you will not discuss the debt or make payments until the collector verifies the debt. Also make this clear in the letter you send requesting the verification.

Once you receive the required verification, you must decide whether you owe or should dispute the bill.

Bills you dispute. If you're sure you don't owe a bill or it's one that you dispute, there is little point in beating around the bush with the collector.

Clearly state the reasons why you dispute all or part of the bill. It could be that you already paid it and the seller or creditor is trying to collect again; the bill may be for goods or services that you ordered but did not receive; maybe it's not your bill; or perhaps the original seller did not live up to the contract and you are entitled to withhold part of the bill.

If you are disputing the purchase, you should already have taken up the dispute with the seller. Explain the steps you have taken to the collector, and send along copies of documents and letters that back up your claims.

Insist on written confirmation of any settlement you propose. If you know you owe part but not all of a bill, you could send a "payment in full" check and write on the back of the check that it can be accepted only as payment in full of the disputed amount.

Your leverage for getting a favorable response is to tell collectors that you will order them to cease all further communications unless they respond favorably to how you asked them to take care of the disputed bill.

If the collector responds by pressuring you to pay instead of trying to resolve the disputed bill as you proposed, the only practical alternative is to order the collector to cease further communications. If the collector insists on not listening to you, it's a waste of time to keep shouting. Tell the collector to get lost.

Alternatively, you could order a collector to cease communications as your initial step. Doing so, however, prevents you from settling the dispute. You could be sued—but that may be exactly what you want if you are absolutely certain you don't owe the bill.

Bills you owe. If you owe the bill but lack the money to pay, it is important not to evade the issue by making up woeful tales or using nitpicking legal technicalities. The collector has likely heard it all before (and then some), and you won't win any sympathy no matter how hard you try.

In all such cases, your first step is to insist that the collector identify the bill as required by the Act. This gives you time to decide what you can do about the bill. Your next and most important step is to decide what you can realistically afford to pay toward the bill. The only thing that helps is to be straightforward about what you can do to pay and demonstrate that you will make a determined effort to do so.

The most important rules here are: Never say you *will* pay if you can't; never say you *can't* pay when you can pay at least something. Ignoring the rules is the surest way to trigger the full collection treatment.

While harassing debt collectors are as likely to disappear as ticks, you should know that the 1977 Act and FTC enforcement—along with some industry self-policy—is probably improving things. In 1996, for example, the FTC fined Pennsylvania-based Allied Bond & Collection Agency $140,000 for various violations of the Fair Debt Collection Practices Act, including contacting consumers at their places of employment even after the firm knew that the consumer's employer prohibited such contact. And it sued Goldman & Levine in New Jersey for telling others about consumers' debts, using obscene language, and using a scales of justice logo on their stationary to falsely imply that collection letters were part of an official inquiry.

The result, says the FTC, has been a downward trend in debt harassment complaints. Which is very nice, but not much of comfort when a collection agency pressures *you* at work.

WHAT TO WATCH OUT FOR

Post-dated checks. A debt collector might pressure you into writing post-dated checks. Then with a stack of post-dated checks in hand, collectors can pressure you to pay by threatening criminal prosecution under bad-check laws. The Act contains specific, limited provisions for taking post-dated checks.

Charges for communications, such as for long-distance collect calls. Collectors sometimes use a ruse such as claiming there is an emergency involving a relative to get you to accept collect charges for phone calls. If you're being hounded by bill collectors, be on guard for this.

Not getting it in writing. We repeat: If the collector has agreed to accept payments lower than those called for by your agreement, get a written confirmation of this fact. If you are already in default on a bill, paying less than you owe without a written agreement could lead to problems later, even if you have an oral agreement with the collector.

THE $MARTER CONSUMER

Don't ignore debt collectors. They won't go away; they'll just come at you harder, convinced you are a deadbeat.

Keep records. Hang on to any written materials collectors send you to document their actions. Document the dates, times, and places of any oral communications, and write up a summary of what happened. Take notes of any discussions, and keep written records to help you prove what happened. In addition, the Act requires you to use written communication to trigger certain rights. Doing otherwise is the same as throwing away the rights the Act created for you. Of course, you should keep a copy of any letters you send a collector.

Deal calmly with collectors. Most encounters with debt collectors will be of the oral kind, whether in person or over the phone. Always stay calm and stick to the point. Be polite but always firmly insist that collectors strictly toe the lines drawn in the Act. Here is an example of how to make collectors heel

THE PENALTY BOX

Violations can cost collectors plenty. The best part? It could be money in *your* pocket. A collector who violates any part of the Act could be liable for the sum of the following amounts:

- All losses you had because of any illegal actions the collector took, such as loss of a job, expenses you incurred, or mental anguish that was caused.
- Up to $1,000 that a court could award for violations even if you had no actual losses. The law allows consumers to collect this money to punish collectors who violated the law when seeking to collect a debt.
- The cost of the legal action plus your "reasonable" attorney's fees (determined by the court).

to when they try to browbeat you in oral confrontations:

"You must be aware that the Fair Debt Collection Practices Act prohibits you from [describe the illegal tactic the collector uses]. . . . If you keep that up, we are not going to have much more to talk about." That's a veiled threat that you will exercise your right to order the collector to cease all further communications.

Making it clear that you won't even talk about payments until you receive the required five-day notice under the Act creates leverage to get the collector to send it. If you still have not received the notice within a few days after the five-day period, there is a good chance the collector has violated the law. Pointing to such violations and the penalties the collector could face gives you leverage in future confrontations.

Answer any lawsuit summons. Otherwise, the creditor will get a default judgment and with it the power to use judicial collection remedies like garnishment and repossession of property. If you appear in court, you may be able to work out a payment settlement with your creditor's attorney on the spot.

H E L P

■ **If you have serious** financial problems, seek professional help. Call the National Foundation for Consumer Counseling to locate the credit counseling agency closest to you; (800) 388-2227.

■ **Where to complain. The Federal** Trade Commission is primarily responsible for enforcing the Fair Debt Collection Practices Act against collection agencies. Send any written complaint to Debt Collection Practices, Federal Trade Commission, Washington, DC 20580.

■ **Struggling to pay** off debt? Read *Debt Consolidation 101: Strategies for Paying Off Debts Faster & Saving Money,* available for $4.50 from Good Advice Press, P.O. Box 78, Elizaville, NY 12523.

■ **Many states also have their own** debt collection laws that are often based on the Fair Debt Collection Practices Act. Check with your State Attorney General's Office to find out about your rights under your state's law.

CHAPTER 42

TAX PREPARERS

Fear of Filing

E ven before Chief Justice Marshall declared in 1819 that "the power to tax is the power to destroy," taxes had been this country's great obsession. Political careers are lost for supporting them; millionaires go to prison for evading them. And the rest of us—the "little people," in Leona Helmsley's immortal words—are left to sweat and fret as April 15 looms near. When asked shortly before Super Bowl XXV if he was afraid of the other team's quarterback, New York Giants coach Bill Parcells replied, "Let me tell you what I'm scared of: spiders, snakes, and the IRS."

Some 115 million Americans dutifully file their income tax returns with the Internal Revenue Service each year. Or try to. As Bill Archer, the chairman of the House Ways and Means Committee, explains, "Mistakes are inevitable so long as we keep our ridiculously complicated tax code." What's the best strategy? Slightly over half of taxpayers choose to go through this painful ritual alone, sitting at the kitchen table with paper, pencil, and eraser or at the computer answering questions from a tax preparation software program, and measuring the extent of the damage. The rest, due to fear or finan-

cial complexity, seek solace or savings by hiring a tax preparer.

Finding the right professional can truly be a taxing task. As Leonard Sloane of *The New York Times* notes, "The industry . . . is diffuse, unstructured, and virtually unregulated." There is no national standard or educational requirement: All you need to do is click your ruby shoes together three times and murmur, "I am a tax preparer"—*et voilà*, you can hang out a shingle and get down to business. Only California and Oregon have qualifying guidelines.

And while fiscal laws are in a constant flux, one in seven preparers has in recent years canceled subscriptions to tax information services that help keep accountants up to date. The result: U.S. taxpayers demanded $100 million in damages from certified public accountants (CPAs) in 1992, according to the chief insurance liability underwriter for the accounting industry. As one industry insider notes, "Most accountants are three to five years behind the laws and regulations. . . . It's like doing carpentry without a hammer."

Therefore you need to take some time to find the right person to take care of your financial health, if you choose not to do it yourself.

THE BASICS

Step one is to decide if you'll prepare your tax return yourself or go for professional help.

If your tax situation changed little since last year, or if you have only a few pieces of information—one or two W-2s, some interest and investment income, and a mortgage deduction—consider sitting down at home one weekend with pen, pencil, coffee, and calculator and slogging through until it's done. As one business journalist who has done his own taxes for 20 years explains, "I go it alone because of an absolute conviction that no outsider will take as much care with my return as I will, no matter how big the fee. Keeping that fee in my own pocket is a big attraction, too, of course. And then there is the buzz that comes from taking on Uncle Sam and his troops at the IRS." Even if you don't enjoy that "buzz," you should be able to knock off your return in an afternoon: According to the IRS, it takes the average taxpayer 3 hours and 27 minutes to prepare a 1040 Form, plus two more hours for forms listing itemized deductions and capital gains and losses.

If you decide to go it alone, the IRS offers free help with publications, phone hotlines, and walk-in centers. While telephone assistance has been notoriously unreliable—one commentator said "you have a better chance of getting accurate information by dialing 1-900-WEATHER"—the rate of technical accuracy had reached 89% by 1993, up from 78% in 1991. If you can show that an error in your return was due to erroneous IRS advice, you'll still be responsible for back taxes and interest, but no penalty. Therefore, keep track of the person's name, the date and time you spoke to him or her, the question you asked, and the answer you received.

In addition, call your local IRS office to find out about Volunteer Income Tax Assistance, a program that offers free assistance to low-income taxpayers, the disabled, non-English speakers, and, in conjunction with the American Association of Retired Persons, low- and moderate-income citizens 60 years and up. Consider also investing in a tax guidebook or, if you have a computer, a software program.

Tax Preparation Software: The Pros and Cons

It may not be the most fun you'll have on your computer, but various companies now offer tax preparation software, both in stores and on the Internet, to replace the pencil and eraser of old.

Three programs dominate the market. Turbo Tax (and its Macintosh counterpart, Macintax) and Personal Tax Edge, both by Intuit, Inc., which controls 80% of the market; and Kiplinger Tax Cut, by the folks responsible for your neighborhood H&R Block storefront. All three follow a question-and-answer interview format similar to how a flesh-and-blood preparer operates; all three are reasonably user-friendly; all three enable you to test different scenarios to maximize your savings; and all three have become quite affordable: Kiplinger Tax Cut could be found in 1997 for as little as $4.95 ($9.95 on CD-ROM), while Turbo Tax Deluxe (the CD-ROM version) was listed for $29.95. Secure Tax, a tax preparation program on the Internet (www.secure-tax.com), is free, though you'll have to pay a fee to print your form (about $10 for a 1040) or file electronically ($4.95).

The downsides: The existing programs can be less than accurate for complicated returns (with Turbo Tax getting the best results in a *Consumer Reports* survey). They take a generally conservative approach to the tax code, which may not suit more aggressive taxpayers. As of 1997, the existing software for state taxes was far more limited than the software for federal taxes (Intuit required additional software for each state, while Kiplinger Tax Cut offered forms for 23 states on a single disk). Finally, as one skeptic points out, "impressive as some software is, it can't put on a suit and wave your receipts in front of an IRS auditor."

In addition, while most software companies offer to pay any IRS penalty with interest due solely to a "calculation error" by the program, there is less here than meets the eye. As an Intuit spokesperson cautiously explains, "If the error is caused by an automatic calculation, then we'll pay. But if it's something where you have a choice as to the calculation or can override it, then it's not covered on the guarantee."

Finally, it is worth noting that in a *Consumer Reports* survey of 26,000 readers, it took software users an average of 9 hours to prepare their taxes, as opposed to 5 hours for pencil-and-paper proponents. However, to be fair, the former often faced more complicated returns.

Ultimately, you should supervise your electronic preparer with the same degree of care as you would a human one, including yourself. Three suggestions to audit your software:

1. Once you print out your return, check your numbers for any erroneous entry.

2. Compare your figures against last year's. Unless your situation (or the tax laws) changed significantly, they should be comparable.

3. If you want an extra level of comfort, hire a professional to review your return.

> "*People get frightened when they look at the forms and booklets. But if a person's situation is fairly simple—just wages, interest and dividends, and no itemizing—there's no reason why he can't do his taxes himself.*"
>
> —JOEL S. ISAACSON,
> Weber, Lipshie & Company,
> accounting firm

A Good Tax Preparer Is Hard to Find

If your tax return is reasonably complex or if you need professional backup, help is available. But not all tax preparers are equally qualified—or equally expensive. Each year, *Money* magazine asks 50 tax preparers to calculate taxes owed by a hypothetical household. In 1997, none of the 45 respondents came up with the same figure—and none came up with the magic number of $42,336, the figure calculated by the expert who prepared the test. Answers ranged from $36,322 to $94,438—i.e., from over 14% too low to 123% too high. Less than one in four respondents came up within $1,000 of the correct answer. In addition, preparers' fees varied by a ratio of 1 to 16.5, and there was no correlation between the fees charged and the accuracy of the returns.

A few pointed queries should help you come up with the right person for the job. First, find out about prospects' professional background. Look for someone with experience (experts suggest five years or more), expertise in your field, and a recommendation from someone in a comparable financial situation. Ask how preparers stay current on tax developments—do they read specialized journals or attend seminars? As always, recommendations from family, friends, or colleagues is a good place to start.

Stay in contact with your preparer year-round, and make sure he or she will be available if you're audited. Find out if your preparer shares your financial philosophy—whether he or she will aggressively push the legal envelope or act in a conservative fashion. Finally, ask how the fee is computed. Storefront preparers generally charge based on the number of forms; enrolled agents and CPAs, on an hourly basis. Steer clear if the fee is calculated based on the size of your income rather than the complexity of your return. Don't forget to ask if your preparer will reimburse you for errors that result in interest or penalties.

Most important, look for someone whose skills match the complexity of your return. Just as you wouldn't hire Albert Einstein to tutor your child in 4th-grade math, you don't need a CPA from one of the Big Six accounting firms to file a 1040EZ (for "easy") form. At the same time, you don't want to hire a rookie if you're playing in the big leagues. Tax professionals break down into four categories:

■ *Storefront preparers* provide the best bang for the buck if your filing is fairly straightforward (only a few documents). Because anyone can claim to be a tax preparer, make sure to check a prospective preparer's qualifications, as suggested above. You're probably in good hands if you go to one of the large national chains. H&R Block, which files one in seven U.S. tax returns, requires all its employees to complete annual 11-week courses. For an average of $50, you can expect a solid, straightforward job—but no fancy accounting to jazz up your refunds. H&R also offers an "executive tax service" for taxpayers earning $40,000 or more. The benefit: nicer amenities—including a private office—a continued relationship with one agent, and year-round planning tips. The down-side: double the fees for the same quality of service.

Unlike enrolled agents, CPAs, and tax attorneys, storefront operators cannot represent you at an IRS audit; large chains, however, will generally send a preparer to accompany you to the IRS if your return is audited.

For business returns or complicated personal returns—if you sold a house, got married or divorced, want to claim depreciation of assets, or had partnership income last year —consider going to a more thoroughly trained professional. There are three kinds:

■ *Enrolled agents (EAs)* are certified to practice before the IRS after having either worked at the IRS for a minimum of five years or passed a rigorous two-day exam (only 30% pass). They are skilled at navigating the system and can handle most functions a CPA would serve, including complex tax returns, financial planning, and representing you at an audit, often for up to one-half to one-third less than a CPA would charge.

Enrolled agents must complete 72 hours of continuing study on tax law every three years. Members of the National Association of Enrolled Agents (NAEA) meet more stringent requirements (minimum

AUDIT TIME

Getting an audit letter from the IRS is about as welcome as getting a "go directly to jail" card would be in real life. Fortunately, less than 1% of returns are subjected to this nerve-wracking process. If fate or fraud singled you out, and if a tax preparer was involved in the return, he or she should generally be involved in the audit as well.

If the issue is straightforward—for example, justifying a high deduction with the canceled check—there's no need for an expert. In fact, 80% of taxpayers who face office audits go it alone;

half face field audits (conducted at home or their place of business) without professional assistance. IRS Publication 556, "Examination of Returns," can help. Key tips: Never lie. Don't volunteer information. And don't rule out a settlement.

If the issues are complex, go to a professional—an enrolled agent, a CPA, or a tax attorney. In particular, you will need a tax attorney if fraud is alleged and also perhaps if the audit involves complex matters like trusts, estates, charitable foundations, or partnerships.

of 30 hours of training a year). Ask your EA to show you an enrollment card and number that you can check with the IRS.

■ *Certified public accountants (CPAs),* like enrolled agents, should be considered for complex filings—especially if your situation involves large investment portfolios, business interests, trusts, or self-employment plans. CPAs may be especially valuable for financial and tax planning. But while all CPAs have some tax training, not all are experts on individual returns. And while they are required to take 80 hours of continuing education courses every two years to maintain their CPA designation, they may do so in a field unrelated to your needs. (Members of the American Institute of Certified Public Accountants [AICPA] must undergo 40-hour brush-up courses on tax law each year.) Make sure that your CPA specializes in your area.

■ *Tax lawyers* are the industry's 800-pound gorillas. They generally do not assist in the preparation of individual returns but rather intervene in complex issues like divorce settlements or more adversarial IRS audits.

Once you decide on the level of expertise you need, narrow your selection to three possibilities. Start the process before January 1, or the right person may not be available to give you the attention you require. Check their history with your local consumer office or Better Business Bureau; the IRS maintains a list of "problem preparers" whose clients face a high chance of being audited.

Tax preparers should be able to give you an estimate of their fee based on your previous year's return and basic information about your current financial situation. You can bring the fee down and make everyone's job easier by keeping careful records year-round and organizing your documents ahead of time instead of dumping a shoebox filled with papers in your tax preparer's lap on April 14. And to avoid trouble down the road, *never* sign a blank return or one written in pencil, and make sure that both you and your preparer signed your return (with his or her social security number) and that you review carefully and understand what you're signing: As the IRS warns, "You are still responsible for the accuracy of every item entered on your return. If there is any underpayment, you are responsible for paying it, plus any interest and penalty that may be due."

The clients of the Tompkins Square Tax Savers (TSTS), a Manhattan tax preparation service learned this the hard way. Imagine their dismay in April 1991 when they called TSTS and got a recorded message saying that the IRS had seized its records *and* their returns after arresting the owner for claiming refunds that taxpayers were not entitled to. Apparently he had forged his customers' signatures. The message warned that TSTS clients were likely to be audited and that they would be well advised "to consult with your attorney."

Ask your preparer for a letter explaining how he or she handled the gray areas of the tax code, with relevant legal support for controversial judgment calls. Finally, you are entitled to—and by law must receive—a copy of your return as well as any accompanying documents.

Electronic Filing

You can also *file* your tax return via computer, as did 14 million taxpayers in 1997. The Internal Revenue Service has been aggressively promoting electronic filing for reasons of efficiency: it hires 21,000 seasonal employees to process paper returns alone. But while electronic filing is clearly a good deal for the IRS, what's in it for you?

First, you'll get your money back a lot faster—16 days on average, as opposed to 38 days for paper returns. Second, you'll get an acknowledgment from the agency within 48 hours that it has received your return. Finally, you're a lot less likely to be the victim of a processing error by feeding your information directly into a computer than by relying on a human go-between to do the job for you. How much less likely? The IRS's own statistics show an error rate of less than 0.5% on electronically filed returns, as opposed to more than 20% on paper returns. As Jeffrey S. Trinca, chief of staff of the National Commission on Restructuring the Interanl Revenue Service, explains, "I've been to IRS service centers, and I've seen the chaos involved with paper filing. I have also observed the computers that receive the electronically filed return, and I know which one I'll choose from here on out."

In other words, there are very few reasons *not* to file electronically. The one big reason: cost. Until 1996, taxpayers could file their returns electronically directly, using a program called CyberFile. No more. Unless you qualify for Telefile (see "The Smarter Consumer"), you must go through a paid tax preparer or a "third-party transmitter," an electronic middleman who at will take your data and translate it into language that is intelligible to IRS computers. Transmitters generally charge a fee of $10 or more (depending on the number of returns), which can be significant if you're only getting a small refund. (One exception exists as of this writing: Drake Software, www.1040.com, offers free filing for Forms 1040A and 1040EZ.)

In addition, even if you file electronically, you will still need to rely on "snail mail" to get to the IRS any supporting documents (like your W-2s), a proof-of-signature form, and, if you owe any taxes, your check. (The IRS is planning for 1999 what Deputy Secretary of Treasury Lawrence H. Summers describes as "a big step forward in our quest to offer taxpayers a suite of electronic options for making tax payments." Starting that year, taxpayers can have the IRS dip directly into their bank accounts rather than mail a check. The IRS is also negotiating with credit card companies to allow payment of taxes by credit card.) If you've heard rumors that electronic filers are more likely to be audited, however, lay your concerns to rest. Such rumors are "just not true," according to an expert at Deloitte & Touche.

Two final points on electronic filing. First, if you do plan to file your return electronically and you are using tax-preparation software, you must use one of the companies approved by the IRS for that purpose. These companies are identified on the agency's Web site (www.irs. ustreas.gov). (The IRS Web site also offers tax forms, instructions, and manuals.) Second, electronic filing is available to *almost* everyone. One of the few exceptions: taxpayers who are sole proprietors of more than three businesses and file a Schedule C for each.

Refund Anticipation Loans (RALs)

Another way to get your refund a lot faster is to go to a tax preparer offering Refund Anticipation Loans. RALs are loans advanced by a financial institution like Beneficial National Bank to a consumer based on an anticipated refund from the IRS. You can generally get these loans within days of filing.

But while these programs have grown popular in recent years—why turn down quick cash, many taxpayers may ask—most financial experts agree with *Newsday* reporter Jerry Morgan, that "unless you need cash right away—within a few days of filing your return to ward off creditors—filing electronically to get a RAL doesn't pay." Some quick math should explain why RALs are an idea whose time should never have come. The average taxpayer refund is $1,227. Fees for RALs typically range from $40 to $90. If you're paying a fee of $65 to get

your RAL of $1,227 four weeks before the refund comes in, you have effectively paid interest of 5.3% over that period, or an exorbitant 69% annual interest rate!

WHAT TO WATCH OUT FOR

Tax preparers often advertise refund anticipation loans as "rapid refunds." They are not—they are short-term loans at exorbitant interest rates. The NYC Department of Consumer Affairs has waged a continuous battle with H&R Block branches in New York City, which culminated in 1997 with H&R agreeing to pay $500,000 for advertising RALs as "rapid refunds" via telephone operators and ads. This settlement—the largest ever under the city's 1969 Consumer Protection Law—followed an earlier settlement for $84,250 for similar deceptive advertising of RALs. Similar actions in Connecticut, Florida, and other states have led to comparable results.

Some preparers also misrepresent the fee they charge for a RAL. In 1992, the NYC Department of Consumer Affairs took action against Beneficial National Bank, a company that made RALs through hundreds of tax preparers for a $29 fee. Beneficial claimed that its interest rate on a $500 loan was 2.5%—but over a ten-day period, that worked out to an astronomical 225% annual rate.

Stay away from preparers who claim a special relationship with the government or who base their fee on the size of the refund they can get you.

The IRS has documented a number of schemes in recent years enabling unscrupulous predators to defraud both the agency and naive taxpayers. Don't fall for them:

- Charging African-Americans $50 for a free phone number to obtain a form that is supposed to entitle the taxpayers to reparation payments for slavery. The scheme originates in post–Civil War legislation enacted by Congress to provide former slaves 40 acres and a mule as a form of redress for their years of slavery. The catch: President Andrew Johnson vetoed the bill, which never became law.
- Promising low-income taxpayers to obtain for them EITC (Earned Income Tax Credit) if they'll provide the perpetrator their name and Social Security number. Don't be surprised if the perpetrator disappears with your money.
- Calling individuals to announce that they have won a prize—that will be theirs as soon as they pay the tax on it. Legitimate prize-givers are supposed to withhold the tax in the case of cash prizes, or provide the lucky winner with a Form 1099 for other forms of prizes.
- IRS agents showing up on a taxpayer's front steps to collect some outstanding payment. Real IRS agents will contact you beforehand and should show you a proper I.D.
- Persuading the taxpayer that taxes are voluntary and that he or she can purchase an "untax package kit" for $49.50. You might like

that idea—but you'll hate the IRS penalties after the agency catches up with you.
- Offering taxpayers a phony W-2 to entitle them to a refund that they can split with the perpetrator. Likely conclusion: The perpetrator will split with the money and leave you facing criminal charges from the IRS.

If you get approached with such schemes, you can protect yourself—and other potential victims—by calling the IRS inspector hotline (800-366-4484) or the Tax Fraud Hotline (800-829-0433).

THE $MARTER CONSUMER

If you are one of the 22 million taxpayers who can file your return on a form 1040EZ (i.e., if you are a single or married taxpayer with no dependent and taxable income typically below $50,000), you can file by telephone using a toll-free number, an option known as TeleFile. However, here again if you owe money, you must mail your check.

Look for a tax preparer before January 1st so that you get the right person for you and to ensure proper attention from him or her.

Organize your documents before visiting your tax preparer. You'll save time—and when you're being billed on a hourly basis, time is money.

Familiarize yourself with tax regulations that apply to you even if you hire a professional to do the calculations and fill out the paperwork.

Never agree to have your tax refund sent to your preparer. It should always be sent to you.

Come out of hiding. If you are among the 10 million Americans who failed to file in the past, don't stay in hiding. The IRS doesn't prosecute taxpayers who voluntarily come forward. But if you don't, you may be getting yourself in more trouble—and missing out on a possible refund. (Seventy percent of persons who file tax returns receive refunds, but refunds must be claimed within three years.)

H E L P

■ **To get free assistance** from the IRS, call (800) 829-1040 or your local IRS office. The hearing impaired with TDD equipment should call (800) 829-4059.

■ **For a list of members of the American** Institute of Certified Public Accountants in your area, call (800) 862-4272.

■ **For a list of members in the National** Association of Enrolled Agents in your area, call (800) 424-4339.

■ **The IRS puts out over a hundred** useful booklets, including Publication 1, *Your Rights as a Taxpayer;* Publication 17, *Your Federal Income Tax;* Publication 910, *Guide to Free Tax Services;* and Publication 579S, *Como Preparar la Declaracion de Impuesto Federal* for Spanish speakers. Call (800) 829-3676 for free copies. Many of them are on the Web at www.irs.ustreas.gov.

■ **Many newspapers publish special** tax sections in February or March with useful tips and information on filing your tax return and where to get help.

■ **Several organizations—such as** *Consumer Reports,* H&R Block, Ernst & Young, etc.—put out annual tax preparation guide/helpers. For $15 to $20, these guides can help you prepare even moderately complex returns.

PART 7

What You Wear

CHAPTER 43

JEWELRY AND WATCHES

All That Glitters Is Not Gold

Everyone should have it as easy as Holly Golightly when she skipped breakfast to go shopping at Tiffany's. She walked out of the store with full knowledge that the ring she just had engraved was made of plastic and came out of a box of Cracker Jack. Meanwhile, most everyone else is left to wonder whether they've gotten their money's worth for the jewelry or watch they bought. Complaints and inquiries of jewelers filed with Better Business Bureaus have increased 40% since 1993. The most common problems involve junky jewelry that breaks after the second or third wearing, deceptions about the quality of gemstones or the gold or silver content, and phony appraisals.

Buying jewelry is like buying works of art: The uniqueness of each gem or piece of jewelry makes it inherently difficult to evaluate without a trained eye. One unhappy man complained about a string of "cultured" pearls he bought as a graduation gift for his daughter. He paid $350 (supposedly 80% off the regular price) and was given what he was told was a "certified appraisal" indicating that the necklace was worth $1,575. An independent appraiser found that the necklace was made of imitation pearls and worth $75.

A suburban couple complained about an appraiser on 47th Street—the heart of New York's jewelry district—who had worked in cahoots with a neighboring jeweler to prop up the jeweler's claims about the quality of the engagement ring they had just bought. Independent appraisers found the ring to be worth two thirds of the $11,000 the couple had been told it was worth. When they confronted the jeweler, he refused to take the ring back or return their money.

THE BASICS

Find a Jeweler You Can Trust

Before you buy anything, ask your friends and relatives for the names of jewelry stores where they have had good experiences. You can also check with the Better Business Bureau (BBB) in your area to find out if the stores you are considering have complaint records. If you buy something from the first store you walk into, you could end up like the 1993 *Primetime Live* undercover producer who paid $3,700 for a diamond ring at Diamond City in Manhattan that an independent expert said was worth not even half that, only $1,700. The store's owner had appraised the diamond at $5,800, more than three times its actual value.

Purchasing diamonds and other true gemstones is a tricky business. Each stone offers a unique combination of the 4Cs—cut, color, clarity, and carat (weight). The average consumer may have a very hard time seeing or gauging these characteristics and therefore judging a stone's true value. Since no two stones are alike, it's hard to comparison-shop even among stones of comparable weights. And since most consumers probably aren't gem experts, you are dependent upon the jeweler's expertise and honesty to make sure you don't get ripped off on a fifth C—cost.

For this reason, a trustworthy, reputable jeweler is a must. Many people in the jewelry industry recommend shopping at well-known, established stores, if not at showplaces like Tiffany's or Cartier. You'll pay more, but you'll almost certainly get exactly what you pay for. And if you don't, you'll probably be able to settle the dispute quickly and satisfactorily. Well-tended reputations depend upon it.

The Jargon

The key to shopping for jewelry is understanding the terms used to describe and value it.

Quality mark. This represents the percentage of gold or silver alloyed with other metals, such as copper and brass. Jewelry industry guidelines require that jewelry marked "silver" or "sterling silver" contain 92.5% silver. On gold jewelry, the quality mark is expressed in karats. The higher the number of karats, the higher the gold content. No jewelry is made from pure gold (24K) or pure silver because neither element is strong or durable enough by itself for long wear.

Manufacturer's registered trademark. Federal law requires this mark to identify the manufacturer if an item has been stamped with a quality mark so that you will know the name of the entity that stands behind the quality of the item.

Gold-filled. A thin layer of gold of at least 10K is bonded to the surface of a base metal, and the gold content is at least 20% of the total weight of the metal. This term must be accompanied by a quality mark.

Gold electroplate. A base metal has been coated with a super-thin layer of gold of at least 10K. Also called "gold-plated." The gold can be as thin as seven millionths of an inch. This term must be accompanied by a quality mark.

Layered in gold. This term is completely meaningless; purveyors who offer such items hope that

KARAT COUNTING

Quality Mark	Gold Content	Notes
24K	*100%*	*Too soft to make jewelry*
18K	*75%*	*Standard in Europe*
14K	*58.5%*	*Standard in the U.S.*
10K	*41.6%*	*Lowest percentage that can legally be called gold in the U.S.*

consumers simply won't ask what it means.

Solid gold. Do not confuse this term with "pure gold." Solid gold simply means that the jewelry has not been hollowed out and tells you nothing about the amount of gold in the piece of jewelry. For example, a 10K solid gold ring cannot be hollow inside. This term must be accompanied by a quality mark.

White gold is usually 14K gold mixed with nickel and zinc.

Platinum must be at least 95% pure to be called platinum. Lesser grades must be marked with the amount of platinum in parts-per-thousand (e.g., 85% pure platinum jewelry will be marked "850 Plat." or "850 Pt.") Less than pure platinum must also be marked with the parts-per-thousand of each platinum group metal it contains (for example, "600 Plat. 350 Iridium").

Four Cs. Gemstones—especially diamonds—have four qualitites that determine their value.

■ *Cut* (also known as the facet). This refers to the small flat surfaces on gems, not just the shape of the stone. The quality of the cut affects brilliance, beauty, and the value of the stone. The price of two stones of similar color and clarity can vary 30% to 50% because of variations in cut.

■ *Color.* Diamonds are graded from colorless (the highest grade) to light yellow or brown (the lowest grade) on a scale between D and Z. D means the diamond is flawless and brilliantly clear. Z means it's yellow in color. Gems other than diamonds also vary in value depending on color.

■ *Clarity.* This scale from F1 (flawless) to I (imperfect or inclusion) grades the stone on the kinds, number, and placement of imperfections. Federal Trade Commission (FTC) rules prohibit any diamond from being called flawless unless no imperfections are visible to a trained eye in good light under 10-power magnification. "Clarity-enhanced" diamonds have been injected with a silicone gel to

485

hide flaws and make the stone sparkle more. Jewelers are required to tell you when a diamond has been enhanced.

■ *Carat.* This is a standard measurement of the weight of the stone. One carat weighs 200 mg. Carats are divided into 100 units, called points. Thus a half-carat diamond is the same as a 50-point diamond.

Kinds of gems. "Natural" gems are found in nature; "synthetic" gems are essentially the same in composition and brilliance as their natural counterparts, but they are made in a laboratory or factory. "Imitation" gems are made of different materials and resemble natural and synthetic gems only in appearance; they must be labeled imitation or simulated.

Gemstone treatments like bleaching, heating, or dyeing can improve a stone's appearance or durability, but some treated gems require special care. The silicone gel in clarity-enhanced diamonds, for instance, might leak when the stone is heated for resetting.

Watches. "Mechanical watches" are operated by a spring inside the watch. "Quartz" or "electronic" watches are operated by a battery.

Appraisals are opinions as to the value, authenticity, quality, and design of jewelry or watches. Since they represent opinions about unique items, there can be a certain amount of variation among competent appraisals. There are two types:

■ *Insurance replacement value* gives you the approximate cost to replace an item, taking into account current market prices, materials, and other costs. You need it to insure your jewelry against loss or damage.

■ *Estate value* estimates what the item would fetch on the open market and is usually lower than the insurance replacement value.

WHAT TO WATCH OUT FOR

All that glitters is not gold. Check the quality markings on both the clasp or hook *and* on the jewelry itself. Each should have a quality mark. A common trick is to put a good clasp on junky jewelry. If you check only the clasp for a quality mark, you may end up with a great clasp—and an inferior bracelet.

It is illegal to mismark jewelry. Most merchants are reliable, but a few may stamp 14K on jewelry that isn't anywhere near it. If you discover that an item you purchased was mismarked—usually through a professional appraisal—you can complain to law enforcement authorities, the local BBB, and consumer affairs officials.

Street vendors. Avoid buying jewelry on the street or take extra precautions. These vendors often use the mismatched markings trick, hoping you will check only the quality mark on the clasp and pay a dear price for cheap jewelry. Be skeptical of street peddlers who offer deep discounts on designer or famous name watches—counterfeits are plentiful (see "Counterfeit and Gray-Market Goods," page 635).

DIAMONDS MAY BE FOREVER, BUT PEARLS ARE MORE POPULAR

The value of pearls is based on shape, color, luster (also called orient), size, surface perfection, and rarity. Since it is a difficult and long process to grow a pearl, larger pearls are rarer and generally more valuable. More symmetrical pearls fetch higher prices, and pink pearls are more valuable than white, which are more valuable than gray. Measurements are across their diameter, expressed in millimeters.

A mollusk produces a pearl when an irritant lodges in its body and deposits of a crystalline substance called nacre form around it. "Natural" pearls result when the irritant gets there by accident (these pearls are virtually unavailable on the market). "Cultured" pearls are formed when an irritant is placed in a mollusk. Anything else that resembles pearls was manufactured, and the FTC requires that it be labeled "simulated" or "imitation." Here are the most common kinds of cultured pearls, according to the Jewelers of America trade association:

- *Akoya* pearls are grown in pearl oysters off the coast of Japan and are the most familiar cultured pearl.
- *South Sea* pearls are large pearls grown in oysters off the coast of Australia. They are usually silvery and less lustrous than Akoya pearls.
- *Fresh water* pearls are cultivated in mollusks other than oysters in freshwater lakes and rivers. They most often come in elongated, irregular shapes.
- *Biwa* pearls are freshwater pearls cultivated in a mollusk found only in Japan's Lake Biwa. They are smoother and more lustrous than freshwater pearls from China.
- *Burmese* pearls are large and grown in oysters off the coast of Burma. Their color tones are warmer than those grown in the South Seas, and they are rare and expensive.
- *Mabe* pearls are large hemisphere-shaped pearls; because of their shape they are usually mounted on rings, earrings, or brooches. They are less expensive than spherical cultured pearls.

When you buy pearls, don't expect any two to match perfectly in size and color—unless they're marked "imitation" or "simulated." However, if you roll a well-strung strand along a flat surface, it should roll evenly without any wobbling. Also, knots between each pearl in the strand will protect you from losing more than one pearl if the string should break.

Beware of jewelers hawking "wholesale" prices. It's just a come-on. By definition, wholesale involves sales to merchants; if a consumer buys something, it is a retail transaction.

Be skeptical of ads that claim an item is discounted by some percent or discounted from "list price." Ask yourself, 40% off what? Merchants who sell brand-name jewelry—a Bulova watch, for example—can honestly say they are selling the watch at a discount (if in fact they are). But in the case of diamonds or other natural, non-synthetic gems, the discount is meaningless. Watch out for dealers touting discounts off a "list price." Each stone is unique, made by nature, and Mother Nature doesn't set list prices.

Look for all four Cs. Many dealers will emphasize a gem's carat weight and downplay color or cut, even though these aspects can seriously affect the stone's brilliance—and value. Diamond buyers also pay extra for stones heavier than certain "threshold" weights. A 50-point diamond can cost 20% more than one that's 49 points—a weight difference that's indistinguishable without a scale.

Never buy gemstones by phone. Many people have been taken in by telemarketers who sell "investment stones," buying them sight unseen. For instance, a Maryland man "invested" $79,000 in tourmalines, tanzanites, an emerald, and a diamond after numerous calls from a dealer promising returns of at least 24% annually. After a year of "reports" from the world's gem markets—all positive, of course—he grew suspicious and had the gems appraised. Their retail value was $25,000, at most.

Misleading displays. In 1997, the Federal Trade Commission accused Zale's, the nation's largest retail jeweler, of advertising its "Ocean Treasures" line of imitation pearl strands, bracelets, earrings, pendants, and rings as made with cultured pearls. Zale's hooked consumers with the line "created by nature, enhanced by man" in ads and displays, but their pearls were made by man, not mussels.

Return policies. Before you plunk down any serious money, find out about the store's return policy. Don't buy from anybody who won't accept a return or be there to take one—i.e., traveling trunk shows at hotels or convention centers.

THE $MARTER CONSUMER

Look for the quality mark and the manufacturer's registered trademark when you're shopping for gold or silver jewelry or watches. Karat quality marks are not required, but most jewelry has been stamped with a quality mark. If there is a quality mark, the National Gold and Silver Stamping Act requires the manufacturer to stamp its registered trademark on the item as a guarantee of authenticity. (Exceptions: antiques and foreign pieces.)

Do not buy a gem without an independent appraisal unless you feel absolutely sure of yourself and your jeweler. A good jeweler who has dealt with you honestly should have no hesitation about allowing you to take a piece of jewelry to an appraiser of your choice. Ask the jeweler if you can charge the item on a credit card and return it if the independent appraisal contradicts what the jeweler told you. Keep in mind that jewelry appraisal is a subjective science; the dollar values don't have to match exactly, but they should be within a reasonable range (about 10%) of each other.

Do not use an appraiser recommended by the jeweler. Find an independent appraiser who has a gemologist's certificate from one of the four major certifying groups—American Gemological Society, American Society of Appraisers, Accredited Gemologist Association, and National Association of Jewelry Appraisers. Using an appraiser from any of these organizations is no guarantee of honesty but it's a good place to start. Get a very specific appraisal, including a written description of the item, an enumeration of each gem's cut, color, clarity, shape, carat weight, and position, and diagrams of all stones. Pay a flat fee or an hourly rate; do not pay an appraiser based on the appraised value of the stone.

When you buy, insist on a detailed, written receipt. The seller should be willing to put on paper every detail promised—the type of setting, quality of the gold or silver, and quality of the gem (specifying each of the four Cs). An honest jeweler should be willing to give you a money-back guarantee that you've bought what you were told you bought. Get it in writing; he or she has nothing to lose if you get an independent appraisal.

Ask for an independent quality report for each piece of fine jewelry you buy. If the jeweler does not have one, ask him or her to submit the item to the Gemological Institute of America (GIA), and get a written guarantee that the jeweler will refund your money if the GIA report shows anything different from what the jeweler promised. Don't try to get the GIA report yourself; the GIA accepts gems only from jewelers.

The best reports include a standard diagram of the stone with its unique internal flaws plotted on the diagram by the gem grader. Since every stone is different, you can use these reports to identify your stone. In a story told on ABC's *Primetime Live,* a Philadelphia woman took a ring with a high-quality diamond to a jeweler for enlarging. When she picked the ring up later, her good diamond had been replaced with an inferior stone. She used the quality report to help prove her case.

Let your budget be your guide. Because high-end jewelry stores want to force potential buyers to talk to a salesperson who can then steer them to even-higher-priced items, they do not mark their jewelry with prices. While a few jurisdictions require that at the very least a range of prices be posted in every display case, most do not. Don't get shifted out of your price range until you're sure there's nothing within it that suits your taste.

Ask about a watch's warranty before you buy. What's covered and for how long? Who will repair it? Where can you get spare parts once the warranty runs out?

H E L P

■ **The Jewelers Vigi-** lance Committee tries to help resolve consumer complaints. Write to: Jewelers Vigilance Committee, 401 East 34th Street, Suite N13A, New York, NY 10016-8578.

■ **The trade association for jewelers** has several free, helpful pamphlets on buying gold, silver, and gems. Write to Jewelers of America, 1185 Avenue of the Americas, 30th Floor, New York, NY 10036.

■ **To get an independent quality re-** port from the Gemological Institute of America, your jeweler has to submit items to GIA's Gemological Trade Laboratory. For information, call (800) 421-7250. GIA created the standardized rating system that is widely used in the U.S. to grade gems.

■ **The Federal Trade Commission will** not intervene in individual disputes, but it will take legal action if it sees a pattern of misrepresentation. Send the FTC copies of your complaint letters to jewelers, manufacturers, or local consumer law enforcement authorities: FTC, Public Reference, Washington, DC 20580.

CHAPTER 44

COSMETICS

The Truth Isn't Even Skin Deep

"For good skin," one dermatologist told the NYC Department of Consumer Affairs, "you don't need much more than a mild soap to wash away the dirt and grime of the day. You don't need masks, scrubs, peels, pore openers, pore closers, etc. It's all bull." Despite all the hype and hope, no cosmetic can iron out wrinkles, crow's feet, or a furrowed brow. Nor can any concoction dissolve those cellulite bulges on the hips and thighs. A new breed of products containing alpha hydroxy acid (AHA) and beta hydroxy acid (BHA) discernibly, but only temporarily, reduce fine line wrinkles and fade age spots, but they are no fountain of youth. None of the lotions, lathers, or cleansers for sale can do anything more than temporarily alter the appearance of the skin. It's that simple.

THE BASICS

The Skinny on Skin and Skin Care

The skin's job is to act as a barrier to bacteria and harmful substances in the environment. At around age 25, the skin begins to age as the naturally occurring collagen fibers that give skin its strength and flexibility begin to deteriorate. The skin then begins to dry out, and gravity's pull creates sagging and wrinkles. Exposure to sunlight and/or ultraviolet (UV) rays hastens wrinkling (and increases the risk of cancer). Avoiding the sun will delay the onset of wrinkling, but it's impossible to completely prevent wrinkles. Only cosmetic surgery and the prescription drug Retin-A (tretinoin) can temporarily stay this process. You'd never know this, though, from the pseudoscientific language and fantastic claims peculiar to cosmetics advertising and promotional pitches at department store counters. Toiletries and cosmetics manufacturers spend several billion dollars a year coaching aging baby boomers in how to stave off the inevitable—the natural and irreversible evidence of aging.

In a brazen attempt to distinguish one similar product from another, manufacturers transform creams in bottles into genies in bottles by implying that various substances like proteins, this or that acid, vitamins, RNA, aloe, and collagen have healing, rejuvenating, or reconditioning powers. A quick

491

flip through some fashion magazines turned up the following typical examples:

- Elizabeth Arden's Ceramide Firm Lift, an "all-in-one firming treatment that helps your skin fight the effects of time . . . *Immediately:* skin looks and feels firmer, 'uplifted.' *With continued use:* <u>firmness</u> and resiliency are measurably <u>improved</u>, the appearance of <u>dark spots</u> is <u>reduced</u>, lines and wrinkles are visibly diminished."

- Shiseido Benefiance Energizing Essence, whose "moisturizing and revitalizing properties are so intense, it actually encourages the skin's own renewal."

- Guerlain Age Defense 12M "ensures younger-looking skin . . . Day and night, 12 months of the year, Age Defense 12M gets to the core of the skin's youthful appearance—the intercellular gel."

Based on 148 undercover inquiries at 14 cosmetics counters at Macy's, A&S, Bloomingdale's, Lord & Taylor, and Saks Fifth Avenue, the NYC Department of Consumer Affairs found that salespeople stretch the truth about cosmetic lotions beyond recognition more than a third of the time. Among the worst sales pitches were:

- Clarins Concentrated "Cellulite" Control Gel. A salesperson described the gel to an undercover investigator as "a natural diuretic" that helps decrease water retention in the area to which it is applied. "It's like medicine," said the salesperson.

- Lancôme Durable Minceur. The salesperson said that rubbing the cream on in a circular motion would help the body flush cellulite away and that it would work even if the consumer didn't exercise, although not as well as it would work *with* exercise.

> "*These anti-aging products were developed under the pressure of the market, not according to scientific principles. . . . There is just no evidence that they work.*"
>
> —FDA OFFICIAL
> (insisting on anonymity) to the
> New York City Department of
> Consumer Affairs

In reality, these and similar products are little more than high-priced moisturizers, and moisturizers accomplish only limited results. They do not actually add moisture to the skin; they work by forming a seal that prevents water already contained in the skin from evaporating. Moisturizers all include the same basic ingredients:

- Water.

- An emollient to prevent moisture from escaping through the surface of the skin, such as the commonly used petrolatum (better known as petroleum jelly or Vaseline) or lanolin (a sheep's wool extract).

- Natural moisturizing factor, a group of ingredients that naturally exist in the body and seem to bind or hold water to the skin, such as urea, lactic acid, collagen,

You may feel all dressed up with no place to go, but the easiest time to get beauty maintenance appointments is midweek, especially Tuesdays, which you might call "Slow Times at Ridgemont Hair." You probably know how hard it can be to get a Saturday haircut appointment, but did you know that you might be able to get a discount on your manicure, or even a free manicure, when you go for a midweek pedicure?

hyaluronic acid, mucupolysaccharids, NaPCA (sodium pyrrolidone carboxylate), and hydroxy acids.
■ Other ingredients (such as aloe, jojoba oil, and allantoin) and triglycerides (such as apricot kernel oil, cocoa butter, and wheat germ oil).

Although you may not like the look of dry skin, it does not cause wrinkles; it only makes them more noticeable. So despite the advice dispensed at cosmetics counters and in glossy ads, using a moisturizer does nothing to prevent aging.

AHA and BHA products cause shedding of the surface skin and expose younger-looking skin underneath—and because of this may diminish fine line wrinkles, age spots and freckles. These effects are temporary; as soon as you stop using the product, your skin re-gresses to its original condition. How well these products work depends upon the formulation: how much acid they contain and its pH level. Early research suggests that BHA works at lower concentrations than AHA. Dermatologists say that the lower the pH, the better the products work, but hasten to add that lower pH also means greater likelihood of irritation.

Few products disclose either their concentration or pH level in ads or labels. "It is absurdly difficult to ascertain exactly the pH of any specific BHA or AHA product. From that standpoint alone, it is almost impossible to make a wise consumer decision as to which is the best product," wrote syndicated cosmetics columnist Paula Begoun.

Safety: More Questions Than Answers

While most cosmetics appear to be safe for short-term use, no one knows conclusively how the sustained use of cosmetics will affect the user.

Regulations governing the manufacture and sale of cosmetics are nowhere near as stringent as those for food and drugs. The Food, Drug, and Cosmetic Act, passed in 1938, gives the U.S. Food and Drug Administration (FDA) jurisdiction over the industry but very little real authority. While drugs must be proven safe and effective before they can be marketed, the FDA does not require testing or affirmative proof of safety before cosmetics hit the market.

This is not to say that manufacturers do not test their products for

Don't Get Burned—or Tanned

Virtually any exposure to the sun contributes to burning, wrinkling, and all forms of skin cancer. And the number of new skin cancer cases grew from 525,000 in 1987 to 940,000 in 1997. Thus the American Academy of Dermatology recommends that, regardless of your skin type, you use a sunscreen with a minimum sun protection factor (SPF) of 15 year-round—and weather reports have added a "solar risk index" or "ultraviolet index" to help you schedule your outdoor activities. No wonder the market for sunscreen has more than doubled since the 1980s and keeps growing year after year by 7%.

Sunscreens shield you from ultraviolet-B (UVB) radiation, which causes sunburning, tanning, and skin cancer. The FDA-approved SPF system refers to the amount of extra time you can spend in the sun without burning if you properly apply the sunscreen. For instance, a person whose unprotected skin burns after 10 minutes in the sun could spend 20 minutes in the sun while wearing an SPF of 2, or 150 minutes in the sun while wearing an SPF of 15.

Many products *also* provide a degree of protection from harmful ultraviolet-A radiation (UVA), which penetrates deeper than UVB rays into the base layer of skin and may contribute to melanoma. There is no rating system. Look for a sunscreen that provides "broad-spectrum" protection, which is the catch phrase for UVA protection.

When choosing sunscreen products, keep in mind that *Consumer Reports* research has shown one sunscreen to be as good as the next. Furthermore, SPF protection does not increase proportionally with the SPF number. While an SPF of 15 shields you from 93% of sunburning rays, SPF 34 adds only an additional 4% to the protection. That said, it makes sense to buy the cheapest waterproof or water-resistant sunscreen of SPF 15 or higher that you can find.

Don't just dab it on. The protective value of the sunscreen was established assuming a uniform and liberal application of goop. Trouble is, most people use only about half as much sunscreen as they need to get the protection level promised on the package and neglect to reapply it after a swim. The average bathing-suit-clad body needs about an ounce of sunscreen to achieve the advertised SPF. Beware claims of "all-day protection." The FDA has not approved this term.

But keep in mind that the only safe way to curtail the risk of skin cancer is to avoid the sun and to wear hats and protective clothing when you're outdoors between the hours of 10 A.M. and 4 P.M.

safety; since they are selling little more than an image, most manufacturers safety-test their products to minimize the likelihood of adverse reactions, adverse publicity, and costly lawsuits. Two problems: these tests are not sufficient to establish that the products or ingredients are not toxic over the longer term; and no regulatory body reviews the tests for adequacy or accuracy.

So what rules does the cosmetics industry have to follow? The Food, Drug, and Cosmetic Act defines "cosmetics" as products that temporarily improve the appearance or feel of the skin; products that affect the body in some physiological way are "drugs." Any cosmetic product cannot contain a disease-causing microorganism or any other substance known to be harmful; it must not be adulterated or stored in unsanitary conditions; it can contain only FDA-approved color additives; it must be labeled with the name of the product, its weight, the name and address of the manufacturer, and an ingredients list organized in descending order of predominance.

In addition, manufacturing plants are subject to FDA inspection. Although cosmetics labels must list the product's ingredients in descending order of quantity, the ingredients of specific flavors and fragrances need not be listed. In addition, the ingredient lists of make-up need only list the colors that *might* be in the product; thus, some colors that are listed in fact may not be in the product at all.

The problem with the FDA's distinction between cosmetics and drugs is that scientific advances have blurred the line between them. Skin is not the impermeable protective layer lawmakers assumed when they wrote the 1938 Food, Drug and Cosmetic Act. In fact, it absorbs many chemical and cosmetic ingredients, allowing some substances whose dangers have not been investigated to enter the body. And aggressive research and development by pharmaceutical and cosmetic manufacturers has created new ingredients and formulations, like AHA and BHA, which appear to have at least some temporary effect on the skin. For the moment, products containing these ingredients are considered cosmetics, and thus their safety was not proven to the FDA before they went on sale.

With wide use have come questions about AHA products' safety and a couple hundred consumer complaints. The adverse effects reported to the FDA range from mild irritation and stinging to blistering and burns. Research also indicates that these products may make people more sensitive to sunlight. The FDA has launched a review of AHA to be sure that it is safe and that, if necessary, consumers get proper warnings about increased ultraviolet sensitivity.

WHAT TO WATCH OUT FOR

Be alert to the technobabble that makes a cosmetic sound like the Fountain of Youth. The government permits puffed-up claims, no matter how meaningless or confusing. However, if a manufacturer makes a therapeutic claim, such as "heals dry skin" or "removes dandruff," the product has strayed into the over-the-counter drug category, and the FDA will demand either retraction of the claim or research proving the product's safety and efficacy. In 1987 and 1988, the government challenged 22 cosmetics companies to prove claims that their products could reverse the process of aging. Given the choice of rewriting the ads or submitting their products to the long, expensive process of FDA testing and approval, the companies, not surprisingly, toned down the rhetoric. But AHA and BHA have made manufacturers particularly brazen, and they still throw the following terms around:

Allergens. Ingredients to which some people have allergic reactions. Any ingredient can cause a reaction, but fragrance is the most common allergen; lanolin, coal tar dyes, and preservatives can also cause allergic reactions.

Hypoallergenic. This is virtually meaningless. No regulatory or even voluntary standard definition has been established. "Hypoallergenic" does not mean the product will not cause an allergic reaction. The same warning goes for terms such as "dermatologist-tested," "sensitivity tested," "allergy-tested," and "non-irritating."

Fragrance-free. Contrary to what you might think, products with this label can still contain fragrances. A more precise term would be "smell-free"—and to achieve this effect the manufacturer probably had to add some fragrance to mask the product's original smell.

Natural. There are no standards for this term; it can mean virtually anything to anybody. Natural cosmetics contain pretty much the same ingredients as the rest, including preservatives. Adding "natural" ingredients like milk, honey, avocado, algae, and vitamins have not been shown to enhance effectiveness.

No animal testing. Products that claim not to have been tested on animals may be splitting hairs. While the product itself was "tested" only on people, the *ingredients* were most likely tested on animals. Both FDA and industry officials say that companies making these claims use well-known ingredients that have already been proven safe—most likely with animal tests, since there are almost no cosmetic ingredients for human use that weren't first tested on animals.

Other ingredients. This catch-all term appears often in ingredients lists and refers to substances that the FDA has allowed manufacturers not to divulge because they are trade secrets.

THE
$MARTER
CONSUMER

Before you next choose between a no-name 19-cent-per-ounce moisturizer and a luxurious $40-per-ounce cream with a designer label—or decide whether to dispense with cosmetics altogether—keep the following in mind:

Don't be taken in by empty promises that a product will "lift the eyes," "firm," "nourish," "recondition," or "retrain" the skin; "relieve," "remove," or "reduce" cellulite; "target" trouble areas, "wash away" free radicals, or "prevent" aging. Cosmetics affect only the outermost layer of skin to temporarily change its appearance. The collagen molecule, for example, is too big to penetrate the outermost layer, the epidermis, to reach the dermis below, where it might rejuvenate the skin. A surgeon can lift sagging eyes; a cream cannot.

Price says nothing about quality. The beneficial ingredients are quite cheap and vary little from one product to another. When you buy expensive products, you pay for advertising, fancy packaging, free samples, perfumes, and all the other razzamatazz that contribute to the creation of the fancy image.

For instance, you could shell out $133 per ounce for Marcella Borghese's Superiore State-of-the-Art lipstick ($20 for a .15 ounce tube) or buy a whole cosmetic kit with what you save paying $7 an ounce for Wet 'n' Wild lipstick ($1 a tube).

All you need to maintain healthy skin is to wash with mild soap; to avoid exposure to the sun or wear a sunscreen; to eat healthy foods, drink plenty of liquids, and exercise regularly; and to refrain from smoking.

If you have skin problems, consult a dermatologist. Do not rely on salespeople or anyone else frocked in a white lab coat at a cosmetics counter for a diagnosis or treatment.

Use cosmetics that are widely distributed and marketed by a well-known firm. At least you'll know the product has a multitude of users who have apparently used it without significant side effects.

H E L P

■ **The Cosmetics Trap:** *When Truth is Only Skin Deep,* an investigative report by the New York City Department of Consumer Affairs, June 1992, available on request from NYC Department of Consumer Affairs, 42 Broadway, New York, NY 10004.

■ **You can look up any cosmetic ingre**dient to determine whether it is safe in *A Consumer's Dictionary of Cosmetic Ingredients,* by Ruth Winter (Crown, 1984).

■ **To find out the latest about cos**metic safety, check the FDA's Web site at www.fda.gov.

■ **Read** *Don't Go to the Cosmetics Counter Without Me,* by Paula Begoun (Beginning Press, 1993), available at bookstores for $13.95. Begoun also edits a newsletter, *Cosmetics Counter Update,* available for $25 a year from 5418 So. Brandon Street, Seattle, WA 98118, (800) 831-4088.

■ **For information on non-toxic cos**metics, consult the *Safe Shopper's Bible: A Consumer's Guide to Nontoxic Household Products, Cosmetics, and Food,* by David Steinman and Samuel S. Epstein, M.D. (Macmillan, 1995), available in bookstores for $14.95.

CHAPTER 45

DRY CLEANING

Don't Get Hung Out to Dry

Everyone seems to have a tale of woe about a favorite item of clothing that went to the cleaner wrinkled and slightly soiled and came back with a conspicuous spot or mysterious tear. One woman tells of picking up a white linen dress from the cleaner and finding blue stains where the receipt had been attached—the ink had bled through the paper. Another day, a favorite rayon dress came back with a hole in the fabric under the arm (not in a seam, where it could be easily fixed). "That was my favorite dress. Every week, it's something else. And the cleaners say it's not their fault," she complains.

Sound familiar? Dry cleaning disputes are one of those common annoyances you probably can't avoid entirely, but you can minimize them pretty painlessly.

THE BASICS

Check the Instructions

If you want to lower your dry cleaning bills, look at the care label before you buy clothing. The Federal Trade Commission (FTC) Care Labeling Rule requires manufacturers and importers to sew care labels that describe at least one satisfactory method of cleaning into most garments. The label must be easily found, designed to last as long as the garment, and give instructions for washing, drying, pressing, and bleaching. All parts of the garment must be able to withstand the recommended care procedure. If an article of clothing cannot be cleaned, the label must also disclose this fact explicitly. These instructions may or may not be easy to understand: Since 1997, the FTC has allowed clothing manufacturers to substitute symbols for worded instructions on care labels (see box on page 501).

This said, the labels are not always accurate. When the New York School of Dry Cleaning surveyed 12,000 garments that had been damaged during cleaning, it found that mislabeling caused half the problems. The case of Venus Enterprises is typical. The company sells imported rayon blouses, skirts, and dresses under the brand names La Femme and Fore Front. The care labels told consumers they could hand-wash the garments instead of having them dry-cleaned, but many of the clothes shrank after washing. The FTC fined Venus Enterprises $4,000 for failing to give proper care instructions.

In the unhappy event that a garment does not withstand the care recommended by the manufacturer on the label, the manufacturer is responsible. Your best bet is to return the item to the store where you bought it. In most cases the store will give you a refund or exchange and then settle up with the manufacturer. The FTC will investigate if it learns of a pattern of mislabeling.

Which Pieces of Clothing Go to the Cleaner?

If you follow the care instructions and the item comes back damaged, you have a right to press your case. If the cleaner followed the care instructions, and they proved to be flawed, the manufacturer must replace the article of clothing (usually accomplished through the store where you purchased it). If the cleaner deviated from the instructions (which they are unlikely to admit), it is responsible. Either way, you're not at fault.

If you want to save the considerable sums dry cleaning bills amount to—and are willing to take the chance, however slight, that you'll ruin the garment—try hand-washing it yourself. Since manufacturers want to avoid liability for replacing clothing that doesn't withstand the prescribed cleaning instructions, their labels are often overly cautious. Thus, many items that say "dry-clean only" can probably be safely hand-washed.

In fact, the FTC is currently considering revising its care label rules to require manufacturers to tell consumers when garments can be hand-washed or wet-cleaned. Meanwhile, it's difficult to guess which ones will hold up and which won't. The fabric content will give you a clue as to how careful you need to be, but it's no guarantee that the item won't

TO WASH OR NOT TO WASH

The dyes and fabric finishes used by manufacturers give clothes luster and sheen, minimize wrinkles and shrinkage, repel stains, and create softness or stiffness. They also make it difficult to generalize about which fabrics can stand up to hand-washing and which can't.

Use the following as a rough guide. Fabrics made of a mixture of natural and synthetic fibers tend to be stronger than natural fibers alone and stand up to hand-washing better. In addition, many woolen and linen things can be hand- or even machine-washed. Silk or rayon with fancy weaves or intense colors should be left for the dry cleaners, but simple silk items can sometimes be hand-washed in cool water. Cashmere sweaters can usually go into cold-water wash if they're first turned inside-out. Dry them flat. Never use water on cotton or silk velvet, unless you like it permanently flat.

shrink and the dye won't run. And unfortunately, if you override the care instructions and your glad rag turns into a dust rag, you have no recourse.

What the Dry Cleaner Does

The cleaner uses solvents rather than soap and water to remove stains from fabric (hence the term "dry" cleaning). Since no water is used, dry cleaning is appropriate for items that would otherwise shrink, fade, or run if washed in water.

Perchloroethylene ("perc"), the solvent most dry cleaners use to clean garments, is toxic and has been linked to leukemia, liver cancer, and neural disorders. In 1995, the International Agency for Research on Cancer upgraded perc from a "possible" to a "probable" human carcinogen, and the EPA lists it as a hazardous air pollutant. Dry cleaners are the largest source of perc emissions—5 million pounds of perc are released into the air each year in New York City alone.

Those who work with perc are at the greatest risk, but people living near dry cleaners are also in danger. In 1995, the New York City Public Advocate's office found at least 100,000 New York City residents were at risk of exposure to the chemical, as most perc-based cleaners were operating in or near apartment buildings. And the stuff can linger: A year after a New York City building that had housed a dry cleaner was renovated into an elementary school, perc levels were still more than 10 times higher than is considered safe. It had to be closed.

People who often wear clothes fresh from the dry cleaners could inhale enough perc to increase their risk of cancer. Properly dried clothes —those left to dry for more than 30 hours—pose much less risk.

If you are environmentally conscious, you may want to cut back on your use of dry cleaning services to minimize your perc contribution. Alternatives include hand-washing (be careful, as noted above) or using a spot remover to clean stains. However, many spot removers contain perc or other toxic solvents and must be used exactly as instructed to avoid exposure and fires.

Another way to minimize perc pollution is to use dry cleaners that dispose of toxic perc filters responsibly. Look for the "We Care" emblem at cleaners that have contracted with Safety Kleen to remove and recycle used perc and filters. Safety Kleen picks up the used perc, removes the clay-like residue, which it turns into pellets that are used to fuel cement kilns. The purified perc can then be reused for dry cleaning. The process costs the cleaner a little more, and the surcharge may be passed along to you. Decide for yourself if the extra expenditure is worth the environmental benefit.

Out, Out, Damned Spot!

Come clean—or your favorite pants may stay dirty.

When you bring your soiled garments to the cleaner, be truthful about where the spot came from and what home remedies you've tried. The cleaner will decide, based on what you say, how to treat the spot.

ART OF WASHING

Question: Do you know what this 🔲🔲🔺 means? If not, and you do your own laundry, you might soon need to learn. (Answer: Wash in warm water, dry medium heat, use only non-chlorinated bleach.) In 1997, the FTC introduced a new system of symbols (see below) that manufacturers can use instead of worded instructions on care labels. A washtub-like figure gives instructions on washing, a square with a circle inside denotes drying, an iron for ironing, and a triangle for bleaching. Dots inside the symbols give instructions on heat settings, and lines underneath stand for cycle settings—one line for permanent press, two for gentle cycles. A freestanding circle means "dry clean." X's over the symbol are warning signs: e.g., a crossed-out iron means "don't iron." Using the symbols is up to manufacturers, but the FTC encourages using them in anticipation of a global labeling standard, expected sometime before 2000.

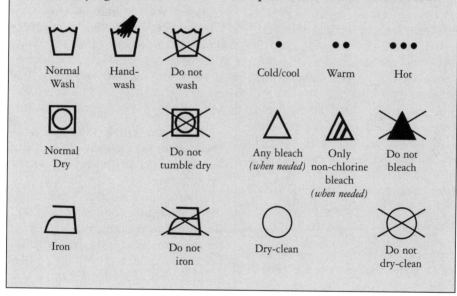

Normal Wash	Hand-wash	Do not wash	Cold/cool	Warm	Hot
Normal Dry		Do not tumble dry	Any bleach (*when needed*)	Only non-chlorine bleach (*when needed*)	Do not bleach
Iron		Do not iron	Dry-clean		Do not dry-clean

An oily stain on silk gets treated one way, but an oily stain on silk that you tried to remove with soap and water calls for different treatment.

In general, you have a better chance of getting rid of a spot if you bring the garment in to the cleaner as soon as you can. And with greasy stains (which means most food stains), there's no point trying to remove them yourself.

If you absolutely can't resist, it's probably safe to blot coffee, tea, or alcoholic beverage spills on non-delicate fabrics, but do so only with cold water, seltzer, or club soda and a white cloth towel. Don't use a napkin—the fibers can migrate to the garment. Don't use soap, detergent, alcohol, or home remedies, since they'll leave residue or rings. And last of all, don't rub, which can cause fading or weakening of the fabric.

WHAT TO WATCH OUT FOR

When buying clothing, and especially when bringing it to the dry cleaner, be on the lookout for trim, buttons, beads, and belts that may require special treatment or that make dry cleaning inadvisable. Polystyrene buttons, for instance, cannot be safely dry cleaned because they dissolve in the solvents, and the cardboard or glue sometimes used in belts that come with dresses or skirts may not hold up. If you have a question about buttons or other decorations, point them out to the cleaner, who'll decide whether dry cleaning them is safe.

And just because you can't see any damage from the lemon-lime soda you spilled on your tie—or the coffee you think you removed—don't assume there is no stain lurking there. It sounds like an oxymoron, but dry cleaners say some spots are invisible until the heat from cleaning brings them out. You can avoid nasty surprises when you pick up your clothes by telling the cleaner about spills, even if there's no visible damage.

THE $MARTER CONSUMER

Have all matching pieces cleaned together. This way any fading or color change will be uniform and the pieces will still match.

Don't go directly to the manufacturer. If an article of clothing did not hold up under the cleaning process recommended by the manufacturer on the care label, return it to the store where you bought it. The store must reimburse you and then settle with the manufacturer.

Be especially careful when buying clothing made from a combination of materials. Talk to your cleaner about whether and how to clean them. Sequins often do not stand up to machine cleaning, and hand-cleaning them can be costly.

Keep your receipts for garments that call for dry cleaning. Should you ever have a dispute with your cleaner over replacement of a damaged or lost item, you will be in a better position to request and receive a refund if you can prove how much you paid for the item. And if the problem was not the cleaner's fault, the retailer will be more likely to reimburse you for a damaged piece of clothing if you can prove you bought it there.

Buy garments made of stain-resistant fabric. For a few extra dollars, you may save yourself more than a few trips to the cleaners: Some wool, silk, and other fabrics now come with a Teflon coating that resists most stains (like red wine and

GREEN CLEANERS

Check to see if anyone in your neighborhood offers a wet cleaning process that uses only heat, steam, and natural soaps and that won't harm you or the environment.

One such process—long used in Europe but only just spreading in the U.S. under the name "Ecoclean"—uses carefully controlled amounts of water and fabric-specific, nontoxic detergents. The EPA has found it works on 80% of garments usually sent to the dry cleaner, from wool to silk to leather. Another new nontoxic method called Dry Wash uses liquid carbon dioxide to remove oil, soil, and other stains better than perc but without perc's harmful effects. (A downside: some synthetics, like the acetate used for many blazer linings, shrink in liquid CO_2.) You should decide for yourself whether the environmental benefit outweighs the slightly higher cost.

While neither method is a complete substitute for dry cleaning, industry experts see dry cleaners of the future offering both conventional and greener processes.

If you're looking for an environmentally safe spot cleaner (that's safe for your clothing, too), try Aveda fabric cleaner made from plants and herb extracts, or Ecover wool wash. Both are available in natural foods stores or, if you live in New York City, at the Ecomat environmentally safe laundries.

---

salad oil) but doesn't change the way garments look or feel. The same stuff that makes pots and pans easy to clean can also keep your silk tie from needing cleaning at all. Look for items marked "Safe Silk" or "Smart Silk," as well as Teflon-treated wool suits, in major department stores.

Inspect your clothing before you leave the dry cleaner. Point out any wrinkles or spots that did not come out. Cleaners are usually happy to take the item back to try again—sometimes the problem can be solved on the spot. If you notice any damage, bring it to the cleaner's attention immediately. Be courteous and firm. Ask to be reimbursed. Most often, cleaners will give you the "current value" of the item and not a full reimbursement of what you paid or what it will cost to replace the item. The cleaner will decide the item's "current value," based on how long you've owned the garment, its condition, and the original purchase price, but negotiating the estimate can be difficult. If you're not satisfied, say so—and take your business elsewhere. As a last resort, you can complain to local consumer affairs officials or go to small claims court.

If you and the cleaner disagree about who's at fault, ask the cleaner to have its trade association's textile analysis lab examine the garment. You cannot send the garment yourself: only the dry cleaner, Better Business Bureau (BBB), or retailer can. If you don't get satisfaction, complain to your local consumer affairs office or BBB.

To be on the safe side, air out your dry-cleaned garments in the yard, garage, or a spare room, especially if they smell strongly of chemicals. Take them out of the plastic wrapping as soon as you get home and let any leftover gases from the solvents escape before you hang your clothes, uncovered, in the closet or in a breathable fabric garment bag.

Keep used plastic wrapping out of the reach of children, who may be tempted to play with it and can asphyxiate themselves. Some cleaners have begun to shun plastic. They wrap dry-cleaned clothes in reusable garment bags. Ask your cleaner about it.

Bring spare wire hangers back to the cleaner. They will be reused.

HELP

■ **If you have a com-**plaint about a dry cleaner, contact:

International Fabricare Institute, a trade association of dry cleaners in the Washington, DC, and surrounding areas, offers textile analysis to its members; call (301) 622-1900.

Neighborhood Cleaners Association, the trade association for dry cleaners in Connecticut, Delaware, Florida, Massachusetts, New Jersey, New York, Pennsylvania, Rhode Island, and West Virginia, offers textile analysis to its members and a complaint mediation service between consumers and cleaners. Main office: (212) 967-3002.

Northeastern Fabricare Institute, 343 Salem Street, Wakefield, MA 01880; call (617) 245-6688.

■ **Write to the FTC's Consumer Re-**sponse Center, 6th Street and Pennsylvania Avenue NW, Room 240, Washington DC 20580. The FTC's Web site, www.ftc.gov, also offers more help on getting the most from your dry cleaner, as well as information on the new care labels.

■ **If a dry cleaning** problem arises from a manufacturing defect and you can't get the retailer to take the item back, ask the retailer for the name of the manufacturer or find the RN number, usually located on the care label. If you tell them the RN number, the FTC can give you the manufacturer's name. The International Fabricare Institute suggests sending the item and an explanation of the problem to the manufacturer via registered mail with a return receipt requested.

■ **For more information on the haz-**ards of dry cleaning and safer alternatives, contact the Pollution Prevention Information Clearinghouse, U.S. Environmental Protection Agency, 401 M Street SW (PM-211A), Washington, DC 20460; (202) 260-1023.

■ **Greenpeace USA offers an online** guide to finding wet cleaners in your area. You'll also find additional information on the dangers of perc, at www.greenpeace.org.

PART 8

Children

CHAPTER 46

CHILD CARE

The Who, What, and Where

What's the problem with child care? There simply is not enough of it. Supply of any child care—let alone affordable, quality child care—has not kept pace with the demand for it. According to U.S. government statistics, one in four families with children have one parent at home, and the number of mothers—traditionally responsible for the prime burden of child care—who work outside the home has increased from approximately 30% to over 60% from 1970 to 1996.

Once you've overcome the problem of quantity, you also have to take on the problem of quality. In what will certainly come as a relief to the nation's guilt-wracked working parents, the largest-ever longitudinal study of the effects of day care on child development concluded that day care kids aren't all that different from the kids who stay at home. Researchers at the National Institute of Child Health and Human Development trace just 1% of the differences among children to factors related to day care—and 32% of the differences resulted from variations in the home life of the children in the study.

However, there was a clear contrast between children in high-quality care and low-quality care. Unfortunately, it can be very difficult to find and afford high-quality care. In a separate study, researchers found that just 15% of day care facilities were excellent, 70% were barely adequate, and 15% were poor. Children in that enormous middle category were found to be physically safe, but they got little or inconsistent emotional support and even less intellectual stimulation.

So it's no wonder you feel bewildered and overwhelmed by your quest to find someone to care for your kids, and you're not alone. Parents often must struggle with long waiting lists for coveted day-care slots, or fees that are higher than one parent's salary.

As a result, many settle for "whatever they can find," which often means a revolving door of child-care providers and arrangements that take an emotional toll on both parents and children. Since your child's health, welfare, and cognitive development are on the line, you can make your search for child care more sane and satisfying by treating it no less seriously than you do other major consumer purchases. "What you want to become is an informed consumer," says Heather Paul, executive director of the National Safe Kids Campaign. "Think of the amount of time people put into purchases like a refrigerator or television set—they check and compare. Yet the most important buying you'll do is selecting a preschool environment for your child, and many people don't do any research at all before they make that decision."

THE BASICS

The Three Child-Care Models

There are many different child-care options, but only three basic models:

Day-care centers care for many children in a group or "school" setting. They are usually staffed by trained professionals under a significant amount of government regulation and oversight. Children can interact with many other children and are exposed to several different organized activities.

The disadvantages? Day-care centers can have child-to-provider ratios as high as 20 to 1; the best day-care centers tend to have extremely long waiting lists and tuition as high as some colleges; and many day-care centers have strict hours, vacation, and sick policies that may not fit in with your work schedule.

DAY-CARE CENTERS PROS AND CONS

UPSIDES	DOWNSIDES
■ Usually have trained professional staff. ■ More state regulation of both staff and facilities. ■ Often more educational and structured programming that has been shown to increase social competence, maturity, and intellectual development. ■ Offers changing experiences as children get older. ■ The opportunity for children to interact with many other children in a school-like setting. ■ More stable, less likely to close or quit than other day-care options. ■ Many center-based facilities offer basic health care.	■ Often high child-to-provider ratios. ■ Often high staff turnover. ■ Often long waiting lists to get in, especially for the best centers. ■ Strict, inflexible hours. ■ Many centers have no provisions for sick children. ■ More interaction with other children also means more exposure to infectious disease and viruses. ■ Centers are often inconveniently located in relation to the child's home and/or parents' place of employment.

FAMILY DAY CARE PROS AND CONS

UPSIDES	DOWNSIDES
▪ Often the least expensive option because of low overhead and reasonable child-to-provider ratios. ▪ More flexible and accommodating of parents' schedules than center-based day care. ▪ More personal care and less provider turnover. ▪ Opportunity for children to interact with a few, but not an overwhelming, number of other children, often of different ages. ▪ Parents often have more input (and control) over the care and may more easily leave special instructions, when necessary. ▪ Caregiver's home is often located close to the child's home.	▪ Little if any government regulation and supervision of staff or facilities. ▪ Often the provider has less training than providers in centers. ▪ Less variety of activities and play materials. ▪ Less structured and possibly fewer educational activities. ▪ Family-based child-care can go out of business unpredictably. ▪ No sick-child facilities or health care. ▪ Since children are still interacting with other, albeit fewer children, there is still an increased risk of contagion.

After you consider the pros and cons of day-care centers, think carefully about the differences between for-profit and not-for-profit centers. About 40% of all centers are for-profit; they're either independent or franchise centers, such as "Kinder Care" or "Children's World." The rest are run by churches, synagogues, co-ops, businesses, research centers, or the government on a not-for-profit basis. According to a 1991 study published in the *Journal of Social Issues,* staff in not-for-profit centers tend to have more training and to receive higher salaries; not-for-profit centers have lower child-to-provider ratios, and parents participate more both as volunteers and in setting policy. Not surprisingly, the not-for profit centers are rated "good" or "superior" twice as often as the for-profit centers.

Family day-care providers typically care for five to eight children in the provider's home. Besides being more personal, they are more flexible and tend to cost less than day-care centers. Another plus is that children are in a home rather than an institutional setting, yet are still exposed to other children.

On the other hand, family day-care providers tend to have less formal training; in many states, they

IN-HOME CHILD CARE PROS AND CONS

UPSIDES	DOWNSIDES
■ Most flexible hours. ■ Children can stay at home when they're sick. ■ Less opportunity for contagion by other children. ■ Most personal form of care. ■ Potentially more continuity of care. ■ Offers parents greatest degree of control over the child's care.	■ Most expensive option. ■ Providers may have little experience or formal training. ■ Lack of accountability; parents are the only enforcement, and there are no legal mandates. ■ Children may not get the benefit of interaction with other children as much as children in family- or center-based care. ■ Providers can quit unexpectedly, leaving parents scrambling.

are unregulated or less regulated than day-care centers. They can be hard to find and have more limited space than day-care centers. And while many are scrupulous about nutrition, hygiene, and safety, some may not be.

In-home child-care providers (baby sitters or nannies) care for children in the child's home on either a full-time or part-time basis. In-home caregivers can live in their own homes or with the family. Their main advantage is that they provide the greatest flexibility for parents and the most continuity of care and personal attention for children. There may also be health benefits—especially for younger children and infants—in staying at home.

Of course, in-home providers are the most costly kind of child care, and typically they are not Mary Poppins—they are often less well trained and they are certainly less regulated than other caregivers. Also, children cared for at home may have less social interaction with other kids than do children at day-care centers or in family-care arrangements, unless their caregiver (or parents) plans regular social activities.

Making the Choice

There are pitfalls in each type of arrangement. You've probably heard at least one of the horror stories that pop up regularly on the evening news: a day-care center employee arrested for alleged child abuse; two children burned to death in a tragic fire in a Queens, New York, family day-care facility lacking smoke detectors and adequate emergency plans; and the British *au pair* Louise Woodward, who was found guilty of killing the 9-

month-old Boston infant she cared for in a case that sparked a national debate about nanny training and mommies working.

Fortunately, tragedies such as these are rare. According to a comprehensive survey of all reported cases of sex abuse in day-care centers from 1983 to 1985, only 5 children out of 10,000 were abused in day care. During that same period, 9 of 10,000 were abused at home. Less than half of the day-care cases involved a professional child-care provider—the others involved janitors, bus drivers, and family members.

To prevent physical or sexual abuse, parents should look for facilities that:

- Allow unlimited access to parents (and other caregivers, like grandparents and trusted friends).
- Keep bathroom doors open while children are using them.
- Do not allow providers to tease or physically punish children.
- Have strict rules about who can pick up children.

Also, parents should be alert and perceptive: Do children at the center look fearful, anxious, or neglected? Be sure to ask plenty of extra questions if they do or if something "just doesn't feel right"; following your instincts may mean insuring your child's safety.

Day-care centers. The three key issues you should consider when you shop for a day-care center are staffing, policies, and facilities. Since day-care centers tend to be heavily regulated by state departments of health, facilities are usually up to par. Most are inspected for building code violations at least once a year. Still, it never hurts to check building maintenance and emergency procedures for yourself.

CHILD CARE FOR CHILDREN WITH DISABILITIES

Kerri D. enrolled her son Michael, who has juvenile diabetes, in a day-care program at the Indian Valley YMCA in Hartford, Connecticut. Even though it took the staff only a minute to check Michael's blood sugar, the YMCA forced Kerri to withdraw Michael because of concerns about liability, insurance, and regulations.

Fortunately, the federal Americans with Disabilities Act should help disabled children like Michael receive care. Centers must now determine whether they are *able* rather than *willing* to care for children with special needs. The Act took effect January 1, 1993, and applies to all child-care homes and centers except those operated by religious groups.

If your child has been unjustly excluded from day care, contact your state attorney general, the disability committee of your state's bar association, or the American Civil Liberties Union.

DAY-CARE CRITERIA

In 1980 the federal government established the Federal Intra-agency Day Care Requirements (FIDCR). Although these standards have never been implemented, FIDCR recommendations are a good guideline for parents. They require day-care facilities to:

■ Have a planned daily program of developmentally appropriate activities to promote intellectual, social, emotional, and physical development.
■ Train caregivers and provide an orientation including health, safety, and program procedures.
■ Give parents unlimited access to the care setting and regular opportunities to discuss the child's needs and participate in policy making.
■ Provide adequate and nutritious meals, as appropriate.

In addition, although there are no federally mandated child-to-provider ratios for day-care centers, and some states allow a ratio as high as 20 to 1, the FIDCR advocates similar caregiver/child ratios as the NAEYC and specifies that a center should have:

■ A maximum of six infants in total.
■ A maximum of 12 toddlers in total.
■ A maximum of eight preschoolers in total.

Staffing is also addressed by most state regulations, but training requirements tend to be loosely enforced and staff-to-child ratios tend to be high. Often, the director of the day-care center is required to have formal education and specialized training in child development, but the day-care workers —who have the most direct contact with your child—must meet far fewer requirements than the director. Some states require only a high school diploma. According to Carolee Howes, a developmental psychologist and professor of education at the University of California at Los Angeles, "When you are in a [day-care] center, you need that specialized knowledge of children to be able to manage groups and do developmentally appropriate activities."

In addition to training, turnover is a key staffing issue. If a well-educated caregiver quits after three months, then the children do not benefit. Often, centers either don't keep or refuse to discuss precise turnover statistics. To find out, ask other parents and get a sense of the work conditions by asking about the caregiver's salary and benefits. The center is less likely to have a revolving door if it treats its care-givers professionally.

But it is not enough for a center to have qualified, committed care-givers if it doesn't have enough of them. The National Association for the Education of Young Children (NAEYC) recommends that all groups of young children have at least two adults at all times with the following staff-to-child ratios:

- One caregiver to three to four infants
- One caregiver to four toddlers
- One caregiver to six to eight pre-schoolers

Family day-care providers. Family day-care providers working in their home appeal to many parents as an ideal middle ground between baby-sitters and full-fledged day-care centers. But according to the Child Care Action Campaign, a nonprofit advocacy group, there are only 1.5 million family day-care providers for the more than 5 million American children whose parents seek this kind of care.

Of central importance for parents seeking this option, about 80% of the family day-care providers are not regulated in any way. According to Barbara Reisman, executive director of the Child Care Action Campaign, this means that "basically, states are saying you're on your own if you use family child care. . . . Parents need to be very well-informed and very vigilant."

First, check with your state's health department to see what, if any, requirements family day-care centers have to meet. Then, if licensing, registration, or certifica-tion is required, make sure the center you're considering is operating legally.

Since any regulation for family day-care centers is likely to be more lax than for formal day-care centers, take more time to check out the facility. Child Care Inc., a New York City referral agency, suggests the following checklist:

- Does the home have smoke de-tectors and fire extinguishers?
- Are medicines and household products kept locked up?
- Are toys safe and appropriate for the child's age?
- Do the children regularly go out-side to play, when weather permits?
- Is there a clear schedule for meals, naps, and playtimes?

You should spend some time in the home observing various parts of the day, and you should spend a good deal of time talking with the child-care provider and checking his or her references. Reisman suggests that if you're not allowed to visit any time during the day, you should move on. Also, according to Sally Ziegler, executive director of the Child Care Council, another non-profit referral group, "If children run hungrily to a visitor, it means they are not getting enough attention."

Finally, as with a day-care cen-ter, you should also check the num-ber and ages of the children being cared for, the provider's vacation schedule (if any), sick day, and late-fee policies. There should be no more than one adult to every five children, including the caregiver's own, and no more than two infants under age one.

In-home child-care providers. Since your child will be cared for in your own home, you will set the rules. The only question is the qualifications of the provider. But finding a qualified provider is far easier said than done—even if you're willing to pay top dollar and particularly if you want to hire a legal worker and pay her or him "on the books."

The question of not hiring illegal aliens and paying Social Security and other taxes became a front-burner issue after the failed 1993 nomination of Zoë Baird for U.S. Attorney General simply because of her "nanny problem." The "Nanny Tax" bill, a.k.a. the Social Security Amendment Act of 1994, does two things: increases the exemption you're allowed before you have to pay taxes to $1,000, and simplifies the process by allowing you to pay your employee's Social Security when you file your income taxes by completing Schedule H.

Most families find caregivers by word of mouth: Once one family's children reach school age, they refer their nanny or sitter to another family. But if you're not so fortunately connected, you have two basic options: place "help wanted" ads or use a nanny agency. If you want to hire someone who is legal *and* willing to pay taxes, you may need to go through an agency. You espe-cially need an agency if you aren't ready to spend lots of time screening scores of applicants yourself. (Remember Diane Keaton interviewing a parade of eccentrics in *Baby Boom?*)

No state specifically regulates in-home child-care providers. If anything, agencies that refer nannies and sitters are regulated as employment agencies, without any special requirements for referring people to care for children. They could just as well be screening gardeners or domestics. So while agencies are certainly helpful with preliminary screening, there is no way to avoid investing a significant amount of time and effort to find the most appropriate in-home child-care provider.

If you don't, the consequences could be disappointing or even tragic. In a story told to the NYC Department of Consumer Affairs, Kate L. said she was horrified to learn that the nanny caring for her infant—whom the agency had called "the perfect person"—had repeatedly lied: The nanny said she had worked for the De Beers diamond-baron family in South Africa and claimed to be a Cordon Bleu chef. The nanny's poor performance tipped Kate off that maybe this wasn't quite the case. And at a dinner party, one of the guests recognized the nanny's "homemade"

> "**W**e tell parents to spend at least as much time choosing child care as you would buying a car—you wouldn't buy a car over the phone. . . ."
>
> —PATSY LANE,
> Child Care Coordinator for the
> City of Los Angeles

gourmet dessert as having come from the bakery around the corner. Before hiring the nanny, Kate had interviewed someone who she was told was Ms. De Beers. But even then she was somewhat suspicious when "Ms. De Beers'" accent slipped from South African to what sounded like Cockney.

And then there's the story of the mother from Westchester County, New York, who found out that her nanny had physically abused her three-year-old son when her son one day asked the new nanny whether she was going to "lock me in my room." The mother then found out that the previous nanny had routinely locked the child in until the mother got home from work.

If you decide to go through an agency, you have to choose one with almost as much care as you choose the actual provider. At anywhere from $500 to $2,000 per referral, it pays to make sure you're getting the referral service you're paying for. Following are some tips:

■ Get a written contract that includes a specific job description for the provider you're trying to find. This will avoid wasting time on inappropriate referrals and also help prevent disputes about fees down the road.

■ Ask specific questions about how the agency screens applicants. Do they do face-to-face interviews? How many references do they check? Do they keep and let you see written records of reference checks?

■ Get and check the agency's own references. If the agency is not able or willing to refer you to other parents who have used their services, you should strongly consider going elsewhere.

Whether you use an agency or go it alone, you have to do two things *yourself*: Interview the nanny and check her or his references. The whole process is so emotional and the stakes are so high that many parents end up relying on their "gut" or "instinct" and hoping they make the right choice. If you don't feel right about an applicant, don't bring that person into your home.

Child Care Inc. suggests asking a candidate the following questions in your interview:

■ What do you like about working with children?
■ How much television-watching do you think is appropriate?
■ What would you do if my child disobeyed you?
■ What would you do in an emergency if I couldn't be reached?
■ Describe your typical day.

Check references after the interview, but be careful, advises Wendy Sachs, a representative for the International Nanny Association. Sachs owns a nanny placement agency and is a parent who employs a nanny. "The references you get are only as good as the person giving the references." One parent interviewed for a NYC Department of Consumer Affairs investigation of the nanny agency business, *Who's Watching the Kids?*, told of checking one reference with whom she shared a mutual friend, and only after an extended personal conversation did she get a true—and most unfavorable—picture of the applicant. One trick to checking references is to ask specific questions based on information you get from the nanny in an interview. If the answers don't agree, you can suspect a problem.

Indeed,. the NYC investigators found widespread problems in reference checking. An undercover nanny "applicant" gave four agencies she visited the names of two Consumer Affairs staff members to call as "references." One of the agencies didn't even try to call the references and the others didn't try very hard, merely leaving messages but never actually talking to both parties. When contact was made, the questions were superficial, and the conversations only a few minutes long. Nonetheless, all four agencies told the undercover "applicant" that they had jobs for her, and two agencies lied to families, telling them that her references had been checked when they hadn't.

Finding the perfect provider is just half the battle: The other half is to retain your child's caregiver. Remember, you're the boss; you've got to take responsibility for supervising your sitter or nanny. The caregiver is a professional; no matter how cordial your relationship, she (or he) is not a member of your family and needs to be treated with professional courtesy. To establish and maintain a professional relationship with your caregiver, you should:

■ Provide a written contract. Include specific job responsibilities, hours, salary, vacation/sick days policy, and car and telephone privileges.

■ Strongly consider providing benefits, such as health care and in-service training, for your provider and putting periodic opportunities for performance reviews and raises into your contract.

■ Meet with your provider regularly, both to give feedback on job performance and to get feedback on your child's development.

WHAT TO WATCH OUT FOR

Special day-care center rules. Before you're satisfied that you've found the perfect child-care center, take a good look at any special rules. Many centers have prohibitively restrictive policies about who can drop off and pick up your child and when, and most charge at least half tuition on personal vacation or sick days, when your child does not attend. Before you sign up, make sure you know and can live within the rules.

Be your own inspector. Few rules govern family care providers and those that do are rarely enforced. It's unlikely your child care dilemma will end as tragically as that of Jeremy Fiedelholtz's parents. Three-month-old Jeremy died in January 1997 at a licensed family care center, where he was one of 13 infants, nine more than the recommended limit, when the director went grocery shopping. She left the children in the care of an attendant who didn't know infant CPR.

Be sure that family day-care facilities provide adequate safeguards against injury and take precautions that will prevent the spread of disease. Look for things like fences around playgrounds and outdoor play areas; be sure that gates have latches (and are latched); watch to see if caregivers wash their hands before and after wiping children's noses, changing diapers and preparing snacks. Check whether there are fire exits, smoke alarms, and an emergency plan. And find out whether care givers have been trained in CPR and whether all facilities—building, furnishings, toys, and educational materials—have been tested for the presence of radon, asbestos, and lead.

Criminal background checks of nannies. Many parents seek criminal background checks before they hire a caregiver. Recent horror stories on the evening news have encouraged the creation of private-eye services that claim to do FBI and other criminal background checks. Unfortunately, no individual or organization has the authority to look at someone's state criminal record or FBI file without that person's permission. The only thing an agency can do is county-by-county record checks, which tend to be both tedious and incomplete.

You'll be an employer if you hire a nanny. Be prepared to give vacation time and pay when your family goes away. Otherwise, you risk losing your nanny to a family that's more generous.

THE $MARTER CONSUMER

Shop around. Regardless of which option you choose—child-care centers, family day care, or in-home day care—both your child and your pocketbook will benefit from shopping around. Like buying a car, reliable and affordable child care requires both comparing the different models and regular maintenance to keep your child-care arrangements working. Here are five basic steps to steer you down the rocky road until your child starts school:

1. Consider your child and your lifestyle before you check out your options. Write out your priorities and take the list with you when you visit day-care centers or interview family or in-home providers. Look beyond the walking tour. Observe what goes on. Pay attention to the number of children, the number of adults, the age of children, and the quality of interaction between caregivers and children.

2. Plan ahead. It's never too soon to start checking out your options. If you wait until a week before you have to go back to work, you'll be stuck with a snap decision.

3. Personally interview and check the references of whoever is going to be caring for your child, no matter what setting the care will be given in.

4. Make the transition as easy as possible for your children by taking extra one-on-one time and leaving them with the caregiver for a few hours at a time when the situation is still new.

5. Drop in unexpectedly every few weeks to make sure that your child is being cared for appropriately. If a center discourages this, think about choosing a different one. Also, meet periodically with your care provider(s) to both give and get feedback on your child and child-care arrangements.

Check-up. Ask a prospective caregiver to get a nationwide criminal check from the FBI. A nanny candidate must initiate the check him/herself by sending her (or his) fingerprints along with a cover letter and a $17 check, to the FBI Identification Division. You can offer to pay for it, but you cannot check without the applicant's go-ahead. It's also a good idea to ask for medical records, including a recent tuberculosis test and proof of childhood immunizations. If the candidate you prefer has no records, you should pay for the shots. Better safe than sorry, for both the caregiver and your child.

HELP

■ **For information on** family day care anywhere in the country, call *Child Care Aware* at (800) 424-2246.

■ **For listings of nanny training programs** around the country, call the *American Council of Nanny Schools* at (517) 686-9417.

■ **For information about your state's** laws and regulations regarding child care, contact your state department of health. Most have a special agency or bureau for child care.

■ **For referrals to local child-care** resource and referral agencies, call the National Association for Child Care Resource and Referral Agencies, (800) 570-4543.

■ **Child Care Action Campaign is an** advocacy group that also publishes a newsletter and other free guides for parents, such as *Finding Good Child Care: A Checklist; Care for Your Child: Making the Right Choice; Questions and Answers About Infant and Toddler Care.* To subscribe to the newsletter ($25/year, including membership) or for a list of publications, write them at 330 Seventh Avenue, New York, NY 10001-5010, or call (212) 239-0138.

■ *How to Choose a Good Early Childhood Program,* and other information, is available from the National Association for the Education of Young Children. Call (800) 424-2460 or (202) 232-8777, or e-mail pubaff@naeyc.org.

■ **Get information on requirements** for safe toys and playground equipment from the U.S. Consumer Products Safety Commission, (800) 638-2772.

■ **To get further information on safe** art materials, contact the Art and Creative Materials Institute via their Internet site at www.creativeindustries.com/acmi or call or write them at ACMI, 100 Boylston Street #1050, Boston, MA 02116, (617) 426-6400.

CHAPTER 47

TOYS

Not Just Child's Play

THE BASICS

Play is the main work of childhood, and toys are the tools of the trade. However, each year some 120,000 children under 14 are injured playing with toys—more frequently than workers in many trades are injured on the job. In addition, many children spend more time watching toy advertisements than their parents spend watching their kids. And many of these ads are misleading, promising kids a product that just doesn't exist. Since kids can't unionize, it is up to parents to make their kids' playroom a safe and satisfying "work site."

The toy industry spends nearly half a billion dollars on advertising to get people to purchase close to $13 billion dollars' worth of toys each year. And more and more of those ads are targeted at kids. The typical seven-year-old sees about 20,000 commercials a year, and advertising in kid-specific media like *Sports Illustrated for Kids* and the Nickelodeon cable channel grew more than 50% between 1993 and 1996, to $1.5 billion. Toys touting commercial logos account for ever more expensive toys. But children are often disappointed by toys that do not live up to their glitzy advertisements. Far worse, while toy manufacturers, consumer advocates, and government regulators agree that toys are safer than ever, thousands of children are rushed to emergency rooms each year because of toy-related injuries. Most emergencies resulted from inappropriate use and/or inadequate adult supervision. Approximately 20 children die annually in accidents with hazardous playthings.

Two-year-old Betsy was playing with a teddy bear when she pulled off its hard plastic nose, popped it into her mouth—and almost choked to death on it. Luckily for Betsy, doctors removed the small toy part from her airway and she was fine. Nonetheless, choking on small parts remains the leading cause of toy-related deaths.

The U.S. Consumer Product Safety Commission (CPSC) catalogs toy incidents like Betsy's and is the federal agency responsible for keeping hazardous playthings from endangering children. Toys are getting increased scrutiny, but the CPSC lacks the resources to adequately monitor and address the thousands of new toys introduced

A Test Tube Too Small

The CPSC defines a small part as a toy or part of a toy that fits entirely into a test tube 1.25 inches wide and 2.25 inches deep. However, children have choked to death on toys that pass the CPSC small-parts test.

In 1990, six children choked to death on the old version of Fisher-Price's Little People, which just barely exceeded the test-tube standard. In February 1991, Fisher-Price increased the size of its Little People. But the CPSC has refused to enlarge the test tube.

Instead of the test tube, parents can use a cardboard tube from a toilet tissue roll, or the child's fist. If the object is smaller than the fist or fits into the cardboard tube, it should not be given to a child who still puts things in his or her mouth.

each year, many of which are imported from foreign manufacturers.

The U.S. Federal Trade Commission (FTC) monitors all advertising, including toy ads, but they too can be outrun by the massive toy industry. The FTC catches a few deceptive ads each year, but many misleading ads go unnoticed—except by the children they target.

The toy industry helps fund two pseudo-trade groups to monitor toy safety and advertising. The American Society for Testing and Materials (ASTM) develops voluntary toy manufacturing guidelines, and the Children's Advertising Review Unit (CARU), which is part of the Better Business Bureau, develops voluntary children's advertising guidelines. But since both the ASTM and CARU get much of their funding from the toy industry, they can be like foxes guarding the henhouse. The bottom line is that *you* need to protect your children from hazardous toys and misleading toy ads.

WHAT TO WATCH OUT FOR

Toy Safety

Don't assume that the toys on store shelves or that your kids receive as gifts from well-meaning friends and relatives are safe. There are just too many toys and not enough toy-safety cops on the beat to check each toy before it goes to market. Toys that are found to be unsafe can take months to recall, and recall notices rarely reach all consumers who have purchased the defective toy. So there's just no substitute for toy-safety vigilance. Here are some things to look for when shopping for safe toys:

Small parts. Choking is the leading cause of toy-related deaths and injuries to children under three. Small parts can be either independent toys, such as tiny trucks or dolls, or parts of toys that can come off, like car wheels or doll shoes. Balloons and small balls are some of the potentially deadliest toys for young children.

Sharp points and edges. These can cut or puncture kids. Some toys have sharp points and edges by design; others are just poorly made. Toys can also develop sharp points and edges when they break. Many stuffed toys have sharp wires inside.

Cords and strings over 7 inches long. These can become a noose around a young child's neck and cause strangulation. Pull toys and crib gyms can be particularly hazardous when children roll around in confined areas, like cribs and playpens.

Loud noises. Noises from toy caps, toy guns, toy phones, radios, and other noisemaking games can injure a child's hearing. The CPSC bans toys that make particularly loud noises, but even quieter toys can impair hearing if used too close to kids' ears.

Electronic toys. These can cause shocks and burns if not properly constructed and maintained.

Toys with hazardous chemicals can be deadly to children. Some toys, such as chemistry sets, must include some chemicals, but others—such as model kits, children's nail polish, and some brands of spray "string"—contain some of the same substances found at toxic Superfund sites.

Toy chest lids have been known to fall onto children, hitting them in the head or trapping them inside the toy chest. Toy chests with hinged lids should be able to stay open in any position. Other options are toy chests without lids or with lightweight removable lids. All toy chests should have ventilation holes in case a child gets trapped inside.

Bikes, in-line skates, all-terrain vehicles, and other riding toys can be very hazardous if they are not the right size for the child and if children do not wear the appropriate protective gear. All-terrain vehicles injure about 23,000 children a year and should not be used by children under 16. No child should use a bike, skateboard, roller skates, or roller blades, etc., without a protective helmet. From 1993 to 1996 the number of injuries related to in-line skates tripled. To help your kids skate safely, make sure they wear the proper protective gear: padded helmets and wrist- and knee-guards.

Backyard play sets are no fun if they're not safe. Unlike many other children's products, there are no mandatory safety standards for play sets. Many are built excessively high, with hard and heavy swing seats, sharp exposed bolts and edges, and overlapping play patterns. The most important aspect of a backyard play set, however, is what is on the ground below. Grass is not a safe play set surface: Kids need at least 6 inches of soft sand or wood chips to break their falls. The rubber mats under some school yard and city park play sets are all right too—as long as they are properly maintained.

Toy Advertising

While some parents and consumer advocates have fought to ban all advertising to children, advertisers have been targeting younger and younger kids with ever more creative messages. Leave aside the scrutiny alcohol and tobacco ads now so deservedly receive. The barrage of commercial messages for products more legitimately aimed at children are even more pervasive and just as insidious. Even parents who try have a hard time keeping kids away from the thinly veiled sales pitches in many books, movies, and TV shows. The average TV show targeted to kids under eight has 12 minutes of advertising, compared with only eight minutes on adult programs. Furthermore, the number of advertisements based on movies, TV shows, cartoon characters, and other celebrities has exploded. As if movies and TV commercials featuring Batman action figures and Pocahontas dolls weren't enough, everything from underpants to sheets to cereal boxes is stamped with toy logos. It's hard enough for adults to keep up with advertisers' antics, let alone help their kids through the maze of consumer messages. Here are some of the more common tricks of the trade to watch out for when watching TV:

Ads that make toys do things only Hollywood can make happen. Hidden wires and invisible hands can make airplanes and stuffed dogs seem to fly, and smoke and mirrors can make action figures conquer all. Each year some advertisers take special effects too far. For example, Mattel paid a penalty of over $150,000 to the FTC for using special effects to enhance the performance of its G.I. Joe action figures and accessories.

Ads that show you more than you will get. Kids who get one set of a toy depicted in an ad with many sets or many different accessories are likely to be disappointed. A 1994 ad for Steel Tec race cars, airplanes, and other vehicles implied that kids could build all nine different vehicles from the kit at once, when in fact they could build only one at a time.

Ads for toys requiring parental supervision that don't show parents. If a child sees an ad for a toy like a ride-on electric car without parents around, then he or she will expect to be able to use that toy alone, even though the manufacturers suggest that safe play with the toy requires parental supervision.

Ads that blur the line between fantasy and reality. Kids, not surprisingly, often expect a toy to do what it does on TV. A Treasure Trolls ad depicted the trolls laughing and making wishes come true. When kids found out the dolls didn't laugh, several complained to *Zillions,* the *Consumer Reports* for kids.

Ads enticing kids to buy toys just because of celebrity logos and look-alikes. Thanks to *Star Wars, Hercules,* and episodes of *Batman* and *Jurassic Park,* almost $5 of every $10 spent on toys in 1997 bought licensed items, up sharply from just $1 in the early 1990s, making up the lion's share of toy profits. For instance, a basketball with Michael Jordan's signature on it can cost three times as much as a basketball without it. Some toys with movie logos are marketed to kids who are too young to see the movies—but aren't too young for the marketing.

Ads that depict toys being used in violent ways. In particular, ads for guns and slingshots that show kids shooting other kids at close range send kids the wrong message for both play and real life.

THE $MARTER CONSUMER

Toy Safety

Read and heed toy age recommendations. Age labels on toys are not just developmental recommendations; they are often safety warnings. The Child Safety Protection Act of 1995 requires clearer and more prominent warning labels on potentially hazardous toys—and stricter penalties for manufacturers who ignore the law's warnings.

- "Ages 3 and up" often means the toy has small (i.e., swallowable) parts.
- "Ages 8 and up" often means the toy has electrical elements or hazardous chemicals.
- "Ages 12 and up" often means that the toy can get excessively hot.

Don't buy a toy intended for an older child because you think that your child is exceptionally bright or will grow into it. Even exceptional two-year-olds put things in their mouths and can choke to death on toys with small parts.

Follow assembly instructions carefully and discard all packaging immediately. Safe toys can become unsafe if improperly assembled. Never allow children to play with packaging that is not part of the toy, or with toys before they are completely assembled and checked.

Check toys carefully and repeatedly for small parts, sharp points and edges, long strings, and other hazards. Not all toys are properly labeled—the "Baby's Fun Infant Gift Set" labeled "for ages 6 months and up" *also* carried the following warning: "CHOKING HAZARD: small parts. Not for children under 3 years." Some gift. And toys that are safe when you buy them can become unsafe with use (and abuse). Be particularly careful with baby rattles, pacifiers, and other toys meant for babies and young children.

Remove crib gyms when infants can get up on their knees. Infants can and have choked to death by falling onto a crib gym strung across a crib.

Keep toys intended for older children out of the reach of younger ones. Teach older siblings about the hazards their toys pose to younger children. *Never* use balloons around young children who still "sample" small objects by mouth or who haven't the coordination to avoid inhaling a balloon while trying to inflate it.

HOW MUCH MORE YOU PAY FOR A NAME

Beauty and the Beast sweatshirt	$12.99
Pink sweatshirt	$ 5.99
	You pay 117% more
Barbie bike helmet	$21.99
Magna Cool Design bike helmet	$12.97
	You pay 70% more
Pooh and Tigger sheet set for a twin bed	$19.99
Colored sheet set for a twin bed	$11.99
	You pay 67% more
Spiderman birthday party set	$24.12
Generic red, blue, and yellow party wares	$15.32
	You pay 57% more
101 Dalmatians plastic child's plate	$ 3.29
Plain plastic child's plate	$ 2.09
	You pay 57% more

Source: Various retail stores, January 1998

Store all toys properly. Many toy-related injuries are caused by falling onto or over toys. Putting toys away can prevent these injuries as well as keep toys from breaking. Outdoor toys need to be protected from the elements to prevent rust and breakage that could cause serious injuries. Do not store toys in unsafe toy boxes or on shelving that children can climb.

Supervise children using toys and teach them to play safely. No matter how safe a toy is, children are creative and resourceful; they will often find ways to use toys in unintentional (and potentially hazardous) ways. Toys are not babysitters; there is no substitute for thoughtful adult supervision.

Check recall notice boards at toy stores and call the CPSC Recall Hotline, (800) 638-CPSC. (You can also check the CPSC's Web site at www.cpsc.gov.) Toy recalls are often poorly publicized, so you have to take the initiative to find out if the toys you have bought are still considered safe. You can also report a potentially hazardous toy to the CPSC by calling the Hotline.

Watch out for toys used as prizes in cereal boxes and fast food kid's meals. These toys are often poorly constructed, overlooked by safety regulators, and almost always are small or made of small parts.

Play with your kids. This is the easiest way to both teach your kids how to play safely and check the toys for hazards. It's also fun!

"Nontoxic" art supplies are not necessarily completely safe. The Consumer Federation of America warns that many ingredients that pose no threat in the short term may be unsafe over the longer term—for instance if a child sucks on a painted surface.

Outsmarting Toy Ads

Watch TV with your kids. Use toy advertisements as tools to explain the difference between fantasy and reality and to teach kids to view advertisements skeptically.

Look—and, when you can, play— before you buy. Encourage kids to play with a toy at a friend's house or to look at it carefully in the store before buying it. The TV image of a toy is often quick to fade in real life.

Fight toy fads. It's tough to resist constant cries of "I want this" or "Buy me that," but a little willpower will teach your kids some valuable consumer skills and could save you a considerable sum of money. Since most kids have short attention spans, one tactic is to wait a couple of weeks or even a month before deciding to buy—as celebrity marketing increases in volume and intensity, the time that particular products stay "hot" gets shorter. When you do give in, try to buy useful items of good quality and teach kids to look more carefully at what they're buying than at the logo that's on it.

Finally, foster creativity. Encourage kids to draw their own "celebrity" logos on T-shirts, notebooks, party cups, and other products so they can identify with their favorite character without paying the premium price.

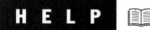

H E L P

■ **The No-Choke Test-** ing Tube, a cylinder you can use to assure that small parts are big enough to avoid a choking hazard, can be purchased for $1.45 from Safety First, Attention Consumer Relations, 210 Boylston Street, Chestnut Hill, MA 02167 (ask for item # 126).

■ **Request the Toy Recall List by call-** ing the CPSC Hotline at (800) 638-2772 or check their Web site at www.cpsc.gov.

■ *A Parent's Guide: Advertising and Your Child* is available free from the Children's Advertising Review Unit (CARU) of the Better Business Bureau, 845 Third Avenue, New York, NY 10022. You will also find it on BBB's Web site at www.bbb.org.

■ *Zillions,* the *Consumer Reports* for kids and their families, can be ordered through *Zillions,* Subscription Dept., P.O. Box 54861, Boulder, CO 80322-4861.

■ **The Art and Creative Materials Insti-** tute in Boston certifies art supplies and materials to be nontoxic. To get further information on safe art materials, look at their Internet site at www.creative-indus-tries.com/acmi or call or write ACMI, 100 Boylston Street, No. 1050, Boston, MA 02116, (617) 426-6400.

P A R T   9

Travel and Vacation

CHAPTER 48

AIRLINES AND AIRFARES

How to Avoid Flights of Fancy

L eaving on a jet plane? It was easier back when Peter, Paul, and Mary first sang their famous song. You simply bought a ticket and left. Since most tickets had no "time of travel restrictions" and didn't require buying a round trip to get a discount fare, you could readily head off without knowing when you'd be back again.

You still can give nary a thought to complicated airline ticket provisos, if you don't mind overpaying. But those who don't wish to make a charitable contribution to the airline industry need to understand the rules. Though several airlines have reported record profits recently, many are only just recovering from the massive $12 billion loss the industry experienced between 1989 and 1993. And start-up airlines are locked in guerilla marketing battles with major airlines which use their size to muscle smaller airlines out of the market. So there is tremendous competitive pressure—thus, all the sales gimmicks, and new ways you can end up paying more than necessary.

THE BASICS

N ext time you're on a plane, look to the left of you, then look to the right. Both your neighbors probably paid a different fare than you did, even though you're seated in the same section of the plane and eating the same microwaved chicken breast and limp salad.

Fare disparities result from sudden changes in published fares, use of restricted discount tickets by some passengers, and from sales, coupons, commission rebates, consolidator tickets, frequent flier plans, and "yield management." What's "yield management"? To make as much money as they can on each flight, airlines use computers to constantly analyze the demand for each flight, with up-to-the-minute information on what's selling and what's not. When demand is low, they lower prices to attract passengers. If demand for a flight strengthens, the airlines curb discount ticket sales.

529

Getting the Lowest Possible Fare

It's a good idea to let a seasoned travel agent search for you. Contrary to popular misconception, airline tickets do not cost more when purchased through a travel agent; the airline simply makes less. Some agents, however, have begun to charge transaction fees of $10 to $20 per ticket. In addition, you have to have your wits about you when using a travel agent, because of:

■ **Computer reservation system bias.** The first thing a travel agent does when you ask to book a flight from Point A to Point B is type your request on a keyboard connected to an airline computer reservation system (CRS) terminal. The CRS is then supposed to list all of the flights departing around the time you want to fly and the available fares. The agent processes your ticket through the same system. More than 80% of airline tickets are purchased through CRSs, and more than half of all airline tickets are purchased via the two dominant CRSs—Sabre, owned by American Airlines, and Apollo, owned by United Airlines.

Studies have questioned the fairness of CRSs. One report issued by the consumer advocacy group Public Citizen estimated that consumers lose up to $1 billion a year because of built-in favoritism toward the CRS-owner's airline. So you may not be getting the absolute lowest fare or easiest connections when you book your flight from East Oshkosh to Podunk.

How can this happen? Lots of ways. CRSs are required to list every flight, and they do. But a 1992 congressional study found that CRS reservation information is typically more current for the owner airline's flights. It can also take longer to confirm a reservation for a seat on a non-CRS owner's airline. And the agent might have to make more keystrokes to book you on a non-owner airline, an important consideration when restless travelers are lined up at your travel agent's. Changes to the system were introduced after Congress's inquiry, but bias still exists, and in 1997 the Department of Justice began a new investigation of CRS bias. Southwest Airlines, an expanding low-fare, no-frills carrier, started its own CRS because its CRS-owning competitors curb travel agents' access to Southwest's schedules and fares.

■ **Agent commissions and perks.** Travel agents earn an average commission of about 8% per flight ticket. No problem with that. But airlines sometimes pay them bonuses (called "commission overrides") and "soft money" commissions (such as VIP club memberships) if they meet a sales target. Or they get permission to overbook, or sell more tickets than the plane has seats. And more tickets mean higher commissions. Such incentives may influence which airline the agent recommends.

Consolidator tickets may offer very significant savings. Consolidators are airline ticket wholesalers that buy large blocks of tickets at substantial discounts. They then resell these tickets to the public, travel agents, and travel brokers at less than the regular fare, pocketing some of the difference as profit. Most retail travel agents don't handle consolidator tickets on a regular basis—usually, you have to go to one of the discount agencies that advertise in the back of travel sections in Sunday newspapers.

Savings are especially significant on international flights, but consolidator tickets are not *always* cheaper. A survey by the Better Business Bureau (BBB) of Metropolitan New York found that on a round-trip New York–Paris flight, a traveler would save a few dollars off Tower Air's lowest fare, about $90 off United Airlines' best fare, $271 off British Airways' best, and $579 off Air France's cheapest ticket. The consolidator's tickets actually cost *more* than the cheapest American Airlines fare and there was no difference for Delta.

Consolidator tickets don't allow you to get an advance seat assignment or order special meals. They typically do not count toward frequent flier accounts, and it may be impossible to get refunds. They also have high cancellation and change penalties. On the other hand, there's a good chance that advance purchase requirements won't apply.

Another way to pay less is by going through a rebater. Rebaters earn the usual straight percentage commission from the airline but pass some of it along to you. For example, the high-volume Travel Avenue agency in Chicago gives customers a 5% cash rebate (less a $15 service fee for one ticket, $20

for two; you can save $8 by getting an electronic ticket) off fares of more than $300. The rebate check is included with your ticket. However, since rebaters might not have the cheapest fares even after the rebate, you should still shop around if you use one.

If you're flexible about the exact date and time of day you fly and can leave on a moment's notice, then an international air courier ticket—which requires you to carry a package for someone else—might be right for you (see **HELP** at the end of this chapter). You'll probably pay half the price of a regular ticket, and occasionally less.

What's the downside? You have to register with a courier company, which may require a small fee. You can't get tickets for two. You probably won't be able to check any baggage, since your baggage allotment is taken up by the courier package—usually, financial documents. And there probably won't be much of a savings off discount fares during peak travel times.

But it is unlikely that you'll do any major schlepping; couriers usually just deliver and pick up documentation at both ends of the journey. What's in it for the company? Personal baggage is handled faster than freight, and probably more reliably. And sending a package with a person means it's far less likely to get waylaid or lost.

Finally, you can save by taking charter flights, for about the same price as a consolidator ticket. Some charter flights leave only once a week and there are few backup planes in case of a schedule disrup-

GETTING THE BEST DEAL FROM YOUR TRAVEL AGENT

Use an agent you know and trust. For tips on finding a good one, see the box on page 551. *The Consumer Reports Travel Buying Guide* recommends working with agents who have the Travel Career Development Diploma on their office wall. The diploma, issued by the Institute of Certified Travel Agents (ICTA), affirms that the agent completed a course in how to get more information beyond that listed in airline CRS data banks.

Be fickle. Even if you have a long-standing relationship with a particular agent, nonetheless double-check whether you can get a better deal elsewhere. Many of the fare deals offered online aren't advertised—or available on agents' CRSs.

Every time you book a flight, re-emphasize the importance of getting the lowest possible fare. Inform your agent that you don't mind making a stop or two or taking a no-meals, no-frills flight, if it will reduce your fare significantly.

Since airlines pay agents a commission consisting of a flat percentage of the fare, it can be tempting to neglect quoting you the super-cheap fare on the no-frills airline. The American Society of Travel Agents responds that agents would soon lose their customers if they started finding out about cheaper flights. Still, airfare structures are complex and fluid. If you don't show some initiative, your regular agent may not put in the extra effort to save you money.

As an antidote to "yield management," ask your travel agent to recheck the lowest fare a few days after you make your reservation or check with the airline yourself. You never know; the fare might have been cut. If it is significantly lower and there are no penalties, or the penalties are minimal, ask to have your ticket reissued.

---

tion. Unfortunately, chores like boarding can drag on for hours, and there are no legal protections for passengers from flight delays.

Airfare Advertising: The Fine Print Says It All

Have you ever tried to read the fine print at the bottom of an airline advertisement? The advertising industry calls it "mice type," and it's so small you practically need a magnifying glass to read it. Since it has line after line of disclaimers about the low fare trumpeted in the banner headline, *ignore it at peril to your wallet.*

The ending of federal oversight of airfares in 1985—as part of President Reagan's federal deregulation—opened the door to these small-print restrictions. Our current bifurcated fare system developed: Business travelers—who need flexibility—pay high fares; other travelers enjoy lower fares but are now subject to many complicated travel time, advance reservation, and refundability restrictions, mostly revealed in the mice type. So either you get a reasonably priced fare and put up with myriad restrictions or pay three to four times as much for an unrestricted seat.

The most common small-print disclaimer, found in almost every low-fare ad, reads something like this: "Fares are each way based on round-trip coach travel. . . . Round-trip purchase required." Of course, most travelers need return flights—the ads halve the real cost just to grab your attention. And if you did want to go one-way, the price would be much higher than the "each way" price listed in the ad.

There are other, less obvious restrictions you'll find in the "mice type." To illustrate, here are some of the small-print disclaimers found at the bottom of a full-page American Airlines advertisement for flights to Europe, the Caribbean, and Latin America published on September 4, 1997, in *The New York Times*. There were 10 lines of small type stretching the entire width of the page.

- *"Fares . . . are nonrefundable."* Watch out, because most bargain

fares require you to purchase at least 14 days—some, 21 days—before departure; your plans could change in the meantime. Lately, airlines have eased this requirement slightly by allowing you a refund (or to reschedule) for a fee of $75 or so.

Proof that competition really does benefit consumers: Southwest Airlines has switched to free refundability for many advance-purchase tickets and also has eliminated its requirement to stay over Saturday night for all but seven-day advance purchase discount tickets. (You still have to stay over one night—but it need not be Saturday.) United Airlines followed suit, but only in areas where it competes with Southwest.

Most airlines will waive refund fees if you are exchanging a ticket for a lower fare on the same flight and you accept a voucher for the difference.

- *"Saturday-night minimum stay requirements apply."* (for London–Paris flights) and *"valid for travel Mondays through Thursdays"* (for Latin America/Mexico flights). Often, the really inexpensive fares are sold for the times that are least desirable.
- Travel time (*"blackout period"*) restrictions, including: *"Three-day minimum and 30-day maximum stay requirements apply"* (for Latin America/Mexico flights). This is a very significant restriction for those lucky enough to be planning a longer vacation. And *"Fares are*

> " **A** *irlines try to do everything they can to make you miserable, then serve it up with a smile.*"
>
> —TOM PARSONS,
> editor of *Best Fares* magazine

INTERNET AVIATOR

If you have an Internet connection, and an infinite amount of patience, you might try planning your next trip through online reservation services like Travelocity (www.travelocity.com) or Microsoft's Expedia (expedia.msn.com), or through the major airlines' Web sites. As with other online research, finding cyberdeals takes time, especially as more people discover the service. But nifty planning tools and cheap fares are out there. In fact, only computer goods sell better than travel online.

Several airlines unload unsold tickets at too-good-to-be-true fares only through their Web sites or e-mail. You have to subscribe to weekly e-mail alerts advertising the following weekend's special deals. Most have tie-ins with hotels and car rental agencies as well, so you can reserve discount packages in just a few mouse clicks.

While these sites also let you plan for travel far in advance, the cheapest rates are only good for spur-of the moment getaways, usually for weekend travel only. Domestic-travel deals aren't posted until Wednesdays, and international flights are posted Mondays. You may have to leave Saturday evening and return the following Sunday or Monday, and fares are offered only to and from selected cities.

Still, compared to last-minute tickets ordered over the phone, that weekend getaway could be ridiculously inexpensive. In March 1997, for example, a quick escape from cold and snowy Syracuse, New York, to sunny Jacksonville, Florida, could be had for just $149 with a Continental COOL (COntinental OnLine) fare. A subcompact car from National Car Rental would have added $21 per day to the trip, a bit cheaper than its going rate of $23.95. From TWA, a weekend roundtrip from Boston to Milan was only $198.

Some airlines won't inform you about these rates over the phone: USAirways and Continental will, while American and Northwest won't. Some consumer advocates call the practice deceptive and unfair to those without Internet access, while the airlines say that offering Net discounts is the same as offering discounts for senior citizens or military personnel. A petition was filed in 1997 by a Florida attorney with the Department of Transportation that protested the Net fares, but as of this writing the DOT hadn't acted. Go to www.1travel.com to find a complete list of "last minute deals."

FLY THE FRIENDLY WEB

Airline	Web Site Address
American Airlines	www.americanair.com
America West	www.americawest.com
Continental Airlines	www.flycontinental.com
Delta	www.delta-air.com
Northwest	www.flynwa.com
Southwest	www.iflyswa.com
TWA	www.twa.com
United	www.ual.com
US Airways	www.usairways.com

valid for travel . . . through midnight 12/10/97." So forget about these lower fares if you were hoping for a *mid-winter* break.

■ *"Tickets must be purchased within 24 hours of making reservations and no later than midnight 9/12/97"* (one week after the advertisement). Such high pressure deadlines have become normal procedure for discount fares. It is still possible to get short-notice discount "bereavement" or "compassion" fares if you are attending a funeral or visiting a gravely ill friend or relative, but according to travel agent Adriane Greene, chairman emeritus of the U.S. Association of Retail Travel Agents, airlines may actually call funeral homes or hospitals for proof because so many travelers have lied. A Delta Airlines official told Ms. Greene about one man who tried to buy a bereavement discount ticket to Denver because his grandfather had passed away; he was charged the full fare at the airport because he was dressed in ski wear and carrying ski poles in the ticket purchasing line.

■ *"Seats are limited. Fares may not be available on all flights."* Variations of this general disclaimer appear in nearly every airfare ad. This is the same as if a department store advertising $40 dresses and the bottom of the ad said in extremely small print, "Dresses at these prices may not be available when you arrive at the store." Department stores can't get away with it, but the federal government allows airlines to.

How easy is it to get a reservation on your preferred flight? *Consumer Reports Travel Letter* surveyed its readers in 1997 and found that about half the respondents were able to get the sale seat they wanted; and only one quarter said they were successful most of the time.

The Department of Transportation requires airlines to reserve at least 10% of its seats at advertised prices, and some sale seats must be available whenever the ad is run. Even so, these seats can be hard to find. A survey conducted by the NYC Department of Consumer Affairs of major airlines' airfare ads in daily newspapers nationwide revealed that many advertised fares for the most popular routes weren't available even *one day* after the ads appeared. For example, on June 28, 1990, Consumer Affairs callers tried to make reservations in response to the previous day's Northwest Airlines ad in the *Los Angeles Times* for low-fare flights to Eastern cities. All flights on most of the days requested for flying from Los Angeles to New York or Cleveland were already sold out. The callers were also informed that most of the flights required connections with stopovers of at least two hours, which wasn't mentioned in the ad.

■ For good measure, just in case the "not available on all flights" disclaimer failed to cover every eventuality, the American Airlines ad mice type also said, *"Other restrictions may apply"* and, *"Fares are subject to change without notice."* Most airline ads have similar all-purpose disclaimers.

Frequent-Flier Benefits

Frequent-flier benefits give the bigger airlines a competitive leg up on their smaller competitors that don't offer them. Giving away free flights is a powerful inducement to fly the same airline time and again.

The major variables to consider when comparing programs are the number of miles required for a free trip; the number of blackout days when you can't fly (average is about 30, mostly around holidays); how

easy it is to use frequent-flier miles for a seat upgrade; how soon the miles expire (either after three years or unlimited); and how many destinations the airline serves.

Understand that airlines are not about to give away free seats on flights likely to be solidly booked with paying passengers. So seats to Hawaii, Florida, and Caribbean destinations are hard to get in the winter without reserving almost a year ahead of time. Europe in the summer is almost impossible.

A 1997 report by the New York City Public Advocate's office found that while getting a frequent-flier seat on a domestic flight was fairly easy, flights to Europe, Mexico, or the Caribbean—especially at popular travel times—would often cost up to two or three times the number of miles normally required. The only available seats on some domestic flights were on the late-night "red eye" flights or on inconvenient dates. You may also have trouble getting seats on days just before and after the official blackout periods. Some airlines do allow free travel during blackout periods, but the mileage requirements may be much higher then. Generally speaking, it is becoming harder to redeem frequent-flier miles—with planes flying close to full in the last few years, there are fewer empty seats, and consequently, even fewer frequent-flier seats.

If you are a very frequent flier, you'll qualify for the elite status most major airlines offer. Among the perquisites these loyal customers enjoy are bonus miles, free upgrades to business or first class,

YOUNGSTERS ON THE GO

Bringing the family along? Here are some basic tips:

- Most airlines offer special children's meals—hamburgers, hot dogs, etc. But, as with any other special meal requests, you have to call ahead of time to arrange them.
- Bring along snacks like granola bars, bagels, and crackers—airline meals are served on a fixed schedule that may not match your kids' appetites. Also bring water and fruit juice.
- Prepare packages with your kids' favorite entertainment, such as markers, paper, travel games, or dolls.
- Check with a flight attendant about the airline's policy on kids visiting the cockpit.
- With younger kids, request a bulkhead seat so they can move around more easily during flight.
- Bring your own child safety seats for small children. They are not required on flights, nor do airlines provide them. You must buy another ticket for your child and safety seat or fly at off-peak times and hope there will be an extra seat.

Here are some travel tips for unaccompanied children, provided by American Airlines:

- Arrive at the airport extra early. Each child will be given a packet to wear around his or her neck with tickets and other important information, such as medical conditions. You'll need time to fill out these forms. Also, it's a good idea to get to the departure lounge with enough extra time to familiarize your child with the airport and the personnel.
- You must stay at the gate with your child until he or she has boarded.
- A flight attendant will introduce himself or herself and make it clear to your child—in a way that nearby adult passengers can hear—that he or she is to be called if there are any problems. Your child *will* be monitored. One enterprising boy asked an American Airlines attendant for a Bloody Mary. She diplomatically asked for identification. He got a glass of tomato juice.
- At the destination, airlines will deliver your child *only* to a person specified previously, and that person must have photo identification. Sometimes people are very sloppy about this. For instance, a woman living on one coast reverted to her own name after a divorce from her husband on the other coast. When their child flew from one parent to the other, there was confusion at the destination because of the name change.

Still, parents need not worry. American Airlines reservation personnel have gone so far as to take kids home for the night.

and greater accessibility to seats that are off-limits to run-of-the-mill frequent fliers. How far do you have to travel in one year to begin to qualify for special benefits?

The airlines giveth and the airlines taketh away: Early in 1995, most of the major airlines increased the number of frequent-flier miles required for free tickets. For example, free domestic flights require 25,000 miles, up from 20,000 miles, on American, Continental, United, and USAirways. (Delta is cutting its requirement from 30,000 to 25,000 miles.) Higher levels cost 50,000 miles at Continental (gold status), 50,000 miles at American (platinum status) and United (premier executive), and 60,000 at USAirways (priority gold plus). You might go even higher. United, for example, offers "100K service" for 100,000 miles or more. Of course, benefits vary from airline to airline; however, regardless of carrier, the greater the number of miles, the greater the benefits.

You don't have to fly to accumulate mileage. Nearly every major airline has teamed up with a Visa or MasterCard issuer to offer one frequent-flier mile for every dollar you charge on a card. Interest rates on outstanding credit card balances are competitive, although annual membership fees are higher than for regular credit cards. American Express's charge card has an advantage; members can choose to apply their mileage to five different airlines, and the miles don't expire as long as you keep your card. But you must pay a $25 fee to participate in the program.

You can also accumulate frequent-flier mileage when you use MCI, Sprint, or AT&T. A stay in certain hotels can earn you 500 miles each stay. When you rent a car, some agencies award 500 to 1,000 miles per rental. Even ordering flowers gets you miles; FTD offers 300 miles for phone orders.

"Ticketless" Travel

Since 1995, the airline industry has been pushing customers to use electronic tickets, or e-tickets, which are cheaper for airlines to manage than paper tickets. The tickets work like this: You make a reservation over the phone, pay by credit card, and get a reservation number. (You'll have to speak up if you want paper; many airlines assign e-tickets by default.) A flight itinerary and receipt is faxed or mailed to you. Once at the airport, you give your reservation number to an agent at the airline counter and pick up a boarding pass. The agent will check your ID and should also ask to see your credit card number—to be sure you are who you say you are.

Forgetful types may like e-tickets. Replacing a lost paper ticket usually costs $70. With e-tickets, there's nothing to misplace but your reservation number—even then, agents can find your reservation using your name and credit card number. And e-tickets save last-minute travelers the $35 express mail charges it would cost to have paper tickets sent.

However, e-tickets are not failsafe. Airlines using e-tickets have

WHAT PRICE SAFETY?

Flying *seems* more dangerous than it is. The chances of ending up in a headline-grabbing accident like the 1996 crash of a ValuJet flight into the Florida Everglades or the explosion of TWA flight 800, which killed over 300 people, are minuscule compared to the odds of dying in a car accident. But if reports of faulty maintenance and aging fleets have you worried, take charge. It's a little-known fact that you can check, model by model, the safety record of the flight you just booked; if you're really concerned, bring your laptop to the airport with you, and using the "tail" number of the plane, you can vet it before you board.

Courtesy of a nifty government Web site, U.S. travelers can now investigate the safety record of any U.S. airline, airport or plane. Simply click on www.faa.gov. You'll find two kinds of reports from the Federal Aviation Administration and the National Transportation Safety Board on everything from broken toilets to engine explosions to fatal crashes. "Incident" reports detail minor events that affect safety—i.e., a wide range of things, including tire prob-

lems and a flight attendant tripping during turbulence. "Accident" reports involve injury, death, or extensive damage to an airplane; but even this isn't exactly what you might think. If a plane backs up into a truck, it's an accident, just the same as if it blew up and all its passengers were killed.

You won't find explicit rankings of the airlines, but you can glean enough information to rank your options. Example: It's more convenient for you to fly into Midway Airport than O'Hare, but what are the safety implications of choosing convenience? There have been almost as many "incidents" at tiny Midway as at enormous O'Hare.

One big caveat: Previous mishaps, and worse, are no indicator of future problems, nor do they correlate to fatal crashes. Some airlines may report problems more assiduously than others; one airport may handle more small planes, which tend to have a higher incidence of problems; and while some "incidents" may in fact be quite, well, incidental compared to serious safety threats, one serious accident can skew all the data.

been known to lose reservations, and computer glitches, airline strikes, and other unforseen problems can give e-ticket holders big headaches. Adele H. was waiting to check in for a United Airlines flight from Los Angeles to Salt Lake City—paper ticket in hand—

when the counter agents' computers locked up. Passengers with paper tickets were able to collect boarding passes, but those with e-tickets stood in line for two hours waiting for the system to unlock. By that time, their flight had gone, and they had to start all over again. There is no way to transfer e-tickets from one airline to another, so if one leg of your flight is delayed or canceled and you're forced to travel on another carrier, you'll have to wait while a paper ticket is issued and then take it to the other airline's counter—delaying you even longer.

Fly Safe

Don't read Ralph Nader's and Wesley Smith's 1993 book, *Collision Course: The Truth About Airline Safety*, while airborne. It could ruin your flight. But anyone who flies should read it when they're back on terra firma.

Actually, airline travel is very safe, relative to other ways of getting to where you're going. But the authors maintain that air travel could be even safer, and they lambaste the federal government for lapses in airline and airport safety. Nader and Smith have plenty of documentation to back up their findings and connect the financially precarious condition of many airlines with a drop in the number of mechanics per aircraft, a rapidly aging fleet, and increasing pilot fatigue. Overwhelmed air traffic controllers working with outmoded equipment don't inspire much confidence, either.

The authors also point out that the hub-and-spoke route system—in which you are likely to be flown to a hub airport and then transfer to a second flight to your destination—has led to more small commuter aircraft on scheduled routes. These smaller planes are not as safe, and their pilots often have less experience. According to the National Transportation Safety Board, propeller-driven "commuter" aircraft have nearly five times the number of fatal accidents per passenger as jets do.

How do you protect yourself? No one airline is appreciably safer than another. But for safety tips when flying any airline, see **The Smarter Consumer** on page 542.

Comfort and Quality

The incredible shrinking seat. Remember the old '50s game of seeing how many people could fit into a phone booth or a Volkswagen Beetle? Well, most airlines play that game, too, seeing how many passengers they can fit into the confines of an airplane fuselage.

Airlines traditionally offered up to 22-inch coach seat widths on their larger planes. The norm now is 19 inches or 20 inches.

Pitch describes how far seats are located from each other front to back; it has been sliced from 34 inches to 31 inches in much of the industry. These few inches make an enormous difference in comfort. In 1993, TWA received just acclaim for adopting a pitch of 34 inches to 36 inches on nearly all its planes.

If you're in a wide-body plane, such as an L-1011, a DC-10, or an MD-11 and the airline has ten seats abreast instead of the formerly standard nine, there's a good chance you'll be very cramped if the plane is more than three-quarters filled. A more comfortable configuration is two aisles with five seats in the center and two on either side.

Other than going on a prolonged hunger strike before you fly, you can minimize discomfort by asking about the width and pitch of the seats on a plane you are considering flying. Remember, since seating configurations are determined by the airlines, the same model aircraft can be relatively spacious with one airline and like a cattle car with another.

Crack open a window? Have airlines been giving you headaches lately? No, not the headaches you might get trying to redeem your frequent-flier miles. We're talking about headaches after spending several hours aloft.

The New York Times reports that all of the air in the cabin is replaced with fresh air every three minutes in aircraft built before the mid-1980s. But newer planes provide only half fresh air—the rest is old air—and it is recirculated only every six or seven minutes. Since fresh air is introduced through the engines and must be cooled, giving passengers less of it saves fuel and money. The airlines, of course, say it makes no difference. But the *Times* reported that flight attendants are complaining of more air travel–related illness, and the Association of Flight

Attendants has commissioned a study. You might want to ask about the aircraft before you confirm your seat; older planes might actually be better for your health.

WHAT TO WATCH OUT FOR

"One-stop" flights. You might imagine your "one-stop" flight from Cleveland to Paris touching down briefly in New York to refuel and board more passengers. Sorry—that probably won't be the case. Some transcontinental or international flights advertised as "one-stop" are really two different flights—including a change of planes—listed under one flight number on your ticket. Your departure from Cleveland and your final arrival in Paris may be listed on your itinerary as plain as day; but the small type at the bottom mentions that you'll be switching planes—and gates, and your luggage will be transferred to the new flight—meaning a greater chance that things will go awry.

Code-sharing. Each airline is assigned a code for ticketing purposes. If you have to change planes, and if the code for the second leg of a flight is the same as for the first leg, then you might reasonably assume you'll continue on with the same airline.

Not necessarily. For the second leg of your trip, you might be scrunched up in a glorified crop-duster said to be owned by a subsidiary of the major airline you started out on. But according to

Collision Course, most of the commuter airlines that share codes with a major carrier are not actually the same company as the major airline. For example, American Eagle—the commuter carrier for American Airlines—is actually four different companies: Executive Airlines, Flagship Airlines, Simmons Airlines, and Wings West Airlines.

Increasingly, you may end up with an entirely different major airline. You might think you're taking KLM all the way from Amsterdam to Indianapolis, but you really are taking it only to Detroit, with a switch to Northwest for the rest of the trip. Or you could begin your journey with Air New Zealand and end up with Quantas. Travel agents and airlines are supposed to identify the name of the second airline, but they often don't.

Getting "bumped." This happens when the airline overbooks—takes more reservations than the plane has seats—and too many people with reservations show up at the gate. The law is on your side. If you are bumped from an aircraft and have to take another flight and you arrive at your destination more than an hour later than your originally scheduled arrival time, the airline *must* give you the cost of a one-way ticket (maximum value of $200). If you are more than two hours late, you get double the one-way ticket (maximum of $400). You should also be able to negotiate long-distance phone calls, free meals, and maybe a free hotel room, although your bargaining power is weak if numerous passengers volunteer to be bumped.

Remember, though, that you get compensated only if you arrived at the gate at least 15 minutes before the scheduled departure time.

THE $MARTER CONSUMER

Take full advantage of airline fare wars. Buy discount "sale" tickets if they are at least 30% cheaper than the non-discount fare. This way, you'll be sure of locking in a good fare. If the fare goes even lower, airlines allow you to exchange for a cheaper ticket by paying a penalty of $75 or so, which may very well be worth it, given the additional savings you would realize.

Save money with upstart (and start-up) airlines. Southwest Airlines' very low fares are giving the major carriers tough competition in markets where they overlap. Among the very cheap new start-up airlines trying to steal business from the major carriers on selected routes are Kiwi Air (based in Newark, New Jersey); Carnival Airlines (Miami); Frontier Air (Denver); and Reno Air (of Reno, Nevada).

Do your homework. While agents are good at finding deals, you may be able to find some of your own. Check the Internet sites listed on page 535. Some start-up airlines aren't on the CRSs used by travel agents, so their low fares might get overlooked. Call the smaller airlines on your own.

WOULD YOU LIKE A BEVERAGE?

If you're feeling a little light-headed while flying, it may not be the altitude; it could be because you're hungry. Airlines spent 27% less on in-flight meals in 1996 than they did in 1992, or about $1.60 less per passenger. Passengers on low-fare airlines usually get low-fare lunches—a tiny sandwich, a half-can of soda, and a small bag of chips. American and United spend the most on flight food, while Southwest spends only 20 cents per person on its peanut snacks.

You may want to order a kosher or vegetarian meal in advance; the food tends to be a little better, though portions aren't any bigger. Perhaps the best option: brown-bag it.

Guard your credit card number. Don't give a travel agent your credit card number without getting a ticket in return. Anne Marie M. called TFI Tours of New York City to inquire about flights to Florida. An employee said it was company policy that no information be given until the caller provided credit card numbers. Even though Anne Marie said she'd pay in cash, she capitulated when pressed. The next morning she called back to say the suggested flight was not convenient. TFI told her it couldn't cancel her "reservation" and that she had to pay the $335 airfare anyway.

Rack up the miles. If you want to benefit from frequent-flier programs, try to concentrate your flying with one airline. Then you'll have a chance not only of getting free flights for you and a companion, but maybe of qualifying for "elite" status—which gives bonus miles and VIP treatment. Also be aware that some airlines require more frequent-flier miles to get a free trip than others; compare requirements carefully and understand that airlines reserve the right to change the rules so long as mileage holders are given reasonable notice.

Plan far in advance if you want to use your miles on popular European or Caribbean flights.

Here's another frequent-flier tip: If there are no free seats between, say, Chicago and Los Angeles, ask if you can go through another city. Sure, it'll take longer—but it's free.

Seniors: Take advantage of discounts. All major airlines sell "senior coupons," which provide a very substantial airfare discount for persons 62 or older on all but short-haul flights. Senior coupons are typically sold in books of four ($596 at USAirways, American, and United) and in books of eight ($1,032 at TWA; $999 at Continental). One coupon is needed for a one-way flight anywhere in the lower 48 states, which comes to as low as $90 or as high as $149 for one flight. You have to reserve 14 days in advance and travel day restrictions could apply. Some airlines' coupons allow discounts for companions as well (grandchildren, children, younger spouses). Travel on the coupons qualifies for frequent-flier miles.

Most U.S. airlines also offer a 10% senior discount off any published fare, except special short-term sale fares.

If using a consolidator, try to pay for the tickets with a credit card in order to preserve your right to withhold payment in case of a problem. Confirm reservations with the airline before and after paying. Make sure you're on a major carrier and not on a charter flight.

Buy split tickets when advantageous, if you don't mind making connections. Instead of buying one ticket from point A direct to point C, it might be cheaper to buy a discount or promotional fare from point A to point B, and a separate ticket from point B to point C.

If you opt for an e-ticket, make sure you bring your receipt to the airport (it should be faxed or mailed to you before you travel). It will serve as proof of your reservation should something go wrong.

Dealing with irretrievably lost baggage. Most lost luggage eventually turns up. But if your baggage is really gone, it's unlikely you'll get much in the way of compensation. By agreement among the airlines, you are entitled only to the depreciated value of what was lost, to a maximum of $1,250 per passenger for domestic flights ($635 per piece of checked baggage for international flights) and then only if you are able to produce receipts and other documents proving how much the lost items are currently worth. If you want more financial protection, you have to pay for it.

Fortunately, most airlines are a little softer when it comes to giving you money for reasonable out-of-pocket expenses caused by losing your baggage. While the airline is searching for your baggage, they don't have to but should advance you some cash for basic necessities—or at least provide you with a toiletries kit. If the news is good and they find your baggage, most airlines will deliver it to your destination address.

Smart seat trick. To increase the likelihood of getting more wiggle room, ask for an aisle seat in the center row. Most of the empty seats on a plane that hasn't been fully booked will be the ones in the middle of the center row. If you're on the aisle, the seat next to you could very well be empty.

Fly safer. Avoid wearing synthetic fibers while flying; they tend to melt on your skin in case of fire. Wear "sensible shoes" you can escape in easily. Scope out the scene as soon as you get to your seat. Where are the emergency exits? Read the safety briefing card. If it is winter and the weather is inclement, look out a window and check the wing for ice buildup; report any to a flight attendant. On March 22, 1992, ice buildup caused USAir flight 405 to run off the runway at New York's LaGuardia Airport, and 27 lives were lost. The local newspapers reported that one passenger noticed ice on the wing before the tragic attempted take-off and said, "We take off like this, we're all dead."

Stay alert during take offs and landings, which is when most accidents occur.

H E L P

■ To complain about airline service, write to the Aviation Consumer Protection Division of the U.S. Department of Transportation, C-75 Room 4107, Washington, DC 20590. You can also leave a recorded complaint on DOT's voice mail, at (202) 366-2220.

■ To complain about airline safety or security, call the Federal Aviation Administration: (800) 322-7873. If it is a pressing safety issue, call the FAA Aviation Safety Hotline: (800) 255-1111; they will assign investigators to look into it. Anonymous calls to the Hotline are accepted, although the FAA encourages you to leave your name and contact information.

■ Want to know more about courier services? If you can't find *The Insider's Guide to Air Courier Bargains* by Kelly Monaghan at your bookstore, order it from Upper Access Books, P.O. Box 4537, Hinesburg, VT 05461. $17.95 includes postage and handling. Or call (800) 356-9315.

■ Order the booklet, *Facts and Advice for Airline Passengers*, and a newsletter from the Aviation Consumer Action Project (ACAP). ACAP was formed by Ralph Nader and his associates to promote air safety, environmental protection, affordable fares, and expanded passenger rights. It distributes passenger information leaflets and advocates passenger interests before regulatory bodies. Send $5 to ACAP, P.O. Box 19209, Washington, DC 20036; call (202) 638-4000.

■ To learn how each domestic air-line ranks on flight delays, mishandled baggage, bumped passengers, and consumer complaints, order the *Air Travel Consumer Report* published monthly by the U.S. Department of Transportation. Write to the Aviation Consumer Protection Division at the address above, left. The report is also posted on the department's Web site, www.dot.gov.

■ For the latest frequent-flier program developments, order the monthly *Inside-Flyer* newsletter ($36 a year) by calling (800) 333-5937.

■ The FAA has airline safety records dating back to 1978, along with on-time arrival rates and lost luggage rates, on its Web site, www.faa.gov.

CHAPTER 49

TRAVEL

Hotels and Tours Without the Fleece

One tour operator nationally advertised a $99 weeklong cruise to the Bahamas that actually cost $700 once surcharges were added. Another operator, Jet Set Travel, used computerized telephone messages and direct mail to tell people they had been "specially selected" for a five-day, four-night Bahamas cruise package for only $328, *and*—if they purchased this package—two round-trip airfares to Hawaii at no additional cost. In fact, consumers taking this bait would have been required to buy 14 nights of lodging in Hawaii in order to get the free airfare. And if they gave the company their credit card number "to verify eligibility," as requested, they would have been billed instead.

These are but two examples of a rapidly spreading way of getting fleeced—travel and tour scams. Deceptive travel promotions are the second-largest consumer rip-off, according to the National Consumers League, behind only fake sweepstakes offers. (Often, the "prize" in these sweepstakes is an expensive travel offer like those above.)

Of course, con artists represent only a small portion of the entire U.S. hotel and tour industry. If you know what to watch out for, you won't become a victim.

THE BASICS

A $mart Consumer Slept Here

If you're paying full price for a hotel or resort room and it's off-season at a not-yet-prime destination, you're doing something wrong. With a little bit of advance work, you can get rooms and even meals on your next trip for half price. Such big price breaks are available because hotel and resort owners spend almost as much running a half-empty hotel as a full one, and they use discounts to fill as many vacant rooms as they can.

But you can't just walk up to the registration desk of a $250-a-night hotel and announce that you'd like to pay only $125 tonight, including a free dinner in their award-winning restaurant. You have to go through a program, buy a voucher, or qualify for a special discount.

Membership programs that negotiate discounts with hotels and then pass most of the savings on to the general public offer what are probably the lowest room rates. Half-price rooms are the norm, and restaurant discounts of 25% are sometimes available as well.

Each program has its own roster of hundreds (or thousands) of hotels, motels, and resorts. You pay an annual fee of $20 to $100 for the roster and an identification card. The programs with lower annual fees tend to specialize in more modest lodgings—the Howard Johnsons, Holiday Inns, and Ramada Inns—while the $100 annual fee gets you discounts at tonier *habiliments*. After you've called ahead to see if discount rooms are available, you show the ID card at the check-in counter to claim your discount.

The modest pitfalls of these programs don't outweigh the potential for big savings. The lowest-priced rooms may be exempt from the program. Discount rooms are always "subject to availability," which typically is only when the hotel's occupancy rate is less than 80%.

The most comprehensive program, according to some travel writers, is "Ultimate Hotel Directory," offered by Entertainment Publications (EP). You pay $59.95 a year for a card entitling you to discounts at any of the approximately 5,500 establishments in EP's worldwide directory. In addition, EP sells different coupon booklets for $20 to $50 each for over 200 cities, offering 50% off room rates as well as restaurant discounts and a cut-rate Continental Airlines airfare. *Consumer Reports Travel Letter* calls the program one

---

BEST TIMES WORST TIMES

To avoid crowds at the airport—and the delays caused by the long line of planes queuing to take off or land—don't go anywhere on Friday afternoon, the busiest travel time of the week. You also might want to avoid the airport from 6 A.M. to 8 A.M., 11 A.M. to 1 P.M., and 4 P.M. to 7 P.M., when most travelers prefer to get away or get home.

---

of the "outstanding values" for travel. (EP's phone number and names and phone numbers of additional discount travel services are listed in **HELP** at the end of this chapter.)

Another way to avoid paying a hotel's "rack" rate—the published full rate—is with vouchers. Here's how they work: You buy vouchers before you leave, either from a travel agent or directly from a voucher program. You make your own room reservations and use the vouchers to pay. Most voucher programs concentrate on hotels in certain areas of the world, such as Europe or Scandinavia. A few, such as the Holiday Inns voucher program, are worldwide. The big downside: You can't automatically assume that the voucher will save you money, because regular "rack" rates may be *less* than what you would pay using a voucher.

Hotel room discounts of 10% to 40% are available through hotel brokers, booking services, or consortiums offering "preferred" rates. Your travel agent might be a member of such a service. The combined buying power of numerous agencies secures the lower rates. Some brokers just make a reservation for a discount-rate room, and you pay the hotel directly when you check out. With others, you buy vouchers that you redeem at the hotel. Two brokers that offer last-minute deals are Accommodations Express (800 444-7666) and California Reservations (800 576-0003). But be careful—you might pay less with a weekend discount or a half-price program. Room discounts can also be realized if you are a member of one of a wide range of organizations—from the American Automobile Association to labor unions—that have group discounts with hotel chains.

Aging has its benefits. Senior citizens—the age cutoff is either 55, 60, or 62, depending on the chain—qualify for 10% to 15% senior citizen discounts at many major hotel and motel chains. The discount may increase to 25% to 30% if you make advance reservations. Some chains' senior discounts require membership in the American Association of Retired Persons (AARP) or give a greater discount to AARP members; you must be 50 or older to join AARP. Even if a hotel chain has no senior citizen discount, individual locations might, so always ask.

Hotel room discounts are available through hotel chains' frequent-stay programs, akin to the airlines' frequent-flier programs. You get credits, based either on the number of nights you stay or how much money you spend, which can be redeemed for room upgrades, complimentary meals, and other perks. Membership is usually free, but a hotel might not advertise its program, so it may be up to you to ask for enrollment forms. Some hotel chains have tie-ins with airlines and car rental agencies. Savings may also be realized by reserving and paying well in advance—sort of like airlines' 21-day advance purchase tickets. Hyatt and Sheraton are two of the chains with such offers.

And don't forget about hotels' weekend rates, when they try to fill rooms that are empty of the usual business travelers.

Online travel guides like Microsoft's Expedia (expedia.msn.com) and Travelocity (www.travelocity.com) can link you to descriptions and customer reviews of thousands of hotels around the world, offer information about different destinations, and book reservations for flights, hotel rooms, and car rentals. Last-minute deals and advance discounts are often featured as well. You can also book rooms through a hotel's Web site, but few offer better discounts than what you might get over the phone.

Getting the Right Package Tour

A package tour is a combination of travel services—hotel, land, and air transportation, sightseeing tours—sold together for one price.

ROOM FOR SAVINGS

You can bypass travel agents, membership programs, and vouchers altogether if you call The Room Exchange, a wholesale agency that offers 20% to 50% off, depending on the season, at more than 23,000 U.S., European, Canadian, and Caribbean hotels. You simply call them at (800) 846-7000 (in NYC, (212) 760-1000) to check availability. Then you reserve by credit card and The Room Exchange mails you a voucher.

Package tours have the potential to save you money because the tour operator purchases services in bulk. And by paying just once, before you leave, package tours make it easier to budget for your vacation and avoid surprise expenses.

Before you plunk down hundreds or thousands of dollars, you still have to have your wits about you, whether you're buying a four-day "weekend" in the Caribbean or going around the world in 80 days. Make sure you know exactly what the package includes, such as whether the airfare is from your home city or if you have to travel to a departure city—at your own expense.

Carefully study the proposed daily itinerary. Note the places you'll actually be visiting rather than just passing through on a tour bus. Be realistic in assessing your feelings about how much time you'll spend at each stop. Can you enjoy ten major European cities in only 15 days? And how much free time will you have? Some travelers prefer a regimented schedule, while others like to have half a day off now and then to do as they wish. What's your style?

Study the descriptions of the lodgings and the meals carefully. Are the proposed hotels in the center of the city you're visiting or close to the beach you hope to sun yourself on? What's their rating? Remember, a "deluxe" hotel in Timbuktu might be barely comparable to a budget chain motel in the U.S. How many meals are included? Are your menu choices limited?

Be sure to read the "conditions" section of the brochure. You'll learn the rules on cancellations, refunds, change penalties, and important restrictions or limits on meals, lodgings, baggage allowance, and extra items that might not be included in the total price.

Ask your travel agent or the tour operator a lot of questions. Far better to get the answers now—when you can still back out—than to find out later that you don't care for yak meat in the middle of the tundra and there's nothing else on the menu or the horizon.

Travel and Tour Pitfalls and Scams

Misleading or outright fraudulent travel offers are booming, and attorneys general and consumer affairs officials around the country report that travel scams are one of the top consumer complaint categories.

While it's very unlikely that you'll encounter any sharks off the beach where you might next be vacationing, you have to watch out for them in the travel industry.

It's early March in a northern city. Over Sunday brunch you scan the newspaper travel section. The pictures of palm trees and couples walking hand in hand on deserted beaches are too alluring to resist. Monday morning, you call the phone number in one of the ads and after a few minutes of explanations you give your credit card number to make a reservation for a vacation package. You work hard. You deserve it.

What you don't deserve is for something to go wrong. It could be relatively minor, like a switch to a hotel not quite as nice as where you were supposed to stay. Or it could be disastrous, like $800 tickets that never arrive.

Let's start with the relatively benign package tour scams and pitfalls and work up to the real vacation-busters.

Understated vacation package prices. Consider the ad for Bermuda vacations by Travel Impressions, a group of 19 New York City travel agencies, that was published in a New York City daily newspaper. It mentioned only the lowest possible prices—"from $523 per person." After legal action by the NYC Department of Consumer Affairs, Travel Impressions paid a fine and changed its ads. A new ad for a Caribbean vacation package more realistically listed prices of "$808 to $1,532."

Even the popular Carnival Cruise Lines was cited by the Department of Consumer Affairs for advertising a four-day Bahamas cruise for $449, when that was the rate for only the smallest, windowless room.

Practically worthless vacation certificates. You may get one of these in the mail as a sweepstakes or contest "prize." Some prize. Here's what will probably happen if you take the bait: You'll have to pay something, possibly as much as a few hundred dollars, for your "resort vacation." There could be a processing fee. It could be hard to actually redeem the certificate, since you get to go on your vacation only on a "space-available" basis. Even after you get a reservation, the trip may be cancelled several times, and it may be difficult to get new reservations because of previously undisclosed time-of-travel restrictions. To add insult to injury, if somehow you manage to take the trip, you'll likely be put up in a second-rate hotel far from any resort.

Take a very close look at the next vacation certificate you see. Chances are, it is very carefully worded to make it *seem* like you'll get something for free, but it never actually says the trip is free.

And if it does say "free," it'll probably be linked to having to buy something. That "something" can be very expensive, cautions *Con-*

FINDING A GOOD TRAVEL AGENT

Too many people have been burned by fly-by-night travel agencies that go out of business before issuing ordered tickets, or by hotel vouchers bought through travel agencies that weren't honored when they presented them at the hotel desk—two examples of the difficulties you could encounter with a disreputable travel agency. The problem is that government only minimally regulates travel agencies. Almost anyone can open a travel storefront and start selling. In fact, only Rhode Island requires travel agents to pass a licensing examination.

So how do you find a well-established agency? Start by getting references from friends, relatives, and business colleagues. Avoid out-of-town agents who advertise locally, especially if their prices seem unusually low; if there's a catch or if something goes wrong, you will want to be able to visit the agency.

At the very least, make sure that the travel agent you use is licensed by the Airline Reporting Company to issue tickets.

Much better, members of either the American Society of Travel Agents (ASTA; its 12,000 member agencies are about a third of all the agencies in the U.S.) or the Association of Retail Travel Agents (ARTA, with about 3,000 members) have been appointed by reputable airlines, cruise lines, or airline coordinating bodies that require agents to maintain a bond of at least $20,000, or $1 million in "errors and omissions" insurance. Both organizations have strict ethics codes. An agency must have at least one agent who has been in business for at least three years before joining ASTA. In addition, ASTA offers a proficiency examination; look for the ASTA diploma on the agent's wall. ASTA can provide you with the names of members in your area, as well as complaint profiles of specific agencies. (See **HELP** for contact information.)

Tip: Find out from the agency if it gives you your money back if a tour operator or airline goes out of business. Some do, some do not, and some will partially reimburse you.

sumer Reports Travel Letter. Consumer Reports gave an example of a department store's offer of free tickets to Hawaii or any one of three Mexican resorts. But you had to purchase seven consecutive nights of over-priced hotel accommodations at these destinations to qualify.

Your travel agent's refund check bounces. When Anu B. of Massachusetts paid Maharajah Travel

$1,190 for an airline ticket to India but failed to get her tickets, the agency sent her a refund. Her bank rejected the check for "insufficient funds." Maharajah told her to redeposit it. It bounced again.

What you get barely resembles what you were promised. Gerry S. paid New Golden Horse Tours a total of $1,040 for a Florida vacation. The agent, the newspaper ad, and the brochure described a comfortable bus ride, a trip to Sea World, and a nice hotel. He got a bus with nonreclining seats and a broken toilet, a smelly hotel room with cockroaches and dirty sheets, and no Sea World.

The travel agent or tour operator doesn't send you the tickets you paid for or sends them late. Shaheen T. of Brooklyn needed to get to Kenya to visit a sick relative. She bought tickets from Maharajah Travel for herself and her four children, paying a total of $6,040 in cash, as required by the agency. She received no tickets—just a printout of her itinerary. Finally, after many phone calls, Maharajah said they'd meet her at the airport on the day of her flight. She went to the airport with her children and all their luggage. Yes, she got the tickets at the last minute. But when she was in Kenya and wanted to return, she discovered she hadn't been given tickets for the second leg of the return trip—London to New York. Eventually, tickets were express-mailed to her in London, but only after she was stuck there for two long days.

WHAT TO WATCH OUT FOR

Hotels, Motels, and Resorts

Travel agent "credential mills." World Class Travel in California offered "travel tutorial kits" that would turn buyers into at-home travel agents, landing them agent discounts and benefits with airlines, cruises, and hotels. But the agent "I.D. cards" issued by World Class are rarely recognized by any travel organization and couldn't get anybody much of anything. World Class, however, made thousands on the scam before the Federal Trade Commission stopped the operation.

Early check-out fees. Recently, hotels have begun charging fees if guests leave earlier than they'd planned. If you made a reservation for four nights but leave after the third, the hotel may charge you a $50 fee or even the full cost of your last night's stay. If your plans aren't concrete, ask about the hotel's policy.

Getting "bumped." An overbooked hotel won't tell you they've assigned too many people to too few rooms; if they have, late-comers, even with "guaranteed" reservations, might be moved to a sister hotel down the block or even across town. When Linda K. arrived with a "confirmed" reservation at a swanky South Beach hotel in Miami, she was told there weren't any rooms left and was moved, in her words, "to a crummy little hotel down the street." Get your reservation confirmed in writing: Waving that piece of paper in front of the concierge gives you an edge in getting the room you paid for.

Using the phone. Hotels make a little extra money on the side by charging you a lot of money for phone calls made from your room. If you charge a call to your room, you'll probably be billed at high operator-assisted rates, even if you dial direct. On top of that will likely be a surcharge of as much as 50%.

Long-distance carriers provide access to their lines via a toll-free "800" number, which would allow you to circumvent the hotel's 75-cent phone-use fee or dollar-per-minute long distance rate. But some hotels are plugging this loophole by charging the fee for all calls, including "800" numbers. Carefully read the surcharge information that should be posted on the phone to find out your hotel's policy. If you're still unsure, ask the hotel desk staff before you dial, or use your phone card at a pay phone in the lobby.

Single supplements. Hoteliers charge single travelers supplements, which are typically 50% or even 100% of the per-person double room rate. *Travel and Leisure* magazine suggests that single travelers sign up for the guaranteed roommate offers of many tour operators

> " *A travel agent can't give haircuts in Massachusetts, but a barber there can open a shop called Nails and Sails and sell travel.*"
>
> —MIKE SPINELLI,
> ASTA president,
> on the government's lack of
> travel agency oversight

and cruise lines. If the hotel doesn't come up with a roommate, you still get the room at the reduced, non-supplement price.

Tour Packages

Adriane Greene, chairman emeritus of the Association of Retail Travel Agents, says that many savvy consumers who pride themselves on their shopping acumen lose their powers of critical judgment when a low-price luxury vacation is dangled before their eyes. Warning bells and whistles should go off in your head when you see or hear any of the following:

Unsolicited telemarketing phone calls or postcards telling you that you "definitely won" a vacation or trying to sell you a discount vacation package. This is the most common travel scam vehicle. If you get such a postcard, rip it up. Hang up on anyone making such a phone call. It only means trouble; no reputable travel firm operates this way.

California-based Design Travel is a good example. They gathered hundreds of names, addresses, and phone numbers from "win a free vacation" booths at fairs and carnivals. Telemarketers then contacted consumers by phone or mail, informing them they had been specially chosen to receive a limited number of cruise vacations in the Bahamas, supposedly worth $1,500 but which could be had for as low as $398—if people bought them right away. Those who took the bait found they were only paying for the *option* to buy the vacation and had to pay an additional $300 to actually take the trip. Customers who demanded refunds had to wait months to get them. Those who paid the additional charge found the "cruise" was just a ferry ride, and the hotels rooms advertised in the package were crawling with cockroaches.

Often, the telemarketer or postcard sender is in business only long enough to rake in hundreds of thousands of dollars' worth of certified checks and credit card charges. Trouble is, if you fork over money without first getting confirmed seats on a flight, confirmed reservations at a named hotel, or confirmed booking on a boat, there is little you can do.

Being "specially selected." Remember that "special" doesn't mean that only a few people were chosen; a million other people may have gotten the same postcard or inviting phone call.

Incredibly low prices. No one gives away $200 five-day Caribbean cruise packages. Any such offer probably doesn't mention a long list of additional fees and expenses, such as charges for ground transportation and processing.

Witness what happened to Cynthia and David Garast, as reported in the *Chicago Tribune.* They responded to a classified ad for a full five-day, four-night Bahamas vacation, including a cruise between Florida and the Bahamas—all for the incredibly low price of $239. Well, it *was* incredible. They soon learned that they would have to pay an additional "reservation deposit" of $139. Even then, their vacation date requests could not be guaranteed. After a year of trying, they were unable to get their $239 back.

Then there's the story of Maggie H., who responded to an ad for a "bargain vacation" that included a three-day cruise from Florida to the Bahamas, plus three days in Orlando, with passes to Disney World and a "free" hotel stay, all for only $400. The package, once bought, was good for one year. After paying by credit card, Maggie waited a few months until she could take a break from work to take the trip. When she called to reserve her spot, she learned that a "reservation fee" of $100 or a $150 "international tax"—to pay for "access to the islands"—weren't included in the original price.

High-pressure sales tactics, forcing you to decide "right then and there," or else the offer expires.

Taking your credit card number over the phone, especially after a high-pressure sales tactic was used. Never give your credit card number to someone asking for it merely to "verify" a free travel offer; it's nearly a sure bet that you'll have bought yourself the offer—whatever it may turn out to be.

Up-front "processing fees" or "refundable" deposits that cost more than the stated price of the trip.

"900" phone numbers. If you have to call a "900" number to learn the details of a vacation offer, typically you'll pay several dollars a minute for a few minutes and find out nothing—not even the "claim number" you were told to call for.

Failure to provide the name, exact address, and phone number of the company making the offer.

THE $MARTER CONSUMER

Call individual hotels to get the lowest room rate. Staff who answer a chain's national reservation number often don't know about the latest local discounts. Always ask about special deals.

Go by the guidebook. Don't rely on tour brochures or advertisements picturing antique-filled rooms and tranquil patios set in verdant gardens. There's nothing stopping any flophouse from calling itself "four star." Consult a reputable ratings guide, like those offered by Mobil, AAA, or Michelin, that rates hotels and restaurants based on in-depth investigations.

In all travel transactions, always try to use a credit card. If you use cash and the agency or operator goes out of business, the chances of getting reimbursed are slim. But if you charged it, the protections for non-delivered merchandise or services afforded by the Fair Credit Billing Act may kick in (see "Credit Cards," page 373).

Book with reputable tour operators; those who belong to the United States Tour Operators Association must have 18 references from a variety of reputable travel agency organizations, must furnish the organization with a $1 million indemnity bond, and must carry at least $1 million in liability insurance with worldwide coverage.

HELP

■ **Half-price programs.** Entertainment Publications can be reached at (800) 477-3234. Additional major discount hotel/resort services include: *The Preferred Traveler's* card offers 50% off rack rates at 10,000 hotels worldwide and discounts on airfares and rental cars; call (800) 638-8976. *Great American Traveler* offers half-off at 1,500 mostly mid-range hotels, such as Ramada Inn, for $49.95 for the first year and $21.95 each year thereafter, (800) 548-2812.

■ **You can obtain** hotel room discounts overseas by booking through your airline. For example, American Airlines offers discount vouchers good for 20% to 30% off at several hundred Best Western Hotels in Europe; call (800) 832-8383. To reach TWA's program, call (800) 438-2929. British Airways, Japan Airlines, Lufthansa, SAS, and Singapore Airlines also have programs.

Continued on next page

Continued from previous page

■ **The annual *Travel Buying Guide*** (issued by *Consumer Reports*) tells all you need to know about getting discounts on airfares, hotels, car rentals, and more. Available at most bookstores, or from *Consumer Reports* for $8.99 by calling (800) 500-9760.

■ **Has a travel agent or tour operator** "taken you for a ride"? Take *them* to the feds by writing to the Federal Trade Commission at 6th Street and Pennsylvania Avenue NW, Washington, DC 20580.

■ **If you've been victimized by a tour** or travel agent, call the consumer affairs division of the American Society of Travel Agents (ASTA) at (703) 739-2782. Or write to them at 1101 King Street, Alexandria, VA 22314. You'll get the most satisfactory result if your complaint is about something specific you were supposed to get and didn't.

Remember, ASTA is not able to force an agent to provide a refund, although a threat to expel them from the organiza-tion may prove persuasive. It exists primarily to benefit its members and is not a consumer advocacy organization. More information is available at www.astanet.com, including a directory of ASTA members and other online travel resources.

■ **If you booked a tour through a** United States Tour Operators Association (USTOA) member and the operator totally fails to perform or goes insolvent, ask for a reimbursement claim form from the USTOA, 342 Madison Avenue, Suite 1522, New York, NY 10173; call (212) 599-6599.

■ **For up-to-date information on how** to best spend your travel dollar, subscribe to *Consumer Reports Travel Letter,* $39 per year. Call (800) 234-1970 or write P.O. Box 53629, Boulder, CO 80322-3629.

■ **For a free copy of a guide to hotel** room safety, send a self-addressed, stamped envelope to American Hotel & Motel Association Tips, 1201 New York Avenue NW, Washington, DC 20005.

CHAPTER 50

CAR RENTALS

Avoid Trumped-Up Charges

I t's never been fun to figure out how much a rental car will cost or to pick it up at the rental counter. And in many ways things are only getting worse. Rental companies have pared down their fleets to cut costs, refuse to rent to drivers with bad records, make up for lost profits with hidden charges, and try to lighten their insurance burden by adding to yours.

On top of all that, the customer service revolution seems to have passed the car rental industry by. Rental volume of 85 million cars a year is up about 20% since the mid-1990s, but staffing at rental counters has not increased equally, so lines are longer than ever; standard information like your driver's license number and frequent-flier or AAA membership number—the kind of information L.L. Bean has been saving and using for years—is collected and laboriously entered into the computer every time you rent rather than stored to expedite future rentals. And the cars get rented more often and are on average several months older than they used to be.

One disgruntled renter summed up the frustrations in *The Wall Street Journal:* "They're like, 'You booked with me. Now drop dead.' "

THE BASICS

Bad Drivers Need Not Apply

S everal years ago, major car rental companies began rejecting customers they judged pose the highest risk of getting into an accident. The policy is in effect in many Hertz, Avis, National, Budget, Enterprise, Thrifty, and Value rental locations in California, Florida, Maryland, New York, Ohio, Pennsylvania, and Washington, DC. And it's likely the policy will continue to spread. About 4% to 6% of rental customers are turned away for things like an invalid or suspended driver's license, conviction for driving while under the influence of alcohol, or multiple recent police citations. The criteria vary slightly from one company to another.

Here's how the system works: You call to reserve a car. When you receive a confirmation number for your reservation, the reservations agent should tell you that your driving record may be checked when you come in to pick up the car. On that day, the counter attendant will ask to see your driver's license and will enter your name, driver's license number, and date of birth into a computer linked to a network of databases containing state motor vehicle records on about 119 million of the 167 million licensed drivers in the U.S. The computer then retrieves your record, analyzes it using criteria supplied by the rental company, and returns a verdict to the rental agent where you are. Some companies will tell you exactly why you were turned down; others will simply give you a list of disqualifying criteria. The whole process takes less than a minute in most cases, a little longer when the driver's record is long.

While the concept is reasonable—no company should have to turn over a $22,000 car to a reckless driver—there is one big drawback. You won't know whether you will definitely get a car until you show up at the counter. Imagine getting off the plane (with your entire family in tow) for a weeks' vacation and finding that you cannot rent a car.

Young Drivers Need Not Apply

Younger drivers in New York won the right to rent cars in court, but most car rental firms in other states will not rent cars to people younger than 21 (sometimes 25), saying that there is a higher chance of younger drivers getting into accidents and they can't get insurance for such "bad risks." People over 21 who have major credit cards or whose employers have corporate accounts with the rental firm generally have an easier time getting a car. Although turning down young drivers may be prohibited by state

or local human rights laws, you'd have to sue the agency to find out— an unlikely vacation occupation. Younger drivers are better off securing an acceptable major credit card or traveling with an older companion who can more easily rent a car.

And younger drivers who can find a rental should be prepared to pay a surcharge of at least $10 to $20 a day. Even after a New York court ruled that rental companies had to serve the under-25 set, many were surcharging so exorbitantly as to deter renting at all. Thrifty topped the list, foisting $145 extra per day on an 18- to 20-year-old renting from a Brooklyn location. Others tacked on daily surcharges of anywhere from $10 to $90. And some cars like vans and premium cars are off-limits entirely.

Collision Damage and Theft Coverage

In most states, the rental company will ask if you want to buy insurance that pays for damage to the car or replacement of the car in the event of theft. The most common option is the collision damage waiver (CDW), also called Loss Damage Waiver (LDW). While this is not technically insurance, it is a provision in rental contracts that for a daily fee absolves the renter of responsibility for damage to or loss of the car. New York outlawed CDWs because most consumers don't need them, and car rental firms coax, scare, and deceive as many as a third of their customers to buy the useless coverage. And California, Indiana, Nevada, and Texas limit how much can be charged for CDW's. Anna A. told *The New York Times* she declined rental car insurance when it was offered at an Alamo counter at Washington, DC's National Airport because she was paying with an American Express card. The agent tried to intimidate her into changing her mind by telling her, "Never mind the credit card. You'll take complete responsibility for the car if anything happens to it." She said, "I still refused the coverage, but left feeling very paranoid."

Most people don't need collision coverage because credit cards or the insurance policy on the car they leave in the garage at home protects them. Credit card coverage, which is not as widespread as it once was, is most often "secondary coverage." This means that any personal automobile insurance kicks in first, leaving the credit card company responsible only for the deductible. For individuals who do not own cars or have their own automobile insurance, credit card coverage is primary.

Rental agents' protestations to the contrary, purchase of the CDW is optional *everywhere*. In Massachusetts, state law requires this fact to be disclosed prominently in all rental contracts. The notice must also inform Massachusetts renters that the CDW may duplicate their insurance, which might already cover them for damages to the rental car from collisions, theft, fire,

> "They like to advertise the lowest rate possible and then sock people with extras."
>
> —EDWARD L. PERKINS, editor *Consumer Reports Travel Letter*

or vandalism. In Florida, the largest leisure car rental market in the United States, state law requires insurance companies to say that they cover collision damage on vehicles rented for private purposes on the insurance identification cards routinely issued to policyholders.

On the small chance that you do not have collision or comprehensive coverage through your car insurance policy, your employer (if you're using the car for business), or the credit card on which you charged the rental, it's a good idea to buy the CDW to protect yourself. You'll pay a steep $10 to $16 a day for coverage, even though it only costs the company about $3 a day. If you got a sweet deal on a weekly rental, this can double the price. A 1994 U.S. Public Interest Research Group study found that the price of the collision damage waiver increased the daily rental bill by 46% on average, and in some cases by as much as 93%.

Liability Responsibility

Most of the major car rental firms—Alamo, Avis, Budget, Hertz, and National—are shifting the responsibility for and the price of liability coverage for injury, death, or damage to others and their property to the renter in many states. Check with each firm about its policy. While in the past, car

PUMP ME UP

Before you return the car, make sure it has a full tank of gas. Many rental companies will charge you more than twice the price at the pump if they have to put gas in the tank. One New Yorker complained to the NYC Consumer Affairs Department that he had returned a rental car to Avis at 5:30 AM. It was too early to find an open gas station. He had used about 10 gallons of gas, which at the time would have cost roughly $13.00 at the pump. Avis's bill for the gas came to $32.37.

rental companies provided primary coverage for liability as part of the package, now your own policy must pay in the event of an accident that leads to a liability claim.

You have several choices: Rent from a company that does not charge for the coverage but provides it, rely on the liability coverage in your personal policy, rely on your employer's coverage if you are traveling on business, or buy the rental firm's coverage. This coverage is separate from collision coverage (CDW), which only covers damage to or disappearance of the car.

Don't go without. Liability claims can involve millions of dollars, putting your entire net worth at risk.

Coverage adds about $7 to the daily rental rate. Ask how much coverage this buys—or how much coverage the company provides if it comes *gratis*. Most rental companies provide only the minimum coverage mandated by the state, and this may not be enough to protect your assets in the event of a large claim against you. Some rental firms sell supplemental coverage to fill in the gap. It's probably worth it if you have major assets that could be at risk.

Fuel's Gold

Because many consumers are skipping the insurance they don't need, car rental companies now try to get you to buy gas you don't use. But the "fuel purchase option" almost never makes financial sense. If you skip it, your rental car comes with a full tank of gas, and you must fill 'er up before returning the car. With the option, you pay for the full tank of gas ahead of time and can bring the car back running on empty. And there's the catch: it's virtually impossible to use up *all* the gas—especially if you are traveling in unknown territory. Even if you leave only a few gallons, that's a few gallons of profit for the rental company. However, you will save yourself the trouble of scouting out a gas station as you rush to make a plane. If you refuse the fuel purchase option, be sure to gas up, or you could pay as much as $3 or $4 a gallon. One stunned renter was charged a staggering $7.25 per gallon.

One last gasoline gimmick: *Consumer Reports* has found that you might not even be getting the gas you pay for. Some rental companies have been known to overstate the capacities of their cars' tanks—so you pay for 13 gallons when the tank holds only 12. And about one in four cars they rented came with less than a full tank. Check the gauge on your way out, and if it registers less than full, get it taken care of before you take off.

WHAT TO WATCH OUT FOR

Hidden costs. The National Association of Attorneys General adopted advertising guidelines for car rental firms requiring them to include all *mandatory* charges and fees in the rates they advertise. Even so, there are plenty of *extra* hidden charges that can raise prices. If you are calling around to try to find the best

NOT SUCH A GREAT DEAL

Here's how a $69/week Florida rental could cost almost three times as much.

Weekly rental:	**$69.00**
Average daily charge for collision damage waiver:	
	$12.95 x 7 days = $90.65
Budget's daily rate for liability coverage:	
	$5.95 x 7 days = $41.65
	TOTAL $201.30

deal, ask how much extra you will have to pay for:

■ *Additional drivers.* This used to be free, but many companies now charge $10, $15, or even $25 per rental for the option of letting someone other than the renter drive. (New York caps the charge at $5.) Many firms waive the charge for spouses and business associates.

■ *Upgrades to a larger class of car.* The prices quoted in ads are most often for the lowest class of car. If you need something bigger, it will probably cost more.

■ *Airport fees.* Many localities tax car renters to pay for airport upgrades or the convenience of picking up cars on airport property. (They figure most renters are from out of town and can't balk at the ballot box.) Phoenix tacks on a total of 26% to the average weekly rental for sales taxes, surcharges, and airport fees. At Newark, renters pay 75 cents to subsidize a new tram. You might be able to dodge some of these stealth fees by renting from a location other than the airport. Take the courtesy shuttle to your hotel and rent from there.

Bias. Car rental companies claim they have to be choosy about which strangers they allow to rent valuable, potentially lethal assets, and at what price. But their rules of thumb —that all the young, the accident-prone, the residents of Brooklyn, Bronx, and Queens should pay more, or not get a car at all—smacks of bias rather than smart business. And several Avis outlets have been accused of racial and religious bias—because they allegedly refused to rent to blacks and Hasidic Jews. Hertz and Budget claim the additional charges for New Yorkers reflect the cost of doing business in each of the boroughs as a result of New York State's vicarious liability law, which holds the rental company responsible for accidents involving its cars even if the renter was at fault. (New York City banned these additional fees for its residents, but while the law undergoes a legal challenge, Hertz and Budget continue to charge New Yorkers who rent anywhere in the metropolitan area extra.)

Mileage caps. Some rental deals give you free mileage—but only up to a pre-set limit. Figure out if your itinerary will keep you within the allowance. If not, you could end up paying high additional charges for every mile you drive beyond the limit. About 30 cents a mile is not unusual. At this rate, if you drive 200 miles over the limit for a $35-a-day rental, you'll almost double the price for a weekend getaway.

Damage. You'll be held responsible for any damage to the car, and car rental companies often pad their repair bills beyond what it actually costs to fix the damage. For instance, they may try to charge you for losses related to not being able to rent the car to someone else while it's in the shop. Hertz once refunded more than $2 million to consumers and insurance companies in 41 states whom it had overcharged for repairs.

Cancellation fees. They don't apply to all reservations—yet. But as of this writing, Alamo, Avis, Budget, Hertz, and National have begun billing a penalty even if you never picked up the car. The policy varies a bit from one company to another, and even from one location to another, but it generally applies to minivans, convertibles, and other special cars. The fees range from $50 to $100. Budget started imposing a penalty charge equal to a full day's rental on people who failed to show up for 1997 summer weekend reservations in Seattle, Boston, and New York.

Reservations clerks are supposed to tell you about the cancellation penalty when you make the reservation. Ask how much notice you need to give in order to avoid the charge; it could be as little as a few hours or as much as a few days.

Debit cards. Rental companies use credit cards as a crude mechanism to avoid risky renters. But debit cards, which banks give to virtually anyone with a bank account, don't provide a similar comfort, and major rental companies do not let people rent cars with only a Visa Check card or Master Money card. If you want to use one of these cards and do not have a credit card to reassure the rental company, you will have to do what people who pay cash do: apply a month in advance and leave a deposit.

Taking the rental off-road is a deal breaker. You'll lose the rental company's insurance coverage if you take a shortcut through the desert or through the woods on an old logging trail.

THE $MARTER CONSUMER

Look for bargains. Since many car rental locations are busiest during the week, serving business customers, they often offer low weekend rates to attract tourists. Just make sure you understand the restrictions. If you rent a car at a special weekly rate and decide you only want to keep it a few days, the price may revert to a much higher daily rate. In the end, you could end up paying significantly more for a few days than you would have paid for the whole week. Likewise, if you take a car for a few days and then decide you want to extend your trip, you probably won't be able to get the lower weekly rate, even if you keep the car a week.

Mileage caps can work against you if you will be covering a lot of territory, but they might work for you if you won't be traveling that far. Ask whether you can get a lower rate if you stay within a mileage allowance. And when the rental company offers two rates, figure out how far you will drive and calculate the most economical rate.

Make reservations ahead of time and get a confirmation number. This locks in the rate. If you reserve far enough in advance, you can avoid getting stung when rental firms boost their prices just before a holiday.

Play your club cards. Chances are memberships in frequent-flier pro-grams, professional associations, auto clubs, and other groups entitle you to a discount at one or another rental agency. But some memberships get you more than others, so be sure to ask about each club at each rental company.

Don't give in to high pressure at the counter. The consumer's interest is in direct opposition to rental counter personnel's: Most companies tie employee pay to sales of extras like insurance and fuel. This is a built-in incentive to intimidate you into buying insurance and fuel extras you don't need.

Liability is a real issue. If you rent cars often and have no coverage, you may want to consider tacking it onto your homeowners insurance. If you don't cover yourself somehow, and you are involved in an accident in which someone is injured or killed, your personal assets may be at risk.

Make sure you have collision damage insurance from one source or another. Don't blindly count on your credit card for collision coverage. For instance, Chase and AT&T Universal Card no longer offer this perk with standard Visa and MasterCards, but their Gold cards cover it. American Express and Diner's Club cards still cover you for collision damage as of this writing. For other bank cards, check with your issuer, and check regularly, as credit card policies can shift on short notice and in small type you might not notice at all.

This is particularly important if you will be renting a car overseas, where policies vary greatly——for example, Amex has stopped providing insurance coverage in Ireland, Israel, Italy, and Jamaica. Don't expect a rental agent to help you figure it out.

If you have a car of your own, double-check that your collision insurance covers rental cars. If it doesn't, or if you wouldn't want to file a claim with your insurance company because you'd have to pay a deductible or your rate would increase, you may want to buy the CDW. In fact, do not count on your personal automobile insurance to cover you in the event of a collision in a car you rent for business travel. Bob M. of Fort Lauderdale was told by his employer *not* to buy the CDW (if he did, the company wouldn't reimburse him

for the expense). Trouble was, Bob's car insurance would only cover vehicles rented for private purposes. In the end, his employer assumed responsibility for damage to the rental car.

Read the CDW. If you buy one, make sure you understand the terms and restrictions, particularly the ones camouflaged in fine print. For instance, the CDW is most often void for accidents involving an unauthorized driver.

Check for scratches before you drive out of the rental lot. You will be charged for any dents or damage, no matter how minor. If pre-existing damage isn't noted in your rental agreement, you may be charged for a previous renter's scrape and your own carelessness.

H E L P

■ **If you have a prob**lem with a car rental: Report it to your state attorney general's office or to your local Better Business Bureau.

■ **For more information, consult:** *Consumer Reports Travel Buying Guide.* It's available at bookstores or call (800) 272-0722.

■ **Find out whether your driving** record will disqualify you at the rental counter. Call Travel Check, the company that links many rental companies to renters' driving records, (800) 388-9099. For $10.77, including tax ($8.61

if you are a member of AAA), they will indicate whether you meet a rental company's criteria. You will have to give your name, driver's license number, state of issuance, and date of birth.

■ **Many car rental companies post** special deals on their Internet sites and take reservations online. Go to www.avis.com, www.budgetrentacar.com, www.dollarcar.com, www.hertz.com, www.national.com. Many also have partnerships with airlines, and it might be worth checking the airlines' sites, too.

P A R T   1 0

Professional Services

CHAPTER 51

LAWYERS

Finding Affordable Representation

The problem of hiring a lawyer can be summed up by a 1973 *New Yorker* cartoon. A distinguished-looking attorney and an anxious prospective client are talking; the caption reads, "You have a pretty good case, Mr. Pitkin. How much justice can you afford?"

High prices for any product or service are a costly burden for cash-strapped Americans today. But paying too much for a TV is one thing. Paying too much for a lawyer, or having to pay so much that you can't afford the day in court due you, is quite another.

One Westchester County, New York, woman (she prefers not to be identified by name) with a doctoral degree in special education from Columbia University found herself in just such a bind: She paid her lawyers $15,000 to get the court to make the deadbeat dad she had divorced pay child support (awarded to her) for their three minor children. After three years she found herself embroiled in a fee dispute with her lawyers over $70,000 in accrued fees. On the eve of trial she refused to sign a note for the debt, and the lawyers abandoned her case. Rather than carrying out their mission of wresting child support from her unresponsive husband, they collected their fees by seizing and liquidating her retirement fund and entire bank account.

The legal profession not only perpetuates an aura of complexity and omniscience, but its esoteric mumbo jumbo—sprinkled generously with arcane Latin phrases like *sui generis* and *pro bono,* which simply mean "unique" and "for the good," respectively—can also hide featherbedding and fee-hiking. It can also silence clients' questions about why three attorneys were needed in court for a seemingly simple case or how a one-hour phone call between lawyer and client could possibly have taken place when the client was atop Mount Kilimanjaro. (For the original, and still the best, book on how the legal profession converts complexity and esoterica into fat fees, see former Yale professor Fred Rodell's 1939 classic, *Woe Unto You Lawyers.*)

And in addition to the language barrier, there's the fabled superior attitude—perceived and proven—that surrounds all things legal. From the mid-19th century until 1975, the bar justified its rule *requiring* lawyers to charge no less than a minimum fee for specific legal services with the explanation that theirs was a profession and therefore not subject to the normal rules of the free market. No matter that the policy precluded price shopping and fee bargaining that might reduce huge fees. But what the bar called an "ethical rule" the Supreme Court unanimously called "price-fixing" and illegal in the *Goldfarb* v. *Virginia State Bar* decision of 1975. It took another unanimous *Bates and O'Steen* v. *State Bar of Arizona* decision from the Supreme Court in 1977 to knock down prohibitions against lawyers advertising —as if the provision of legal services were somehow not a commercial transaction. (Because many members of the established bar consider the *Bates* decision's "commercialization" of their "profession" demeaning and declassé, they often denounce TV, radio, print, and direct-mail ads for lawyers. The issue, however, should not be whether advertising offends their lawyerly sensibility but whether the ads tell the truth. As with any other product or service, legal advertising is fine unless it deceives or misleads.)

The laws may change, but the attitude lingers on. Florida legal secretary Rosemary Furman created a small business providing men and women with help filling out the legal forms necessary to obtain a divorce. The Florida bar challenged the legality of her business on the basis that she was not a lawyer and therefore should not be allowed to give what they perceived to be legal advice. The case dragged on for ten years; representation by the Public Citizen Litigation Group kept Rosemary out of jail, but it could not save her business.

By the mid-1980s, however, the Florida bar and Supreme Court had relaxed their requirements enough so that people like Rosemary can now assist litigants with filling out forms. To the extent that courts require lawyers to do things that paralegals, court clerks, legal secretaries, or you yourself could easily do, you are paying these professionals something for nothing.

Such incidents fuel the current wave of anti-lawyer jokes and negative references in our popular culture—such as the lawyer-eating dinosaur in *Jurassic Park,* which provoked cheers in movie theaters in the mid-1990s around the country.

While the trend in the lawyer –client struggle may favor clients, it's also true that two-thirds of the public can't afford to hire a lawyer when they need one. In fact, new legal problems crop up in more than 40% of low- and moderate-income households each year—disputes between landlords and tenants or families and their health insurers over disallowed charges—but, according to a 1994 study by the American

> " *I heard my lawyer tell another attorney he was filing a counter motion to increase his billable hours, and I realized he was looking for money, not solutions.* "
>
> —DANA H.,
> a former divorce client

Bar Association, most people choose to avoid the formal legal system because they fear that it won't help them or that it will cost too much. Hence this chapter, which will guide you through the process of buying the best representation you can for whatever price your budget can bear, even if it means you represent yourself. (Nothing in the chapter should be construed as a *substitute* for legal advice, but instead as advice on how to pursue, procure, and evaluate professional legal services.)

THE BASICS

Finding a lawyer is easy—there are almost a million of them in the U.S. But finding the right one is something else again. Purchasing legal services should be no more mystifying than buying any other product or service—a lawyer is there to serve you and help you get a job done. But getting good legal advice at minimal cost takes careful management of your own case and your relationship with your attorney—including choosing your lawyer carefully, hammering out a fair working (and billing) relationship, setting realistic goals, keeping track of your case, judicious use of telephone calls, and careful review of lawyers' bills.

Do You Need a Lawyer?

Many situations obviously require professional legal advice—Your dog bites the U.P.S. man and you are sued; your husband is charged with driving while intoxicated; you are about to enter the hospital for open-heart surgery and need to draw up a will and guardianship papers for your three young children; you need to seek redress for serious injuries your wife sustained in a car accident; you and your husband are splitting up or adopting a child.

And there are many less obvious situations in which a lawyer's advice or review of documents can easily pay for itself in avoided headaches and expenditures—contracts for renovating the kitchen or other significant home improvements or insurance agreements, for instance. But there are also situations in which a lawyer may not be necessary, for example in a dispute over a bill or a service. (For more on handling your own disputes, see the final chapter "How to Complain," page 701.)

The Selection Process

When you begin your search for an attorney, the two most important things to keep in mind are finding someone you feel comfortable working with and finding someone knowledgeable about the area of law with which you need assistance. Doing so will probably require talking to more than one attorney to see how each of them would treat both you and your matter. Even if you have to invest some money in these meetings (some lawyers charge for an initial consultation), it's probably worth the investment.

The most common ways to find a lawyer include asking friends, family, and other attorneys. Surveys show that seeking names from such friendly sources is the most common way people find lawyers, and we recommend it, too. But make sure the recommendation fits your needs. Just because the client on *Ally McBeal* was comfortable with Ally McBeal and happy with the divorce settlement McBeal got for him doesn't mean his sister would be just as well-served by her, particularly if her sister wanted to bring a medical malpractice suit. McBeal might, however, be able to refer the injured woman to an appropriate colleague. Be sure to choose a lawyer who knows the field your case falls in—for instance, if you want to adopt a child, pass over the kindly woman who wrote your mother's will (unless, of course, she also works as an adoption lawyer) and keep up the search for an attorney who specializes in adoptions.

Referral services. In the best of all worlds, using legal referral services, which are offered on a non-profit basis by virtually every state bar association, would give you the benefit of talking to experts who could assess your situation and make a referral to the appropriate attorney or another non-legal provider. "Most [bar association] referral services act as clearinghouses for social service agencies, government offices, and other services that may even be free," says Carol Woods, director of the San Francisco Bar Association's legal referral service. "What we provide is a knowledgeable person who can help you define your problem and help you figure

out what resource is best. We get 85,000 calls a year, and only 25% of them are referred to lawyers."

Each bar association runs its referral service differently. The basic service involves listening to your situation and referring you to the appropriate place. If you need an attorney, the service will give you the name of one who has agreed to participate and will provide you with a half-hour initial consultation at a fixed charge (anywhere from free to around $25).

Virtually all bar association referral services require their lawyers to carry malpractice insurance, and the best programs—like those in San Francisco, Los Angeles, and New York City—require attorneys to demonstrate a certain level of experience in a given area before giving their name out. But there is a lot in between. Some have lawyers or specially trained interviewers answering the phone and making referrals, while others use paralegals or clerical staff.

To further confuse matters, for-profit referral services operate in Texas, Florida, California, and many other areas of the country. Some states—California, for instance—regulate them, but others don't. The danger lies in being referred to a lawyer who signed up with the service for a hefty monthly fee in return for getting every call—whether or not the lawyer is qualified and appropriate to handle the case—that comes from a designated zip code.

When using either kind of referral service, ask the following questions before you call any offered names:

■ How did this lawyer get on your list? What were the specific qualifying criteria?

■ Are the attorneys on your list required to have malpractice insurance?

■ What happens if I'm not happy with the representation I receive? To whom would I complain or address grievances?

The first meeting of the minds. Take advantage of the free or low-cost initial consultations many lawyers offer to get information about the lawyer and a feel for his or her style. But don't feel obligated to hire the lawyer—if the consultation is free, it's free. Even if the lawyer charges for the consultation, it may be worth it if the lawyer spends a couple of hours with you going over the facts of the case, the documentation, where things stand now, and tries to apply the local law to the facts of your case.

To make the most of your visit, get organized before you go:

■ Put together a file of all the relevant documents and study them. Bring copies with you to the initial meeting. For instance, if you want to declare bankruptcy, bring copies of all the bills you've received and a list of your assets and their fair market value; for a divorce, bring copies of all deeds, recent bank statements, and life, property, and health insurance policies.

■ Write down a chronology of events, and make a copy to leave with the attorney.

Once you are there, you are simultaneously trying to size up the attorney's expertise, benefit from whatever advice you may be offered, and figure out how well you will work together. Here are some tips to make your evaluation easier:

■ Ask how long the attorney has been in practice, how much experience he or she has with similar cases, how busy he or she is, and who else may be working on your case.

■ Review the facts of your case and your document file. Run through the process step-by-step, and ask whether the lawyer anticipates any problems.

■ Ask about the fee arrangement. An hourly fee is standard for most divorces, but bankruptcies or house closings are so rote that many lawyers charge a flat fee. If you will be billed by the hour, ask who will work on the case: The attorney? Other attorneys in the firm? Paralegals? Legal secretaries? Don't walk out in a huff if others will be working on your case; you might want an agreement that lets the expensive hot-shot do the expert legal work and uses a less experienced associate or legal secretary for more routine efforts, at an hourly rate that reflects their level of expertise. Less-skilled help could cost up to 50% less.

■ Ask for an estimate of what it will cost to resolve your legal situation—pre-trial, trial (if there is to be one), and possible appeal. Lawyers may be reluctant to give an exact dollar amount, but they ought to be able to give you a range.

■ Make sure you will receive a monthly, itemized bill.

■ Ask for references.

The Written Fee Agreement

Once you have chosen a lawyer, work out an agreeable employment and fee arrangement, and get it in writing. Make sure you understand the fee arrangement—read it carefully, ask questions about it, read it again when you get home, and ask more questions if you need to. Vague language can hide expensive traps. One retainer agreement we examined said, "It may be necessary to spend substantial amounts of time in obtaining the file." But it never defined "substantial amount," or what specific motions might be needed to fulfill this prediction, or what those motions usually cost. Another agreement included the following statement: "Because of mounting costs, it may be necessary from time to time for the applicable time charges to be increased, and such adjustments will be reflected in your billing." So the rate quoted could change at any time without advance warning and was essentially useless for the client trying to gauge future fees.

"It's truly remarkable how many people don't know how much they are being charged," says Allen Charne, director of the Legal Referral Service jointly sponsored by the New York City bar associations. That's why it's unremarkable that fee disputes sour so many lawyer–client relationships.

Make sure the written agreement accurately reflects your discussions and covers these crucial areas (explained in detail below): fees, expenses, retainer, billing procedure, dispute resolution procedures, and lawyer–client rights and responsibilities.

Fees. Lawyers use three billing methods: hourly fees, contingency fees, and flat fees.

■ *Hourly fees* are just what they sound like—you pay a set price for every hour (or fraction thereof) the lawyer spends on your matter. Lawyers most often bill in 15-, 10-, or 6-minute increments. So no matter how long you meet or talk on the phone, the length of each conversation will be rounded up to the next increment. Thus, a five-minute phone call with a lawyer who charges $150 an hour will cost you $37.50 in 15-minute increments, $25 in 10-minute increments, or $15 in 6-minute increments.

This arrangement provides a financial incentive for lawyers to put in time on your case. It may encourage them to do so even if the case doesn't warrant it.

If you will be billed by the hour, be sure your agreement stipulates reduced hourly fees for work done by associates, paralegals, or legal secretaries.

■ *Contingency fees*, most often used when the client cannot afford to pay the attorney if the case is lost, mean that the attorney "gambles" on the likelihood of winning. If you win, your lawyer gets an agreed-upon percentage of the settlement or judgment; if you lose, the lawyer gets no fee. Contingency fees are the norm for product liability, medical malpractice, and class action cases. Many states do not allow contingency fees for divorce and criminal cases, based on the belief that attorneys should be somewhat more objective and dispassionate on such matters.

While the percentage can be great (anywhere from 15% to 50%, but most often 33%), it theoretically makes up for the cases the lawyer works on but doesn't win (no fee). Still, you can usually negotiate a declining percentage for increasing damages. For instance, 33% of the first $500,000 in damages, 25% of the second $500,000, and 15% of anything beyond $1 million.

Even if you lose the case, you may be required to pay your lawyer's expenses. Make sure to investigate this ahead of time—ask the lawyer to estimate what the bills might be—and hammer out an agreement about when these expenses will be payable.

■ *Flat fees* may be charged for routine matters that will take a fairly predictable amount of effort—for example, incorporating a business, drawing up a simple will, and uncontested divorces. Just be sure you ask about additional costs for expenses and court filing fees.

Expenses. No matter what kind of fee you pay, you will most likely be asked to also pay expenses for things like court filing fees, court reporters and transcripts, photocopies, postage and messengers, long-distance phone calls, private investigators, and expert witnesses. Make sure you understand which expenses are included in the fee and which will cost you extra.

Retainer. It is common practice for a lawyer to ask you to pay a sum of money up front from which he or she can draw payment as it's earned or pay court filing fees and other expenses. Ask whether this "retainer" is an advance on fees, expenses, or both and what happens if any is left at the end. Look for an agreement that refunds whatever is left.

If you don't, you could end up like the unhappy couple who sued Long Island, New York, matrimonial attorney Joel R. Brandes. He refused to refund a $15,000 retainer after the couple reconciled only a few weeks after the agreement was signed. The non-refundable retainer agreement was eventually struck down by the court, which found it "grossly excessive and shocking to the court's conscience," since "not one document was generated during the tenure of the agreement. Not one pleading or letter was prepared by counsel. No appearance in court was made. No conference among counsel was scheduled, nor does it appear from the time-sheets submitted that the plaintiff was involved in negotiating a settlement with adverse counsel. . . . Thus to permit counsel to retain what he characterizes as the minimum fee would be to lend judicial approval to an hourly rate of $3,571.43 ($15,000 divided by 4.2 hours)."

Over the last two decades, nonrefundable retainers have become prevalent in domestic, criminal, and, to a somewhat lesser degree, bankruptcy cases. New York is the only state that prohibits non-refundable retainers. If your lawyer insists on a non-refundable retainer, take your business elsewhere. And if your lawyer does no work, challenge him or her in court or through the disciplinary system run by the state bar associations.

Billing procedure. Ask to get an itemized monthly bill and get this spelled out in your fee agreement—not only that you will get a monthly bill but what it will include. You want a precise, itemized bill that lists each piece of work done on your case, the service performed, the individual who performed it, and the time it took, along with precise accountings of the amount of expenses and their purpose. An accurate monthly bill allows you to keep track of your case and keeps the lawyer accountable to you. A bill saying merely "For Services Rendered" should have gone out with hand-cranked adding machines.

Complaint resolution procedure. Make sure the fee agreement spells out how you and your lawyer will work out any possible disputes between the two of you. This part of the negotiation may have an awkwardness like that between potential spouses who want a prenuptial agreement, but it can come in handy later. It also tells you something about the lawyer you are about to hire. Ask that you be allowed to discuss fee disputes without being billed for the time the discussion takes. And in the event you can't come to terms, ask if the lawyer will agree to fee arbitration or mediation.

Lawyer–client rights and responsibilities. This section of the written fee agreement should outline each of your rights and responsibilities.

For instance, this is the place to get in writing the agreement that your attorney send you copies of all documents related to your case, that you receive periodic updates on how things are going, or that you have agreed to do some of the legwork yourself. It is also a place for the attorney to outline your responsibility to review your bills and pay promptly and keep him or her up-to-date on any developments that may affect your case. You also might want to ask your lawyer to append the "Client Bill of Rights" to the agreement (see the box on the facing page). New York requires a similar "Divorce Client Bill of Rights and Responsibilities" to be discussed with prospective clients and appended to all divorce retainer agreements.

Legal Service Plans

Legal service plans operate much like insurance—you pay an annual "membership fee" or "retainer," similar to an insurance premium, for access to legal services whenever you need them. Coverage varies from plan to plan and state to state, but most plans are geared to very basic legal needs—landlord–tenant disputes; bankruptcies; basic family matters (adoptions and simple divorces); and buying and selling homes. In addition to helping find a lawyer, they promise unlimited legal advice and counsel by phone, routine document drafting (wills and house-closing contracts, for instance), document review, and access to lawyers who have agreed to work within a specified fee

CLIENT BILL OF RIGHTS

1. You have the right to discuss the proposed rates and retainer fee with your lawyer and you have the right to bargain about the fees before you sign the agreement, as in any other contract.

2. You have the right to know how many attorneys and other legal staff will be working on your case and what you will be charged for their services.

3. You have the right to know in advance how you will be asked to pay legal fees and expenses at the end of the case. If you pay for a retainer, you may ask reasonable questions about how the money will be spent or has been spent, and how much of it remains unspent.

4. You are under no legal obligation to sign a Confession of Judgment or Promissory Note, or agree to a lien or mortgage on your home to cover legal fees. You are under no legal obligation to waive your rights to dispute a bill for legal services.

5. You have the right to a reasonable estimate of future necessary costs. If your lawyer agrees to lend or advance you money for preparing your case, you have a right to know periodically how much money your lawyer has spent on your behalf. You also have the right to decide, after consulting with your lawyer, how much money is to be spent to prepare your case. If you pay the expenses, you have the right to decide how much to spend.

6. You have the right to ask your lawyer at reasonable intervals how the case is progressing and to have these questions answered to the best of your lawyer's ability.

7. You have the right to make the final decision regarding the settlement of your case.

8. You have a right to any original documents that are not a part of your attorney's work product. For instance, if you gave your present attorney documents prepared by another attorney, you have the right to those documents. You have a right to ask your attorney to forward copies of documents to you in a timely manner as he/she receives them from the opposing attorney.

9. You have the right to be present at court conferences relating to your case that are held with judges and attorneys, and you also have the right to bring a family member or friend to all court proceedings, unless a judge orders otherwise.

10. You have the right to know the cost of bringing a motion. The cost may vary depending on the lawyer's rates and the circumstances of the case, but you have a right to a general estimate.

If at any time, you, the client, believe that your lawyer has charged an excessive or illegal fee, you have the right to report the matter to a disciplinary or grievance committee that oversees lawyer misconduct.

Source: Revision of the New York City Department of Consumer Affairs' Divorce Client Bill of Rights

schedule for non-routine work. And like a health maintenance organization (HMO), most legal service plans promote preventive care by encouraging you to get advice before you find yourself with a significant legal problem.

And, not surprisingly, many middle-income consumers prefer to pay a couple of hundred dollars *a year* on the chance they'll need legal help rather than a couple of hundred dollars *an hour* when they actually do. There are now about 98 million people covered by legal service plans, most through their employers, up from 15 million in 1985.

Pre-paid legal service plans started out as group benefits for union members that were paid for by employers. There are now also individual plans available, most often sold through the mail, telemarketing, or door-to-door. Group plans—which may be offered through your employer, union, or other membership organization—often cost little or nothing to join. Because they spread the risk over a large group, their operating costs are relatively low and they can pass the savings on to you. Many offer "comprehensive" benefits that cover practically anything and everything, including reimbursing you for things like expenses related to representing yourself in traffic court. Individual plans cost anywhere from $80 to several hundred dollars a year and most often provide "access" benefits—i.e., the basic consultations and services described above. For more complex matters, individual plans will refer you to a lawyer who has previously

agreed to provide legal services at a reduced price to the plan's members. Plans that give you more choice among lawyers typically cost more.

Whether a legal service plan makes sense for you depends upon your situation. If it's offered through your employer at little or no extra cost, it may be the perfect alternative to close the deal on a new house or to draw up a simple will. However, if you have to pay hundreds of dollars a year (commonly in monthly installments) just to join, ask yourself a few questions before you write the check:

■ Do you have frequent or occasional legal questions?
■ Do you have pre-existing legal problems? (Most plans exclude covering them.)
■ Do you understand fully what out-of-pocket expenses you may incur or the difference between a "simple" matter and a more complicated one, for which you will have to pay? For instance, how simple is that will? Will your divorce *truly* be uncontested?
■ Can you switch lawyers if you are unhappy with the one assigned to your case?
■ Is there a satisfactory process for resolving any complaints you may have about the plan?

The laws governing legal service plans vary from state to state. Some 25 states, including Florida, Texas, and Washington, have comprehensive statutes that either regulate legal plans as though they were insurance or assign jurisdiction to a state insurance department, since the plans operate so much like insurance plans. The laws require financial security, bonding, and reasonable complaint handling procedures. For more information, contact your state's Insurance Commissioner.

How to Avoid Lawyers

Small claims court. Small claims court was designed to allow a lay person to get a quick decision from a judge without paying big fees for minor disputes. The maximum amount disputable averages $2,000 but varies from state to state. (For more information on how to use small claims court effectively, see "How to Complain," page 701.)

Alternative dispute resolution. All parties have to be willing, and you may still want an attorney's legal advice, but practically any conflict can be resolved more quickly and cheaply through mediation or arbitration than through litigation. Mediation and arbitration can also be more effective because they offer a less adversarial, non-judicial process that encourages deal-cutting and compromise rather than winning at all costs.

In arbitration, participants present their arguments to an impartial third party whose decision is final, binding, and most often not appealable. Parties are not bound by the rules of evidence, and the arbitrator is under no obligation to explain the final decision. Parties choose an arbitrator mutually, with the help of a judge, or through the American Arbitration Association. Since you usually cannot appeal an arbitrated decision, if you think you'll have trouble living with the result, arbitration isn't for you.

In mediation, parties work through the conflict themselves with the guidance of an impartial third party who simply facilitates a negotiation and allows the parties to hammer out a reasonable resolution.

WHAT TO WATCH OUT FOR

Get a second opinion. As with your physical health, a fresh evaluation can make all the difference.

Take the case of a New York City delicatessen worker who lost most of his arm when it got caught in a meat grinder. He went to one of the best-known personal injury lawyers in New York, who investigated the possibility of a product liability suit. Because the grinder was 30 years old and had been manufactured in Italy, the lawyer believed that the deli man had nothing but a worker's compensation case, through which he could receive only a minimal settlement. A few years went by. When the deli man needed a lawyer to help with some trouble with his worker's compensation, he called the Legal Referral Service. (As it happened, there was just a week left before the statute of limitations was to run out on the case.) He was referred to a second personal injury lawyer, who promptly filed a complaint and, after considerable legal maneuvering, settled the case out of court for over $1 million.

Pro Se: Flying Solo

If your financial situation limits your options—or to avoid legal featherbedding—you are allowed to represent yourself, which is called going *pro se* in legal lingo. Ask the clerks in the courthouse how to fill out paperwork and to review the court's procedures with you. They may even help you prepare motions. Use local law libraries for legal research and local courthouses for records searches. Consumer activists have fought successfully in California, Florida, and Georgia to allow non-lawyers to assist people with simple legal matters, and Arizona has some of the most user-friendly courthouses in America. You can actually sit at a computer in a court clerk's office in Phoenix to fill out the necessary forms yourself!

Just don't forget Justice Louis Brandeis's commentary on an old axiom: "Long ago it was recognized that 'a man who is his own lawyer has a fool for a client.' The reason for this is that soundness of judgment is easily obscured by self-interest."

One way to do some of your own legal work is through computer networks. You can find lawyer listings and legal forms and bulletin boards on America Online, CompuServe, and the Internet. The state of Florida has even put complaints against lawyers on the Internet. You can swap advice (or horror stories) and perhaps get a referral. You can even find your way into an electronic law library. In the end, it's best to double-check whatever you've found out or done for yourself with a lawyer, but you may well prune back your bill by going solo at least part of the way.

Take Miles E. Crawford, for example. He used the Washington State Legal Ease library to draw up the papers necessary to set up a corporation. He then asked an attorney to review the matter. "He wasn't exactly pleased. I think he was expecting to make more money," Crawford told *The Wall Street Journal*.

Overcharging, hidden charges, and phony bills. First, the profit motive behind the hourly billing fee structure encourages excess. "Most lawyers will prefer to leave no stone unturned—provided, of course, they can charge by the stone," wrote Stanford University Law Professor Deborah Rhode. And, effectively, they can. Efficiency is rewarded with lower fees, so where's the sense in keeping things moving as quickly as possible? A 1992 study of divorce actions by the New York City Department of Consumer Affairs found this to be particularly problematic for the non-moneyed spouse (typically women) in matrimonial cases. Excessive litigation, motion churning, and other delaying tactics drive up fees and delay justice. Take the observation of Justice Kristen Booth Glen of the New York State Supreme Court:

"They come in for the conference, and one lawyer says 'I want this and I want this' and the other lawyer says 'Why didn't you ask me?' And then the first lawyer says, 'Because seven weeks ago I tried to call you and you didn't call me back.' And I say to him 'Well, will you give it to him?' and he says, 'Of course I will.' They've just spent three hours of the client's time over something that was not an issue at all—it was an absolute non-issue."

Second, it's relatively easy to bury hidden charges in bills or retainer agreements: One woman in the Consumer Affairs divorce study was billed for the time she spent organizing her own file at the lawyer's office; another was billed for phone calls she never received because she wasn't at home; and another told about a clause hidden in her lawyer's retainer agreement that would require her to pay a "penalty fee" if she and her husband reconciled.

Third is the fudge factor. Professor Rhode cites such abuses as billing two clients for the same time, charging for unnecessary work, or failing to disclose the basis of a bill. She cites a national survey of lawyers which revealed that a quarter of respondents had billed more hours than they actually worked. About half of those who responded denied that they had padded bills but believed that other lawyers did.

Unreturned phone calls and general unresponsiveness are among the most common and deserved complaints clients have about their lawyers. This can particularly be a problem with legal service plans. Ask whether the plan has lawyers on staff who actually handle members' questions or whether you'll simply be referred out to a lawyer on a list. Not surprisingly, the latter situation does not always provide the best incentive for the lawyer to answer your calls. John Prince of Fort Walton Beach, Florida, told *The Wall Street Journal* that he called his lawyer three times in one week identifying himself as a member of Montgomery Ward's Signature Group legal services plan. He was told the lawyer was "out" each time and never received a return call.

On the other hand, at a price upward of $2 a minute and a minimum billing time of six minutes, ignoring your possibly overzealous calls may actually be saving you a bundle. Take the San Francisco man who complained to the San Francisco Bar Association's Legal Referral Service, from which he'd gotten his lawyer's name. He claimed the lawyer not only wouldn't return his calls but also that his bill was climbing too high too fast; when the director of the referral service called to investigate, the lawyer said that the man insisted on calling at least every other day and that there was no movement on the case because of the opposing party's delaying tactics. The lawyer wasn't returning the calls because he didn't want to add needless charges to the man's bill.

Fee-based arrangements, essentially kickbacks, between lawyers, doctors and lawyers, or mental health professionals and lawyers. If a professional of one kind or another recommends a lawyer to you, ask about the basis of the recommendation. It may be hard to get the truth, but you certainly won't get it if you don't ask. Look for legitimate recommendations: the lawyer who tells you that she's opposed her colleague yet been impressed with his understanding of the relevant legal precedent; the doctor who says that he's been an expert witness on cases the lawyer was arguing (and that he understands the medical aspects of cases like yours); the therapist who tells you that the lawyer has a good sense about how to deal with soon-to-be ex-husbands like yours and respects the privacy of clients. Ethical guidelines prohibit doctors from taking fees for making referrals, but lawyers' guidelines merely require that they affirmatively divulge the fact they are getting a fee.

People impersonating lawyers. Courts, bar associations, and attorneys general across the country receive complaints each year about people who misrepresent themselves as lawyers. Call your local courthouse or bar association to confirm that your lawyer is licensed to practice and in good standing. Or consult the *Martindale-Hubbell Law Directory*, available in your local library.

Legal services plans. Since the advantages of legal services plans are similar to those of HMOs, it's not surprising that some of the pitfalls are, too.

Ask about the qualifications of the plan's lawyers. If the plan will take any lawyer who agrees to the set fee schedule without screening them, you're simply paying a finder's fee rather than getting a well-thought-out referral to an appropriate professional. And don't sign up for a plan that won't let you switch lawyers if you are not satisfied with the work being performed on your case. Beware of additional charges; for instance, what happens if the contract you need reviewed runs over the eight-page limit?

Gerald Mann, former president of the American Bar Association–affiliated American Pre-Paid Legal Services Institute, cautions people to read the plan carefully: "Some plans never do a 'simple' will or divorce, which would be free, because the definition of what constitutes a simple matter takes virtually all wills or divorces out of the classification."

Lawyers disciplining their peers and other deterrents of adequate lawyer discipline. If your attorney cheats or misadvises you, you have a right to sue for malpractice or breach of contract, complain to the bar association grievance committee, or submit to fee arbitration or a fee hearing in court. However, be forewarned that real redress through any of these means is rare.

More than 90,000 complaints are filed against lawyers each year, yet the vast majority are dismissed by bar-controlled attorney discipline committees that most often operate in secret and at a snail's pace. Even if your complaint gets heard and you "win," you won't get any money back. Sanctions run from private admonishment to disbarment, but your conflicts-of-interest-poisoned divorce settlement won't get any larger.

As for vengeance—or justice—know that just a handful of states have open disciplinary proceedings or records. Only Florida, Oregon, and West Virginia offer the public unrestricted access to prior complaints about lawyers. At least 32 other states open the proceedings only after a finding of probable cause. Bar associations object to openness for fear of sullying individual lawyers' reputations. But in 1991, an American Bar Association commission found "in Oregon, Florida, and West Virginia ample evidence to demonstrate the public proceedings or public records of dismissed complaints do no harm to innocent lawyers' reputations. On the contrary, secrecy does great harm to the reputation of the profession as a whole."

As for initiating a lawsuit, if the root of your lawyer–client problem is that you couldn't afford your lawyer's legal fees, it's unlikely you'll be able to afford *another* lawyer to press charges. In any case, before you go ahead with another legal action, ask yourself if you have the stamina to withstand more motions, more court dates, and inevitably, more lawyers.

THE $MARTER CONSUMER

Finding a lawyer you feel comfortable with and can trust is only the beginning. Managing the attorney–client relationship and looking out for your rights is just as important.

Approach your legal health the way you would your physical health. Don't wait until a legal crisis looms to seek counsel. A general practitioner can give you general advice and steer you to a specialist when a crisis arises. Many people end up overpaying "because they usually arrive in a panic" at a lawyer's doorstep, Ralph Warner, president of the consumer legal information publisher Nolo Press of Berkeley, California, told *The New York Times*.

Monitor the level of hostility between your lawyer and opposing counsel. Lawyers can sometimes increase the level of hostility between parties—and legal fees might increase along with it. This is often a problem in matrimonial cases, but it comes up in business and other kinds of cases, too. Keep in mind the story of a prominent hotel. A cleaning woman for the hotel was accused of stealing $30 from a hotel room. She insisted she didn't do it, and she took (and passed) a lie detector test. A hotel manager insisted on pressing charges. The woman was acquitted in a criminal trial. The hotel then sued the woman to get back the $30—and $15,000 in punitive damages. The cleaning woman countersued the hotel for malicious prosecution and won. The hotel was forced to pay her $300,000 over a $30 dispute.

Try to negotiate the fee. You lose nothing by asking. And although it's rare to get a truly uncontested divorce, if yours is, ask if the lawyer will do it for a flat fee.

Keep phone calls to a minimum. Instead, write down your questions and save them for a meeting. Limit your questions and discussion to legal matters; your attorney is a legal specialist, not a financial consultant or psychotherapist. One focused, half-hour meeting could easily replace 20 random phone calls.

Put your goals or positions in writing and give a copy to your lawyer. For instance, if you are involved in a personal injury case, write down a realistic minimum below which you will not settle. If you are involved in a divorce, note the home, shared custody, or whatever else you consider non-negotiable. This decreases the possibility of a misunderstanding between you and your lawyer, and it protects both of you later. If necessary, you could show the court or a grievance committee that your lawyer ignored your wishes and, as well, counsel can remind you of what you said was a satisfactory settlement.

Work things out between yourselves if possible. If you and your ex-spouse are trying to work out a new visitation schedule for your children, for instance, try to come to terms without counsel and use the attorneys solely to draw up the papers. What's the point of threatening your ex with a schedule drawn up by an attorney if you know you won't be able to reach agreement?

Stay away from any lawyer who bills by the quarter hour. At $200 per hour, getting her on the phone (even for three minutes, to hear that there's no news on your case) will run you a minimum of $50. The most common billing interval is a sixth of an hour (10 minutes).

If your lawyer is working on a contingency basis, maximize your settlement or judgment by asking that

Expenses Before Fee:		Expenses After Fee:	
AWARD	$100,000	**AWARD**	$100,000
EXPENSES	-$10,000	**LAWYER'S THIRD**	-$33,333
BALANCE	$90,000	**BALANCE**	$66,667
LAWYER'S THIRD	-$30,000	**EXPENSES**	-$10,000
YOUR SHARE	$60,000	**YOUR SHARE**	$56,667

expenses be deducted from the award *before* calculating the lawyer's fee—and get this understanding written into your fee agreement. To illustrate how much you can save, take the example of a $100,000 award in the chart on the opposite page.

Be your own legal researcher or legal secretary. Don't be shy. You can do some of the legwork and trim your legal bills. For instance, you could ask your lawyer if you could go to municipal or local law school libraries to research the pertinent laws, or if you could go to the local courthouse to research and photo-copy the incorporation papers of a local business.

Computer users can find legal forms and resources on the Internet or buy reasonably priced kits for bankruptcies, wills, and other sim-ple legal forms. It doesn't make much sense to spend $400 to hire a lawyer when the computer can help you do the same thing for less than $40.

H E L P

■ **Most local bar as-**sociations offer a legal referral service through which you can get the names of lawyers who specialize in the area of law you need. Usually, listed lawyers will see you for an initial consultation at no cost or for a relatively low fee of about $25. Check your phone book or call your courthouse for a listing.

■ **If you want information on prepaid** legal plans, write the American Prepaid Legal Services Institute, 541 North Fair-banks Court, Chicago, IL 60611.

■ **Call or write to HALT: An Organiza-**tion for Legal Reform, 1612 K Street NW, Suite 510, Washington, DC 20006, (202) 887-8255; www.halt.org. In addition to many other books, they distribute a basic guide written by Kay Osteberg, *Using a Lawyer . . . And What to Do if Things Go Wrong: A Step by Step Guide* (Random House, 1990). It's free to people who join HALT ($20/year) or $8.95 plus $3.95 for shipping and han-dling for non-members.

■ **Need information about a family** matter? Call the National Coalition for Family Justice, a self-help group that was founded by and is staffed by people (mainly women) who have been through difficult divorces and other domestic matters. The group of-fers information, advice, and support groups. Write to them at 821 North Broadway, Irvington-on-Hudson, NY 10533, or call (914) 591-5753.

■ **Want more information about alter-**native dispute resolution? Contact your local bar association or the American Ar-bitration Association at 140 West 51st Street, New York, NY 10020; (212) 484-4000; www.adv.org.

■ **Refer to** *The Consumer Reports Law Book: Your Guide to Resolving Every-day Legal Problems,* by Carol Haas and the editors of Consumer Reports Books, 1994, $29.95.

■ **Your local bar association most** likely has a grievance committee and/or a fee arbitration panel. Call your county courthouse or the bar association to in-quire about the options in your area.

Continued on next page

Continued from previous page

■ Get *Representing Yourself: What You Can Do Without a Lawyer*, by Kenneth Lasson and the Public Citizen Litigation Group. (Plume/Penguin, 1995.) It's available in bookstores or for $13.95 + $3.50 shipping and handling by writing to Public Citizen, Publications Department, 1600 20th Street NW, Washington, DC 20009.

■ **Nolo Press, 950 Parker Street,** Berkeley, CA 94710; e-mail, noloinfo @nolo.com, is the largest publisher of self-help legal guides. Look for them in bookstores or call for a free catalog: (800) 992-NOLO. The catalog and ex-cerpts of various publications are on the Web, www.nolo.com; and you'll also find lawyer jokes.

■ **You'll find loads of legal informa**tion, tools, and resources on the Internet. A few good places to start are Consumer World, www.consumerworld. org, which provides many useful links to resources useful to consumers; the Nolo Press Self-Help Law Center, www.nolo.com, can help with simple legal issues and excerpts some of its books like the *Everyday Law Book* and *Mad at Your Lawyer;* an electronic version of the *Martindale-Hubbell Law Dictionary* can be found at www.lawyers.com.

CHAPTER 52

FUNERALS

The High Cost of Dying

Dying is a very profitable business for two reasons—ignorance and distress. Since the average family "purchases" this service just a couple of times every 50 years, there's a steep learning curve to know what to buy. In addition, caskets and gravesites are often purchased while the consumer is grief-stricken and least likely to bargain hard—and funeral homes and cemetery owners know it.

For these reasons—and because it's also a big expenditure, with the average funeral costing $5,400 in 1995, up 27% since 1991—it makes special sense to plan ahead, however difficult and distasteful you may find it.

The elaborate funeral familiar to most Americans is a fairly recent tradition. Until the 20th century, funerals were considered intimate affairs, arranged mostly by the family of the deceased. But as Jessica Mitford, the Ralph Nader of the funeral industry, wryly noted, "We've come a long way, baby."

"Undertakers" became "funeral directors." Their responsibilities have expanded from supplying the coffin and transporting the body to the gravesite to protecting the public health and acting as grief therapists and planning directors. They brought back a practice dating to the Age of Pharaohs—embalming—in response to both alleged public health concerns and the emerging practice of "viewing" the body of the deceased, which was supposed to facilitate the healing process. Often, survivors bought package deals and entrusted most decisions to the funeral director or were pressured into purchasing expensive caskets and glorious flower arrangements as a final show of affection and respect for their loved one. A typical funeral, according to Mitford, came to include:

"The display of the embalmed and beautified corpse reposing on an innerspring or foam-rubber mattress in an elegant 'casket'; 'visitation' of the deceased in the mortuary 'slumber room'; an open-casket ceremony at which the mourners parade around for a last look; a burial vault that allegedly affords 'eternal protection'; elaborate 'flower tributes' from family and friends; a 'final resting place' in a 'memorial park' or 'mausoleum.' "

In 1963, Mitford published *The American Way of Death,* an exposé of abusive practices in the funeral trade that brought to light the myriad ways in which funeral directors foisted regal funerals on hard-up families. Mitford's landmark study generated seismic changes in the industry. After a 12-year battle, the Federal Trade Commission (FTC) in 1984 enacted the so-called Funeral Rule, for the first time establishing federal standards for funeral directors. The Rule is comprehensive and puts the onus on the provider to inform consumers of their rights. Consumers must be given a copy of a general price list of services offered when they enter; they must be able to purchase only some of the services, not locked into a package deal; and they must receive an itemized list of goods and services actually selected.

Still, *having* these rights is not as good as *knowing* these rights, especially when for years in the late '80s and early '90s, less than a third of funeral parlors were in compliance with FTC regulations. And the Rule still does not apply to cemeteries, crematoria, or casket retailers.

Faced with a rising tide of complaints and non-compliance, the FTC began to enforce the 1984 Rule (amended in 1994). In the mid-90s, for example, it sued and forced Lewis & Ribbs Mortuary, a San Francisco–based funeral home

operator, to pay a $20,000 penalty to settle charges that it failed to give consumers general price lists and itemized statements. And in the largest Funeral Rule settlement ever, Restland Funeral Homes of Dallas paid a whopping $121,600 fine for the same infractions.

Probably as a result, an enforcement sweep in 1995 found that compliance had improved from one-third to two-thirds. But the glass is still a third empty—i.e., to avoid being fleeced and to shop smart, consumers need to know and use the powers—and the new choices—given them.

> "**A** *funeral is, for most people, the third most expensive purchase they're going to make after a house and a car. Yet in no other case are consumers at a greater disadvantage. They're beset by grief, for the most part ignorant about funerals . . . and under pressure to act quickly.*"
>
> —THOMAS NELSON,
> American Association of
> Retired Persons

THE BASICS

The range of choices for consumers has exploded in recent years. A lavish last homage or a minimalist memorial? Cremation or burial? Pre-plan, pre-pay—or procrastinate?

For the industry, the stakes are high. Remember the scene in *A Christmas Carol* where Scrooge visits the dying Marley and finds the undertaker already there? Scrooge asks him, "You don't believe in letting grass grow under your feet, do you?" The undertaker replies, "Ours is a highly competitive profession, sir."

LIFE-GIVING GIFTS

According to the United Network for Organ Sharing, six patients die each day awaiting a liver or heart because no suitable donor is found. One of your lasting legacies could be the gift of life, or health, to one of the 31,000 Americans on waiting lists for organs around the country. Organs that can be transplanted are the kidneys, corneas, heart, heart/lungs, liver, pancreas, bone, bone marrow, and skin.

If you would like to donate your organs, inform your family and complete a Uniform Donor Card (signed by two witnesses) that can be attached to your driver's license. The card can be obtained from the Living Bank or the National Kidney Foundation (see **HELP** at the end of this chapter). The Bank also maintains a national registry of potential donors. All expenses are paid by the recipient and his or her health insurance.

Funerals are a big business: Americans arrange over 2 million of them a year and spend over $10 billion annually on funeral and cemetery services, according to the National Funeral Directors Association.

But the stakes are no less high for consumers. The average funeral costs about $5,000. Yet three quarters of families, when arranging a funeral, don't bother comparing prices and may end up spending far more than they should. For this reason, most experts, including the American Association of Retired Persons (AARP), strongly suggest that you plan your funeral in advance. Despite the awkwardness involved, if fiancés can negotiate "pre-nuptials," older married partners can—and should—"pre-plan" their funeral arrangements. Doing so has four benefits.

■ It ensures that the ceremony will reflect your and your family's wishes.

■ It lifts a tremendous weight from your survivors and leaves them free to grieve and mourn.

■ It enables you to "comparison shop."

■ It also lifts a burden from the person who is or may be ill to have funeral plans in place—one less worry.

"Pre-planning" your funeral means making a series of decisions regarding the disposition of the body, the type of ceremony you want, the selection of a site, and funding arrangements. You should strongly consider involving your family as well as a religious advisor or trusted friend, who may not be as emotionally involved and can help you make clear decisions. Write down your arrangements in a place easily accessible to relatives (*not* in your will—it won't be read until *after* the funeral).

Disposition of the Body

The most prevalent way to dispose of a deceased's body is burial in a cemetery, either in the ground (interment) or above-ground in a mausoleum (entombment). The latter is usually more expensive.

A second option is cremation. It's on the rise—14% of all deaths in 1985, 21% in 1996—because of price: the average cremation costs just $800. The body is reduced by burning to ash and "cremains," small bone fragments that are in turn pulverized into small particles. The ashes can be scattered—from the air, in the water, or over a field—or stored in an urn, to be buried in a cemetery, placed in a columbarium, or kept by the family.

Cremation can reduce your funeral expenses in a number of ways. By opting for "direct cremation," in which the body is taken directly from the place of death to a crematory, you eliminate the costs of embalming, cosmetic preparation of the body, use of the funeral home's facilities, and purchase of a casket. (Under the Funeral Rule, the funeral home is required to offer you in writing an inexpensive container in which the body will be placed for the cremation.) If you want a viewing prior to cremation, you may be able to rent an elegant casket for the ceremony for a third of its sale price.

A third option is donation of your organs or body to a medical school or hospital. Organ and tissue donation does not affect the need for funeral arrangements. But you may be able to eliminate almost all funeral expenses by donating your body to a medical school. However, you should make alternative funeral arrangements in case your body cannot be accepted. (See the box on the previous page for more information.)

Choosing a Ceremony

Whether you are planning your funeral or organizing the funeral of a loved one, don't meet with a funeral director until you have some idea of the type of funeral that suits you best.

The AARP recommends that you call or visit a minimum of two funeral homes to compare services and, especially, prices. Funeral directors are required to provide price information over the phone, and price lists of itemized services, caskets, and outer burial containers in person. The Funeral Rule gives you the option to buy only those services you want—not just "prix fixe" but also "à la carte." If a funeral provider claims that a certain good or service is required under state law, he or she must disclose the specific law requiring the purchase. Before you sign an agreement, the funeral director must provide you with an itemized statement of the total cost, including a "good faith" estimate of any "cash advance" item, described below.

Here are some of the things to think about:

What type of service do you want? A funeral service can be held prior to the final disposition of the body (with or without viewing) or as a memorial service after burial, or both. The funeral service generally takes place at the funeral home, a place of worship, or the gravesite; the memorial service at the funeral home, a place of worship, or a private home.

Care of the body. Embalming—the replacement of bodily fluids with chemicals to slow the deterioration of the body—has long been routinely performed on public health grounds. It is, in fact, unnecessary. Embalming remains mainly as part of the process to prepare the body for one last display, or "viewing," before final disposition, along with clothing the body, or "dressing," hair dressing, and other cosmetic services.

The Funeral Rule prohibits funeral directors from falsely representing that embalming is required, except, of course, for those rare cases where it is—such as when a body will be transported across state lines, if a funeral is delayed for a few days after the death, or when death occurred from a communicable, contagious disease. Some funeral homes require embalming to delay decomposition when a viewing is planned. If embalming was done without legal requirement or prior consent of the survivors, you don't have to pay.

Other services. All funeral homes charge a mandatory basic service fee that typically includes consultation with the family, preparation of legal documents and notices, care and shelter of the body before disposition, and overhead costs. Other charges may include transportation of the body, use of the facilities, or rental of tents and chairs if a gravesite service is held.

Caskets. Caskets vary based on their visual appeal, protective features—and price. Caskets can amount to half the cost of a funeral. According to Matthew Daynard of the FTC, they are a source of considerable profit for funeral directors, some of whom mark up the wholesale price by as much as five- to tenfold. So since 1994, the FTC has prohibited funeral providers from charging a "casket-handling fee" to consumers who buy a casket from another seller.

Consider doing just that. The happy result is that competition has broken out among cut-rate casket sellers. You can now shop in a showroom, call a toll-free number, or order on the Internet—with most places providing 24-hour delivery. Direct Casket, for example, which has six stores in New York and California and is growing, offers 40 models, from basic steel at $595 to solid bronze at $3,495. Consumer Casket USA is a successful retailer selling through stores and on the Net, with a brisk sideline in cut-rate cremation urns.

And remember, most caskets are made of metal or wood; some are fiberglass or plastic. While some sealed models can slow deterioration of the body, none preserve the body indefinitely. However, a Gallup poll found that 30% of customers had been told just that by funeral directors, in violation of the Funeral Rule.

Outer burial containers. Most cemeteries require a burial vault or concrete grave liner (or "rough box") to enclose the casket in a grave and prevent the ground from caving in as the casket deteriorates. (Arlington National Cemetery does not.)

Vaults are usually more visually elaborate (and twice as expensive) than grave liners and offer more protection—but here again, ignore all claims that a sealed vault will preserve the body indefinitely. It won't.

"Cash advance" items. These include flowers, fees for pallbearers, honoraria for clergy, memorial books, and obituary notices. Funeral directors, if they provide these items, must disclose any fee they charge or discount they receive.

Selecting a Site: The Final Resting Place

There is no Funeral Rule for cemeteries, and only 37 states require a license. Cemetery "pre-need" arrangements are typically far less regulated than funeral pre-need arrangements. Check with the Better Business Bureau (BBB) for a reliability report. The BBB also suggests that you look for a cemetery that has been in operation for a number of years. *Visit* several cemeteries yourself, not only to compare prices and make sure you like the setting but also to ensure that they are well cared for. (The prime complaint regarding cemeteries concerns maintenance.) In particular, walk around to find out how well maintained older graves are, and

ask the cemetery for an audit of its perpetual care fund.

Read the fine print in your contract. If you buy a plot under a pre-construction plan, what happens if death occurs before the site is developed? If you purchase on time payments, what happens if death occurs before final payment is made? If you're shown a plot in a cemetery, your contract should specify whether you're buying the specific plot you were shown or merely the right to be buried in the cemetery.

Cemetery costs range from $1,000 to $10,000 and up, including space, container, and marker. (A plot in the Westwood cemetery where Marilyn Monroe is buried will cost you $20,000.)

Most states require that the consumer make provision for maintenance of the grave. The "perpetual care" fee may be included in the sale of the plot, or you may be required to buy into a "memorial fund" or "special care fund" separately, payable up-front or annually. But, caveat emptor! Because here "perpetual" really means "for a while." For "perpetual care agreements" are actually endowments in interest-bearing accounts paid to cemeteries to cover the cost of maintenance of a grave. Care continues only as long as funds last. And usually the interest generated doesn't cover the cost of maintenance. So once the interest and principal are exhausted, the consumer gets a bill that plays heavily on guilt: "In order to allow us to continue to care for the grave of your loved one in the proper manner and as tradition requires, please remit an additional thousand dollars immediately." Who can say no?

Ideally, state legislation should require cemeteries to change the name of "perpetual care" arrangements to "endowed care" because it would be less likely to mislead normal customers.

Finally, if you are arranging the burial of a loved one, find out before you buy a plot if the deceased already owns a funeral plot—60% of the 65-plus population does. Veterans, their spouses, and their minor children are eligible for burial at one of the nation's national cemeteries, as well as a marker and a flag.

Funding Arrangements: Caveats About Pre-Paying

Life ain't cheap. But if the truth be told, neither is death. Carefully reviewing your assets, setting ample money aside, and shopping around may prevent an emotional heartache from becoming a financial heartburn.

First, find out if you can receive financial assistance for your funeral or that of a close relative by checking with Social Security, the Veterans Administration, a local General Assistance program, pension funds, or fraternal organizations.

The fastest-growing trend in the industry is pre-payment, especially among senior citizens. A million pre-paid (or "pre-need") funeral contracts were sold in 1990, up from 22,000 30 years ago. (Though on the rise, only one in four Americans arranged some detail of his or her funeral or burial in 1995, according to the Funeral and Memorial Information Council—compared to 50% to 70% in the Netherlands, Belgium, and Spain.)

Such arrangements may bring you a certain peace of mind, but remember that you are making a major investment, and make sure that you know what you're paying for—and that you'll be getting it when the time comes.

Pre-payment takes two forms. You can plan the funeral with a funeral director, assess the cost, and pay the value of the funeral, which is then placed in a trust account. Or you can purchase an insurance policy from a funeral director or an insurance company in the amount of your planned funeral, name the funeral home as its beneficiary, and pay an annuity. Such plans are prohibited in certain states, including Georgia, Maryland, and New York.

Here's why: While the AARP strongly recommends that everyone "pre-*plan*" their funeral, it cautions consumers about pre-*payment*. Jessica Mitford was more blunt: "Stay away from them. You don't know what's going to happen to either your money or the company." Memorial societies offer the same advice.

Instead, you may want to sign a non-binding pre-arrangement agreement to indicate your preferences. Lisa Carlson, a leading consumer advocate in the field and no friend of pre-payment, suggests only two reasons to pre-pay: First, depending on state law and the terms of your pre-payment contract, its value may

591

not be counted against the asset ceiling for S.S.I. or Medicaid eligibility, whereas an individual account will; second, you may consider pre-paying if you have no survivors.

Still, setting funds aside can be a reassuring prospect for you and your survivors. Your safest bet may be to create a type of trust account, called a "Totten Trust" or "revocable living trust," which remains under your control but will upon your death pay funds for your funeral to a named beneficiary. (You may need an attorney to set up such a trust.)

You can also set aside money in an interest-earning savings account designed as "payable on death" to the funeral home or your survivors, or open a joint savings account with a family member who has a "right of survivorship." Each of these options enables you to earn interest and lets your survivors keep any excess funds in the account. The interest earned, however, is taxable.

If you decide to pre-pay, read your contract carefully; make sure that it states clearly what goods and services you are paying for. And find out the following:

Is the contract "revocable"? If you change your plans, can you cancel your contract and get your full deposit back—and any interest earned? Is there a cancellation fee? Consumers who attempt to cancel a life insurance policy, in particular, may be severely penalized.

Is the contract "portable"? If you move out of state, can you transfer your plan to a funeral home in your new area? Again, will you be charged a fee?

Is the price of your funeral "guaranteed"? Will your estate be required to pay additional money if funeral inflation exceeds the interest earned on your payment?

Is your money secure? The main consideration is peace of mind: Are you getting what you paid for? When you contract with a funeral director, all states except Vermont, Alabama, and the District of Columbia require that all or part of your payments—from 50% in Mississippi to 100% in most states—be placed in a trust account. But trust accounts are no panacea. Consumers in Ohio and Pennsylvania were left in the lurch after morticians in those states invested the trust funds in diamonds and rare coins.

While such investments are generally prohibited, regulations, investigations, and auditing are minimal in most states. The California Cemetery Board and Board of Funeral Directors, for instance, came under attack for lackluster supervision after a series of exposés in the *Sacramento Bee*—despite having among the toughest enforcement and auditing provisions in the country.

Ask your state funeral board if trust accounts are subject to regular audits, as in California, and if they are protected by state guarantee funds, as they are in Florida and a few other states. Life insurance policies are regulated and guaranteed in all 50 states—but not in the District of Columbia.

IF YOU'RE HIV POSITIVE

Lisa Carlson, author of *Caring for Your Own Dead,* found that early in the AIDS epidemic, funeral parlors frequently refused to care for the bodies of persons with HIV or AIDS. In addition, a 1989 study by the Gay Men's Health Crisis (GMHC) found that a lot of excessive billing and other abuses were taking place. AIDS activists and industry insiders believe that the industry has mostly cleaned up its act in recent years, but some establishments may still charge a higher fee for certain services (for example, extra disinfecting). The GMHC believes that the bodies of persons with HIV require no special handling or procedure, but individual state laws may require embalming.

Because the funeral director is likely to see the HIV status of the deceased on the death certificate, you may want to disclose the condition when planning for the funeral to avoid any last-minute complications. If you do not want the death certificate to mention the deceased's HIV status, most physicians will likely accommodate you—for instance, by listing instead the specific illness that was the immediate cause of death. (Most people with AIDS actually succumb to an opportunistic infection or invasive neoplasm.) If the physician refuses to change the death certificate, it can be appealed, but the process may take up to six months.

WHAT TO WATCH OUT FOR

Don't succumb to high-pressure sales tactics. Some funeral directors, for instance, will typically conceal from view or disparage as "welfare caskets," their lower-priced caskets, to lure consumers to the highest-priced items. Ask to be shown the full variety of caskets available. Others may try to sell you an expensive memorial service if you opt for an inexpensive cremation.

Beware the door-to-door sales-person. Mary B. of Phoenix, Arizona, and her husband both decided to pre-pay when a door-to-door salesman came to their house. Total cost: $10,000. Shortly afterward, they read an advertisement for the same funeral for $1,500 each. If you suspect fraud, you have three days to cancel your contract under the FTC's door-to-door cancellation rule.

Get ready for the "Home-Depoting" of your neighborhood funeral homes. There is a growing trend toward national firms—called "consolidators"—taking over your local funeral homes and cemeteries. Because demand is expected to surge in the next 20 years as the huge baby boom generation ages—and since there are economies of scale in centralizing casket sales and transportation services—bigger means more profitable.

So although the faces and facades of traditional mom-and-pop funeral homes may look the same, the hidden new owners are increasingly SCI of Houston (with $2.3 billion in annual sales based on 2,800 funeral homes, 330 cemeteries, and 140 crematoriums) and the Loewen Group ($908 million in annual sales).

What are the implications for consumers? Much higher prices. Playing on the guilt that stops folks from price-comparing the day before burying a loved one, consolidators jack up fees and replace an acquired home's lowest price offering with expensive substitutes. In Amarillo, Texas, for example, a Loewen home post-acquisition charged $425 for embalming and $1,638 for the basic services of its funeral director and staff (the "cover charge" in industry parlance); but nearby independent homes averaged only $185 and $863 for the same services, respectively.

In the consolidator era, it pays even more to shop around and plan.

THE $MARTER CONSUMER

If you find a casket you like, get the exact brand and model and call other sellers to find out about the price. Compare caskets and outer burial containers from various providers—the retailer you went to may not offer lower-priced items.

Consider memorial societies, which are volunteer-run, non-profit groups dedicated to dignified but inexpensive funerals. They can help you arrange the funeral of your choice at a significantly reduced cost. Membership usually requires a one-time $25 fee.

Forty-one states let you bypass funeral homes altogether. You will have to fill out a host of legal documents, arrange for final disposition with a crematory or cemetery, and attend to countless details on your own. Both Lisa Carlson's *Caring for Your Own Dead* and Ernest Morgan's *Dealing Creatively With Death: A Manual of Death Education and Simple Burial* provide useful information and checklists.

If you opt for cremation, the container with your remains will be destroyed during the process; you might prefer to buy an inexpensive container or unfinished wood box.

Save the cost of embalming and other cosmetic expenses with a closed-casket funeral.

Eliminate expenses for the use of the funeral home's facilities with a gravesite service. A memorial service at home will eliminate funeral expenses altogether.

Consider a weekday funeral, if your religious practice permits and if you're trying to keep costs down. Many funeral homes and cemeteries charge extra for services on weekends and holidays.

If you are concerned about relocating, don't pre-pay for a cemetery plot. Cemeteries are usually unwilling to buy back property. Or ask if the cemetery participates in a credit-exchange program, which enables you to transfer the value of your plot to another participating cemetery. Some 525 members of the American Cemetery Association in every state participate in such a program, but may impose restrictions.

HELP

■ **To complain about** a funeral parlor, contact your state regulatory board and the Federal Trade Commission, 6th Street and Pennsylvania Ave. NW, Washington, DC 20580; (202) 326-2222. For mediation (free) or binding arbitration, contact the Funeral Service Consumer Assistance Program, 2250 East Devon Avenue, Suite 250, Des Plaines, IL 60016; (800) 662-7666.

■ **To complain about a cemetery,** contact your state regulatory board, attorney general, or local consumer agency. For free, non-binding mediation, contact the Cemetery Consumer Service Council, Box 2028, Reston, VA 20195-0028; (703) 391-8407 or (800) 645-7700.

■ **Organ donation. The Living Bank,** P.O. Box 6725, Houston, TX 77265; (800) 528-2971, and the National Kidney Foundation, 30 East 33rd Street, New York, NY 10016; (800) 622-9010. These organizations give out universal donor cards and provide information on organ donation and transplants.

■ **Memorial societies. To find a memo**rial society close to you, contact Funeral and Memorial Societies of America, P.O. Box 10, Hinesburg, VT 05461; www.funerals.org/famsa or call them at (800) 765-0107.

■ **Body donation. The National** Anatomical Service, (800) 727-0700, will provide complete information about donating your body to science.

■ **The International Cemetery and** Funeral Association provides information on intrastate cemetary plot credit-exchange programs. Call (800) 645-7700.

■ **Read** *Caring for Your Own Dead,* by Lisa Carlson, (Upper Access Publishers, 1998). $29.95. Call (800) 356-9315 to order.

■ **The American Association of Re**tired Persons has several free booklets: *Cemetery Goods and Services, Product Report: Funeral Goods and Services,* and *Product Report: Pre-Paying for Your Funeral.* Call (202) 434-2277 or go to www.aarp.org.

■ **The FTC** *publishes Funerals: A Con*sumer *Guide* and *Caskets and Burial Vaults;* call (202) 326-2222 or write FTC Consumer Response Center, Washinton, DC 20580; or go to www.ftc.gov.

CHAPTER 53

EMPLOYMENT AGENCIES

Doing a Job on You

The Clinton years have witnessed what one *New York Times* financial reporter described, with only a touch of hyperbole, as "the hottest economy practically since Columbus's once-celebrated landing." Productivity is up; the stock market sets one new record after another; the federal budget is balanced, or about to be; inflation is now so low that economists are worrying about the potential effects of deflation; and employment is at the highest since 1948, when the federal government first kept tabs on the job market.

But while the job market is larger than it has been, it is also less stable. Lester Thurow, the noted M.I.T. economist, rightly noted that "the era of lifelong company jobs with regular promotions and annual real wage increases are over." Americans who are now entering the workforce can expect to change jobs an average of eight times during their working lives. And many of the jobs being created are part-time or "temp" jobs. Case in point: U.P.S. employees went on strike in

1997 because 38,000 of the 46,000 jobs the company boasted of creating in the four years prior to the strike were part-time jobs.

In such a fluid market, employment agencies fulfill a critical function; they bring together employer and job-seeker to the benefit of both. But some have unconscionably chosen to hit people when they're down and out: The district attorney's office in Orange County, California, reports that employment agencies are one of the top ten categories of businesses about which it gets the most complaints. Having to look for a new job is difficult enough without the added insult of being tricked into paying a fee up-front for no service or interviewing with an intermediary when you think you're talking to an actual potential employer.

THE BASICS

Unfortunately, you can't expect Uncle Sam to help you sort things out. Although federal laws

596

govern such areas as employment discrimination and the minimum wage, employment agencies aren't subject to any federal regulations beyond basic consumer laws on deceptive trade practices. And regulations at the state level run the gamut from nonexistent (Florida) to comprehensive (Pennsylvania and Illinois).

Therefore, if you're not ready to familiarize yourself with your state or local laws—always a good idea—your best bet is to be vigilant and get to know the tricks of the trade. For all the complexity and diversity of the industry, it all comes down to one question: Who's offering what, and for how much?

Have You Found What You're Looking For?

The first issue is, what services does the company offer you? Agencies can help you obtain jobs in two different ways:

- *Employment agencies* will put you in touch with actual employers and/or provide job listings.
- *Career counseling services* generally try to help you sharpen your appeal to potential employers and become more "marketable." Services they provide include teaching you how to write a strong cover letter and resumé, helping you interview better, and counseling you in a new career path. They may require a fee for those services independently of finding a job.

Some companies, of course, offer both types of services. You should look for a firm with a track record in your line of business. If an agency actually presents you with lists of jobs or companies, find out where the listings are coming from. While most agencies will put you in touch with legitimate employers who are currently looking to fill positions that match your skills, beware of the following schemes:

- Some agencies offer little more than a "resumé service"— meaning they'll mail bundles of your (unsolicited) resumés to companies selected more or less at random. It doesn't take a genius to put together a lot of names: All you need to do is to go to the library and photocopy pages from corporate directories. If that's all the agency does for you, you can probably save yourself a fee by doing the job yourself.

> "*Victims of downsizing need a job, credit, and to save their home from foreclosure. You would think that these would be the last people con artists would prey upon. But because they are especially vulnerable, they're prepared to take risks to get the things they need, and that's what con artists take advantage of.*"
>
> —STEPHEN BROBECK, Executive Director, Consumer Federation of America

■ An agency may present you with a list of actual job openings that fit your profile. The question is, how current is the list? Are the referrals to employers with *current* job openings or employers who listed job openings in the past? Where did they get the listings? Were they contacted by employers, or did they simply pull the jobs from last Sunday's classified or other publicly available lists?

■ Finally, as the National Association of Consumer Agency Administrators and Consumer Federation of America have reported, "some companies sell unemployed workers lists of jobs that don't exist, and charge these individuals several hundred dollars each." Be especially wary of agencies that promise you the moon in some faraway land for a "modest fee." All you'll get is a castle in the air: Only an estimated 2% of customers of companies promising a job paying $70,000 or more in an exotic locale ever get one, and refunds are rare. Consumer watchdogs estimate that overseas-job scams rake in at least $100 million a year.

Shortly after the Persian Gulf War, at the height of a recession, Pennsylvania's attorney general at the time, Ernie Preate, went after two such companies, Jobs Overseas and Patriot Promotions, for selling lists for up to $24.50 that supposedly contained thousands of skilled and unskilled job opportunities in Kuwait, paying up to $87 an hour. In fact, the only link between the jobs listed and the Kuwaiti desert was mirages in both. The state's investigation revealed that most of the companies listed did not have contracts for work in the Persian Gulf, and the few that did hired only for highly specialized positions like oil field firefighter.

But don't be lulled into thinking that these scams happen only in bad times when jobs are scarce. In July 1997, two companies based in Seattle agreed to pay an estimated $288,000 into a redress pool for a number of schemes perpetrated on students, such as charging them fees up to $69.95 for lists of nonexistent, high-paying summer jobs in the Alaskan fishing industry or on cruise ships.

Your Treat or Mine?

Before signing anything, be clear about who'll pick up the tab.

Contingency-fee or retainer-fee agencies: The company looking to fill a position usually pays a fee to find someone for the job—often, a percentage of the new employee's first year's salary (25% to 45%). These are the so-called "headhunters," the executive-search companies that are an integral part of the bubbly 1990s.

Employer-pay agencies are typically subject to little regulation. The theory, as one Michigan official explains, is that "businesses who pay the fees have the wherewithal to investigate companies and don't really need state government looking out for their interest in hiring a legitimate firm."

Be aware that if you obtain a job through a retainer-fee agency, you may be required to stay on the job

WHO'S THE BOSS?

You may end up contacting an employment agency without realizing it. In 1991, the NYC Department of Consumer Affairs revealed that many agencies run classified ads identical to those placed by employers. The goal: to lure job-seekers with a nonexistent job listing, then redirect them to another, perhaps less desirable, job opportunity. Some agencies failed to identify themselves even after undercover inspectors called.

But the *chutzpah* award goes to the Career Resource Center, which placed ads in newspaper "help wanted" sections for job openings with the Pennsylvania Turnpike Commission and U.S. Postal Service that were simply not available. Job-seekers who responded to the ads were asked to pay $40 for a job application and other purported employment information, and they got nothing in return.

for a certain duration—usually a year—or you will be responsible for all or part of the fee.

Applicant-pay agencies: Some agencies expect the job seeker to pay a fee—as much as 15% to 20% of the first year's salary. If you are required to pay, make sure you know what you're paying for. For instance, do you pay the fee to get your resumé in shape—or to find a job? Do you pay before or after the services are provided? Do you have to pay even if you don't find a job? What if you find a job and it's not satisfactory? What is the agency's refund policy?

State governments are a lot more likely to regulate agencies when the applicant pays the fee. Regulations include licensing requirements, mandatory posting of bonds, refund requirements if the employee is terminated within a certain time, employment advertising disclosure requirements, and bans on advance fees or mandatory tie-ins with services like resumé preparation.

Finally, some agencies require *both* employer and employee to pay a fee.

Temp Agencies

Temporary help agencies are a breed apart in the world of employment agencies, even though many agencies offer both job referrals and temporary assignments. You can become a "temp" by registering with a temp agency, filling out an application, taking any qualifying tests—such as word processing skills, for example—and receiving whatever training is required. You are then sent on assignment with another corporation. But as the fee structure makes clear, the "temp's" contractual relationship remains with the agency: The company for which the person works pays a fee to the temp agency, which in turn pays the worker.

One of the most striking phenomena of the changing labor market is the growth of temp services. Temporary employment, which barely existed two decades ago, accounts for nearly 15% of new job growth in recent years.

Why are companies increasingly turning to temp work? For one, it gives corporations the flexibility to adjust their workforce to shifting economic conditions. But corporations also turn to temps to eliminate the costs of fringe benefits like vacations, pensions, and health care; federal mandates like equal opportunity and family leave; union representation; and other staples of a permanent workforce. Bank of America, for instance, is restructuring its work force so that a mere 19% of its employees will remain full-time.

One consequence of this shift is that temps increasingly receive long-term assignments—and if the company that contracted for their services is afraid of losing them, they may get a permanent job offer. In a National Association of Temporary Services (NATS) poll, 54% of temps reported being asked to continue full-time at the company or organization where they were employed. As an agency manager explains, "It's kind of like dating before getting married."

Another consequence is that temp services are attracting a more qualified pool of workers: "temporary professionals." As John Fanning and Rosemary Maniscalco explain in their book, *Workstyles to Fit Your Lifestyle: Everyone's Guide to Temporary*

Employment, "No longer the domain of clerical staff, today's temporary workers include physicians and executives as well as word processors, bookkeepers, and data-entry clerks." Professional or highly skilled workers now account for 24% of temp workers, according to the NATS.

WHAT TO WATCH OUT FOR

Employment agencies have become increasingly sophisticated in their strategies to attract potential job seekers—and cash in on their credulous prey. In particular, watch out for:

Firms charging an advance fee. Chances are, you won't get a job, and you won't get your money back either. Diane Callis, president of the National Association of Personnel Services, argues that "no agency should accept a fee up front. No fee should be paid until the individual actually accepts a job through an agency."

Many states ban the practice, although agencies can get around the regulation by allocating the fee for a specific service. But Florida has no such regulations. The result: Cedric Gathwright of Mississippi answered an ad for a construction job after being several months out of work. He called a toll-free number and was offered a welder's job in Bermuda for $70,000 a year—more than he had made in the past five years combined. All he had to do to secure the job, he was told, was send a $295 security deposit to a

Florida address. He borrowed the money from his parents and sent it to the company—but got neither a job nor his money back.

Other similar scams involve agencies offering job lists or access to some hidden job market for an advance fee of $2,000 to $10,000.

The FTC also cautions consumers to be wary of firms that require them to provide credit card or bank account information but promise that no immediate charges or debits will occur.

Classified ads by employment agencies.

Classified ads are appealing, if only because your only up-front expense is the cost of the newspaper. But they're not always what they appear to be. Many employment agencies place alluring ads that appear to originate from a potential employer, then bait-and-switch the caller.

Stanley Wolfal answered such an ad touting a $9-an-hour job at the Tallahassee, Florida, airport. Expecting an interview for a food-service job, he found out that the ad was placed by Florida Employment Inc., an agency that charges cash fees for job leads. A representative of the agency promised him a job within a week in return for a $95 fee. What he got were job leads that had nothing to do with the original ad and that in many cases did not exist or that he didn't want.

The contract Stanley signed was heavy on jargon, promising access to "value-added data," but short on specific guarantees. The agency's oral promises, of course, were of little value.

Temp agency ads that don't deliver.

According to Temple University professor Maureen Martella, workers are often lured to temp services by ads promising high wages and then pressured by recruiters to accept less. Often the advertised jobs are nonexistent.

"900" numbers offering job openings or job skills. Calling a "900" number is a de facto advance fee, regardless of the opportunities for job placement. You may not be able to find out how much the fee is before calling and could get a nasty surprise. In addition, if you're charged fraudulently, the phone company may not be able or willing to delete the charge.

In June 1996, the FTC took action against Career Information Services, Inc., and CIS Associates, Inc., two Atlanta, Georgia, firms engaged in such a scheme. The companies would place ads for postal service and government jobs, falsely touting wages exceeding $20 per hour. When consumers called the "800" number in the ads to apply, they were directed to call a "900" number, but were not told that they would be billed $34.95 for that call, in violation of FTC rules. The companies eventually paid nearly $2.3 million in redress.

Nanny-gate.

Here's a situation that turns the tables, leaving the potential employers at risk rather than the job applicants. Long before the British au pair trial captured America's attention, consumer advocates were warning against laggard standards in the industry. Wanting to find out exactly whose

Bias at the Job Bank

Some employment agencies have come under scrutiny in recent years for discriminatory practices or for accommodating discriminatory requests by employers. New York's attorney general and New York City officials found agencies using codes in job offerings, in clear violation of federal and state laws—for example, "all American," "front-office appearance," "mom-and-apple-pie," or "corporate image" meant white applicants only. In addition, CBS' *60 Minutes* sent a black and a white tester with similar resumés and skills to Cosmopolitan Care, a Manhattan employment agency, in 1989. You guessed it: The white candidate was given several referrals while the black candidate was told no positions were available.

hand rocks the cradle, the Department of Consumer Affairs in 1992 surveyed 50 nanny agencies in New York City. The result: 45 (90%) were in violation of state employment agency laws. The undercover investigation revealed that some companies lied to families by telling them that they had checked a potential nanny's references when they had not, and that they guaranteed replacements for two months. Some companies also failed to even interview the nannies and illegally charged the family non-refundable registration fees (see Chapter 46, "Child Care," page 507).

THE $MARTER CONSUMER

After you've sorted out all the issues involved with using an employment agency, take a few extra steps to verify that you're dealing with a reputable firm.

Visit the premises to make sure that the agency is legitimate and not a fly-by-night operator or other scam artist. As *Time* magazine reporter Cathy Booth Hollywood explains, "even a small-time boiler-room operation with just three phones can take in $5,000 a day."

Get references. Ask if you can speak to a few clients who recently obtained jobs.

Check the agency's professional affiliations. Reputable associations include the National Association of Personnel Services (NAPS); the National Association of Temporary Workers; the Society for Human Resource Managers; and the American Management Association. The NAPS, for instance, offers a two-day certification exam for personnel consultants with at least two years' experience.

Take a copy of the contract home and read it carefully before committing to anything or making any payment. Again, make sure that all the promises and guarantees you received are in writing.

Before signing on with a temp agency, keep a few things in mind:

Look for a temp agency in your field of work. Some agencies are becoming highly specialized in such fields as health care support workers or electronics technicians.

Find out what benefits the agency offers. If you temp, the temp service *is* your employer. Therefore, you should look not just at how much cash you'll be making but what, if any, benefits you'll receive—vacation, health insurance, bonuses, pay raises, etc. The package you get will typically depend on the number of hours worked. While most temp services provide access to group-insurance policies,

you may have to pay for it yourself. However, some agencies, trying to encourage the professionalization of the temp industry, are offering more generous benefits packages.

Manpower Inc., for instance, pays 50% of health insurance premiums for employees who have worked at least 300 hours. And MacTemps offers full benefits—health, dental, long-term disability, a 401(k) retirement plan, paid holidays, and vacation bonuses—to full-time temps (over 2,000 hours a year) and partial benefits to temps working at least 1,000 hours a year.

Keep looking for full-time employment. Unless you need flexible assignments for personal reasons, temp work is at best an inadequate substitute for a permanent position. Temps often receive lower wages and fewer benefits than full-time workers and lack the security of full-time employment—relative as that has become.

HELP

■ **Don't forget about** free sources for employment opportunities: *legitimate* newspaper classified ads, local human resource agencies, library listings, and college placement offices. And possibly the most valuable of all: networking—with friends, former colleagues, or alumni groups, for instance.

■ **To complain or launch an investigation,** contact your state attorney general, local consumer office, Better Business Bureau, the consumer office where the firm is located, or the Federal Trade Commission's Bureau of Consumer Protection.

■ **If you suspect that** you've been dealing with a fraudulent service firm, report the company to the National Fraud Information Center's Telemarketing Fraud Hotline at (800) 876-7060. You can also request the FTC's consumer brochure, "Help Wanted . . . Finding a Job" from the FTC's Public Reference Branch, Room 130, 6th Street & Pennsylvania Avenue NW, Washington, DC 20580, (202) 326-2222, TYY for hearing-impaired (202) 326-2502. The brochure is also available on the FTC's Web site at http://www.ftc.gov.

PART 11

Shopping

OUTLET SHOPPING

Don't Go Broke Saving Money

With baseball on the wane as the national pastime, Americans have taken up a new sport. No, it's not soccer. It's bargain hunting. And nowhere is this more evident than the explosion in factory outlet stores. Once only adjacent to the factories themselves, now manufacturers have multiple stores, often located near vacation hotspots. A trip to the birthplace of our nation in Williamsburg, Virginia, can double as a rebirth for your closet; when your muscles are too sore to pull on your ski boots, you can always try on discounted Timberland or Joan and David shoes; and if you need your faith restored after a visit to Opryland, there's even a Bible factory outlet in Nashville. The Sawgram Mills outlet mall in Sunrise, Florida, is the state's second most popular tourist attraction, trailing only Disney World.

But if you have a sneaking suspicion that those sneakers aren't any cheaper than at the local mall or that blouse you've been eyeing isn't quite silky enough to sell in the upscale department store you usually shop in, you may be right. Sorry to rain on the outlet parade: As many as 50% of the stores in some outlet

malls aren't outlets at all; and despite the labels, most of the merchandise sold in outlet stores has never seen, and was never meant to see, the sales floor at Saks, Neiman Marcus, or Bergdorf's.

THE BASICS

Manufacturer's outlet stores first appeared in New England in the early part of the 20th century when fabric mills set up shop next door. Then the sewing plants in the South did the same thing. And by the 1970s, the first full-fledged manufacturer's outlet center emerged—in Reading, Pennsylvania. By the end of the 1980s, entire malls centered around off-price merchandise had mushroomed beyond the outskirts of out-of-the-way places, close enough to major cities to snag day-tripping shoppers but far enough away to keep department store competitors' noses in joint. There are now more than 300 outlet centers in the U.S.—three times what there were ten years ago.

Today, there's even cut-rate Armani, and many of the department stores the manufacturers' outlets tried so hard not to compete too di-

607

rectly with have set up their own outlet stores—with names like Saks Off Fifth, Neiman Marcus's Last Call, and Nordstrom's The Rack.

Bargain hunters rang up sales of $13 billion at outlet stores nationwide in 1996. As recently as 1990, outlets sold only half that much merchandise. Prices are anywhere from 20% to 60% lower than retail prices, but generally about 30% off—which is not the bargain it used to be; before the outlet boom, prices averaged about 50% off.

But did you ever stop to wonder where, exactly, the surfeit of sweaters and tube socks that fills up the nation's 12,000 outlet stores comes from? Logically, it can't *all* be manufacturers' overruns or leftovers from last season. And it isn't.

At clothing designer's outlets, you'll usually find only the narrowest selection of the real thing. One industry watcher estimates that just an eighth of the items you see in outlets are actually seconds or irregulars or overruns (see opposite page for definitions). The large majority of merchandise is manufactured specially for the outlet and tends to be of lower quality for a lower price than items made for regular retail sale. This is especially true of designers with lots of outlet stores. As retail analyst Eileen Byrne puts it, "Do you think a manufacturer could stay in business if it made enough mistakes to keep its factory outlets stocked?"

> " *As long as the label is there, as long as the fantasy is there, that inveterate shopper looking for the bargain will keep coming back.* "
>
> —ALAN MILLSTEIN,
> retail analyst

Hiding a few true bargains among specially manufactured merchandise helps outlet retailers skirt the truth. The cut of a suit may look similar to the real thing, but it's sewn from different, cheaper fabric. Ubiquitous "compare at" price tags make it seem like the outlet undercuts department stores' full price. But "compare at" is a sign that the item was manufactured expressly for sale at outlets—and you won't find another item like it to compare it with, except at another outlet. That's exactly what happened when a producer for the *Prime Time Live* television news magazine bought a shirt at a Gant outlet for $14.99. The "compare at" price tag suggested the retail price would be $38. But after striking out at 10 stores, *Prime Time Live* called Gant and was told that the shirt was available only at Gant outlet stores.

And even if you find the real thing, the way department stores discount these days, you don't have to wait that long before the latest designer fashions are available at a discount in a store close to home. During one fall week in 1997, both a Donna Karan outlet and a tony department store in Cherry Creek, Colorado, were selling the exact same trousers for $55, marked down from $90.

Decoding the Price Tag

Truth in packaging is lacking, but here's what you need to know:

- *As is:* There's a major imperfection, and you can probably see it. Be sure to check these items very carefully before buying.
- *Close-out:* The item has been discontinued, and the manufacturer will not produce anything more in that style, exact color, or line.
- *Compare at*: The item was never sold in full-price stores. It was manufactured specifically to be sold at outlet stores. Most likely it's a knock-off of a more expensive line—for example, a dress cut from cheaper fabric—and intended to be sold for less than the real thing.
- *First quality:* These items are without flaws and identical to those found in full-price stores.
- *Irregular:* These items have barely noticeable flaws that shouldn't affect fit or durability.
- *Multiple markdowns.* A tag with lots of cross-outs and price markdowns probably means the item languished on retail racks before landing at the outlet. That can mean an item is a year old.
- *Overruns and overstocks:* These are items that are left over after the manufacturer has sold all it can to wholesale customers.
- *Past season:* These items are offered after the traditional department store season is over—winter coats in February, bathing suits in August, Christmas decorations when you'd rather not be reminded how big your credit card bill is for Christmas shopping.

BEST TIMES WORST TIMES

Go outlet shopping on Fridays, Saturdays, and Sundays. Many outlets run promotions and deeper discounts on weekends, because they know that's when most consumers are doing their shopping. To beat fellow bargain hunters to the best deals, go first thing in the morning.

- *Sample:* These items were used for display or to sell the product to wholesalers and retailers. They may not match other items in the line, and there are probably very few of them.
- *Seconds:* These items have small flaws, usually minor but more serious than irregulars. The color isn't quite what the designer ordered, say, or they are misshaped or mismatched.

WHAT TO WATCH OUT FOR

Not every store in an "outlet mall" is actually an outlet. Some malls mix in full-price stores and discounters with outlets. So no, you're not crazy if the prices seem the same as at your local mall. A Today's Man in an outlet center sells virtually the same clothing as one in New York City—and a shopper with a good eye might even find that a sweater for sale for $29 at the store in the outlet center costs just $19 at the store in New York City.

Outlets do not always have the lowest prices. An ABC *Prime Time Live* exposé found a "compare at $27.50" tie at a Geoffrey Beene factory outlet for $19.99. The identical tie was also for sale at Macy's that week—for just $16.50.

To get good bargains, you have to know what you are buying. Prices don't only fall at outlet stores. They may rise, in tandem with the arrival of a big holiday (and shopping) weekend. One young man told the *Washington Post* the story of buying a pair of shoes on sale at a Bass outlet for $20 (marked down from the outlet price of $50). A few weeks later he saw the same shoes for sale at the outlet for $60. That's about the same price he would have paid at retail. It was Memorial Day weekend.

Discontinued patterns at housewares outlets can be a boon for people who need to replace broken pieces of china or fill gaps in a set. But don't buy a few starter pieces figuring you'll build up to a full set later. It's likely that you'll never see the stuff again—except maybe at a garage sale.

THE $MARTER CONSUMER

Allow plenty of time. You'll likely have to rummage through rack after rack before you find much worth considering. But don't stay too long. After a while, you lose perspective and the ugliest stuff starts looking good.

Know what you are looking at. It takes knowledge of designers, fashion trends, and good workmanship to get good outlet deals. Even if you can't ordinarily afford top fashions, do some browsing and trying on at regular retail stores before you go outlet shopping. That way you'll know a bargain from a bad buy.

It's only a bargain if you gain. Who cares if an item is from last year's collection if it's well-made and wearable? On the other hand, fashion-forward items bought a year later are by definition fashion-backward. The best buys tend to be on the most garish colors and oddball designs. You'd probably like to forget balloon skirts and grunge, but they seem worth mentioning as a reminder of how fast trendy turns silly.

Don't fall for designer labels alone. You'll be wearing that off-white suit, not the label. Your dry cleaner may be the only one happy to see it. And even the most gifted tailor may not be able to make a size 12 suit hang well on your size 8 frame. They don't call fashion the "rag trade" for nothing.

Look for off-prices in the off-season. You'll find the best bargains on multiple markdowns and clearance items. Fill in blanks in your summer wardrobe in the fall and buy winter leftovers in spring.

Does it work? Try out all buttons, zippers, snaps, and hooks. On hard goods like televisions, test every control knob.

Confirm the store's return policy ahead of time. More and more outlets are relaxing their no-return policies. But find out ahead of time, and keep receipts. Without the receipt, you may be stuck with the item or at best a store credit for a store that's hundreds of miles from home. Ask if you can return items to a full-price branch of the store. For example, with a receipt, Ann Taylor accepts returns from its outlets; the Gap doesn't.

Get on the mailing list. If you shop outlets regularly, ask if there is a mailing list. This way you'll get a heads up about sales and new arrivals.

HELP

■ *The Outlet Bound Guide to the Nation's Best Outlets* and its Web site list 13,000 outlets around the country by location and designer or manufacturer. Call (888) OUTLET2 or go to www.outletbound.com. The book costs $9.95 plus $3.50 delivery charge.

■ *The Joy of Outlet Shopping* guide is available for $6.95 plus $1.50 for delivery. Call (800) 344-6397, or write The Joy of Outlet Shopping, P.O. Box 17129, Clearwater, FL 34622.

CHAPTER 55

HOME SHOPPING

Stamping Out Fraud

How does a Robot Culinaire food processor for just $12.79 sound? Or the luxury motorboat you've just "won"— that you can claim for a mere $159 freight charge? Or a telephone call saying you've won a free vacation in Hawaii? Maybe you are tempted by the Svelt-Patch, a purported transdermal skin patch that promises to melt away the pounds.

Too good to be true? You bet. These are true offers—and truly scams. The "food processor" turned out to be a hand-operated gizmo with a rotary blade, and the motorboat was really just an inflatable raft with a battery-powered motor. The vacation in Hawaii didn't materialize—unless consumers first spent thousands of their hard-earned dollars on merchandise. All the patch did was look silly.

Catalogs, telemarketing, TV shopping channels, and the Internet have changed the way Americans shop. The advantages are obvious: convenience, efficiency, no crowds, no parking problems, no tax for out-of-staters. All from the comfort of your couch. The drawbacks may not be so clear: delayed orders, ill-fitting garments, the hassle of returning damaged or disappointing merchandise, and, alas, fraud.

While outright misrepresentation is the exception rather than the rule, it's an all-too-frequent exception. The Federal Trade Commission estimates that telemarketing and mail-order fraud of all kinds steal upward of $40 billion from consumers every year. Still, it's easy enough to avoid the scams if you shop from home sensibly and defensively.

THE BASICS

Your Rights

Over 100 million people order products or services by phone, mail, or computer each year. Most of these transactions go smoothly, thanks in part to FTC regulation. The FTC's Mail or Telephone Order Rule requires companies to send your order within 30 days or within the time frame promised in advertising or catalogs. The clock starts ticking as soon as the company receives payment from you, whether you order by mail, phone, fax, or computer. If the company cannot meet this schedule, it must notify you and send you a postage-paid reply card giving you the choice between canceling the order and getting a refund or agreeing to the new shipping date. If you cancel, the company must send your refund within seven days or credit your account within one billing cycle. If the company will miss the second shipping date, it must notify you again and give you the postage-paid option of canceling the order. (Transactions involving magazine subscriptions, book and record clubs, seed and plant purchases, photo processing, and C.O.D. orders are not subject to the Mail or Telephone Order Rule.)

If you pay for your purchase with a credit card, you are also covered by the Fair Credit Billing Act, which permits you to withhold payment of charges you dispute. You have 60 days to write to the credit card company explaining that you will not be paying the charge until the billing dispute is resolved. If the dispute is resolved in your favor, you do not have to pay the charges or any finance charges that accrued during the resolution process. If you were wrong, however, you have to pay both.

For the time being, you only have to pay sales tax if the mail order or telemarketing company has a "physical presence"—for example, a store or distribution facility—in the state in which you live, or if the laws of your home state require taxation. Thus, if you live in New York or Virginia and order something from the Lillian Vernon catalog, you'll owe sales tax: Lillian

Vernon has its headquarters in New York and a distribution center in Virginia Beach. However, if you live in any other state that does not require sales tax, you won't owe any sales tax on a Lillian Vernon order.

As for protection from scam artists, Congress passed and the President signed the Telemarketing and Consumer Fraud and Abuse Prevention Act of 1994, and the FTC drew up stricter rules requiring telemarketers to give their names and aims promptly, along with the precise cost and terms of a sale; banning calls before 8 A.M. and after 9 P.M.; requiring telemarketers to maintain "do-not-call lists"; and allowing state attorneys general to sue telemarketers on behalf of consumers.

> "*In the hands of a con artist, a phone is an assault weapon.*"
> —HUBERT HUMPHREY III, Minnesota Attorney General

WHAT TO WATCH OUT FOR

Mail or phone orders. Better Business Bureaus (BBBs) around the country handled over 22,000 complaints about mail, telephone, and computer solicitations in 1996. The most common problems were non-delivery of merchandise and goods or services that didn't live up to their advance billing—e.g., the "food processor" mentioned earlier.

When ordering, skip the postal "insurance." It's perfectly legal for firms to try to pass this charge on to you, but it's redundant. The company is legally responsible for making sure the merchandise arrives at your doorstep safely.

Also, be on the lookout for shipping and handling charges. Some firms calculate the charge based on the weight of your order; others charge a flat fee or calculate the fee based on how much you spend.

Take, for instance, the Pottery Barn (though Pottery Barn is by no means alone). A ribbed cotton pillow costs a tempting $24, but delivery at $6 adds another 25% to the price. If you order an $18 whisk from Williams Sonoma, the delivery charge is $5.75, adding 32% to the price. Oddly, a cheap item that weighs a lot usually costs less to ship than an expensive item that is very light—a pizza baking stone versus a Victoria's Secret fancy silk nightgown. When you take these fees into account, you might find you'd do just as well driving over to the mall.

Sweepstakes and prize promotions. You've seen these schemes. Perhaps you've even been taken in. You receive a call or a letter in the mail congratulating you on "winning" or being "chosen." All you have to do is buy something, or send a check, or call a "900" telephone number (at a rate of $10 per minute) to claim your reward. Ha!

One elderly Wisconsin man was told he had won a big prize, either a new car or a large pot of cash. To claim his prize, he had only to help kids get off drugs—which would cost $398 for materials to distribute at schools. He sent a check, but neither car nor cash came his way. All he got was 15 plastic Frisbees printed with an anti-drug slogan.

Federal and state laws make it illegal to require a fee or purchase in a legitimate sweepstakes. All you legally have to do is lick a stamp. That's why you often find the disclaimer "no purchase necessary" somewhere in the mailing. And the odds of winning do not increase if you buy something. By law, everybody's chances must be the same.

Here's an example of how sweepstakes and prize promotion scams work. An outfit calling itself First National SweepsBank of America sent consumers a "facsimile passbook account that represents a worth of $10,000," according to the company. The mailing was designed to induce people to buy things like jewelry and coupon books. No purchase was necessary, but Alfred Raffo, Jr. of Brooklyn, New York, didn't realize that. Raffo sent $15, as the mailing requested, to cover "venture processing, shipping, and handling" to collect what the mailing also said was a $10,000 prize. Raffo got a zirconia "diamond" ring.

Not every sweepstakes is a swindle. If you read every word carefully, you'll often find that clever lawyers and layout artists have prefaced the enormous CONGRATULATIONS with a hardly noticeable "If you return the grand-prize-winning entry, we'll say . . ." Publishers Clearinghouse and American Family Publishers give away millions of dollars this way each year. Yes, someone really does become a millionaire overnight. But the chance that it will be you is infinitesimal. For one *Time* magazine sweepstakes, the odds were 1 in 900 million.

Chain letters. Any letter, telephone solicitation, or Internet offer that requires you to send money to someone in return for more money later on should sound your alarm bells loud and clear. Since you can't win, don't even bother trying. These schemes typically induce you to send money to a person at the top of a list of names with the promise that you will receive many times the amount of money you lay out several weeks later. Lay off. Often the list is bogus, the names are fictitious, scam artists get the money, and your name never reaches the top of the list.

Online shopping. The same laws that protect you when you shop by phone or mail protect you on cyber-shopping sprees. Unfortunately, many of the same scams also apply. Between 1996 and 1997, the number of complaints tripled. Consumers have reported problems with Internet auctions, pyramid schemes,

BEWARE OF BOGUS CHARITIES

Americans gave away $143 billion in 1995, and high-pressure telephone appeals on behalf of charities, known as "telefunding," take advantage of this goodwill. About $1.4 billion of the largesse may have been misused or unknowingly directed at fraudulent solicitors.

"You are talked into donating large sums of money for what you believe are worthwhile causes. Too often, the bulk of the money goes to the company doing the soliciting, rather than to a charitable program," says Bennett M. Weiner, the director of the Council of BBB's Philanthropic Advisory Service.

To avoid getting taken in, know who you are giving to before you make a contribution. There's no need to suspect all charitable telephone solicitations, but do ask for additional facts, such as how much of your contribution or what portion of your purchase will be received by the charity and how much of the charity's income actually supports its programs and how much supports more fund-raising. Consumer watchdogs suggest that an acceptable minimum ratio is 60% program to 40% fund-raising, but many charities put a larger portion of your money to work toward their mission. Ask for a copy of the charity's annual report or financial statement before you contribute and ask for an explanation of the solicitor's relationship to the charity. Send a check, rather than giving a credit card number.

You can check the charity's reputation with your local BBB or with your state's charity registration office (usually within the attorney general's office).

615

ARMCHAIR SHOPPING

Don't confuse television home shopping with smart shopping. It's pure entertainment. No matter how the shows pitch the products, it's rare to find a real deal. Unless, of course, you would pay anything to live in Englebert Humperdink's house, which was put up for sale on QVC, or have a hankering for a Volkswagen painted by Peter Max (price tag: $100,000).

These examples are clearly publicity stunts, but home shopping has become a serious business. Home shopping channels QVC, HSN, and other shopping shows reach over 61 million cable subscribers. In all, the 5 million viewers who are watching during any one hour ring up bills for as much as $1 million an hour. The industry racks up sales of more than $3 billion a year on mostly low-quality luxury items. More than 40% of the business is jewelry sales, but there are also cosmetics, perfume, cookware, clothing, and exercise equipment to be watched and had.

Many of the pitfalls of TV shopping are the same as those of catalog shopping—the consumer can't see or touch the merchandise without first buying,

what you expect isn't always what you get, and returns can be a hassle. But there are other things to watch out for, too.

Quantities are limited, or so they say. Each item is offered for only a few minutes, and buyers are warned to act fast. A clock on the TV counts down the seconds remaining. The time pressure keeps consumers from thinking through purchases carefully. One QVC addict confesses to *Ladies Home Journal:* "I would feel victorious at having grabbed that watch or scarf just in the nick of time."

Products are shown to their best advantage through the use of lighting and camera angles. Hosts reinforce the favorable treatment by gushing about every aspect of every product in repetitive and painstaking detail.

The pitch seems hokey, but it's clever and alluring, especially for a group of frequent home shoppers who are hooked. Celebrities like Victoria Principal, Marie Osmond, Joan Rivers, Regis Philbin, and Susan Lucci all have their own lines of merchandise. They not so subtly suggest that buyers can have their glamorous lives simply by buying their products.

prizes and sweepstakes, as well as difficulties buying merchandise, including computers and Internet

services themselves. According to the National Fraud Information Center, the most common signs of

The merchandise may not be worth what it sells for. One day in 1993, the HSN barkers were selling baseballs autographed by Johnny Bench for $129. A moment or two later, Johnny Bench himself came on the show and said the balls could be had for just $59.95. Then the HSN host lowered the price to an "absolutely unbelievable" $49.95. Unbelievable was right. Turns out the same baseball was available from the leading baseball collectibles dealer for only $35. HSN buyers could have overpaid by 40%.

Claims about products may be overblown. In 1995, the Federal Trade Commission caught HSN making unsubstantiated health claims about four products. For example, Lifeway Vitamin C and Zinc spray purportedly prevented colds and healed mouth lesions, cold sores, and cracking lip corners, and Lifeway Vitamin B12 spray was supposed to treat hangovers and increase energy. In fact, HSN had no scientific evidence to support the claim that spraying vitamins in the mouth is as effective as taking a vitamin pill (already a bit suspect, as you can see in "Nutritional Supplements" on page 100). And Washington Mint, which aggressively mar-

kets special silver and gold coins to "serious collectors" via home shopping channels and newspapers, is neither in Washington, nor an actual mint. It is a Minneapolis-based marketing company. The coins are worth only the silver or gold used to manufacture them; Boston area coin dealers said they would pay only $40 to $50 for a Washington Mint half-pound silver eagle coin the Washington Mint was selling at the time for "a special discount price" of $139.

It can become an obsession. *The Washington Monthly* reported in 1995 about a man who died in a retirement community in Fairfax, Virginia, leaving behind a house crammed with kitchen gadgets, costume jewelry, bed linens, and many unopened packages. The man had bought about one item a day, and someone who worked at the retirement community said the lonely man had simply been happy to have someone to talk to for a half hour or so at a time.

If you are wondering about your rights, the FTC's mail order rule rules. To be a smarter TV home shopper, you need only be on the lookout for these pitfalls and to follow the advice elsewhere in this chapter.

fraud are, as with lower-tech scams, extravagant promises of profits, guarantees of credit regardless of bad credit history, incredibly low prices, and "prizes" that require upfront payments.

THE $MARTER CONSUMER

Ask telephone solicitors for a name and number to call back, or ask them to mail you more information. If they refuse, don't buy.

Never give your credit card number, bank account number, or Social Security number unless you are familiar with the company or have checked it out.

Check a company's reputation with the local BBB before you order anything in response to an unsolicited offer or from an unfamiliar company. Since mail and telephone orders are one of the BBB's top complaint categories, they are likely to know about bad companies.

Keep records about everything you order, including the date, a tear sheet of the ad, the page out of the catalog, or a printout of the Internet page, and either a copy of the order form or a written record of the items ordered, how much you paid, and the company's name, address, and telephone number.

Familiarize yourself with the return policies. They vary from one company to another; some, like L.L. Bean and The Company Store, offer lifetime guarantees, while others have extremely limited return policies. This also means investigating who pays the shipping charges for returned items. Most often, you'll have to pay, especially if the problem is the item's fit. In cases where the product arrives damaged, significantly different than pictured, or in error, the company should pay the return postage.

Open your packages promptly and make sure that you got exactly what you paid for and that it is in perfect condition. If you need to return anything, send it back by insured or registered mail with an explanation of the problem and your method of payment.

Try not to buy. Once you buy, you are likely to be inundated with more calls, catalogs, and commercial e-mail—you are now a proven home shopper and word gets around fast.

If you receive a notice that you have won a fabulous prize, read it very carefully. If you've won *anything*, it's almost certainly of considerably lower value than is likely to be represented in the headlines.

HELP

■ **The National Fraud** Information Center, a project of the National Consumers League (800) 876-7060, www.fraud.org, provides information and help in filing complaints.

■ **The Direct Marketing Association's** Mail Order Action Line (MOAL) mediates disputes between consumers. Contact the Direct Marketing Association, MOAL, 1101 17th Street NW, Suite 705, Washington, DC 20036-4704.

■ **Address complaints about solicitors** of charitable contributions to your local BBB or your state's charity registration office, often found within the attorney general's office.

■ **Fraudulent direct** mail pieces may be under the jurisdiction of the U.S. Postal Service. Address complaints to the local postmaster or postal inspector. Look under "Postal Service U.S." in the U.S. Government listings in your local phone directory.

■ **Complain about what you think are** deceptive telemarketing practices to the Federal Trade Commission, Consumer Response Center, 6th Street and Pennsylvania Avenue NW, Washington, DC 20580, www.ftc.gov. The FTC also publishes several free fact sheets and brochures on telemarketing fraud, shopping by phone and mail, and credit billing.

CHAPTER 56

INSTALLMENT LOANS

Buying on Time, at a Price

A generation or so ago, few Americans bought on credit except when buying houses or, perhaps, cars. Credit cards were a novelty, and cash on the barrelhead was the norm.

Look at us now! The total amount of consumer installment credit outstanding (not counting mortgage loans) rocketed from $100 billion in 1970 to $700 billion in 1997, a 600% increase in only two and a half decades.

All this credit hasn't come cheap. A decent $13,000 used car paid for with a five-year loan at 12.5% annual interest would end up costing $17,548.80.

THE BASICS

Credit Sales and Money Loans

Installment borrowing, also called closed-end credit, is a loan for a fixed amount that is to be repaid within a specific time in regular installments. Such loans are typically used to buy cars, furniture, or mobile homes, or to finance home renovations. A contract spells out the borrower's rights and obligations and the consequences of default. *Credit sales* and *money loans* are the two basic ways to obtain installment credit.

With a credit sale, you enter into a "retail installment contract" with the seller, who extends the credit that you use to make a purchase—say, a new car. In most cases, this contract is immediately sold to another creditor to whom you then owe the money. In effect, the seller is the go-between for a creditor that the consumer has never met.

One important feature of a credit sale is that the sales terms and financing terms are tied together in one contract. This means that your obligation to pay the money back is conditional on the seller's obligation to live up to the terms and conditions of the sale, including warranty obligations.

For many years creditors were able to use various legal dodges to make consumers pay even though the seller failed to honor the sales terms. The Federal Trade Commission (FTC) finally put an end to these practices by adopting what is called the "Preservation of Consumers' Claims and Defenses" rule. This rule applies to all credit sales for $25,000 or less and to any credit sale secured by your dwelling or real property. It requires that the seller include this clause in every credit sale agreement printed in boldface type:

NOTICE

ANY HOLDER OF THIS CONSUMER CREDIT CONTRACT IS SUBJECT TO ALL CLAIMS AND DEFENSES WHICH THE DEBTOR COULD ASSERT AGAINST THE SELLER OF GOODS OR SERVICES OBTAINED PURSUANT HERETO OR WITH THE PROCEEDS THEREOF. RECOVERY HEREUNDER SHALL NOT EXCEED AMOUNTS PAID BY THE DEBTOR HEREUNDER.

If this notice is absent, don't sign and don't buy. If a seller is prepared to violate a federal mandate that creates important protections for you, what makes you think you can count on the seller to honor any other promises?

Tens of thousands of homeowners —mostly in lower-income, inner-city neighborhoods—have learned this the hard way. As described in earlier chapters, a wave of "equity theft" has swept the nation; dishonest home-improvement contractors sell renovated kitchens, roofs, and newly created basement apartments by promising unrealistically low monthly payments. The work is rarely completed or is so shoddy that it has to be ripped out. To add insult to injury, the homeowners are often conned into signing a separate loan agreement for much more money than they were originally told—as well as a mortgage document.

In money loans, a creditor lends you money that you then use to pay for purchases. Banks, credit unions, and finance companies are the most common sources of such credit.

Since the loan and a purchase you make with the money are separate transactions made under different agreements (and usually with different companies), the sales terms and financing terms are not locked together in the same closed-end loan agreement. This usually means that if you have a dispute about the purchase with the seller, you would have to repay the loan and separately settle up with the seller.

The FTC "Preservation of Consumers' Claims and Defenses" rule carves out an exception that can help you lock the terms of the sale into the loan agreement just as in a credit sale. This rule covers loans made in the following circumstances:

- The seller engages in a pattern or practice of referring purchasers to the creditor who makes the loan used to pay for the purchase, as when the seller arranged the loan, made out the papers for you, or sent you to the lender; or
- The seller and the creditor are affiliated for the purpose of making loans, as when the same company owns both.

The FTC locks the loan and sales terms together by requiring the seller to make sure that the lender includes the following clause in the loan agreement, as shown below:

NOTICE

ANY HOLDER OF THIS CONSUMER CREDIT CONTRACT IS SUBJECT TO ALL CLAIMS AND DEFENSES WHICH THE DEBTOR COULD ASSERT AGAINST THE SELLER OF GOODS OR SERVICES OBTAINED WITH THE PROCEEDS HEREOF.

RECOVERY HEREUNDER SHALL NOT EXCEED AMOUNTS PAID BY THE DEBTOR HEREUNDER.

This rule is likely to help you lock the sales and the loan terms together *only* if the lender includes the required clause in your loan contract.

Secured or Unsecured Installment Credit

Installment credit can be either secured or unsecured.

Secured credit simply refers to an extension of credit that is backed up by personal or real property or by a co-signer. With secured credit, a creditor has more than just your signature and income to fall back on to collect the debt. In case of default, a secured creditor can use legal procedures to recover the collateral and sell it to pay off the debt. If the collateral brings more than the amount owing, it must be paid back to you; if not, the creditor could sue for the remaining amount, which is usually called the "deficiency balance."

The type of collateral used determines the legal procedures a creditor must employ to obtain the collateral upon default. The three most commonly used types of collateral are:

■ *Personal property,* like a car, boat, furniture, refrigerator, or household goods. A creditor obtains such collateral by getting what is called a "security interest" in the goods. The agreement that puts such goods up as collateral must be in writing, and is referred to as a "security agreement." In the case of credit sales, the retail installment sales agreement almost always includes the clauses a creditor needs to obtain a security interest in the goods you buy.

■ *Real property,* such as a home. To obtain such collateral, the creditor secures a first or a second mortgage on the property. A mortgage must be in writing. Someone, such as a contractor who makes improvements to your home, can, however, obtain a lien on it to secure payment. This lien does not have to be put in writing; the creditor acquires it because the law allows it.

■ *Liquid assets,* such as a bank savings account or a stock account at a brokerage firm. The creditor acquires a right to obtain the money or the stocks put up as collateral, and the assets are usually frozen until the loan is repaid. Such an arrangement must be in writing if the lender is not also the financial institution holding the account(s) you're using as collateral. If the lender is your own bank, however, a bank usually has what's known as a "right of set-off," which allows it to take from your accounts amounts for defaulted debts.

Borrowing with a co-signer is another way to obtain secured credit. Creditors usually require co-

> "**E**asy credit paves the road to bankruptcy."
>
> —ANONYMOUS

signers when an applicant doesn't have an acceptable credit record. The person who co-signs is then just as obligated to repay the debt as the person who actually received the money or the goods bought on the credit. If and when default occurs, it's the creditor's choice as to who will be made to pay.

Unsecured credit means the creditor has no additional collateral backing up the debt aside from your promise to pay. To collect, a creditor would first have to sue and then use legal procedures to enforce payment, such as garnishment of wages or attachment of property.

What the Law Says: Truth in Lending Act Disclosures

The federal Truth in Lending Act (TILA) requires creditors to clearly and conspicuously disclose in writing key credit terms. These disclosures must be made *before* you are legally bound to go through with the transaction.

TILA does not regulate the actual terms of a credit agreement. Such regulation is left to state law, and all states have various laws regulating the different types of credit you can get, such as bank loans, installment loans, finance company loans, retail installment contracts, and the like. TILA has, however, simplified and standardized how creditors must disclose important financial terms. See the box on the next page for the key up-front disclosures creditors must make about closed-end credit transactions.

How Creditors Compute Finance Charges

Actuarial method. With this method, finance charges are computed bi-weekly or monthly by applying a periodic rate to a declining balance. A periodic rate may be expressed as "1.2% per month," for example.

The actuarial method can be used to calculate the unpaid balance after any scheduled payment or the amount due in interest as of any payment. It can also be used to allocate what portion of pre-computed finance charges a creditor has to "rebate" if a loan is paid off early (see below).

When the actuarial method is used, finance charges are computed and owed as each payment becomes due.

Since the actuarial method calculates finance charges based on the time *between* scheduled payments, finance charges do not keep accruing if you pay late. But you also don't owe less if you pay early.

"Pre-computed" finance charges. Creditors "pre-compute" finance charges for many types of installment debts. This simply means they figure out in advance, assuming that all payments will be made on the scheduled due dates, the amount due for finance charges for the entire loan period and add it to the total amount owing under the contract. Finance charges do not accrue if you pay late, but you don't get credit for paying early. Creditors, however, collect late charges if payments are delayed beyond a

KNOW THE LINGO

Here are the key terms decoded that lenders must include in any credit agreement:

The "finance charge" and the "annual percentage rate" (APR). The finance charge is the cost of credit as a dollar amount for the entire loan period. The APR tells you the cost of credit expressed as a percentage of what you borrow. The rate is annualized so you can easily compare how much different creditors are charging regardless of differences in the amount borrowed or the length of the payment period.

The "amount financed" tells you the total dollar amount of credit being extended to you. This is the amount you must fully repay, regardless of whether you pay the loan back before the originally scheduled term.

The "total of payments." This is the sum of all the payments scheduled to repay the debt. It is the sum of the amount financed plus the amount of the finance charge, or interest.

The "total sale price," in the case of credit sales, is the sum of the total of payments plus any down payment.

The "payment schedule" is the amount, the number, and the date of the payments scheduled to repay the loan. If your sched-ule includes a balloon payment —one that is more than twice as large as other scheduled payments—it must be specifically identified.

Security interest. If the creditor is taking a security interest in products other than those being sold on credit, the property must be described in writing.

Late charges. Creditors assess such fees when your payment is late by between 10 to 15 days, depending on the law in your home state. The fee is usually 5% of the payment or a flat dollar amount, whichever is greater.

Prepayment consequences. What could happen if you pay your loan off early? This information also lets you know how the creditor computes finance charges on your debt.

The creditor indicates that you either "may" or that you "will not" have to pay a penalty if you pay the debt off early. Consumer credit laws in many states prohibit creditors from penalizing consumers for paying off installment debts early. If penalties are allowed in your state, this disclosure tells you if you would have to pay the creditor an extra charge just to pay the debt off early. If the disclosure statement indicates there could be such a penalty, find out what the charge would be.

specified payment grace period (usually 15 days).

When finance charges are pre-computed, you could technically be obligated to repay the amount borrowed *plus* all the pre-computed finance charges. For example, in the car financing illustration given at the beginning of this chapter, the creditor who pre-computes finance charges adds the $4,548.80 that would be due in finance charges over five years to the $13,000 amount financed, to come up with $17,548.80—the total amount that is to be repaid in 60 payments of $292.48 each. Of course, creditors would collect huge windfalls if they could make you pay the entire $4,548.80 in finance charges even if you paid the loan off after only 30 months, for example. Here's why they can't:

Most state laws require creditors to "rebate" the portion of the pre-computed finance charges that are unearned by the creditor when a loan is paid off ahead of schedule. When a pre-computed debt is paid off early, you must pay the outstanding unpaid debt balance plus unpaid finance charges, only as of when you pre-pay. To come up with the right number, creditors must allocate how much of each $292.48 payment went to reduce the debt balance and how much went to pay finance charges. Since the loan balance is highest at the beginning of the loan, a much higher portion of each payment goes to pay finance charges at the beginning of the loan term than at the end; the amount due in finance charges is not directly proportional to the fraction of

all payments that you had paid. For example, if you paid the loan back in full after making half the scheduled payments (30 out of 60, in our example), you would owe much more than just half of the $4,548.80 due in finance charges over the full term of 60 months.

The "Rule of 78s" is one method that's often used to figure out how much of the pre-computed interest a creditor has earned and how much the creditor must rebate upon pre-payment of the loan. The Rule of 78s produces a higher payoff figure than the actuarial method described above, especially when the loan term is longer than five years and the APR is over 15%. That's why some states prohibit creditors from using the Rule of 78s to compute the rebate; others allow creditors to use it only for certain types of loans.

Daily simple interest method. With this method, creditors calculate the interest due on the debt on a daily basis by applying a periodic rate to the outstanding balance, as with credit cards. When using this method, creditors deduct from each payment the amount due for finance charges since the last payment and apply the remainder to reduce the debt balance. Most commonly used for computing interest due on mortgages, this method is becoming more widespread for other fixed-term installment debts because the increasing use of computers makes the calculations easier for creditors.

Since the finance-charge meter keeps running each day from the last payment until the next one is made, your payment habits will affect how much you end up paying in finance charges. Borrowers who habitually pay early end up paying less than the amount disclosed as the total finance charges—the principal balance is reduced more quickly than estimated. On the other hand, borrowers who habitually pay late will end up owing more at the end of the loan term because the principal was reduced more slowly than estimated, especially if late payments occurred during the early part of the loan period.

WHAT TO WATCH OUT FOR

Loan consolidations and refinancing. Avoid consolidating or refinancing closed-end installment debts unless the APR for the finance charge on the consolidated loan is significantly lower than the rates charged for the debts you are consolidating. It's costly to consolidate installment debts because the payoff amount for each account that you consolidate usually includes some leftover finance charges from the old contract —unless the old creditor computes finance charges on the unpaid balance on a "daily basis" method.

Adding new purchases to existing installment debts. It is seldom a good idea to add new purchases to an existing closed-end installment contract. First, the old purchases end up securing the new ones, sometimes long after you have repaid the amount owed for the old purchases. Second, it becomes very difficult to untangle what you owe

for each purchase in case of a dispute about some of them; you can't safely withhold payment as you might be entitled to do if the disputed purchase was the only item financed under the contract.

Now you see it, now you don't: the "instant credit, no finance charges" trap. Newspapers, mail, and the Internet are full of advertisments touting the availability of instant credit with no finance charges for from one to three months. These offers are made for both closed-end loans (such as for furniture) and open-end "revolving" loans (such as credit cards).

The hook is that you get the instant credit, but the "no finance charges" part disappears unless you repay the entire amount in full within the time allowed for "no finance charges"—that is, you have to pay it all back within one to three months of the date you made your purchase. If you don't do this, you will usually find you owe finance charges from that date.

Don't let the instant credit/no finance charge sugarcoating lure you into this credit trap. These deals are worth taking *only* if you are certain you'll pay the balance in full within the time allowed or if you have deliberately decided to assume the additional credit obligation that will result if you don't pay in full. Andy E. did this when he bought a $2,800 personal computer at New York City's J & R Music World. If he didn't pay the entire balance within three months, he would owe interest at an astounding 21.84% APR, starting from the *date of pur-*

chase. Fortunately, he did pay it all in time, in effect giving himself a free three-month loan. If he hadn't paid when he did, he would have immediately owed $52.14 in interest on his purchase.

Credit life or credit disability insurance. This insurance pays off the outstanding balance of the debt in case of the death or disability of the borrower. Creditors must include premiums for credit insurance in the finance charge unless they offer such coverage as an option. Disclosure documents, therefore, almost invariably include a statement indicating that you are aware you are not required to purchase the coverage, and a space where you must sign to indicate you have opted to buy any coverage that is included.

Credit insurance is almost always a bad buy. Stephen Brobeck, executive director of the Consumer Federation of America, summarizing his group's 1996 study of this product, called credit life insurance "the nation's worst insurance rip-off." The study found that borrowers who buy this insurance get gouged—by $400 million a year, an amount equal to $1 for every $6 spent on premiums. Life insurers pay out in claims an absurdly small 42% of the money they take in. If you really think you need such coverage, you can almost certainly get much more protection for far less by purchasing a term life insurance policy; credit life usually costs about three times as much as basic life. (See Chapter 39, "Life Insurance," page 440.)

Credit disability insurance is even more expensive than credit life

coverage, and is rarely worthwhile if you have sick leave at your job.

Property insurance. This insurance typically covers the property you have to put up as collateral against damage or loss. Creditors will invariably require you to obtain it for a car or other substantial collateral. While creditors can require you to have the coverage, they must give you the option to purchase it from other sources. You are better off shopping for your own coverage.

Some creditors are now pushing casualty insurance covering almost any collateral against loss or damage. Get such coverage through a homeowner or renter's policy rather than from your creditor.

THE $MARTER CONSUMER

Lessen the bite of auto and other closed-end loans. First, shop around for a lower interest rate or do whatever you have to to scrape together a bigger down-payment and finance less of your purchase. Take the example of the $13,000 car in the introduction. As explained, finance charges would add another $4,548.80 if the interest rate was 12.5% over a five-year period. You would have to devote $292.48 a month to pay back that loan, and the car would end up costing you $17,548.80.

Assuming the loan period remains at five years, reducing the amount financed on the car to $10,000 would slash $1,050 from your total finance charges. Reducing the interest rate on $13,000 financed from 12.5% to 10% would slash total finance charges by $975.

Measure number two: Cutting the loan period from five to four years *lowers* the total finance charges from $4,548.80 to $3,585.92, a savings of $962.88—even if the interest rate remains the same. The car will end up costing $16,585.92. However, the period reduction *raises* each month's payment by $53.06, from $292.48 to $345.54. If you can handle the extra $53.06 a month, you can save a total of $962.88 in finance charges.

Reducing the dollar amount of monthly payments (instead of the actual number of payments) only makes the loan *seem* easier on your budget. So be careful about ads touting "low monthly payments."

With money loans, make sure you have the loan before you commit to buy. Be sure that your purchase agreement includes a condition that obligates you to buy *only* if you obtain *acceptable financing* within a specified period. Alternatively, you could first obtain the loan and then make the purchase, knowing you have the money to pay.

Doing it backwards can be costly. Suppose, for example, you put down a deposit and sign a purchase agreement expecting to pay for a new dining room table and chairs with a loan but without including the financing condition in your purchase agreement. If you don't get the loan, you can't pay for the furniture; the seller will almost certainly treat it as a breach of contract and keep your deposit.

Wait at least 10 days after obtaining credit on any installment loan or purchase agreement before purchasing any products that you will pay for out of funds other than the credit being extended to you. The Uniform Commercial Code (UCC) section that governs security interests involving personal property in every state except Louisiana allows creditors to obtain a security interest in any personal property a debtor acquires after he or she receives the money. Creditors call this a security interest in "after acquired" property. In consumer transactions, however, the UCC sets a time limit on how many days "after" the agreement is signed a creditor can use this clause to reach personal property you acquire. This time limit is usually set at up to 10 days after, but can vary depending on your state's law. A little patience is all it takes to beat "after acquired" security interest clauses that creditors exploit to get hidden leverage on consumers.

Don't co-sign for anyone . . . unless you won't mind having to pay. Since you will, if the primary signer does not, you are essentially extending that person credit but getting none of the benefits of the loan. If the creditor—a professional judge of creditworthiness—is unsure about the primary signer's ability or willingness to pay, you must be doubly certain that the person you sign for will honor the debt.

Avoid late fees if at all possible. Make up skipped payments even if you have to get a cash advance on your credit card to do it. With late fees of 5% of each monthly payment, the creditor who "pyramids" late charges over the entire remaining loan period levies a finance charge at an incredible 60% APR.

Look beyond the APR to the total cost of the entire deal. The APR the creditor discloses does not tell the whole story, especially when there's a rebate involved. Manufacturers' rebates do not have to be counted as part of the finance charge. This practice makes it easy for credit sellers to team up with manufacturers to hide finance charges in the sales price. For example, if a bank charges 8% APR to finance a $12,000 car loan over four years, is that a better deal than the 6% APR deal the car manufacturer offers through a dealer on a car that would cost $13,000 if you financed it, but on which you would get a $1,000

rebate if you paid cash? The 8% loan on $12,000 would be cheaper (by $592.80) than the 6% rate on $13,000 you would have to pay without a cash-purchase rebate. It's smarter to borrow from the bank, pay in cash, and enjoy the rebate.

Always ask for an itemization of the charges for goods or services you are buying and/or payments the creditor is making on your behalf out of the credit being extended to you. For example, if the creditor is supposed to pay off an outstanding loan on a car you are trading in, make sure that's clearly identified as the creditor's obligation. Itemizing is also the only way for you to make sure the lump sum adds up to the prices you negotiated for each item. If there was an addition "mistake" but the lump sum is the only amount shown, that's what you will owe. But if the costs are itemized, you will almost certainly owe no more than the sum of the itemized amounts, not the mistaken total.

HELP

■ **The pamphlet "Paying Off a Loan Early"** explains the methods creditors use to calculate the payoff amount when a loan is paid off ahead of schedule. Call 215-574-6115 to order, or write Federal Reserve Bank of Philadelphia, Public Information/Publications, P.O. Box 66, Philadelphia, PA 19105-0066.

■ *Surviving Debt* **(1996), a publication** of the National Consumer Law Center, will help you work your way out of a financial jam—there are chapters explaining the various kinds of debt, your legal rights, strategies for reducing debt,

and how to handle debt collectors. Cost: $15. To order, call (617) 523-8010.

■ **For more information about credit** life insurance, contact Consumer Federation of America, 1424 16th Street NW, Suite 604, Washington, DC 20036, (202) 387-6121.

■ *The Consumer Handbook to Credit Protection Laws* is available from the Board of Governors of the Federal Reserve System, Publications Services, Washington, DC 20551, or on the Worldwide Web, http://www.pueblo.gsa.gov.

CHAPTER 57

LAYAWAY AND RENT-TO-OWN

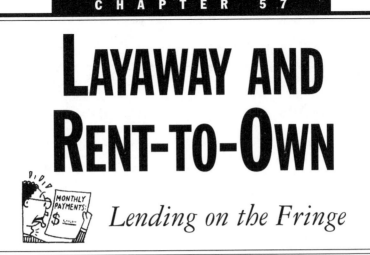

Lending on the Fringe

lthough layaway plans should be a relic from the distant past, when consumer credit was not yet widely available, signs urging shoppers to "Ask about our convenient layaway plan" are still commonly seen in some discount furniture and clothing stores.

Rent-to-own (RTO) is a more recent phenomenon, a way to market primarily appliances, video and electronic equipment, and furniture to people who have trouble getting credit. Despite astounding markups and astronomical rental charges, the RTO industry makes sales of $4 billion to 2.8 million customers a year, even though it is probably the worst consumer deal of the 1990s. Even when everything goes according to plan, a more accurate translation of RTO would be "Rip Them Off."

THE BASICS

Layaway Plans

Layaway plans allow you to pay in installments, but you don't get the goods until all the payments are made. It's the flip side of buying on credit—pay now, buy later. With layaway, *you* extend the credit to the retailer. That makes layaway plans risk-free for the seller and financially risky for consumers—the retailer could go out of business before you pay off the balance on your bill, or you could face unexpected bills to repair your car or leaky roof that keep you from completing your payments.

So protect yourself. If you really must sign up for layaway, make extra-sure the seller spells out these terms in writing:

Description of the goods. The goods should be described in detail. Be sure to include the brand name and model number.

Firm purchase price. The price should be firmly fixed in writing without the seller having any option to raise it later. Hijacking consumers for more money when they have completed their payments is like increasing the number of bombing missions needed to leave the service in *Catch-22*. It's unfair, and it's one of the main tricks of this trade.

Payment period. The number of payments and the amount of each should be clearly spelled out. Also, the plan should indicate how long the seller will hold the layaway once you start making payments.

Refund rights. Your right to a refund if you don't complete the payments within the specified payment period, or if you change your mind about the purchase, should be made explicit. State laws that specifically govern layaway plans and laws banning unfair and deceptive practices require that sellers clearly and conspicuously disclose their layaway refund policies. You are entitled to a refund of any payments made before the seller actually sets the product aside for you.

The Uniform Commercial Code (UCC), which governs the sale of goods, sets 20% of the purchase price or $500, whichever is less, as the maximum the seller can keep if you do not make all the required payments under a layaway plan. Sellers can keep more for seasonal items, such as winter clothing, or specially ordered goods, such as custom-designed furniture.

Rent-to-Own Plans

Angela P. "rented" a used four-head RCA videocassette recorder from a Long Island rent-to-own company for 70 weekly payments of $19.99 each, plus tax. After making her 70 weekly payments, she would own the VCR. While it would have cost a few hundred dollars to buy new in a store, the VCR *cost $1,399.30 plus tax under rent-to-own.* This massive markup is the norm in the RTO business.

In RTO plans, you lease an appliance or furniture for a period of weeks or months and make low payments weekly or monthly. The low payments mask the inflated price. Once all of the scheduled rental payments are completed, you either own the product outright or have the option to buy it, for a nominal additional amount or for a substantial balloon payment (a large single payment at the end of the rental period). The RTO industry came up with balloon payments to avoid laws under which the transaction would otherwise have been deemed a credit sale, which would have triggered certain consumer protection laws the industry sought to avoid so as to keep their effective interest rates secret.

When the U.S. Public Interest Research Group surveyed 124 RTO stores in 17 states in 1997, they found interest rates as high as 275% and averaging 100% nationally. As if the interest rates weren't punishing enough, purchasing items from RTO stores costs two to five times as

> " **G** enerally speaking, when a store fails, there is no recourse for the layaway customer."
>
> —SUSAN KASSAPIAN,
> former general counsel, NYC
> Department of Consumer Affairs

much as purchasing them at a department or discount store.

How can they get away with all this? The RTO industry is woefully under-regulated. No federal law requires RTO outlets to disclose their usurious interest rates. Only seven states (Iowa, Michigan, Minnesota, Nebraska, New York, Ohio, and South Carolina) place a ceiling on lease charges. In these states, a portion of each payment, ranging from 45% to 55%, must be applied toward the actual purchase of the product. This still works out to an effective annual interest rate of 90% to 180%—a far cry from the 15% to 20% typically charged by most credit card issuers.

If you sign up for rent-to-own anyway, be sure the lease includes clauses with:

An accurate description of the item to be rented.

A payment schedule. This spells out the amount and timing of each rental payment.

The total cost. This identifies the total number of payments and the total amount you must pay to become the owner of the leased property. Compare total costs from RTO businesses to find out where you can get the best deal.

Additional charges. This usually includes taxes and charges for other services or insurance. Be sure you really want or need any additional services.

Late charges. Most states that regulate RTO transactions limit late charges. In New York, for ex-

ample, it's $3 or 10% of the delinquent payment for weekly rentals, and $5 or 10% for monthly rentals, whichever is greater. You are usually allowed a grace period, generally a few days' duration.

Liability for loss. This spells out what you would owe in case the rented product is stolen or destroyed. RTO companies now sell "liability waiver" coverage under which they agree not to hold you liable for the theft or destruction of the product if you pay an additional charge. These charges can be high, but you could also owe a lot if El Niño floods your home or other harm comes to the item under RTO contract.

What happens in case of "excess wear and tear." Charges for excess wear and tear (usually defined in the contract) only matter if you cancel the lease and return the product or if you default and it is repossessed.

Ownership rights. What you have to do to become the owner of the leased product. Usually, you must keep up with the scheduled payments.

Cash price, which is what the RTO company would ostensibly charge if you bought it from them without renting. The rental charges are computed on the basis of it. The cash price is usually inflated. In the case of Angela P., believe it or not, the cash price for the used VCR was $699.95, probably three times what it would have sold for elsewhere.

Only a few states require that the cash price be disclosed. The difference between the cash price and

RENTING TO OWN, AKA RIPPING THEM OFF

A $250 TV costs $1,014 if you choose rent to own instead of paying with a credit card.

	Rent to Own	Credit Card
Amount financed	$250	$250
Payment	$13/week	$16.17/month
Number of months	18 (78 weeks)	18
Total paid	$1,014	$291.06
Annual Percentage Rate	265%	19.8%

Source: Consumers League of New Jersey

the total cost of all the rental payments tells you how much extra you are paying in order to buy the item over time.

Early purchase option. Some states' laws, like New York's, entitle you to purchase the item at any time upon payment of the early purchase option price. Having an early purchase option is a big plus; you could save a lot in lease charges if you can buy yourself out of the lease early.

Reinstatement right. Explains how you can reinstate a lease after defaulting on the payments. This right usually lasts for only a few days unless you voluntarily return the merchandise. RTO companies are quick to repossess goods after payment defaults, which could result in losing all the payments made toward buying the product. The law in each state then spells out how many days you have to reinstate the lease after returning the merchandise.

RTO leases allow you to cancel the rental at any time. But then the company will cart the item away, and all the rent you paid just goes with it.

WHAT TO WATCH OUT FOR

Old goods passed off as new. One of the most frequent RTO complaints is that a company furnished a used product when the consumer was supposed to get a new one. Under the laws in most of the 31 states that separately regulate RTO transactions, the item you are leasing should be fully and clearly described, especially whether it is new or used. Insist that the agreement include a requirement that the product be delivered in its factory-sealed container.

Balloon RTO payments or other conditions you would have to satisfy beyond making the periodic rental payments to become the owner. If there are any, the deal is worse than bad.

Used or missing manuals and warranties. These should be properly packed and sealed in their original envelope or wrapping. Booklets should not show any evidence of prior use.

THE $MARTER CONSUMER

Layaway Plans

Layaway your money for a rainy day. Since a layaway plan means saving money until you have enough to buy with cash, why let the seller hold your money without paying you interest? Instead, set up a bank deposit account that you use only for big-ticket purchases.

Use only well-known and established companies for layaway plans, since you are lending *them* your money until you get the goods.

Rent-to-Own

Stay away. The smartest thing you can do is not to get involved with RTO in the first place. They're never a good deal.

If you return an RTO-leased item, have the company give you a written condition report that accurately describes the condition of the product when you returned it.

Promptly tell the dealer about defects or malfunctions. If the dealer cannot or will not quickly and properly correct the problem, the product will not improve with age. Your right to cancel at least gives

you the chance to bail out quickly, before you get in too deep.

Immediately put your complaints in writing, clearly and fully spelling out the problems and making it clear that you expect the product to be promptly and properly serviced.

If you cancel early because of product malfunctions or defects, you should also insist on a refund of rental payments. If the dealer refuses, you could try to sue in small claims court. You have little to lose except the payments you have already made.

Canceling early and quickly may cost you the rental payments you have already made, but that's better than making more payments and getting nothing but grief.

Be sure you will be covered by the manufacturer's warranties. If such warranties are not extended to you until after you actually buy the product, be sure the agreement specifies that the dealer is responsible for servicing and repairing the product in the interim.

H E L P

■ **Check with your state attorney** general's office to find out about local RTO transaction requirements.

■ **You can find U.S. Public Interest** Research Group's Rent-to-Own exposé on the Web at www.pirg.org. and for more information you can call or write U.S. PIRG, 218 D Street SE, Washington, DC 20003, (202) 546-9707.

CHAPTER 58

COUNTERFEIT AND GRAY MARKET GOODS

You Get What You Pay For

Several years ago, the New York City Police Department confiscated 130 cases of ersatz Halston and Aramis fragrances in a Brooklyn warehouse. They looked exactly like the real thing, but any discerning nose would have known they were cheap knockoffs. And NYC residents weren't meant to be the only victims; the operation intended to ship to 30 different states.

Counterfeiting of high-quality luxury products has become a big business. But when buying name-brand products, counterfeits aren't the only scam to watch out for. You need also to be aware of "gray market" goods—products made by the manufacturer on the label but that are still not up to the manufacturer's usual standards.

THE BASICS

What Are Counterfeit Goods?

The counterfeiter we normally hear about prints bogus bills and tries to use them to purchase genuine merchandise. Product counterfeiters do the reverse, producing bogus merchandise that they try to turn into genuine cash. Bogus goods or bogus bills, the result is the same—the person stuck with them usually ends up with garbage.

Product counterfeiters are really trademark pirates who slap counterfeit labels of respected manufacturers on their own products. They do a booming business, especially in places where tourists concentrate to look for bargains. In New York City alone, counterfeit sales amount to more than $2 billion annually.

And just as currency counterfeiters ignore the small stuff to concentrate on bigger bills like $20s, $50s, and even $100s, product counterfeiters go for high-priced, easy-to-move, high-demand items like watches, videotapes of first-run movies, national sports teams' T-shirts and caps, or high-fashion apparel and accessories like sunglasses and handbags. According to the head of Rolex watches, over a third of all "Rolexes" sold are fakes!

As with most scams, trademark pirates try to hook consumers with the "bargain-of-a-lifetime" lure—the Gucci handbag for $50 or "make me an offer"; Oakley sunglasses for $10; the latest Bruce Willis action thriller on tape for only $5. The list is endless, but it's the same scheme—an incredibly low price for the genuine article, which is usually an inflated price for phony goods.

The only sure thing about buying counterfeit goods (assuming that you are unaware that you are buying a fake) is that you will be disappointed. The quality of the imitation is always vastly inferior to the genuine article. The $15 "Rolex" watch stops ticking after only a week. The bad stitching on the "Chanel" handbags is only one of the myriad quality differences from authentic Chanel handbags. The only way that you can effectively protect yourself is to avoid falling into the trap in the first place.

> ## "The gray market is the sale of goods with genuine brand names, but which are not intended for sale in the United States. It's actually legal, but it can hurt consumers badly."
>
> —BETTY FURNESS,
> the late WNBC Consumer
> Reporter

"Gray Market" Goods

Mary W. of Tulsa, Oklahoma, was upset when jewelers told her that parts for the watch she bought were unavailable because the watch had not been manufactured for distribution in the United States. William S. of Cincinnati, Ohio, was furious because the camera and equipment he purchased by mail did not have warranties. Gerry C. of Durango, Colorado, was perplexed because the owner's manual for the product she bought was printed in French. Although they lived far apart, these consumers had one thing in common—each had unknowingly bought "gray market" goods.

Unlike counterfeit goods, which have phony brand names, "gray market" goods are genuine brand-name products. But the goods are manufactured for sale outside the United States and are imported into the United States through illicit channels—that is, those other than the manufacturer's authorized distributor. The problem of gray market imports first cropped up in 1985, when price discounting came into fashion and their importation became more widespread.

Here's the rub: Because gray market goods are not made to be sold in the U.S., such products may not measure up to the standards that American consumers expect for the same brand-name product. So while the label is genuine, consumers can't immediately tell the quality of the product by the label consumers have come to know.

Consumers can stumble onto gray market goods in a wide range of consumer products—from toothbrushes and toothpaste to photographic equipment, soft drinks, and outboard motors. Cameras, batteries, electrical products, cosmetics, and watches are the most common.

Here is how consumers can be shortchanged by shoddy gray market goods:

Warranties. The product is not covered by the manufacturer's warranty, is not eligible for warranty servicing by authorized repair sources, or is not covered by manufacturer's rebates.

Product differences. The product is not manufactured according to applicable U.S. health and safety standards, lacks qualities American consumers expect from that product, or includes parts or ingredients not found in the domestic version. Examples: Gray market cosmetics may contain additives like red dye #2 that are banned in the U.S.; Johnson & Johnson talc made in Brazil contains talc that is different from the U.S. version; detergents may have been formulated for water with a different mix of minerals than is usually found in the U.S.; or an electrical product may not operate on U.S. current, or may not be set for our radio frequencies.

Ingredient labels. The ingredient or contents labels may provide less information than is required for American products.

Is it ever worthwhile to buy gray market goods? Not if the price is close to what you would pay for a product made specifically for the U.S. market—why take a chance?

But if the price of a gray market product is significantly lower than the product made for the U.S. market, it may be worth the risk of some difference in performance, unless the difference could matter a lot. It's unlikely to be worth gambling on possible quality or performance differences in the following situations:

The product interacts with your body, like food and cosmetics. Here you're taking chances with your health, and that's never a good gamble.

The product has moving parts that may require repairs, or you may need accessories to upgrade it. Everything you save on price could disappear with the first breakdown.

WHAT TO WATCH OUT FOR

Counterfeit Goods Warning Signals

Two surefire early-warning signals usually go together: The price is "too good to be true." (In these cases, it always is.) And the product is sold by street vendors, at kiosks or small hole-in-the-wall-stores, or are not on display. The hallmark of quality products is that they are sold by established merchants from fixed locations. After all, the seller and manufacturer both seek to maintain an image for the product that matches its quality. You simply won't find high-quality products sold through shady locations.

The product lacks labels or hand tags that provide information about the company, the product's qualities, or references to licensing agreements (if it involves a licensed product, such as a fictional character, sports team, or movie). If the product is clothing, it should have sewn-in labels identifying the legitimate manufacturer.

Any sports product that uses a college athlete's name or likeness is automatically a fake—the National Collegiate Athletic Association prohibits the sale of such items.

The packaging is flimsy, the labels are made of inferior grade material, the printing on the package or labels is not sharp and detailed.

Written warranties are absent when you would normally expect them to be included, such as for a watch or a radio.

Gray Market Goods Warning Signals

Unfortunately, gray market goods do not come neatly labeled. New York is one of the few states that requires retailers to alert consumers that they might be buying gray market goods. But even New York's law only requires retailers to post signs telling consumers that some of the products they sell may not be covered by warranties valid in the U.S., may not be accompanied by instructions in English, or may not be eligible for manufacturer rebates. Here are warning signs that should alert you:

■ The product is not sold through a manufacturer's official or authorized representative.

■ The product is priced significantly lower than what you would expect to pay when purchasing from authorized sources.
■ The product labels or printing on the package is entirely in a foreign language.
■ The owner's manual or other written instructions are entirely in a foreign language.
■ No warranty information is given for a product that would usually be covered by such a warranty.

THE $MARTER CONSUMER

You can't do much if you bought counterfeit goods. The manufacturers of the genuine articles might express their regrets, but they won't fix your problem—it is, after all, not their product. If you can find the seller, you could then try to get your money back because the seller engaged in deception or fraud by selling a product that was not, in fact, what it was represented to be. Sadly, this is easier said than done.

If you find out that you purchased gray market goods only after opening the package—such as by finding only foreign language instructions or a product that only runs on current not generated by your electric utility—take the product back to the seller and demand a refund, pronto. Tell the seller that the product is not fit for the usual purpose for which it is intended. In legalese, you can say that the product is "not merchantable" and the seller has "breached the warranty of merchantability" created by the Uniform Commercial Code.

HELP

■ **To report suspected** counterfeit goods, write the Federal Trade Commission, Consumer Response Center, 6th Street and Pennsylvania Avenue NW, Room 240, Washington, DC 20580.

■ **If you buy an item that does not live** up to the Uniform Commercial Code's requirement that it be fit to be used for the purpose for which it was sold, report the incident to the attorney general of your state.

■ **If you buy an item whose lack of a** proper ingredient label leads you to suspect it to be counterfeit or from the gray market, report it to the Food and Drug Administration by calling (800) 532-4440.

CHAPTER 59

CONSUMER PRIVACY

Who's Watching?

The word "privacy" never appears in the U.S. Constitution, yet it is "the most comprehensive of rights and the right most valued by civilized men," as Justice Louis D. Brandeis so aptly put it in his 1928 dissent in *Olmstead* v. *United States*. This is where the "right to be left alone" was first formulated, rooted in the Fourth Amendment protection of "persons, houses, papers and effects against unreasonable searches and seizures" and in various other parts of the Bill of Rights.

In the computer age, it's nearly impossible to mind your own business without giving over all manner of personal information to people who are only too happy to mine your personal business for all it's worth. In the normal course of applying for a mortgage or a credit card, registering for a professional conference, filling out the warranty for a new television, renting an apartment, applying for health or life insurance, or registering to use an Internet Web site, you surrender many of the most private details of your life. You also—largely unwittingly—part with control over who has access to this information.

No wonder public opinion surveys consistently show that most people—74% in a 1997 poll conducted by *Money* magazine—believe they have completely lost control over who sees personal information about them and how the data are circulated and used. They're right. Charles Z. of West Roxbury, Massachusetts, was charged 25% more than the standard rate for disability insurance because of a notation in his medical history that he was an alcoholic. Problem: He wasn't—but he had told an insurance investigator about attending meetings of Alcoholics Anonymous, for help in other areas of his life. Take advantage of the low-cost or free cholesterol testing at the local mall, and you may begin receiving solicitations from local hospitals and clinics for special diet programs.

Credit bureaus, government agencies—federal, state, and local —marketers, and Web sites collect all kinds of information. Investigators for people like landlords, insurance providers, employers, and salespeople cull these public records and data banks to assess your value as a customer, adequacy as an employee, or risk as a loan.

They keep track of information like how much you make, what magazines you read, how many children you have, where you went to school, where you live and work, your medical and psychiatric histories (and one day, perhaps, your genetic profile, including your tendency to inherit certain diseases), how creditworthy or trustworthy you are, whether you've sued or been sued, how much debt you carry, your phone number (even if it's unlisted), which Web sites you visit, and the last time you used a credit card. The list is endless. (For more information on Internet privacy, see page 257.)

Most often, you turned over the information for a legitimate purpose, but it's tempting—and in many cases legal—for data keepers to resell information for secondary purposes. You probably can't completely undo what's already been done to collect this information, but there are several steps you can take now to better protect your privacy. You can review the accuracy of the information that's out there, avoid giving too much more information to people who don't need it, and learn about your legal rights to privacy.

THE BASICS

At least 10 federal laws are supposed to protect individual privacy, but they are riddled with loopholes. Meanwhile, advances in computers, telecommunications, and other technologies have made it relatively simple to pass all kinds of information around. Such advances cut down the time it takes to approve a credit card purchase or process an order from a catalog—

which means you get what you want faster. However, new threats accompany the convenience. The same tools that speed your transactions also efficiently spread information about you. So without realizing it, you may have consented to this free flow of personal information when you signed release forms on credit card applications or health insurance claims.

Your Credit History

Credit reporting agencies, or credit bureaus, keep libraries of credit histories on 170 million individual Americans, anyone who uses credit to buy anything. These files come from public records as well as credit grantors, such as banks and department stores, which periodically update the bureaus. Employers and credit grantors—banks, stores, or finance companies—use the information to evaluate the risks of lending you money or hiring you based on your history of making payments.

The Fair Credit Reporting Act (FCRA) gives individuals the right to see and correct their credit reports and limits the rights of others to look at them. It also requires grantors of credit to explain to loan applicants why their requests were denied. The same goes for banks, landlords, merchants, insurers, and others who take adverse action based on a credit report. The FCRA prohibits credit bureaus from divulging your credit record to just anyone, but it allows them to release it to those with a "legitimate business need." This is a large exception: For a small fee, a *Business Week* magazine reporter once got a copy of then-Vice President Dan Quayle's credit record. One group that is explicitly prohibited from getting your credit report without your permission is employers. A FCRA requirement that went into effect in 1997 requires that employers get an employee's or job applicant's written permission before they can acquire a report.

Furthermore, as we've seen, some of the information in these reports just isn't true, and it can be damaging. *Consumer Reports* once found that 48% of the 161 reports it examined contained errors, and 19% contained errors serious enough to cause the denial of credit, employment, or insurance. A larger survey undertaken by a credit bureau found errors in 43% of its own files.

Mrs. Lawrence of Boston had a typical complaint: She was denied credit because a complete stranger's bad debt appeared on her report. Just a few months earlier, her son's and daughter's credit had been threatened when Mrs. Lawrence and her husband's entire credit history appeared in their children's reports. "Mistakes like these threaten 40 years of hard work, and it has been a terrible ordeal trying to correct them," Mrs. Lawrence told the Massachusetts Public Interest Research Group.

> "**W**ith relative ease and for very little cost, anybody can learn anything about anybody."
>
> —ROBERT ELLIS SMITH, privacy advocate

It's likely that one or more of the three major credit bureaus—Equifax, Experian (formerly TRW), and Trans Union—is tracking you. Periodically checking your records for inaccuracies will enable you to correct any mistakes before they can hurt you when you apply for credit, insurance, or a job. It's especially important to check your credit history before you apply for a mortgage or other major loan. Since each bureau may have a slightly different profile of you, you need to contact all three of the major bureaus. (You'll find their addresses and telephone numbers in the **HELP** section at the end of this chapter.)

In your request, include your name, address, previous addresses for the past five years, Social Security number, your spouse's name (if you're married or divorced), signature, and a daytime telephone number. If you have been denied credit in the last 60 days or are the victim of credit fraud, the report is free, as required by the FCRA. Equifax, Experian, and Trans Union charge $8, payable by check or major credit card, for residents of every state except Connecticut ($5) and Maine ($2). In Colorado, Georgia, Maryland, Massachusetts, New Jersey, and Vermont, consumers can request one free report each year. A copy should arrive within two to three weeks.

Your credit report may look like gobbledygook at first. Each agency uses its own coding system rather than plain English. Use the printed explanations they send with the report to help you decipher it. Essentially, these codes describe the status of your various credit accounts and your history of making or missing payments—what your credit limits are, whether you routinely pay late or scrupulously pay on time, etc. In addition to your credit record, the report will list every organization that has requested your report in the last two years.

If you want to dispute any part of your credit record, write the bureau, explaining the inaccuracy. Under the FCRA, the bureau must reverify the information within 30 days. And under new rules that went into effect in 1997, the three major credit bureaus are required to operate a joint error reinvestigation system to prevent incorrect information from finding its way back into your credit history.

Negative information will remain in your file for seven years, bankruptcy information will stick around for ten. You may attach a written explanation to any negative information in your file that is in dispute. Keep your side of the story to fewer than 100 words and send it to the bureau.

Your Driving Record

You probably haven't a clue about C.L.U.E. Personal Auto, but automobile insurers sure do. And as a consequence, they have plenty of clues about you and your driving record. Equifax Inc. compiled this database, short for Comprehensive Loss Underwriting Exchange, which contains encoded information on claims going back three to five years—the policyholder's name, the driver's name, the vehicle involved, the nature of the claim, the status, and the cost to the insurer, no matter how small or large. These claims histories are among the factors insurers use to help decide whose premiums to raise, whose policies not to renew, and who among new applicants is too big a risk or too costly to insure. C.L.U.E. catalogs eight out of ten personal automobile insurance policyholders in the country—about 134 million drivers covered by liability insurance.

As with the credit bureaus that spawned it and that it resembles, C.L.U.E. offers a valuable service to consumers. It helps insurers to quickly figure out who to take on and who to slough off based on people's driving records and claims histories rather than on artificial and discriminatory factors, such as where people live or their marital status. It also helps insurers to avoid frauds and fibbers, who raise premiums for honest and good drivers.

However, as with other databases, the files are only as useful as they are accurate. Since very few people know about the files, even fewer check their records for accuracy—and it's nearly impossible to measure how straight the stories are. Furthermore, C.L.U.E. files contain *no* facts concerning the circumstances of any claims. "The amount of property damage and whether the

WHAT TO DO IF YOUR IDENTITY HAS BEEN STOLEN

In the last few years, there has been an alarming rise in so-called identity theft—in which someone steals personal financial information—identifying data like an individual's Social Security number, mother's maiden name, credit card and bank account numbers, etc.—and creates a double who uses this good name to do bad things. With fake IDs, an impostor can open credit card accounts, rent a home, and charge expensive items to credit cards without paying for them. The true owner of the name gets the bills, the ruined credit record, and the headache of straightening out the mess. It probably won't end like *Face/Off,* but it's "a nightmarish experience that can devastate lives," says David Medine, associate director of the FTC.

If someone steals your identity, you'll need to take several steps immediately:

1. Report the theft to local police, postal inspectors, and the U.S. Secret Service.

2. By phone and in writing, notify each bank or other institution with whom your name has been used fraudulently. Send each a copy of the police report and any documentation that shows you are a victim of fraud.

3. Call all three credit bureaus' fraud departments to get free copies of your credit reports. Check for fraudulent accounts and have fraud flags and statements added to your credit report asking all potential creditors to check with you before approving credit applications. (Their toll-free numbers are listed in **HELP** at the end of this chapter.)

You may get the runaround—and the distinct impression that you are the guilty one rather than the victim. Identity theft victims told the U.S. Public Interest Research Group, "You are guilty unless you can prove otherwise. The assumption is that it is not fraud, since the thief gave the correct information"; and "Stores where checks were accepted didn't stop harassing me for payment even after I sent them lists of our bad checks, a copy of the police report, and whatever else they requested." Still, the only way to clear your name is to write letters, make follow-up calls, and periodically check your credit report to be sure that it has been restored. Are you sitting down? This process could take months —many months.

person was at fault gives us a hint," said one underwriting supervisor at State Farm Insurance, "but it doesn't give us any facts." One Long Island, New York, woman was denied insurance after she had already canceled her old policy, thinking she'd found a better deal. On the basis of one spurious claim that was cheaper for the insurance company to pay than to fight on her behalf, and two large vandalism claims that she filed when she lived in a dangerous neighborhood she had long since moved away from, she couldn't get auto insurance.

Clearly, it's a good idea to check your C.L.U.E. record *before* you apply for auto insurance. Requests must include your name, address, signature, date of birth, Social Security number, name of your present insurance company, policy number, insurance companies for the last five years, your driver's license number, and the state that granted the license. If adverse action has been taken within the last 60 days, the report is free. For others, it costs $8.

When You Use a Credit Card or Pay With a Check

Many states have passed laws that make it more difficult for merchants to collect personal information when you pay for a purchase with a check or credit card. Some states prohibit a store from recording a credit card number on the back of a personal check. If the merchant insists, you can allow him or her to compare your signature, but no one can demand to write down your credit card number as a condi-

tion of making a sale. Another law prohibits a merchant from requiring excessive amounts of personal information, such as your address and phone number when you use a credit card to buy something. If your state does not have a similar law, remind any stubborn retailers that the major credit card companies actually *prohibit* a vendor from refusing a sale to a person who won't provide his or her address or telephone number.

Telephone Privacy

Many marketers have your phone number—credit card companies, catalog companies, insurance salespeople, banks, etc. They got it because you gave it to them at an earlier time, or they bought it from another database. They can frequently get it even before they answer the phone, when you call their "800" or "900" numbers. Telephone technology, called Automatic Number Identification (ANI), records your number for identification and future marketing purposes as soon as their phone starts ringing. Some organizations use this information immediately to link the number with a computer file describing you and previous purchases you've made. Used this way, this technology can help you order the right size of clothing or the right piece of luggage to match others you've bought in the past. Its efficiency also saves the vendor precious time, which means money. But without your consent, this service forfeits your anonymity and opens you up to aggressive future sales pitches.

Residential customers in many states can get a service similar to ANI to help screen local calls. Known as Caller ID, it enables you to see the phone number from which a caller is calling before you pick up the phone. If you decide not to answer, you can let an answering machine record a message and decide later whether to return it. That way you won't miss important calls from numbers you don't recognize.

GETTING YOUR NAME OUT OF THE JUNK MAIL X-FILES

The Direct Marketing Association (DMA), a trade group representing many of the nation's largest users of mail, telephone calls, and computers to sell things, also offers several services to the public. The DMA Mail and Telephone Preference Services give you the option to have your name removed from the lists used by DMA member companies. This move may thin out your bundle of mail, but it will not unclog your mailbox entirely. Plenty of businesses do not subscribe to the service, and the program is entirely voluntary, allowing a subscriber to participate as conscientiously as it wishes. However, a powerful incentive works in your favor: Because direct marketing costs a lot, it makes sense for a marketer to avoid contacting people it knows will junk unwanted mail.

To take yourself off the lists, send your name and address to the DMA address listed in the **HELP** section at the end of this chapter. Specify whether you would like to be removed from commercial or nonprofit lists or both, and also whether you would like to have your phone number deleted from telemarketing lists.

Under the Telephone Consumer Protection Act of 1991 and Federal Communications Commission rules, telemarketers who solicit you in your home must keep lists of people who do not want to be called again. The law allows you to file suit and collect damages for violations. Also be on the lookout for boxes you can check off on catalog order forms to indicate your wish *not* to have your name sold. And if your wallet is already stuffed with enough credit cards, you can ask financial firms to stop sending you pre-approved credit card offers. The three credit bureaus are required to maintain "opt out" lists, and each offer must explain how to add your name to the list. Toll-free numbers you can call to opt out are in **HELP** at the end of the chapter.

Conversations you have on wireless communications devices such as cellular and cordless phones, or baby monitors and mobile radios are not secure because they are transmitted over radio frequencies. What's more, federal law *permits* eavesdropping on all of the above—except cellular calls. (Not that this ban has stopped many busybodies. Just ask Newt Gingrich.) If you use a baby monitor or a cordless phone, be aware that anyone with a scanner radio can listen in on the goings-on.

Swollen Mailboxes, Clanging Phones

Marketers—credit card companies, catalog houses, diaper services, or the local hardware store—cull mailing and telephone lists from a wide variety of data bankers who eagerly scoop up information from sources as varied as magazine subscription lists, warranty cards, market research surveys, and public records. For example, for the last 50 years New York State has made motor vehicle registrations available to whichever company would pay the highest price. Women who checked into the hospital to give birth to a child probably signed a release form allowing the hospital to sell their names to marketers of infant formula, diaper services, and other baby products. Many nonprofit groups and charitable organizations add significantly to their contributions by selling their lists. Catalog companies routinely sell their lists to other companies; the names of people who have bought a product or service by mail

are especially prized because these people have proven willing to shop through the mail.

Once they get your name, these marketers take to the phone (and mail) to deliver their pitch. You can keep these solicitations to a minimum by asking marketers you do business with or magazines you subscribe to *not* to sell your name to others. You can also minimize the amount of personal information they have on you by giving only that which is essential to do business with them.

Your Medical Records

Although no federal law protects the privacy of your medical records, many states have their own laws. In assessing this patchwork of laws and proposing federal standards, Health and Human Services Secretary Donna Shalala summed up the situation like this: "The way we protect the privacy of medical records right now is erratic at best, dangerous at worst." Video rental records are harder to get.

In recent years, the combination of computerized records and managed care have created a powerful threat to the few protections that existed. Managed care companies now have both the ability and financial incentive to collect, analyze, share, and sell data that reveal some of people's most intimate secrets. Drug makers want to identify potential customers for their products; employers could get information from pharmaceutical-benefits managers on their employees' drug use; medical personnel in many managed care networks have access to full paient records rather than only those they need to review to keep costs in check. In a 1995 study of the privacy practices of 84 Fortune 500 companies by David Linowes, a University of Illinois professor and privacy expert, 35% of employers said they use medical information to help make hiring, promotion, and firing decisions.

In a particularly egregious example, the Southeastern Pennsylvania Transit Authority (SEPTA) paid Rite-Aid Pharmacy to see the drug purchase records of SEPTA employees. It wasn't hard to identify people with HIV/AIDS or other conditions that lead to high drug bills.

The Clinton administration has been pushing to establish minimal federal standards to control the use of medical information:

- Disclosure would be allowed for health care purposes only (with a large exception for law enforcement personnel, who could get records without patient consent or even notification).
- Patients would be able to get copies of their medical records and correct any inaccuracies; and patients would be able to find out who had looked at their records.
- Employers would be prohibited from using medical records for business decisions like hiring, firing, and promotion.
- People who improperly disclose records would be subject to criminal penalties.

Most people sign their insurance company's standard waiver that allows the insurer to obtain access to their health background and anything affecting it. If they don't sign, they don't get insurance.

You might be surprised to know what kinds of details your medical records can include. Along with notes about physical health and medical treatment, these records may include information about family relationships, sexual behavior, substance abuse, and perhaps even the private thoughts and feelings that are expressed in psychotherapy. Most often, this intimate diary is filed under one widely known and used number—your Social Security number.

Some of that information may wind up with the Medical Information Bureau (MIB). Similar to the credit bureaus, MIB acts as a clearinghouse for 650 to 700 of the largest insurance companies in the U.S. and Canada. MIB stores both medical and non-medical information on more than 15 million people that helps insurers ferret out fraud and determine eligibility and premiums for life, health, and disability insurance. About 15% of insurance applications result in a report to the MIB. Once again, mistakes can creep into people's files. For instance, Jim G. of Palo Alto, California, once told a doctor during a routine physical exam that he drank a couple of six-packs of beer *a month,* which somehow wound up in his file as two six-packs *a day.* "Guess what happened when I applied for a disability insurance policy," Jim told *American Health* magazine.

Your medical records are sensitive personal information and are vulnerable to misuse. Do you want a potential employer to know that you are a recovering alcoholic or that you are HIV-positive?

It's a good idea to review a free copy of your file for errors. If you find any, write to MIB explaining the problem. The bureau will go back to the insurance company that supplied the information for verification. But if you and the insurance company disagree, it can be difficult—sometimes impossible—to get a correction. It's possible, however, for you to add a statement to your file disputing or explaining the questionable information.

You also might want to check with your doctor(s) and insurer(s) to see what they have on you in their files and to get them to correct any mistakes you find.

When applying for insurance or filing a claim, try to revise the information release form, which most often is broader than the legal mumbo-jumbo suggests. Try to limit access and dissemination of information and add an expiration date after which information can no longer be collected or released.

Think twice before you give out any information about yourself that isn't absolutely necessary to complete a specific transaction. Do not write your driver's license number or credit card number on your personal check. Do not give your Social Security number unless absolutely necessary. Legally, you only have to give your number for tax or Social Security matters. However, there's nothing stopping a merchant from denying you service if you refuse to give the number.

To guard your name and numbers from equity thieves, opt out of pre-approved credit mailings; review your credit report once a year; and use care when buying over the Internet—either have your correspondence encrypted or call the seller's toll-free instead.

Take a look at your file. Get copies of your credit reports from credit bureaus. Get copies of your medical records from insurance companies, your doctor(s), and the Medical Information Bureau. Check out your driving record on your C.L.U.E. report. If there's any information in any of the files that you dispute, write a brief letter explaining the error for inclusion in your file.

Don't send in warranty cards. Mailing and telephone marketing lists are culled from the cards. Virtually all warranties are valid as long as you have the receipt for the item.

Keep your name off the lists. Ask organizations whose mail you want to receive *not* to sell your name to others. This includes magazines, catalogs, and charities.

Send out your own change of address notes. Information from the U.S. Postal Service change of address form is sold to direct marketers, who use it to update their mailing lists.

H E L P

■ **If you want to** check your credit report, contact all three major credit bureaus to catch any and all errors. It will cost $8 for each report in most states. The report will come with instructions for correcting inaccuracies. Contact:

Equifax National Consumer Center
P.O. Box 105873
Atlanta, GA 30348
(800) 685-1111

Experian (formally TRW)
P.O. Box 2104
Allen, TX 75013-2104
(800) 682-7654

Trans Union Corp.
P.O. Box 390
Springfield, PA 19064-0390
(800) 916-8800

■ **Report credit fraud (identity theft)** immediately to each credit bureau:

Equifax
P.O. Box 740241
Atlanta, GA 30374-0241
(800) 525-6285

Experian
P.O. Box 1017
Allen, TX 75013
(800) 301-7195

Trans Union
P.O. Box 403
Springfield, PA 19064
(800) 680-7289

■ **To have your name removed from** pre-approved credit mailing lists, contact each of the credit bureaus at the following numbers:

Equifax
(800) 556-4711

Experian
(800) 353-0809

Trans Union
(800) 680-7293

■ **If you have a problem** with a credit bureau, report it to your state attorney general or to the Federal Trade Commission, Consumer Response Center, Washington, DC 20580; (202) 326-3761.

■ **The FTC also has a Credit Practices** Hotline offering recorded information about consumer rights: (202) 326-3758. Much of this information is also available on the Web at www.ftc.gov.

■ **To see what's in your C.L.U.E.** auto claims report, call (800) 456-6004.

■ **To have your name removed from** many mailing lists, contact Mail Preference Service, Direct Marketing Association, P.O. Box 9008, Farmingdale, NY 11735-9008.

■ **To have your name removed from** many telemarketing lists, contact Telephone Preference Service, Direct Mail Association, P.O. Box 9014, Farmingdale, NY 11735-9014.

■ **To see your MIB file, contact** Medical Information Bureau, P.O. Box 105 Essex Station, Boston, MA 02112; (617) 426-3660.

■ **You'll find lots of good resources** regarding consumer privacy issues on the Web. Here are a few sites to get you started: Electronic Privacy Information Center, www.epic.org; Privacy Rights Clearinghouse, www.privacyrights.org; Center for Democracy and Technology, www.cdt.org.

CHAPTER 60

ENVIRONMENTAL CLAIMS

Not Always Friends of the Earth

B iodegradable? Compostable? Ozone-friendly? Recyclable? Don't bet on it. The most degrading aspect of some products making these claims is often the claims themselves.

THE BASICS

E ver since Earth Day first energized consumers in 1970 to seek out and buy earth-friendly products, "green marketing" has become big business. The green marketing industry's revenues were reportedly worth $95 million by 1997. And as of 1996, environmental concerns were among the top five factors consumers considered when making a purchase. And 10% to 15% of all new products make some sort of environmental claims.

By the mid-1990s, at least 300 stores across the country exclusively sold green products: earthsafe tile cleansers, earth-friendly cookbooks, bathrobes, and slippers made of organically grown un-bleached cotton, home composters, water-saving toilet flushers and shower heads, and super-efficient fluorescent lightbulbs.

While some of these products actually reduce solid waste, eschew dangerous chemicals, or save energy as they promise, the proliferation of green products has brought with it a cottage industry into misleading environmental advertising—what some consumer advocates call "greenwashing" or "green-collar fraud." Green-collar fraud poisons the well of public trust by making cynics out of consumers who want to be environmentally sensitive but can't distinguish between honest and false environmental claims.

WHAT TO WATCH OUT FOR

T here are commendable exceptions, but too many companies have recognized consumer interest in the environment simply by changing what they say about their products rather than changing the products themselves.

Remember the plastic garbage bags that were supposed to be biodegradable? Turned out that garbage dumps, designed to be dark, don't allow enough sunlight to get to the plastic to degrade it. And even in the few dumps where the bags were exposed to enough light to break down, the wind picked up the scraps of plastic and blew them over the countryside.

How about government-mandated reformulations of aerosol products that contained chlorofluorocarbons (CFCs)? The CFCs—complex chemicals that cause the ozone layer to thin, weakening the natural shield against harmful ultraviolet rays—*are* for the most part gone. Nonetheless, virtually all aerosol cans that boast their ozone-friendliness actually contain harmful, flammable hydrocarbons, which contribute to smog.

The list goes on and on. Procter & Gamble touted disposable diapers as compostable —so that they would transform into "a soil conditioner to enhance plant growth . . . so we can help feed the earth"—when readers of the ad had virtually zero chance of finding a composting program near them, since only 14 facilities existed in the entire country. Orkin Exterminating Company called its lawn pesticides "practically nontoxic." Amoco said you could recycle its packaging materials and polystyrene products. And ARCO Chemical Co. labeled its Sierra Antifreeze "essentially nontoxic," "environmentally safer," and "biodegradable."

The Federal Trade Commission, attorneys general around the country, and local consumer offices like the Department of Consumer Affairs in New York City put a stop to these examples of "greenwashing." But others keep cropping up.

> "**T**o say a product is 'environmentally friendly' is inherently misleading. By virtue of its very existence, a product has had negative environmental ramifications."
>
> –JOHN TREVOR,
> Rhode Island environmental
> advocate and recycling official

Recycled/Recyclable

Cities across the country are closing landfill sites and are scrambling to find ways of reducing the amount of garbage their citizens produce. Recycling is a great way to reduce solid waste. But in the rush to promote their products as recyclable or recycled, many companies stretch the truth. Virtually any material is recyclable under the right conditions and at some cost, but items like the polystyrene (styrofoam) cup are not recycled at anywhere near the level that would render a recyclable claim truthful: in 1992, less than 1% of polystyrene packaging and products were recycled, according to the Environmental Defense Fund.

Be on the lookout also for recycled paper products. Much of "recycled" paper actually contains wood shavings and scraps from paper mills, *not* true recycled paper. This method of "recycling" has been practiced for years by efficient paper mills and does not represent environmental progress. If you want to use a product made from materials that people and businesses have used and discarded, look for a label saying it contains a high percentage of "post-consumer" waste.

Don't assume the familiar "three chasing arrows" denotes that a product has a high percentage of post-consumer waste. Without explanation, the symbol could convey that the item is recyclable or that it is made from recycled material, or both, or it could convey that the item's packaging is made from recycled material. Think about a package of coffee filters. Does the chasing arrows symbol on the package mean the filters are made of recycled material? Are they recyclable? Or is the package they come in recyclable or made from post-consumer waste?

"Clean" Power

After years of local monopolies, consumers have begun to gain more freedom to choose their power supplier. With that freedom comes an inevitable marketing blitz as one power company struggles to distinguish its electricity from the next company's—sort of like AT&T, MCI, and Sprint battling to make you think their long-distance service is the best. And greenness may be one of the few ways to distinguish one power source from another. Companies participating in deregulation pilot programs in the Northeast and Minnesota have already begun offering consumers "clean energy."

Unfortunately, the supply of wind power and other renewable sources of energy is extremely limited, and it's impossible for consumers to trace their power back to its source to test the truthfulness of the claim. One Minnesota power company is simply reselling existing wind-generated power at a higher price—so consumers are getting the same power they would have gotten anyway, but they are paying more for it. It would be helpful if governments required companies to provide a breakdown of the energy source mix on customers' bills and in promotional materials. Meanwhile, forewarned is forearmed.

THE $MARTER CONSUMER

Here are seven things you can do to be a green consumer and help preserve the environment:

Reduce solid waste. If you're an average American, you generate about 1,200 pounds of solid waste each year—about 25% of which gets recycled. That's garbage the size and weight of a small car, and a third of it is packaging you toss out immediately. One easy way to reduce waste is to carry a string shopping bag with you at all times, and ask for recyclable paper bags instead of plastic at the supermarket. If you're buying just one item or there's room in your backpack, say "No bag, please."

Recycle paper. The American paper industry actually started as a recycling industry. The first paper mill, built in 1690 near Philadelphia, manufactured paper from secondhand linen and cotton rags. We now recycle only about 29% of the paper materials we use. Recycling would go a long way toward reducing our apparently insatiable appetite for trees: The average American uses about 700 pounds of paper each year, twice as much as in 1960; in total, we consume over a billion trees per year for paper.

So recycle those newspapers: One run of the Sunday edition of *The New York Times* consumes 40 acres of trees. Making new paper from old paper is also a great way to save energy. Turning old paper into new uses 30% to 55% less energy than making paper from trees—and it reduces air pollution produced by the manufacturing process by 95%.

Recycle aluminum and glass. Green consumers recycle all the aluminum cans and bottles they use—even the ones without deposits. And don't forget to recycle other types of aluminum—foil, pie plates, frozen food trays, window frames, and siding. Also, be sure to recycle any aluminum used in packaging: 40% of all aluminum used in the U.S. is used for packaging.

Recycling these materials reduces solid waste *and* saves energy.

The process of manufacturing aluminum from bauxite consumes so much energy that molten aluminum is "affectionately" known as liquid electricity. Making an aluminum can from recycled aluminum uses 90% less energy than making aluminum from scratch, and the energy saved will operate a television set for three hours.

Making new glass from recycled glass uses 32% less energy than starting from scratch, reduces air pollution created in the process by 20%, and cuts water pollution by 50%. The energy saved by recycling one glass bottle will light a 100-watt light bulb for four hours. And since glass doesn't crush that easily in a garbage dump, bottles tend to take up a lot of landfill space. So recycle every glass bottle you've got —clear, green, or even colored wine bottles. Some cities such as New York City actually crush colored glass, mix it with asphalt, and pave the streets with it. The result is that the streets sparkle with the new, brightly reflective surface, and the city preserves precious landfill space.

Convert to a green economy. The word "economy" originates in an ancient Greek word that means "the arrangement of a household." You can only hope political leaders will implement green policies in the national economy—and you can encourage those policies by lobbying and voting. Here are some things you can do to convert your own household to a green economy:

■ *Avoid household toxics.* You don't have to clean your oven with harsh

REDUCE, REUSE, RECYCLE

Instead of this	Use this
1,000 paper towels	One cloth kitchen towel Crumpled newspapers
1,000 paper coffee filters	One gold-plated filter
1,000 polystyrene coffee cups	One ceramic mug
14 incandescent lightbulbs	One compact fluorescent bulb
Toxic household cleaners	Vinegar, baking soda
Drink boxes	Thermos
Disposable diapers	Reusable cloth diapers

Comparisons based on expected useful life.

oven cleaner (usually containing lye); baking soda works fine. Use cedar chips instead of paradichlorobenzene, better known as mothballs, to winter-proof closets and drawers.

■ *Use unbleached paper coffee filters.* If you use coffee filters for your morning brew, be aware that the process of bleaching paper creates dioxin, a deadly toxic by-product, which often gets dumped into American waterways. You could also consider switching to a gold-plated coffee filter that doesn't require paper inserts at all. Depending on how much you like coffee, you could avoid using hundreds (if not thousands) of coffee filters over the life of the coffee maker.

■ *Use reusable containers* to save leftovers, rather than plastic wrap, which you'll just throw out afterward. If you must wrap a sandwich, use waxed paper instead of foil or plastic; it biodegrades.

■ *Use cloth kitchen towels* to dry hands and dishes instead of paper towels. They do the job better— and they won't wind up in the trash. You'll eventually save money by buying fewer paper goods.

■ *Here's a thrifty recycling tip:* Crumpled-up newspapers actually work a lot better at cleaning windows than paper towels, which can streak or leave little fibers. Spray your glass windows with a liquid glass cleaner, and wipe clean with yesterday's sports section.

Avoid using pesticides and insecticides on your lawn. Eventually, they will wind up in the water supply—yours, your neighbors', or both. Often, many lawn problems can be solved just by allowing your lawn to grow a little taller. It's not natural for a lawn to be as short as a putting green. Let it grow two or three inches; it'll be healthier and more resistant to fungus and insects. And if you leave the grass clippings after you mow, they help your lawn retain water naturally.

Keep a ceramic mug on your desk at work. Use less Styrofoam—it's completely nondegradable. Even 500 years from now, that Styrofoam cup will still be a Styrofoam cup.

Let your voice be heard. You're not limited to voting once every four years. You can cast a vote for the environment when you write a letter, make a phone call, or send a fax or an e-mail communiqué. Urge legislators to pass stronger bottle bills. Urge your favorite fast food restaurants to reduce their use of packaging.

A massive letter-writing campaign convinced recording companies to abandon bulky cardboard CD packaging for less-wasteful shrink-wrap packaging. Never underestimate the power of the pen. And don't forget to send congratulatory letters, too. For example, if your neighborhood McDonald's is making an effort to reduce the packaging it gives to customers, let it know you notice.

Either way, keep in mind the corporate executive's rule of thumb: Every letter a company receives represents the views of 100 customers. So don't be shy, write to the CEO or President, and rest assured, your letter will get attention.

HELP

■ **For green kitchen** products by mail, contact Seventh Generation, 10 Farrell Street, South Burlington, VT 05403; (800) 456-1177.

■ **For information on recycling** contact: The Environmental Defense Fund, (800) CALL-EDF, www.edf.org.

EPA Nationwide Recycling Hotline, 800-cleanup, www.1800cleanup.org.

The Aluminum Association, 900 19th Street NW, Washington, DC 20006; (202) 862-5100.

Glass Packaging Institute, 1627 K Street NW, #800 Washington, DC 20006; (202) 887-4850.

Paper Recycling Committee, American Forest and Paper Association, 1111 19th Street NW, #800, Washington, DC 20036; (800) 878-8878, http:/www.afsandph.org.

American Plastics Council, 1801 K Street, #701-L Washington, DC 20006, (800) 243-5790.

■ **Report questionable environmental** claims to your attorney general or the Federal Trade Commission, Consumer Response Center, 6th Street and Pennsylvania Avenue NW, Washington, DC 20580, www.ftc.gov. Addresses and phone numbers for the nation's attorneys general are in the appendix at the end of this book.

Bias in the Marketplace

WOMEN

Gypped by Gender

The incomes of women relative to those of men have crept up a bit since 1979, when a woman made 63 cents to a man's $1. Now women earn 75 cents to men's $1. That's progress in the *workplace,* however slow. But adding injury to injury, study after study has shown that American women in the *marketplace* pay more than men for many goods and services. Women, simply because of their gender, suffer the double financial blow of making less and paying more.

THE BASICS

The evidence of this gender gap is all around us. A New Jersey woman, for example, once wrote:

"Why is it that certain hair salons charge more to cut women's hair than men's? A friend of mine once asked a stylist why they insist on pursuing this practice, and he replied that it was because most men have shorter hair than most women.

"This, of course, is untrue; Manhattan is home to thousands of men with shoulder-length hair or longer, just as it is home to many women with short hair. These long-haired men require just as much shampoo, conditioner, and attention as their female counterparts."

One Phoenix woman who runs a van shuttle service opened a garage that caters to women because she was so fed up with male mechanics ripping her off. And legal challenges in Boston, Los Angeles, New York, San Francisco, and Washington, DC, have shown that women have been losing their shirts because of dry cleaners' discriminatory price policies.

These sometimes-minor, day-to-day injustices don't "harm" women as obviously as workplace harassment, job bias, or discriminatory lending practices, but these overcharges add up to additional per-capita expenditures of hundreds of dollars a year. They create a commercial environment that simultaneously woos women with smooth sales pitches and targeted advertising but then discriminates against them in practice. Say we were talking about a car wash: Would anyone be able to get away with charging women more than men for a car wash? So why tolerate gender-based pricing for dry cleaning, haircuts, auto sales, clothing or other products?

WHAT TO WATCH OUT FOR

A mixture of outdated stereotypes, unscrupulous salespeople, "traditional" policies, and a lack of information conspires to require women to bargain harder to get the same deal a man would get more easily or to pay extra for identical service. This bias lurks beneath the rules of the supposedly impartial marketplace. So *caveat emptor*—let the buyer beware—applies especially if you're female.

Unfortunately, women face a lack of information about the prices paid by other consumers. If women car buyers, for example, have no way of knowing what prices men negotiate, they may not realize they are overpaying.

Similarly, service providers in many cities are not required to post their prices, making it nearly impossible for women to know that they pay more than men for identical service.

Don't Get Taken for a Ride

Car manufacturers and dealers have belatedly woken up to an economic truth: women not only drive cars, they buy them, too. Women buy and are the principal drivers of almost half the cars sold every year, and they participate in at least four out of every five new-car purchases. In an effort to appeal to this crucial consumer segment, the automobile industry developed special ad campaigns, offered training programs for the largely male staff of dealerships, and even used fewer shapely blondes in ads and annual automobile show promotions.

Still, women have good reason to dread car buying. Stereotypes persist: Dealers frequently assume women are pushovers and reward men, not for their superior knowledge or bargaining skills, but simply for being men. In a study conducted in Chicago, men were usually offered better deals on new cars than women, even at the outset before haggling began. And the women's disadvantage did not disappear as the negotiation continued. In the end, the prices for women included an extra 52% profit for the dealer, as compared to the price offered to white men for identical cars. Male and female "testers" used an identical bargaining strategy, designed to alleviate any advantage a superior bargainer would have.

A similar study of used-car dealers in New York came to the same conclusion. Undercover female car shoppers were quoted higher prices for used cars 42% of the time. When women were quoted higher prices, they were quoted an average of $396 more than men for the identical vehicle. In the 22% of cases when men were quoted higher prices, their additional charge averaged only $183. In one case, a female "buyer" was offered the same car as the male "buyer" but at a price nearly 11% higher.

While the evidence is indisputable, the motive is not. Car dealers and other vendors who use bargaining to set prices argue that they don't explicitly discriminate

UNEQUAL TREATMENT

Awoman posing as a prospective car buyer was sent by ABC's *PrimeTime Live* to test for discrimination; she was quoted a price $500 higher than a man was for the same Geo Tracker at a Cincinnati car dealership with the slogan, "Where salespeople treat gals as well as guys."

on the basis of sex—the seller's goal is to get the highest price possible and the buyer's goal is to pay as little as possible, no matter what the gender of either party is.

Don't Get Fleeced

Long or short hair, straight or curly, elaborately styled or simply cut, women usually pay more than men for haircuts according to surveys in Boston, New York City, and California. In California, for instance, the State Assembly Office of Research estimated in 1994 that 40% of haircutters charged more for basic women's cuts than for men's. In a more extensive survey, two out of three New York City haircutters charged women more than men for a basic shampoo, cut, and blow dry. And more recent studies confirm that nothing has changed. Undaunted by media exposure and anti-bias laws, haircutters in New York City were found to be charging women 20% more than men for a shampoo, ½-inch

cut, and blow dry. In a typical case, a young man paid just under $20 for the same service that cost a young woman $31.

The practice is so prevalent and widely accepted that haircutters routinely splash their disparate prices in huge type across their shop windows. Millions of men and women walk past these displays daily never even thinking to question the price difference—or to question their own haircutter the next time they need a trim.

But, as the letter quoted earlier points out, the boundary between men's and women's hairstyles is fuzzier than ever today. Think about Kenny G, the pop music star. Leave aside perms, coloring, or other special styling, and focus on the most basic service. It's hard to see much difference between putting a few layers in Bob Kostas's hair and blowing it dry and doing the same for Katie Couric. Or how trimming a guy's tresses so they can be pulled back into the perfect ponytail is any different from doing the same for a woman. Is the woman getting several dollars' worth of extra time? More mousse? Is her blow dry consuming extra electricity? Or is she just getting clipped?

Most haircutters dismiss challenges to the dual price structure with flimsy excuses they can't back up: "Women are fussier," they say; or "women take longer"; or "women want a consultation before their cut." If these explanations were true, haircutters ought to happily give rebates to women with short hair and no need of a consultation. Or they'd collect a surcharge from men with complicated hairstyles. But they don't.

"How much time a client takes depends on how much hair they have," says the owner of a pricey Manhattan salon. "And I'm not referring only to length. A man's cut is just as much work as a woman's." A Boston haircutter gave a similar explanation to the *Boston Globe*: "We schedule just as much time for a man as for a woman. . . . Most men's cuts are short, but there are just as many details to attend to as a woman's. There's the back of the neck, the sideburns, etc."

The price gap seems to be a vestige of the days when men paid a barber a quarter for a cut and shave and women paid a few dollars to have their hair "done." Those days are long gone, but the discrimination often isn't.

Don't Get Taken to the Cleaners

Laundries in New York City charge women an average of 27% more than men to launder and press a basic white cotton shirt. For suits, women pay 5% more to have a lightweight dark wool suit dry-cleaned than men. Surveys in Boston, Washington, DC, San Francisco, and the state of California have shown similar price disparities. In a 1994 survey of 25 dry cleaners, the California State Assembly Office of Research found that 64% charged more to launder women's cotton shirts than men's, and 28% charged more to dry-clean women's suits.

A few cents here or there may not seem like much, but discrimi-

natory cleaning and laundering prices cost American women millions of dollars a year. New York City women alone pay between $1 million and $2 million extra every year. For example, the annual bill for a man who has three suits and ten shirts laundered monthly at one of the most biased shops in Manhattan would add up to only half what a woman with the same cleaning needs would pay: $828 vs. $432.

Cleaners say it's a pressing problem. Because of such fancy details as ruffles, pleats, tucks, fabrics, and linings, women's clothing requires some hand ironing that men's clothing does not. Even a plain white, man-style woman's cotton shirt is more bother because, cleaners say, the pressing machines used by most cleaners and launderers were designed for men's shirts. But in fact, most women's shirts fit on the pressing machines, and some very large or small men's shirts do not. One Washington, DC, dry cleaner who has charged men and women the same for years says that skirts, even if lined, are easier to dry-clean than pants. He told Frances Cerra Whittelsey, author of the book *Women Pay More*, "I don't see any justification for charging more for women's suits than men's."

The deciding factor should be the characteristics of the shirt, not the gender of the character who brings it in, as was the case with Barbara Sobel of San Francisco. Her regular dry cleaner charges $2.50 to launder and press her button-down shirts when she brings them in. But when her boyfriend once brought the exact same shirts in for her, the same cleaner charged him *half* that price.

Don't Get Hemmed In

Although many in-house tailors at department stores and boutiques have changed their policies, word does not seem to have filtered down to the salespeople that women qualify for the same alteration policy as men. In a 1996 survey of New York City department stores, sales clerks quoted women alteration prices 50% to 190% higher than for men. Store management, however, insists that they have adopted gender-neutral pricing even though women's clothes are put together in ways that make them harder to alter and that female consumers would not actually have been charged differently from men. But this doesn't do women much good—once a salesperson quotes a ridiculous price for alterations, it's natural for a woman to skip buying the item or to buy it and take it to an outside tailor.

Moral: don't rely on salespeople for alteration information; ask to speak to the alterations department directly. And if women are quoted higher prices than men, they should complain to the higher-ups.

Product Parity, Price Disparity

The gender tax is levied on brand-name products, too. You'd think that a pair of jeans was a pair of jeans, or that shaving cream was shaving cream. But re-search by Shop! Information Services (SIS), an advertising-free consumer magazine on the Internet, turned up virtually identical garments, made by the same manufacturer, costing 10% to 20% more when made for her rather than him. Barbasol Shave Cream for Women costs an incredible 342% more than the men's version. That makes Skintimate Shaving Gel, her version of his Edge—both manufactured by S.C. Johnson and containing the same top four ingredients—look like a bargain at only 15% more than Edge per ounce. And women get something, however lame, for this premium: a plastic cover that fits over the bottom of the can to guard against rust stains on the tub. Shop carefully and you can avoid paying this tax: Gillette, for instance, charges the same whether you buy men's or women's shaving gel.

Divorce Lawyers Deplete the Marital Pot

Women are often denied a fighting chance for their rightful share of marital assets. The American adversarial legal system and equitable distribution laws in effect in many states (that result in lengthy investigations or litigation to evaluate marital assets) encourage enormous legal fees and financial exploitation of women when marriages are dissolved. Too often, divorce lawyers care more about fees than clients; consequently, the matrimonial legal system either impoverishes women or prices them out of fair divorce settlements. A 1992 investigation of New York's divorce process by the NYC Department of Consumer Affairs (and a flood of responses to it since) identified the following trouble spots:

- Nonrefundable legal retainers;
- Overcharges and underperformance;
- Excessive litigation, delaying tactics, and motion churning;
- Perjury regarding assets valuation;
- Faustian bargains on the eve of a trial, when the client has no choice but to sign a promissory note; and
- "Retaining liens," which essentially hold a client and her file hostage, even after the lawyer has been dismissed.

In response, the state's highest judge appointed a panel to examine the conduct of lawyers in matrimonial actions and eventually enacted a sweeping set of reforms that should protect women from losing their homes when their marriages end. (The chapter on "Lawyers," page 567, offers a more detailed discussion of this problem—and how to guard against it.)

Don't Get Denied Credit

Women, especially widows or divorcées, often have a difficult time getting credit because they don't have a "visible" credit history. Even though most have made responsible credit transactions, their husband's name, not theirs, is the one on file with the credit reporting agencies that often serve as unworthy gatekeepers of credit.

To avoid becoming invisible in the financial world, married women should make a point of building their own financial history and credit ratings. Most credit card companies don't charge extra to put two names on an account. Even better, you can put some of the household bills—telephone, gas, electric, water, etc.—in your name. Be responsible and pay on time to build your own solid and independent financial history.

Savings Gender Gap

Since most women earn less than most men and are more likely to work part-time, they contribute less to pensions and Social Security. This, combined with the fact that women tend to outlive men, increases women's need to save for their retirement.

Odds are that women will live seven years longer than men (to 79 as opposed to 72) and need an additional seven years of retirement money. But it turns out single women are much worse off than married people or single men when it comes to retirement planning, according to Arthur D. Little financial consultants. And since social scientists predict that perhaps half of the marriages made since 1983 will end in divorce anyway, marriage does not necessarily provide cover.

Women must address this issue intelligently. Beware two pitfalls:

- Don't be overly cautious. A 1996 study by the U.S. General Accounting Office found that "women tend to invest their pension funds in safer and lower-yield assets than men."

Since stocks have historically outperformed bonds, this means women's nest eggs don't grow as fast.

■ In your enthusiasm to catch up on savings, don't entrust your savings to fast-talking investment advisors who are more concerned about their own bottom-line performance than yours. Special seminars designed to help women learn about investing may be helpful, but don't buy anything without doing your own *independent* research. The sponsors of these seminars tend to favor their own products, which may not be the best for you.

Good places to look for information are the chapters in this book on mutual funds and retirement investing. You may also want to contact the National Center for Women and Retirement Research and the Mutual Fund Education Alliance, which sells a women's investment kit. Their numbers are in the **HELP** section at the end of this chapter.

THE $MARTER CONSUMER

Civil rights laws enacted by the U.S. in the 1960s outlaw discrimination on the basis of race and gender in employment and housing. However, federal civil rights laws governing the sale of goods and services don't specifically protect women. State and local human rights laws, where they have been enacted, fill in the gap.

But even in places like New York, California, and Boston, where laws prohibit *de jure* gender-based bias, price disparities persist. Since every customer strikes her or his own deal, the nature of the car-buying process makes it difficult to document discrimination; although many haircutters post disparate prices on signs and in windows for all to see, the status has been quo for so long that it barely registers as bias, even to its victims.

Educating yourself and speaking up for yourself are your best defenses against discrimination.

Buy on the merits of the deal, not the gender of the seller. A woman won't necessarily be any more sympathetic than a man, and she could be just as greedy as the next guy.

Don't go to a car dealer until you've done your homework, and don't be bashful about making it clear you know what you're talking about. (Read the chapters on buying new and used cars, pages 309 and 321, to get started.)

Understand before you sign. Don't sign any contracts to buy a car, retain a lawyer, or engage a home improvement contractor unless and until you have added clauses to protect yourself and understand every word. If you have any doubts, have someone you trust give it a second read.

Get an estimate before you authorize repair work on your car or home. And never sign a blank work order.

Don't be afraid to speak up. If you aren't happy with the price or the service being provided—whether it's a haircut, a routine transmission replacement, or a major legal matter like a divorce—you have an absolute right to complain. The provider will often drop the price or work a little faster to assure your repeat business or good reference, and to avoid having irate customers complaining to legal authorities or the media. If you can't settle the disagreement satisfactorily, go over the provider's head to the manager or to local and state consumer authorities, if you have to.

As for haircuts, dry cleaning, and tailoring, demand that you pay the same price a man would for the same service. If the establishment refuses, take your business elsewhere. You can also file a complaint with your state attorney general; and you could also file a lawsuit.

Do your research. And don't invest your money in anything you haven't thoroughly checked out. But at the same time, try not to be overly cautious. Taking greater risks can yield greater financial rewards.

HELP

■ **Check out the** Shop! Information Services Web page at www.sis.org. You'll find contributions from Frances Cerra Whittelsey, author of *Women Pay More*, and all kinds of useful information targeted to women.

■ **To get started on a retirement savings** plan, the National Center for Women and Retirement Research can be reached at (800) 426-7386. And a women's investment kit costs $21.50 from the Mutual Fund Education Alliance, (816) 354-9422.

■ **If you think you've** been turned down for a loan on the basis of your sex, complain to your state's banking department.

■ **If you think you've been treated** unfairly simply because of your sex, report it to your attorney general's or other appropriate office. Consumer and attorneys general office addresses and phone numbers are in the appendix at the end of this book.

CHAPTER 62

SELLING MINORITIES SHORT IN THE MARKETPLACE

The Money of Color

In the movie *Boomerang*, in an example of art imitating life, Eddie Murphy received a chilly reception at a Fifth Avenue boutique—"We don't do layaway," says a salesman to Murphy and a group of young black executives as they walk into the store.

There's not much economic literature on the subject, but a bias operating throughout the marketplace injures consumers of color in their everyday commercial interactions. Just to shop for groceries, buy a compact disc, or get a haircut, people of color often encounter discriminatory prices, racial stereotypes, considerable inconvenience, and none-too-subtle surveillance. Take an instance in which the Manhattan restaurant check for a group of African-American diners included a 15% gratuity when the check for a white patron at the next table didn't, or the discovery by a

female black lawyer shopping around for a haircut that several salons in Fairfax County, Virginia, charge African-Americans more than whites for a basic haircut.

When it comes to larger transactions like finding a home or buying a car, injustice is heaped upon insult because of blatant bigotry or de facto redlining (in which companies draw a "red line" around certain areas and refuse to sell to people who live in those areas solely because of where they reside rather than how safely they drive or how big a down payment they've put aside to buy a house).

For example, a 35-year-old male who lives in a comfortable New York City suburb pays $624 for mandated automobile insurance coverage, but a similar driver who lives in a poor, minority Brooklyn neighborhood pays $777, or 25% more. When producers for the tele-

INVISIBLE PEOPLE

When corporate advertisers were surveyed in 1992, seven national firms—Calvin Klein, Perry Ellis, Gucci, Estée Lauder, Lancome, Giorgio Armani, and NordicTrack—had zero minorities in over 800 ads.

vision show *Prime Time Live* sent "testers" to look for apartments in St. Louis, the white man was given keys to an apartment to look at and was encouraged to apply; when the black man came to look, he was told the only available apartment had been rented earlier in the day.

Then there are the tens of thousands of elderly black women, living alone in the inner city, who are subjected to repeat visits from home-improvement and furniture salesmen who trick them into buying expensive services or products at "low monthly rates."

Pura C. in Washington Heights, New York, for example, twice refused an offer in 1996 of $14-a-month payments for an elegant living room set but finally relented to the persistent pitch of the Credit Express Furniture salespeople. Big mistake. The furniture was flimsy junk, the cost was $60 a month, and bill collectors began harassing her.

Over in Oakland, California, widow Mattie A. in 1997 lost ownership of the house she had lived in for 35 years to foreclosure when she couldn't pay off or refinance a $162,000 balloon payment that came due 12 months after she signed a high-interest second mortgage to pay for home construction work. She sued First Capital Finance because, according to the *San Francisco Examiner,* the firm "targeted plaintiffs for an unfair loan with excessive fees, a high interest rate, and a balloon payment because of their race."

THE BASICS

It was just this kind of day-to-day consumer abuse of African-Americans that President Johnson's National Advisory Commission on Civil Disorders (commonly referred to as the Kerner Commission) cited back in 1968 as a significant contributing cause of riots in places like Watts, Newark, and Detroit in 1967. The applicable section of the commission's report could just as easily describe South-Central Los Angeles and, indeed, parts of most American cities today:

"Grievances concerning unfair commercial practices affecting Negro consumers were found in approximately half of the cities. . . . Beliefs were expressed that Negroes are sold inferior-quality goods (particularly meats and produce) at higher prices and are subjected to excessive interest rates and fraudulent commercial practices."

The cost of such explicit or subtle marketplace bias is that those who have the least income too often pay the most; even those who have money but are not white have a hard time buying the things they want or need. These irritating, frustrating, and humiliating marketplace practices compound the more well-known effects of poverty, educational inequity, and job discrimination.

This racial reality contradicts the popular assumption that capitalism is a judgment-free system that rewards merit and rejects private prejudices. Praising the market's "invisible hand," conservative business leaders attack government intervention in the economy as unnecessary and counterproductive, while they engage in private-sector prejudices that disadvantage nonwhite consumers.

For example, although people of color make up a sizable minority of magazine readers, they are practically invisible in magazine advertising. (The few minority figures to appear in magazine ads are either superstars, such as Michael Jordan, or children or people cast in stereotypical roles of athlete, musician, menial worker, or object of charity.)

This visual belittling and virtual invisibility reinforces the small and large racial prejudices already operating throughout society and the marketplace. Not seeing minorities in ads as consumers of clothes, cars, and computers contributes to the perception that they are an undifferentiated mass of bad credit risks and check-bouncers, with limited disposable income.

In fact, a third of America's blacks are middle-class and live in the suburbs, and over the last 20 years the aggregate annual income of African-Americans has grown sixfold, to almost $270 billion. The black, Latino, and Asian communities spend over $500 billion a year on goods and services. Rather than cater to this market, however, advertisers and ad agencies bombard minorities with specially targeted ads for harmful products like cigarettes and malt liquor.

WHAT TO WATCH OUT FOR

Many businesspeople have answered that the only color they care about is green—as in dollars. But the market cannot operate efficiently or freely if the immutable fact of skin color determines the outcome of everyday negotiations and situations.

People of color often face discrimination in the following six areas: grocery shopping, buying cars and car insurance, banking, finding and financing housing, making home improvements, and shopping for clothing and other durable goods.

Shopping for Groceries

Because there are no supermarkets in her south-central Los Angeles neighborhood, a 69-year-old retired hospital worker walks 15 minutes to catch a bus to get to the nearest supermarket. She buys small bags of flour or sugar, even though bigger packages give better value, because she can't manage heavy grocery bags on the overcrowded bus trip home.

This anecdote illustrates the situation that residents of America's poor neighborhoods find themselves in day after day; they have so few choices about where to buy food that, as a result, they pay more and get less. The NYC Department of Consumer Affairs (DCA) found that while the most affluent areas in Manhattan had one supermarket for every 6,500 people, the most destitute neighborhoods of Brooklyn—populated mostly by people of color—had one supermarket for every 17,000 people.

Because residents of lower-income neighborhoods are forced to shop in small convenience stores with higher prices and limited selection, DCA calculated that residents of poor New York City neighborhoods pay an average of 8% more than people living in middle-class communities for a shopping cart loaded with the same grocery staples. That's an extra $350 a year for a family of four. One A&P in Harlem charged 13% more overall than an A&P in middle-class Queens. For example, in Queens, one pound of Oscar Mayer bacon cost $2.49; in Harlem it cost $3.29; in Queens, 13 ounces of Maxwell House coffee cost $2.69; the same can cost $3.59 in Harlem.

> "*Ideals about equality and inferiority and superiority are not simply figments in people's minds. Such sentiments have an impact on how institutions operate, and opinions tend to be self-fulfilling.*"
>
> —ANDREW HACKER,
> in *Two Nations: Black and White, Separate, Hostile, Unequal*

Buying a Car and Auto Insurance

A study of scores of car dealerships in Chicago found that neatly dressed, articulate black testers were routinely quoted higher prices on new cars than neatly dressed, articulate whites, despite the fact that both customers used identical, rehearsed negotiating strategies to price a car of the same make and model with the same options. Based on over 550 visits to Chicago area car dealers by testers posing as middle-class car buyers, the study, published in the *Harvard Law Review*, found that black men were quoted prices that included more than double the markup offered white men, and black women were quoted an average price with a markup three times higher than that offered white men. So blacks pay as much as $150 million a year more for cars than whites.

Even after buying a car, minorities face an "insurance ghetto." In spite of a New York State law prohibiting *de jure* redlining, in 1992 DCA found de facto redlining by car insurers. Simply by keeping company sales offices and agents out of low-income areas, car insurers force drivers who live in these neighborhoods to buy insurance from independent brokers who only sell the exorbitantly priced "auto insurance plan," which was designed to insure people with bad driving records. This practice penalizes good drivers with clean records who happen to live in what the insurance industry considers "high-risk" *communities* and perverts the intent of the auto plan, which was designed to insure "high-risk" *drivers*.

As a result, many minority customers pay extra for state-required auto insurance based on their residence rather than their record. Aetna, for example, had one agent for every 22,000 registered vehicles in Queens and one for every 26,000 in Brooklyn; yet across the border, in suburban Nassau County on Long Island, Aetna had one agent for every 8,000 cars. Insurance that costs $669 a year in Brooklyn costs only $213 in Ithaca, New York. When New York City officials called insurance agents for an explanation, one with Allstate said, "Would you want to put *your* office in one of those neighborhoods?"

This problem is not peculiar to New York. The California Insurance Department has also found that car insurance is more expensive and more difficult to obtain in minority, low-income, and inner-city communities than in other communities in California. (See "Automobile Insurance," page 349, for tips on getting the best deal.)

Basic Banking Services

In 1992, 13 banks served the more than 250,000 residents of South-Central Los Angeles; in neighboring Melrose, which is 90% white, 15 banks served a community of 25,000.

The story is similar in minority and low-income communities across the country. The consolidation of the banking industry has left large, populous areas with few banks and extremely limited competition. In the Anacostia neighborhood of Washington, DC, for instance, only two banks serve the 69,000 mostly black and mostly poor residents, a resident-to-bank ratio six times worse than the national average of 5,000 residents per branch.

Even if people try opening a bank account at a branch in another neighborhood, they may well be thwarted by the "ten-block" rule. A study of major New York City banks by two state legislators found that most required applicants for checking accounts to live or work near the branch—most often within ten blocks. In effect, this rule deprives many minorities of one of the key tools for participation in the consumer economy—a checking account and an ongoing relationship with a bank that could be useful later for getting a loan.

All too often, no local bank means no savings accounts, no check-cashing, and no loans for individuals and businesses located in the area. When Bank of America closed a branch in the Vernon-Central neighborhood of South-Central Los Angeles in 1988, it shut down the last bank within a three-mile radius. The customers, who had $31 million on deposit, had little choice but to use pawnshops and

THE COLOR OF CREDIT

Income	Mortgage approval rates*	
	Whites	Blacks
LOW TO MODERATE (50–79% MFI**)	65%	47%
LOWER MIDDLE (80% TO 99% MFI)	74%	54%
UPPER MIDDLE (100% TO 119% MFI)	79%	59%
HIGH (MORE THAN 120% MFI)	84%	68%
ALL INCOME GROUPS	68%	40%

*Conventional mortgages approved in 1997; from U.S. Federal Reserve data.
**MFI = Median family income (of the area in which property is located).

corner check-cashing outlets—which do not provide checking, savings, or lending services—for high-priced, bare-bones service.

Both pawnshops and check-cashing services have flourished since banks started fleeing the inner cities in the 1980s. Check-cashing businesses now outnumber banks seven to one in neighborhoods like South-Central L.A., but at an enormous cost to consumers. Checks worth some $45 billion annually were cashed at check-cashing outlets in 1990, for fees ranging from 3% to 20% of the check's value.

If you think the interest rate on your credit card is high, you haven't had to hock your watch lately. Pawn shop customers pay annual interest rates of 36% to 240% for short-term loans they can't get anywhere else. Here's how pawnbrokers rake in such astounding returns: You find yourself short of money for diapers and formula for your infant;

the pawnbroker spots you $10 in return for your watch; 12 weeks later you exchange $14 for the watch; voilà, you've paid 40% interest to borrow $10 for less than three months.

The number of pawnshops in the country has grown more than 60% since 1990, and outstanding loans have tripled to about $2 billion.

Finding and Financing a House

An annual Federal Reserve survey of 1991 home-mortgage data found that African-Americans were roughly twice as likely as whites to have their mortgage applications rejected. A *Washington Post* investigation of 130,000 deeds of sale also showed that Washington-area banks and savings and loans extend mortgages in white neighborhoods at twice the rate they do in comparable black neighborhoods. What's more, a separate study by the Federal Reserve Bank of Boston found that even after adjusting for differences in credit history, debt-to-income ratios, and many of the other considerations that determine mortgage qualification, black mortgage applicants were 60% more likely to be rejected than similarly situated whites.

The disparity might be explained by income differences among groups, but the Federal Reserve's survey data showed that 21% of *high-income* blacks were turned down, compared with only 14% of *lower-income* whites. The Federal Reserve analysis also showed that as the percentage of minorities living in a community increased, the number of loan denials also increased, regardless of income levels.

"Everyone here has stories of being rejected [by local bankers]. After a while, you just give up trying to deal with them," said Neil G. to *The Washington Post* about Kettering, Virginia, a high-income, predominantly black suburban community. "In my whole block, I don't know anyone who has gotten their mortgage from a regular bank."

Making Home Improvements

Unscrupulous home improvement contractors and finance companies prey on lower-income, largely minority homeowners and trick them into taking high-interest second mortgages for shoddy and incomplete home repairs. An extensive DCA investigation of "equity theft" by contractors found that salesmen acting, in effect, as agents for finance companies and banks, go door-to-door in areas of New York City where they know that homeowners can't afford repairs without financing and can't get reasonably priced financing directly from banks. As a result, many millions of dollars in equity have been transferred from the homes of poor and minority families to the ledgers of banks via 20% mortgages or actual foreclosures.

Ironically, the banks that end up with the high-interest mortgages are many of the very same banks that wouldn't lend money to the homeowner in the first place. This has created a dual home-improvement-lending system—one for whites in middle-class neighborhoods and another for people in lower-income and/or minority neighborhoods. For instance, at the same time Citibank was charging 10% to 11% for mortgages it originated in middle-class neighborhoods, it was purchasing 16% mortgages from finance companies doing business in poor or predominantly minority neighborhoods. (See the next chapter, "Seniors as Consumers," page 677, for more details on this scam and how to avoid it.)

Going Shopping

Shopping malls located in predominantly minority communities have trouble finding tenants, regardless of the income of area residents. Even though local family incomes averaged $38,522, southern California's largest shopping center developer had great difficulty filling a renovated 800,000-square-foot mall located in a predominantly minority community. A mall in Atlanta found similar resistance.

No wonder that 51% black Prince George's county, Maryland, lost out to 85% white Baltimore county for new Macy's and Nordstrom stores, even though Prince George's residents' median household income is 15% greater than Baltimore's.

If the stores won't come to you, go to the stores, some may suggest. But stores sometimes keep African-Americans out or follow them around as they shop, and not because the salesperson has any intention of helping them find what they are looking for. While such discrimination has usually been shrugged off in the past, recently it's led to litigation and even a new moniker to describe it—*consumer racism.* In the most famous and publicized case, the Denny's restaurant chain in 1995 paid $46 million to 300,000 customers who said they were subject to various forms of racial discrimination—not being seated, suffering poor service, or paying higher prices. Included in the class action settlement, for example, were six Secret Service agents who waited to be served for an hour at an Annapolis, Maryland, restaurant while their white counterparts received second helpings.

Denny's is the leading, but not the only, example of consumer racism:

■ When Shawn Jackson wrote out a check for $168 to buy a Washington Redskins jacket at a Foot Locker store in Columbia, Maryland, the store manager said the store didn't accept checks from District of Columbia banks. So Jackson, who's black, sent her white roommate to buy the coat a few minutes later with a DC check, which the store manager accepted. Jackson sued and won an undisclosed settlement.

■ Three black male teens were confronted by two security guards at an Eddie Bauer outlet store in Ft. Washington, Maryland; when one couldn't produce a receipt for a shirt he was wearing, it was confiscated, despite a cashier's recollection of selling the shirt to him the day before. A federal district court jury decided in October 1997 to order Eddie Bauer to pay $3 million in damages.

■ In December 1997, a federal jury in Kansas City awarded $1.56 million to a woman because she had been stopped and searched by store security guards merely because she was black. The court concluded that the Dillard's department store routinely put black customers under surveillance even when they had done nothing suspicious.

■ Ted Williams, an attorney for two minority residents who sued a women's lingerie store near Baltimore over a strip search, told the *Washington Post* that his office receives about 15 calls a week from young black men with similar complaints about retailers. "In the past, young black males were discouraged to do anything," said Williams.

"But because of cases like Eddie Bauer, they now believe a wrong can be righted."

THE $MARTER CONSUMER

As for underserved minority communities, there are some small positive signs that the marketplace may correct this shopping gap. Pathmark has announced it will open some new stores in low-income areas of New York City. Chemical Bank (now merged with Chase), too, opened the first new branch in 30 years in Harlem. As crime falls faster in the inner city than elsewhere, the historic avoidance of high-crime and high-cost retailing is beginning to subside. Two businessmen writing in *The Wall Street Journal* in late 1997 laid out the rationale for reinvesting in communities of color: "Households in America's inner cities possess . . . far more retail spending power that Mexico's entire formal retail market. Inner-city markets are attractive because they are large and densely populated. Despite lower household incomes, inner-city areas concentrate more buying power in a square mile than many affluent suburbs do. . . . Approximately 30% of inner-city retail demand is unmet within the inner city."

For retailers, the message should be clear. America's inner cities are the next retailing frontier and they are growing right in our own back-

yard. As for explicit anti-minority discrimination of the Denny's and Eddie Bauer kind, there is also slow progress, case-by-case. But most marketplace discrimination is not explicitly prohibited by existing law. The civil rights laws of the 1960s outlaw discrimination in a few specific and important areas—employment, housing, and public accommodations—but leave other markets for many goods and services uncovered.

Until there's a national debate on whether to extend civil rights laws to cover economic segregation generally, people must push for:

■ Strong enforcement of existing laws, such as the Community Reinvestment Act, the Fair Housing Act, and the Equal Credit Opportunity Act.

■ Stronger state insurance laws requiring insurers to charge based on driving record rather than personal residence, and financial penalties for firms that pull agents out of lower-income areas.

■ Broadening the use of local human rights laws against, say, haircutters or restaurants that explicitly charge minorities more than whites for the same services.

Individuals can arm themselves with the information they need to shop knowledgeably and wisely and band together to exert the strength of numbers:

Learn the law. Familiarize yourself with local human- or civil-rights laws. Know where to complain if you think your rights have been abridged.

Vote with your feet. If you're choosing between banks that are otherwise equal, pick the one with the best community reinvestment record. Avoid car dealers, haircutters, or other service establishments that base prices on race.

Use community groups or religious organizations to take your concerns to local officials and business leaders who may be in a position to help bring supermarkets, department stores, and banks to your neighborhood by getting zoning variances or offering incentives to the owners of these kinds of establishments.

H E L P

■ **The Federal Reserve Bank's** annual survey of home mortgage data is released every October. Look for summaries in *The Wall Street Journal*, or you can check the Feds' Web site at www.bog.frb.fed.us.

■ *Consumer Reports* **publishes an** annual car-buying issue in April of every year. Look for it in your library, or send $5 to Back Issue Department, *Consumer Reports*, P.O. Box 53016, Boulder, CO 80322-3016. You'll also find lots of useful information on *CR*'s Web site; go to www.consumerreports.org.

■ **Ask your state attorney general** or local consumer office about civil rights laws that may be in effect where you shop or live.

CHAPTER 63

SENIORS AS CONSUMERS

Scamming the Elderly

Virtually every shady deal-maker targets seniors—telemarketing scam artists announcing phony prizes, corrupt home improvement contractors selling overpriced financing, fast-talking insurance agents selling worthless policies. The stories are straight out of the tabloids—or your worst nightmare. Victimizing seniors is so commonplace that con artists have a name for it: "Getting Granny."

Take the following scam, clearly designed to appeal to seniors' deepest fears about medical emergencies: Life Alert Emergency Response, Inc. used scare tactics and high-pressure in-home demonstrations of personal emergency response systems to dupe elderly California and Arizona consumers into buying their exorbitantly priced systems. In extensive television advertising and sales presentations, the company claimed that it was staffed with former policemen and air-traffic controllers who had special access to "911" emergency services and that emergency services person-nel reacted faster to Life Alert calls than to regular 911 calls. Not so. In addition, the company set prices artificially high so that they could be "dropped" for "special" customers. Finally, Life Alert failed to inform customers that they had the right to cancel the contract.

THE BASICS

Fraud against the elderly, especially women, is a growth industry. (Con artists are avid readers of obituary pages.) The Federal Bureau of Investigation estimates that there are 14,000 illegal telemarketing operations bilking senior consumers out of some $40 billion a year. It can happen to anyone. A study by the American Association of Retired Persons found that most elderly fraud victims were college educated, owned homes, and had annual household incomes exceeding $30,000.

Why are seniors thought to be such easy targets? Two congressional investigations concluded that seniors are perceived as more vulnerable than younger consumers for the following reasons:

- Seniors tend to live on fixed incomes, which makes many people more intent on cutting corners and getting bargains.
- Seniors can be lonely and isolated, which makes them more susceptible to doting salespeople.
- Many seniors live alone and can't easily turn to trusted family or friends for objective feedback and advice on consumer purchases.
- As a group, seniors have more health problems and are often willing to try new things to alleviate pain and feel "young again."

To make matters worse, seniors often ignore or dismiss consumer fraud when it happens to them. Like anyone else, they feel humiliated and don't like to admit they've been had.

In addition, many seniors are struggling to maintain their independence. Keeping up appearances is so important to seniors that in case after case, seniors admit that they didn't ask for help because they couldn't bear to tell their children or other loved ones what happened. This gives the swindlers a second shot at them; in their desperation to replace some of the money they've lost, seniors fall victim to new scams, especially the so-called "recovery room." In this scam people posing as government agents or lawyers approach elderly fraud victims and offer to recover money they lost in earlier scams —for a large fee that must, of course, be paid up front.

How can you and your loved ones be less vulnerable to consumer scams? First, recognize your own weak points— are you sometimes overzealous about saving money? Do you have access to a second opinion before you make major purchases? Do you try to get redress if you've been wronged, or are you more likely to turn the other cheek?

Second, learn to recognize the warning signs of various scams. According to former FBI Director William Sessions, "illegal schemes are only limited by the imaginations of their perpetrators and by the susceptibility of the consuming public." It's certain that the schemers have proven their imaginative prowess, but you *can* make yourself less susceptible.

> "*The elderly are vulnerable because their memory is poor, they rarely take notes on phone conversations, and only occasionally ask for written guarantees. . . . Their most notable weakness is that once they recognize the deceit, they are often too embarrassed to relay the events to their offspring, friends, counsel, and law enforcement.*"
>
> —CONVICTED TELEMARKETER, testifying before a congressional committee

AARP's Rx for Spending Less

Surveys of hundreds of pharmacies across the country by the American Association of Retired Persons (AARP), the NYC Department of Consumer Affairs, the General Accounting Office, and the Visiting Neighbors Program, found startling disparities in prescription drug prices—even in the same community. Prescription drugs can cost more than twice as much from one pharmacy to the next and as much as 14 times more.

Since many elderly people aren't covered by prescription reimbursement plans, it's no wonder that prescription drug prices led the list of complaints in NYC's *Senior Consumer Watch*

Survey. Seniors can end up with bills for hundreds, or thousands, of dollars a year for pills. The AARP offers this checklist to help seniors get the best buy and the best care from pharmacies. Does your pharmacy have:

- Weekend hours
- 24-hour service
- After-hours emergency service
- Free delivery service
- Personal medication records
- Medicine-management aids
- Special labels and containers
- Free educational materials
- Prescription drug leaflets
- Free health screenings
- Discounts for senior citizens
- Generic drugs

WHAT TO WATCH OUT FOR

Medical Quackery

A congressional report cited medical quackery as "a $10 billion scandal" and called it "the single most prevalent and damaging of the frauds directed at the elderly." Promotion and sales of useless remedies and cures for chronic and critical health ailments predates snake-oil merchants and covered wagons. No matter how many times quack remedies are exposed (there was an attempt in 1994 to crack down on claims made by dietary supplements), vulnerable consumers—desperate for relief, or sometimes just hope—continue to spend their dollars on worthless do-nothing drugs.

Worse than do-nothing drugs that cost huge sums of money are quack cures that can actually damage your health. While most "miracle" remedies are harmless, some can be deadly. Algamar, for instance, was hailed by its hawkers as a wonderful new cancer cure, but it actually contained two potentially lethal bacterial organisms. The manufacturer raked in about $120,000 from 5,000 credulous customers before the U.S. Postal Service intervened.

TELEMARKETING FRAUD

Chances are you've received a call from a company telling you that you've been randomly selected as a winner of a car or a vacation in Hawaii, or a large chunk of cash—but before you can have it, you have to pay a fee. Typically, you'll be asked to send a check for hundreds or thousands of dollars by overnight mail to cover taxes, postage, and handling for the prize. Smooth salespeople point out that if the taxes are this high, the prize must be fantastic. But the prize never arrives.

These offers are especially tempting to seniors—many of whom are overly trusting and grateful to have someone to talk to. One 80-year-old woman who sent thousands of dollars to telemarketers because she had become "addicted" to the attention from her callers told *The New York Times:* "I've been a widow for 19 years. It's very lonely. They were nice on the phone. They became my friends." In fact, nearly 80% of the victims in the prize promotion and loss-recovery scams investigated in a special U.S. Department of Justice effort were elderly.

Why? The perpetrators can best explain. Convicted telemarketers testified before a congressional committee:

"Retirees were easily accessible by phone, usually at home during the day, and thus easy to resell. We found the elderly intent on enlarging their nest egg, their limited income, and often interested in generating money for their grandchildren."

Quack treatments can also inspire seniors to stray from the health regimen prescribed by their physicians. Lena R. of Philadelphia told a congressional committee that she spent over $2,000 and ignored the instructions of her husband's physician because "when he got sick, I was looking for magic." But the regimen of wheat grass juice, watermelon rind juice, and the juice of green vegetables prescribed by Dr. Haasz (who was actually a doctor of *engineering*) at a clinic called "The Beautiful Temple" did not cure her husband's cancer.

The Arthritis Foundation suggests the following tips for spotting unscrupulous promoters of phony cures:

■ Beware of "special" or "secret" formulas or devices to cure ailments that are considered incurable.
■ Be skeptical of case histories and testimonials from satisfied patients. Look instead for confirmed results from clinical tests. If the promoter

Another convicted telemarketer said: "Because most senior citizens are more trusting of supposedly 'caring' strangers, because they grew and matured in less threatening times, they are incredibly easy to con out of everything they have."

Once someone falls for a scheme, they're more likely to be targeted again and again. Telemarketers buy and sell "mooch" lists of people who have taken the bait before. So how can you end the cycle? Here are some tips:

- **Don't talk to sales agents who call you first.** If you want to buy something, seek it out yourself.
- **Keep your name off the lists.** Ask any organizations you deal with not to sell your name.
- **Be very skeptical** of anyone who requests money for deposits, to prepay taxes, or to cover delivery; asks for overnight delivery of checks; wants your credit card numbers; or insists on immediate action.
- **Look before you leap.** Before you reply to an offer, get the company's name, address, phone number, and references. Beware of companies with only a P.O. box. Before you send any money or give out your credit card number, check out the company with the Better Business Bureau (BBB), your state attorney general, or your local consumer protection office.
- **Avoid making calls to 900 numbers** to claim a prize. These calls cost much more than a toll call.
- **If you do get scammed, don't be embarrassed, get mad**—and get even! Report incidents of telemarketing fraud to the National Fraud Information Center at (800) 876-7060.

won't allow the remedy to be tested, don't use it.

- While there is a legitimate controversy between established and alternative medicine, watch out for promoters who accuse the medical establishment of deliberately thwarting their progress or persecuting them.

Mortgage Credit Scams

Millions of seniors are house-rich but cash-poor. Over 11% of all homes owned free and clear are owned by people who are at least 80, according to SMR Research Corp., and the average age of the 23 million debt-free homes in America is 64.3. Since many of these people live on relatively low fixed incomes, they have trouble qualifying for conventional loans. Faced with mounting medical bills, costly home repairs, or just an eroding standard of living, these house-rich seniors are easily hooked by the promise of converting their castle's capital into cash.

But senior homeowners can quickly become poorer and even homeless if they don't read the fine print on their reverse mortgages home equity loans. For example, the Landbank Equity Corp. offered 79-year-old William J. a home equity loan to refinance delinquent medical bills. But after paying $7,731 in upfront points and fees and refinancing several times, William faced a $48,000 debt and imminent foreclosure on his home. The federal bankruptcy trustee suspects that Landbank stole some $17 million from vulnerable consumers before it went bankrupt.

Home equity loans and reverse mortgages offered by responsible lenders can be a good deal for millions of homeowners of all ages. However, home equity loans turn into lifetime losses when legitimate lenders turn seniors down and a convincing con artist comes along to fill in the gap.

Seniors—especially minority seniors—have been particularly victimized by a recent wave of home equity theft by disreputable home-improvement contractors working hand in glove with shady finance companies. Here's how it works when seniors are the targets: The senior citizen is visited at home by a home improvement contractor who offers to renovate the kitchen or bathroom or fix the roof or porch for very low monthly payments. Once the homeowner agrees, the contractor pulls out a thick sheaf of legal documents and asks, typically, for "a few signatures . . . just to get the work started." Only the lower right-hand corner of each document

is lifted, preventing the soon-to-be-victim from reading the full page. What the homeowner unwittingly signs, besides a home improvement contract, may be an application for a high-priced mortgage from the finance company.

"These folks really work them," says Manuel Duran, a counselor who helps seniors with home-equity fraud at Bet Tzedek Legal Services in Los Angeles. They call them 'Grandma,' and say that the smells here remind me of when I was a kid, and the senior citizens love that."

These loans are often for far more than the homeowner had agreed to (typically, the contractor gets the homeowner to sign blank forms and an amount is filled in later). Interest rates of an extraordinary 18% to 21% have been the norm. And the contractors usually fail to complete the promised renovation work or do it so shoddily that it actually decreases the value of the house.

For example: In the Bedford-Stuyvesant neighborhood in Brooklyn, New York, an African-American woman named Louise B. was struggling to get by on a housekeeper's salary. She owned a home that needed repairs to the roof and kitchen, and she wanted to remodel to create a rental unit. A home improvement contractor trolling the low-income minority neighborhood agreed to do the work and arranged financing with Citibank. The contractor did $6,000 worth of work— and $15,000 worth of damage, rendering the home unlivable and unsafe. The contractor was paid in full by the bank, and Louise B. struggled to make the $760 monthly loan payments and eventually faced foreclosure.

There are several home equity scam warning signs: First, beware of unsolicited offers, particularly from door-to-door home improvement salespeople who conveniently carry around second mortgage applications. Be even more skeptical if the solicitor seems to be too much aware of your financial plight—some companies appraise your home and then send you an unsolicited loan offer. Many home equity scams begin with the scam artist promising to give the senior a break or "do them a favor." Before any money changes hands the senior is made to feel in the huckster's debt. Finally, watch out for lenders who say that they're not concerned with your ability to repay the loan. Catch phrases like "no income or credit check" or "approval guaranteed" might be enticing, but they're sure signs of a scam. Reputable lenders want you to repay the loan; hucksters want your house.

In addition to staying alert to these warning signs, you can avoid home equity scams by:

■ Going to a reputable lender if you are interested in a home equity loan. Don't do business with lenders that come to you.
■ Having an attorney or a trusted financial advisor review your loan agreement before you sign. Even sophisticated consumers have trouble deciphering the financial jargon and tedious technicalities of most loan papers. Have an outside expert recalculate the annual percentage rate

(APR) to make sure it's accurate and to get a "bottom line" of how much your loan is going to cost.

In some states, certified public accountant associations and/or Elder Law Bar Associations provide some free services to seniors—check your telephone book for local listings. Low-income seniors can also try their local Legal Services for help. If you can't find a professional to help you for free, you can also ask finance professors at local colleges if they (or their students) would review your contract.
■ Always check the reputation of your lender or home improvement contractor with your state attorney general, local consumer protection office, or the BBB *before* you sign on the dotted line. If the lender can't or won't wait, it's a sure sign that the loan has serious loopholes.

Credit Repair Scams

Seniors who can't get a home equity loan, credit card, or auto loan are often vulnerable to credit repair scams. But there is nothing a credit repair service can do that you can't do for yourself—for free.

Credit repair services that promise "a new credit identity" or a "clean credit record instantly" are either lying or illegal. "New credit identities" are actually stolen personal identification numbers or Social Security numbers; using someone else's credit identity can land both you and the number dealer in jail.

There's simply no legal way to erase true records of missed payments or bankruptcy. You can start building a better credit profile by paying bills on time and taking on a manageable amount of debt. And if you dispute the accuracy or completeness of the information in your credit file, the Fair Credit Reporting Act entitles you to add to your file a short explanation of your side of the story.

The best way to avoid credit scams? Know your rights. If you have been denied credit, you are entitled to a free copy of the credit report the lender used to make its decision. The lender legally has to tell you which company it used, where to call, and the fact that you can get a free copy of your credit report if you call within 30 days. (See "Consumer Privacy," page 640, for a discussion of how to fix errors on your credit report.) If you believe that you've been discriminated against because you're a senior, contact the elder law committee of your state's bar association or your local legal services office. They'll help you file a complaint with the appropriate agency or initiate legal action.

Finally, you can watch out for senior credit discrimination by being aware of what creditors are and are not allowed to do under the federal Equal Credit Opportunity Act (ECOA):

- Creditors cannot discourage applicants from applying for credit because of age, race, color, religion, sex, marital status, or source of income.
- Creditors cannot have a blanket policy based on age alone and cannot deny credit because the appli-

cant is "too old" to qualify for credit insurance.

- If creditors use age as one characteristic in a credit scoring system, people 62 and over cannot be scored lower for their age than people under 62.
- If the consumer already has an account, creditors cannot change the terms of the credit or require a new application for credit when the account holder retires or reaches a certain age.
- Creditors cannot assume that retirement income is always insufficient to repay a loan, or discount or exclude income from part-time employment, annuities, retirement benefits, or public assistance benefits like Social Security.
- Creditors *can* ask about and evaluate the applicant's source(s) of income.
- If the credit is going to be used to buy or refinance a home, creditors *can* ask an applicant's age.
- Creditors *can* give seniors more favorable treatment.

Investment Fraud

Unscrupulous financial advisors promise sky-high investment returns—but the only thing that's aloft are the advisor's commissions. With 3% to 5% interest earned on bank certificates of deposit, many seniors are finding they can't cover their bills. Anxiety about paying bills over longer life expectancies and leaving something for heirs can push lifelong savers to become first-time investors. But since many seniors may be unaware of the risks associated with investing—and un-

SOCIAL SECURITY SCAMS

Two words get the attention of almost every American over 65: Social Security. Every politician—and every scam artist—knows that a threat to Social Security will mobilize thousands of seniors to fight it. While there have been many legitimate threats to Social Security, and legitimate organizations formed to lobby to preserve seniors' interests, there have also been many phony threats and phony funds set up to steal from scared seniors.

Many of these groups are intended more for profit than politics. The Seniors Coalition and the Taxpayers Education Association have raised tens of millions of dollars by sending direct mail to seniors with such claims as "All the Social Security Trust Fund Money Is Gone!"

Before you contribute to any cause, political or charitable, contact your state attorney general or the Better Business Bureau. Beware of political groups' claims that contributions are tax deductible—support for most lobbying activities is not. Finally, while money can be key to political victories, don't forget to exercise your other political powers: attend political forums, vote, and write letters to your elected representatives.

---

familiar with the ways and wiles of Wall Street—investment scammers find them easy marks for their fly-by-night financial services. Many of them fish for customers at churches or senior centers. They all promise high, safe, and quick returns; require large investments, sometimes as much as $100,000; and involve complicated prospectuses or forms that consumers are told they must sign but "don't have to read."

The Murphys of Missouri, for example, thought they were getting a great deal on a piece of retirement property in south Florida. But when it came time to retire, they found that their investment was literally underwater—and their retirement savings with it.

"If you blow it when you're 30, you've got 35 years to make it up before you retire. If you blow it at 65, you may have to go back to work for the rest of your life," warns Barbara Roper, director of investment protection at Consumer Federation of America.

An economy fueled by low interest rates is always tough for people who depend on interest income. Still, seniors who have to earn more on their money can find reasonable risks without falling for frauds. The most important thing to remember is that for every investor who's made a million overnight, there are likely to be many more who have lost as much as quickly. Don't be greedy. Increase your return with calculated risks that meet your investment objectives. To lower your risk:

Always read the fine print and understand what you're getting into before you move your money. Ask an attorney or a trusted financial advisor for help understanding mutual fund prospectuses and other financial contracts.

Be wary of financial fads. Like fads in fashion, various investment strategies tend to fall in and out of favor as quickly as poodle skirts and tie-dye. You'll be better off with an investment that's proved its performance over the long term.

Don't put all your eggs in one basket. Even the best pundits can't predict what the market will do tomorrow. Hedge your bets; accumulate a diversified portfolio that balances investments that do well under one set of market conditions with others that will do well under opposite conditions.

So many different frauds are targeted to seniors, it's impossible to watch out for all of them all the time. Here are some general safeguards to make you a harder target for con artists of all stripes.

Avoid direct solicitations. If you want something, seek out merchants yourself. You will steer clear of both scams and costly impulse purchases.

Thoroughly investigate your reverse mortgage options. Reverse mortgages turn the equity you've built up in your home into cash you can live on without paying anything back for as long as you live in the home. Not all of these loans are created equal, and the perfect one for homeowner A can be disastrous for homeowner B—and the real cost to you can vary by tens of thousands of dollars. The National Center for Home Equity Conversion can help you figure out which loan makes most sense for you, based on your age, the value of your home, current loan rates, and your preferences. They'll also help you find qualified lenders that have agreed to abide by basic consumer protection guidelines. For contact information, see **HELP** at the end of the chapter.

Beware of home improvement contractors who say your house needs repairs for problems you never noticed. They may offer you a "deal," saying they have materials left over.

Do your homework. Being a smart shopper is like being a smart student—but failing the "test" has a higher price than it did in school. Don't play multiple choice with your financial future or your health. Read the chapters in this book on prescription drugs, telemarketing, eyeglasses, financial services, and long-term care to find out how to be a $marter consumer of the products and services you buy.

Get a second opinion. Regardless of what they may claim, few salespeople put your interests above their own. If the seller won't give you time to get advice and think over your purchase, don't give him or her the time of day, especially when fat commissions are at stake.

Complain if you get taken. Don't you wish someone had blown the whistle on the scam artist who scammed you? If you don't know whom to call, look up your local consumer affairs office or state attorney general listed at the back of this book (they're also listed in the government section of your phone book), or contact one of the advocacy groups listed below.

HELP

■ **The American As**sociation of Retired Persons is both a potent lobbying force and resource for people over 50. Call (800) 424-2277 or write to 601 E Street NW, Washington, DC 20049, for a list of publications, campaigns, and local offices. The *AARP Guide to Internet Resources Related to Aging* lists and describes Internet sites of interest to older people and those concerned with aging-related issues. You can find it and lots of the AARP's own information at www.aarp.org.

■ **Report telemarketing fraud to the** National Fraud Information Center at (800) 876-7060.

■ **For good nuts-and-bolts advice on** reverse mortgages, contact the National Center for Home Equity Conversion. This independent, not-for-profit publishes *Your New Retirement Nest Egg: A* *Consumer Guide to the New Reverse Mortgages* ($24.95, plus $4.50 for shipping) and also offers an individualized analysis of 12 loan choices keyed to your age, your home's value, and current loan costs and benefits ($19 from NCHEC or free from any NCHEC-preferred lender). Contact NCHEC, 7373 147 Street West, #115, Apple Valley, MN 55124, (612) 953-4474.

■ **To check a stockbroker or invest**ment firm's credentials, call the North American Association of Securities Administrators (202) 737-0900. It will give you the phone number for the correct office in your state.

■ **Most state bar associations have** Elder Law committees that will help seniors use the courts to get redress. Look in the phone book for the number of your state bar association.

CHAPTER 64

CONSUMERS WITH DISABILITIES

Battling Barriers

The disabled encounter ignorance and an unwillingness to communicate with them on the part of the general public, as well as physical barriers that impede their ability to get around. These two factors conspire to raise prices and limit choices for disabled consumers. The good news, however, is that this virtual wall is being torn down brick by brick, assisted by technology.

As we approach the 21st century, reports of machines that read to the blind, "talk" to the deaf, and grant movement to the paralyzed seem to appear in the media almost daily. There was the day Bernice Connor turned on her television set and flicked a special switch. Words—the dialogue spoken by the actors, called closed captioning—appeared in white letters against a black band. For the first time in her life, as reported in a *TV Guide* article by her daughter Linda, the hearing-impaired Mrs. Connor could follow and understand all that was happening on the screen.

Computer smarts helped Chicago couple Bob and Joanne Greenberg, both completely blind, score with their business, the Bob Greenberg Sports Reports. They use a scanner that electronically captures printed information and stores it in the computer. They call up information on the computer as they need it, and additional technology, including a speech synthesizer, reads aloud what appears on the monitor. "Tasks such as billing and accounting," reports *The Wall Street Journal,* "which once could have taken them hours, can now be completed in minutes."

THE BASICS

As individual consumers, the disabled must chant the same mantras as anyone else: Comparison shop, get it in writing, beware the deal that sounds too good to be true, beware managed care, etc. But as a group, the disabled suffer from ignorance—not their own but that of the non-disabled.

The technology part is easy compared to public attitude. Although growing social awareness has opened doors for the disabled and led to empowering legislation, it has not yet led to a new age of enlightenment.

Many people with disabilities have been called "shut-ins," but they have really been shut out—of employment, education, mobility, expression, experience, and dignity. Education and economics have started to change this picture, as various state and local governments have passed laws that give access to the disabled.

ADA is A-OK

A major advance is the federal Americans with Disabilities Act of 1990 (ADA). Its major provisions started to take effect in 1992. In essence, this law says that people who are disabled cannot be treated differently than others. It also covers people who are in a situation associated with someone with a disability (e.g., the parent of a child with a disability), and it includes people who are perceived as being disabled (e.g., cancer survivors). They can't be barred from jobs for which they are qualified. They can't be refused hotel and restaurant accommodations that they can afford. They can't be refused transportation, state and local government services, telephone and

> "**D**emand and they must provide. If you can't access the goods or services, they must be brought to you."
>
> —Jim Weissman,
> Policy Counsel, Eastern Paralyzed
> Veterans Association

telecommunications service, or even the right to go into a store and buy what they please.

The first item on a disabled consumer's agenda is simply to get waited on. For example, for someone using a wheelchair, a store with steps and no aisle space in which to maneuver is truly a little shop of horrors. The ADA requires making barrier-free "if readily achievable" all "places of public accommodation"—which includes (but is not limited to) restaurants, bars, hotels, theaters, physicians' offices, pharmacies, retail stores, museums, libraries, parks, private schools, and day-care centers. Private clubs and religious institutions are exempt. Whether modifications are "readily achievable" depends on the ability of the establishment to reasonably afford them and on the difficulty in carrying them out. (If the establishment leases the premises, both the landlord and the tenant are responsible for complying with the ADA.) Installing offset hinges to widen doorways, making curb cuts, lowering pay telephones, and installing grab bars near toilets are examples of modifications that would probably be deemed "readily achievable." A modification that would probably not be deemed "readily achievable" in most cases is installing elevators.

In 1993, in the first legal settlement involving the ADA's hotel guidelines, New York's swank Hotel Inter-Continental agreed with the U.S. Justice Department to make $1.7 million worth of modifications, such as adding ramps, widening doorways, and reconstructing rooms for the disabled.

All newly constructed buildings must be accessible. And any renovations must make a facility accessible to the maximum extent feasible. For example, reconstructed bathrooms must be handicapped-accessible. The law caps the added accessibility expense at 20% of the total cost of the initial alteration.

At first, businesses groaned about compliance; many still do. Then some glimpsed an alluringly large "new" population of consumers—an estimated 43 million Americans have activity-limiting disabilities—to woo. Trade organizations and publications in such fields as banking and the hotel and retail industries talked about the new legislation and stressed two points: Here's how you comply, and here's how you market. People with disabilities are now featured in all sorts of Madison Avenue cross-section-of-America ads.

Compliance can also come from creative solutions rather than from spending money. For example, if steps lead to a dry cleaner's entrance, the merchant can arrange for curb drop-off and pick-up. Instead of printing menus in Braille, a restaurant can have an employee read from a menu to visually impaired patrons.

Try to work it out with the establishment. Jane D. loves to dine at her favorite Manhattan restaurant, but as her diabetes began to worsen, she had to give herself insulin shots before starting to eat. So one evening she neatly and discreetly laid out her hypodermic needle and supplies on her restaurant table and proceeded to do what she had to do. The management was upset; she had "repulsed" the other diners and the staff.

Jane contacted the NYC Mayor's Office for People With Disabilities. They mediated an acceptable alternative: The restaurant would provide Jane with a clean, private space

DID YOU KNOW?

■ According to the 1994 National Health Interview Survey, an estimated 15% of Americans of all ages had a limitation on activity—about two thirds of them were limited in a major activity and one third in a non-major activity. Some 7.8 million people aged 16 to 64 had a disability severe enough to keep them from working

■ Companies offering telephone service to the general public must offer telephone relay services to individuals who use telecommunications devices for the deaf (TDD) or similar devices.

■ Almost all TV sets now sold must contain a decoding chip. The chip provides access to closed-captioned programs.

—not an unsanitary bathroom—to administer her injection. And she can continue to enjoy her favorite meals.

Know What You Buy

The world of the disabled is loaded with bureaucracy—government and private insurers;

nonprofit organizations; federal, state, and local agencies; and the medical establishment. In this rules-and-regs jungle, disabled consumers need to have sharp navigating skills and to know that they don't have to accept what they are told and how they are treated.

Take, for example, buying a wheelchair. A wheelchair is a hefty, complex, and expensive piece of machinery that can cost thousands of dollars. It is customized and equipped with all sorts of appropriate appurtenances that fulfill the user's needs. Like a fine made-to-order garment, it must be fitted to the user's body.

The wheelchair purchase process starts rolling when a doctor, occupational therapist, or physical therapist writes a prescription. Be sure to double-check with the professional to make sure that the prescription includes every item that is needed.

The consumer (or the consumer with his or her doctor) has to decide between motorized or manual. Motorized chairs are easier to use and less physically taxing to the user. But they cost more. And they're not really portable, since they can't be folded. They're also heavy—maybe too heavy to be tilted by another person, which can be a problem when negotiating curbs.

Another potential drawback to electric wheelchairs may be electromagnetic interference—from cellular phones, radio and TV stations, and CB radios. According to Food and Drug Administration (FDA) tests, radio waves caused brakes to release and wheelchairs to move un-

CREATIVE COST-CUTTING

An ingenious cost-cutting tactic has emerged at the grassroots level—the equipment exchange. As the name suggests, people can borrow or purchase needed equipment and accessories (such as hospital beds) at substantially reduced costs.

The equipment exchange also helps people who need "loaners" while their own equipment is being repaired or readied. This means they don't have to be home- or bed-bound while waiting. Also, people who want to try out a brand before they purchase it get the opportunity.

Find out from your state or local office for people with disabilities if there is an equipment exchange in your area. Exchanges also advertise on the Internet and in the classifieds of national publications for the disabled.

controllably. The FDA has required warning labels on motorized wheelchairs since December 1994, including a numeric "rating" that indicates the wheelchair's radiowave resistance.

Even when all the decisions are made, the process is not over.

TRAVEL SUPPORT

Disabled people who wish to go it alone might contact the Society for the Advancement of Travel for the Handicapped (SATH) at 347 Fifth Avenue, Suite 610, New York, New York 10016; by phone (212) 447-SATH or fax (212) 725-8253. SATH can give limited information over the phone—such as whether a particular hotel claims to be handicapped-accessible—and provides information sheets with more extensive information for $5. An annual membership is $45 ($30 for seniors and students), which entitles you to free help for a year and the quarterly magazine, *Open World*. You might have to call a few times to get through to someone who can assist you. They are unable to return long-distance calls.

Another source for disabled travelers is the bimonthly *Access to Travel* magazine, P.O. Box 43, Delmar, NY 12054, (518) 439-4146. Subscriptions cost $16 a year.

Wheelchair dealers sometimes neglect to give a warranty at the time of purchase. This means that customers have no idea for how long they can repair the chair without spending their own money. Be sure to ask.

When selecting a vendor for any product specially designed for the disabled, check their references. If the vendor is licensed, check with the licensing agency to see if any complaints have been filed. Be sure to find out how long it will take for the product to be delivered. When getting repairs, get an estimate that details costs for parts and labor and a completion date. Also try to get a ceiling on the price—it should not exceed the estimate by more than 10%. Request a loaner wheelchair or other product if the repairs will take time.

Disabled and on the Go

When following a daily routine, disabled people learn what obstacles they'll encounter and how to surmount or avoid them. But disabled travelers have to deal with all sorts of unanticipated obstacles—physical ones, such as a supposedly "accessible" hotel that really isn't, and human ones, namely discrimination against serving disabled people.

Fortunately, the situation is improving. The ADA is beginning to remove barriers on the ground, and the U.S. Air Carrier Access Act of 1986 (ACAA) is removing barriers to air travel. To start with, all terminals must be made fully accessible. Practically speaking, this means that disabled people must be able to use the primary ticketing area, that baggage areas—including gates and turnstiles—and the plane loading bridges and mobile lounges must be barrier-free. Each terminal must have a clearly marked tele-communications device for the deaf (TDD). Commuter aircraft with fewer than 30 seats are the big ex-ception to the level-entry boarding requirement.

The ACAA also requires that all airplanes ordered after April 1990 or delivered to the airline after April 1992 be wheelchair accessi-ble. If the plane has more than one aisle, it must have a restroom acces-sible to someone using a wheel-chair. Planes with more than 60 seats and an accessible restroom must have their own wheelchairs available—chairs that must have removable footrests and armrests to make transferring to the seat easier. If the plane has at least 60 seats and an inaccessible restroom, the dis-abled passenger must provide ad-vance notice of the need for an aisle chair. By law, airlines are required to tell callers about rest-room ac-cessibility as well as any other per-tinent information about disabled accessibility.

The ACAA prohibits airlines from requiring advance notice as a condition for receiving services and accommodations, other than what is required of all customers. The exceptions can be reasonably antici-pated, such as connecting a respira-tor to the airplane's electrical system and carrying "hazardous ma-terial" packaging for a wheelchair battery.

Once a disabled passenger is on the plane, the ACAA prohibits air-lines from denying them seats in rows next to exits unless necessary to meet federal safety regulations. This means that such seats *can* be denied if it appears that the dis-abled person would be unable to perform the duties required by law of a person sitting in an exit row—basically, following oral and written instructions, opening the exit door, and moving quickly through it.

Disabled people are allowed to stow assistive devices, which are not counted in the carry-on quota, close to their seats. Mechanical wheel-chairs get priority in the airplane's in-cabin stowage area, but electric wheelchairs have to travel with the baggage.

If an airline refuses to serve an individual because of a disability, it must provide a detailed written ex-planation within 10 calendar days of the refusal.

Accessibility improvements for train travel are still being phased in. According to Amtrak, at least one car on every train meets ADA accessibility requirements, which includes a handicapped-usable rest-room. And all new Amtrak cars now on order will be barrier-free—although people who use wheel-chairs will still be limited to the lower level of the new Superliner cars. Amtrak has until the year 2010 to make their stations fully accessible.

A number of Amtrak stations now have lifts to get disabled, mo-bility-limited passengers up off the ground and into the cars. Am-trak suggests that disabled people

GUIDE TO GROUPS AND GOVERNMENT

Disabled consumers can get savvy advice from organizations that provide advocacy or assistance services. If you cannot find a local chapter, check with its national headquarters.

The National Council on Independent Living, an advocacy group with chapters around the country, is headquartered in Alexandria, VA; call (703) 525-3406.

Disability Rights Education and Defense Fund in Berkeley, California, provides information, assistance, and legal advice regarding civil rights laws and protections related to disabilities; call (510) 644-2555.

Eastern Paralyzed Veterans Association at 75-30 Astoria Boulevard, Jackson Heights, NY 11370-1177 provides direct services and technical assistance; call (718) 803-EPVA.

The International Center for the Disabled in New York provides outpatient rehabilitation services, helps people with disabilities achieve independence, and provides informa-

tion and training; call (212) 679-0100.

The Lighthouse in New York City serves the visually impaired by providing information, training, assistance in acquiring devices to aid employment, and an array of other services; call (212) 821-9200.

The National Association of the Deaf emphasizes communications skills, employment rights, and works in advocacy and legislation. Write to 814 Thayer Avenue, Silver Spring, MD 20910, or call (301) 587-1788.

The President's Committee on Employment of People with Disabilities provides educational materials and technical assistance. Write them at 1331 F Street NW, Washington, DC 20004, or call (202) 376-6200; TTY (202) 376-6205 or go to www.pcepd.gov/.

Department of Justice, Civil Rights Division, Office on the ADA provides legal and technical assistance. Write them at P.O. Box 66738, Washington, DC 20035.

with special travel needs—such as the wheelchair lift—call 24 hours before their trip to make arrangements.

Many disabled people take vacations with tours organized especially

for the disabled. The number of such tours has declined lately. Why the decline? Curiously enough, two factors may be the ADA and ACAA, which are making domestic travel easier for the disabled. Another reason is that regular travel agencies are becoming more proficient at serving the disabled. A final factor in the decline of special tours for the disabled is that more disabled people wish to travel with the non-disabled.

When Bad Disallowances Happen to Good People

Life would be much simpler if insurers just approved all the invoices for reimbursement that landed on their desks. But they may limit your choices of wheelchairs, hearing aids, and braces; and they employ people whose job it is to review paperwork and routinely disallow, disallow, disallow. Plus, there are the errors that can occur. (For more information, see "Health Insurance," page 39, and "Doctors and Hospitals," page 68.)

You needn't accept the insurer's decree. Be meticulous about preparing your paperwork before submitting it. Then check the insurer's response against your records. Private insurers may have an internal appeals mechanism. If not, contact the local regulatory agency. The appeals process can be frustrating and time-consuming, but it is necessary to ensure that you get the full benefits of your coverage.

THE $MARTER CONSUMER

A sweet momentum favors the disabled. ADA is taking hold.

So is the development and marketing of targeted helpful products. Both forces bring more disabled persons into the workplace and marketplace. And with a growing contingent of $mart disabled consumers holding fistfuls of dollars, the barriers will continue to fall. Here are some tips to help you advance the process:

Scout in advance. When getting ready to vacation, have your travel agent learn which hotels, restaurants, landmarks, etc. are accessible; where to get oxygen if needed; and what the ground transportation situation is. It can be difficult to obtain exactly what you want in a country where you don't speak the language. A useful book for you or your travel agent to consult is Helen Hecker's *Directory of Travel Agencies for the Disabled* (Vancouver, Washington: Twin Peaks Press, 1993, $19.95). It reports on 360 travel agencies that specialize in assisting the disabled.

You also can call the Convention and Visitor's Bureau, Chamber of Commerce, or government office for people with disabilities in the area you're planning to visit for a list of hotels, restaurants, theaters, and other establishments that are accessible to the disabled. A word of caution about the reliability of accessibility guides: Because standards vary and things change, always call first and ask *lots* of questions. Almost everyone who uses a wheelchair has arrived at an ostensibly "accessible" hotel only to discover steps at the entrance.

Speak up for your rights. If a restaurant or retailer is not wheelchair-accessible, tell the management about ADA. Let the proprietors know they can modify their establishment with advice from a local, federally funded technical assistance center. Point out that tax incentives might also be available.

File a complaint with the Feds if educating merchants doesn't help elicit ADA compliance. Mail written complaints to: Office on the Americans With Disabilities Act, Civil Rights Division, U.S. Department of Justice, P.O. Box 66738, Washington, DC 20035-9998. While there is no legal deadline, the Justice Department recommends doing this within 180 days of the alleged violation. It's a good idea to first write a letter to the offending establishment and give them time to answer. The person filing the complaint need not be the victim, but can act as a spokesperson or liaison.

Letters to the Justice Department should state the name and address of the establishment, the names of the owners and manager (if available), the violation (failed to provide accessible toilet, failed to provide a ramp, refused to allow a seeing-eye dog into the facility), how the establishment could remedy the situation, and whether the writer has spoken with and/or written to the owner to no avail. Enclose a copy of any such letter. If you are alleging failure to remove archictectural barriers, try to include photographs or diagrams.

Don't expect a quick reply. Advocacy groups for the disabled have been complaining about extensive delays in conducting investigations. They urge that complaints also be filed with local or state human rights law enforcement agencies, if there are any where you live.

Insist on your air rights. First contact the airline. If that doesn't help, complain to the Department of Transportation about airlines that violate the ACAA. (Send the complaint to U.S. Department of Transportation, Aviation Consumer Protection Division, C-75, Room 4107, Washington, DC 20590, or call (202) 366-2220.)

Phones for people with disabilities. If a disability makes it difficult for you to use a regular telephone and your income is under certain limits ($50,000 with Bell Atlantic, for example), the phone company will provide adapted equipment for free through its equipment distribution program. If your income is higher, there is a small co-payment. The equipment includes large-button or large-number telephones, TDDs, hands-free phones, artificial larynxes, and more.

Vote with your wallet. The National Council on Independent Living says it's a powerful act to spend your money at a business that is accessible. Let other disabled people know which shops do the right thing. Reinforce the good behavior by telling the new recipients of your patronage why you have become their customer.

More and more toy manufacturers sell special and modified versions of their toys—for example, Barbie now has a friend who is in a wheelchair, named Share a Smile Becky, and Little Tykes' patio doll houses are accessible to children in wheelchairs. To find out where you can learn about toys appropriate for children with specific disabilities, see the **HELP** section.

Go for the right fit. If a wheelchair or prosthesis doesn't "feel right," it's not. Disregard retailers' suggestions that you will get used to it. Advise the insurer that it's not a good fit. The manufacturer probably will say that they made it according to the prescriber's specifications and the prescriber will counter with a reasoned "did not." Bring them together and make them iron it all out—in your favor.

The "if it doesn't feel right" manifesto also applies to such equipment as crutches. The "notches" that make crutches adjustable are separated by different intervals, such that one brand might fit you better than another. Even if you can get used to it, a poorly fitting crutch can do more harm than good.

Try before you buy. When buying specialized equipment, don't accept just the word of the salesperson. You need to know if the equipment works well for you. Try it out in a congenial setting—preferably at an organization or an equipment exchange that has the equipment up and running or with someone who already has the equipment.

Find out what the technical support includes: Is there training? Is there a toll free number to call? Is there *any* number to call? Does the manual come in a format that *you* can use and refer to with convenience, such as large print, Braille, or on audiocassette?

Check the warranty. What are the terms? Is there a service contract? How does that work for you?

Is your wheelchair a "lemon"? Try to get the manufacturer or seller to fix the problem or replace the chair. If that doesn't work, see what your rights are under your state's laws. A number of states, including California, Georgia, Massachusetts, New York, and Wisconsin, have "Wheelchair Lemon Laws" that protect disabled consumers the same way vehicle lemon laws protect car buyers.

The laws vary, but generally they cover both leased and purchased wheelchairs and are triggered after the wheelchair has been out of service several times or for at least 30 days (not necessarily consecutively). Hang on to your receipts and letters of complaint; the consumer must be able to document repeated attempts at repair. Some states, such as New York, require you to be furnished with a loaner to replace the out-of-service chair.

697

H E L P

■ **To complain about** a business or public agency you think is violating the ADA, write the U.S. Department of Justice, Civil Rights Division, Disability Rights Section, P.O. Box 66738, Washington, DC 20035-9998.

■ *We* **magazine focuses on the** lifestyles of consumers with disabilities. An annual subscription to the bimonthly costs $14.95. Contact (800) WEMAG26, Coppola Publications, 372 Central Park West, Suite 6B, New York, NY 10025, or www.wemagazine. com. *We* is also available on cassette for people who are blind or unable to read print.

■ *Enable,* **the official magazine of the** American Association of People with Disabilities, is a free bimonthly lifestyle magazine. Call (888) 4ENABLE.

■ **Wheelchair Access is a not-for-**profit organization that helps people with disabilities buy, sell, or rent wheelchair-accessible homes. The agency publishes listings monthly and includes practical resources on obtaining used wheelchairs, specially outfitted vans, and other services and equipment. For a free copy of the newsletter, write Frank Gomez, P.O. Box 12, Glenmoore, PA 19343.

■ **The Abledata Database of Assis-**tive Technology gives equipment descriptions, prices, and manufacturer information for 23,000 products for people with disabilities and 2,600 manufacturers. The database is searchable and can be found at www.abledata.com. For more information call (800) 227-0216. The TTY is (301) 608-8912.

■ **To get further information about** toys suitable for children with disabilities, call Toys R Us toll-free at 888-2-GEOFFREY. The Toy Manufacturers of America, in association with the American Foundation for the Blind, offers a guide to toys for children who are blind or visually impaired; send a postcard to Toys for the Blind, c/o TMA, 1115 Broadway, Suite 400, New York, NY 10010 or go to www.toy-tma.com.

■ **Easy Street offers a catalog that** features products aimed at making daily life easier. Items include "reachers" to extend one's reach (high or low) and doorknob levers that let you open a door by pushing instead of grasping; kitchen products that require the use of only one hand; wheelwalkers; and telephones for the hearing-impaired. Most products are low-tech and all are thoroughly tested before going into the catalog; call (800) 959-EASY.

■ **L.S. & S. Group offers a catalog** with over 1,000 products for the visually impaired. These items include computer software, magnifiers, canes, "talking" kitchen scales, and liquid level indicators; call (800) 468-4789.

Last Resort

CHAPTER 65

HOW TO COMPLAIN

Talking Back

An ounce of preventive consumer education is worth many pounds of cure. But what should you do when disappointment invades even the smartest purchases? For instance, salespeople and advertisements make promises their products can't keep, an item that looks to be of superior quality turns out to be inferior, or a merchant's seemingly good intentions go bad. In fact, a federal study indicated that approximately one in four purchases results in a consumer problem—yet only one in 25 people with problems actually takes the time and effort to complain. But based on a company's usual impulse to resolve complaints to maintain good word-of-mouth and repeat sales, *it pays to talk back in order to get your money back.*

THE BASICS

Better Business Bureaus (BBBs) around the country handled 1.8 million consumer complaints in 1996. Be especially careful when you deal with the following businesses, which had the most complaints lodged against them: retail sales, home improvement companies, service firms, auto repairs and services, and ordered product (catalog, telephone, and mail order) sales.

You have a good chance of getting redress if you take the trouble to address the problem. But you may never get what you paid for—and you might end up more frustrated than if you hadn't complained at all—if you don't complain in a firm and organized way. Wheels that know how to squeak will get the grease.

Correcting your problem helps others as well as yourself. When you complain to a business, your action may motivate merchants and manufacturers to improve their ways. When you alert and seek help from a government or nonprofit agency, you help them target the worst offenders for law enforcement and consumer education initiatives.

If you are fortunate enough to have a local or state government office with law enforcement authority, you have the extra benefit of legal clout and a better shot at speedy resolution of your problem. For instance, New York City has some of the broadest consumer protection laws of any local government in the country. Every year, the city's Department of Consumer Affairs agency responds to some 150,000 New Yorkers and visitors with questions and problems, and formally handles an average of over 10,000 complaints. About 90% of consumers who file complaints get some satisfaction after Consumer Affairs staff helps them and the merchants work out mutually acceptable solutions to their disputes. Consumers receive an average of more than $1 million each year in money refunded and debts canceled. The one in 10 complaints that are not resolved through Consumer Affairs mediation are referred to courts or dropped by the consumer. (See the appendix on page 709 for consumer offices or the attorney general's office in your state.)

The first step in becoming a $marter complainer is checking a seller's "return policy" *before* making a purchase—otherwise, your complaint may be pointless from the start. Such policies should be posted on store premises and on sales receipts. They usually require that products be returned within a given time, in good condition or in

BUSINESS GROUPS RANKED BY COMPLAINTS

Type of Business	1996 Rank	1996 No. of Complaints
AUTO DEALERS, FRANCHISED	1	14,668
AUTO REPAIR SHOPS	2	9,728
HOME FURNISHINGS STORES (E.G., MATTRESS, WINDOW, FLOOR COVERINGS)	3	7,792
SERVICES, MISCELLANEOUS	4	7,129
HOME REMODELING CONTRACTORS, GENERAL	5	6,829
AUTO DEALERS, USED CARS	6	6,164
COMPUTER SALES/SERVICES	7	5,733
TELEPHONE COMPANIES	8	5,682
RETAIL STORES	9	4,898
DRY CLEANING, LAUNDRY COMPANIES	10	4,649

Source: Council of Better Business Bureaus, 1997

the original packaging, and with a receipt.

The Art of Complaining

Identify the problem. Go through the events leading up to your problem, including any attempts you made to resolve it.

Decide on an acceptable remedy. Do you want the item repaired? Replaced? Your money back? If you used credit, do you want your debt canceled?

Decide on the best strategy: Whom should you contact first, or last? It varies. For example, when Martha C., a financial analyst, purchased a lemon of a computer, she repeatedly called the company's technical support line. No response. "It suddenly occurred to me, who has the most interest in keeping me happy?" said Ms. Crawley. "The company's salespeople, of course! I got through immediately to the sales staff, and the replacement part I needed was in my hands within three days."

Gather your records. Include all sales receipts, credit card statements or canceled checks, and contracts, and repair bills. You'll need them to support your case.

Start where you made the purchase. Call the business that sold you the item or performed the service. Describe the problem calmly and thoroughly. Politely tell the retailer how you would like the problem resolved. If you end up talking to the customer service representative, remember that you are dealing

with someone other than the person actually responsible for your problem. So be firm while being polite and try to win them over. Ask for the manager or owner if the person you are speaking with is not helpful. You may need to move up the chain of command and call the company's headquarters to get satisfaction.

Contact the maker. To deal with a manufacturing defect, contact the manufacturer—ask for the consumer affairs director, the president, or the chief executive officer. (Phone numbers, sometimes toll-free, and addresses can be found on warranty cards, product boxes, or at the library.) A national firm may have spent millions of dollars to create brand-name goodwill and could be more concerned about not jeopardizing that good name than a local retailer would be. Before you contact the manufacturer, become familiar with the terms of your warranty. You also have rights under implied warranties that apply to all goods: Under the Uniform Commercial Code, which all 50 states have enacted in some version, a product must be fit to be used for the purpose for which it was intended—or you're entitled to restitution. You may also be protected by other local, state, and federal laws and regulations.

Put it in writing. If your problem cannot be settled over the phone, write a letter. Be brief and to the point. Let the company know that you believe the complaint can easily be resolved without any need for publicity or law enforcement ac-

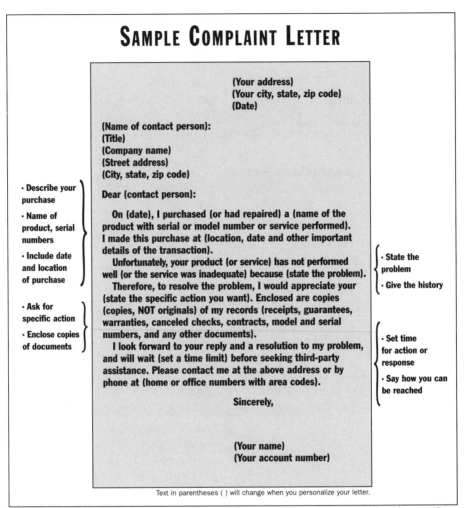

SAMPLE COMPLAINT LETTER

(Your address)
(Your city, state, zip code)
(Date)

(Name of contact person):
(Title)
(Company name)
(Street address)
(City, state, zip code)

- Describe your purchase
- Name of product, serial numbers
- Include date and location of purchase

Dear (contact person):

On (date), I purchased (or had repaired) a (name of the product with serial or model number or service performed). I made this purchase at (location, date and other important details of the transaction).

Unfortunately, your product (or service) has not performed well (or the service was inadequate) because (state the problem).

Therefore, to resolve the problem, I would appreciate your (state the specific action you want). Enclosed are copies (copies, NOT originals) of my records (receipts, guarantees, warranties, canceled checks, contracts, model and serial numbers, and any other documents).

I look forward to your reply and a resolution to my problem, and will wait (set a time limit) before seeking third-party assistance. Please contact me at the above address or by phone at (home or office numbers with area codes).

Sincerely,

- Ask for specific action
- Enclose copies of documents

- State the problem
- Give the history

- Set time for action or response
- Say how you can be reached

(Your name)
(Your account number)

Text in parentheses ( ) will change when you personalize your letter.

Source: U.S. Office of Consumer Affairs

tion. But be prepared to escalate—and politely mention your options of going to consumer groups, the media, or the government—in order to prod performance. In other words, adopt the admonition about a steel fist within a velvet glove.

Your complaint letter should include all the important facts about your purchase, the problem, and what you've done to try to resolve it:

- Your name, address, daytime and evening phone numbers, and account number, if appropriate.
- All important facts, including the date and place you made your purchase, and the serial and model numbers of the item, or the type of service you received and who performed it.
- A complete description of what you've already done to try to fix the problem.

- Exactly what you want as a remedy, such as a replacement, repair, or your money back.
- A reasonable time frame for the merchant to respond and correct the problem.
- Copies—*not originals*—of all related receipts, invoices, and warranties.

Maintain a file. Keep copies of all your correspondence and make notes about the content of phone conversations with retailers and manufacturers. Be sure to get the names of everyone with whom you speak and the dates and outcomes of your conversations. Pay a little extra and send the letter by certified mail. Request a return receipt—it's evidence that the letter was received and shows the name of the person who signed for it. For extra protection against the letter being lost in the mail, you can pay a bit more to send the letter by registered mail.

Surf the Net: The "information superhighway" is not only a convenient place to shop for the best buys but also a way to complain effectively. Consider:

- Financial writer Wayne Harris tells how Ed K. tried to use a discount coupon at Wendy's for a quick burger but the harried staff refused to accept it. Kennedy turned to Personal Advocate, a computer program for aggrieved consumers. Since Wendy's headquarters was listed in the software's address book, all he had to do was copy the location into Personal Advocate's standard business complaint letter, print, and mail it. He got a prompt apology and a new coupon.
- Yale law student Jonathan Kay was assured when he joined a Bally Health Club in Virginia in the summer of 1996 that he could get out of the remaining months of his monthly contract upon his return to school. When Bally refused to release him from the remaining $1,150 in payments, a frustrated Mr. Kay told *The New York Times,* "The cost of litigating was too high, but I realized the most valuable asset for a company is its good name." So he posted a complaint on an Internet bulletin board. Bally released him from his contract.

> "*Complaining is important because you can not only help yourself but you can trigger an investigation, which can help many others as well.*"
>
> —BARBARA BERGER OPOTOWSKY, Former President of the Better Business Bureau of Metropolitan New York

The Next Step

If you still don't get satisfaction, it's time to contact your government consumer affairs office, trade association, or the Better Business Bureau. Send a brief cover letter outlining the problem and your attempts to resolve it on your own; include copies of your correspondence with the offending company. Send the company a copy of your letter to government authorities and you may get results even before the consumer affairs agency, trade group, or BBB takes action.

The government is there to help you. Really. In most parts of the country, local and state consumer affairs or attorneys general offices will be able to help you resolve your problem. These offices typically have the legal muscle—or at least the official letterhead—to persuade a firm to provide a fair result, or even to fine the company if it broke any laws or violated regulations. Federal agencies do not generally handle individual consumer complaints, but they keep track of your letters to help them target troublesome industries.

Tell the relevant trade association how you were tricked or unfairly treated. Some trade associations sponsor dispute resolution programs involving arbitration, conciliation, or mediation. Since the outcomes of these programs may be binding, get a copy of the program's rules *before* you file your case. (See **HELP** at the end of this chapter for information on these programs and refer to relevant chapters earlier in the book.)

Tell it to the judge. In those rare instances when all of the above efforts fail, consumers have one more option: suing the business in either small claims or civil court. Don't wait too long to exercise your legal

rights: The laws where you live may limit the amount of time you have to file a lawsuit.

State and local consumer affairs offices usually offer advice on how to proceed in court, including how to get affordable legal help. Small claims courts handle disputes involving relatively small amounts of money, while civil courts handle cases involving bigger bucks. In small claims court, most people represent themselves without the help of lawyers. Civil court procedures can be complicated, and even though you may be allowed to represent yourself, you may not get very far without a lawyer.

Most often, the small claims process is convenient, fast, and saves you from having to pay a lawyer (although you can hire a lawyer simply to review your case with you or accompany you to court, if you like). Typically, small claims court is the place to take up cases involving broken contracts, negligent behavior that caused damage to your property, violation of your rights, and redress for purchases of defective merchandise or services. However, it's only worth the effort if the person or business you are suing can pay. The maximum amount disputable in small claims courts in the U.S. averages $2,000, but some states have a higher threshold: Alaska, California, Georgia, New Mexico, and Pennsylvania have raised their limits to $5,000; and in parts of Tennessee, the limit is $10,000.

To prepare your case, document your efforts to resolve the dispute

PLACES TO SEEK RESOLUTION

If you run into trouble with a product or service, there are a number of places to seek resolution.

- **Store.** Speak to or visit the original salesperson, the supervisor, a customer service representative, the manager, or the owner of the store.
- **Manufacturer.** Write to the president or chief executive officer.
- **Media.** Contact a consumer reporter, a letter-to-the-editor section, or media action line.
- **Self-policing groups.** Convey the problem to the BBB, a trade association, or an industry-specific resolution group (for example, bar association grievance committee, medical society, auto arbitration panels).
- **Consumer groups.** Report the incident to one of Ralph Nader's groups, Consumers Union, or the Consumer Federation of America.
- **Public agencies.** Inform the local consumer office or attorney general's office.
- **Court.** Depending on the size of the claim, go to small claims or civil court.
- **District attorney.** If the matter involves willful fraud, consider reporting it for possible criminal prosecution.
- **Legislature.** Go to your city council or state legislature if a new law is needed.

yourself. Keep photocopies of all correspondence and a written log of all phone conversations. Before you go into court, get organized:

- Prepare a written outline of the chronology of events. Keep it short and to the point.
- If you have a problem with a local business, go to the County Clerk's office to research the full name, address, and owner of the business.
- Make your own detailed estimate of what you are owed. Then, itemize your expenses and bills to determine what you think is fair compensation.

- If visible evidence is relevant, photograph the place or item at issue for the judge.

When you go to court:

- Before the judge, present your case and all the evidence. Listen to the story told by the opposing party and point out misstatements, misinterpretations of fact, and memory lapses. But don't lose your temper; the judge may take it as a sign that you're missing solid evidence.
- Again, don't forget to bring all the supporting documents for your case with you to help the judge come to a fair decision.

■ Submit any evidence you have of your efforts to resolve the dispute outside court—i.e., letters to the contractor who skipped town before finishing the job, canceled checks for payments you made that you thought were fair, notes to neighbors who insisted on letting their daughter practice the drums at 6:30 A.M.

Speak Up and Out

If *The Consumer Bible* offers you anything, it's this—$marter consumers can save thousands of dollars a year if they compare prices and complain when aggrieved. Yet an estimated 24 of 25 purchasers who are dissatisfied but silent underestimate their power. Reputable stores and manufacturers survive and thrive if they (a) get good word-of-mouth, (b) avoid bad publicity and liability claims, and (c) treat customers as advisors, not adversaries. Says a shrewd Tim Hicks, Blockbuster's VP for Operations, "Every complaint is a gift."

These three elements actually stack the deck *in favor* of a committed complaint, so long as he or she energetically works through the alternatives described earlier. The goal of this book was to educate and empower you in the marketplace. Ultimately, only *you* can stand up for your rights as a consumer.

HELP

■ **To find listings of** local, state, and federal agencies, corporate consumer contacts, Better Business Bureaus and trade associations, consult the free *Consumer's Resource Handbook*, published by the U.S. Office of Consumer Affairs. Write to Handbook, Consumer Information Center, Pueblo, CO 81009; it's also on the Internet at www.pueblo.gsa.gov/, and the federal government's Internet gateway to all its consumer resources and agencies is at www.consumer.gov.

■ **Trade associations and their con**sumer functions are also listed at your local library in *National Trade and Professional Associations of the United States*, published by Columbia Books, Inc.

■ **If you just need the address and/** or phone number of a company, call the reference desk of your local library and ask them to look the company up in AT&T's directory of toll-free numbers or other directories of corporations they have, such as *Standard and Poor's Register of Corporations, Directors and Executives*, the *Standard Directory of Advertisers*, or the *Trade Names Directory*.

■ **The "Consumer World" Web site at** www.consumerworld.org has gathered over 1,700 of the most useful consumer resources on the Internet and categorized them for easy access. This well-designed site not only helps you find buying advice and bargains, it also leads you through the process of filing consumer complaints with company consumer affairs offices, the Better Business Bureau, and government officials.

STATE CONSUMER OFFICES

Alabama

Office of the Attorney General
Consumer Affairs Division
11 South Union Street
Montgomery, AL 36130
(334) 242-7334
(800) 392-5658 (toll-free in Alabama)

Alaska

The Attorney General's Office refers complaints to the Better Business Bureau, small claims court, and private attorneys.

Better Business Bureau
2805 Bering Street, #2
Anchorage, AK 99503-3819
(907) 562-0704

Arizona

Office of the Attorney General
Consumer Information and Complaints
1275 West Washington Street, Room 259
Phoenix, AZ 85007
(602) 542-5763
(800) 352-8431 (toll-free in Arizona)

Office of the Attorney General
Consumer Protection and Advocacy
400 West Congress Street
South Building, Suite 315
Tucson, AZ 85701
(520) 628-6504

Arkansas

Office of the Attorney General
Consumer Protection Division
200 Tower Building
323 Center Street
Little Rock, AR 72201
(501) 682-2343 (voice/TDD)
(800) 482-8982 (toll-free voice/TDD in Arkansas)
www.ag.state.ar.us

California

California Department of
  Consumer Affairs
400 R Street
Suite 3000
Sacramento, CA 95814
(916) 445-1254
(916) 322-1700 (TDD)
(800) 952-5210 (toll-free in California)

Office of the Attorney General
Public Inquiry Unit
P.O. Box 944255
Sacramento, CA 94244-2550
(916) 322-3360
(916) 324-5564 (TDD)
caag.state.ca.us/piu

Bureau of Automotive Repair
California Department of
  Consumer Affairs
10240 Systems Parkway
Sacramento, CA 95827
(916) 445-1254
(800) 952-5210 (toll-free in California, auto repair only)
(916) 322-1700 (TDD)

Colorado

Office of the Attorney General
Consumer Protection Unit
1525 Sherman Street, 5th Floor
Denver, CO 80203
(303) 866-5189
(800) 332-2071 (toll-free in Colorado)

Connecticut

Department of Consumer Protection
165 Capitol Avenue
Hartford, CT 06106
(860) 566-2294
(800) 842-2649 (toll-free in Connecticut)
www.state.ct.us/dcp

709

Delaware

Division of Consumer Protection
Department of Community Affairs
820 North French Street, 6th Floor
Wilmington, DE 19801
(302) 577-8600

District of Columbia

Department of Consumer and Regulatory
Affairs
614 H Street, NW, Room 1120
Washington, DC 20001
(202) 727-7120

Florida

Department of Agriculture and Consumer
Services
Division of Consumer Services
407 South Calhoun Street
Mayo Building, 2nd Floor
Tallahassee, FL 32399-0800
(850) 488-2221
(800) 435-7352 (toll-free in Florida)
www.fl-ag.com

Office of the Attorney General
Consumer Division
110 S.E. 6th Street
Fort Lauderdale, FL 33301
(954) 712-4600

Georgia

Governor's Office of Consumer Affairs
2 Martin Luther King Jr. Drive
Suite 356
Atlanta, GA 30334
(404) 656-3790
(800) 869-1123 (toll-free in Georgia)

Office of the Attorney General
40 Capitol Square, SW
Atlanta, GA 30334-1300
(404) 656-4585

Hawaii

Department of Commerce and Consumer
Affairs
Office of Consumer Protection
235 S. Beretania Street, Room 801
Honolulu, HI 96813
(808) 586-2636

Department of Commerce and Consumer
Affairs
Office of Consumer Protection
75 Aupuni Street
Hilo, HI 96720
(808) 974-6230

Department of Commerce and Consumer
Affairs
Office of Consumer Protection
54 High Street
Wailuku, HI 96793
(808) 984-8244

Idaho

Office of the Attorney General
Consumer Protection Unit
P.O. Box 83720
Boise, ID 83720-0010
(208) 334-2424
(800) 432-3545 (toll-free in Idaho)
www2.state.id.us/ag/index.html

Illinois

Office of the Attorney General
Consumer Protection Division
100 West Randolph, 11th Floor
Chicago, IL 60601
(312) 814-3000
(312) 793-2852 (TDD)

Indiana

Office of the Attorney General
Consumer Protection Division
402 E. Washington Street
5th Floor
Indianapolis, IN 46204
(317) 232-6330
(800) 382-5516 (toll-free in Indiana)
www.state.in.us/hoosieradvocate

Iowa

Office of the Attorney General
Consumer Protection Division
1300 East Walnut Street
2nd Floor
Des Moines, IA 50319
(515) 281-5926
www.state.ia.us/government/ag

Kansas

Office of the Attorney General
Consumer Protection Division
301 West 10th
Kansas Judicial Center
Topeka, KS 66612-1597
(913) 296-3751
(800) 432-2310 (toll-free in Kansas)

Kentucky

Office of the Attorney General
Consumer Protection Division
1024 Capitol Center Drive
Frankfort, KY 40601

(502) 573-2200
(808) 432-9257 (toll-free in Kentucky)
www.law.state.ky.us/cp/default.htm

Office of the Attorney General
Consumer Protection Division
9001 Shelbyville Road
Suite 3
Louisville, KY 40222
(502) 425-4825
(800) 432-9257 (toll-free in Kentucky)

Louisiana

Office of the Attorney General
Consumer Protection Section
1 American Place
301 Main Street, Suite 1250
Baton Rouge, LA 70801
(504) 342-9638
(800) 351-4889 (toll-free in Louisiana)
www.laag.com

Maine

Bureau of Consumer Credit Protection
State House Station No. 35
Augusta, ME 04333-0035
(207) 624-8527
(800) 332-8529 (toll-free in Maine)

Office of the Attorney General
Consumer Mediation Service
State House Station No. 6
Augusta, ME 04333-0035
(207) 626-8849 (9 AM to 1 PM)

Maryland

Office of the Attorney General
Consumer Protection Division
200 St. Paul Place
Baltimore, MD 21202-2021
(410) 528-8662 (9 AM to 3 PM)
(410) 576-6372 (TDD in Baltimore area)
www.oag.state.md.us

Eastern Shore Branch Office
Office of the Attorney General
Consumer Protection Division
201 Baptist Street
Suite 30
Salisbury, MD 21801-4976
(410) 543-6620

Western Maryland Branch Office
Office of the Attorney General
Consumer Protection Division
138 East Antietam Street
Suite 210
Hagerstown, MD 21740-5684
(301) 791-4780

Massachusetts

Department of the Attorney General
Consumer Protection Division
200 Portland Street
Boston, MA 02114
(617) 727-8400

Executive Office of Consumer Affairs and
Business Regulation
1 Ashburton Place, Room 1411
Boston, MA 02108
(617) 727-7780
www.consumer.com/consumer

Michigan

Office of the Attorney General
Consumer Protection Division
P.O. Box 30213
Lansing, MI 48909
(517) 373-1140

Bureau of Automotive Regulation
Michigan Department of State
208 North Capitol
Lansing, MI 48918-1200
(517) 373-4777
(800) 292-4204 (toll-free in Michigan)

Minnesota

Office of the Attorney General
Consumer Services Division
1400 NCL Tower
445 Minnesota Street, Suite 1400
St. Paul, MN 55101
(612) 296-3353
www.ag.state.mn.us/consumer

Mississippi

Office of the Attorney General
Office of Consumer Protection
P.O. Box 22947
Jackson, MS 39225-2947
(601) 359-4230
www.ago.state.ms.us/consprot.htm

Missouri

Office of the Attorney General
Division of Consumer Protection
P.O. Box 899
Jefferson City, MO 65102
(573) 751-3321
(800) 392-8222 (toll-free in Missouri)

Montana

Consumer Affairs Unit
Department of Commerce
1424 Ninth Avenue
Box 200501
Helena, MT 59620-0501
(406) 444-4312

Nebraska

Consumer Protection Division
Department of Justice
2115 State Capitol
P.O. Box 98920
Lincoln, NE 68509
(402) 471-2682

Nevada

Commissioner of Consumer Affairs
Department of Business & Industry
1850 E. Sahara Avenue
Las Vegas, NV 89104
(702) 486-7355
(800) 326-5202 (toll-free in Nevada)
www.state.nv.us/fyiconsumer

Consumer Affairs Division
Department of Business & Industry
4600 Kietzke Lane, B-113
Reno, NV 89502
(702) 688-1800
(800) 326-5202 (toll-free in Nevada)

New Hampshire

Office of the Attorney General
Consumer Protection and
   Antitrust Bureau
33 Capitol Street
Concord, NH 03301
(603) 271-3641
www.state.nh.us/oag/ag.htm

New Jersey

Division of Consumer Affairs
P.O. Box 45025
124 Halsey Street, 7th Floor
Newark, NJ 07101
(201) 504-6200
www.state.nj.us/lps/ca/home.htm

New Mexico

Office of the Attorney General
Consumer Protection Division
P.O. Drawer 1508
Santa Fe, NM 87504
(505) 827-6060
(800) 678-1508 (toll-free in NM)

New York

Office of the Attorney General
Bureau of Consumer Frauds
   and Protection
State Capitol
Albany, NY 12224
(518) 474-5481
www.oag.state.ny.us

Office of the Attorney General
Bureau of Consumer Frauds and Protection
120 Broadway
New York, NY 10271
(212) 416-8345

New York State Consumer Protection Board
5 Empire State Plaza, Suite 2101
Albany, NY 12223-1556
(518) 474-8583
(800) 697-1220 (toll-free in New York)
www.consumer.state.ny.us

North Carolina

Office of the Attorney General
Consumer Protection Section
Old Education Building
P.O. Box 629
Raleigh, NC 27602
(919) 716-6000

North Dakota

Office of the Attorney General
Consumer Protection
600 East Boulevard Avenue
Bismarck, ND 58505
(701) 328-3404
(800) 472-2600 (toll-free in North Dakota)
www.state.nd.us/ndag

Ohio

Office of the Attorney General
Consumer Protection
30 East Broad Street
State Office Tower, 25th Floor
Columbus, OH 43215-3428
(614) 466-4986
(614) 466-1393 (TDD)
(800) 282-0515 (toll-free in Ohio)

Office of Consumers' Counsel
77 South High Street, 15th Floor
Columbus, OH 43266-0550
(614) 466-8574
(800) 282-9448 (toll-free in Ohio)
www.state.oh.us/ans/

Oklahoma

Office of the Attorney General
Consumer Protection Division
4545 North Lincoln Boulevard, Suite 260
Oklahoma City, OK 73105
(405) 521-2029

Department of Consumer Credit
4545 North Lincoln Boulevard, Suite 260
Oklahoma City, OK 73105
(405) 521-3653

Oregon

Financial Fraud Section
Department of Justice
1162 Court Street NE
Salem, OR 97310
(503) 378-4320
www.doj.state.or.us/finfraud/welcome3.html

Pennsylvania

Office of the Attorney General
Bureau of Consumer Protection
Strawberry Square, 14th Floor
Harrisburg, PA 17120
(717) 787-9707
(800) 441-2555 (toll-free in Pennsylvania)
www.attorneygeneral.gov

Office of Consumer Advocate
Forman Place, 5th Floor
555 Walnut Street
Harrisburg, PA 17101-1921
(717) 783-7152 (utilities only)
www.oca.state.pa.us

Puerto Rico

Department of Consumer Affairs (DACO)
Minillas Station, P.O. Box 41059
Santurce, PR 00940-1059
(787) 721-0940

Department of Justice
P.O. Box 902192
San Juan, PR 00902
(787) 721-2900

Rhode Island

Office of the Attorney General
Consumer Protection Unit
150 South Main Street
Providence, RI 02903
(401) 274-4400
(401) 274-4400, ext. 2354 (TDD)
(800) 852-7776 (toll-free in Rhode Island)

South Carolina

Department of Consumer Affairs
P.O. Box 5757
Columbia, SC 29250-5757
(803) 734-9452
(803) 734-9455 (TDD)
(800) 922-1594 (toll-free in South Carolina)
www.state.sc.us/consumer

State Ombudsman
Investment Division
1205 Pendleton Street, Room 308
Columbia, SC 29201
(803) 734-0457
(803) 734-1147 (TDD)

South Dakota

Office of the Attorney General
Division of Consumer Protection
500 East Capitol
Pierre, SD 57501-5070
(605) 773-4400

Tennessee

Division of Consumer Affairs
500 James Robertson Parkway
Nashville, TN 37243-0600
(615) 741-4737
(800) 342-8385 (toll-free in Tennessee)
www.state.tn.us/consumer

Texas

Office of the Attorney General
Consumer Protection Division
P.O. Box 12548
Austin, TX 78711
(512) 463-2070

Office of the Attorney General
Consumer Protection Division
714 Jackson Street
Suite 800
Dallas, TX 75202-4506
(214) 742-8944

Office of the Attorney General
Consumer Protection Division
6090 Surety Drive, Room 113
El Paso, TX 79905
(915) 772-9476

Office of the Attorney General
Consumer Protection Division
1019 Congress Street
Suite 1550
Houston, TX 77002-1702
(713) 223-5886

Office of the Attorney General
Consumer Protection Division
916 Main Street
Suite 806
Lubbock, TX 79401-2905
(806) 747-5238

Office of the Attorney General
Consumer Protection Division
3201 North McColl Road, Suite B
McAllen, TX 78501
(210) 682-4547

Office of the Attorney General
Consumer Protection Division
115 East Travis Street
Suite 925
San Antonio, TX 78205-1605
(210) 225-4191

Texas Department of Insurance
Consumer Protection MC 111-1A
P.O. Box 149091
Austin, TX 78714-9091
(512) 463-6500
(800) 252-3439 (toll-free in Texas)

Utah

Division of Consumer Protection
Department of Commerce
160 East 3rd South
P.O. Box 146704
Salt Lake City, UT 84114-6704
(801) 530-6001
(801) 530-6601 (fax)
(800) 721-7233 (toll-free in Utah)

Vermont

Office of the Attorney General
Public Protection Division
109 State Street
Montpelier, VT 05609-1001
(802) 828-5507

Consumer Assistance Program
104 Morrill Hall UVM
Burlington, VT 05405
(802) 656-3183
(800) 649-2424 (toll-free in Vermont)

Consumer Assurance Section
Department of Agriculture, Food and
  Market
116 State Street
Montpelier, VT 05620-2901
(802) 828-2436

Virginia

Office of the Attorney General
Antitrust and Consumer Litigation Section
Supreme Court Building
900 East Main Street
Richmond, VA 23219
(804) 786-2116

State Division of Consumer Protection
Department of Agriculture and Consumer
  Services
Washington Building, Room 101
P.O. Box 1163
Richmond, VA 23218
(804) 786-2042
(800) 552-9963 (toll-free in Virginia)

Washington

Office of the Attorney General
Consumer Protection Division
P.O. Box 40118
Olympia, WA 98504-0118

(360) 753-6210
www.wa.gov/ago

Office of the Attorney General
Consumer Protection
900 Fourth Avenue, Suite 2000
Seattle, WA 98164
(206) 464-6684
(800) 551-4636 (toll-free in Washington)

Office of the Attorney General
Consumer Protection
West 1116 Riverside Avenue
Spokane, WA 99201
(509) 456-3123

Office of the Attorney General
Consumer Protection
1019 Pacific Avenue, 3rd Floor
Tacoma, WA 98402-4411
(206) 593-2904

West Virginia

Office of the Attorney General
Consumer Protection Division
812 Quarrier Street, 6th Floor
Charleston, WV 25301
(304) 558-8986
(800) 368-8808 (toll-free in West Virginia)

Wisconsin

Division of Trade and Consumer Protection
Department of Agriculture, Trade and
  Consumer Protection
P.O. Box 8911
Madison, WI 53708
(608) 224-4949
(800) 422-7128 (toll-free in Wisconsin)

Department of Agriculture, Trade and
  Consumer Protection
10930 West Potter Road, Suite C
Milwaukee, WI 53226
(414) 226-1231
(800) 442-7128 (toll-free in Wisconsin)

Wyoming

Office of the Attorney General
Consumer Protection Division
123 State Capitol Building
Cheyenne, WY 82002
(307) 777-7874

SOURCES

FOOD

1. GROCERIES

Better Business Bureau A to Z Buying Guide. New York: Henry Holt & Co., 1990.

Chase, Marilyn. "Pretty Soon the Word 'Organic' on Foods Will Mean One Thing. *Wall Street Journal*, Aug. 21, 1997.

"Chicken: What You Don't Know Can Hurt You." *Consumer Reports*, March 1998.

"A Common Sense Approach to Pesticides." Center for Science in the Public Interest's *Nutrition Action Healthletter*, September 1993.

Environmental Defense Fund, California Department of Health, Office of the California Attorney General. *What You Should Know About Lead in China Dishes.* San Francisco: 1992.

Feeney, Sheila Anne. "Milk Date Law Flouted." *New York Daily News*, Oct. 24, 1997.

Garman, Thomas E. *Consumer Economic Issues in America.* Boston: Houghton Mifflin, 1991.

Gerth, Jeff, and Tim Weiner. "Imports Swamp U.S. Food Safety Efforts." *New York Times*, Sept. 29, 1997.

"Greener Greens?" *Consumer Reports*, January 1998.

Jacobson, Michael, Ph.D., Executive Director, Center for Science in the Public Interest. Comments made at Ralph Nader's Frugal Shoppers Week press conference. Aug. 31, 1992.

Murphy, Kate. "There's Big Green in Organic Food." *Business Week*, Oct. 6, 1997.

Newman, Stephen A. and Nancy Kramer. *Getting What You Deserve: A Handbook for the Assertive Consumer.* Garden City, NY: Doubleday, 1979.

New York City Department of Consumer Affairs. *Caveat Eater.* New York: May 1991.

————. *A Consumer Guide to Waxes on Fruits and Vegetables: Safer Choices for a Healthful Diet.* New York: Autumn 1991.

————. *Dangerous Dishes: Lead in Ceramics and What We Can Do.* New York: January 1993.

————. *Federal Trade Omission: False Nutritional Claims in Food Advertising.* New York: April 1992.

U.S. Federal Trade Commission. *Milk: Does It Measure Up?* July 17, 1997.

————. *Price Check: A Report on the Accuracy of Checkout Scanners.* Oct. 22, 1996.

U.S. Food and Drug Administration. "Focus on Food Safety." *FDA Consumer*, September/October 1997.

U.S. Food and Drug Administration, with the American Heart Association. *How to Read the New Food Label.* (AHA 51-1052 (CP) and FDA 93-2260). Washington, DC: FDA, 1993; Dallas: AHA, 1993.

————. *Reducing Exposure to Lead from Ceramic Ware.* Washington, DC: November 1991.

"Winning the Grocery Game." *Consumer Reports*, August 1997.

2. FAST-FOOD OUTLETS

"The Eating-Out Boom." *U.S. News & World Report*, Dec. 9, 1996.

"Fast, Yes, But How Good?" *Consumer Reports*, December 1997.

"The Fattening of Fast Food." *Consumer Reports*, October 1996.

Jacobson, Michael F., Ph.D. and Sarah Fritschner. *Fast Food Guide*, 2nd ed. New York: Workman Publishing Co., 1991.

Mulrine, Anna. "Psst. About That Veggie Pita..." *U.S. News & World Report.* July 7, 1997.

Nutrition Action Healthletter. Washington, DC: Center for Science in the Public Interest, September 1996.

Nutrition Action Healthletter. Washington, DC: Center for Science in the Public Interest, November 1993.

Pitts, Myron B. "The Latest on What to Feed Kids." *USA Today*, Mar. 30, 1997.

Sugarman, Carole and Sandra Evans. "'Low-Fat': Heavy Promises, Light Performance." *Washington Post*, Mar. 15, 1995.

3. WATER

Blumenthal, Robin Goldwyn. "Water Bottlers Tap Resources to Prepare for FDA Label Rule; Consumers at Stake." *Wall Street Journal*, Mar. 12, 1993.

Brand, Rick. "33 Contractors Caught in Sting." *Newsday*, Dec. 12, 1996.

"EPA Study of Watersheds Finds More Than Half Are Polluted." *Wall Street Journal*, Oct. 2, 1997.

"Fit to Drink?" *Consumer Reports*, January 1990.

Get the Lead Out. Oakland, CA: Environmental Law Foundation.

Hays, Constance L. "Now, Liquid Gold Comes in Bottles." *New York Times*, Jan. 20, 1998.

"How to Reduce Lead in Drinking Water." *New York Times*, Mar. 2, 1991.

Ingersoll, Bruce. "FDA Finds Bunk in Bottled Water Claims." *Wall Street Journal*, Apr. 10, 1991.

Ingram, Colin. *The Drinking Water Book.* Berkeley, CA: Ten Speed Press, 1991.

"Is There Lead in Your Water?" *Consumer Reports*, February 1993.

Milius, Susan. "Tapped Out." *Organic Gardening*, April 1988.

New York State Department of Law. *Consumer Guide to Water Treatment Devices.* New York: July 1990.

1991 Drinking Water Guide. San Diego: California Public Interest Research Group, January 1991.

"Quenching the Thirst for Safe Drinking Water." *NCL Bulletin*, March/April 1993.

Shabecoff, Philip. "EPA Adopts Stiffer Regulations to Protect Drinking Water Supply." *New York Times*, June 23, 1991.

"Should You Use a Water Filter?" *Consumer Reports*, July 1997.

Terry, Sara. "Troubled Water: Episodes in Milwaukee, New York and Elsewhere Show America What Must Be Done to Turn the Tap With Confidence." *New York Times Magazine*, Sept. 26, 1993.

U.S. Environmental Protection Agency. "Safe Drinking Water Hotline Factsheet." Washington, DC: February 1993.

Wald, Matthew L. "High Levels of Lead Found in Water Serving 30 Million." *New York Times*, May 12, 1993.

HEALTH

4. HEALTH INSURANCE

Anders, George, "Polling Quirks Give HMOs Healthy Ratings." *Wall Street Journal*, Aug. 27, 1996.

Auerbach, Stuart, "How Can Patients Judge Their HMOs? Nonprofit Group Offers Guidelines for Ranking Health Plans, But It's Not an Easy Task." *Washington Post Health*, Aug. 6, 1996.

"Are HMOs the Answer?" *Consumer Reports*, August 1992.

Bunis, Dena. "Medical Review Services Assailed." *New York Newsday*, Sept. 18, 1991.

Capel, Kerri Y., "When Your HMO Says 'No Way.'" *Business Week*, May 17, 1997.

Cropper, Carol Marie, "The HMO Says the Doctor Is In. Is He?" *New York Times*, Nov. 10, 1996.

Findlay, Steven, "Trend in Managed Care is Flexibility." *USA Today*, April 16, 1997.

Freudenheim, Milt. "Many Patients Unhappy With HMO's." *New York Times*, Aug. 18, 1993.

Garland, Susan B., and Keith B. Hammonds, "How Good Is Your HMO? More Employers Offer Ratings of Medical Plans and Doctors." *Business Week*, Nov. 19, 1997.

Jack, Lyon; Jones, P.A., "In-Depth Analysis of Regulations Governing the Health Insurance Portability and Accountability Act." *Arkansas Employment Law Letter*, September 1997.

Jeffrey, Nancy Ann, "How to Tell if an HMO's 'Quality' Promise is for Real," *Wall Street Journal*, June 13, 1997.

Kilborn, Peter T., "Trend Toward Managed Care is Unpopular, Surveys Find," *New York Times*, September 28, 1997.

Kramon, Glenn. "Health Insurers in Trying to Save Find New Costs in Managing Care." *New York Times*, Aug. 25, 1991.

Polzer, Karl, and Patricia A. Butler, "Employee Health Plan Protections Under ERISA." *Health Affairs*, September/October 1997.

Quinn, Jane Bryant, "Is Your HMO OK—Or Not?" *Newsweek*, Feb. 10, 1997.

Ruffenach, Glenn. "Firms Use Financial Incentives to Make Employees Seek Lower Health-Care Fees." *Wall Street Journal*, Feb. 9, 1993.

Schultz, Ellen E. "Employees Find There Is Little Recourse When Denied by Company Health Plans." *Wall Street Journal,* Oct. 25, 1993.

——. "Medical Data Gathered by Firms Can Prove Less Than Confidential." *Wall Street Journal*, May 18, 1994.

Spragins, Ellyn E., "How to Choose an HMO." *Newsweek*, Dec. 15, 1997.

United States Department of Health and Human Services, Office of the Inspector General. *Medicare HMO Appeal and Grievance Processes.* Report. December 1996.

Winslow, Ron. "Health Care: HMOs May Impair Ties to Specialists." *Wall Street Journal*, July 9, 1993.

——. "Quality of HMOs in U.S. Varies Widely, Report by Accreditation Group Finds." *Wall Street Journal*, Oct. 2, 1997.

5. PHARMACEUTICALS AND PHARMACISTS

"Another Way to Overtreat the Symptoms of a Cold." *Consumer Reports*, February 1991.

Colburn, Don. "How Drug Prices Vary." *Washington Post,* Dec. 15, 1992.

——. "Drug Prices—What's Up?" *Washington Post,* Dec. 15, 1992.

Consumers Union. *The New Medicine Show.* Mount Vernon, NY: Consumers Union of the United States, 1989.

"Do You Need a Financial Makeover?" *Consumer Reports*, March 1997.

Gutfeld, Rose. "FDA Attacks Drug Makers' Ads to Doctors." *Wall Street Journal,* Aug. 3, 1993.

"How to Buy Drugs for Less." *Consumer Reports*, October 1993.

Long, James W., M.D., and James J. Rubacki, Pharm. D. *The Essential Guide to Prescription Drugs.* New York: HarperCollins, 1993.

Miller, Roger W. "Doctors, Patients Don't Communicate." *U.S. FDA Counselor,* July/August 1983.

New York City Department of Consumer Affairs. *Don't Be Left Out in The Cold: A Comparison of Cold and Flu Remedies.* September 1991.

——. *Pills and Potency—Why Prescription Drugs Need Expiration Dates.* New York: January 1993.

——. *Comparison Shop for Less Expensive Prescription Drugs.* New York. February 1993.

New York City Public Advocate's Office. *Compromising Your Drug of Choice.* December 1996.

——. *Pharmaceutical Payola: How Secret Commercial Deals Are Dictating Your Next Prescription and Harming Your Health.* Aug. 13, 1997.

Pins, Kenneth. "Running Drugs—to Fill Prescriptions." *The Des Moines Register*, May 11, 1997.

Pressler, Margaret Webb. "A Prescription for Trouble?" *The Washington Post*, July 22, 1997.

Public Citizen Health Research Center. "Colds: How to Treat Them." *Health Letter*, February 1993.

Smith, Tammie. "Dealing with Drugs: Shopping Around Can Save Consumer Money on Prescriptions." *The Tennessean,* June 8, 1997.

Spalding, B.J. "Is Pharmacy Counseling a Myth?" *American Druggist,* May 1990.

Washington Post. "Cold Remedies Are a Hot Market." *New York Newsday*, Apr. 13, 1993.

Weber, Joseph, and John Carey. "Drug Ads: A Prescription for Controversy." *Business Week,* Jan. 18, 1993.

Wolfe, Sidney, M.D. *Worst Pills, Best Pills.* Washington, DC: Public Citizen Health Research Group, 1988.

6. DOCTORS AND HOSPITALS

Aiken, Linda H, Ph.D., Herbert L. Smith, Ph.D., and Eileen T. Lake, MPP. "Lower Medicare Mortality Rate Among a Set of Hospitals Known for Good Nursing Care." *Medical Care*, August 1994.

American Nurses Association. Report. *The Acute Care Nurse in Transition.* August 1996.

Bunis, Dena. "The Nursing Revolution (series): Nurses Fight Back/RNs Seek to Stop Unlicensed Aides From Taking Jobs." *Newsday*, May 3, 1996.

Crenshaw, Albert B. "Making Fairness Part of Hospital Bills." *New York Newsday,* May 7, 1992.

Duerksen, Susan. "For-Profit Hospitals Cut Costs; But Dangerously?" *San Diego Union-Tribune*, Dec. 8, 1996.

Goad, Meredith. "Hospital Horror Stories Bound for Your Enjoyment." *Central Maine Morning Sentinel* (Gannett Service), July 14, 1997.

Grady, Denise. "Some Routine Lab Tests May Be Unnecessary." *New York Times*, Nov. 20, 1996.

Graedon, Joe, and Teresa Gordon. "Drug, Dosage Errors a Common Hospital Hazard." *Raleigh News and Observer*, Feb. 2, 1997.

"Hospital Costs." *Primetime Live,* ABC News. August 15, 1991.

"How Good Is Your Doctor?" *Consumer Reports*, April 1996.

Inlander, Charles B., and Ed Weiner. *Take This Book to the Hospital With You*. Allentown, PA: People's Medical Society, 1993.

————. *150 Ways to Be a Savvy Medical Consumer*. Allentown, PA: People's Medical Society, 1992.

Jaklevic, Mary Chris. "Medical Groups: AMA's Seal of Approval: Group Plans to Start Universal Accreditation of Docs This Summer in Massachusetts." *Modern Healthcare*, March 17, 1997.

Korman, Richard. "Hospitals: Choosing Well to Get Well." *Business Week*, Feb. 26, 1996.

Lagnado, Lucette. "Ex-Manager Describes the Profit-Driven Life Inside Columbia/HCA." *Wall Street Journal*, May 30, 1997.

McVicar, Nancy, and Glenn Singer. "Guide Aims to Detail Hospitals' Strong, Weak Points; Patients Should Make Choices With Doctor's Help, Experts Say." *Ft. Lauderdale Sun-Sentinel*, Feb. 28, 1996.

Meckler, Laura. "Survey Nixes For-Profit Hospitals." *Associated Press*, Oct. 30, 1997.

Meehan, Mary. "How to Survive a Hospital Stay." *Better Homes and Gardens*, February 1997.

Millenson, Michael L. "'Miracle and Wonder': The AMA Embraces Quality Measurement." *Health Affairs*, May/June 1997.

New York State Department of Health. *Cardiac Surgery in New York State, 1989–1991*. Albany, NY.

New York State Nurses Association. "Statement to the New York State Assembly Standing Committees on Labor, Health, Higher Education and Social Services on the Understaffing of Professional Nurse Positions in Health Care." May 9, 1995.

————. "Statement to the Standing Committees on Higher Education and Health on Non-Nurses Performing Nursing Services." Feb. 6, 1997.

Nicholson, Joe. "Doctors of Disaster." *New York Post*, Aug. 25, 1993.

Public Citizen Health Research Group. *Ranking of State Medical Licensing Boards Serious Doctor Disciplinary Actions per 1,000 MDs—1995. Health Letter,* May 1996.

————. "Unnecesary Casarean Sections: Halting a National Epidemic." *Health Letter*, June 1992.

————. "Medical Records: Getting Yours." *Health Letter*, September 1992.

Rosenthal, Elisabeth. "The Alert Consumer: Confusion, Errors and Fraud in Medical Bills." *New York Times,* Nov. 14, 1993.

————. "Confusion and Error Are Rife in Hospital Billing Practices." *New York Times*, Jan. 27, 1993.

Sharpe, Anita. "The Operation Was a Success; the Bill Was Quite a Mess." *Wall Street Journal*, Sept. 17, 1997.

Sloane, Leonard. "Health Costs: Checking Bills Carefully to Catch Costly Errors." *New York Times,* Nov. 28, 1992.

Twedt, Steve. "A Question of Skill: Is a Cheaper Hospital Staff More Costly?" *Pittsburgh Post-Gazette*, Feb. 11, 1996.

Winslow, Ron. "California Group Publishes Ranking of Physicians Based on Patient Surveys." *Wall Street Journal*, Sept. 17, 1997.

7. LONG-TERM CARE

Brookings/ICF Long-Term Care Financial Model. Washington, DC: The Brookings Institute, 1993.

"Elder Care: The Insurer's Role." *New York Times*, Mar. 16, 1994.

Eisler, Peter. "Home Health Care Opens Door to Abuses." *USA Today*, Nov. 11, 1996.

Estes, Carroll L., and Thomas Bodenheimer. "Paying for Long-Term Care." *The Western Journal of Medicine*. Vol. 160, No. 1. January 1994.

Hinden, Stan. "Taking Cover From High Nursing Home Costs." *Washington Post*, July 13, 1997.

"How Will You Pay for Your Old Age?" *Consumer Reports*, October 1997.

Medicare: Entitlements and Advocacy Training. New York: Brookdale Center on Aging of Hunter College, Institute on Law and Rights of Older Adults. January 1992.

New York City Department of Consumer Affairs. *Promise Them Anything: The Selling of Long Term Care Insurance for the Elderly*. New York: 1993.

Nursing Home Input Price Index. Philadelphia, PA: The Wharton Business School of the University of Pennsylvania, 1993.

Nursing Home Insurance: Who Can Afford It? Washington, DC: Families USA. February 1993.

Overby, Stephanie. "Pricey Protection." *Smart Money Interactive,* 1997.

Pomeroy, Earl R. *Testimony of the National Association of Insurance Commissioners Before the Labor and Human Resources Committee, U.S. Senate.* Washington, DC: NAIC, 1992.

Tahmincioglu, Eve. "The Catch-22 of Long-Term-Care Insurance." *Kiplinger's Personal Finance Magazine,* May 1997.

U.S. General Accounting Office. *Long-Term Care: Current Issues and Future Directions.* April 1995.

————. *Long-Term Care Insurance: Risks to Consumers Should Be Reduced.* Washington, DC: GAO. December 1991.

————. *Older Americans Act: More Federal Action Needed on Public/Private Elder Care Partnerships.* Washington, DC: GAO. July 1992.

U.S. House Select Committee on Aging. *Abuses in the Sale of Long Term Care Insurance to the Elderly.* Washington, DC: June 1991.

Weissenstien, Eric. "Survey Casts Shadow on Long-Term Care Plans," *Modern Healthcare,* Apr. 27, 1992.

8. NUTRITIONAL SUPPLEMENTS

Barrett, Stephen, M.D., and the editors of Consumer Reports. *Health Schemes, Scams and Frauds.* Mount Vernon, NY: Consumer Reports Books, 1990.

Brody, Jane. *Jane Brody's Nutrition Book.* New York: W.W. Norton, 1981.

Burros, Marian. "Testing Calcium Supplements for Lead." *New York Times,* June 4, 1997.

Condor, Bob. "Pill Drill: Supplements Have Their Place, But You First Need to Find Out What You're Missing." *Chicago Tribune,* Mar. 19, 1997.

Herbert, Victor, F.A.C.P., and M.S., Subak-Shurpli, eds. *Mt. Sinai School of Medicine Complete Book of Nutrition.* New York: St. Martin's Press, 1992.

Hovey, Sue. "One Pill Makes You Larger." *Women's Sports and Fitness,* April 1997.

Howe, Maggy. "Blue-Green Algae." *Country Living,* March 1997.

Marsh, Barbara. "Commission Asks FDA to Regulate Diet Supplements." *Los Angeles Times,* June 25, 1997.

Neergaard, Lauran. "Herbal Pills Face Limits." *Dayton Daily News,* June 3, 1997.

New York City Department of Consumer Affairs. *Magic Muscle Pills!! Health and Fitness Quackery in Nutrition Supplements.* New York: May 1992.

Podolsky, Doug. "Nature's Remedies." *U.S. News & World Report,* May 19, 1997.

Turk, Michelle Pullia. "Ephedrine's Deadly Edge." *U.S. News & World Report,* July 7, 1997.

U.S. Congress, Health and Environment Subcommittee of the House Energy and Commerce Committee, *Hearing: Regulation of Dietary Supplements, July 29, 1993.* 103rd Congress, 1st Session, Washington, D.C.: GPO, 1993.

9. WEIGHT-LOSS PRODUCTS AND PROGRAMS

Barrett, Stephen, M.D. "Weight Control: Facts, Fads and Frauds," in *The Health Robbers,* Stephen Barrett, M.D. and William T. Jarvis, Ph.D., eds. Buffalo, NY: Prometheus Books, 1993.

Brody, Jane E. "Obesity Drugs: Weighing the Risks to Health Against the Small Victories." *New York Times,* Sept. 3, 1997.

————. "Panel Criticizes Weight-Loss Programs." *New York Times,* Apr. 2, 1992.

Burros, Marion. "Eating Well." *New York Times,* June 16, 1993.

Kolata, Gina. "2 Top Diet Drugs Are Recalled Amid Reports of Heart Defects." *New York Times,* Sept. 16, 1997.

Langreth, Robert. "Critics Claim Diet Clinics Misuse Obesity Drugs," *Wall Street Journal,* Mar. 31, 1997.

————. "Next Generation Obesity Drugs Are Still Many Years Away." *Wall Street Journal,* Sept. 16, 1997.

"Losing Weight: What Works — What Doesn't." *Consumer Reports,* June 1993.

National Institutes of Health. *Methods for Voluntary Weight Loss and Control.* Washington, DC: Technology Assessment Conference Statement, Mar. 30–Apr. 1, 1992.

New York City Department of Consumer Affairs. *A Weighty Issue: Dangers and Deceptions of the Weight Loss Industry.* New York: June 1991.

Schwartz, John. "Weighing the Data on Yo-Yo Dieting: No Major Risk Found," *Washington Post*, Oct. 19, 1994.

"Top-Selling Diets. Lots of Gimmicks, Little Solid Advice." *Consumer Reports*, January 1998.

U.S. Food and Drug Administration. "Health Advisory on Fenfluramine/Phentermine for Obesity." Aug. 27, 1997.

10. HEALTH CLUBS

Felton, Bruce, "Resolving to Sweat, At Least Until Feb.," *New York Times*, Dec. 29, 1996.

"Health Clubs: The Right Choice For You?", *Consumer Reports*, January 1996.

Howard, T. J. "Gym-Dandies: The Latest Craze in the Fitness Movement Is Not a Machine, But Personal Trainers Who Give TLC." *Chicago Tribune*, May 13, 1992.

"Indulgers to Join Fitness Scene," *Dallas Morning News*, Dec. 29, 1996.

IRSA, The Association of Quality Clubs. *50 State Summary: Sales Taxes, Bonding Regulations & Consumer Protection Laws Affecting the Health, Fitness & Racquet Sports Industry.*

—————. *The Economic Benefits of Exercise.*

—————. *The Guide to Choosing a Quality Health Club.*

Leichter, Franz S. "Leichter Survey Shows Health Club Ads Are Deceptive; Calls for Passage of Needed Health Club Regulations." Press release. New York: Jan. 18, 1987.

Martin, Douglas. "Strictly Business: Fitness Clubs Vie for Market Share." *New York Times*, Feb. 1, 1993.

McCarthy, John. "IRSA's Quality Initiative— A Marketing Opportunity." *Club Business International*, August 1992.

New York City Department of Consumer Affairs. *Choosing a Health Club: "Exercise" Caution.* New York: 1989.

Sloane, Leonard. "Making Sure a Health Club Is on Strong Financial Ground." *New York Times*, Feb. 2, 1991.

U.S. Centers for Disease Control and Prevention & American College of Sports Medicine. *Summary Statement: Workshop on Physical Activity and Public Health.* Washington, DC: 1993.

Valdes, Alisa. "Home Sweat Home: Boomers Who Are Too Busy to Make It to the Club Fuel a Trend in Fitness," *Boston Globe*, July 10, 1997.

Whitford, Ellen. "How to Pick a Health Club That is Just Right for You." *Atlanta Journal and Constitution*, Jan. 1, 1992.

Yaqub, Reshma Memon. "Need a Lift? Here's the Skinny on Choosing a Personal Trainer," *Chicago Tribune*, Jan. 2, 1997.

11. INFERTILITY SERVICES

Dunkin, Amy, ed. "In Vitro Fertilization: Delivering that Ray of Hope." *Business Week*, Sept. 3, 1990.

Greenberg, Jon. "In-Vitro Fertilization Needs Regulation." National Public Radio's *All Things Considered*, Apr. 14, 1992.

Gutfeld, Rose. "FDA Says Labels of Fertility Drugs Must Warn Users." *Wall Street Journal*, Jan. 14, 1993.

Hopkins, Ellen. "Tales From the Baby Factory." *New York Times Magazine*, Mar. 15, 1992.

Kong, Dolores. "Clinics Get Little Oversight." *Boston Globe*, Aug. 5, 1996.

—————. "The Painful Quest for Fertility." *Boston Globe*, Aug. 4, 1996.

Miller, Annetta. "Baby Makers Inc." *Newsweek*, June 29, 1992.

Muller, Joanne. "Making a Baby. Part II." *Boston Globe*, Sept. 8, 1996.

New York City Department of Consumer Affairs. *Consumer Guide to Fertility Services.* New York: Fall 1992.

Pear, Robert. "Fertility Clinics Face Crackdown." *New York Times*, Oct. 26, 1992.

Resolve National Office. "Questions to Ask About Assisted Reproductive Technology (ART) Programs."

Rothman, Barbara Katz, Ph.D. "The Frightening Future of Baby-Making." *Glamour*, June 1992.

U.S. House of Representatives, Subcommittee on Health and the Environment of the Committee on Energy and Commerce. *Hearing: Fertility Clinic Services,* Feb. 27, 1992.

Wozencraft, Ann. "It's a Baby, Or It's Your Money Back." *New York Times*, Aug. 25, 1996.

12. EYEGLASSES AND CONTACT LENSES

Blau, Melinda. "I Can See Clearly Now." *New York*, Mar. 10, 1997.

Brooks, Andree. "Yet Another High-Tech Innovation: Eyeglasses to Shake, Rattle and Roll." *New York Times*, July 31, 1991.

Contact Lens Council. *What You Need to Know About Safe Contact Lens Wear.*

Debare, Ilana. "Computer-Related Eyestrain a Growing Problem." *San Francisco Chronicle*, July 15, 1997.

Ervin, Keith. "State Sues Two Optometrists." *Seattle Times*, Apr. 20, 1996.

"Eye-Popping Price for New Contacts." *New York Newsday*, June 17, 1993.

Johannes, Laura. "Bausch & Lomb Agrees to Stop Selling Duplicate Contact Lenses." *Wall Street Journal*, Aug. 20, 1997.

Korman, Richard. "Eye Surgery? Take a Close Look." *Business Week*, Jan. 27, 1997.

"Q & A: Eye Protection." *New York Times*, Nov. 16, 1993.

"The Spec On Specs." *Consumer Reports*, July 1997.

U.S. Federal Trade Commission. "Dallas Eyecare Center Agrees to Settle FTC Charges." Press release. May 3, 1996.

Wessel, Harry. "Laser Eye Surgery: Is It Worth a Look?" *Orlando Sentinel*, Apr. 29, 1997.

HOME

13. HOUSES, CONDOS AND CO-OPS

Brooks, Andree. "Picking the Best Broker." *New York Times*, June 12, 1994.

——. "Getting a Home Inspected." *New York Times*, Jan. 23, 1994.

Bruss, Robert J. "Not All House Inspectors are Qualified." *Chicago Tribune*, Aug. 7, 1992.

Byrnes, Nanette. "How to Sell Your House at the Highest Price." *Smart Money*, July 1997.

Catalano, Joe. "What's Your House Worth?" *New York Newsday*, Dec. 11, 1993.

Eisenson, Marc. "25 Steps to a Penny Pinching Home Closing." *The Banker's Secret Bulletin*, Spring 1994.

Freedman, Alix M. "Power Lines Short-Circuit Sales, Homeowners Claim." *Wall Street Journal*, Dec. 8, 1993.

Glink, Ilyce R. *100 Questions Every First-Time Home Buyer Should Ask.* New York: Random House, 1994.

Goodman, Beverly. "Having a Mortgage in Hand Can Help You Land a House." *Money*, August 1997.

Harney, Kenneth. "Now You Have The Right to See Home Appraisals." *New York Newsday*, Jan. 1, 1994.

Irwin, Robert. *Tips & Traps When Buying a Home.* New York: McGraw Hill, 1997.

Romano, Jay. "Http:// Buyandsell Online.com." *New York Times*, July 27, 1997.

Rothstein, Mervyn. "When the Broker Works for the Buyer." *New York Times*, Sept. 19, 1993.

Smith, Anne Kates. "Heads Up, House Hunters —Here's a Guide to Recent Changes Affecting Buyers and Sellers." *U.S. News & World Report*, Apr. 5, 1993.

U.S. Environmental Protection Agency. *Radon Health Risks: Frequently Asked Questions.* Jan. 14, 1997.

"Your Home: Buy? Sell? Refinance?" *Consumer Reports*, May 1996.

14. HOME IMPROVEMENT CONTRACTORS

Brooks, Andree. "Repair Rip-Offs: Looking for Signs of a Scam." *New York Times*, July 4, 1993.

Buggs, Shannon. "Midwest Anticipates Flood of Out-of-State Contractors; Officials Expect Price-Gouging and Scams to Multiply." *Dallas Morning News*, Aug. 6, 1993.

Capell, Kerry. "The Nuts and Bolts of Hiring a Contractor." *Business Week,* July 7, 1997.

Costanzo, Christie. "How to Pick a Remodeling Contractor." *Los Angeles Times*, Aug. 25, 1990.

Crowe, Rosalie Robles. "Building Cases Against Builders: Investigator Tracks Unlicensed Contractors." *Phoenix Gazette*, May 5, 1993.

Daspin, Eileen. "Contractor Catfights Plague Wealthy, Too." *Wall Street Journal,* June 20, 1997.

Fried, Carla. "Everything You Want." *Money,* April 1997.

"Fixing Things Around the House." *USA Today,* July 1, 1997.

Giorgianni, Anthony. "Before You Hire a Contractor, Know What You're Getting Into." *The Hartford Courant*, May 22, 1993.

Locy, Toni. "Handymen Did a Job on Elderly D.C. Woman." *Washington Post,* Aug. 10, 1997.

McCullough, David. *Truman.* New York: Simon & Schuster, 1992.

Melia, Marilyn Kennedy. "Rehab Resources: Funding Your Remodeling Project." *Chicago Tribune*, July 16, 1993.

Nader, Ralph, and Wesley J. Smith. *The Frugal Shopper*. Washington, DC: Center for Study of Responsive Law, 1992.

New York City Department of Consumer Affairs. *A Consumer's Guide to Home Improvement*. 3rd ed. New York: 1987.

—————. *The Poor Pay More for Less, Part III: Predatory Home Improvement Lending*. New York: February 1993.

Your Money: Home Improvement Scam Could Cost Homeowners Big Bucks. Cable News Network, July 10, 1993.

15. THE ENERGY EFFICIENT HOME

"Bulbs that Won't Charge Up Your Bills. *Business Week*, Sept. 16, 1991.

Consumer Guide to Home Energy Savings. Berkeley: American Council for an Energy-Efficient Economy. 1996.

"Cool It: A Survey of Energy and the Environment." *The Economist*, Aug. 31, 1991.

The Earth Works Group. *Fifty Simple Things You Can Do to Save the Earth*. Berkeley, CA: EarthWorks Press, 1989.

Fowler, Deborah. "Energy Saved Is Money Earned." *Houston Chronicle*, June 10, 1996.

Goldstein, Eric A., and Mark D. Izeman. *The New York Environment Book*. Island Press, 1990.

Incantalupo, Tom. "Oil or Gas? Burning Question Doesn't Have Easy Answer." *Newsday*, Sept. 9, 1990.

New York Public Interest Research Group. "Conservation Tips" on Water, Appliances, Insulation, Cooling, Transportation, Heating, Lighting. New York: 1992.

—————. "Weatherstripping and Caulking Tips," 1990.

Romano, Jay. "Conducting an Energy Audit." *New York Times*.

U.S. Department Of Energy. "Energy Efficient Windows." October 1994.

16. HOME SECURITY SYSTEMS

Better Business Bureau A to Z Buying Guide. New York: Henry Holt & Co., 1990.

"Coping With Lighting: Tips From the Experts on How to Make the Home Safe, Inside and Out." *New York Times*, Oct. 27, 1990.

Hanley-Goff, M.J. "Guarding The Castle." *New York Newsday*, Feb. 28, 1997.

Insurance Information Institute. "Home Security Basics." New York: April 1990.

Maxwell, Helen. *Home Safe Home: How to Safeguard Your Home and Family*. Far Hills, N.J.: New Horizon Publishing, 1992.

"Protect Your Home." *Consumer Reports*, May 1994.

"To Catch a Thief." ABC News *20/20*. Feb. 5, 1993.

17. FURNITURE AND MATTRESSES

Crane, Margaret. "Stay Wide Awake When Buying a Mattress." *St. Louis Post Dispatch*, Feb. 1, 1997.

Crenshaw, Albert B. "Congress Eyes Curbs on Rent-to-Own Industry." *Washington Post*, 1993.

Gilgoff, Henry. "Carpet Scams Cited by City." *New York Newsday*, Aug. 11, 1993.

Hayes, David. "Perpetual Sales Alleged in Levitz Investigation." *Kansas City Star*, June 26, 1996.

"Home Style: Getting the Right Home Furniture Takes Planning, Shopping Savvy, But You Can Have Fun Too." *Atlanta Journal and Constitution*, Oct. 3, 1992.

Kahn, Eve M. "To Pick a Sofa, Lift It, Squeeze It and Don't Forget to Sit on It. *New York Times*, Aug. 1, 1992.

New York City Department of Consumer Affairs. *Furniture: From Purchase to Delivery*. New York: April 1992.

—————. *Mattress Buying: How Product Proliferation Confuses Consumers*. New York: March 1993.

Seymour, Liz. "Returning Furniture: Repent at Leisure." *New York Times*, Apr. 29, 1993.

U.S. Federal Trade Commission. "Guides for the Household Furniture Industry." Washington, DC: 1973.

Waresh, Julie. "When Is a Sale Not a Sale?" *Palm Beach Post*, Mar. 9, 1997

18. PETS

American Society for the Protection and Conservation of Animals. *Selecting the Family Dog: How to Find the Dog of Your Dreams*.

Bennefield, Robin M. "When a Pet Dies." *U.S. News & World Report*, June 30, 1997.

Capuzzo, Mike. "Reptile-linked Salmonella Cases Rising." *Rocky Mountain News*, June 21, 1997.

Finnegan, Lora J. "Flying With Fido: Traveling With a Pet." *Sunset*, March 1993.

"Going Out in Style: Casketmaker Dennis Hoegh Sends Pets Packing in a Box of Their Own." *Time*, Feb. 1, 1993.

Green, Rany. "Is This You? — University of Oregon Study Reveals Psyches of Owners." *Seattle Times*, Apr. 8, 1993.

Jaegerman, Megan. "The Cost of that Dog in the Window." *New York Times*, June 13, 1992.

Kelley, Tina. "See Spot Run. See Spot Fall. Call Spot's H.M.O." *New York Times*, July 20, 1997.

Kopecki, Dawn. "D.C. Dogs Live in the Laps of Luxury: Devoted Owners With More Money than Time Unleash Boom in Services." *Washington Time*, July 7, 1997.

Navarro, Mireya. "After Movies, Unwanted Dalmatians." New York Times, Sept. 14, 1997.

"Pet Health Insurance: Should You Bite?" *Kiplinger Online*, July 1997.

"Picking the Best Vets." *St. Petersburg Times*, June 5, 1993.

Randolph, Mary and Guy Murdoch. "Your Rights When Buying a Dog." *Consumers' Research Magazine*, June 1994.

Seremet, Patricia. "Putting on the Dog—or Cat." *Hartford Courant*, Nov. 10, 1994.

19. LAWN AND GARDEN CARE

Damrosch, Barbara. *The Garden Primer.* New York: Workman Publishing, 1988.

Hayes, David. "In Plain English, Please." *Kansas City Star*, Sept. 21, 1997.

"Lazy Lawnmowing." *Consumer Reports*, June 1997.

Rodale, Robert, et al. *Lawn Beauty—The Organic Way.* Emmaus, PA: Rodale Books, 1970.

Schneider, Keith. "Senate Panel Says Lawn Chemicals Harm Many." *New York Times*, May 10, 1991.

Sharkey, Joe. "Not in My Backyard." *New York Times*, June 8, 1997.

Slatella, Michelle. "Masters of the Turf; If You Love Your Lawn (and We Know You Do), You Either Fret Over it Yourself, or Pay a Professional to Do It for You." *Newsday*, July 29, 1992.

Squires, Paula. "One-Fifth of Us Hire Services for Lawn Work." *Richmond Times Dispatch*, June 8, 1997.

Stocker, Carol. "A Few Timely Facts About Fertilizer; Gardener's Notebook." *Boston Globe*, Apr. 8, 1993.

20. MOVING COMPANIES

Adelson, Andrea. "Boxing Up a Life and Moving It Requires Caution and Cash." *New York Times*, Dec. 31, 1995.

American Movers Conference. Household Goods Carriers' Bureau. *Intrastate Regulatory Requirements.* May 21, 1993.

Crispell, Diane. "Movers of Tomorrow." *American Demographics*, June 1993.

Fields, Robin. "Movers Leave Some Customers in a Lurch." *Sun Sentinel* (Fort Lauderdale), Mar. 24, 1997.

Fink, Ken. "Best Moving Deal Is to Do It Yourself." *Chicago Tribune*, May 1, 1993.

Gilgoff, Henry. "A Cheap Move Can Be Costly." *Newsday*, July 7, 1996.

Gilje, Shelby. "Relocating? Some Tips That Will Move You." *Seattle Times*, May 16, 1993.

Goldberg, Jeffrey. "All the Wrong Moves." *New York Magazine*, June 7, 1993.

Schwartzman, Paul. "How to Avoid Rip-Off Hauls." *New York Daily News*, Mar. 31, 1996.

—————. "Movers Take You for a Ride." *New York Daily News*, Mar. 31, 1996.

Simross, Lynn. "Selecting a Reputable Moving Company Requires Homework. 'Get Everything in Writing,' Experts Advise." *Los Angeles Times*, June 12, 1991.

"Surviving Your Next Move." *Consumer Reports*, August 1990.

U.S. Senate. Committee on Investigations, Taxation, and Government Operations. *Abuses in the Moving Industry — Reforming a Troubled Business.* Washington, DC: 1992.

21. PRODUCT SAFETY

Asch, Peter. *Consumer Safety Regulation: Putting a Price on Life and Limb.* New York: Oxford Univ. Press, 1988.

Claybrook, Joan, and David Bollier. *Freedom From Harm*. New York: The Democracy Project, 1985.

Coalition for Consumer Health and Safety. *The Nation's Health and Safety: A Status Report 1997.*

Fise, Mary Ellen R. "Testimony Before the U.S. Senate Subcommittee on Consumer Affairs, Foreign Commerce and Tourism." Apr. 23, 1996.

Green, Mark, et al. eds. *Changing America: Blueprints for the New Administration*. New York: New Market Press, 1992.

Lief, Louise. "Shocking! Bogus Safety Labels." *U.S. News & World Report*, Mar. 3, 1997.

"A Major Recall of Ceiling Fans." *Consumer Reports*, February 1994.

Meier, Barry. "Product Safety Commission Is Criticized As Too Slow to Act." *New York Times*, Sept. 21, 1991.

U.S. Consumer Product Safety Commission. "Alert: Hidden Hazards in the Home: Large Buckets Are Drowning Hazards for Young Children." Washington, DC: April 1992.

—————. *National Electronic Injury Surveillance System Product Summary Report for 1996.* Washington, DC: 1994.

—————. "Product Safety Fact Sheet on Riding Lawnmowers," Publication No. 588. Washington, DC: revised spring 1988.

TECHNOLOGY

22. COMPUTERS

Armstrong, Larry. "Gadgets: Pumping Up Your Old PC." *Business Week*, Feb. 16, 1998.

Carlton, Jim. "Computer Support Lines Fail to Click OK in Industry Study." *Wall Street Journal*, Aug. 25, 1997.

"Do Computers Have to Be Hard to Use? *New York Times*, May 28, 1998.

Flynn, Laurie J. "Just Drive a Used PC Off the Lot and Save." *New York Times*, Feb. 23, 1997.

Heating, Peter. "How to Buy a Computer." *Money*, November 1995.

"How Much Computer for $1,000? For $2,500?" *Consumer Reports*, June 1998.

National Association of Attorneys General. "22 Attorneys General Obtain $1.5 Million Settlement With Packard Bell." *Consumer Protection Report*, September 1996.

Mossberg, Walter S. "The PC Buying Guide: Bargains Packed With Power." *Wall Street Journal*, Apr. 23, 1998.

Overby, Stephanie. "The Cure for an Aging PC." *Smart Money Interactive*, Jan. 27, 1998.

Pearson, Olen R. *Consumer Reports Guide to Personal Computers*. Yonkers, NY: Consumer Reports Books, 1997.

Peterson, Tami D. "10 Tips for Direct Success." *Computer Shopper Net Buyer*, 1998.

Simons, John. "Take this PC and..." *U.S. News and World Report*, May 5, 1997.

"Sure, My PC's Insured." *Computer Shopper*, October 1996.

Thomas, Susan Gregory. "New Cut-Rate PCS." *U.S. News and World Report*. June 16, 1997.

Turner, Rob. "Do Warranties Compute" *Smart Money*, July 1997.

23. THE INTERNET

"A Parent's Guide to Cyberspace." *Consumer Reports*, May 1997.

Better Business Bureau. *Choosing an Internet Service Provider*. New York: 1997.

Cortese, Amy, Steve Hamm, and Robert D. Hof. "Why Microsoft Is Glued to the Tube." *Business Week*, Sept. 22, 1997.

Frank, Stephen E. "Inside a Get-Rich-Quick Plan on the Web." *Wall Street Journal*, July 9, 1997.

"Internet Service Providers." *PC Magazine*, Sept. 9, 1997.

"Is Your Computer Spying on You?" *Consumer Reports*, May 1997.

Kennedy, Nancy Boyd. "Authorities Endeavor to Deal With Investment Spam' Scams." *Wall Street Journal*, Oct. 24, 1997.

Kristof, Kathy. "Web Rife with New Twists on Old Scams." *New York Newsday*, Sept. 28, 1997.

Lewis, Peter H. "Many Users of Commercial On-Line Services Are Getting a Steady Diet of Spam.'" *New York Times*, Oct. 20, 1997.

—————. "WebTV—Bigger Is Better for Viewing, but Remote Buttons Aren't on the Same Scale." *Seattle Times*, Oct. 26, 1997.

Naik, Gautam. "Do I Have Privacy?" *Wall Street Journal*, Dec. 9, 1996.

National Consumers League. "Top 10 Internet Frauds for 1997." Press release. Sept. 10, 1997.

Sandberg, Jared. "What Do They Do On-Line?" *Wall Street Journal*, Dec. 9, 1996.

Schiesel, Seth. "America Online Backs Off Plan to Give Out Phone Numbers." *New York Times*, July 25, 1997.

——. "Now That You're On Line, Check for the Bottom Line." *New York Times*, Apr. 3, 1997.

Sorkin, Andrew Ross. "2 Popular Web Sites Report Breaches in Their Security." *New York Times*, July 10, 1997.

Tejada, Carlos. "Are My Kids Safe?" *Wall Street Journal*, Dec. 9, 1996.

24. CABLE TELEVISION

Bauman, Risa. "Selling in the Long Form." *Direct*, January 1993.

Brinkley, Joel. "Cable TV in Digital Push to Get More Channels." *New York Times*, Nov. 11, 1997.

Consumers Union. *Testimony of Gene Kimmelman on Antitrust and Competition Issues in the Cable and Video Markets before Antitrust, Business Rights and Competition Subcommittee of the Committee on the Judiciary, United States Senate*. Oct. 8, 1997.

Cooper, Jean Duggan. "Cable Cuts." *New York Newsday*, Apr. 2, 1993.

Farhi, Paul. "TCI Memo Called for Price Hikes." *Washington Post*, Nov. 16, 1993.

——. "Television's Great Gray Area." *Washington Post*, May 13, 1994.

Feder, Barnaby J. "Some Local Cheers for 'Creeping Socialism'." *New York Times*, Oct. 4, 1997.

"FTC Promises Close Regulation to Ensure Infomercial Standards." *New York Newsday*, June 22, 1992.

Gilgoff, Henry. "You Might Not Get Lower Price for Cable." *New York Newsday*, Aug. 18, 1993.

Glastris, Paul, Julian E. Barnes, Kent Jenkins Jr., and Nancy Shute. "Hang on to Your Wallet." *U.S. News & World Report*, Apr. 14, 1997.

Gruley, Bryan. "Cable Companies Are Finding Days of Monopoly Are Over." *Wall Street Journal*, Sept. 22, 1997.

Jefferson, David J. and Thomas R. King. "Slice It, Dice It: 'Infomercials' Fill Up Air Time on Cable, Aim for Prime Time." *Wall Street Journal*, Oct. 22, 1992.

Kimmelman, Gene. "Time to Put a Lid on Cable Rates." *Consumer Reports*, March 26, 1998.

Kolbert, Elizabeth. "States Act on Cable Rate Rises." *New York Times*, Nov. 19, 1993.

Landler, Mark. "F.C.C. Is Urged to Keep Close Eye on Cable Rates." *New York Times*, Sept. 24, 1997.

——. "The Infomercial Inches Toward Respectability." *Business Week*, May 4, 1992.

Lipman, Joanne. "Infomercials Attract Some Big Sponsors." *Wall Street Journal*, Jan. 14, 1992.

Meier, Barry. "Standard Parts Debate Clouds Choices for Users of Cable TV." *New York Times*, July 7, 1990.

Nussbaum, Bruce. "'I Can't Work This Thing!'" *Business Week*, Apr. 29, 1991.

Robichaux, Mark. "Scrambled Picture: How Cable-TV Firms Raised Rates in Wake of Law to Curb Them." *Wall Street Journal*, Sept. 28, 1993.

"Satellite Broadcasters Face Higher Programming Fees." *New York Times*, Oct. 28, 1997.

U.S. Federal Communications Commission. *Annual Assessment of the Status of Competition in the Market for the Delivery of Video Programming*. Dec. 26, 1996.

25. ELECTRONIC GOODS AND APPLIANCES

Brinkley, Joel. "F.C.C. Approves 2nd Channels for High-Definition Television." *New York Times*, Apr. 4, 1997.

——. "A Gulf Develops Among Broadcasters on Programming Pledge." *New York Times*, Aug. 18, 1997.

——. "Home Box Office Will Offer High-Definition TV Programming Next Year." *New York Times*, June 11, 1997.

——. "TV Sales Weaken on Fears New Sets Will Soon Be Obsolete." *New York Times*, June 27, 1997.

——. "Under Pressure, 2 Broadcasters Decide They Will Now Run HDTV." *New York Times*, Sept. 18, 1997.

——. "Warning to Broadcasters that Renege on Running HDTV." *New York Times*, Sept. 15, 1997.

Creno, Glen. "Static Over Digital Confuses Consumers About What to Buy." *Arizona Republic*, July 13, 1997.

Flores, Delia. "Tug of Warranties: Deciding Whether Peace of Mind Justifies the Extra Cost." *Chicago Tribune*, Aug. 26, 1993.

Glover, Mark. "Consider Value of Your Purchase Before You Pay for a Service Contract; The Stakes are High on Extended Warranties." *Chicago Tribune*, Mar. 23, 1993.

Major Appliance Consumer Action Panel. *Put New Appliances "To the Test" Soon After Installation* (Consumer Bulletin #3). Rev. ed. May 1985.

O'Malley, Chris. "HDTV Stirs Fears of TV Sales Slowdown; Industry Worried Buyers Think Today's Sets Will Be Obsolete Soon." *Indianapolis Star*, July 3, 1997.

Saladyga, John S. "Are Extra Warranties Worth It?" *New York Newsday*, Jan. 21, 1993.

Silverman, Fran. "Going Digital: Learn About Next-Generation Digital TV Before You Buy New Set." *Hartford Courant*, June 8, 1997.

Somerfield, Harry. "Getting Set: Shopping for a TV Doesn't Have to Be a Marathon Event." *San Francisco Chronicle*, July 15, 1992.

Walker, Dave. "Revolution's Impact or Cable More Unknown than Known." *Arizona Republic*, July 13, 1997.

Wolfe, Phyllis. "Say No to Most Extended Warranties." *Des Moines Register*, Feb. 15, 1997.

26. TELEPHONES

Brooks, Andree. "Who's the Phone For? Depends on the Ring." *New York Times*, Feb. 29, 1992.

Cordes, Henry J. "So Far, Consumer the Losers in Battle for Dial-Tone Dollars." *Omaha World-Herald*, July 17, 1997.

Crenshaw, Albert B. "Making a Call for Saving on Telephone Service; Study Shows Most People Don't Know Costs of Choice." *Washington Post*, Dec. 6, 1992.

Dahl, Jonathan. "Before You Use the Hotel Phone, Read This." *Wall Street Journal*, Aug. 2, 1994.

Elstrom, Peter and Catherine Young. "It'll Be Good for Competition, Honest." *Business Week*, June 30, 1997.

Keller, John J. "Are They Safe? Nobody knows. But Studies Are Underway to Determine the Health Effects of Cellular Frequency Radio waves." *Wall Street Journal*, Feb. 11, 1994.

——————. "Decisions, Decisions." *Wall Street Journal*, Feb. 11, 1994.

Koss-Feder, Laura. "A New Labyrinth for Phone Customers." *New York Times*, Sept. 14, 1997.

Landler, Mark. "Rising Phone Bills are Likely Result of Deregulation." *New York Times*, Mar. 30, 1997.

——————. "Most Residential Phones Are from Local Monopoly." *New York Times*, May 22, 1997.

Martin, Justin. "Phone Card Boom." *Fortune*, Aug. 23, 1993.

Meier, "Speak Your Phone-Card Number Softly." *New York Times*, Aug. 15, 1992.

Sturm, Paul. "Phoning Home Without Going Broke." *Smart Money*, August 1993.

27. CALLING LONG DISTANCE

Consumer Action. *1997 Prepaid Phone Cards Survey*, Mar. 21, 1997.

Davis, Kristin. "1-800 Collect Calls: Cheap, but Not the Cheapest." *Kiplinger's Personal Finance Magazine*, November 1993.

"If Your Phone Card Disconnects ..." *Consumer Reports*, September 1996.

Keller, John J. "Best Phone Discounts Go to Hardest Bargainers." *Wall Street Journal*, February 13, 1997.

Landler, Mark. "Big Restructuring of Phone Charges Approved by F.C.C." *New York Times*, May 8, 1997.

New York State Attorney General's Office. *Pre-Paid Phone Cards: The Facts*, February 1997.

Norris, Floyd. "Want Lower Phone Rates? Don't Dial 0." *New York Times*, Mar. 2, 1997.

Quinn, Jane Bryant. "'Dial-Arounds': Giving AT&T the Runaround." *Washington Post*, June 22, 1997.

——————. "Local & Long-Distance Together Again, But ..." *New York Daily News*, June 1, 1997.

Ramirez, Anthony. "Battle Is Fierce on the Phone Front." *New York Times*, Nov. 27, 1993.

Schiesel, Seth. "AT&T Will Simplify Its Pricing Structure." *New York Times*, Nov. 5, 1997.

Tele-Consumer Hotline. Press release. "Consumers Urged to Read the Fine Print Before Using Dial-Around Codes." Apr. 23, 1997.

Telecommunications Research & Action Center. *Residential Long Distance Comparison Chart No. 34*, Sept. 1997.

"Telephone Service: Don't Fall Prey to the Slam Scam." *Consumer Reports*, October 1996.

AUTOMOBILES

28. NEW CARS

"Annual Auto Issue," *Consumer Reports*, April 1995, 1996, 1997, 1998.

Bennet, James. "Buying Without Haggling as Cars Get Fixed Prices." *New York Times*, Feb. 1, 1994.

Bradsher, Keith. "Collision Odds Turn Lopsided as Sales of Big Vehicles Boom." *New York Times*, Mar. 19, 1997.

Brown, Warren. "Selling Cars by the Cart." *Washington Post*, Feb. 9, 1997.

"Finding a Safer Car." *Consumer Reports*, April 1997.

Gillis, Jack. *The Car Book*. New York: Harper Perennial, 1997.

Greater New York Automobile Dealers Association. *Car Buying or Leasing Made Simple: A Step by Step Consumer Guide*. New York: 1993.

"How to Buy or Lease a Car." *Consumer Reports*, April 1997.

Insurance Institute for Highway Safety. *Shopping for a Safer Car: 1996 Models*. Arlington, Virginia: September 1997.

Levin, Doron. "When It Pays to Complain: Detroit's 'Secret Warranties'." *New York Times*, June 23, 1992.

National Automobile Dealers Association. *1993 NADA Data*. McLean, VA: 1997.

Naughton, Keith. "Buying a Car? Steer Clear of 'the Bump.'" *Business Week*, Apr. 28, 1997.

New York State Consumer Protection Board. *The Lemon Owner's Manual*. Albany, N.Y.: 1978.

Ross, James R. *A Former Car Salesman Tells All: How to Buy a Car*. New York: St. Martin's Press, 1992.

Sherman, Debra. "Ex-Car Dealer Tells All." *Ms.*, November 1988.

U.S. National Highway Traffic Safety Administration. "Questions and Answers Regarding Airbags." March 1997.

29. USED CARS

"Buying Used: How to Avoid the Lemons." *Consumer Reports*, April 1992.

Gillis, Jack. *The Used Car Book*. New York: Harper Perennial, 1997.

Herring, Hubert. "Adding Up the Savings of Buying a Used Car." *New York Times*, May 21, 1995.

"How to Buy a Used Car." *Consumer Reports*, April 1996

"How to Buy or Lease a Car." *Consumer Reports*, April 1997.

Kaye, Steven D. "Why Buy New?" *U.S. News and World Report*, May 12, 1997.

Knight, Jerry. "Lost but Not Leased? A Used-Car Glut Looms." *Washington Post*, June 5, 1994.

Lavin, Douglas. "Stiff Showroom Prices Drive More Americans to Purchase Used Cars." *Wall Street Journal*, Nov. 1, 1994.

Lucchetti, Aaron. "Used Car Sales Soar, Fueling Mileage Scams." *Wall Street Journal*, Aug. 19, 1996.

Meier, Barry. "Buying Almost-New Cars With a Past." *New York Times*, Jan. 25, 1992.

Nader, Ralph, and Clarence Ditlow. *Lemon Book: Auto Rights*. Mount Kisco, New York: Moyer Bell Limited, 1990.

Quinn, Jane Bryant. "Lease a Used Car?" *New York Daily News*, May 22, 1994.

—————. "Stay in the Driver's Seat When Buying a Used Car." *Washington Post*, Jan. 19, 1992.

Ross, James R. *How to Buy a Car: A Former Car Salesman Tells All*. New York: St. Martin's Press, 1992.

30. CAR LEASING

Crenshaw, Albert B. "5 Car Firms to Curb Ads for Low-Cost Lease Deals." *Washington Post*, Nov. 22, 1996.

"Get a Smart Lease That Beats Buying." *Smart Money*, March 1997.

Gillis, Jack. *The Car Book*. New York: Harper Perennial, 1997.

Gottschalk, Earl C., Jr. "When to Re-Lease or Release Your Leased Car." *Wall Street Journal*, Aug. 19, 1994.

Greater New York Automobile Dealers Association. *Car Buying or Leasing Made Simple: A Step by Step Consumer Guide*.

"How to Buy or Lease a Car." *Consumer Reports*, April 1997.

New York State Department of Law. "Abrams Announces Agreements Curbing Deceptive Auto Lease Ads" Press release. Apr. 8, 1993.

Suris, Oscar. "New Data Help Car Lessees Shop Smarter." *Wall Street Journal*.

U.S. Federal Reserve. "Revisions to Regulation M to Implement Amendments to the Consumer Leasing Act." Mar. 27, 1997.

U.S. Federal Trade Commission. "FTC Drives to End the Blur in Car Leasing Ads." Press release. Nov. 21, 1996.

—————. "Look Before You Lease." FTC Consumer Alert, November 1996.

Woodruff, David. "Is It a Deal? The Arithmetic of Leasing." *Business Week*, Feb. 7, 1994.

31. GASOLINE

Arendt, Phil. "How Octane Can Do a Number on You." *Chicago Tribune*, Aug. 16, 1992.

Brown, Warren. "Gasoline Ads Overstated, FTC Says; Sun Ordered to Stop Touting High Octane." *Washington Post,* Dec. 18, 1991.

"Does America Have an Energy Strategy?" *Consumer Reports*, July 1996.

Peyla, R.J. "Additives to Have Key Role in New Gasoline Era." *Oil and Gas Journal,* Feb. 11, 1991.

U.S. Federal Trade Commission. "Exxon Settles FTC Charges." June 24, 1997.

—————. "Penny Wise or Pump Fuelish?" FTC Consumer Alert, May 1996.

Wald, Matthew, "Amoco Begins the Sale of Cleaner Fuels," *New York Times,* Nov. 2, 1990.

—————. "It Burns More Cleanly, but Ethanol Still Raises Air-Quality Concerns." *New York Times,* Aug. 3, 1992.

"What's Happening to Gasoline?" *Consumer Reports*, November 1996.

32. AUTOMOBILE INSURANCE

"Are You Paying Too Much for Auto Insurance?" *Consumer Reports*, January 1997.

Crenshaw, Albert B. "No-Fault Car Insurance May Be Making a Comeback." *Washington Post*, February 9, 1997.

Delaware, State Department of Insurance. *The Guide to Delaware Automobile Insurance.* Wilmington: 1991.

Gillis, Jack. *The Car Book 1997.* New York: HarperPerennial, 1997.

Larson, Jane. "Fall Car Insurance Comparisons Released; A Little Shopping Can Save a Shopper Hundreds." *Arizona Republic*, Dec. 3, 1996.

Nader, Ralph, and Wesley Smith. *The Frugal Shopper.* Washington, D.C.: Center for the Study of Responsive Law, 1992.

—————. *Winning The Insurance Game.* New York: Knightsbridge Publishing, 1990.

Stutz, Terrence. "Auto Insurance Rates Vary Widely." *Dallas Morning News*, July 30, 1997.

Taylor, Barbara. *How to Get Your Money's Worth in Home and Auto Insurance.* Insurance Information Institute, McGraw-Hill, Inc.: New York, 1991.

33. CAR REPAIR

Berner, Robert. "Lawsuit Claims Sears Sold Used DieHard Car Batteries." *Wall Street Journal*, Aug. 26, 1997.

California Department of Consumer Affairs. "Bureau of Automotive Repair Suspends Three So. Cal. MIM Auto Centers for Ten Days." Press release. April 25, 1997.

California Department of Consumer Affairs. "Sears Auto Repair Registrations in Jeopardy Statewide." Press release. June 11, 1992.

Clemens, Kevin and Peter Gregoire. "Can You Fix My Car?" *Reader's Digest*, October 1997.

Gillis, Jack. *The Car Book: Maintenance.* New York: Harper Perennial, 1997.

Incantalupo, Tom. "The Auto Service Schedule Debate." *New York Newsday*, July 20, 1993.

Kaye, Steven D., and Richard J. Newman. "Made-Up Maintenance." *U.S. News & World Report*, Sept. 14, 1992.

Konrad, Walecia. "Ten Things Your Mechanic Won't Tell You," *Smart Money*, August 1993.

Spring, Justin. "How to Avoid Tow Trouble." *New York Times*, Jan. 6, 1994.

FINANCES

34. CREDIT CARDS

"Airline Charge Cards — Who Has the Best Deal?" *Consumer Reports Travel Letter*, August 1993.

Associated Press. "Credit Cards Out of Control/Group Puts Blame on Bank Campaigns." *Newsday*, Dec. 17, 1997.

Bankcard Holders of America. *Credit Cards: What You Don't Know Can Cost You.* Report. June 18, 1992.

Bryant, Adam. "It Pays to Stick to Basics in Credit Cards." *New York Times*, Oct. 31, 1992.

Castaneda, Laura. "Card Rate Linked to Credit History," *San Francisco Chronicle*, July 21, 1996.

Coulton, Antoinette. "Activist Group Targets Ford Unit, Calling Its Card Rates Excessive." *American Banker*, Jan. 12, 1997.

—————. "Aggressive Ford Unit Now a Driving Force." *American Banker*, Feb. 20, 1997.

—————. "Ameritech's Twist: Drop Grace Period, Earn Higher Rates." *American Banker*, Feb. 18, 1997.

Frank, John N. "Platinum Panache," *Credit Card Management*, October 1996.

Frank, Stephen E. "Savvy Consumers Thwart Credit-Card Partners." *Wall Street Journal*, July 1, 1997.

——. "Credit Card Pitches Promise More, But Not All Deliver." *Wall Street Journal*, Apr. 18, 1997.

——. "Are New Fees for Canceling an Account in the Cards?" *Wall Street Journal*, June 11, 1997.

Greenberg, Herb. "The Trouble With Credit Cards: Banks Pushing Plastic May Be Headed for a Fall." *Fortune*, May 26, 1997.

Hansell, Saul. "Credit Industry Tightens Terms on Many Cards." *New York Times*, July 6, 1997.

"House of Cards." *Consumer Reports*, January 1996.

Kantrow, Yvette. "Banks Press Cardholders to Take Cash Advances." *American Banker*, Jan. 28, 1992.

Kristof, Kathy M. "Smart Money—Secret and Costly Credit Card Fees." *New York Newsday*, June 18, 1992.

Lipin, Steven. "'No Fees Ever! Low Rates!' Firms Besiege Consumers With Credit Card Offers." *Wall Street Journal*, Nov. 10, 1993.

Meece, Mickey. "Suddenly, Cobranding Is Music to Wachovia's Ears." *American Banker*, May 21, 1997.

Pae, Peter. "Watching for 'Traps' on Lower Rate Cards." *Wall Street Journal*, Feb. 21, 1992.

——. "Credit Card Issuers Give Consumers Holiday Incentives. " *Wall Street Journal,* Nov. 25, 1992.

—— "Bank Robbers' Latest Weapon: Social Security Numbers." *New York Times*, Sept. 27, 1992.

Ramirez, Anthony. "A Citibank Promise to Shoppers." *New York Times*, Apr. 1, 1991.

Schultz, Ellen E. "Credit Card Crooks Devise New Scams." *Wall Street Journal,* July 17, 1992.

Simon, Ruth. "Make Sure Your Rebate Card Still Delivers the Goods." *Money*, August 1997.

Sloane, Leonard. "Secured Credit Cards: Ask Before You Leap." *New York Times*, Mar. 16, 1991.

—— "How Thieves Try to Horn in on Your Credit Card Accounts." *New York Times*, Oct. 3, 1992.

U.S. Congress, House Committee on Banking, Finance and Urban Affairs, Subcommittee on Consumer Affairs and Coinage, *Hearing: Credit Card Disclosure Amendments of 1991.* 102nd Congress, 1st Session, Washington, DC: GPO, 1991.

——. *Give Yourself Credit (Guide to Consumer Credit Laws).* 102nd Congress, 2nd Session, Washington, DC: GPO, 1992.

U.S. Federal Trade Commission, Office of Consumer/Business Education. *Choosing and Using Credit Cards.* Washington, DC: November 1991.

Willette, Anne. "Credit Cards Are Cash Cows for Issuers." *USA Today*, Apr. 28, 1994.

35. BANKING ON BANKS

Asinof, Lynn. "Looking for Better Rates and Lower Fees? Credit Unions Are Favorites These Days." *Wall Street Journal*, Sept. 2, 1992.

Bacon, Kenneth H., and Steven Lipin. "Under New Bank Law, More Large Depositors Face Losses in Failures." *Wall Street Journal*, Oct. 22, 1992.

Blykal, Jeff. "Finding the Best Bank for Your Dollar." *New York Magazine*, Dec. 7, 1992.

Federal Trade Commission, Office of Consumer/Business Education. *Lost or Stolen: Credit and ATM Cards.* Washington, DC: June 1987.

Haady, Robert. "The Deal on Debit Cards." *Chicago Tribune,* Apr. 13, 1993.

Lamiell, Patricia. "MasterCard Caps Customer Liability." *Associated Press*, July 30, 1997.

LRP Publications. "$2.2 Million Settlement Reached With CoreStates Bank," *Consumer Financial Services Law Report,* June 26, 1998.

Mierzwinski, Edmund, and Paige Blankenship. *Up! Up! Up! ATM Fees Up!* Washington DC: U.S. Public Interest Research Group, 1991.

Morrow, David L. "Is Your ATM Ripping You Off?" *New York Times*, May 4, 1997.

New York Public Interest Research Group. Report. *Charging Consumers Twice/ATM Surcharging Survey*, October/November 1996.

Quinn, Jane Bryant. "Private Deposit Insurance May Not Be Worth Cost, Risks." *Washington Post.* Apr. 11, 1993.

Replansky, Dennis. *Truth-in-Lending and Regulation Z/A Practical Guide to Closed-End Credit.* Philadelphia: American Law Institute, 1985.

Reyes, Sonia. "Banks May Up Price to Get Cash at ATMs." *New York Daily News*, Dec. 7, 1997.

Tobias, Andrew. "A Primer on Market Pitfalls." *Time*, May 3, 1993.

Updegrave, Walter L. *How to Keep Your Savings Safe*. New York: Crown Publishers, 1992.

United States General Accounting Office. *Automated Teller Machines/Banks Reported That Use of Surcharge Fees Has Increased*. Report to the Chairman, Committee on Banking, Housing, and Urban Affairs, U.S. Senate, May 1997.

36. MUTUAL FUNDS

Antilla, Susan. "Alternatives to CD's: The Ads Skip the Risks." *New York Times,* Nov. 7, 1992.

Belsky, Gary. "Avoid These Eight Mistakes and Save $1,000 or More." *Money*. December 1996.

Black, Pam. "Reinvesting Your CD Without Leaving the Bank." *Business Week,* Apr. 19, 1993.

Clements, Jonathan. "Investors Can Benefit From Categories When Building a Diversified Portfolio." *Wall Street Journal,* Oct. 5, 1992.

Jasen, Georgette. "Be Wary When Buying Funds From Ads." *Wall Street Journal*, June 16, 1992.

Landerman, Jeffrey, and Geoffrey Smith. "The Power of Mutual Funds." *Business Week,* Jan. 18, 1993.

—————— . "The Best Mutual Funds." *Business Week*, Feb. 15, 1993.

Morris, Kenneth M., and Alan M Siegel. *Wall Street Journal Guide to Understanding Personal Finance*. New York: Simon & Schuster, 1992.

"Mutual Funds 1997, Part 1, Stock Funds." *Consumer Reports,* May 1997.

Myerson, Allen R. "No Front or Back Fees, But Watch That Middle." *New York Times*, May 29, 1993.

New York City Department of Consumer Affairs. *Making Sense of Mutual Funds*. Report. September 1993.

Quinn, Jane Bryant. *Making the Most of Your Money*. New York: Simon & Schuster, 1991.

Savage, Terry. *New Money Strategies for the '90s*. New York: HarperCollins, 1993.

Tobias, Andrew. *The Only Investment Guide You'll Ever Need*. New York: Harcourt Brace & Co., 1996.

U.S. Securities and Exchange Commission. *Invest Wisely: An Introduction to Mutual Funds*. Oct. 21, 1996.

—————— . "SEC to Consider Mutual Fund Prospectuses at Open Meeting." Press release. Feb. 27, 1997.

Wayne, Leslie. "Concern Over Bank Sales of Funds." *New York Times*, Dec. 31, 1993.

37. RETIREMENT NEST EGGS

Clements, Jonathan. "The Roth IRA Will Show Investors It Pays to Wait." *Wall Street Journal*, Sept. 16, 1997.

Damato, Karen. "U.S. Gives Investors a Gift, But How Do They Open It?" *Wall Street Journal*, Aug. 1, 1991.

Editors of Consumer Reports Books. *The Consumer Reports Money Book*. Mount Vernon, NY: Consumers Union, 1992.

Kaye, Stephen D. "Have I Got an Annuity for You." *U.S. News & World Report*, Feb. 17, 1992.

Morris, Kenneth M., and Alan M. Siegel. *Wall Street Journal Guide to Understanding Personal Finance*. New York: Simon & Schuster, 1992.

O'Brian, Bridget. "Owner's Guide to the Variable-Annuities Rush." *Wall Street Journal*, June 2, 1997.

"Retirement Guide." *Business Week*, July 21, 1997.

Savage, Terry. *New Money Strategies for the '90s*. New York: HarperCollins, 1993.

Schultz, Ellen. "Leaving Your Job? Think Twice Before Stuffing Retirement Money Into an IRA." *Wall Street Journal,* June 20, 1997.

Stevenson, Richard. "Expanded Options for Salting Away Money to Retire." *New York Times*, Aug. 10, 1997.

Williamson, Gordon K. *All About Annuities: Safe Investment Havens for High-Profit Returns*. John Wiley & Sons, 1993.

38. MORTGAGES AND HOME EQUITY BORROWING

Asinof, Lynn. "How to Avoid the Pitfalls in Mortgage Refinancing." *Wall Street Journal*, Mar. 12, 1993.

Catalano, Joe. "There Are More Home Loan Options Than Ever — and More of a Chance for Trouble." *New York Newsday*, Aug. 22, 1992.

Dougherty, Timothy R. "Home Buyers Should Be Prepared to Do the Paperwork Shuffle." *New York Newsday*, May 16, 1992.

Eisenson, Marc. *The Banker's Secret*. New York: Villard Books, 1991.

Gerlin, Andrea. "Mortgage Maze: How to Cash in on Ever Lower Rates." *Wall Street Journal*, Nov. 22, 1996.

————. "Pressure Increases on Issuers of Home Mortgage Insurance." *Wall Street Journal*, Jan. 16, 1997.

Glink, Ilyce R. *100 Questions Every First-Time Home Buyer Should Ask.* New York: Random House, 1994.

Gottschalk, Earl C. "What You Need to Know About Mortgage Brokers." *Wall Street Journal*, Apr. 9, 1993.

Harney, Kenneth R. "Homeowners Notice Many Fees Piled On By Mortgage Companies." *Washington Post*, July 27, 1996.

HSH Associates. *Understanding Mortgages—A Guide to Home Financing.* Butler, NJ: HSH Associates, 1989.

Irwin, Robert. *Tips & Traps When Buying a Home.* New York: McGraw Hill, 1997.

Kass, Benny L. "In Loan Terms, How 15 and 30 Add Up." *Washington Post*, Apr. 17, 1993.

Mandel, Mike. "Don't Jump Too Fast for That 15-Year Mortgage." *Business Week*, Sept. 20, 1993.

Morris, Kenneth M., and Alan M. Siegel. *Wall Street Journal Guide to Understanding Personal Finance.* New York: Simon & Schuster, 1992.

Pinder, Jeanne P. "Owners Refinancing Homes to Cut Debt, Not Payments." *New York Times*, Aug. 9, 1993.

Romano, Jay. "Easy Money From Your House (If It's Paid Back)." New York Times, July 6, 1997.

————. "125% Loan: Blessing or Bane?" *New York Times*, July 13, 1997.

Savage, Terry. *New Money Strategies for the '90s.* New York: HarperCollins, 1993.

39. LIFE INSURANCE

Abelson, Reed. "When the Best Policy May Be No Policy at All." *New York Times*, Nov. 3, 1996.

Belth, Joseph M. *Life Insurance: A Consumer's Handbook.* Midland Books, 1985.

Chatzky, Jean Sherman. "Everything You Ever Needed to Know About Insurance." *Smart Money*, October 1993.

Clements, Jonathan. "Four Questions You Should Ask Yourself Before Purchasing an Insurance Policy." *Wall Street Journal*, July 1996.

Damato, Karen Slater, and Leslie Scism. "Insurer Warns of Premiums That 'Vanish'." *Wall Street Journal*, June 30, 1994.

Dugas, Christine. "Low-Load Insurance May Save Time, Money." *USA Today*, April 26, 1996.

Geer, Marilyn. "What Every Investor Should Know About Life Insurance." *Forbes,* June 22, 1992.

Harrigan, Susan. "Turning the Tables on Insurers." *New York Newsday*, Nov. 28, 1993.

Kaye, Barry. *Save a Fortune on Your Life Insurance.* New York: Simon & Schuster, 1991.

Lawrence, Jill. "The Pitfalls of Credit Life Insurance." *New York Newsday,* June 5, 1990.

Lieberman, Trudy, and the editors of Consumer Reports Books. *Life Insurance/How to Buy the Right Policy From the Right Company at the Right Price.* Mount Vernon, NY: Consumers Union of the United States, Inc., 1988.

"Life Insurance—How Much Coverage Do You Need?" *Consumer Reports,* July 1993.

"Life Insurance, Part 2, Choosing a Universal Life Policy." *Consumer Reports,* August 1993.

"Life Insurance, Part 3, Should You Buy a Whole Life Policy?" *Consumer Reports*, September 1993.

Nader, Ralph, and Wesley Smith. *Winning the Insurance Game.* New York: Knightsbridge Publishing, 1990.

New York State Insurance Department. *Consumers Guide for Life Insurance.* New York, 1989.

Quinn, Jane Bryant. "Insurance You Can Do Without, Maybe." *Good Housekeeping*, March 1997.

Rowland, Mary. "Your Own Account; A Little Caution in Life Insurance." *New York Times,* Dec. 15, 1991.

Savage, Terry. "Life Insurance Policy Check Up Worth Your While." *Denver Post*, Mar. 30, 1997.

————. *New Money Strategies for the '90s.* New York: HarperCollins, 1993.

"Woe May Not Be to You." *Newsweek*, Nov. 30, 1995.

40. HOMEOWNERS INSURANCE

Brooks, Andree. "Hiring an Adjuster for Damage Claims." *New York Times*, Apr. 24, 1993.

Evans, Judith. "Looking for Cover When an Insurer Refuses to Renew." *Washington Post*, July 6, 1996.

Hagstrom, Suzy. "Homeowners to Pay More After Storms." *Orlando Sentinel*, May 4, 1997.

"Homeowners Insurance: Do You Have the Right Coverage?" *Consumer Reports*, September 1997.

Insurance Information Institute. "12 Ways to Lower Your Homeowners Insurance Costs."

Insurance Information Institute. *Tenants Insurance Basics.* Pamphlet. 1989.

"Insuring Your Home." *Consumer Reports,* September 1989.

Kristof, Kathy M. "Beware of Holes in Earthquake Coverage." *Los Angeles Times,* Jan. 17, 1997.

Marino, Vivian. "Homeowners Insurance Puzzles Many Who Must Purchase It." *Associated Press,* Sept. 7, 1993.

Morris, Kenneth M., and Alan M. Siegel, *Wall Street Journal Guide to Understanding Personal Finance.* New York: Simon & Schuster, 1992.

Razzi, Elizabeth. "Yikes!" *Kiplinger's Personal Finance,* November 1996.

Sherry, Christina. "Florida Homeowners Feel Pinch As Insurance Companies Bail Out." *Washington Post,* June 13, 1993.

Stettner, Morey. "Consummate Consumer: Insuring Success." *Washington Post,* Mar. 12, 1996.

Whitaker, Barbara. "Small Claims, Big Price in Homeowner Insurance." *New York Times,* Aug. 17, 1997.

41. DEBT COLLECTORS

DeParle, Jason. "Poor Find Going Broke Is Too Costly." *New York Times,* Dec. 11, 1991.

Eiler, Andrew. *The Consumer Protection Manual.* New York: Facts On File, 1984.

Fair Debt Collection, 2nd ed. Boston: National Consumer Law Center, 1991 and supplement.

Feder, Barnaby. "The Harder Side of Sears." *New York Times,* July 20, 1997.

New York City Department of Consumer Affairs. *Merchants of Menace: Debt Collector Harassment.* New York: June 1993.

U.S. Federal Trade Commission. *Fair Debt Collection Practices Act.*

——————. "Debt Collection Agency Agrees to Pay $140,000 Civil Penalty." Press release. Feb. 13, 1996.

——————. "FTC Continues to Target Consumer Harassment by Debt Collectors." Press release. May 16, 1996.

42. TAX PREPARERS

Allen, Al. "Scam Artists Resurface as Tax Deadline Approaches." *Courier-Journal,* Mar. 9, 1997.

Block, Julian. "Tax Preparers Respect IRS—and Its Penalties." *Chicago Tribune,* Feb. 17, 1992.

Dougherty, Timothy R. "Tips to Ease the Taxing Task of Filing." *Newsday,* Mar. 14, 1993.

Esanu, Warren H., et al. *Guide to Income Tax Preparation.* Yonkers, NY: Consumer Reports Books, 1993.

Freierman, Shelley. "Bypassing the Post Office: Alternatives in Tax Filing." *New York Times,* Mar. 30, 1997.

Good Morning America. Interview with Tyler Mathisen. NBC, Feb. 5, 1992.

Griffith, Stephanie, and Evelyn Hsu. "Financially Strapped Residents Are Filing Early for Fast Cash." *Washington Post,* Feb. 24, 1992.

Herman, Tom. "Electronic Filing Is Slick, But You'll Still Need a Stamp." *Wall Street Journal,* Mar. 7, 1997.

Hershey, Robert D., Jr. "Coming in '99: Another Way to Pay I.R.S." *New York Times,* Sept. 10, 1997.

Jasen, Georgette. "If You're Confused by the Tax Forms, Here's Where to Find Professional Help." *Wall Street Journal,* Feb. 27, 1992.

Johnston, David Cay. "Tapping into the Internet to File." *New York Times,* Feb. 23, 1997.

Leaf, Clifton. "Ten Things Your Tax Software Won't Tell You." *Smart Money,* March 1997.

MacDonald, Elizabeth M. "Many Preparers Make Errors on Returns Because They Haven't Kept Up With New Rules: Why Great Tax Pros Are Scarce." *Money,* January 1993.

Mansnerus, Laura. "Facing the I.R.S. Audit: When to Get an Expert." *New York Times,* June 26, 1993.

McLeod, Ramon G. "IRS Gears for Fake Tax Claims." *San Francisco Chronicle,* Apr. 13, 1996.

Morgan, Jerry. "Fast Tax Refunds Could Lead to Many Unhappy Returns." *New York Newsday,* Mar. 15, 1992.

——————. "IRS Arrests Tax Preparer in Phony Refunds Case." *New York Newsday,* Apr. 16, 1991.

Siegel, Joel. "Biz to Pay 500G in Refund Scam." *Daily News,* Jan 14, 1997.

Sloane, Leonard. "Doing Taxes for the Lazy, the Nervous and the Rich." *New York Times,* Mar. 3, 1991.

"Tackling Your Taxes." *Consumer Reports,* March 1997.

"Tax Bytes." *Consumer Reports,* March 1997.

Tritch, Teresa. "Keep an Eye on Your Tax Pro." *Money,* March 1993.

——————. "Why Your Tax Return Could Cost You a Bundle." *Money,* March 1997.

WHAT YOU WEAR

43. JEWELRY AND WATCHES

Better Business Bureau A to Z Buying Guide.
New York: Henry Holt & Co., 1990.

"Everyone's Best Friend." ABC News *PrimeTime Live*, Nov. 4, 1993.

Jewelers of America. *What You Should Know About Buying a Diamond.* New York: 1992.

———. *What You Should Know About Colored Gemstones.* 1992.

———. *What You Should Know About Cultured Pearls.* 1992.

———. *What You Should Know About Karat Gold Jewelry.* 1992.

———. *What You Should Know About Jewelry Appraisals.* 1976.

Kristof, Kathy M. "Gem-Dandy Lesson." *New York Daily News*, Aug. 17, 1997.

Liu, Caitlin M. "The Stone-Cold Facts Gem Buyers Should Know." *Washington Post*, July 27, 1997.

Sloane, Leonard. "Jewelry: Admire Glitter, but Count Karats." *New York Times*, Jan. 18, 1992.

U.S. Federal Trade Commission. *Facts for Consumers: About Fine Jewelry.* Washington, DC: GPO, June 1989.

———. "FTC Updates Guides for Advertising of Jewelry." Press Release. May 21, 1996.

44. COSMETICS

American Academy of Dermatology. "Facts About Sunscreens." Shaumburg, IL.

Begoun, Paula. "Sorting Through the BHA, AHA Confusion." *Houston Chronicle*, Aug. 7, 1997.

Being Beautiful: Deciding for Yourself: Selected Readings on Beauty, Beauty Products, Health, and Safety. Washington, DC: Center for Study of Responsive Law, 1986.

Better Business Bureau A to Z Buying Guide. New York: Henry Holt & Company, 1990.

Bouchez, Colette. "Nobody Does It Beta." *New York Daily News*, Apr. 24, 1997.

Brumberg, Elaine. *Save Your Money, Save Your Face: What Every Cosmetics Buyer Needs to Know.* New York: Facts On File and Perennial Library, 1986, 1987.

"Choosing a Lipstick." *Consumer Reports*, July 1995.

Day, Kathleen. "Screening Sunscreens." *Washington Post*, July 12, 1997.

Foulke, Judith E. "Cosmetic Ingredients: Understanding the Puffery." *FDA Consumer*, May 1992.

New York City Department of Consumer Affairs. *The Cosmetics Trap: When Truth Is Only Skin Deep.* New York: June 1992.

Schoen, Linda Allen, and Paul Lazar, M.D. *The Look You Like: Medical Answers to 400 Questions on Skin and Hair Care.* New York: Marcel Dekker and sponsored by the American Academy of Dermatology, 1990.

Stehlin, Dori. "Cosmetic Safety: More Complex Than at First Blush." *FDA Consumer*, November 1991.

U.S. Food and Drug Administration. "Alpha Hydroxy Acids in Cosmetics." FDA Backgrounder, July 3, 1997.

Winter, Ruth. *A Consumer's Dictionary of Cosmetic Ingredients.* New York: Crown Publishers, 1984.

45. DRY CLEANING

Collins, Clare. "Wash It or Clean It? Read the Fine Print." *New York Times*, Mar. 21, 1992.

Codrington, Andrea. "Laundry-Care Labels: Can You Break the Code?" *New York Times*, Sept. 25, 1997.

"Cutting Clothing Care Costs." *Consumer Reports*, February 1997.

International Fabricare Institute. *Trouble Spots.* Silver Spring, MD, 1991.

"International Road Signs for Clothing Care." *Consumer Reports*, July 1997.

Lord, Mary. "You Can Be Dressed to Spill." *U.S. News & World Report*, May 19, 1997.

"Natural Clothes Cleaning Presses Case." *New York Times*, Nov. 29, 1993.

Neighborhood Cleaners Association. "Questions and Answers About the Ecoclean Alternative." New York: May 1993.

New York City Office of the Public Advocate. *Clothed in Controversy.* New York: Aug. 30, 1994.

———. *Clothed in Controversy II.* Report, Mar. 18, 1997.

U.S. Federal Trade Commission. "Closet Cues: Care Labels and Your Clothes." July 1997.

———. "Court Upholds FTC Charges Against New Jersey Clothing Company." Press release. Washington, DC: Oct. 7, 1992.

CHILDREN

46. CHILD CARE

Buchholz, Barbara. "Small World: Know What to Look for When Choosing a Child-Care Provider." *Chicago Tribune*, Aug. 28, 1996.

Child Care Action Campaign. *Care for Your Child: Making the Right Choice*. Information Guide 13.

————. *Finding and Hiring a Qualified In-Home Caregiver*. Information Guide 20.

————. *Finding Good Child Care: The Essential Questions to Ask*. Information Guide 19.

Clarke-Stewart, Alison. *Daycare*. Cambridge, MA: Harvard University Press, 1993.

Collins, Clare. "Nanny Background Checks Have Big Limitations," *New York Times*. Mar. 17, 1994.

Healy, Melissa. "Study Says Day Care Affects Bonding But Not Learning; Development." *Los Angeles Times*, Apr. 4, 1997.

Johnson, Kirk. "The Nanny Track: A Once-Simple World Grown Complicated." *New York Times*, Sept. 29, 1996.

Kagan, S.L. "Examining Profit and Non-Profit Child Care: An Odyssey of Quality and Auspices," *Journal of Social Issues*, Vol. 47, 1991.

Kassler, Jeanne. "The Great Nanny Hunt: The Definitive Guide to Finding Someone You Can Trust." *New York Magazine*, July 19, 1993.

Lauerman, Connie. "Who's Watching the Children?" *Chicago Tribune*, Apr. 26, 1992.

New York City Department of Consumer Affairs. *Who's Watching the Kids?* New York: 1992.

O'Connell, Martin and Amara Bachu. *Who's Minding the Kids? Child Care Arrangements: Fall 1988*. Washington, DC: U.S. Department of Commerce, Economics and Statistics Administration, Bureau of the Census, 1992.

Pelletier, Elaine S. *How to Hire a Nanny: A Complete Step-by-Step Guide for Parents*. New York: Andre & Lanier, 1994.

Thomas-Lester, Avis. "The Consummate Consumer; Choose Day Care With Great Care; Selecting a Preschool Isn't Child's Play." *Washington Post*, Aug. 30, 1996.

Yale University. "Quality of Child Care for Infants and Toddlers Compromised by Inadequate Regulations." Press release. Oct. 23, 1997.

47. TOYS

Better Business Bureau A to Z Buying Guide. New York: Henry Holt & Co., 1990.

Brooks, Andree. "Warnings on Toys Are Often Ignored, Causing Injuries." *New York Times*, Mar. 13, 1997.

Children's Advertising Guidelines. New York: Childrens' Advertising Review Unit (CARU) of the Council of Better Business Bureaus Inc, 1994.

Clear & Present Danger: Statistical Support for Choke Hazard Warning Labels. Trenton, NJ: New Jersey Public Interest Group, 1991.

"Playing for Keeps: Kids, Toys, and Danger." *Consumer Reports*, November 1990.

Standard Consumer Safety Specification on Toy Safety, Designation F 963-86. Philadelphia, PA: American Society for Testing and Materials, 1986.

Thomas-Lester, Avis. "The Consummate Consumer; Choose Day Care With Great Care; Selecting a Preschool Isn't Child's Play." *Washington Post*, Aug. 30, 1996.

Toy Industry Fact Book. New York: Toy Manufacturers of America. 1992–3; 1993–4.

"Tricky Ads." *Penny Power, A Consumer Reports Publication*. Vol. 7, No. 3, December 1987/January 1988.

Trouble in Toyland. Washington, DC: U.S. Public Interest Group, 1994.

U.S. Consumer Product Safety Commission. *For Kids' Sake Think Toy Safety*. Washington, DC: U.S. CPSC, 1994.

————. *National Electronic Injury Surveillance System (NEISS) All Products Summary Report*. Washington, DC: 1997.

Wechsler, Pat. "Hey Kid, Buy This." *Business Week*, June 30, 1997.

"The Zap Awards." *Zillions, The Consumer Reports for Kids*, November 1992.

TRAVEL AND VACATION

48. AIRLINES AND AIRFARES

"The Best Airlines." *Consumer Reports*, June 1995.

Better Business Bureau of Metropolitan New York, Inc. *Airline Ticket Consolidators: Bargain or Bombast?* Press release. New York: July 28, 1992.

Buchholz, Barbara. "You've Earned a Free Ticket. Just Try Getting It." *New York Times*, June 1, 1997.

Busche, Linda. "Airlines Stretch to Give More Room in Coach." *USA Today*, May 11, 1993.

Coleman, Calmetta. "Fliers Call Electronic Ticketing a Drag." *Wall Street Journal*, Jan. 17, 1997.

Dahl, Jonathan, and Lisa Miller. "Which Is the Safest Airline? It All Depends." *Wall Street Journal*, July 24, 1996.

"Frequent Flier Programs—The Pick of the Pack." *Consumer Reports Travel Letter*, November 1992.

Goetz, Thomas. "FAA's New Web Site on Safety Is No Mere Flight of Fancy." *Wall Street Journal*, Apr. 3, 1998.

──────. "How Safe Is That Airplane?" *Wall Street Journal*, Apr. 3, 1998.

Hirsch, James S. "Code Sharing Leaves Fliers Up in the Air." *Wall Street Journal*, Mar. 11, 1993.

──────. "Some Clever Travelers Beat Sky-High Fares By Knowing Where to Look on the Ground." *Wall Street Journal*, Mar. 12, 1993.

──────. "Frequent Flier Plans: Turbulence Ahead." *Wall Street Journal*, Sept. 20, 1993.

"How to Beat Sky-High Fares." *Consumer Reports*, July 1997.

Keates, Nancy. "Boosting the Odds for Cashing in Miles." *Wall Street Journal*, July 25, 1997.

Martinez, Andres. "Airline Web Surfers Learn Love Can Reach New Heights." *Wall Street Journal*, Oct. 10, 1997.

Nader, Ralph, and Wesley Smith. *Collision Course/The Truth About Airline Safety*. Blue Ridge Summit, PA: TAB Books, 1994.

New York City Public Advocate's Office. *Consumer Alert: Airline Frequent Flier Miles Can Be Hard to Redeem*. July 1997.

Perkins, Ed. "Beat the Crunch, Few Airlines Respect Your Kneecaps." *Chicago Tribune*, Aug. 22, 1993.

Public Citizen Health Action Group. "Pilot Fatigue Could Kill You." *Health Letter*, May 1992.

Rice, Faye. "Be a Smarter Frequent Flier." *Fortune*, Feb. 22, 1993.

Scherreik, Susan. "An Upgrade for Air-Courier Travel." *Business Week*, Aug. 23, 1993.

"Snug Seats in the Sky—Avoiding the Coach Crunch." *Consumer Reports Travel Letter*, July 1993.

Tolchin, Martin. "Frequent Fliers Saying Fresh Air Is Awfully Thin at 30,000 Feet." *New York Times*, June 6, 1993.

Wade, Betsy. "Frequent Fliers Feeling Squeezed." *New York Times*, May 22, 1994.

Weiner, Eric. "Decoding Ads for Special Fares." *New York Times*, Nov. 18, 1990.

Warner, Gary A. " 'Bump' Season Is Here; Know Rules on Overbooking." *Ft. Lauderdale Sun Sentinel*, June 22, 1997.

49. TRAVEL

Adler, Jack. "If the Deal Sounds Unbelievable, Don't Believe It." *Los Angeles Times*, Oct. 25, 1992.

American Society of Travel Agents. *Hotel Tips*. Alexandria, VA: 1989.

──────. *Avoiding Travel Problems*. Alexandria, VA: 1990.

Andrews, Michelle. "Ten Things Your Hotel Won't Tell You." *Smart Money*, August 1997.

Grossman, Kathy Lynn. "Beware of Those Selling Cheap Trips." *USA Today*, July 8, 1992.

"Hotel Vouchers: Deals and Gouges." *Consumer Reports Travel Letter*, June 1993.

Kobliner, Beth. "How To Complain on the Road." *Money*, December 1992.

McGinley, Lauri. "Offers of Luxury Trips at Low Prices Lure Many Consumers Into First-Class Scams." *Wall Street Journal*, May 13, 1992.

New York City Department of Consumer Affairs. *Travel Scams: The Road to Nowhere*. Report. New York City: June 1993.

Perkins, Ed. "Consumer Reports." *Newsday*, Oct. 5, 1997.

Potter, Everett. "How Much Will You Pay for This Hotel Room?" *Smart Money*, August 1993.

Sansoni, Silvia. "Are Travel Clubs Really Worth the Fee?" *Business Week*, Aug. 19, 1996.

U.S. Federal Trade Commission. "FTC, States 'Trip Up' Travel-Related Scams in Latest Joint Fraud-Enforcement Sweep." Press release. Mar. 13, 1997.

U.S. Federal Trade Commission. FTC News. *FTC Charges Florida Firms in Deceptive Travel Certificate Scheme*. Washington, DC: Apr. 6, 1992.

Wade, Betsy. "Dialing Away Dollars in Hotels." *New York Times*, July, 18, 1993.

──────"Rebating Travel Agencies: For Plan-It-Yourselfers." *New York Times*, July 25, 1992.

————"Tightening Up On Agencies."
New York Times, Apr. 18, 1994.

————. "Who's Minding the Agents?"
New York Times, Sept. 14, 1997.

Why Won't Travel Scams Go Away? Transcript of a
conference by the American Society of Travel
Agents. Dec. 3, 1992. Washington, D.C.

50. CAR RENTALS

Dahl, Jonathan. "Car Rental Firms Leave Drivers
Dazed by Rip-Offs, Options, Misleading Ads."
Wall Street Journal, June 1, 1990.

————. "Rental Counters Reject Drivers
Without Good Records." *Wall Street Journal*,
Oct. 23, 1992.

Felton, Bruce. "Rental Car Insurance: Staying
Out of Financial Potholes." *New York Times*,
Mar. 23, 1997.

Hirsch, James. "Chase Cuts Off Its Car-Rental
Insurance Perk." *Wall Street Journal*, June 8,
1993.

Knox, Noelle. "Cars Available! But With More
Strings Attached." *New York Times*, Jan. 11, 1998.

Meier, Barry. "When a Reservation Doesn't Get
You a Car." *New York Times*, Jan. 18, 1992.

Miller, Lisa. "Car Rental Companies Say There's
a Better Road Ahead." *Wall Street Journal*,
July 17, 1997.

Pearl, Daniel. "Airport Shuttles and Limos
Compete With Rental Cars." *Wall Street
Journal*, Sept. 20, 1993.

"Renting a Car: A Survival Guide." *Consumer
Reports*. June 1996.

Shea, Barbara. "Economy Class: Car Insurance
Limits." *Newsday*, June 22, 1997.

Sims, Calvin. "Bias by Age and Credit Is Found in
Car Rentals." *New York Times*, Aug. 20, 1994.

U.S. Public Interest Research Group. *Taking
Consumers for a Ride: A Report on Collision
Damage Waivers*. Washington, DC: May 1990.

Wade, Betsy. "Car Renters Pass or Fail." *New
York Times*, July 20, 1997.

————. "Liability Is Being Shifted to Auto
Renters." *New York Times*, Aug. 8, 1993.

Wald, Matthew L. "Car-Rental Computers
Rejecting High-Risk Drivers." *New York
Times*, Sept. 9, 1993.

————. "Car Rentals Hide Welcome Mat."
New York Times, Jan. 15, 1992.

PROFESSIONAL SERVICES

51. LAWYERS

Adelson, Andrea. "Getting Legal Advice,
Without Billable Hours." *New York Times*, May
26, 1996.

American Bar Association Public Education
Division. *The American Lawyer: When and How
to Use One*. Chicago: ABA Press, 1993.

Brooks, Andree. "To Get Legal Advice Without
Overpaying, Handle Some of the Tasks
Yourself." *New York Times*, Mar. 26, 1994.

Burghardt, Linda F. "Instead of Hiring Lawyers,
Couples Look to Mediators." *New York Times*,
Aug. 11, 1996.

Casteneda, Laura. "How to Pick an Attorney."
San Francisco Chronicle, Aug. 5, 1996.

Green, Mark, and John F. Berry. *The Challenge
of Hidden Profits: Reducing Corporate Bureaucracy
and Waste*. New York: William Morrow
and Co.

Haas, Carol and the editors of Consumer Reports
Books. *The Consumer Reports Law Book: Your
Guide to Resolving Everyday Legal Problems*.
Yonkers, NY: Consumer Reports Books, 1994.

Hernandez, Raymond. "The People's Court—
Notes From the Small Claims Front: Wringing
Justice, With Peace, From the Maddening
Fabric of Everyday Life." *New York Times*,
Mar. 20, 1994.

Johnson, Daniel. *The Consumer's Guide to
Understanding and Using the Law*. Cincinnati:
Betterway Books, 1994.

Knight-Ridder Report. "Lawyers, Clients
Discover Safety Net of Prepaid Claims." *Tampa
Tribune*, May 20, 1997.

Lasson, Kenneth, and the Public Citizen
Litigation Group. *Representing Yourself: What
You Can Do Without a Lawyer*. New York:
Farrar Straus Giroux, 1983.

Leeds, Dorothy, with Sue Belevich Schilling.
Smart Questions to Ask Your Lawyer. New York:
Harper Paperbacks, 1992.

New York City Department of Consumer Affairs.
*Women in Divorce: Lawyers, Ethics, Fees &
Fairness*. New York: March 1992.

Pedersen, Laura. "Minding Your Business:
Divorce, Can You Get It for Me Wholesale?"
New York Times, May 19, 1996.

Pinckney, Michael J. "Arguing Your Case: Some Counsel From the Bench," *New York Times*, Mar. 20, 1994.

Simon, Christopher. "Disgruntled Legal Clients Read Small Print to Avoid Hefty Fees." *Wall Street Journal*, Oct. 3, 1997.

Simon, Stephanie. "Mixed Verdict: Prepaid Legal Services Draw Plenty of Customers and Criticism," *Wall Street Journal*, Aug. 6, 1991.

Tharpe, Gene. "The Best Defense." *Atlanta Journal and Constitution*, Aug. 5, 1996.

Torry, Saundra. "Airing Disciplinary Laundry in Full View of the Public." *Washington Post*, May 27, 1991.

————. "Many With Legal Needs Avoid the Court System." *Washington Post*, Feb. 6, 1994.

Woo, Junda. "Electronic Bulletin Boards Furnish Legal Information to Non-Lawyers," *Wall Street Journal*, Jan. 18, 1994.

Yeh, Emerald, and Christine McMurray. "When Your Lawyer Lets You Down." *San Francisco Chronicle*, May 5, 1996.

52. FUNERALS

American Association of Retired Persons. *Product Report: Pre-Paying Your Funeral?* Washington, DC: AARP, August 1992.

Babbitt, Wendy. "A Business You'd Rather Ignore—But Shouldn't." *Public Citizen*, July/August 1991.

Burkins, Glenn. "Protecting the Bereaved." *Chicago Tribune*. Mar. 10, 1993.

"The Business of Bereavement: An Expensive Way to Go." *Economist,* Jan. 4, 1997.

Colburne, Don. "Need Spurs Study of New Sources of Organ Donors." *New York Newsday*, June 22, 1993.

"Death and Deception." Editorial. *Sacramento Bee*, Apr. 11, 1993.

"Debate Rages Over Funeral Rules." *Chicago Tribune*, Jan. 9, 1989.

Fairclough, Gordon. "Casket Stores Offer Bargains to Die For." *Wall Street Journal,* Feb. 19, 1997.

Friedman, Dorian. "Caskets: Compare and Save." *U.S. News & World Report,* June 2, 1997.

Gilje, Shelby. "Before That Final Exit, Make Your Disposal Wishes Known." *Seattle Times,* Dec.15, 1996.

Glover, Mark. "A Fresh Approach to Funeral Prices." *Sacramento Bee,* May 9, 1993.

Larson, Erik. "Fight to the Death." *Time,* Dec. 9, 1996.

Long, Scott A. "Basic Consumer Tips Apply When Arranging a Funeral." Gannett News Service, Apr. 28, 1993.

Mitford, Jessica. "The Funeral Salesman." *McCall's*, November 1977.

National Kidney Foundation. *The Organ Donor Program*. New York City: National Kidney Foundation, Inc.

Norrgard, Lee E, and Jo DeMars. *Final Choices: Making End of Life Decisions*. Santa Barbara, ABC-CLIO Inc., 1992.

Siwolop, Sana. "Mortality Wears a Profitable, Noncyclical Edge." *New York Times,* Mar. 30, 1997.

U.S. Federal Trade Commission. "FTC Announces Results of the First Year of the Funeral Rule Offenders Program." Press release. Jan. 27, 1997.

————. *Funerals: A Consumer Guide.* 1994.

————. "San Francisco Funeral Home Agrees to Pay $20,000 Civil Penalty to Settle Funeral Rule Violations." Press release. June 14, 1996.

53. EMPLOYMENT AGENCIES

Berkowitz, Harry. "Nanny-Agency Violations: City Survey Finds Deceptive Practices at 45 out of 50." *New York Newsday*, Nov. 25, 1992.

"'Contingent' Workers Deprived of Benefits, Wages, Senate Panel Hears." *Pension Reporter*, June 21, 1993.

Diesenhouse, Susan. "In a Shaky Economy, Even Professionals Are 'Temps.'" *New York Times*, May 16, 1993.

Furfaro, John P., and Maury B. Josephson. "Temporary Employees." *New York Law Journal*, May 7, 1993.

Gilgoff, Henry. "City Targets Job Agencies." *New York Newsday*, Mar. 5, 1993.

Granelli, James S. "Backlash Hits Job-Hunting Companies." *Los Angeles Times*, July 27, 1997.

Kane, Mary. "More People Forced to Turn to Temporary Work." *Minneapolis Star Tribune*, Apr. 18, 1993.

Kilborn, Peter T. "New Jobs Lack the Old Security in a Time of 'Disposable' Workers." *New York Times*, Mar. 15, 1993.

Myerson, Allen R. "There Went the Holidays. Woopee." *New York Times*, Jan. 4, 1998.

Ozemhoya, Carol U. "Agencies Charged With Deceptive Practices." *South Florida Business Journal*, Feb. 9, 1993.

Pennsylvania Office of the Attorney General. "Lists of Job Opportunities in Kuwait Were Bogus, Preate Alleges." Press release. Harrisburg, PA: July 8, 1991.

————. "Telephone Carriers to Block Pay-per-Call Job Information Services." Press release. Harrisburg PA: Oct. 23, 1991.

Rosen, Jan. "Looking for Work." *New York Times*, May 23, 1992.

Ross, Sherwood. "Temp Agencies Mislead Workers, Study Finds." *Reuter Business Report*, Dec. 29, 1992.

Suris, Oscar. "Check Out Job Services Before You Pay." *Orlando Sentinel Tribune*, Oct. 27, 1992.

Uchitelle, Louis. "370,000 Jobs Added to Rolls in Dec." *New York Times*, Jan. 10, 1998.

————. "What's Ahead for Working Men and Women." *New York Times*, Aug. 31, 1997.

SHOPPING

54. OUTLET SHOPPING

Brown, Suzanne S. "Outlet Shopping." *Rocky Mountain News*, Oct. 6, 1997.

DeCaro, Frank. "Looking for an Outlet." *New York Times Magazine*, Apr. 6, 1997.

Levey, Bob. "Outlet Malls: Bargains or the Opposite?" *Washington Post*, June 10, 1997.

"Outlet Malls." *Consumer Reports*, August 1998.

Schoolman, Judith. "Outlet Shopping Myths and Realities of Bargain Hunting." *Reuter Business Report*, Jan. 24, 1996.

Simons, Janet. "Myths and Realities of Factory Outlet Shopping." *Rocky Mountain News*, Feb. 17, 1996.

Slater, Pam. "Thrill of the Hunt." *Sacramento Bee*, Sept. 5, 1996.

55. HOME SHOPPING

Andrews, Edmund. "New Rules to Require More Disclosure by Telemarketers." *New York Times*, Aug. 17, 1995.

AT&T. *Be Aware of Phone Fraud*. New York: 1993.

Better Business Bureau. "Dialing for Dollars: Advice on Holiday Phone Appeals." Press release. Nov. 19, 1996.

Cummins, H.J. "Check Out Charitable Organizations." *New York Newsday*, Dec. 9, 1993.

Gilgoff, Henry. "Watch the Mail—and Fine Print." *New York Newsday*, Apr. 5, 1993.

Jay, Sarah. "The High Price of Shipping for Mail-Order Shopping." *New York Times*, July 13, 1997.

Louis Harris and Associates. "Telephone-Based Fraud: A Survey of the American Public. New York: April/May 1992.

Meier, Barry. "FTC Adds Safeguards for Shoppers." *New York Times*, Sept. 21, 1993.

National Fraud Information Center. "1996 Telemarketing Scam Statistics."

U.S. Federal Trade Commission. "Charitable Donations: Give or Take" April 1997.

————. "Cybershopping. Protecting Yourself When Buying Online." June 1996.

————. "Is There a Bandit in Your Mailbox?" FTC Consumer Alert. September 1997.

————. "Shopping by Phone or by Mail." December 1996.

"You've Won, Or Have You?" *Consumer Reports*, January 1998.

56. INSTALLMENT LOANS

Eiler, Andrew. *The Consumer Protection Manual*. New York: Facts On File, 1984.

National Consumer Law Center. *Truth in Lending* (and 1993 supplement). Boston: 1989 and 1993.

U.S. Federal Reserve Board of Governors. *Consumer Handbook to Credit Protection Laws*. Washington, DC: December 1991.

57. LAYAWAY AND RENT-TO-OWN

Better Business Bureau A to Z Buying Guide. New York: Henry Holt & Co. 1990.

Oldenburg, Don. "Items of (100 Percent) Interest." *Washington Post*, June 18, 1997.

Schwadel, Francine. "For Many Budget-Conscious Consumers, Layaways Can Turn Into Throwaways." *Wall Street Journal*, Dec. 18, 1991

Unfair and Deceptive Acts and Practices, 3rd ed. Boston: National Consumer Law Center, 1991.

U.S. Public Interest Research Group. "PIRG Charges 'Rent-to-Own' Stores Rip Off Consumers." Press release. June 12, 1997.

Warren, Ellen. "Layaway Is Only Way or Some in Age of Plastic." *Chicago Tribune*, Dec. 8, 1996.

58. COUNTERFEIT AND GRAY MARKET GOODS

"Importing of 'Gray Market' Goods Upheld; Decision Likely to Save Consumers Millions of Dollars." *Los Angeles Times*, May 31, 1988.

"Inside the Gray Market." *Time*, Oct. 28, 1985.

Ioannou, Lori. "Shopping the Gray Market." *New York Daily News*, Sept. 29, 1985.

New York City Department of Consumer Affairs. "Green and Designer Companies Launch Biggest Anti-Counterfeit Sweep." Press release. Feb. 27, 1991.

Thurow, Roger. "Logo Cops Confront and Bust Peddlers of Bogus Merchandise." *Wall Street Journal*, Oct. 24, 1997.

59. CONSUMER PRIVACY

"Auditing Your Records." *Consumer Reports*, Nov. 1996.

Bernstein, Nina. "On-line, High-Tech Sleuths Find Private Facts." New York Times, Sept. 15, 1997.

——————. "Personal Files Via Computer Offer Money and Pose Threat." *New York Times*, June 12, 1997.

Carnevale, Mary Lu. "Fighting Fraud." *Wall Street Journal*. May 18, 1992.

Chandrasekaran, Rajiv, "Public Files Open to Profit Potential." *Washington Post*, Mar. 9, 1998.

Consumer Action. *Consumer Alert on ChexSystems*. San Francisco: September 1991.

Crenshaw, Albert B. "Consumers Can Get a Look at Insurers' Big Data Bank." *Washington Post*, June 25, 1995.

Louis Harris & Associates and Dr. Alan F. Westin. *The Equifax Report on Consumers in the Information Age*. Atlanta: 1990.

Miller, Annetta, and John Schwartz. "How Did They Get My Name?" *Newsweek*, June 3, 1991.

Miller, Michael. "Patient's Records Are Treasure Trove for Budding Industry." *Wall Street Journal*. Feb. 27, 1992.

New York City Department of Consumer Affairs. *Prying Eyes*. New York: November 1991.

——————. *Secret Files and Consumer Rights*. New York: April 1992.

"Plan Would Protect Medical Records." *USA Today*, Sept. 11, 1997.

Ramirez, Anthony. "Name, Resume, References. And How's Your Credit?" *New York Times*, Aug. 31, 1997.

U.S. Public Interest Reserch Group. *Don't Call; Don't Write; We Don't Care*. Washington, DC: October 1993.

——————. *Identity Theft II*. Report. Sept. 1997.

Weigl, Andrea. "New Credit Report Rules Should Aid Consumers." *Wall Street Journal*, Sept. 29, 1997.

"What Price Privacy?" *Consumer Reports*, May 1991.

"Who's Reading Your Medical Records?" *American Health*, November 1993.

60. ENVIRONMENTAL CLAIMS

Center for Science in the Public Interest. "Worst Ads of the Year Named." News release. Washington, DC: Jan. 27, 1994.

Dold, Catherine. "Green to Go: Shopping Well Is the Consumer's Best Revenge Against Environmental Degradation." *American Health,* April 1990.

The Earth Works Group. *Fifty Simple Things You Can Do to Save the Earth*. Berkeley, CA.: EarthWorks Press, 1989.

Eleven Attorneys General. *The Green Report II: Recommendations for Responsible Environmental Advertising*. May 1991.

Environmental Action staff. *Solid Waste Action Paper # 5: Drink Boxes*. Washington, DC: Environmental Action Foundation, 1991.

Environmental Defense Fund. "Recycle. It's the Everyday Way to Save the World." Washington, DC: 1990.

Goldstein, Eric A., and Mark D. Izeman. *The New York Environment Book*. Washington, DC: Island Press, 1990.

Holusha, John. "Industry Seeks U.S. Rules Covering Environmental Ads." *New York Times*, Feb. 20, 1991.

——————. "Learning to Wrap Products in Less—Or Nothing at All." *New York Times*, Jan. 19, 1992.

——————. "So What Is 'Environmentally Friendly?" *New York Times*, Jan. 26, 1991.

——————. "Some Smog in Pledges to Help Environment." *New York Times*, Apr. 19, 1990.

Horovitz, Bruce. "'Green' Honeymoon is Over." *Los Angeles Times*, May 12, 1992.

Meersman, Tom. "Has Your Electric Bill Been Greenwashed?" *Minneapolis Star Tribune*, June 9, 1997.

Miller, Molly. "The Color of Money: Green Marketing." *Mother Earth News*, February 1996.

"Old Cans Get a New Life, in Sleek Automobiles." *New York Times*, Feb. 20, 1991.

Rule, Sheila. "Smaller CD Boxes Promised Amid Clamor About Waste." *New York Times*, Feb. 28, 1992.

Schneider, Keith. "As Recycling Becomes A Growth Industry, Its Paradoxes Also Multiply." *New York Times*, Jan. 20, 1991.

U.S. Federal Trade Commission. "FTC Updates the Green Guides." Press release. Oct. 4, 1996.

BIAS IN THE MARKETPLACE

61. WOMEN

Ayres, Ian. "Fair Driving: Gender and Race Discrimination in Retail Car Negotiations." *Harvard Law Review*, Vol. 104, No. 4, February 1991.

Burns, Judith. "Gender Gap in Retirement Investments Is Cited, With Women Too Conservative." *Wall Street Journal*, June 20, 1997.

Commonwealth of Massachusetts. "Attorney General Harshbarger Warns Dry Cleaners Not to Charge Women Higher Prices." Press release. Sept. 12, 1991.

Myerson, Allen R. "Wall Street Addresses Women's Distinct Needs. *New York Times*, July 31, 1993.

New York City Council. *The Price Is Not Right.* Report, Sept. 27, 1996.

New York City Department of Consumer Affairs. *Gypped by Gender: A Study of Price Bias Against Women in the Marketplace.* New York: June 1992.

—————. *Women in Divorce: Ethics, Fees & Fairness.* New York: March 1992.

Perlman, Ellen. "The Gender Gyp." *Governing,* January 1996.

Rigdon, Joan E. "State May Ban Bias in Pricing Hairdos, Wash." *Wall Street Journal*, May 11, 1994.

Swisher, Cara. "Pressing Charges: Law Students Fight Discriminatory Fees." *Washington Post*, June 29, 1989.

Whittelsey, Frances Cerra. "How Women Can Stop Paying More Than Men for the Same Things." *Money*, June 1996.

—————. *Why Women Pay More: How to Avoid Marketplace Perils.* Washington, DC: Center for Study of Responsive Law, 1993.

62. SELLING MINORITIES SHORT IN THE MARKETPLACE

Ayres, Ian. "Fair Driving: Gender and Race Discrimination in Retail Car Negotiations." *Harvard Law Review*, Vol. 104, No. 4, February 1991.

Braitman, Ellen. "As Pawnshops Thrive, Banks Steer Clear." *American Banker*, Nov. 15, 1991.

Brenner, Joel Glenn, and Liz Spayd. "A Pattern of Bias in Mortgage Loans." *Washington Post*, June 6, 1993.

Canner, Glenn B., and Dolores S. Smith. "Bias in Home Lending." *Federal Reserve Bulletin*, November 1991.

Dent, David J. "The New Black Suburbs." *New York Times Magazine*, June 14, 1992.

Milbank, Dana. "Finast Finds Challenges and Surprising Profits in Urban Supermarkets." *Wall Street Journal*, June 8, 1992.

New York City Department of Consumer Affairs. *Banking on Merging.* New York: October 1991.

—————. *The Poor Pay More for Less, Part 1: Grocery Shopping.* New York: April 1991.

—————. *The Poor Pay More for Less, Part 2: Automobile Liability Insurance.* New York: July 1992.

—————. *The Poor Pay More for Less, Part 3: Equity Theft.* New York: February 1993.

New York City Public Advocate's Office. *The Poor Pay More for Less, Part 4: Financial Services.* New York: April 1994.

Quint, Michael. "Racial Gap Detailed on Mortgages." *New York Times*, Oct. 22, 1991.

Schwadel, Francine. "Poverty's Cost: Urban Consumers Pay More and Get Less, and Gap May Widen." *Wall Street Journal*, July 2, 1992.

Siverstein, Stuart, and Nancy Rivera Brooks. "Shoppers in Need of Stores: South Los Angeles Has Been Tagged by Businesses as a Place to Avoid." *Los Angeles Times*, Nov. 24, 1991.

Spayd, Liz, and Joel Glenn Brenner. "Area Blacks Have Worst Bank Access." *Washington Post*, June 7, 1993.

Taylor, Betsy. "Poverty, Race and Consumerism." *Poverty & Race.* July/August 1997.

Thomas, Paulette. "Persistent Gap: Blacks Can Face a Host of Trying Conditions in Getting Mortgages." *Wall Street Journal*, Nov. 30, 1992.

63. SENIORS AS CONSUMERS

American Association of Retired Persons. "Credit Discrimination: Knocking Down the Barriers." *Senior Consumer ALERT*. Washington, DC: March/April 1989.

————. "If It Quacks Like a Duck, Don't Trust It: Fraud in the Sale of Health-Related Products." *Senior Consumer ALERT*. Winter 1990/91.

————. "Investment Fraud: The Subtle Scam." *Senior Consumer ALERT*. Spring 1990.

Church, George J. "Elderscam." *Time*, Aug. 25, 1997.

Eckholm, Erik. "Alarmed by Fund-Raiser, the Elderly Give Millions." *New York Times*, Nov. 12, 1992.

Harney, Kenneth. "Reverse Mortgage 'Services' Rip-Off Seniors." *Los Angeles Times*, Apr. 6, 1997.

Hays, Constance. "If the Hair Is Gray, Con Artists See Green." *New York Times*, May 21, 1995.

Hendrix, Anastasia. "Pressure Builds to Protect Seniors' Equity." *San Francisco Examiner*, Apr. 14, 1997.

Locy, Toni. "Handymen Did a Job on Elderly D.C. Woman." *Washington Post*, Aug. 10, 1997.

Lohse, Deborah. "Help for Cash-Poor, Home-Rich Seniors—At a Price." *Wall Street Journal*, Nov. 24, 1995.

New York City Department of Consumer Affairs. *Seniors As Consumers: An Analysis of the Senior Consumer Watch Survey*. New York: April 1993.

"Phone Swindlers Dangle Prizes to Cheat Elderly Out of Millions." *New York Times*, June 29, 1997.

Tanouye, Elyse. "Prices of Drugs Increase Faster than Inflation." *Wall Street Journal*, Feb. 13, 1997.

Tsiantar, Dody, and Annetta Miller. "Dipping Into Granny's Wallet: Marketers Woo Seniors." *Newsweek*, May 10, 1992.

U.S. Federal Trade Commission. "Telemarketing Fraud Against Older Americans."

U.S. House of Representatives Select Committee on Aging, Subcommittee on Health and Long Term Care. *Quackery: A $10 Billion Scandal*. Washington, DC: May 31, 1984.

64. CONSUMERS WITH DISABILITIES

Bureau of National Affairs. Title II of the Americans With Disabilities Act: Technical Assistance Manual. Washington DC: April 1992.

Canedy, Dana. "More Toys Are Reflecting Disabled Children's Needs." *New York Times*, Dec. 25, 1997.

Eastern Paralyzed Veterans Association. "Removing Barriers in Place of Accommodation." Jackson Heights, NY: 1992.

Field, Robert. "Phones Drive Wheelchairs Up the Wall." *New York Post*, Aug. 3, 1994.

Goldstein, Amy. "President Acts to Curb Home Health Care Fraud." *Washington Post*, Sept. 16, 1997.

New York Lawyers for the Public Interest, Inc. *Your Rights Under the Americans With Disabilities Act to Access to Public Accommodations*. New York.

U.S. Equal Employment Opportunity Commission and U.S. Department of Justice, Civil Rights Division. *The Americans With Disabilities Act—Questions and Answers*. Washington, DC: September 1992.

LAST RESORT

65. HOW TO COMPLAIN

Better Business Bureau A to Z Buying Guide. New York: Henry Holt & Co. 1990.

Furchgott, Roy. "Surfing for Satisfaction: Consumer Complaints Go Online." *New York Times*, June 8, 1997.

Harris, Wayne. "Software Helps Wronged Consumer Write for Action." *Home PC*, Mar. 1, 1997.

Klein, David, Marymae E. Klein and Douglas Walsh. *Getting Unscrewed and Staying That Way*. New York: Henry Holt & Co. 1993.

Nader, Ralph, and Wesley J. Smith. *The Frugal Shopper*. Washington, DC: Center for Study of Responsive Law, 1992.

New York City Department of Consumer Affairs. *Resolving Consumer Complaints 1990–1993: Who Complains, Why, and With What Results*. New York: February 1993.

Stewart, Joyce M. "Art and Science of Making a Complaint." *New York Times*, October 1997.

U.S. Office of Consumer Affairs. *Consumer's Resource Handbook*. Washington, DC: 1997.

INDEX

Q, R